The Strange Nation of Rafael Mendes

The Strange Nation of Rafael Mendes

Moacyr Scliar

Translated by Eloah F. Giacomelli

Harmony Books/New York

Published by Harmony Books, a division of Crown Publishers,
Inc., 225 Park Avenue South, New York, New York 10003, by
arrangement with Ballantine Books, a division of Random
House, Inc.

HARMONY and colophon are trademarks of Crown
Publishers, Inc.

Manufactured in the United States of America

Book design by Richard Tassone

Library of Congress Cataloging-in-Publication Data
Scliar, Moacyr.
    The strange nation of Rafael Mendes.
    Translation of: A estranha nação de Rafael Mendes.
    I. Title.
PQ9698.29.C54E8713   1988   869.3   87-17598
ISBN 0-517-56776-8

10 9 8 7 6 5 4 3 2 1
First Hardcover Edition

Books by Moacyr Scliar

The Centaur in the Garden

The One-Man Army

The Carnival of the Animals

The Gods of Raquel

The Ballad of the False Messiah

Old at daybreak

What time is it? What time is it?

It's six o'clock.

Six o'clock in the morning and everything is fine. Time, so to speak, flows slowly; History, so to speak, follows its course—and the urge to urinate is driving me crazy. No, not crazy. Nothing could drive me crazy at this point in my life, not even this wild urge to urinate. True, I do feel discomfort on account of my full bladder; but at least I have a bladder, at least I can hold in the urine. Which at the age of seventy-two is quite something, isn't it? I am the master of my bladder. I challenge it, and except for some occasional leakage, I always get the upper hand. It doesn't control me, this clepsydra, this organic timepiece that inexorably keeps filling up. Time, yes, now that's something that controls me; but not its agents. Does my bladder fill up? I empty it. Not as quickly as I would like to, but I succeed in emptying it. I should go to the bathroom now. . . . But I don't feel like getting up. I spend most of the day lying here. It's true that today is a very special day; if I were younger I would be jumping out of bed eagerly, singing. But I'm too old now, even for the special days, which are few and far between, by the way. Besides, this is such a good bed. So prodigal of surprises. Under the bedcovers I find everything: crumbs of the cookies that I ate yesterday, and the day before yesterday, and last week, cookies being invariably part of my meals, always taken in bed. And there are books here as well, and newspaper clippings, and letters that I've written and never mailed; some dirty clothes, empty bottles, a knife, some twine. . . . A survival kit. If the city were to be invaded by the waters again, as happened in 1941, and if the floods were to transform this bed into a boat, I wouldn't be a desperate castaway; I would have the means to survive both physically and spiritually. Enough to keep me alive until the waters entrusted me to some Mount Ararat.

It's not a boat, though. It's a bed. The bed that my wife and I picked in a small store in Bom Fim, almost fifty years ago. *Give me your warmth, my beautiful girl, give me your warmth, which is balm to my sorrow.* Beautiful, hardly; kind, yes; gentle. When she fell ill, I was struck by the certainty that she wouldn't live much longer, she was much too frail. She died in the Public Charity Hospital, notwithstanding Dr. Débora's efforts to save her. A very serious case—and very uncommon, too, according to that kind lady doctor. My wife wasted away until she died. She left me with a young son, whom I raised with sacrifice, and he too died when still a young man, what a pity. A victim of the rat race, too eager to rise to the top quickly. Had he been more moderate, had he spent the day—or the morning at least—in bed, he might perhaps have survived. Even though he would have had to live on crumbs.

She understood me, my wife did, and life in her company was good. Lying on this very bed, surrounded by books and sheets of papers, I would work ceaselessly on my historical research. What I earned then was a mere pittance, but she never held it against me; on the contrary, for as long as she was able to, she provided for the household by making artificial flowers and knitting pullovers for a store. Then all of a sudden, there she was, in my arms, dead. She died and the days went by.

And now, what time is it? Hm? What time is it?

Ten past six. I've been awake since four o'clock, ruminating thoughts. Things happen while I lie here: wars and coups d'état, cases of people coming suddenly into a fortune, and devastating love affairs. But me, I'm old and I'm lying down. If I got up, it wouldn't be to take over power, but to urinate. I'm aware of my own limitations. Yes, I'm an educated man; I've studied a great deal, which, however, hasn't done me any good. Not until today, that is, because today I intend to change things; the historical moment has arrived. I'll seize this opportunity, one in a lifetime. I won't be a fool like that descendant of Jonah's who, wanting to identify himself with the prophet, used to plunge into the waters of Lake Tiberiades, and remain underwater—intensive training it took!—for a long period of time, waiting for the gigantic fish that would come to swallow him. One day this man, while submerged, raised his eyes and what did he see through the clear waters? The soles of two feet walking on the lake. Did he think that it was Jesus walking toward a transcendent destiny? No. He concentrated on examining the skin on the soles of those feet. A smooth, rosy skin; from this the man inferred that the walker must be someone given to contemplation, someone so much above reality that it was possible for him to walk on water. Jesus, a contemplative? The man was mistaken. It was neither the first nor the last error in a long line that has come down to our times.

To whom am I speaking? To God? I don't know. I don't know whom I'm speaking to, but I speak as a person of commanding knowledge: I'm an educated man, an historian. I don't hold a university degree, of course; I'm self-taught. I know more about History than many a university professor. Nobody knows more about the *cristãos-novos,* the New Christians, as the Christianized Jews became known, than I do. Nobody has studied their genealogy so thoroughly. I've returned to the biblical roots of these strange individuals, hybrids of Christians and Jews.

It's true that this knowledge hasn't done me much good. . . . It has made me neither rich nor famous. I've tried to profit from my knowledge—but without success. At least until now. At least until today, until this very hour.

What time is it? What day is today? How is the weather? What is the exchange rate on the dollar? Has Franco died yet? Who has died? What kind of pain is this in my chest, or in my belly, or in my hand, or in my head?

Why ask? Why ask so many questions when time keeps running out, faster and faster? And by the way, how much time do I have left? Little? How much is little? Months, years? Minutes? How many minutes?

The morning dawns, as usual; and, as usual, there are questions. What else can a solitary old man do but ask questions? Questions, questions. Always.

5

Today, however, it is going to be different. Today I'll get an answer to my tortured questionings. In the rough sea of anguished uncertainties, peace and tranquility will finally reign. A speck of order will be introduced into chaos because now there is a plan, a program, an objective; a goal: ten thousand dollars.

Money is the answer. The answer is money. A short, distinct, definitive answer—dollars.

A man is going to pay. Although innocent, he'll pay. Innocent? He can't be all that innocent: if he's going to pay it's because he's not innocent. And he'll pay. He doesn't know yet that he will, of course; at the moment he is unaware; he dreams. At the moment he lies asleep, like many other citizens of Porto Alegre. Soon, however, he'll wake up, and then the countdown will start. By the time the sun goes down today, the goal will have been reached: ten thousand dollars. Funny: I've never laid eyes on a dollar bill, I don't even know what one looks like. But there's no need to. All I have to do is ask. No, not ask—demand. I'm glad I'm convinced of this fact: I can demand. They owe me a lot of money, at least ten thousand dollars. Even more, for sure; a minimum of ten thousand. Dollars. I'll demand. Rafael Mendes will pay.

What time is it? What day is today?

It's six-fifty—Monday, November 17, 1975. The parcel is now probably being delivered. The parcel for Rafael Mendes.

And Rafael Mendes? What does he see upon waking up?

Rafael Mendes

The eyes of the prophet? Hm? The eyes of the prophet?

No. Neither the eyes of the prophet nor the bonfires of the Inquisition, nor the caravel, nor the decapitated head of Tiradentes, none of this does Rafael Mendes see upon opening his eyes. And yet it was a night of adventures, of love affairs and of betrayals; a night of fire and of blood, of wine and of annato; it was a night of harps and of drums. It was a night that lasted for centuries. And from which he might never have awakened: for in the last of a succession of terrifying dreams and nightmares he was being attacked by a knight in medieval armor who kept tightening his iron gauntlets around his neck to the point where he could no longer breathe; to the point where—although aware that it was but a nightmare—he felt he was dying. He was saved by the pale dawn; the first flash of light of this day woke him up, startled, gasping for breath, drenched in sweat. But alive. And the first thing that he does upon being reborn is to look at the clock.

Six-fifty. With his hand still shaking, he pushes the alarm button in before the small electronic clock goes off. Then, with a sigh, he lies back again. Little by little he calms down—a serious matter these nightmares, these ghastly apparitions. Where do they come from? Rafael doesn't know, he doesn't have the vaguest idea. By and large, he used to sleep well and it was even hard for him to wake up—on the day of his university entrance exams his mother had to splash him with cold water in order to wake him up. But now—now everything has changed. He doesn't sleep much, he doesn't sleep well. But why not? An acquaintance of his who also suffers from nightmares speaks of *anxiety. Anxiety.* Yes, but is there anyone who doesn't feel *anxiety?* Is there anyone who doesn't worry every now and then about a promissory note in the bank—or speaking more broadly, about the meaning of life, about death? Everybody feels anxiety. Rafael Mendes doesn't think that he's any more anxious than the average man of his age, thirty-nine.

Helena lies asleep beside him. Helena, who used to suffer from insomnia, who used to complain of anxiety—Helena is asleep. Asleep and even snoring. It's true that hers is not a normal sleep, it's sleep induced by the pills that the doctor prescribed—she does sleep, however, and sometimes won't get up until ten o'clock. It's not that Rafael begrudges her her sleep. Helena *has to* sleep, she has earned sleep; she's been through quite a lot, poor thing. Because of their daughter: *What will become of her, Rafael? Of our Suzana?* Rafael tries to reassure her; she shouldn't worry so much, she shouldn't take matters to heart so much; yet, the fact is that he too worries about their daughter. She's probably the cause of his nightmares. Although she doesn't appear in them, she must be the reason behind them. Suzana and everything else, of course, but mostly Suzana. Helena used to take things in stride. Even in moments of adversity—of which there were many, God knows there were—she remained stoically calm, bearing the hardships with exemplary resignation. Now, this state of affairs with Suzana. . . . It has really upset Helena. Ever since this trouble started, she's been unable to eat or sleep properly; she has fits of crying; she's been going from doctor to doctor; she has consulted psychologists; and under the pseudonym "A Distressed Mother," she even wrote a letter to a newspaper. A letter that the editor described as being *anguished.* A letter that was given prominence by being printed in boldface and which, except for its last paragraph ("Hoping this will receive the traditional welcome," etc.), was published in its entirety. A letter that, however, did not receive a response worthy of it. "Nobody is willing to help me!" she cries out in moments of utmost distress. "Nobody!"

And not even in her sleep can she find rest. Which is substantiated by the way her face screws up in pain at intervals. She must be dreaming about Suzana. What else could she be dreaming about, poor thing? The bonfires of the Inquisition? The decapitated head of Tiradentes? Maybe. It's possible that married couples share the same nightmares; but this wouldn't be fair. The bonfires of the Inquisition? Why? Isn't Suzana causing her enough heartache as it is? Poor Helena.

With pity, and with tenderness too, he gazes at her. He loves her. He is sure he does, or almost sure. To be perfectly honest, he doesn't really know what it means, this thing called *love*. If he were pressed to come up with a precise definition of this feeling, he would hesitate. It was with admiration that he once overheard one of his office workers saying: "I love my wife almost as much as I loved her on the day we were married; some twenty percent less, maybe, but I still love her." A mere subordinate, yet cocksure about his feelings, cocksure about many things. Unlike Rafael, who doesn't feel sure. Not at all sure. And with each new day—a day like this one now breaking, for example—he grows less confident; less and less so by the hour, by the minute. It's six-fifty-five. With a sigh, he pushes the bedcovers aside, gets out of bed, goes to his daughter's bedroom.

Empty. Even before entering her room, he was sure that's how he would find it, and yet, up to the moment of opening the door, he was still hoping he would find her there, asleep. Cradling the plush cat in her arms, just as she used to when she was a little girl. The plush cat is now hanging by the neck from the chandelier.

As it has been for the last three months. The maid, horrified, wanted to take it down. Suzana wouldn't let her. It was a symbol of oppression, and its punishment well-deserved, she explained. Which didn't make any sense to the maid, the daughter of farmhands in the interior. And ever since, the maid has refused to set foot in the bedroom. Which suits Suzana just fine: she doesn't want anyone tidying up her things. This accounts for the amazing disarray: clothes strewn over the chairs and on the desk, lying in a heap in a corner; books and records scattered everywhere. On the walls, torn posters: a Guevara, an Einstein sticking out his tongue, a Christ with the caption JOIN THE NEW ESSENES. That's the sect she belongs to: a group of young people, some living in communes, others not; all of them believing in a primitive form of Christianity mixed with paganism. Christ, they claim, has a double identity—male and female. As a man, he attracts women with his purity, with his gentleness; under the form of a beautiful woman called Sophia he entices male proselytes. Through copulation with her they reach truth—orgasm standing for Passion, death, and resurrection. The ancient Essenes lived in communes, true, but they would remain chaste until they reached a certain age; the contemporary Essenes use sex as a form of initiation. The New Essenes? The old indecencies, that's what it amounts to, mutters Rafael. How disgusting, how stupid. What bothers him the most in this bedroom is the smell, a mixture of incense, alcohol, mustiness, marijuana. Enough to make him dizzy. Abruptly he gets out of the room, closes the door behind him, returns to his room, goes into the bathroom, turns on a switch and—there is light. Bright light: several lightbulbs shine in this spacious bathroom, reflecting themselves on the chrome-plated metals. Pure light, abundant light; such things, trivial though they are, touch Rafael Mendes. Darkness instantaneously chased away thanks to light! Thanks to the anonymous workers who at this very moment are moving about silently and diligently in a distant hydro-electric power plant!

In spite of everything, this country has vitality, energy; it's a country of contrasts, an irritating country, yet a great country, no doubt about it. And with this thought he takes off his pajamas, steps into the shower stall, and at one stroke, turns on the cold-water tap. The jet of water hits him violently, he has to stop himself from stepping out of the shower, but anyway, that's what he wants—a stimulating, ice-cold shower. Then, turning off the tap, he grabs a towel and vigorously rubs himself dry (a piece of advice from his Latin teacher in high school: Boys should take a cold shower and rub themselves dry vigorously with a rough-textured towel. His towel is not rough; anyway, the Latin teacher is already dead, and so are many of his former teachers). He feels better. Not *well,* not one-hundred percent well, yet better. As his employee would put it, twenty percent better; but how close to feeling really well is he? Not close at all. If only Suzana.... *I'd better shave and listen to the news.* He turns on the radio.

ARE YOU READY FOR THE GREAT ADVENTURE OF YOUR LIFE? asks the announcer in a grave voice, which is, however, neutral, devoid of excitement, of promises. The question remains unanswered: The radio goes silent, the station is off the air. A power failure. An event not entirely unexpected, yet unexpected enough to annoy Rafael Mendes: Such exorbitant rates they charge us, these people at the Electricity Company, they charge the highest rates in the world and look at the service they provide. A real ripoff it is. In the United States, in Europe, the person responsible would have long been fired.

ARE YOU READY FOR THE GREAT ADVENTURE OF YOUR LIFE? The question keeps reverberating in his ears. What kind of adventure could that be? A voyage around the world in a flimsy caravel? An outer space exploration? An expedition to Africa? A meeting with a mysterious woman? A plunge into the past in search of childhood ghosts or even historical roots? The probing of the future in a daring exercise in perspective? No, of course not. More likely a plot of land by the seaside. Or a new car model. The station is back on the air, and the announcer is apologizing; it was indeed a power failure, he informs his listeners with no apparent grudge. But without saying what kind of great adventure it is, he moves on to the next commercial, and soon the news is on.

Preparations for the establishment of the Petrochemical Pole are underway. Rio Grande do Sul can no longer remain an essentially agricultural State, somebody, a politician, declares; we have to enter the industrial era even at the price of causing some harm to the environment. A Federal Decree putting into effect the National Alcohol Plan has been made public—and again someone makes a statement: We cannot remain at the mercy of petroleum, we must become self-sufficient in energy. West Germany's Minister of Foreign Relations arrives in Brazil to put into effect our nuclear agreement; Brazil announces that it will resist any pressures against this agreement; and yet another statement: It is, somebody says, our last chance (last chance of what? It's not clear). Water in gasoline causes the crash of a Cessna in Minas Gerais—two dead and two wounded. In São Luís, the explosion of an oxygen container kills thirteen people and leaves twenty wounded. In São Paulo, the implosion of the thirty-story-high Mendes Caldeira Edifice takes place. The Government will grant homeowners a twelve-percent rebate on their monthly mortgage payments to the National Bank of Housing; someone, a labor leader, voices his opinion that even so the dream of owning a house is becoming less and less real for millions of Brazilians. Petrobrás will ask a financial consortium headed by the Libra Bank for a one hundred-million-dollar loan. Ford launches its luxury models for 1975. It is hot: Yesterday the temperature rose to 37 C. Commenting on the decision made by the Brazilian Government to establish diplomatic relations with Mozambique at the embassy level, a spokesman declares: Brazil is a sovereign country that follows its own independent line of foreign politics; besides, we have interests in common with the Third World countries, which like us, are fighting a severe international crisis. Uleanto won the Great Bento Gonçalves Prize for 1975.

Next, a commercial, soon followed by the last news item: Generalissimo Franco remains in a coma. Gosh, mutters Rafael. He's not in the habit of talking to himself; but like all the citizens of Porto Alegre, and like everyone else, generally speaking, he can't help being amazed at the dictator's stamina. Why doesn't this fiend die, everybody wonders (or at least he imagines that everybody does). Not that he's particularly interested in this matter; he isn't; he doesn't like Franco, he doesn't have any particular regard for the Spanish caudillo, but—he's a human being. Anyhow, human or not, it doesn't matter. What does matter is the fact that there was nothing in the news about the financial market. Proof that the rumors haven't reached the media yet. Fortunately, Rafael thinks to himself, relieved. He finishes shaving, turns off the radio, goes to the living-room, sits down on an armchair, and lights a cigarette. He shouldn't, not so early in the day: The doctor has already advised him to cut down on smoking, there's something wrong with the T-wave of his electrocardiogram and the chest X-Ray doesn't look too good, either. Top executives can't afford to get ill, says Boris, half-way between a joke and a veiled warning; although Rafael doesn't like his tone, he agrees that top executives have to stay healthy and maintain a high level of energy, so he has cut down on smoking, and he has his first cigarette only after the morning coffee. Today, however, he's making an exception. Because of the nightmare, or because of Suzana, or even because of Franco being in his death throes, whatever the reason, he feels restless, and only a cigarette can help. Besides, the maids haven't brought in the coffee yet. Disgraceful. There are two of them and they can't even handle the work that Helena handled all on her own when they lived in the small apartment in Floresta. If Helena knew about this. . . . But no, Rafael doesn't want her to get upset about a trifling thing. Anyway, the maids are now moving about, and Rafael can hear them talking in the kitchen. Curiously enough, they are discussing Franco. Isn't it something, says one of them, the way this man is hanging on. Right, replies the other, these old folks are really strong, not like us who can be knocked down by any slight breeze. Well, reasons the first maid, it can't be much fun, hanging on to life like that, we have to make room for other people. The second maid—who always agrees with the first one—agrees again, and adds another well-considered statement, to wit, what kind of life is that, thrown on a hospital bed, unaware of what's going on around him, relieving himself in bed—that's no life. And what is life?—Rafael feels like asking. You who are so smart, come on, tell your boss here what life is! They know nothing, no, they don't. They don't even know how to brew coffee properly.

He stands up, opens the door leading to the balcony, then steps outside. He loves this balcony; it's the one place in the house where he can feel better. Because of the beautiful view that unfolds from there: Not as magnificent as the enthusiastic advertisement claimed ("Spectacular apartment with a gorgeous view, located in aristocratic urban neighborhood," etc.), but the view is beautiful, anyhow: the hills, the river. A small strip of the river—and what else would he want to see from there? A beach, the vast ocean, the shores of Africa, who knows? The apartment is spacious, comfortable (besides being, as Boris remarked at the time when Rafael first bought it, right for his social position). He likes the apartment, he likes Porto Alegre, a city he doesn't know much about. That is was founded by sixty Azorian couples in the eighteenth century he learned in elementary school; but he learned very little else about it. The little he learned, however, is enough for the current exigencies of his existence. Sixty couples: all he needs to know.

It's not the city that occupies Rafael's mind now, it's his daughter. Where in the world is she? He doesn't have the slightest idea. When it comes down to it, he doesn't have the slightest idea about anything relating to Suzana. Which leaves him perplexed rather than hurt. How did this all come about? How did the little girl that he used to rock to sleep become transformed into this stranger he can't even communicate with?

"Good morning, Senhor Rafael."

It's one of the maids, a little mulatto girl with a pert face. Although Rafael dislikes her, he doesn't say so; he doesn't want to make things any more difficult for Helena. Poor thing, she's already got plenty of problems: The last thing she needs is to have to go hunting for another maid, a species that's becoming more and more rare, even in this city of Porto Alegre, where all these girls from the interior converge in search of opportunities and guiltless sex.

"And Dona Helena?"

Trying to vex me, she is, this little hussy. She knows that Helena sleeps late in the morning, and yet she has to ask.

"Later."

"I see. And Suzana?"

"Dona Suzana," he corrects her dryly.

"What?" Her face wears an expression of surprise.

"Dona Suzana, do you hear? All right, you may leave the coffee here."

Crooning to herself, the maid walks away.

For a few moments Rafael Mendes sits staring at the stainless steel coffee pot in front of him; a dark drop hangs from its spout. Spellbound, he watches it: Will it fall? It does. It falls and a dark stain forms on the white tablecloth. The sight of this stain brings to his mind something that happened to Suzana once. She was two years old when he and Helena finally managed one evening to go out for the first time. Until then it had been impossible, his mother refused to look after her grandchild, saying she wasn't a babysitter; finally, they got hold of someone reliable, an old servant who used to work for Helena's mother—a fat, quiet woman who had difficulty breathing; she suffered from high blood pressure. But she was extremely devoted to the little girl, so one evening they decided to go out for dinner and then take in a movie. They returned home late. Upon opening the apartment door they were horrified at what they saw. Suzana was sitting on the floor, very quiet. Before her, lying face down in a pool of blood, was the servant—dead. She'd been dead for hours, according to the doctor they sent for; she must have felt suddenly indisposed, and as she fell down, she hit her head. And Suzana? What had happened to her during all that time? Impossible to find out. An incident long relegated to a catalogue of obsolete things. Except that such things will haunt you. They always do.

Rafael Mendes raises his eyes and looks at the front door.

(Later he'll wonder what made him get to his feet and open the door. In retrospect, he may come to the conclusion that it was a presentiment, but this explanation will neither satisfy nor reassure him, because he doesn't really believe in presentiments. After all, there are plenty of people who, moved by strange presentiments, rise to their feet, open the door—and find nothing. But if it wasn't a presentiment, what was it then? Yet another unknown factor to increase his perplexity.)

He rises to his feet, walks to the door, and with an abrupt gesture, opens it. *There is* something.

There is a box in front of the door.

A cardboard box, old and tattered, crudely tied up with some grimy string. Who placed it there? wonders Rafael, intrigued. It couldn't have been the maids; they know their boss dislikes untidiness and wouldn't leave things lying in the corridor of the building. Moreover, the box is for him, Rafael; his name is written on the lid in big, carefully traced letters. Both his name and address.

Rafael Mendes's initial reaction is to open the box. He even steps forward—but stops short, suddenly suspicious: What if it is a trap? A . . . bomb? A box-bomb?

Ridiculous. A bomb? Why? Who in the world would send him a bomb? Who would go to the trouble of plotting an attempt against the life of a man who is interested in nothing but his work and his family, a man who hasn't harmed a soul, a man who, in addition, suffers from nightmares that wake him up gasping for breath? As far as he knows, he doesn't have any enemies. And he stays away from politics; as a matter of fact, he doesn't understand a thing about politics and doesn't even want to. Now Boris, yes, he has connections in the two national parties—the National Renovating Alliance and the Brazilian Democratic Movement, he has financed electoral campaigns, he must have made political enemies—not to mention other enemies, and there must be quite a few of them. But that's Boris's problem, Rafael doesn't want to get involved, notwithstanding his own high position in the firm (for how much longer Rafael will manage to keep himself apart from certain, let's say, scabrous matters is another story. But this is not what is at stake at this moment. At this hour in the morning, in this place, and under these circumstances).

Rafael knows nothing about the underworld of crime. He hasn't engaged in any shady deals; the brokerage business doesn't preclude the occasional wheeling and dealing, but there has never been anything amounting to embezzlement. He merely tries to survive, that's all. Like everybody else, he too is caught in the rat race. He fights to keep himself afloat, he keeps flailing his arms, his legs, and if in the process someone gets hurt, it isn't on purpose—and it certainly wouldn't warrant a bomb. At least not a bomb *this* big.

Neither does he have any dangerous connections. Once he met a man in a bar, and this fellow, an elderly mulatto with a carioca accent, after saying that he had been a member of former President Getúlio Vargas's Department of Journalism and Propaganda, began telling him some muddled story about the killing of Indians in Rio Grande do Sul. If I'm bumped off, the man said, write to the newspapers and tell them everything. A rather strange situation; but they were both drunk, and anyhow, the incident took place a long time ago; Rafael couldn't have been more than thirty years old at the time.

Could the box be the result of one of Suzana's mix-ups, somebody with a grudge against her, a rival group perhaps? Possible, but rather unlikely. The left-wingers she's been hanging around with, or used to, are basically fun-loving types, who speak of rivers of blood but wouldn't harm even a fly. Anyhow, as far as Rafael knows, his daughter is now going through a mystical phase, and mystics don't send bombs.

However—whether or not it contains a bomb—how did the box

get there? Who brought it? Who succeeded in walking across the lobby, where day and night—and at no small cost to the condominium (not that Rafael minds, though it's expensive)—there is always a doorkeeper who even carries a weapon? He goes into the kitchen (*a modern, spacious kitchen*) and under the questioning eyes of the maids, he picks up the intercom phone. The doorkeeper answers.

"Yes, Senhor Rafael."

"What's this box in front of my apartment?"

The man hesitates:

"I put it there, Senhor Rafael. It was too early, I didn't want to wake you up. I was just about to. . . ."

"Who brought it?"

"To tell the truth, Senhor Rafael, I wasn't here when it was delivered. It was the other doorkeeper, he's off at six o'clock, who received it. He said that a young man had come with a box for you."

"And this young man—did he say who sent the box?"

"No."

A pause. From the kitchen Rafael can see the box through the half-open front door.

"Senhor Rafael . . ." begins the doorkeeper, embarrassed. "I'm sorry, sir, but when I took the box upstairs to your place, it burst open. I did my best to tie it up, but I must say that it opened."

"And what's inside?"

"Some clothes and books . . . I'm sorry."

"That's all right, young man. This can happen."

He puts the receiver down, suddenly relieved, euphoric even; he could say to the maids, Imagine, darlings, somebody sent me a box and I was afraid to open it because I thought it was a bomb—a bomb, imagine! But without saying anything, he makes for the front door, and picks up the box. Heavy, but not too heavy. Nothing that would strain his heart or his backbone. With some difficulty, he places the box on the balcony outside the living room. Getting a knife from the table, he cuts the string. And he opens the box.

Clothes, just as the doorkeeper had said. Old clothes: old shirts, old pants. Two old suits in an old-fashioned style—dating back to the thirties or forties. A Panama hat. A Borsalino cap. Bow ties—three of them. A pair of shoes with woven vamps. And oddly enough, a pair of combat boots of the kind soldiers used to wear a long time ago. Taking these articles out of the box, Rafael carefully stacks them in a pile on the balcony.

At the bottom of the box he finds some old, yellowed books, most of them historical texts: *The Inquisition in Portugal and in Brazil, The Sugarcane Cycle,* among others. A notebook with annotations. Inside Rafael finds a photograph. An old snapshot taken by an itinerant photographer; the caption reads: *Porto Alegre-Rua da Praia—1938.* It shows a couple, the man holding a child on his lap. . . .

For some seconds, Rafael gazes at the photo; then his eyes brim with tears. The little boy in the sailor suit is himself. And the man in the white linen suit, smiling shyly, is his father, Rafael Mendes, who in 1938 walked out on his family never to come back.

The door opens.

"Hi."

Rafael turns around, startled. It's Suzana.

Beautiful, his daughter. Rafael has to admit that she is beautiful, despite his displeasure at seeing how grubby and slovenly his daughter has become: her hair dishevelled, her dress tattered, her feet in rawhide sandals—not to mention the cigarette dangling from the corner of her mouth. She's beautiful despite her slenderness and small frame, despite her stooping posture. As beautiful as Helena; the same beautiful mouth and big dark eyes. Eyes now staring at him with an expression of insolent defiance.

Defiance? Yes. But there's also weariness on her face. Weariness and a certain perplexity. The same perplexity that Rafael sees on his own face when he looks at himself in the mirror upon getting up in the morning. And wasn't it perplexity too that he saw in the eyes of the little boy in the photograph?

"What's that?" asks Suzana, pointing to the snapshot.

"None of your business," Rafael replies, quickly putting the photograph into his pocket. Irritated; irritated and aggrieved; it's the same aggrieved irritation that his mother could barely conceal whenever he asked about his father. "Besides," he adds, "don't you think that I'm the one who should be asking the questions? Where have you been?"

She sighs.

"So here we go again. It's going to start all over again, the same old fight. Why, Father? I could say it's none of your business where I've been, but then you'll say that you're my father, that you have the right to know whose company I keep, and I'll say I'm now eighteen years old and can damn well choose my own company, and then you'll say that as long as I live here and eat your food I owe you explanations, and I'll say you can stick your food up your ass, and then you'll be furious and tell me to hold my tongue, and I'll say no way and then I'll run to my room, slam the door shut, throw myself upon the bed and start crying while you remain here muttering 'how shameless, how shameless.' No, Father. We're not going to watch this rerun again, are we? Maybe we could try to change ourselves, what do you say? Why don't you begin by telling me about that photograph? Why don't you try to tell me everything? Hm, Father?"

He doesn't reply. He keeps staring at her in silence.

"All right," she says. She goes to her room, slams the door shut. Rafael plops himself into an armchair. In a daze. It's eight o'clock and so many things have already happened to him since he managed to extricate himself from the gauntlets of the warrior. He tries to sort out his thoughts, to make sense of things—without success, for he's far too disturbed. Fortunately, the maid walks in; fortunately, she reminds him that the coffee is getting cold; fortunately, he comes to his senses. After all, it's Monday, and he has to go to work, he has to earn a living, there are all these bills to pay, the mortgage, the condominium fees, the maids' wages, the supermarket, Helena's psychiatrist. He sits down at the table: it's important to eat, even if he's not hungry. At least a slice of bread, a cup of coffee, a small one, but with milk and sugar—he can't go to the office on an empty stomach, it would make him dizzy, trigger palpitations, the doctor has already warned him about such things. Before sitting at the table, though, he carefully folds the clothes, puts them back, together with the books, into the cardboard box. He carries the box to his study and locks it in a cabinet. As for the photo and the notebooks, he puts them in his briefcase. He'll examine them leisurely in the office, away from the prying eyes of the nosy maids.

He sits down at the table, turns on the radio. The last chords of a soothing melody, and soon afterward the announcer repeats his previous question: ARE YOU READY FOR THE GREAT ADVENTURE OF YOUR LIFE? in the same grave, emotionless voice. It refers, as Rafael had suspected, to a plot of land you can own by the seaside, a place near the town of Laguna, in the state of Santa Catarina. A dream place. The sea breeze, the charming landscape, etc., everything yours for low monthly payments. Rafael pours himself some coffee, takes a sip. Cold. Even so, he drinks it.

Another newscast. Generalissimo Franco remains in a coma, and the doctors have given up any hopes of saving him.

Franco, Spain: his father. In 1938 Rafael Mendes abandoned everything—family, friends, his medical practice, his government job—to go to Spain, where a civil war was raging. Why? He has never found out; his mother is tight-lipped about this subject. Understandably so, but the fact is that she is tight-lipped. When Rafael was a child, she used to tell him that his father had gone away on a trip and that he would come back one day (like King Dom Sabastião returning to the Portuguese people?). Later she told him that his father had fought in the war and had been killed. And she would say nothing else:

"I don't know, Rafael. I don't know why he had to get mixed up in it."

"But was he a communist?"

"No. He was never involved in politics."

"Was he upset at the time?"

"No. A bit eccentric, perhaps; but I wouldn't say upset."

"But then. . . ."

"I don't know, Rafael. I just don't know. It was the war, that's all. Many people were . . . idealists."

Other people, both friends and acquaintances of Dr. Rafael Mendes's, were equally evasive. The old bacteriologist Cuvier de

Souza, known in the medical circles as *Dr. Microbe,* once talked to him at length about his former classmate at the Faculty of Medicine:

"He was a very kind man . . . I liked him a lot. Do you know that the two of us were the very first people to test penicillin in the state of Rio Grande do Sul? Penicillin which I produced, my friend, in a lab I had at the far end of my backyard!"

But when Rafael Mendes wanted to know about Spain, the doctor became reticent:

"Well, such things do happen. Who knows what was going on in his head. Or in anyone else's mind, for that matter."

Then slouching over the microscope, he changed the subject:

"Bacteria. . . . They've always fascinated me, ever since the day when I first looked at them through a microscope. It's a whole world, my friend. A world of tiny creatures that live, flit about—and don't talk. Talking is not always necessary."

Disconcerted, Rafael took leave of him. And as time went by, he stopped asking questions; he had resigned himself to the fact that it would be impossible to throw light upon this mystery—until the moment when, opening the door, he came across the box.

Could this box have been sent from Spain? Could it be that Franco's imminent death had encouraged the anonymous guardian of his father's belongings to ship them to Brazil? But if this were the case, who was the bearer? Who in Porto Alegre saw to it that the box got to Rafael Mendes without any advance notice?

Picking up a crust of bread, Rafael pierces it with a toothpick, into which he then inserts a small piece of the paper napkin. And behold, a hull, a mast, a sail—the small boat is ready. Rafael pours coffee on the saucer and there he places the tiny vessel to sail away. Blowing upon it, he creates a favorable breeze; the tiny boat glides away but soon keels over and sinks in the dark liquid. Sighing, Rafael looks at his watch. It's late, he must be going.

He goes into the bedroom, finishes dressing; Helena stirs in bed.

23

"Where did I go wrong?" she murmurs. "Tell me Rafael, where did I go wrong?"

Poor Helena. Raised in a straitlaced family—her father was a Lutheran minister—and given to hard work and to the pursuit of virtue, she just can't comprehend her daughter's metamorphosis. From a gentle, attentive girl into a rebellious, wild beast: How did it happen? Helena has good reasons to feel hurt; she was always a good mother, she did everything she was supposed to do. She breastfed her daughter at regular hours, kept her tidy and clean, taught her to follow good hygiene habits; helped her with her schoolwork, gave her some sensible advice when she turned into an adolescent. The result of all this? Rebelliousness. Rebelliousness and uncleanliness. Rebelliousness, uncleanliness and licentiousness. Weird ideas. Atrocious behavior. Vices aplenty. A constant stream of foul language, even in the presence of guests. Venereal disease—who knows? Who knows what's been happening to this girl?

The worst of all is the idleness. Suzana doesn't *do* anything—she doesn't study, she doesn't work, she doesn't even have a hobby like playing the piano or sewing. And to Helena, nothing could be worse than laziness. Not nowadays, not since the sleeping pills, but until recently she would get up early in the morning to go shopping at the supermarket, at the fruit stalls; she would look after all the needs of the household, leaving nothing to the maid (having two servants is something new—Rafael's decision, which she but reluctantly accepts). She still looks after her husband's clothes, and if it weren't for the tremor in her hands, she would darn the holes in his socks too— before marrying him she had taken sewing lessons. A fine woman.

And Suzana? She mocks. She sneers. Soon after joining this sect, The New Essenes, she started taunting her mother: "Christian! Some Christian you are! What are you willing to do for Jesus? Would you fuck an atheist if that's what it takes to turn him into a believer?" "May God forgive you," Helena, shocked, would mumble. "May He save you because there's nothing I can do anymore to help you, except pray and pray a lot." "Phony prayers!" Suzana would reply. "Jesus doesn't want your prayers! You pharisee!" She has now toned down her hostility toward her mother; she ignores her, which is much worse. Poor Helena.

Rafael sits down on the bed by his wife, and leaning over, kisses her on the face. Again, he thinks: *My wife, she's beautiful.* Still beautiful, despite the expression of contained suffering. Beautiful. There are other women more beautiful; more intelligent, more fun-loving, more sensual. But Helena is *his* wife. This really counts. A lot. She has been important to him ever since they first met at a dancing party.

A mutual friend had introduced them to each other:

"Helena, I'd like you to meet Rafael; Rafael, Helena is the daughter of our pastor. You may dance with her, but see that you treat her with respect. And no necking!"

Rafael had laughed then, but ever since he met her, he has always treated her with respect: Throughout the two years of courtship, the two years of engagement, the nineteen years of marriage. To him, love and respect are intertwined. Boris, who is a bachelor, often remarks with a tinge of mockery mingled with a certain admiration:

"I asked you to work for me, Rafael, because any man who stays married for such a long time is bound to be faithful to the company he works for."

He is faithful. He's had a fling or two, of course; more out of need than wantonness. Since the problems with Suzana began, Helena has lost interest in sex. "I'm sorry, Rafael, but I'm not in the mood, I just can't," and so he was forced to turn to someone else; nothing serious, however. Because there are things that carry more weight than sex. Like spending nineteen years together, struggling and suffering together—this carries weight. Even if there is no love, there's still friendship. There's tenderness. It's with tenderness that he now sits gazing at his wife. Such a kind woman. So affectionate, so attentive. No, she couldn't have failed as a parent. If someone has failed, it's him, Rafael. There must have been an occasion when he failed—or many, perhaps. How many? Two, three? One hundred and twenty? In what way did he fail? By beating his daughter? To the best of his recollection, he has never beaten her. Some light spanking, for sure, but that's not damaging, it's even recommended by modern child psychology, according to what he has heard. Did he yell at Suzana? But who hasn't yelled at their kids? It's unlikely that he inflicted traumas upon his daughter by yelling at her, or by using a sharp tone of voice, or by frowning at her. It must have been something more serious. Something like the incident that occurred on that winter night.

It was a freezing cold night, and the *minuano,* the cold dry wind that blows from the southwest, was hissing furiously. Around midnight, Suzana, who was then three years old, woke up crying. She was afraid of the wind. "Go and bring her here," said Helena; Rafael, sleepy, didn't want to get up, so Helena went to the child's room, picked her up and put her on their bed between the two of them. Suzana laughed, happy. All three of them were laughing, frolicking, singing children's songs. Meanwhile, under the blankets—

Under the blankets *things* were happening. Rafael's foot kept searching for Helena's foot, his hand on her thigh. *I want you,* he whispered, his voice cracking with the sudden, violent desire. He turned off the light, and moving over his daughter, he lay on top of his wife. "Not now," she protested feebly, "the child is awake, Rafael, this is crazy." He, however, wasn't listening, he was already entering her: a quick, nervous act of copulation. Then still panting, he slipped back to his side of the bed.

Groping about, Helena found the light switch. "Don't," he whispered, but too late: in the raw brightness created by the lightbulb he saw Suzana's eyes fixed on him. There was no accusation in her gaze, not even sorrow; perplexity, maybe, but not the innocent perplexity of children, it was something else, something disturbing. Disturbed, he got out of bed, went to the small living room of the apartment and there he remained smoking, shivering with cold, determined not to go back to bed until his daughter had fallen asleep. Once in a while he peered through the door—and there she was, staring at him. "Oh, shit," he kept muttering, overcome by guilt and embarrassment. Guilt, embarrassment, and irritation as well; he was sleepy, he had to get up early in the morning. Finally the little girl fell asleep and he could slip back into bed. "I told you so," murmured Helena, still upset, "I told you we shouldn't have done this."

Could this incident have been the cause of everything? Could it have been the seed, which after being latent for a long time had finally germinated to grow into this carnivorous plant of hatred? A good metaphor—but does it correspond to reality? Helena believes it does. After talking to psychologists and to her own psychiatrist, she firmly believes that this incident was the cause of everything. Rafael, initially skeptical about such interpretations, is now beginning to think that she might be right. A childhood trauma, it could well be. Otherwise, how to explain this transformation in the girl, a transformation that makes her seem possessed? A trauma. It could well be.

And if he assumes the blame for his daughter's strange behavior, shouldn't he also assume the blame for his father's behavior, a behavior no less strange than his daughter's, and for his mysterious disappearance? What did he do to make his father leave home so abruptly? Did Rafael make fun of him, did he irritate him with his shrill screaming? Did he spill soup on his books? (His father had a huge library, a haven he repaired to whenever he could, there to submerge himself in reading. What did he read, that kept him so engrossed? Rafael has never found out: Soon after his father's disappearance, his mother sold all his books to the owner of a secondhand bookstore. When Rafael was a teenager, he was once stopped on the street by an elderly gentleman who asked him if his father was still interested in genealogy. "My father is dead," Rafael replied, and he walked hastily away so that he wouldn't cry in front of a stranger. He ran home, locked himself in his room, and cried for a long time; then he wiped his eyes and consulted a dictionary. He wanted to know the meaning of genealogy.) So? What had he done to displease his father? Did he cry a lot at night? Suzana would bawl all night long, keeping him awake. Rafael, at that time, was trying to finish an evening course in Economics; always tired, he would nod off in class. The teacher would wake him up: "What have I just said, Senhor Rafael? What did I say about Marx's mother?" Rafael didn't know. He knew absolutely nothing about the fact that Marx's mother had demanded that her son stop talking about capital and that he start doing something about earning the said capital. His classmates would grin. Rafael ended up dropping the course. But he didn't walk out on his wife and daughter; he continued to work hard as a real estate salesman and he didn't make much money. After meeting Boris, his life changed. But it was then too late to go back to college.

He sacrificed a career because of his daughter. They have sacrificed many things, Helena and he. But apparently they haven't absolved themselves from the mistakes they've made, from the traumas they've inflicted.

And on his father—what kind of trauma did Rafael inflict? It would be more logical to think that it was Rafael's father who had inflicted a trauma upon Rafael as a result of a trauma his grandfather had inflicted upon his father, and so on and so forth in a succession of traumas transmitted from generation to generation; a distressing picture it is, but isn't this just like the history of humanity? Julio, who used to work with him at the office, had always maintained that it was; but Julio had been a depressive who ended up by killing himself, who knows, maybe to interrupt an anguishing sequence of events that affected his life. Now, is Rafael so powerful that he can inflict traumas on both his daughter and his father? Can he generate traumatic waves that might be transmitted with reverberations to the past and to the future, upward and downward, leftward and rightward? Rather unlikely. Besides, not everything was a trauma. Not where Suzana was concerned. They have a photo album that bears witness to the beautiful moments: Helena, at the maternity hospital, breastfeeding Suzana; Rafael pushing Suzana in a stroller; Rafael on all fours with Suzana riding astride his back; Rafael on the beach, building a sand castle for her. And the pictures taken at birthday parties, with all the children in their clown hats standing around the table, and the birthday cake with two small candles, four small candles; seven, ten; and also all the other pictures showing Suzana in school, at dancing parties, during a trip to Rio (the Sugar Loaf Mountain, the Corcovado); and also a snapshot that caught her unawares as she stood by the window, a dreamy expression on her face. Many pictures; many moments. Good moments. Good pictures: As Rafael bettered himself, he kept upgrading his photographic equipment. He was paid a good salary, they lived comfortably. . . .

Suddenly Suzana changed. The artless smile gave way to the mocking, bitter expression; the childish remarks to the ironic observations; the peaceful family life to the almost daily fights. A sudden transformation—as sudden as the transformation that Rafael imagines his father underwent. Why? Could it be that Suzana inherited something of her grandfather's character, a predisposition to sudden instability? Could this be something genetic, inevitable?

There is no time now for any further lucubrations; it's eight-fifteen. Kissing his wife once more, he gets to his feet, puts on the jacket, picks up the briefcase, and leaves. He takes the elevator down to the underground parking lot, where at that hour there is already much activity: The roar of powerful engines echoes in the spacious precinct, cars pull away, the tires screech on the cement. Rafael walks toward his parking stall. He greets a neighbor: A top functionary at City Hall. Another neighbor: The manager of a large pharmaceutical laboratory. A third one, a doctor, waves and comes over to him to talk. He is still young, this doctor (a neurologist, it seems), and usually cheerful; there is, however, an undisguisable tone of anxiety in his voice as he asks:

"What are these rumors flying about, Rafael? People are saying that the situation of your finance company is not good—is it true?"

Rafael reassures him: of course not, everything is fine, it's only the market that has been a bit jittery.

"I bet it's the franc. Not the Swiss franc, the other one. The franco with one foot in the grave," he quips.

The joke falls flat; the other man forces a smile: "Well, Rafael, I have quite a bit of money invested with you people, see that you don't let me down, you'll tip me off, won't you, if things are really on the skids. I want out before it's too late."

"Don't you worry," Rafael assures him. "I'd do anything to help out a neighbor."

Saying goodbye, Rafael gets into his Opala and starts the engine. The doctor also gets into his car, and waves to him: "You won't forget, will you, Rafael?" and drives away. Rafael, too, pulls out; after leaving the parking lot, he drives up a quiet street until he gets to the Avenida, then plunges himself into the stream of cars. The usual traffic jam, with horns blasting in the air. Rafael whistles softly. No use losing his temper. What for? To have a heart attack, an ulcer? Not worth it. Besides, his schedule is flexible. He's no longer a mere employee who has to clock in at a regular time. Now that he's an executive, he doesn't have to quit or start work at any fixed time.

The man in the car next to his, a battered Corcel, stares at him with a threatening scowl. Why? Is this man, like the neurologist, another suspicious investor? Rafael doesn't know him, has never seen him before. There was a time when he knew almost all of the clients of the finance company, but since the expansion he no longer has contact with them, he now deals only with documents, with balance sheets. Maybe the man is indeed an investor. Then again, maybe not: there are so many people who go about scowling for no reason at all. So many people ready to pick up a fight with anyone. If Rafael were to scowl back, the man would probably ask: *What are you staring at me for? Don't you like my face?* And Rafael would have to (what else?) retaliate with an insult, and the man would then open the door, step out of his car with an iron bar in his hand, and Rafael would have to open the glove compartment and take out the gun . . . except that he doesn't have a gun. Luckily: This way he won't get mixed up in turmoils, he has enough problems of his own to harass him. The traffic starts moving again, the Corcel turns into a sidestreet. Luckily.

He turns on the radio. Another newscast (there's no shortage of them, for sure, at this hour). But it's the same news he's already heard: Franco remains in a coma. He'll remain in a coma, for sure, until Rafael gets downtown, and until the following day, and the following, and the following, generation after generation. . . . That's a good idea for a book, he thinks to himself. He's not much of a reader, he has neither the time nor the inclination to read; however, here's a novel he would like to read—the story of a man who, despite being in a coma, still wields power.

Next to him now is a big cattle truck. Twenty or thirty or forty steers travel behind bars—to the slaughterhouse, surely. They seem perplexed, the poor animals (what's happening? what happened? what's going to happen?). Rafael is reminded of something Boris once told him about his relatives in Europe, who were taken to concentration camps like cattle to the slaughterhouse. A fate Boris, born in Brazil, had escaped. As a matter of fact, Boris would even have somehow escaped from a cattle truck like this one transporting him to his annihilation. Initially—for the first couple of kilometers—he might be perplexed or frightened; soon, however, he would find a way to reverse the situation. By bribing the guards, for instance. By offering them partnership in some business enterprise—say, public transportation. ("Why transport people to their death? These are passengers with a one-way ticket, passengers who don't pay for their tickets. A much better deal would be to transport workers and farmhands to the fields.") Guards and prisoners would escape with the truck, already transformed into the first vehicle of a large fleet that would eventually cover Europe, the Americas, and Africa. Boris is shrewd. Rafael has no doubt about it. He'll find the means to get over the problems besetting the finance company. But how, Rafael doesn't know.

He stops for a red light. A girl comes up to him, gestures to him to roll down the window (he always keeps the windows up—as a precaution against assaults). She must be Suzana's age, and dresses like his daughter: a long tunic, rawhide sandals, necklaces and bracelets. And the same dishevelled hair. A member of The New Essenes, for sure. "Jesus loves you, darling!" she shouts, holding a brochure out to him. Even without looking, Rafael knows what it is: a comic-strip story about an atheist ("I didn't believe in anything. All I wanted was money and power"), who is converted ("I returned to the arms of my sweet Jesus") and who finds happiness (". . . and now I'm happy"). So that's what Suzana does: She accosts drivers, calls them *darling*. The shamelessness. And why is she home, sleeping? If at least she got up early in the morning, like this girl. But no, she'd rather sleep in the daytime and go out at night. The shamelessness.

"I'm not interested," he says dryly.

"It doesn't matter, darling." The girl smiles; it's a somewhat forced smile, but a smile nevertheless. "Jesus still loves you. And I love you too. A kiss."

Taking hold of his head, she kisses him on the face, almost on the mouth. Then laughing, she steps back, and walks toward the car behind his. Embarrassed, he smoothes down his hair, glances around him. The truck driver is grinning:

"Why didn't you take advantage, buddy? The chick was giving

you the come-on and you missed the chance! You're a real fool, man."

The light turns green, Rafael, irritated, drives off revving the engine; he cuts in front of a sports car (what do you think you're doing, hey oldster, yells the driver, a young man wearing sunglasses), the traffic now flows freely, he passes car after car, still irritated, such shamelessness, such shamelessness.

Downtown, he leaves the car in a parking lot. He'll have to walk a few blocks to the finance company. So much the better. The walk will calm him down a little.

Carrying his briefcase, he walks along Rua da Praia. It's a beautiful day—that's something: a beautiful day—and he strolls down the street. It's a luxury he can afford, there's no need for him to hurry: less haste, more speed is what Julio used to say—poor Julio. Not so these office boys in their gaudy shirts, or these salesgirls with folded arms and a bewildered expression on their faces as they walk toward their place of work, the Lojas Brasileiras or Lojas Americanas or Casas Pernambucanas, or some other department store; or unlike these plainly dressed gentlemen heading for their offices or government bureaus. As he saunters along Rua da Praia, he searches for a familiar face; to greet someone on this street is almost a need, it would be a solace, particularly on this morning, a morning so replete with threatening omens.

But Rafael doesn't recognize a soul. He no longer knows anyone. The city has grown, there are no streetcars anymore on Rua Borges de Medeiros, no photographers at the entrance of Galeria Chaves. And no paperboys hollering out the headlines as they run down the street. Instead, there are now newsstands exhibiting, in addition to newspapers (*Franco remains in a coma*), brightly colored pornographic magazines. And the café once located in this old building, the café where he used to be a regular, is now a video arcade, and despite the early hour it's already jampacked. A group of young people stand admiring the skill with which a boy with an Afro wields an electronic weapon. The agonized repeating howls of the bear he's shooting mean the boy must be a good marksman. Rafael is familiar with this game, he's seen it played at another such establishment in Camboriú, a town in the state of Santa Catarina: The beast is shot at, it turns around, it's shot at again, it turns around—endlessly, relentlessly, until a sudden silence signifies that the player has used up all the shots entitled by the token he'd inserted into the machine; with a bored sigh he drops the weapon. Rafael walks on but soon stops again in front of a show window displaying adding machines. Now, that's something he likes; he knows everything about adding machines, he keeps himself well-informed about every new model that comes on the market. And these *are* new models, state-of-the-art machines. He'll come back at another time to talk to the manager and find out about prices. Now he can't, it's getting late, and he hurries away. He arrives at the headquarters of the finance company. An old but respectable-looking building, utterly unlike those buildings so common downtown, with their maze of large and small rooms housing companies that are often mere fronts for dens of racketeers, drug traffickers, and drug addicts. Boris knew what he was doing when he chose the *Dom Furtado de Mendonça Edifice* for the headquarters of his finance company. Boris always knows what he is doing.

Rafael gets into the elevator. He greets a company employee (arriving late for work, is she? No, she probably went out on an errand and is now back), who smiles at him obsequiously. And the elevator operator greets him effusively, then comments on the beautiful day: in his opinion the good weather will hold, the days will become increasingly more beautiful, will probably reach an almost unbearable level of beauty—an excessively radiant sun, a tremendously blue sky. No more clouds. Rain? Don't even think of it. Were Rafael to suggest, however, the possibility of losses that could be caused by the drought, the elevator man would immediately correct himself and say it's going to rain, it won't be long before it starts. A nice fellow, this old man; usually garrulous, yet unassuming. He's a black man. Whenever he talks about his ancestors—one of his favorite topics, by the way—he remarks that many of them were slaves. He mentions Palmares, a hideout for runaway slaves in the seventeenth century, and recalls his grandmother eulogizing the *Lei Áurea,* the law that abolished slavery in Brazil. His grandfather worked in the fields from sunrise to sunset, but he operates an elevator, forever marveling at this wonderful technology: "You press a button, and it starts working." Besides, he is in contact with important people, businessmen as well as beautiful women who leave a subtle scent in the elevator cab. Sometimes matters whispered about in the elevator have hit the headlines. He has already said to his wife that he could make a fortune with the things he knows; however, he admits that he hasn't mastered the art of piecing together a coherent picture from fragments of information; he hasn't been initiated into this game of power and money, which is full of unknown factors. Slavery still casts its shadow upon him. This, though, doesn't prevent him from saying at the moment when they get to Rafael's floor: "I've heard that the company is going down the tubes, Senhor Rafael." There's no time now to clarify the implications of this remark, made in a casual tone; nor to find out the reason behind the new way of addressing him, the reason why the *Doutor Rafael* of a few days ago gave way to the *Senhor Rafael*. The elevator doors open, others are waiting, he has to step out. He gets out, followed by the woman employee.

So people are already talking, he thinks to himself as he walks down the corridor. Even the elevator operator is talking, and if he is, it must be an open secret, probably the talk of the street, what's astonishing is that the newspapers haven't reported it yet (right below FRANCO REMAINS IN COMA: *Rumors about Situation of Finance Company Shake Stock Market*). Maybe it will hit the headlines tomorrow. Maybe there's already something on the radio.

"Good morning, Doutor Rafael."

The doorman, deferential, holds the large glass door open. On the wall opposite the entrance, right above the head of the pleasant, smiling receptionist, is the name of the company, *Pecúnia S.A.,* written in letters of burnished metal. Three thousand and six hundred square meters; three floors decorated by the famous Ballestra, of São Paulo. The image of strength and sobriety that Boris has always wanted his business enterprise to project is evident in the hardwood panels, the crystal chandeliers, the marble, the red carpets. The company emblem, designed by a heraldry expert, alludes to Boris's family name, Goldbaum: It depicts a gold tree against a blue background, with the legend *Arbor Aurea*. Something Rafael has always thought rather tacky, but the clients apparently go for it.

Walking past the reception area, he enters the waiting room; except for Boris's office, which has a private entrance, access to all the directors' and managers' offices is through this room. This large room (approximately ten meters long by eight meters wide) is known as the Coin Room. One of Boris's ideas: Near the farthest wall, dangling from ceiling-suspended metallic strings, are huge reproductions of ancient coins—the smallest one being nearly half a meter in diameter. The cruzado, the doubloon, the talent, the louis d'or, the penny—they swing in currents created by hidden fans, casting whimsical reflections about the room as they swirl in the spotlights aimed at them. (There's a rumor, which Boris hasn't refuted, that he owns several other collections of the same coins, in a smaller size but minted in gold and silver.) In the middle of this room stands the main attraction, again a reminder of Boris's family name: The gold tree. Small, with a thick furrowed trunk and sparse foliage, it resembles a bonsai. Hanging from the branches are half-open pods containing seeds like the ones found in bean pods, except that these are metal seeds and glow intensely in the spotlights. "Gold?" the visitors wonder, amazed. Boris has always left them wondering; they *must* be gold, though. Proof of this belief is the fact that the tree is kept inside an unbreakable glass dome. Embossed in gothic letters on an acrylic plaque is—by way of explanation—the history of the Gold Tree. The Gold Tree, the inscription informs, is one of the three trees mentioned in the Bible, the other two being the Tree of Life and the Tree of the Knowledge of Good and Evil. Unlike the first two, the Gold Tree was not in Paradise, but somewhere in the vast territory that stretched to the east of Eden, where it waited for dauntless and enterprising men to find it. The Gold Tree, the inscription goes on to explain, "derives its name from the powerful tropism of its roots toward this most precious of metals. Avidly searching for subterranean lodes, the roots infiltrate themselves into the hardest rocks. They solubilize the ore by secreting a certain liquid and then they absorb the ore; after circulating in the sap, the liquified gold is then deposited into the seeds in the pods, and eventually they become grains of the purest gold, their shape perfectly spherical. Although the Gold Tree can live for millennia, their total number nowadays probably doesn't exceed ten. This is because the adventurers that

35

come upon them are interested only in seizing the seeds in order to sell them. What they do not know is that these seeds, surprisingly enough, are capable of germinating, thus generating—after a long period of time—new Gold Trees. Wisdom, patience, discernment are thus richly rewarded." As a matter of fact, the family name Goldbaum was adopted by Boris's great-grandfather in Europe under the conviction that a name or a family name can condition one's destiny. In this case, the conviction came true: Boris does have his Gold Tree. Or if not the Gold Tree, the material possessions that gold can buy: real estate property, cars, land. He has even invested in art: Adjacent to the Coin Room is an art gallery with paintings and sculptures by famous Brazilian artists, and even a small Frans Post—not a widely known painter, but unquestionably the painting is an authentic piece of work by this Dutch master. A good collection worth several million dollars. However, what has made Boris Goldbaum famous throughout the country—he has even been profiled in the TV program *Fantástico*—is the Coin Room. The guest book has the autographs of distinguished visitors, among them, the Minister of Finance and the Minister of Projects. In the financial circles, the whole thing is regarded as an eccentricity, if not a publicity gimmick, but Boris says that the Coin Room is intended as some kind of homage to the all-time great financiers. Among them, he particularly admires the Rothschilds, to whom he claims to be distantly related. To verify the existence of this family connection, he had German genealogists do some research, which although far from finished, has already cost him a fortune; the initial findings, however, are encouraging—the experts believe that Boris's great-grandmother might have been a cousin of the first Rothschilds. It is the founders of the dynasty that Boris would dearly love to have as ancestors. He's not interested in any of the more contemporary Rothschilds: The barons who live in castles in France, who devote themselves to horsemanship, to philanthropy, to the cultivation of certain exclusive varieties of grapevines—these don't interest him at all. The Rothschilds he admires are the first ones, the five brothers. In every major European capital, each brother laid the foundations upon which a financial empire was to rise. Of the five, Boris's favorite is Nathan of London. In sharp contrast to his elegant brothers, Nathan was pudgy and unattractive. With his hands stuck into his pockets, he would stand by one of the pillars—Rothschild's pillar—in the London Stock Market. From there he would follow the bidding, and it was there that he pulled off the coup that was to increase the wealth of the family overnight.

Thanks to the speed with which his brothers' agents moved across Europe, he had been informed about Napoleon's defeat at Waterloo even before the British government knew anything about it. So what did he do with this valuable piece of information? Did he rush into buying English bonds and shares? No. On the contrary, he began to sell them, thus triggering a run on the stock market. *Rothschild is in the know,* the speculators thought, *if Rothschild is selling, it means that Napoleon has won.* The price of bonds and shares kept plummeting; then, at the eleventh hour, Nathan Rothschild made one final bid and everything was his for a ridiculously low price. A huge fortune made in a matter of minutes.

What a master stroke, says Boris with a sigh. That's art, my friend, pure art. It takes a genuine dramatic talent to pull off something like that. Full control of one's emotions is essential. The face: impassive, stony. The voice: steady, confident. The eyes: fixed. The trace of a smile, a tremor in the voice, a fleeting glitter in the eyes, and all is lost.

In those days, Boris goes on, the stock market was an adventure, it was life itself. Not anymore. Nowadays, it's the telex, the computer. Of course, personal abilities are still important, but intensely developed awareness, quick reasoning, a deep genuine knowledge, no longer count. Among the Rothschilds, it was Amschel, the founder of the dynasty, who first gave signs of having this special talent. He started out as a coin dealer. He would carefully keep his collection of ancient coins in small cases lined with velvet; to collectors, he would then send beautiful gothic-lettered catalogs illustrated with pictures of his coins. It was this passion of his that brought him and Wilhelm, the Prince of Hanover, together as friends: power now allied to money. With the prince's approval, he opened a small money-exchange house, the *Wechselstube*, where the currency of all the German feudal states could be exchanged.

Mayer Amschel Rothschild was not avaricious. He realized that money had to circulate. However, it wasn't without pain that he disposed of his coins. Before handing them over to a buyer, he would cast one last lingering gaze upon them, trying to fix in his mind the stylized drawing of a tree, the firm profile of a prince, the fancifully embossed number—a five, or a two, or a seven.

Boris has a portrait of Mayer Amschel, painted in the style of the Dutch masters. It depicts him as an old man, together with his wife, Gutele.

Boris has contradictory feelings about the matriarch of the Rothschild clan. On the one hand, he respects her: He can feel in her not only the age-old strength of Jewish mothers, but also an additional component—the firm determination of a Roman matron, could that be it? The end result was this woman's remarkable ability to lead her children along the road to victory. On the other hand, her presence in the Rothschild clan irritates and even repels Boris. It seems to him that the ship that so dauntlessly braved the treacherous sea of international finances could well dispense with a female figure. Money is a man's business. Only men possess the capacity for abstraction necessary to discern the face of the Goddess of Fortune in the numbers hastily jotted down on scraps of paper. To women, money represents merely the ordinary: a home, food, clothes. At best, jewelry, and not always real: low-carat gold, flawed diamonds. Costume jewelry. Boris definitely doesn't take women seriously. He acknowledges that the women's movement has made progress; in his publicity campaigns he addresses the female sex— *Women investors, at the Pecúnia you are given special consideration*—but that's about it. This Boris, whom gossip columnists refer to as *our most eligible bachelor* wants women only in bed, and then for a short period of time: a week, a month—until the moment when they start mentioning marriage. Then, gently but firmly, he sends them packing.

Of course, he pays a price for this attitude. There are investors, and good ones too, who won't entrust their money to the Pecúnia because they disapprove of what they consider frivolous behavior. And even Boris's own family puts pressure on him to grow up and get married. His mother and sisters are always phoning to tell him about various charming, intelligent—and even wealthy—young ladies. But Boris doesn't want to hear about them:

"I've already got all the charm I need, Mother," he shouts over the phone: The old woman is practically deaf. "I said that I've already got all the charm that I need! That's right! And all the intelligence too! And money I have too, Mother! That's right! I'm loaded with money!"

Boris doesn't like his mother and sisters too much; of his father, however, he has fond recollections. His father was a communist tailor who would spend his meager earnings on books. He knew Marx by heart and was able to answer such questions as: Can you quote paragraph two, page three, of the German edition of *The Eighteenth of Brumaire?*—and: Karl's first dog was called Toddy; what was the name of his second dog? His father was a first-class tailor, but had no personal ambitions. On the contrary: He hoped one day to use his expertise to get finally even with the bourgeoisie. He had even devised an incrimination scale based on the various kinds of fabric favored by the bourgeoisie: English cashmere indicated a ruthless despoiler (the sentence: death by hanging); S-120 linen, a bribetaker (the sentence: execution by firing squad); radiant alpaca wool, a crafty politician (the sentence: imprisonment in a cage for public exhibition) and so on. "Thank goodness," says Boris, "that my father died before he saw his son rich. He would never have forgiven me for my silk shirts; I'd get a life sentence, at the very least."

Rafael greets his secretary and goes into his office. Big, not as big as Boris's, but much bigger than the offices of the other directors; after all, Rafael is a trusted man: His rank is reflected in his desk (hardwood), in his chair (with a high back, not as high as Boris's, but still quite high, with five centimeters of the backrest protruding from his head), in the telephones (five of them, including a red phone for direct access to Boris), in the comfortable armchairs, in the thick carpet. The pictures on the walls are not worth millions like the ones in Boris's art gallery but they are signed by the most prominent painters in the arts community of the southern part of the country.

Rafael sits down, places the Samsonite briefcase—a gift from Boris, who purchased it in New York's Fifth Avenue—on the desk. A beautiful briefcase—solid, dependable, really impressive; it's true that for a while Rafael fantasized about this briefcase: a fantasy about opening it one day and finding a rattlesnake lying on his papers; but that's already in the past. His fears are now of a different kind.

He opens the briefcase: There's the notebook. He takes it out, puts it on the desk, sits staring at it.

An old notebook with a torn, stained cover. The kind that school children use for their homework and that adults sometimes like to use. Heaven knows why. Out of a yearning for their own childhood, perhaps.

No, Rafael doesn't recall seeing this notebook before. But then he hardly remembers anything from his childhood; it's amazing how other people can recall so many things from their first years of life; he can't: It's as if he were looking at the past through opaque glass. Shadowy forms, nothing but shadowy forms. Slowly he leafs through the notebook. A journal? No, more like a record of scattered annotations, phrases and words that a person jots down almost at random, for reasons known only to him. As for the handwriting, he can't say if it's his father's. As a matter of fact, he has never seen much of Rafael Mendes's handwriting, except for his signature. Besides, there's nothing unusual about this handwriting he is now looking at, quite ordinary it is, in the lilac ink popular in his father's time. A graphologist would probably be able to disclose a little more about his father's character, and even throw light upon the reasons behind his abrupt departure ("Your father, although a physician, was really a potential warrior. Notice the way he crosses his T's with a violent stroke—like someone wielding a sword. He had an uncontrollable vocation for action—these curlicues, don't they look like smoke rising from a burning city?" "Could this description apply to a revolutionary?" "Yes. A revolutionary. Why not? Trotsky's handwriting looks pretty much like his. Are you familiar with the life of Trotsky, sir?" "No, I'm afraid I'm not very interested in such matters." "Neither am I—please, don't get the idea that I'm a subversive or something like that. I happen to be familiar with Trotsky's handwriting because I have a book with a specimen of his signature. There is a resemblance between the two signatures, I can assure you.") On the surface, none of the annotations makes much sense. What does it mean, for instance: *The Prophet Jonah—glass?* And what or who is *Maimonides? The Inquisition*: This he knows what it is, of course, and ditto for *The Dutch Invasions*. Both must be related to his father's interest in History; ditto for *Colombo and Palmares*, the colonies established by fugitive slaves; but *the treasure of the Essenes* is again a mystery (a legend? something like the legend of the Gold Tree?). And there are also small drawings: ancient weapons (a bow and an arrow, an apple, a halberd), escutcheons, flags that Rafael has never seen (but what does he know about flags, anyway?). Finally, the following verses:

Malato está el fijo del rey, malato que no salvaba,
siete dotores lo miran, los mijores de Grenada.
Siete suben y siete abajan, ninguno le face nada
ainda manca de venir el de la barba envellutada.
Calentura fuerte tiene, las tripas tiene danadas.
Tres horas de vida tiene, hora y media han pasadas.
En esa horica y media—hasedle bien por su alma.

And the words of a lullaby:

Duerme, duerme, mi angelico,
hijico chico de tu nacion.

In Spanish: Meaningful to someone who went to Spain. But what kind of Spanish is this? It doesn't resemble the kind spoken nowadays in Buenos Aires, for instance, the kind of Spanish Rafael is familiar with from several visits to that city. He has never heard anyone recite this poem, nor has he ever seen it in print anywhere. It seems to be a Spanish dialect, but where is it spoken? In which *nación*? Why did his father write down this particular poem? What does it mean? Rafael heaves a sigh. The notebook hasn't really been of much help. At least the photograph helped him recall his father, the face he had forgotten; when he was a teenager he used to imagine his father as having the face of a soldier photographed by Robert Capa, a photograph Rafael had seen in a book about the Spanish Civil War. A dramatic photograph: Hit square on the chest by a Falangist bullet, the man is falling backward, his arms wide open: his right hand still holds the rifle, but the weapon is now useless because he is about to die, no doubt about it; and because he died, Rafael appropriated that man's face on which pain and surprise were stamped, and superimposed it upon his father's face. Now Rafael no longer needs this borrowed face for he has a face, although it is old and out of focus; a face but still no answers. To sum up, what does he know about his father at his hour, on this day? That he was a physician and a humanitarian—which he learned from an old lady, one of the many old ladies who entrusted their savings to the Pecúnia: "Your father was very kind, Doutor Rafael. I consulted him once; very charming and kind he was; a bit eccentric, but kind."

Eccentric. That's what his mother also says, her husband was eccentric. Yes, but what does she mean by *eccentric*? That Dr. Rafael was crazy? That he was different? And why different? Because he didn't say much? Because he read a lot? True, he did read a lot. According to the owner of the secondhand bookstore who bought Dr. Rafael's library, he had amassed a large number of fine history books. Mostly Braziliana, but also some World History. And in a large cabinet with glass doors he kept a collection of assorted curiosities: ancient maps, astrolabes, sextants, telescopes, compasses, retorts, hourglasses, clepsydras.

His mother hadn't wanted to keep any of it; she offered all those objects to an antiquarian: "Take everything." "But I'm rather embarrassed, ma'am, they are real treasures." "I don't care. Take everything." "Wouldn't you like to think it over, ma'am?" "Take everything. Or I'll throw them away." "For heavens' sake, please, don't do that! I'll take them." He did. And of his father's belongings there is nothing left.

Yes, that's about all Rafael knows. There are some memories, too. ...Dim images...Sensations...A mustache brushing gently against his face when he was a little boy...A deep baritone voice singing a lullaby. . . But it's difficult to recall such things clearly.

There's a knock on the door. Startled, Rafael hastily puts the notebook away in a drawer and locks it.

"Come in."

"Excuse me, Doutor."

It's the office boy coming in with a long computer printout: the balance sheet showing the transactions of the previous day. Still upset, Rafael thanks him. The young man stands looking at Rafael:

"Are you feeling all right, Doutor? Is there anything you need?"

Rafael thanks him: No, he doesn't need anything. He's fine, a slight headache, that's all. It will soon go away. The young man, however, still lingers at the door. Finally, he is bold enough to ask:

"Doutor Rafael . . . Is it true what they are saying?"

Rafael looks at him, surprised.

"What? What are they saying?"

"That this company is about to close down."

He takes one step forward:

"Look, Doutor Rafael. If it is true, I want to let you know, sir, and Senhor Boris too, that you can count on me for anything at anytime. Senhor Boris—"

He stops abruptly, wipes his eyes.

"Senhor Boris has been like a father to me. He got me this job, he helped me buy a small house out there in Alvorada, he paid for the medicine that my wife had to take when she was ill. I'm deeply grateful to Senhor Boris for everything I have, Doutor. Really grateful."

Rafael stares at him, surprised. This man, deeply grateful to Boris? That's news to me! Well, well, was Boris then helping this insignificant, boring little man, so insignificant that Rafael can't even think of his name, and so annoying that people call him Sticky? That's news, disconcerting news; it shows that he doesn't really know Boris as well as he thought he did, despite their long acquaintanceship. Definitely, there are things that the computer printouts don't tell.

"All right, St— All right, young man. Thank you for your concern. It's quite comforting to know that we can depend on such dedicated employees."

As soon as the man leaves, Rafael unfolds the long printout and begins to peruse it. He does his own calculations; for the next half hour he presses the keys of the calculator with annoyance, at times cursing under his breath. When he is finished, he flings the mechanical pencil on the desk, leans back in the chair. It's worse than he thought. The crack, which began to widen a month before, has become a huge hole. The situation is now unmanageable. The fears of the neurologist, of the office boy are well founded; the Pecúnia is indeed in the red. The deficit, just taking into account the bills of exchange without coverage, amounts to thirty million dollars. Besides, there are all those floating checks, and the bank loans, and the fat payroll. "I have the highest rate of profit potential in the market," Boris has often boasted, and indeed he has, but this situation has its price too, and then there is the matter of the disastrous mismanagement of the company, and all those parties given to entrepreneurs and investors—the whiskey and the champagne in bottles carrying the emblem of the Pecúnia, the Gold Tree. It's all over now.

Picking up the red phone, he dials Boris's number. "He's not in yet," his secretary informs. "Let me know as soon as he comes in," says Rafael. He can barely control his annoyance: Here's the ship springing leaks everywhere and Boris doesn't even put in an appearance. He might be the financial wizard people say he is, but he is intrinsically irresponsible. Like Suzana. "Oh, shit," he mutters.

He rises to his feet, paces about the office; he opens a cabinet, takes out a bottle and a glass, pours out a shot of whiskey, then sits down on an armchair, sipping the drink while looking at the view absentmindedly: The heart of the city, the shimmering river, a freighter slowly sailing away. I wish I were on that ship, he thinks. Traversing the sea. Toward some far-off region.

The phone rings. A woman's voice, husky, sensual.

"It's me. Celina."

Celina Cordeiro. Ex-Miss State of Rio Grande do Sul, ex-wife of a wealthy industrialist, a well-known socialite. Boris hired her as the company's public relations person: Her job consists in making contacts with various people, in finding potential investors, such as wealthy farmers; she's very good at what she does. Rafael's admiration for Celina is independent of the affair he's having with her. An educated, intelligent woman with class. No longer as beautiful as she was in the days when every newspaper carried her picture; she was in a car accident that marred her face; the scars, despite several plastic operations, are still visible on her beautiful, altered face. But she still has a gorgeous body, and in bed she's an ardent lover. Her affair with Rafael has obviously nothing to do with love; it's part of a plan, but so far she hasn't made any demands on him. They usually meet at noon, at a very convenient place—a kind of hotel located downtown, a place with an interesting detail: Access to this building is either through a door that opens onto a tranquil side street or through a tobacco shop. A tobacco shop! The elegant gentleman seemingly looking for fine tobaccos is actually on his way to a tryst. He is not interested in the pipes with fanciful bowls. Nor is he interested in the amber cigarette holders; nor in the Cuban cigars, the cigarillos, the table top models of chrome-plated cigarette lighters; nor in the pocket knives, the daggers with etched blades; nor even in the lottery tickets. This gentleman is about to discreetly enjoy a minor affair of the heart. Without glancing at the shop owner, who leans on the counter reading a newspaper, Rafael draws aside the velvet curtains at the back of the small store, walks down a narrow, dark corridor, reaches an inner, Spanish style courtyard with a small public fountain: a peaceful, picturesque place right in the heart of a city that grows at a vertiginous pace. Another corridor starts from this courtyard leading to three apartments set aside exclusively for the use of a few, selected customers. Celina prefers the apartment in the middle, the one with mirrors.

An artist in sex, this Celina. With her, it's never the same: There are always new positions, new techniques—for she has studied the subject thoroughly: Under the name of her dead sister Cornélia, she gets all the books she needs to keep herself up-to-date from a mail-order catalog, or else, disguised behind dark glasses, she buys them from newsstands located in distant neighborhoods. She is an expert in the Oriental modes of copulation (these people are really well versed in this subject. Who would have thought so by looking at them, slightly built, with slanted eyes); one mode she particularly fancies requires that the man and the woman do it on a horse galloping across a vast meadow—being a city dweller, though, it's unlikely that she'll ever find the opportunity to try it out.

"There's no need to identify yourself, Celina." He tries to make a wisecrack: "This aphrodisiac voice of yours—"

"It's been a long time since we last talked, Rafael."

The tone of voice is aggrieved; contained, but bitter.

He makes excuses:

"I'm bogged down with work, as you know. I haven't had time to see you."

"It's not as if I were living on some other planet. . . . Oh, forget it. I've got to talk to you, Rafael. Today."

"Today, Celina? But I can't today, I'm really awfully busy."

"All right," she says, with impatience. "Then it'll have to be over the phone. I want to know everything there is to know about the situation of the Pecúnia, Rafael. Tell it like it is. In black and white."

Ah, so that's what it is. She too has got wind of the situation. Which is not surprising, considering that even the elevator operator and the office boy are already discussing the matter. Rafael tries, senselessly, to sound unconcerned: "Now then, Celina, it's just a rumor. We've had some problems with cash flow, but this—"

She cuts him short—and her tone of voice is now ominous, threatening:

"Let me tell you something, Rafael: You can't bamboozle me, do you hear? Don't think that you and Boris can take me to the cleaners. I happen to know that the Pecúnia is hanging by a thread, and everybody is saying that the government is about to step in, and that you and Boris are decamping, heading for Paraguay. But I'm warning you: If you're actually thinking of pulling off this swindle, I want compensation, Rafael. Substantial compensation for everything I've done for you, and I've done a lot, as you well know. I demand an indemnity, I want a year's salary as severance. Otherwise I'll raise a howl. I'll spill the beans, and you know that I have plenty of friends in the press who can concoct some really scabrous story. And I have connections in the area of security too. I'll smear you, Rafael. You'd better believe me."

Rafael reassures her, saying there's nothing in the rumors; the company is going through a difficult phase, but has the means to weather the difficulties; it's not true that the government is going to step in; on the contrary, the government is interested in preventing any panic in the stock markets, something like this would only tarnish the image of the country abroad, and frighten away the foreign investors.

"Watch out, Rafael," she says, still rather suspicious. "Watch out. You I can trust, you're a decent guy. Boris, however—"

"Don't worry about Boris."

"All right. We'll wait and see."

She hangs up. Almost immediately another phone starts ringing. It's Boris's secretary: He won't be in this morning; he wants Rafael to have lunch with him at his house; his chauffeur is at Rafael's disposal.

"All right."

Typical of Boris. That's how he settles everything: with a lunch or dinner invitation, with a small intimate party; with a phone call to Rio, or to Brasilia, or to New York, or to Zurich; with a tip, substantial or not; or with a gift, expensive or not. Resigned, Rafael folds the computer printout, opens the briefcase—and it's then that he sees the piece of paper. A leaflet, now yellowed; it must have been among his father's belongings:

> "Read to the end! You might find it useful! The occult sciences—genealogy—chiromancy—graphology—astrology—phrenology—sensibility to electromagnetic waves—telepathy—spiritual healing. Genealogy is a positive science. Who was your father? Who was your grandfather? Our ancestors determine our fate—the living will always be, and increasingly so, governed by the dead. Bring us your old photographs—letters—notebooks—family documents. By consulting Professor Samar-Kand you will be able to find out about the most important facts of your life. Alchemy too. Cabala, the science of numbers. Porto Alegre has never seen anything like this. Unheard of in the metropolis of the pampas. Modern Tarot cards. If you are disheartened, spiritually upset, if you are faced with disharmony in your blessed home,

with bad business deals, with lawsuits, with separations, or if you are having difficulties in succeeding in life, etc., don't forget: Professor Samar-Kand has the solution."

Followed by an address. But what is this? wonders Rafael, intrigued. What kind of nonsense is this, the occult sciences? Did his father have anything to do with this?

He turns the leaflet over and, oh, yes, there it is: a message. It seems that this professor something doesn't have any stationery for he had to use the back of the leaflet to write his message:

"Dear Senhor Rafael Mendes. These things belonged to your father. I have some other objects and papers that might interest you. Please get in touch with me." Rafael heaves a sigh. Now he knows: There is someone in Porto Alegre who can talk to him about his father.

Who is this professor? The leaflet suggests a con artist; could his father have been in any way involved with a con artist? But he can't make suppositions based on a leaflet; besides, con artist or not, he intends to seek out this man, so he had better wait before passing an opinion on him. Moreover, there's a far more pressing matter right now: He must talk to Boris. He picks up the briefcase and walks toward the door. The phone starts ringing. It's not the red phone, it's the one on the PBX system. With his hand on the doorknob, Rafael hesitates. Finally (*shit!*), he turns back and answers the phone. "Your wife," says the secretary. He heaves a sigh; and then he sighs again (how many times has he already sighed this morning?).

"Okay, I'll take the call."

A click, a silence, and soon after:

"Hello! Rafael? Hello!" says Helena, sounding anxious.

"Yes, it's me, Helena." Rafael tries not to lose his temper. "It's me, you can talk. Is something wrong?"

"Ah, Rafael," she says tearfully, "this telephone of yours is so complicated! Rafael, what will become of her, Rafael? Tell me, what will become of her?"

"But what happened?" asks Rafael, torn between impatience and alarm.

"She didn't sleep home last night, Rafael. Again. She didn't come home until early this morning, the maid told me. Did you know that she came home only this morning?"

"Yes."

"And why didn't you tell me, Rafael? I'm her mother, Rafael, I've got to know about it!"

"Listen, Helena." Rafael tries to remain cool and collected, somebody has to. "You were asleep, and you know what the doctor said . . ."

"What the doctor said!" She blows up. "I don't give a damn about what the doctor said! I want to know where my daughter spent the night, Rafael."

"Probably with those friends of hers, the ones from the sect—"

"Sect, my foot! They haven't seen her for a month, they keep phoning all the time, asking about her!"

"Then—"

"Then what, Rafael? We've got to know what's happening to her, Rafael! I'm afraid she got herself into a jam, Rafael."

"What do you want me to do?" says Rafael, already annoyed.

"What do I want you to do?" She's now shouting. "Rafael, for heavens' sake, you're her father!"

"Listen, Helena, I can't talk to you now, an urgent problem has come up and I have to see to it. But I'll find a solution for this situation with Suzana, I promise you, Helena, I will."

"You will, Rafael?" She's in tears. "But how, Rafael? How?"

"Leave it to me, Helena. I'll find a solution somehow, I've already told you."

Silence.

"Helena?"

"Yes, Rafael. I've heard you. Bye now, Rafael."

"Bye, Helena. I love you, did you hear? I love you. Bye."

He hangs up, picks up the briefcase again, and again walks toward the door.

Boris next.

R afael first met him during his college days. Boris would show up at the school quite often; he represented various publishers of technical books, so he would say, but in fact he was a salesman. And what a salesman he was, that slightly-built Jew with bright eyes and a rather ironic smile. He was good at persuading the instructors to recommend his textbooks to their students, he offered gifts to anyone who bought over a certain minimum amount of books, he sponsored dinner parties to welcome first-year students. And Rafael himself was unable to resist his sales pitch: He bought several books on economics and mathematics. They were good books actually, Rafael had no complaints. The two of them had hit it off right away; after class they would go somewhere for a beer and talk late into the night. The stock market was already Boris's hobbyhorse. He would say modestly that he knew nothing about the subject—he was a high-school dropout—and he would ask Rafael to explain to him the theory behind the stock market. In fact, Boris's knowledge, empirical though it was, was far superior to his; Rafael was amazed at the vivacity, at the sharpness of Boris's mind. "You'd make it in the stock market," Rafael would say. But Boris would dismiss the idea with a gesture:

"I don't think so, Rafael. Such things are not for me. They're for people with a long tradition in this line of work, not for the son of a communist tailor."

After quitting college, Rafael lost touch with him; when they ran into each other again years later, Boris already owned a small brokerage firm; from there to opening his own finance company, it was one single leap, a quick trajectory that Rafael followed, already in his capacity as director of the company. And as friend. At least once a week Boris would have lunch at Rafael's place. He felt at home there; you're my family, he would say, and it was true—he couldn't stand his relatives, who, he claimed, were only after his money. He was very fond of Suzana, would bring her gifts, take her to the circus, or to a movie in the afternoon. But he never married. And nowadays, a hardened bachelor, he leads the life of a mogul, of a tycoon, living in a big house in Vila Assunção, a veritable manor with swimming pools, tennis courts, huge garages for his imported cars, kennels for his Dalmatians. He entertains frequently and is constantly surrounded by gorgeous and famous women. With his arms around them, he lets himself be photographed for the gossip columns, something that Rafael disapproves of, not because of moralism, but because this kind of behavior could mar the image of the finance company. Paradoxically, this hasn't been the case: on the contrary, the more Boris's name appears in the newspapers and magazines, the more he gets new clients; it seems that people want to partake of the secret of this successful social-climber by investing their money in his company.

On the other hand, Boris himself seems to attach little importance to all this luxury surrounding him. He says that he remains a simple man, the difference between his present lifestyle and his lifestyle at the time when he was a book salesman being merely a matter of degree. The Mercedes Benz is just a bigger, more comfortable Volkswagen; as for women—whether it's one, two, or three—what difference does it make? One single woman can offer as many varied and exciting experiences as three or four of these actresses everyone so admires. A swimming pool? Just an outsized bathtub in the open air. Imported wines? Some of them can't hold a candle to our own white rum. Caviar? In the stomach, digested, it's just like any other food. People starving to death? Sure, it happens; it's not his fault, though. There's no use feeling guilty. What's important is to keep money in circulation, to create jobs for these wretchedly poor people. The greatest satisfaction that one can derive from an enterprise such as the Pecúnia, he argues, is to be able to accomplish—and what's more, accomplish in an atmosphere of constant excitement—a job that has no pre-set routine, a job that brings in daily surprises, as if it were a game. He pays a price for this: he is distrusted, envied, even hated; besides, there are few people whom he can trust. "I have no friends," he says, "just contacts."

In the Mercedes, Rafael is taken to Boris's house. The chauffeur, a likeable mulatto, chatters away, he talks about the weather, he discusses soccer, and before he starts commenting on the situation of the finance company, Rafael asks him to turn on the radio—he wants to listen to the noon newscast. Franco remains in a coma, a minister

51

(not the Minister of Finance) arrives in Rio Grande do Sul to sign agreements, there was an accident on Highway BR-101. The newscast ends with the signature tune. Nothing—luckily—about the Pecúnia. Soon after the ARE YOU READY FOR THE GREAT ADVENTURE OF YOUR LIFE? the chauffeur, at Rafael's request, turns off the radio.

They arrive at Boris's mansion, the gatekeeper opens the wide gate to let them in. The butler conducts Rafael to Boris. Wearing dark glasses and a spiffy wine-colored robe, he lies stretched out on a deck chair by the swimming pool. By himself, Rafael can see, relieved. Well, that's something. No gossip columnists or women in scanty bikinis. By himself, sipping whiskey. Boris signals to him to sit down. Rafael sits down uncomfortably on the edge of a deck chair; dressed in a suit and tie, he feels rather ridiculous sitting on a deck chair by a swimming pool. Boris doesn't notice. He seems rather withdrawn today.

"I'm glad you asked me to come over," begins Rafael, "because I really must talk to you. In private."

"All right, Rafael, and I must talk to you too." Boris's *r*'s have a pronounced trill—the kind of articulation Rafael used to think of as being typically Jewish, until he met Julio, who also rolled his *r*'s heavily. Not being Jewish, Julio looked upon this peculiarity of his as a lucky sign: "Maybe I'll get to be as rich as the boss," he would say, alluding to Boris in a slightly mocking tone. Poor Julio. Not even his *r*'s saved him.

The butler approaches.

"What are you having?" asks Boris.

Rafael hesitates: Another whiskey at this time of a working day seems unadvised. However, he asks for one. The butler serves him with measured, but in a way, elegant gestures. Rafael waits until he moves away, then he begins:

"Well now, Boris, it's this matter with—"

He is cut short by a clamor that comes from the house, where some heated argument is going on. Soon afterward a woman bursts through the back door:

"Ah, there he is! I knew he was home! What a pack of liars, finks, all of them!"

Rafael recognizes her; she's Lina Andrade, a television actress with whom Boris was involved for a long time; she was in Rio recently, playing a minor role in a soap opera. Fuming, she advances toward them:

"You told them to tell me you weren't home, Boris! You wanted to deceive me! Me, of all people! Me, who has never played dirty tricks on you!"

Embarrassed, Rafael rises to his feet; Boris, however, doesn't even budge; impassive, he watches the woman shouting, her finger raised:

"I want my money, Boris! I want my money and the apartment that you promised me! A shelter in Leblon, remember? I want them now, Boris! Everybody's saying you're on the brink of bankruptcy. Whether you're broke or not, I don't give a damn, but if you try to double-cross me, I'll go to the newspapers, Boris, you bet I will. I'll tell all about your little parties, do you hear?"

Boris is unfazed. The young woman, furious: "You scoundrel!" Grabbing a glass, she hurls it at him. Boris ducks; then, leaping from the deck chair, he slaps her on the face so violently that she staggers, loses her balance, and falls into the swimming pool. She sinks—her wig is afloat—but soon she rises to the surface, flouncing about and shouting that she'll come down with pneumonia, the water is ice-cold.

"A lie," says Boris. "It's a heated swimming pool."

He asks the servants to get her out of the water and to drive her to her hotel. Then he turns to Rafael, who stands dumbfounded.

"But go on with what you were saying, Rafael."

"Later," says Rafael. "Not now, not under these circumstances. . . . You can see for yourself, Boris. It's impossible under the circumstances."

Boris sits straight up on the deck chair, takes off his glasses:

"Listen, Rafael. We've got to talk. About a very serious matter."

"At the Pecúnia, then."

"No, not there." Boris hesitates. "Are you staying for lunch?"

"No." Rafael can barely disguise his irritation. "I can't, Boris. I'm up to my neck in work."

That's a clear accusation, which Boris chooses to ignore:

"All right," he says. "But listen, we really have to talk. I'll phone you later, Rafael."

Rafael rises to his feet: "I'm leaving now," he announces. They gaze at each other for a moment, and what is in their gaze? Trust, and at the same time, distrust. Affection, and at the same time, anger. And—perplexity. In Rafael's gaze, perhaps more distrust; in Boris's gaze, perhaps more affection, an affection generated by a long friendship. But in Boris's gaze there's also a minute component of mockery; and mockery, irony, are alien to the makeup of Rafael's character. Perplexity, yes, it has to do with him, especially under the present circumstances. But the perplexity doesn't neutralize the irony, and if their gazes were, say, laser rays, and if the outcome of the fight between the two men were to depend on the intensity of such rays. . . .

No. They do not fight against each other. Occasionally Boris challenges Rafael to a game of tennis, which is played according to a veritable ritual, with Boris in an impeccable outfit, holding his excellent racquet by the handle, and Rafael, rather awkward in his bermuda shorts and old tennis shoes, marching abreast toward the tennis court, and then taking their positions, like real gentlemen; true, once the game starts, it's the usual frenzied scramble, with Rafael, a poor player, running like crazy for the ball, hitting it frantically, trying to get rid of it at all costs. Today, though, there won't be a tennis match, just an exchange of glances full of minute components. Saying goodbye, Rafael departs.

Rafael goes into his office, sits down, stares dejectedly at the stack of papers before him. I'm not up to it, he concludes. He decides he'll get out of the office, take a walk about the premises, sound off the morale of the staff. He walks down the halls past several departments. Through the open doors of the offices he sees the employees absorbed in their work. Are they aware of the situation? Quite likely. However, they are probably not very worried.

After all, to them the Pecúnia represents merely a job; a good job—Boris pays them very well—but nothing more than a job. At the end of their working day they turn off the calculators, cover the typewriters with dust covers, and leave in a hurry. They go home to play with their children, to watch television. If the Pecúnia goes under, chances are they'll find another job with another finance company; or with a store or a bank. From the office previously occupied by Julio, his replacement, an accountant, greets Rafael deferentially.

Poor Julio. In his early thirties at the time of his death. A thin young man with intense eyes. On second thought—a bit crazy, but always properly dressed. His neckties perhaps a touch too bold, but not bold enough to attract attention or to rouse suspicion.

An only son, his father had wanted him to study medicine or engineering; Julio, however, had other plans. This country is booming, he would say, and anyone with a keen nose will make a fortune. Julio believed in his personal magnetism; he had taken a course in the psychology of salesmanship, he had memorized good jokes, which often fell flat because of a certain anxiety in his voice. Ever since joining the finance company in 1968, Julio had been waiting for the big chance. When prices in the stock market began to rise, he believed that the right moment had come. He sold his house, persuaded his father to lend him his savings, and even went as far as—this came to light later—to embezzle money from the finance company. He drew on the dollars—quite a large sum it was—that Boris had given him for safekeeping. But Julio had every intention of making restitution of everything.

Prices in the stock market were skyrocketing. Sell, his friends would say. Sell, certain shadowy forms kept saying in his dreams. Sell, his wife said timidly and he slapped her in the face for meddling in his affairs. A while longer, he would say, just a little while longer, and I'll be a millionaire, and then yes, then I'll sell my shares and start my own investment company.

And then prices began to fall.

At first Julio wasn't fully aware of what was really happening. His contacts in Rio and São Paulo informed him that it was nothing serious, that the stock markets were having the jitters, that they would soon recover.

The markets didn't recover. Prices kept plummeting. There was still a moment when Julio could have sold without suffering a loss; but he was unwilling to lose even one cent of his profits. To exclude himself from the winner's team? No way. Later, it was no longer a matter of profits, but a matter of saving something, anything, a matter of handing over the rings in order to keep one's fingers; and in the end, not even the fingers could be saved. Julio was growing thinner and thinner; his eyes now looked hallucinated; at times he would show up for work unshaven, without a necktie. He confided in Rafael what was happening; even knowing that things were pretty bad, he still wouldn't sell his shares. There must be some manipulation going on behind the scenes, he would say; investors are waiting for prices to hit bottom before they buy everything back. Then, lowering his voice: *I know from a reliable source that the multinationals are about to invest zillions in the stock market.*

One Friday Julio announced to his wife that he intended to spend the weekend at the seaside. "In this rainy weather?" she asked. "I have to do some thinking," he said. She offered to go with him, but he rejected her suggestion.

He didn't return home on the following Sunday, nor on the following Monday and Tuesday. On Wednesday his car was found abandoned on a deserted beach; but there was no sign of Julio. The possibility of suicide was raised; it was expected that the Atlantic would eventually return the body, although changed beyond all recognition. The newspapers reported briefly on the incident and soon dropped the subject, much to the relief of Julio's widow, who didn't want any scandal. The only relative to show up at the finance company was his brother-in-law, who came to collect Julio's personal belongings; before leaving the premises, he told Rafael that he held Boris responsible for what had happened.

Rafael was outraged: "Why didn't you tell him, Boris, that Julio had stolen thirty thousand dollars from you?"

"What for?" said Boris with a shrug. "Julio is dead. We'll respect his memory. I liked him, Rafael, I really did. A nice fellow. Serious, dedicated, he could have had a brilliant career as a financier—but he was irresolute, he vacillated. And in this business, as you know, moral fiber is needed. Besides, we mustn't lose our cool over thirty thousand dollars."

He hesitated for a while, then he added:

"Besides, it was counterfeit money."

"Counterfeit?" Rafael was flabbergasted.

Boris lit a cigarette.

"It can happen. Even to me, it can happen. Somebody passed me bogus dollar bills. Somebody I trusted. On the day when Julio disappeared I got a phone call from Miami saying that I had been taken in. I still tried to find the whereabouts of this person, but with no success. . . . Fate, Rafael."

Respect his memory. Rafael wondered, had the dollars been genuine, would Boris still have felt the same way? He came to the conclusion, reached first with sorrow, then with anger, that he didn't know. And he didn't want to know.

He never brought up this subject again.

Rafael goes back to his office, takes the notebook out of the drawer, opens it at random. *Malato está el fijo del rey.* What does it mean? Yes, something like *the king's son is ill*; but which king? Why did his father write down this poem? He opens the briefcase to put the notebook inside—and there it is, Professor Samar-Kand's leaflet.

I've got to see this man, Rafael thinks. I've got to see him to get to the bottom of this matter. What do you know about my father, sir? Why did he go to Spain? How did he die? Where is he buried?

Questions, questions: he needs the answers. Today. This very day. At least these questions will have answers. That is: maybe.

The phone rings. It's his secretary.

"There's a newspaper reporter here."

Rafael dials Boris's secretary:

"What's going on? What's this reporter doing here?"

"He's been coming every day. He wants information about the Pecúnia. I've spoken to Boris, he wants you to see the man."

"But where is Boris?"

"At home. He said he would be in later."

Shit, mutters Rafael, hanging up. That's all he needs now: a newsman. And Boris doesn't want to talk to him. Boris, who knows how to deal with newsmen, who often boasts about being favorably portrayed in the press—the intrepid financier who started from scratch and worked his way up—Boris now doesn't want to talk to the press. Rafael sighs, then tells his secretary on the interphone to send the newsman in.

A young man in shabby clothes, but wearing a necktie, walks in. Pencil and paper at the ready, he wants to know—what else?—about the situation of the Pecúnia. Any truth behind these rumors afloat throughout the city?

Before replying, Rafael considers him for a moment. What is this young man trying to do? What kind of a reporter is he? A left-winger searching for a scandal that will expose the evils of capitalism? An opportunist using his position to gain access to the financial circles? Or an impartial drone who bureaucratically carries out the task he has been assigned? Impossible to tell. He won't know until the story appears in the newspaper—if it does. Because Boris might already be pulling strings.

For half an hour Rafael discourses on the situation of the financial market; he chooses his words carefully, and successfully parries the more embarrassing questions. The reporter scribbles. At the end of the interview, he says goodbye with a smile and leaves.

Wiping his forehead, Rafael sits back in the chair. Boris will have to do something, he will have to use his connections. It's not the first time that the finance company is going through a tumultuous phase;

Boris has always managed to find a way out, either with the help of some politicians or of certain friends in Zurich, in South Africa—gold in the first instance, diamonds in the second. But now Rafael doesn't even want to think about this. He's had a bellyful. With an abrupt gesture, he closes the briefcase and gets to his feet.

"I'm going out," he announces to his secretary on the interphone. "I don't know if I'll be back in the afternoon."

But he doesn't head straight for the address in the leaflet. He decides to stop at his mother's house, which is on the way out there. He doesn't quite know yet what he'll do at his mother's: Should he tell her that he has received a box containing his father's belongings? Show her the notebook? What for? To upset her? Why should he make her rake over old ashes?

He arrives at her house—the same old house of his childhood days. His mother lives there with an old servant, despite Rafael's and Helena's efforts to persuade her to move closer to them. Once they even rented a small-but-decent apartment for her in a building with a caretaker and electronically monitored main entrance. In vain. Alzira Mendes, who is over sixty, remains as stubborn as ever: She says she doesn't want to live near her son and her daughter-in-law, that there's no reason why she should, and that she's not afraid of burglars—a fact reaffirmed now as Rafael finds her front door wide open. And there she is, seated before the television set, a small woman, thin and prim, wearing an old (but clean and befitting) dress. Standing next to her—for Alzira has never allowed her servant to sit down in her presence—is the black old woman who was only a young girl when she first came to work for Alzira; now she's almost blind, which is why she keeps asking: "And now, Mother, what's happening now on the television, Mother?" She calls Alzira mother, which Rafael used to find amusing; now, however, it strikes him as merely sad.

"Good afternoon, folks."

The face of the old servant lights up. "Look who's here, Mother!" Groping about, she draws closer to Rafael, then embraces him effusively.

"Our boy, Mother! Our little Rafael!"

She touches his face with the tips of her tremulous fingers.

"Getting more and more handsome, this boy! Don't you think so, Mother? Don't you think so? You can see better than me."

Alzira doesn't reply. It's part of the game: For a few minutes she'll ignore the presence of her son, her eyes fixed on the television screen; then she'll finally turn to him, asking abruptly: "So, what brings you here, glad or sad tidings?"

But Rafael doesn't feel like following the usual ritual. He removes the notebook and the photograph from the briefcase.

"What's that?" she asks, suspicious.

"Something I received early this morning, Mom. I think they were Dad's."

She is startled, but she controls herself and feigns indifference.

"Your father's? I doubt it. Who would have your father's things in his possession?"

"A man. A genealogist—"

"A what?"

"A genealogist. A person who studies family history."

"I see," she says, cagey. "And what has he got to do with your father?"

"That's what I intend to find out. Listen, Mom, I've got to know: Did these things belong to Dad?"

"I don't know." She averts her eyes.

"How can you say you don't know when you haven't even looked at them? There's this notebook with annotations. . . ."

Again, she flinches; and again, she controls herself.

"Looking at them wouldn't make any difference. Not without my glasses."

"What happened to your glasses?"

"I broke them."

It's now Rafael's turn to become angry:

"Is that so? You broke your glasses. And why didn't you let me know?"

She hesitates, shifts in her chair. And when she finally replies, it is with sullenness, like a child who's been scolded by her father; but at the same time, she's obviously pleased to have attracted the attention of her son—of her only son, her little Rafael.

"I couldn't. The phone is out of order."

"Out of order? But I talked to you on the phone several times last week!" Rafael, too, is now pleased. A dialogue with mutual reproaches? He'd rather have it so, at least there is a dialogue now and not just silence.

"There's . . ." she hesitates again, she's obviously telling a fib, like a child, "there's something wrong with the rotary dial. It won't dial."

He walks over to her, lays a hand on her shoulder.

"Come on, now, Mom. Couldn't you have gone to the grocery store and phoned me from there? I would have come right away, you know I would."

She bursts into tears.

"No! You wouldn't! You never worry about me, neither you nor your wife, nobody cares."

He heaves a sigh, decides to steer the conversation back to the original subject matter.

"This man says he has some of Dad's writings. Do you have any idea what they could be?"

"No, I have no idea. Whatever I know, you know it too, I've already told you a thousand times your father all of a sudden made up his mind to go to Spain and fight in the war there. I did everything I possibly could to make him change his mind, but with no success, he went and got himself killed, he's buried in a common grave near Madrid. . . ." She turns to him, her eyes brimming with tears. "But why bring up this subject again, Rafael, why talk about such painful things? Isn't it enough what I had to go through, what both of us had to go through? Isn't it enough all the sacrifices I made to raise you single-handedly, a woman all alone?" Taking a handkerchief tucked inside her sleeve, she wipes her eyes with a trembling hand. Rafael kneels down by her side and hugs her:

"All right, Mother. We won't talk about it anymore."

Annoyed, she struggles free.

"Leave now, Rafael. Go away."

He makes for the door.

"Rafael."

He turns around.

"What is it?"

Now she stares at him, pathetic:

"Rafael," she says in a quivering voice, "look after Suzana. Look after your daughter."

"Why, Mom?" he asks, suddenly alarmed. "Why do you say so? Has something happened? Tell me, Mother! Is there something you know?"

"No...I know nothing, Rafael, you know that she's just like you, she hardly ever comes here. But one night last week she came. She was out of her wits, Rafael."

"And what did she tell you?" says Rafael, anguished. "Tell me, for heavens' sake!"

"Nothing, she told me nothing, Rafael. All she did was cry. She cried for a long time. And then she left. There's something the matter with this girl, Rafael. Something really serious. That's why I'm telling you: Look after her. We must look after our own, Rafael."

He opens the door and leaves.

Rafael wanders about the streets of the Lower City, walks up to Praça da Matriz, sits down on a bench, and there he remains watching the children at play. A certain peace descends upon him; at this hour, two o'clock in the afternoon, birds twitter in the treetops and the public square is peaceful, surrounded by austere and imposing façades: the Government Palace, the Legislative Assembly Building, the Cathedral, Courthouse, São Pedro Theater, Public Library. Yielding to a sudden impulse, Rafael rises to his feet and goes to the Cathedral.

Not too many people there. The usual women dressed in black, naturally (Azorian widows?); three schoolgirls who whisper, giggling; an old man wearing sunglasses. Rafael kneels down, something he hasn't done in a long time; a Catholic, or rather a lapsed

Catholic, he rarely thinks of eternal life. Now, however, he feels like praying: *Our Father*, he murmurs, *who art in heaven*. They comfort him, these words that generations upon generations have murmured in the demi-dusk of chapels, catacombs, cathedrals. It's good to have faith, to be part of something greater than yourself, something transcendent; it's good not to depend exclusively on a strange Jew, on a rebellious daughter.

He finishes his prayer, crosses himself, leaves. He is bedazzled by the afternoon light, but only for a moment; soon he starts climbing down the steps, then walks along Rua Duque, heading for Alto da Bronze. He is going to the house of one Professor Samar-Kand.

An old house, squeezed between two tall apartment buildings. The faded paint, and the broken panes in the windows with tattered lace curtains, give the impression that the house is abandoned. Who knows, maybe it is. Maybe it's now the dwelling of vagrants or petty criminals—who can say? Rafael hesitates. Finally he pushes the iron gate, which creaks open; he follows a narrow path paved with slimy flagstones and trimmed with a row of neglected plants in ancient pots. He searches for the doorbell but can't find it, so he knocks on the door, on which are tiny windows with bars. Nothing. After a while he knocks again, then stands waiting with his head lowered, eyes fixed on the shriveled wisps of grass growing amid the stones. With a start, he raises his head; from behind one of the tiny windows two eyes peer at him curiously. A moment of tension—and then the door is opened. Standing before Rafael is a short, pudgy man in a shabby wine-colored dressing-gown that is so long that it trails on the floor. He's quite old, this diminutive man: The hair, although foppishly long, is completely white, but the blue eyes behind the metal-rimmed eyeglasses have an expression that is curiously child-like; and the voice, wispish and nasal, is also childlike.

"Is there something you want, friend?"

All of a sudden, Rafael finds this situation so comical, so unreal, that he can barely refrain himself from bursting into laughter. However, he manages to control himself:

"Are you professor—"

"Samar-Kand. That's me."

"I received your note . . . My name is Rafael Mendes."

63

The words produce an immediate response: The face of the old man lights up, a smile replaces the air of suspicion.

"Oh, yes. So you're Rafael Mendes, sir. Why didn't you say so right away? Come in, please, do come in."

Rafael follows him down a long corridor. On either side are shelves crammed with books—and articles of clothing, and jars of preserves ("I'm partial to preserves," explains the old man as they walk past, "I practically live off preserves and cookies.") and bottles of medicine, stuffed animals, bibelots. The farther they advance into the house, the stronger the smells—dust, mustiness, old paper, food gone bad.

The corridor ends in a large room, poorly-lit by the low-wattage light bulbs of a chandelier decorated with glass beads. It's a big, spacious room; there are shelves, similar to the ones in the corridor, and like them, cluttered with books and all kinds of strange objects— among them, the skeleton of a snake and the heads of three dolls. The walls are lined with pictures: maps of the sky, Zodiac symbols, the Tree of Life, everything rather vulgar. However, the big round table of dark wood occupying the middle of the room and the set of old chairs padded with red velvet are magnificent. "Please, sit down," says the old man.

Both of them sit down. There's a crystal ball on the table. The old man looks at it, first casually; then he takes it in his hands, examines it attentively, a frown creasing his forehead; with a sigh, he puts it back where it stood before—on a pedestal made of dark granite:

"Chipped. Practically a brand-new crystal ball—and already chipped. And it cost me quite a bundle, let me tell you. Believe me, they don't make crystal balls as they used to do in the old days. Actually, it's good that they don't—then we are forced to innovate."

He has a plan for developing an electronic crystal ball to be operated by the client himself. It looks like an ordinary crystal ball, but it contains electronic sensors capable of detecting and registering various characteristics of a person's hand. Starting with the lines of the palm: the line of life, the line of fortune, the line of the head, the line of the heart, the line of the liver. Then, the presence or absence of callosity or other signs that might indicate the person's occupation. The presence of gold rings. The size of the fingers. The pressure exerted by the fingers—thus revealing what some would call claws. The temperature of the hands, the amount of perspiration: important psychological clues. The data thus collected would then be fed into mini-computers and transformed into visions of the future, which would appear inside the crystal image itself in the form of images of liquid quartz, like the ones in the Japanese watches.

"Yes, I could develop this plan and many others as well—I am well-versed in many branches of human knowledge. I understand the way systems work, I know the theory of play. I can mount a flow chart in seconds, no matter how complex the situation. I'm a psychologist, a parapsychologist, and a physiopsychologist. Have you ever heard of physiopsychology? It's a relatively new science, it studies the psyche through the body functions. I can tell everything about a person by noting the volume of a tear, the degree of viscosity of the saliva, the arching of the jet of urine into a urinal; the amount of tension a wisp of hair can withstand and for this purpose I use a small device I myself have developed, I call it a psychocapillarymeter. I can interpret a person's character by examining his—pardon me the word—feces. Pencil-thin feces indicate a situation of anxiety, of self-consciousness, generally a result of dependency on calculations done with a pencil. Small, hardened feces, like a goat's, point to a temperament which is—can you guess?—that's right, similar to the goat's: reserved, self-centered, suspicious. Well-formed feces are indicative—which is only logical—of a well-formed soul. As for diarrhea, it's nothing more than the result of a storm—such as the storm that forced the frightened seamen to cast the prophet Jonah into the sea—except that this storm is internal."

He becomes vehement all of a sudden, shaking the crystal ball:

"I know all of this might seem in bad taste. But I can assure you, sir, it's superior to the old way of predicting the future, examining the viscera of birds as the Romans used to do, a method which some people would like to see reinstated. I'm not going to mention any names, I don't want to give the impression of being unethical, sir, but you have probably been approached by people who use such methods. Some people even use chicken for this purpose, imagine! That's a method with no scientific basis whatsoever. Yes, I know that Father Vieira used to say in his sermons that the ancients were right to have chosen the viscera and not the head to read fate: *He who is able to love is a better prophet than he who is able to reason.* Well, it was the seventeenth century then, and Father Vieira was a fanatic, a Quixote, a romantic ahead of his time. Whereas I, my dear sir, I work only with science. I'm always studying and researching, as you can see by the amount of books I have here; a lot of it is old stuff, but there are also many recent publications to keep myself abreast of what is going on. I'm old, but not old-fashioned, my friend. I'm all for progress, it's wonderful, I've been thinking of introducing Porto Alegre to the computerized horoscope and the computerized family tree, using the Cobal and the Fortran languages. Would you be interested in financing one of these projects, sir?"

Rafael, dumbfounded, doesn't know what to say. The little man puts the crystal ball back on its pedestal, and sighs.

"No, you wouldn't. You don't believe in such things, sir. Never mind. Anyhow, I'm not a fortune-teller by profession, I tell fortunes just to bring in a little money on the side. My specialty is genealogy—now that's something serious. An old science. Consider, for instance, the Bible: What is it if not a monumental family tree, illustrated with stories of a religious nature? And from biblical times down to today, genealogy has never stopped growing. Ah, never. In Europe it's wonderful, every city and town, no matter how small, has its own genealogist—every one of them highly competent. True, they have all kinds of resources over there, such as historical archives. Whereas here I have to overcome the greatest difficulties in order to do my research. The worst of it is that very few people appreciate this kind of work. Rio Grande do Sul, my friend, doesn't have a history. Nobody here knows a thing about their ancestors, and they don't want to know. There are exceptions, of course; Celina Cordeiro, have you heard of Celina Cordeiro, sir?—you must have, everybody in Porto Alegre has heard of her—she was one of my clients. I reconstructed her family tree. We became good friends, she still visits me. But she's an exception. There isn't much chance of genealogy ever succeeding here. That's why I've branched out into other areas."

He hesitates before adding:

"Successfully, if I may say so. I have several irons in the fire, I can assure you."

Rafael stares at him, stunned; stunned and dejected. Where in the world did I end up? he thinks to himself. The little man, coming to his senses, realizes that his impassioned harangue might have created a bad impression:

"Pardon me, sir. I allowed myself to be carried away with my enthusiasm. That's how I am, don't mind me. Let's go back to the main point: So you received your father's belongings, did you? And my note as well?"

"That's the reason why I'm here, sir," says Rafael, cautious. "As you know, my father deserted us many years ago; I was only a little boy then, and I can hardly remember him. Ever since—"

He stops short. The little man looks at him with sympathy, with interest, even with affection. How long has it been since someone has looked at him in this way? There's a lump in his throat, he tries to go on but can't, and then he breaks down and weeps convulsively: He cries not just because of his father or the memory of his father, it's because of everything: his daughter, the predicament of the finance company, all the tension he's been under—the torrent has burst through the barriers and he cries unrestrainedly before the astonished little man. Finally, Rafael manages to pull himself together; he takes a handkerchief out of his pocket and wipes his eyes.

"I'm sorry. I'm not in the habit of breaking down like this. I'm a restrained man, believe me. I don't get upset easily. But lately I've been through some difficulties. And just now as I remembered my father. . . ."

"I understand," says the old man. His sympathy seems genuine; whether madman or con artist, he feels compassion. And who wouldn't at the sight of a man's tears?

They remain silent for a few moments. Then the old man clears his throat:

"Let me explain about that note. I met your father many years ago. He was interested in genealogy, that's why he came to me. I did some research—and I was astonished."

Then, waxing enthusiastic again, he says:

"What a family tree it was, Senhor Rafael! One of the most magnificent I have ever come across. An oak tree, a sequoia, a veritable genealogical forest! The Mendeses have roots all over, in

67

several countries, in several continents. We spent months researching your ancestors. We would work until the small hours; sometimes
he would stay overnight; those clothes I sent you, he left them behind
when he went to Spain. . . . Did you know, sir, that he went to Spain
at the time of the civil war there?"

"Yes, I knew. But I don't know why—"

The old man cuts him short with a gesture:

"I'd rather not go into any explanations. Look: Your father left
two other notebooks with me, in addition to the one with the
annotations already in your possession. The first contains stories of
your ancestors, or rather, stories that he wrote about your ancestors.
Your father was endowed with imagination, Senhor Rafael. He was a
man who would marvel at the things that happened in life and in the
world, and for this reason, he had to write. The first notebook, then,
contains Genealogical Stories—the title is his own. The other notebook is about himself; he tells about something that happened to
him, something that changed his life, and this notebook even
provides an answer to your previous question about his journey to
Spain. Valuable material, I'd say. Valuable in general, and valuable
in particular to a son.

"Interesting," mumbles Rafael. He feels odd in this place, a bit
nauseous; it must be the smell, he concludes. He decides to end this
conversation:

"Yes. And how can I have access to these notebooks?"

The old man shows him a parcel wrapped in brown paper:

"Here they are. And they can be yours. . . . "

He pauses.

"For ten thousand dollars."

"What?" says Rafael, incredulous: It is so bizarre to hear the old
man mention dollars, ten thousand dollars, in this archaic, phantas-
magorical setting that Rafael thinks he didn't hear it right:

"Ten thousand dollars, did you say, sir?"

Ten thousand dollars? Does the old man know what he's talking
about? Does he know how much the exchange rate on the dollar is
right now? Ten thousand dollars: It's the sum Rafael has in the safe
hidden behind a painting in his study. Money that he keeps for
emergencies. Ten thousand dollars? He feels like sending the old

man to the devil. Barely controlling his indignation, he forces a smile:

"You know, strictly speaking, this material doesn't belong to you. You yourself said, sir, that it was my father who—"

"Your father left these notebooks in my possession, Senhor Rafael. They are, therefore, my property." Then, conciliatory: "But I don't intend to make a mountain out of a molehill. After all, the contents of the notebooks concern you. They are, let's say, a message. A message from the hereafter." Then, pleased with this figure of speech: "And I'm willing to hand this message over to you. Except that I'm charging for the storage and the delivery of the material. Isn't that what the post office does?"

"But ten thousand dollars, that's absurd!"

The old man smiles.

"That's what you say. However, these are the writings of your father, about whom you claim to know so little. If people want information, they'll have to pay—in cruzeiros, dollars, or any other currency. I prefer dollars."

He shifts in his chair.

"There's something else too, which I haven't mentioned yet. I never got paid for my services, for your father died before he could have done so. He was a friend of mine, of course, and I didn't bear a grudge against him, but the fact is that he owed me an honorarium for the fruits of my labor."

A pause.

"Besides, genealogical work is not easy. In the case of your family, I had to consult dozens of books I have in my library, which is really huge, the only library of its kind here in our country—it's worth a fortune. Climbing up and down stairs and handling dusty books can really kill a person. Not to mention the mental effort. Genealogy is pretty much like a detective's work, Senhor Rafael. Sometimes we have to start from negligible details: a coat of arms engraved on flatware, an old painting, or mythological allusions—to the Gold Tree, for instance. Also, in the case of your family—well, it wasn't a minor job. It wasn't a mere 'family shrub' I had to deal with, Senhor Rafael, I can assure you."

"But—" Rafael isn't convinced. "Why dollars?"

The old man shrugs.

"Strong currency, that's why, naturally. You're in the money business, sir; you know that we cannot put our trust in the cruzeiro. Pay me in Swiss francs or German marks, if you want, it doesn't matter as long as it's a strong currency. Ten thousand dollars, let's agree, is not all that much for someone in the financial market. Ten thousand dollars for the evocation of a father? Please, do me a favor, Senhor Rafael. Don't repeat Judas's mistake. Don't betray a loved one for thirty coins."

The slur angers Rafael, but he's now set on continuing with this dialogue to the very end—he wants the notebooks, and he also wants to find out what's behind this whole story.

"How do you know, sir, that I can pay?"

The old man shifts again in his chair.

"Because of the crystal ball." He breaks into histrionic laughter, then becomes serious: "I know a lot about your life, Senhor Rafael. My son used to talk about you."

"Your son?"

"Julio." The little man smiles sadly; all of a sudden, he looks much older than his years, an old gnome of a man, shriveled, melancholic. "Julio, Senhor Rafael. He worked with you."

So he's Julio's father, this old man. Rafael's suspicions are now confirmed: There was something fishy there, something more than just the notebooks and the dollars. Julio, of course. How else could the old man have met Celina Cordeiro? Julio. This clears up the mystery. Rafael now recalls the stockbroker occasionally talking about his father. A weird old man, he would say, I don't get along very well with him, he has never forgiven me for working for a finance company.

Julio's father! But this complicates matters. There could be something else behind this sensational deal that has just been proposed to him—revenge. Revenge taken on the Pecúnia, which the old man must surely hold responsible for his son's misfortune. Revenge taken on Boris and on Rafael.

As if guessing at Rafael's thoughts, the old man says:

"But that's all in the past, Senhor Rafael. My son is dead, may God keep his soul, and I bear no grudges against anyone or anything. Besides . . ."

He hesitates for a moment; then shaking his head as if to free himself from a disturbing thought, he goes on:

"But let's get back to the main point: I'm making you the following offer: Take the notebooks with you, examine them as much as you like. And then, if you want to keep them, you'll pay me ten thousand dollars. Agreed?"

Rafael, still wary, can't help smiling:

"Aren't you afraid, sir, to trust me with the notebooks?"

"No," replies the old man. "I know you're a decent man. That's what my son used to say: This Rafael Mendes, he's a decent guy. I trust you, sir, and I'd be happy to have your friendship too, as I had your father's."

He pauses for a moment, then goes on:

"Besides, there's something else I'd like to offer you as a token of my regard for you. There's a third notebook."

"What? A third notebook?" says Rafael, creasing his forehead. What kind of trick is he trying to pull off now?

"Yes. Or rather, there isn't one yet. Not yet, but there might be: I can start writing it at any moment."

"You?!"

"That's right. Me. And furthermore: It will be a notebook entirely devoted to you."

"To me?"

"To you. Are you skeptical? Don't be." Then leaning forward, he says: "There's a lot I could write about you, Senhor Rafael: About things that happened, things that are happening, things that *will* happen."

He straightens up in his chair and stares at Rafael, triumphant. *I bet,* thinks Rafael, he's now going to bring up the electronic crystal ball.

"Don't worry," the little man hastens to say, "for this notebook I won't charge you a cent. It's included in the ten thousand dollars. Let's say it's a genealogical gift thrown in."

Rafael looks at him, not knowing what to say.

"This third notebook will be of great importance to you," the old man goes on. "As important as the other two. After all, I do know a lot about you. I've been following, although indirectly, it's true, a good part of your life; therefore, I believe I know you thoroughly, more than you think I do. Even your gestures are predictable to me, Senhor Rafael. This morning I could imagine your astonishment when you came upon the box I sent you—"

"By the way," Rafael cuts in, "you could have phoned me first, sir. You would have spared me a shock."

"Mystery and uncertainty add to the value of things," retorts the old man. "You, who operate on the money markets, must know this better than I do. But to answer your previous question: You'll come back, Senhor Rafael, I'm sure you will. You'll come back because you're honest; and you'll come back because you want to know more. More than what you know now; and I'm in a position to tell you what you want to know, sir."

"Well," says Rafael, "if you, a fortune-teller, are so certain that I'll be back, then surely I'll be back. And if you mentioned ten thousand dollars. . . ."

He falters, but it's too late to backtrack, he's now at the point of no return, he'll have to go on all the way to the end:

"If you mentioned ten thousand dollars, it's because you know that I'll pay you ten thousand dollars. And I will indeed. If I find at least some of the answers I've been searching for, I'll pay you, sir."

Rafael shakes the hand—small and delicate like a child's—that the old man holds out; for a moment they gaze at each other, smiling, until they come to their senses, both of them embarrassed. Picking up the parcel, the old man says:

"Let's get down to business."

Quickly he unwraps two old notebooks:

"Here they are. The notebooks of Dr. Rafael Mendes, your father."

He adjusts his eyeglasses, then leafs through one of the notebooks:

"This one here is particularly interesting, genealogically speaking. It begins with the most distant of your ancestors—a biblical prophet."

"A prophet?" asks Rafael, with disbelief.

"A prophet, yes. And many other distinguished figures. For instance, a famous Hebrew philosopher and physician who lived in Moorish Spain . . ."

"Wait a minute," protests Rafael. "Where did you get this idea that I'm a Jew?"

"I didn't say that you are a Jew," corrects the old man. "What I said was that you come from a Hebrew lineage. A noble lineage, by the way, as you'll see."

"But I was baptized a Christian."

"New!" exclaims the genealogist. "A New Christian, a cristão-novo, you, and your ancestors: They converted to Christianity, they were the New Christians, a term applied to Christianized Jews. Haven't you ever heard of it? Very common here in Brazil. Many of us are of Jewish descent because the first Portuguese settlers who came here were mostly Jews. Didn't you know, sir, that soon after the Portuguese discovered Brazil, the entire Brazilian territory was conveyed by charter to a group of New Christians headed by Fernão de Noranha?"

"I didn't know that," says Rafael.

There is a silence. A tense silence.

"I bet I know who you're thinking of now," says the old man. "Boris. You're saying to yourself that the two of you after all have something in common. Even though this Jew—"

"I ask you," Rafael cuts him short, "to drop this subject. I don't know what kind of grudge you might have against Boris, but he happens to be a friend of mine."

"Well," says the old man, sour. "There's no disputing about tastes, or friendships for that matter. My opinion about Senhor Boris—"

"I'm not interested," Rafael says. He rises to his feet: "Excuse me, I'm late. Can I have the notebooks?"

"Of course, of course." The old man wraps them up, hands them over to Rafael.

With the parcel in his hand, Rafael hesitates:

"And . . . how do I get in touch with you, sir?"

"I'll phone you," says the old man. "Tonight, or if not, tomorrow."

"For an historian, you sure are in a big hurry," remarks Rafael, bitter.

"With financiers one has to be in a hurry," retorts the old man not less bluntly. "After all, I'm giving you credit, my friend. Full credit—in your trustworthiness."

He suddenly seems so very old and frail. Ashamed, Rafael feels the blood rise to his face. Without a word, he puts the notebooks in the briefcase and leaves.

Getting out of this house feels like emerging from an unreal subterranean world: Suddenly bedazzled by the brightness outside, Rafael Mendes, his head swimming, hesitates, not knowing what to do next. He looks at his watch: three-fifty. He decides to go home to read the notebooks he's carrying in the briefcase.

To go home, however, is not all that simple. He goes into a bar, orders a cognac, drinks it down in one gulp. He orders another one. The bar owner, a fat bald man with a mustache, watches him in silence.

"Rough going, is it?"

"Yeah. Very," Rafael agrees.

"I know how it feels," the man says. "There are times when I need my shots of cognac too."

He smiles sympathetically. Rafael smiles back, pays. He walks back to the parking lot where he left the car and drives home.

He enters the apartment. Helena is sitting in the living room, watching television.

As soon as she sees him come in, she leaps to her feet, her eyes wide open:

"What happened, Rafael? Did something happen to Suzana?"

"Relax," he says. "Nothing happened, it's just that I've come home early, there are some documents I have to look over and I decided I'd work here."

She lets herself fall into the armchair:

"What a scare you gave me, Rafael! That was quite a turn you gave me."

He strokes her hair, does his best to soothe her. Then he heads for his study. Before going in, he turns around: "Helena, I don't want to be disturbed, tell the maids not to knock on my door."

"All right," she murmurs feebly.

Sighing, Rafael goes into the study and locks the door behind him. He sits down in his armchair, opens the briefcase, takes out the parcel containing the notebooks, unwraps them.

Two old composition books, exactly like the one that came in the box. On the covers are the titles *The First Notebook of the New Christian* and *The Second Notebook of the New Christian*. Strange titles. As strange as Rafael Mendes, his father, must have been.

He leafs through the notebooks. Pages and pages covered with a small, regular handwriting. Is it his father's script? Again, he isn't sure. But the notebooks are certainly quite old: The sheets of paper are yellowed, moth-eaten, and the lilac ink has faded, rendering the words almost illegible in some passages.

Rafael Mendes opens the first notebook. He plunges into it just like the prophet Jonah must have plunged into a billowy sea. He travels swiftly inside the belly of time, like the prophet inside the fish, heading for a destination still unknown.

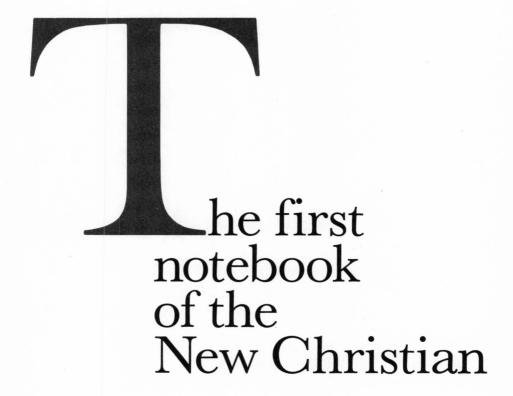

The first
notebook
of the
New Christian

Perplexed, Jonah received from the Lord the gift of prophecy and the mission of denouncing the corrupt city of Nineveh.

My name is Raphael Mendes. I am a physician and a genealogy enthusiast. By searching the roots of my family—a search that involved the study of documents, of old books, of coats of arms engraved on flatware, and even of lullabies—I was able to track down someone named Jonah as the most distant of my known ancestors.

My conclusion is based on various clues: in the twelfth century, the coat of arms of the Mendes family displayed the effigy of a whale, but the typical spout of water had been replaced by a stylized tree— the Gold Tree, undoubtedly. This association of the whale with the legend of the tree, which had been with the family for generations, is certainly very significant. And as with Jonah, perplexity is a distinguishing trait of the Mendeses, too: What is happening? What happened? What will happen? Like other people, they, too, searched for the Gold Tree, but without great conviction; in fact, they would have much preferred peace of mind and tranquility—which they never succeeded in attaining—to riches. Throughout the ages, they fled from place to place, from country to country; they crossed oceans, they scaled mountains, living strange adventures, sensing a disturbing summons.

N ews spread quickly that Jonah had received the gift of prophecy from the Lord. People found it strange: Jonah? Why Jonah? An ordinary man, unendowed with any sort of clairvoyant abilities, incapable of even predicting the weather for the following day—so, why him? In public, however, they tried to rejoice at the news. After all, it was a distinction for the village to have a prophet among its inhabitants. But that's not how Jonah's wife felt; dejected, she foresaw a bleak horizon for her husband. She was partly right: True, prophets were respected in those days—but they were hated, too. They would *say* to the rich and the powerful things that ordinary people hardly dared to *think*. If some potentate had a banquet, the prophets had to hasten to his place, burst into the premises, assail with fiery words all persons present and curse their food, which would punctually spoil—such a waste, because then not even would the poor, who were usually the recipients of any food left over from the love feasts, be able to eat. Hence prophets, while feared by the powerful, were also abhorred by the humble: "Prophets? They're useless. They are only interested in foretelling the future, and what do we care about the future? In the future we'll all be dead."

This, however, didn't prevent numerous people from seeking out Jonah to ask him to intercede with the Lord on their behalf. Desperate women wanted him to help them get pregnant; discredited priests yearned to share the divine word with him. Grain speculators offered him money in exchange for harvest predictions; soldiers consulted him about the advisability of certain military operations. And when Jonah's father began to urge him to find out from the Lord the location of the Gold Tree—you owe it to your family, to your community, Jonah, we've had enough of this life of poverty—Jonah decided to renounce his mission and run away: After all, Jonah thought, I have nothing to do with Nineveh. Are the Ninevehites fornicating? Let them fornicate, I couldn't care less. Nineveh there, I here: Why should I hitch my fate to a city I've never even been to? I'm going to run away.

He ran away. At Yafo he boarded a boat bound for Tarshish. The sea was tranquil, at first; then came the storm. The sailors believed that someone on board was attracting the divine wrath. They drew lots; Jonah was pointed out as the culprit. He was thrown into the sea. A fish swallowed him.

A fish swallowed him. Jonah found himself inside a huge stomach, full of undigested remains. A terrible smell, total darkness. Groping about, Jonah found sand, two silex stones, and some old rags. He managed to produce sparks, which ignited the rags. On a surface of sand and stones he made a fire, and felt better: pleasantly warm, even sheltered.

He could—should—stay there and wait for the fate that Jeovah had in store for him; instead, he began to explore the insides of the fish. He improvised a torch and began his expedition. The stomach extended to the narrow tunnel of the intestines; a short way down the intestines, however, there was something resembling a chamber, where, to his surprise, he came upon a group of people, eleven men and one woman seated around a small fire. Jonah's arrival didn't surprise them. One of them, an old man with a long beard, addressed the prophet in Aramaic; he welcomed Jonah and invited him to sit down.

These people were there for different reasons. Like Jonah, some had been punished for having run away from missions that Jeovah or other deities from the Fertile Crescent had entrusted to them; others were well-known sinners, thieves, murderers. To many of them the belly of the fish was a prison where they were serving sentences whose duration—and this added to the harshness of the punishment—was unknown to them. The old man had been there— he guessed—for over twenty years. He could only guess because he had no way of measuring time:

"When I was first swallowed, this fish was so small that I could barely fit in its stomach. Now, this hollow can house a legion. That's the way dishonesty, hypocrisy, and above all, indecision and perplexity, keep growing in this world."

Jonah was no longer listening. His eyes were fixed on the woman.

Still young and very beautiful, she had a dark complexion, long black hair, dark eyes. A woman of haughty bearing. A priestess of Astarte, as he was to find out later.

The old man invited Jonah to have lunch with them. How did he know it was lunch and not dinner? How could he tell daytime from nighttime in that place? Maybe he was a prophet. "We have fish," said the old man, "fish swallowed by our fish." The way he stressed the *our* showed irony, yes, but also pride—as if the fish were his master, his god.

"The smaller fish are swallowed by the bigger fish, which, in turn, are swallowed"—said the old man with pride—"by the biggest of them all (again: pride). It's a war waged by all against all. But why should we concern ourselves with this war when it's thanks to it that we survive?"

Jonah declined the invitation. He felt uneasy among these people; he was especially disturbed by the presence of the beautiful priestess, who kept looking at him with a smile. Excusing himself, he went back to where he had come from.

A surprise awaited him: The fire had died. Lying amid the ashes he saw a blade of some transparent substance, glittering in the light of the torch. Jonah had discovered glass.

(It was quite simple: the stones upon which Jonah had built the fire were—although he knew nothing about this—soda, which had been the cargo of a boat swallowed by the fish. Through the action of the fire, the soda and the sand changed into glass.)

Jonah examined this material, but because he wasn't actually an inventive or creative man, he never imagined even one of its thousand practical uses. It never occurred to him, for instance, to cut an opening through the flank of the fish and fix the blade of glass there, thus creating some kind of a scuttle, which would become hermetically sealed by the healing process triggered along the edges of the wound. Through it he would have been able to sight the sunken ships lying on the bottom of the sea, ships that might contain treasures. He could have become rich! But this possibility never occurred to him. Neither did he think to use the glass to make lenses, or mirrors. Mirrors—what wouldn't the women have given to see themselves! The mirrors then in use were made of silver; they were expensive and the image they reflected wasn't very accurate, which afforded the opportunity for deceptive practices. Thus, to their rich customers, merchants would sell mirrors that flattered their physical appearance, either by eliminating wrinkles or by slimming down waistlines. Whereas the women who were poor had to satisfy themselves with any scrap of metal more or less polished. These paupers, however, would sometimes look at the rich women and, much to the women's consternation, burst into laughter. Was the laughter of the destitute women yet another sign of the age of debauchery in which they lived, or was it triggered by some grotesque defect that the imperfect mirrors failed to reveal? Who could the rich women trust to help them clarify such agonizing self-doubts? Not their husbands, who made only flattering remarks; not the servants. Only good, faithful mirrors. Jonah could have manufactured and sold such mirrors, thereby not only revealing the truth—which is expected from a prophet—but also earning lots of money. But precisely because he wasn't a prophet yet, he couldn't foresee this possibility. A prophet? Not when it came to glass and mirrors.

"Prophet Jonah!"

Startled, he turned around. It was one of the men he had just met, a thin bald fellow with a big scar on his face: a sinister type, more like a bandit than a prophet. Really strange, the way Jeovah and other gods selected their envoys.

"Could we talk?"

Jonah invited him to sit down. The man went straight to the matter:

"Would you like to get rich, Jonah? Really rich?"

For a moment Jonah thought that the man wanted to talk to him about the Gold Tree. But that wasn't the case; he wanted to disclose a plan of his, a plan to bilk wealthy Ninevehites out of their money:

"Everything points out to the fact that you'll be in Nineveh soon. The city has reached the sum of its corruption; Jeovah must be eager to punish it."

He leaned forward—terrible, his breath, worse than the emanations from the stomach of the fish—then he spoke in a low voice:

"Now listen carefully: As soon as you arrive in Nineveh, you prophesy that because of its sins, the city will be destroyed, and its inhabitants will die amid excruciating pains; in short, you'll make a really good prophecy, and in this way you'll fulfill your mission. Soon afterwards, however, you offer to placate the divine wrath by acting as a go-between. Naturally, you'll charge for this service, and you'll ask them to pay in advance; and the more frightened they are, the more you can charge."

Appalled, Jonah listened to him.

"With this money," the man went on, "you'll hire boats and good fishermen. They'll catch this fish here and set us free. Now, you may ask: Why should I save a man I barely know? Can't you guess why?" Smiling, he added: "Some prophet you are!"

He paused, then went on:

"Because I happen to know where the Gold Tree is," he whispered, his eyes glittering. "And I'm willing to lead you to it in exchange for my freedom. So? Is it a deal?"

Ah: So at last, he came out with it—the Gold Tree. But under the guise of an offer, which was surprising and merely raised Jonah's suspicions. As if anticipating them, the man was ready with an enticing offer, which he announced with a leer:

"The priestess of Astarte. She'll be very grateful to you, Jonah— and mind you, she really knows how to please a man she's grateful to. ...So? Is it a deal?"

Jonah remained silent, which disconcerted the other man:

"Of course, you don't have to give me an answer right away. Think about it. But I ask you not to wait too long to make up your mind."

Suddenly he was entreating, clinging to the prophet:

"Don't let us down, Jonah! Please, don't let us down! I—"

Then pulling himself together, he wiped his eyes, got to his feet, and left. Jonah sat there, deeply disturbed by what he had heard.

Jonah wants to mull over this matter, to sort out his thoughts. All of a sudden, soft arms encircle his neck. It's the priestess of Astarte: already naked, lustful. Jonah heard that these priestesses worship sex, but he had no idea they would go this far. He wants to repel her, it's not the right place nor the right time—he is on a divine mission—besides, he is afraid the others will show up. Lust, however, wins out; he returns the woman's caresses and ends up by taking her right there in the moist, slimy entrails of an enormous fish traveling at an incredible speed across the depths of the ocean.

Later on, lying side by side, they talk. The young woman tells him that she's there as a punishment: Destined for the High Priest, she had, however, fornicated with a wealthy Babylonian merchant. She was then cast into the sea and swallowed by the fish.

"I have nothing to do with Jeovah," she says. "But I know that your God is powerful . . . that he can summon up plagues, that he can part the waters of the sea. Therefore, he'll be able to rescue us from this place too. *You* will be able to. Take me out of this place, and I'll be yours. So, what do you say to my proposal?"

What can he possibly say now, having held the woman in his arms, having shared with her the fruit of sin? Only that he'll think about it:

"I'll think about it."

"I depend on you," she murmurs. She rises to her feet, puts on her tunic, and departs, leaving Jonah once more to his guilt and to his doubts. They want him to give in, these people in the belly of the fish; they want him to humble himself before Jeovah, they want him to obey His command—which amounts to sowing death and destruction throughout an entire city. Yes, the Ninevehites have sinned, but then who hasn't? They are human beings, worthy of compassion. On the other hand, the people inside the fish—who have defied the Lord—they, too, are human beings, they, too, are worthy of mercy. What a dilemma. But, damn it, why did Jeovah have to choose him for this mission? Why doesn't He change his plans—being God, he could—and send him, instead, to some unknown country? A country with beautiful landscapes (a bay, that's what he envisions, a beautiful bay, with waves lapping on the pure white sand of the beach; coconut trees, brightly colored birds wheeling in flight, a gloriously blue sky), a country inhabited by friendly people (bronze-skinned men, women and children, their faces painted in gaudy colors, their long black hair adorned with feathers), in such a country he would at the most have to admonish a few naughty pranksters for their small offenses. In such a country it would be easy to be a prophet. But Jeovah is cruel. Cruel to sinners, cruel to His chosen people.

Inside the belly of the fish there is no concept of time. Holding the blade of glass in his hand, Jonah meditates, he tries to. But the man with the scar on his face is back, he wants to know if Jonah has come to a decision about his earlier proposal. "I'm thinking about it," replies the prophet, already annoyed. "All right," says the man, "but don't forget that we're waiting for an answer."

"We?" asks Jonah, intrigued. "We, who?"

Then it dawns on him: The two of them are in collusion, the beautiful priestess and the man with the scar are in cahoots, they're trying to pull a fast one on him. Incensed, Jonah asks the man to go away: "Go away, you scum! Go and enjoy your courtesan!"

Muttering insults, the man leaves. Jonah, overcome by a sudden rage, drives the blade of glass into the stomach of the fish. Blood spouts out, extinguishing the torch; he is tossed about in the darkness: The fish, driven insane by pain, thrashes about in the sea frantically. Finally, the fish spews up Jonah, who, as if catapulted, flies up into the air, then flops down into the water. Free! At long last, daylight and fresh air! After swimming a few hundred meters, Jonah comes ashore. Exhausted, short of breath, he remains lying on the beach.

Then rising to his feet, he sets out on his way. He walks and walks. And finally he arrives in a big city surrounded by walls. White-washed houses, temples, palaces glitter in the sun; through the main gate, caravans of camels flow in and out of the city.

Nineveh.

In Nineveh Jonah denounced lust and prophesied, as the Lord had commanded, that in forty days at the most, the city would be plunged into chaos and destruction. The people believed him, and began to fast and to pray; nobody was fornicating anymore. Such things were not enough for Jonah: "It won't do you any good," he thundered in the main squares, "you've sinned and now you're doomed." Much to Jonah's chagrin, however, Jeovah didn't make the threats come true: The days went by and nothing happened to Nineveh. Jonah was deeply disappointed. Addressing the Lord, he voiced his complaint:

"I knew I was doing the right thing when I ran away to Tarshish. There's no way the two of us can ever work together: I, perplexed, and you, enigmatic, it just won't work. I've had enough."

He went outside the city walls and there he remained, seated on the ground, waiting to see what Jeovah would finally do to Nineveh—or to him, His prophet. The rays of the sun, hitting him squarely on the skull, made him ill with calenture. He felt his brain boiling, and had terrifying visions: The gentle, bronze-colored men, whom he had imagined he could see in the country of the beautiful landscapes, were now being attacked and massacred by warriors in steel armors. Blood stained the white sand. . . .

God then took pity on Jonah.

On the parched soil before him, a tiny plant sprouted, and it soon began to grow into a small, but leafy, tree. Disturbed as he was, Jonah didn't see in this occurrence a sign of Divine mercy; he didn't lie down in the shade of this tree so that he could rest and get well again. Instead, he began to rave like a madman:

"It's the Gold Tree! I've found the Gold Tree!"

And he began to tear out its branches, searching for the pods with their precious seeds. Jeovah, angered, then sent a grub of the desert, and in the twinkling of an eye, it devoured the entire tree, and then it transformed itself into a butterfly, which flew away and disappeared.

At first Jonah couldn't believe it. When he finally realized what had happened, he burst out laughing. He laughed and laughed; he was rolling about on the ground, laughing; he laughed so much that his belly ached; he would stop laughing for a moment, wipe his eyes, and then succumb to another fit of laughter.

Finally he stopped laughing, rose to his feet, and heaving a sigh, set out on his way; he was going back home, to Judea. On the way he walked past a craggy mountain, situated south of Jericho, near the Dead Sea. In that bleak landscape, perhaps because of the intense heat, he had a premonition: One day, he murmured, a descendant of mine will climb this mountain in search of his destiny. Centuries later, the prophecy was fulfilled.

He is young, this man now climbing the mountain, this Habacuc ben Tov, my ancestor.

He wears a coarse tunic, and rustic sandals. Tied to his waist, a goatskin pouch. Empty: the last of the water drunk hours ago. Covered with dust, his mouth dry, he labors up the steep cliffs. And he is thinking not of Jonah's prophecy but of an incident that happened to his father. One summer day, this man, a humble farm worker, decided to take a break from his tedious work and go for a dip in the cool waters of the Sea of Galilee. He was enjoying his swim, when all of a sudden the area was hit by a violent storm. Frightened, and interpreting the phenomenon as a sign of divine disapproval of his self-indulgence, the man dived into the water: There he stayed submerged, fearful of being struck by lightning. He endured the situation for as long as he could; finally, unable to hold his breath much longer, he lifted up his eyes in a mute request for mercy—and what did he see through the clear waters? Feet walking upon the surface of the lake. *A man was walking upon the waters.* He didn't suppose at that moment that it could be Jesus Christ walking toward a transcendent destiny; as a matter of fact, he didn't suppose anything at all. Instead, his attention was focused on the examination of those feet. Beautiful, well-shaped feet; the skin on their soles was smooth, with no callosities. From this fact he concluded—erroneously, as it turned out—that those feet belonged to a contemplative, to a person capable of floating above reality. When he finally emerged from the water, there was no one in sight; however, the image of the feet upon the water was to haunt him, and on his deathbed, he said to Habacuc: "Search for men who are above." "Above what, Father?" "Above everything." Respectful but disappointed, Habacuc listened to him in silence; he would have preferred that the old man had relayed to him, say, the secret of the Gold Tree. Being a poor man, with a family to support, Habacuc ben Tov was forced to think of prosaic matters, such as earning his daily bread. However, hidden in the enigmatic words of his father was a message, whose validity circumstances would soon demonstrate.

I n Roman-occupied Palestine, intrigue, corruption, wretched poverty, discontent, are rampant. The small farmers are bankrupt; their wheat cannot compete against the Egyptian wheat, which is much cheaper. The small farms are being taken over by the owners of latifundia, who prefer to use slave labor, much to the shame of the people of Israel. The impoverished masses flock to the cities, and there they live in constant struggle. In Jerusalem, where Habacuc lives, there is a succession of political and religious crimes, the result of confrontations among various factions. Sadducees, Pharisees, and others. Hired assassins, high on hashish, mingle with the crowds. Suddenly, a scream, and a man, covered with blood, collapses: A merchant, suspected of collaborating with the invaders. Or a priest who has adopted Greek practices. Sickened by all this madness, by all this fury, Habacuc decides to leave, deserting his wife (who has been betraying him with a Roman legionnaire) and three children. He goes away in search of purity, of redemption. In search of the legendary Essenes, the sect that holds the key to the harmony of the soul and to eternal life.

Finally, he sights the holy city—an assemblage of austere stone houses, strategically built on the top of the mountain. A man comes to meet him; he supports him, gives him a drink of water. He is Eliezer, the friend who had joined the Essenes many years before, and with whom Habacuc exchanged secret messages.

Before being accepted into the community, Habacuc has to go through a period of initiation: fastings, prayers, meditation. His mentor is Eliezer, who offers him support when he loses his courage. With the help of his friend, Habacuc surmounts one by one all the stages of his painful initiation. Finally, the great day arrives. Before the entire community gathered in the main square, Habacuc takes an oath. He promises to obey the law of Moses exactly as it was revealed to the sons of Sadoc—the Essenian priests. And during the final battle against the Children of Darkness, he will stand side by side with the Children of Light. He will follow the Angel of Truth against Satan. It will be a terrible battle, when even the dead will rise from their graves to fight: their decomposed bodies brandishing swords of light. Finally, Good will triumph, and the Messiah will reign sovereign. "Blessed be the Lord!" shout the priests when Habacuc is through with the ceremony. The believers break into applause: Habacuc has been accepted as one of their own. Since he is still a novice, he is not yet a full-fledged member of the community of the definitively pure; but God willing, one day he will be.

That night—and what prompted him to do so? A test of confidence? A daring gesture? A residue of his former Jerusalemite arrogance?—Eliezer invites Habacuc to go with him to a cave located on the outskirts of the city. With great difficulty, the two of them push aside a huge stone—and Habacuc can hardly contain an exclamation of surprise: In the light of the torch that Eliezer carries, he sees bangles, necklaces, bracelets, statuettes; gold, silver, diamonds, rubies. So it is true! The legendary treasure of the Essenes does exist! But Eliezer has something even more surprising to show his friend: a phial containing small, glittering metal grains.

"Do you know what they are? Seeds from the Gold Tree."

Then Eliezer adds, "The fact that we don't sow these seeds and that we keep our jewels in this cave is proof of our selflessness." He seems convinced of the truth of what he is saying and yet, Habacuc detects in his voice a faint, yet definite, tone of falsehood: No, Eliezer doesn't really believe in what he's saying. But why, wonders Habacuc, perplexed. After so many years amid the Essenes, after so much fasting and so many hardships, shouldn't Eliezer have attained that degree of moral superiority that reflects itself in a tranquil disregard for material possessions? It doesn't seem that this is the case. . . . Hm, there's something wrong here. . . . Unaware of Habacuc's suspicions, Eliezer continues to talk about the treasure. "All this wealth," he says, "is reserved for the Messiah. His arrival will be celebrated with a huge, fabulous banquet. The partakers of this love feast will make their entrance into a spacious hall, lit up by scores of gold candelabra, in the following order: the High Priest; the priests in general; the Messiah in person; the heads of family. The High Priest will then bless the bread and the wine; the Messiah will also bless the bread; and then delectable choice dishes will be served."

W ho is the Messiah?" Habacuc wants to know. "The Messiah is the Master of Justice," explains Eliezer. "A long time ago, he lived amid the people, preaching the divine word; but they didn't listen to him; aggrieved, he then went away. But riding a beautiful white horse, he'll be back one day, in search of the righteous—that's us." "But," persists Habacuc, "how will we know that he is indeed the Messiah and not an impostor?"

"Because," says Eliezer, beginning to feel annoyed at all these doubts, "he has the divine commands engraved on his tongue."

"On his tongue?" Habacuc is stunned.

"On his tongue."

"On his tongue, well, who would have guessed," murmurs Habacuc, quite impressed. He remains silent for a moment, but is soon asking another question:

"Is the Messiah this Jesus, the one who was crucified?"

"Jesus?" Eliezer laughs. "No. Jesus was a kindly man, but he wasn't the Messiah. Do you think the Messiah would have let himself be crucified? No way. With a single glance he would have exterminated thousands of those Romans before they even had a chance to touch him." Impassioned, he adds: "Ah, all the traitors will be exterminated! Woe to anyone who has drawn away from the divine word, from the Well of the Spring Tide!"

His vehemence surprises and disturbs Habacuc. From a holy man he would expect meekness and gentleness, not this outburst of ferocity. However, he says nothing. He helps Eliezer replace the stone. Then, in silence, they walk back to the small stone house that they share with another five or six people. Habacuc undresses and lies down on his hard cot. His first night amid the Pure is haunted by terrifying nightmares.

I t's a grueling existence. The Essenes get up very early; the sky is still dark when they leave for work. On small terraces they cultivate vegetables, making the best of the scanty amount of water that has been carefully collected in reservoirs—it hardly ever rains in this region. The sun rises, the heat becomes unbearable. Down below lies the Dead Sea, dense, saturated with minerals, whose crystals, encrusted on the logs that lie about the shore, glitter in the shimmering light.

Habacuc and Eliezer have been assigned an arduous task: the building of cisterns. They have to cut stones, transport and put them in place, then seal the cracks with bitumen and pitch. In the distance, they can see the women baking bread in round-shaped ovens.

Habacuc would like to ask questions about the women. He doesn't dare; he knows, however, that many of the men are single and chaste. Eliezer is one such man; he is forty years old, and has never known a woman. One day he confided to Habacuc that he would like to take the daughter of one of the priests as his wife. But the girl is only fifteen years old, and according to what the Law prescribes, she can't marry until she's twenty—even though she already has the body of a woman, with breasts bulging under her tunic. Eliezer's sleep is restless, he moans. Habacuc knows why. He, too, secretly desires this same girl, this Naomi.

O ne night Habacuc gets out of bed and goes for a walk. A huge yellow light shines upon the hills of Judea. The air is saturated with dust and odors. From the distance the wind carries strange sounds—laughter, moaning. In the Holy City, the Essenes lie asleep. They rest their exhausted bodies after a day of hard work, a day that has brought them closer to the Great Happiness. Only Habacuc, driven by anguish, has to walk on and on, the sweat running down his face, his chest.

Suddenly, the feeling that he is being watched. He turns around. Did a window close quickly? Perhaps. Habacuc keeps on walking, now at a slower pace. His ears, pricked, detect footsteps. Habacuc stops: Somebody is following him, he wants to know why. Is he doing something wrong? Does walking at night make him one of the Children of Darkness?

A figure approaches. A small, delicate hand takes him by the arm. To his astonishment, Habacuc is being led to a cave near the one with the treasure. The cave has a narrow entrance, but soon reveals itself to be spacious, like a hall with a domed ceiling, faintly lit by the moonlight that barely penetrates this place.

They stand, the two of them, face to face. An abrupt gesture, and the cloak drops to the floor, revealing a girl to Habacuc's surprised eyes. Naked! It's the priest's daughter, and she is naked! Naked and quivering! "We haven't got much time," she whispers, and throws herself upon Habacuc. They roll on the ground, she tears away his tunic, kisses him ravenously on the mouth, the neck, the chest, and then on her knees, she takes his member in both her hands, gazes at it with near fervor—and then proceeds to perform fellatio on him, the sinful practice introduced by the Romans. "No," protests Habacuc, "don't," but his terror is already giving way to pleasure and he lets himself go. What a tongue, oh, God in heaven. What a lecherous demon she is with this tongue of hers!

Habacuc possessed her one, two, three times. Both of them insatiable: He, full of lust that has been accumulating in deep, invisible cisterns ever since he left Jerusalem; and she, she seems demoniac. She must be an incarnation of Lilith, the she-devil—Adam's first wife, the one who chose to live among demons; or an incarnation of Potiphar's wife.

Suddenly, she rises to her feet. She wraps her tunic about her. Habacuc tries to hold her back, but she extricates herself free and leaves, not before murmuring: "Here, tomorrow."

They meet every night. She, always lustful, ardent. "You're a real man," she says, "the only man amid all these sanctimonious fools." She makes it quite clear that she doesn't believe in anything, neither in the Messiah nor in the last battle; she was even considering running away from the Holy City. "And then you came, my love. You, my savior, my Messiah! My inexhaustible well of love!"

Although flattered, Habacuc can't help feeling apprehensive. What if they find out, he wonders. And even if they don't—how is all of this going to end? What makes him feel even guiltier, however, is his betrayal of his friend Eliezer, who continues to talk to him about Naomi in the most glowing terms. Doesn't he suspect anything at all? Habacuc can hardly believe that anyone could be so naive; maybe Eliezer is plotting something, maybe he is leading Habacuc on, just to see how far he'll go. So, when one night Eliezer invites him to go for a walk—we have a lot to talk about—Habacuc is in a near panic: It's now, he thinks, it's now that he's going to get even with me. He can't, however, decline the invitation. Tense, he accompanies his friend. Under his tunic, Habacuc firmly holds his dagger by the handle, the dagger he never got rid of, not even after opting for an ascetic lifestyle. But Eliezer doesn't have a clue about what is going on between Habacuc and Naomi. What he wants is to confide an astonishing plan to Habacuc: He can't stand this existence among the Essenes anymore, the fastings, the penances, the waiting for a Master of Justice who will never come.

"This banquet!" he shouts, enraged. Then controlling himself, he lowers his voice: "For years now I've heard them talk about this banquet with the Messiah, Haba. For years I've been preparing myself for the arrival of the Master. I'm fed up with all of it."

A pause, then he goes on:

"I can't bear being without a woman anymore. I just can't, Haba. Every night I have these dreams, I ejaculate in bed. I'm wasting my semen, I'm getting weak. And old. I want the priest's daughter,

Haba. And I'm sure that she wants me just as badly. The way she looks at me . . . She's crazy about me, Haba. Crazy. And I'm just as crazy about her. I want her now. And I'm willing to go to any lengths to get her."

He discloses his plan. He will go down the mountain, search out the Roman troops, which are camped nearby. He will reveal the location of the treasure. In exchange for the information, he will ask their commander for a share of the riches—and for Naomi.

Habacuc listens, horrified: "But it'll be a bloodbath," he exclaims. "Nobody here knows how to wield a weapon, all you hear is this talk about swords of light." Eliezer shrugs. "I couldn't care less," he says in a dull tone of voice. "I've made up my mind, I want this woman, I'll have her no matter how." He holds Habacuc by the arm: "Can I count on you, Haba? You'll get your share of the treasure, too. I'll be generous, I promise you."

Habacuc stares at him, at a loss for words.

"Even without your help, I'm going ahead with my plan," threatens Eliezer. "In two days' time I'll approach the Romans. Until then, you have time to think it over."

That night Habacuc and Naomi leave the Holy City. Behind them are the quiet houses. On a cot, his eyes wide open, lies Eliezer—dead, with Habacuc's dagger buried in his chest.

Walking during the night and hiding by day, they finally reach the coast. They run into a group of refugees, who like them, want to flee the country. They will have to charter a ship; there's a Greek captain who is willing to oblige, but for a high sum of money. But neither of them has any money. As Habacuc argues with the Greek, Naomi begins to pull him by the arm. "What is it?" he asks, annoyed, "can't you see I'm busy trying to solve this problem?" "Come over here," she says, smiling, "there's something I want to show you." After they step aside, she removes the pouch that hangs from her neck, and opens it: rings, necklaces, tiaras; gold, diamonds, rubies.

"How beautiful," marvels Habacuc, "where did you get them?"
Then it dawns on him—and he blurts out:

"And what about the seeds of the Gold Tree? Did you bring the
seeds of the Gold Tree? With the Gold Tree—"

He stops short: By the expression on her face, he realizes that he
has made a mistake. He tries to apologize, but it's too late. From now
on things won't be the same between them. They will no longer be
able to surrender themselves to each other with their former passion.
Greed has poisoned their lives. Like Adam and Eve after eating the
fruit of the Tree of the Knowledge of Good and Evil, they, too, won't
have any peace.

The small ship sailed from an anchorage at Yafo on a
dark moonless night. The campfires of a nearby Roman encampment glowed in the blackness; the fugitives could even hear the
laughter of the legionnaires as they celebrated their latest victories
over the fanatically insurgent Jews. Carried by favorable winds, the
ship glided rapidly away; by dawn they had left the coast far behind.

Two days later, as they coasted some islands, a sudden lull took the
wind from the ship's sails. Seated on the deck, the crew and the
passengers traded worried looks. What did it bode, this unexpected
change in the weather? Nobody knew, not even the experienced
Greek captain.

Night fell. The ship swayed gently in the dark. The silence was
broken only by the squealing sound of the vessel's timbers. Snuggled
against Habacuc, Naomi slept. The others, apprehensive, sat waiting.

Suddenly a voice, from afar: *Habacuc! Habacuc!* Twice. Roused
from their sleep, the voyagers, terrified, whispered: "Answer, Habacuc, answer." But he kept shaking his head stubbornly. Only when
the voice called him for the seventh time did he rise to his feet:

"I am Habacuc! Who calls me? Why do you call me?"

"Your crime didn't go unnoticed," replied the voice. "Because of the sins you and others have committed, a god has died, Habacuc. As punishment, your descendants will wander the earth until they finally hark to the word of the Children of Light. Have I made myself understood?"

"Yes," murmured Habacuc, livid, his forehead damp with perspiration. "This is my message," said the voice. There was a silence; and then the wind rose. Reassured that this matter didn't concern them, the sailors then hoisted sail.

Six days later the boat arrived in Sefarad (later called Spain). There Habacuc and Naomi joined a small Hebrew settlement. They prospered, thanks to the jewels Naomi had brought with her. To the end of his life Habacuc suffered pangs of remorse for having deserted the Essenes, for having drawn away from the Well of the Spring Tide, and for having robbed a father of his only daughter even though it had been with her consent. For having forsaken the land of Israel. For having killed a man. For having caused the death of a god. Despite his guilt, however, Habacuc drank and ate well and was in good health; he lived to a "ripe old age." His children, grandchildren, and great-grandchildren lived in Spain, in cities like Toledo, whose name comes from *Toledoth*, meaning the city of the generations, first under the rule of the Romans, then of the Visigoths, and later of the Moors. Among the Moors lived a famous ancestor of the Mendeses: Moses ben Maimon, better known by the Greek form of his name: Maimonides.

Born in 1135, when the Iberian Peninsula was under Arabic rule, Maimonides was educated by his learned father and by Muslim masters. From an early age he dedicated himself to philosophy. He wrote treatises in which he wondered about the meaning of life, which filled him with anxiety—but by and large, he was happy.

In 1148 the Omayyads, who had until then ruled over Arabic

Spain, were overthrown by the fanatical Almohads. This was followed by the expulsion of both Christians and Jews. Maimonides's family moved to Northern Africa, and later settled in Cairo. After their father died, Maimonides and his brother David set up a jewelry business. David, who loved jewels, would spend hours lovingly stroking necklaces, bracelets, rings. It was painful for him to part with these precious objects. "If I could," he would say with a sigh, "I'd spend the entire day admiring these. The more I look at a precious stone, the greater the wonders I find therein. Some stones have the warmth of the sun, others have the mysterious glow of the moon. Signs, my brother—signs of fate. And the Gold Tree! Ah, if only I could find the Gold Tree!"

Maimonides, however, was completely indifferent to jewels. He would take them to their customers, who were noblemen in the court of the sultan Saladin. Reclining on silk cushions, they would examine the goods while Maimonides stood lost in thought. What is the meaning of the human condition? What is the relationship between God and the universe? The customers would ask him about the price of the jewels; the question had to be repeated three or four times before he came to his senses, and then, in a flurry, he would blurt out something: either a preposterously high or a ridiculously low price, which made the noblemen burst loudly into laughter. Some, irritated, would send him away, saying they didn't want to do business with such an idiot. As a result, his brother David's workload increased. It even fell to him to charter ships and to travel to Cyprus, to Byzantium, in search of new customers. It was in the course of one such voyage that David died in a shipwreck. His body was never recovered.

His brother's death was a severe blow to Maimonides, who for several days sat on the beach, staring out at the sea, grievously striking at his chest with his fists. He had to be taken home against his will. Then, shutting himself up in his room, he began to write his masterpiece, *The Guide for the Perplexed*, which was an attempt to guide himself, and others, through the major issues of life and death.

There were, however, far more pressing worries. Now that his brother was dead, the support of the family became his responsibility. What should he do? He disliked the jewelry business, and with

David gone, he wouldn't have the slightest chance of succeeding in this line of work. So he decided to take up medicine, a respected and lucrative profession. Besides, medicine was close to philosophy: Maimonides secretly expected that in the humors secreted by the diseased bodies, in the whispered words of the dying, in the hallucinations of the lunatics, he would find the answers to the questions that kept disturbing him.

At that time Arabic medicine was flourishing under great physicians, such as: Avicena! (or Ibn Sina.) Avenzoar! (or Ibn Zurh.) Averroes! (or Ibn Rushid.) Maimonides—or Musa Ibn Maimun, as he was known—became Averroes's favorite disciple.

Maimonides learned how to prepare infusions of medicinal herbs. With a sharp knife he was able to remove a cataract in a matter of minutes; he would then examine the tiny lens, milky and opaque like the pearls his brother used to admire so much, and with a sigh, he would discard it, unless the patient requested to have it as a souvenir; in this case, he would put it in a phial with alcohol.

In accordance with the best Hippocratic tradition, he learned how to interpret the signs of disease. By examining urine, he was able to tell from its appearance, smell, taste, and the deposits it left, whether the patient was going to die or get better. If the fever went down fast, he would sigh with relief; but if a low-grade fever lingered for days or weeks, or if at twilight the cheeks of the patient flushed, Maimonides would be alarmed, for he was well familiar with the disguises of tuberculosis. Like Joseph in the Bible, he, too, was interested in dreams; he could tell which particular remorse was tormenting a person by analyzing the shapes of the figures that appeared in his dreams. And he also had a special interest in the pathology of the unusual or exotic.

He became respected and well-known. He settled in Fostat, near Cairo; soon afterward, he could write to his relatives: "Due to my reputation as a physician, the powerful hold me in high regard. My antechambers are always crowded with patients. I arrive in the morning, dismount my horse, wash my hands, and proceed to attend to the sick, who keep streaming in until sunset. I'm so tired at night that I can barely talk—tired but happy."

He was making a lot of money. His former doubts about the meaning of life still obsessed him, but to a lesser extent. The lives he saved absolved him from his faults. He was . . . happy. Happy. He was married to a beautiful, gentle, understanding woman. It's true that at times, after they made love, Maimonides had difficulty falling asleep; restless, he would toss about in bed. When he finally drifted off to sleep, it was to find himself submerged in a deep sea, confronting what he was afraid of finding: the body of his brother. Fish swam through the empty eye sockets, crustaceans sidled out of the mouth. Tied to his dead brother's neck, a pouch with precious stones: pearls, emeralds, rubies. *Take the jewels,* whispered a distant voice. A series of muffled bangs began to reverberate in the depths of that sea, growing louder and more distinct until they finally woke him up; it was someone battering away at the door. Someone calling him to attend to a sick person.

Throughout the Jewish community in Egypt, the *Rambam* (an acronym standing for Rabbi Moses ben Maimon) was truly venerated. People came to him not only because of his medical skill but also because of his great wisdom. "Me? a sage?" he would say. "But I'm the most ignorant of the ignorant." But they thought otherwise. They all came for comfort and advice, gathering at his door.

One day a stranger came to see him.

He walked in disguised in a long mantle, which he didn't take off; he declined the wine that a servant had offered him, and when Maimonides asked what had brought him there, he ignored the question and started to fire questions of his own at the physician: Wasn't Musa Ibn Maimun overworking himself? Wasn't he getting tired of looking after so many patients? Intrigued but not angry, Maimonides replied to each one of his questions. He knew human nature too well to be offended by such impertinence. Besides, he knew that the sick tend to be suspicious, demanding explanations before submitting themselves to the care of a physician.

When the stranger was through with his questioning, he proffered a remarkable opinion: He believed that the physician was overworking himself, he had too many patients. "Wouldn't it be better to have fewer patients?" he asked. "Say, ten, or five—or, even better, just one patient willing to pay him royally for his services?" "I don't think so," replied Maimonides, wary. "A physician should attend to anyone who needs him. Now, if you'll excuse me, I have to get back to my work."

He rose to his feet. The man rose too, and flinging aside his mantle, he revealed his opulent attire. He identified himself as one of Saladin's ministers: He was offering Musa Ibn Maimun the position of personal physician to the sultan.

Maimonides quivered. The proposal amounted to an official recognition, the greatest recognition to which he could aspire; however, despite being the physician of many a dignitary, he now hesitated about accepting responsibility for the health of a ruler of empires. The minister noticed his uncertainty. "Allow me to remind you that the sultan's invitation amounts to an order," he said.

The man's authoritarian tone of voice and arrogance angered Maimonides; his first impulse was to reply haughtily *then take me with you, but you will have to kill me first;* however, he knew it would be impossible for him to say this. He was responsible not only to his family but also to the Jewish community in Egypt, of which, in the eyes of the Arabs, he was the official representative. He couldn't take a stand that might put other people in jeopardy. "All right, I accept the offer," he said. The minister, pleased, outlined the details of the proposal: Maimonides would move to the sultan's palace, where he and his family would live in private lodgings. He would have as many servants and assistants as he needed, as well as books, medical instruments, medicines. He mentioned the payment—a sum so high that even Maimonides was impressed: "Am I worth all this much?" The minister smiled: "The sultan pays handsomely for what he wants."

Finally the minister mentioned the main stipulation: Musa Ibn Maimun was to be at the sultan's beck and call. He was not to attend to anyone else—one of the reasons being the risk of his hands transmitting another person's disease to his employer. Then, rising to his feet, he said:

"Is everything clear?"

Sighing, Maimonides said it was. "Let's go then," said the minister, "I have camels waiting outside."

"But I need some time," said Maimonides, "to look after a few matters; there are also the patients waiting to see me—"

"They will be informed," said the minister with impatience. "Call your family and let's go without any further delay."

And so Maimonides is taken to the palace: On a camel, shielded from the stares of the populace by a richly ornamented baldachin. As soon as they arrive, the minister takes him to the sultan.

A corpulent man, this Saladin; vitality exudes from the piercing eyes, from the vigorous gestures. He looks Maimonides up and down: "So, this is the physician then? Welcome, physician, welcome." Respectfully, and choosing his words carefully, the minister suggests that the sultan submit himself to a physical examination right away, for he is scheduled to start out on a journey very soon. Good-humored, Saladin acquiesces. Everybody leaves the hall, and he remains alone with the physician. Maimonides questions him about his dietary habits, his bowel movements, his sexual drive, the shape of his feces and the force with which the stream of urine comes out. Saladin, willingly but rather impatiently, replies to every question: "I've never been ill, physician, why all these questions?" Intimidated, Maimonides proceeds to the clinical exam: "Would you, Your Excellency. . . ."

"Take off my clothes?" Laughing, the sultan undresses, lies down on the cushions.

Maimonides recognizes at once the sultan's excellent physical condition, but being in a fluster, he makes mistakes typical of a greenhorn; however, he has no trouble noticing that the sultan's forehead is cool, that his mucous membranes are pink and moist, that there is no furring on his tongue, that his pulse is regular, a touch too full, perhaps, a touch too strong, but taking into account his age, still within normal range. No signs of disease, Maimonides concludes, nothing to prescribe, and so he informs the sovereign. "Aren't you afraid you'll lose your job now?" asks Saladin, laughing. Both physician and patient laugh together. The sultan's laughter is deep, he laughs slapping his hands on his thighs, he laughs until he gasps for breath. Finally, he asks Maimonides if everything is all right with him, if Musa Ibn Maimun is happy.

Maimonides is suddenly serious. He doesn't reply right away. He thinks for a while, his eyes fixed on the rug. Finally—surprised at his own frankness—he says that everything is not all right. He feels honored by his position as royal physician, but he would rather attend to many patients, not just one.

"I'm not 'just one,'" Saladin says dryly. "I'm many. I'm everybody. And now leave. You're dismissed."

Maimonides leaves.

Days, months go by. Maimonides sees Saladin but occasionally. Claiming he doesn't have the time, the sultan refuses to see the physician. Maimonides has to turn to Saladin's closest associates for information: Does he sleep well? How is his appetite? Does he pass wind? Does he belch? He neatly writes down the answers in a special logbook, then spends hours mulling over his notes, trying to guess at the condition of the humors, of the pneuma, of the pituitary from the observations that he wrote down. On his desk, thick volumes written in Latin, in Arabic, in Greek, in Hebrew, keep piling up; these books, brought by Saladin's envoys, who travel all over the world to get them, epitomize the medical knowledge of those days. They contain descriptions of exotic diseases, of new forms of treatment. Maimonides doesn't read them. What for? He lacks the opportunity to put this knowledge into practice. Motionless, he sits staring at the books. At times his fingers twitch—the fingers are eager to touch a wrist, to palpate the contours of a tumor. There are no wrists, there are no tumors. There is nothing.

In the evening Maimonides locks his office and goes to his private lodgings. His wife waits for him. Ever since her husband became the sultan's physician, she has experienced contradictory feelings. On the one hand, she's proud of the envy that her status causes in the friends that come to visit her and to whom, with affected insouciance, she relates the latest gossip of the court. On the other hand, she is worried, for she realizes that her husband is unhappy. But she chooses not to say anything to him, hoping that it's just one of those ephemeral depressions that from time to time afflict Maimonides, a melancholic man by nature.

Affecting unconcern, she asks her husband about his day. "So, so," he says. "And how's the sultan?" "Fine," he says, then correcting himself: "I think he's fine. It seems that his headache is better."

Trying to cheer him up, she tells him about the flattering remarks that the Jewish community keeps making about the Rambam, their greatest representative. Maimonides listens in silence. He rises to his feet, goes to his room. He sits there, leafing through his own books, especially *The Guide for the Perplexed*. In this work he advocates applying Aristotelian logic to the Jewish religion itself—which perplexes the more Orthodox Jews, who are, as a matter of fact, invariably suspicious of any Greek trend: Logic, in religion? How? And now Maimonides himself wonders: Under the present circumstances, what good does logic do to me? Could there be something deeper, something not on a conscious level, that would explain what happens? Perhaps supra-individual forces, or historical laws? Such ruminations are cut short by the arrival of his wife, who comes in with a glass of milk: "Go to bed," she says, "it's late, you'll have to be in your office tomorrow."

On the following day everything starts all over again.

Maimonides devotes himself to treating imaginary patients. At first there's only one, a young man afflicted by mysterious fevers; then, Maimonides adds a woman with jaundice, a man with tuberculosis, and an old man with an abdominal tumor. They moan, they call for him. He imagines that he is examining them, that he is looking at their tongues, for example; and so vividly does he imagine the scene that he can actually see the furring on their tongues, the blotches with contours that suggest maps of mysterious countries. Then leaning over, he places his ear on imaginary chests, listening to the beating of hearts that have never existed—and he is amazed at their strange rhythms, rhythms that no Ibn Sina has ever described. To him, it is music, music of the spheres. From this reverie he is roused by the voice of his wife:

"Moses! Dinner!"

At the sound of her voice, he sighs. Does a person who doesn't work, who doesn't help others, have the right to eat bread? However, in his case it's not bread, but delectable dishes—so, he rises to his feet to eat dinner.

One day the sultan agrees to see him, but only reluctantly, making it quite clear that he has acceded to the requests of his ministers, but he doesn't believe in medicine or in physicians.

"I only want to make sure that you are in good health," says Maimonides somewhat apologetically.

An idea occurs to Saladin; his eyes glitter; he smiles lewdly:

"So, you really want to see if I'm in good health, is that right, Musa Ibn Maimun? Well, let me show you."

Grabbing the physician by the arm, he drags him through the corridors of the palace as far as a pavilion with an iron door, at which stand two armed guards. Maimonides is puzzled: that's the harem. What is Saladin up to? The sultan pushes him indoors: "Go in, physician, there's no need to be afraid, there aren't any lepers in here."

Around a fountain in the hall, there are some twenty or thirty women wearing transparent silk; reclined on cushions, they talk, they sing. Upon seeing Saladin, they fall silent, puzzled: A man here? And brought in by Saladin?

"You'll see how healthy I am," says the sultan, taking off his clothes.

He looks around, then calls one of the women: "You! Lie down here!" The young woman complies, and Saladin throws himself upon her, and takes her. Then he gets up and calls another woman. Again, he has sex with her, and then with a third woman—afterward, he rises to his feet. Then he asks the shocked, embarrassed Maimonides: "So, what do you think? Am I in good health or not?"

Maimonides doesn't reply. Saladin puts on his clothes. "There's no need for my ministers to worry anymore," he says grinning. "Wouldn't you agree, physician?"

Maimonides agrees. Excusing himself, he then leaves. He locks himself up in his room: to cry. More than perplexed, he feels lost. Hopelessly lost. Not even God can help him.

He cannot leave the palace. It's forbidden. But from a small window he watches the city, the crowds that fill up the streets, the market. Small dark creatures enveloped in rags. What does he know about them, about the populace? Nothing. To distract himself, he makes diagnoses from a distance: That man over there has scabies . . . that woman there is chlorotic . . . that other man there seems to be suffering from dropsy. It's A.D. 1192. On April 6 Maimonides notes a certain restlessness in the city, a certain disturbance that keeps growing during the following days; observing the panic displayed by the people, he deduces that something very grave must be happening. Masses of people begin to leave the city, taking their possessions with them. Cloaked figures appear on the streets, carrying stretchers on which lie corpses, which are then thrown into the fires that burn everywhere. "There's some terrible disease going around, Musa Ibn Maimun," his valet tells him confidentially. And he disappears: he, too, has fled the city.

It's cholera, concludes Maimonides, what the Hebrews called *chole ra*, the cruel disease, the ancient plague of the Orient. It's cholera, and nothing can be done, except what Saladin himself—without deigning to consult him—has already ordered: Burn the corpses. As a matter of fact, consulting Maimonides would have been useless. Maimonides doesn't know. Nobody knows. The cause of the disease is unknown, and so is the manner by which it is spread. With a sigh, Maimonides closes the window and returns to *The Guide for the Perplexed*.

In the third week of this epidemic, he wakes in the middle of the night with a sudden and extraordinary intuition: *The disease stems from the water.* From the water in the great communal well near the market, a well used by most of the townspeople. In the darkness of the room he can clearly see the depths of this well, the subterranean rivulets that feed it; into this crystalline water flows a muddy liquid: excrements, the copious fecal discharges from the cholera victims. A deadly vicious circle is thus established.

The day is barely dawning when he hastens to see the minister to request an audience with the sultan. The minister wants to know why. Maimonides says he wants to see him about the cholera; he outlines his ideas about the disease, claims that he can save the townspeople from this plague—at least he can try. The minister listens to him with a frown, and says nothing. "So?" says Maimonides. "Forget it," says the minister, "you're the sultan's physician, the diseases of the rabble are none of your business." Maimonides still tries to reason with the minister, but he puts an end to the interview, saying he's much too busy. He's making preparations for a military expedition: Saladin is going to confront the Christians in Palestine.

Devastated, Maimonides returns to his lodgings. However, he manages to pull himself together; he won't let himself feel depressed. He spends that night writing nonstop; what he writes amounts to a treatise on cholera: causes, manner of transmission, treatment. But in the morning, in a frenzy of despair, he throws the manuscript into the fire. From then on, his state of mind deteriorates quickly. He shuns his wife, he doesn't want to talk to his children. He has frequent fits of crying. He prays and prays, but even religion cannot give him solace. He considers putting an end to his life. . . .

One night there is a loud banging on the door. Alarmed, Maimonides gets up, opens the door. It's a guard: Maimonides is being summoned to the palace. The physician dresses in a hurry and follows the man. They walk across the inner courtyards of the palace, which are bathed in moonlight. Maimonides shivers in the cold wind. What's in store for him at the palace?

He is taken to the Council Room. All the ministers and court dignitaries are gathered there. Also present is a messenger who has just arrived from Saladin's encampment in Damascus. He is the bearer of bad tidings: The sultan is ill.

Maimonides interrogates the man quickly; from what he hears, he is convinced that the sultan's illness is serious. Orders are given to make preparations for a journey; Maimonides is to leave for Damascus immediately. He returns to his lodgings to pack a few articles of clothing, his medical instruments, a few books; then saying goodbye to his wife, he joins the escort already waiting for him. They'll travel by sea as far as Palestine; from there they'll proceed on horseback to the encampment.

Three days later Maimonides arrives at his destination. He is met by Saladin's generals; their worried faces convey to the physician that his arrival represents their last hope. Little information is given out. Saladin had just ended his campaign against the Christians, who were led by Richard of England. Even though he had been defeated twice at Yafo, he was negotiating a highly advantageous peace treaty. Upon returning to Damascus, he was suddenly taken ill.

Maimonides is taken to a large tent, where there is only a couch. The man he sees lying on it, the seriously ill man who at times tosses about deliriously, this man is Saladin.

Maimonides removes the mantle that covers him, exposing the ailing body: a strange, unknown country. He is gripped by terror, the same terror of the nightmares in which he sees his dead brother. Clumsily, his hands palpate Saladin's abdomen; the sick man moans, the hands hastily withdraw. The hands hesitate, not knowing whether they should take the pulse or percuss the thorax. Relax, Maimonides murmurs to himself, stop acting like a madman; think, damn it, think.

He tries to coordinate his thoughts, to reach a diagnosis. There's lethargy, he notes, there are tremors; the muscle tone is weakened, the eyes are sunken, the abdomen, depressed and sensitive. What could it be? He doesn't know.

He glowers at his patient: It's his own fault, Maimonides says to himself. He took me away from my practice, he shut me up in a palace, away from my patients. I've lost my skills, my insights. But he's now paying for it: He has condemned himself to death, this Muslim dog.

Maimonides leaves the tent. Alone, he wanders among the soldiers' tents, comes to the well, stands staring at the moon reflected in its dark waters.

Somebody grabs him by the arm. It's the minister.

"The man is very sick, Musa Ibn Maimun."

A statement or a question? Maimonides chooses not to reply. The minister looks at him; it's a look that disturbs the physician. What next?

"I'm not going to beat about the bush, Musa Ibn Maimun," says the minister in a low, ominous voice. "I don't know whether you can cure Saladin or not; the point is, he must not survive. He must not, understand?"

He stops talking: A group of soldiers walks by. The minister waits until they are out of earshot before he goes on: "This treaty with the Christian king . . . this treaty is going to be fatal to us. And it will affect you too, as a Jew. The blood of your people will flow, Musa Ibn Maimun. In Palestine, and everywhere else. Therefore, it's imperative that Saladin die."

Maimonides says nothing. He wants to leave, but the minister seizes him by the arm: "Remember what I've told you," he says. And then he threatens: "It's either Saladin's life—or yours."

Maimonides returns to the sultan's tent. The ministers and the generals are gone; only Saladin's old nursemaid is there, pressing compresses on the sick man's forehead. Dismissing her with a gesture, he sits down by the couch, and there he remains, immersed in deep, sorrowful contemplation.

Suddenly he is aware of Saladin's wide-open eyes fixed on him. There's mockery in the dying man's eyes; the physician is transfixed by this look. "You don't know what's wrong with me," he murmurs. "Of course I do," says Maimonides in a trembling voice. "It's a pretty common illness—congestion, biliousness." "It's none of it," says Saladin, "you're lying." His voice shows no rancor; on the contrary, there is even a certain tenderness in it. "You don't know what's wrong with me," he repeats, "and I'm going to die. Today."

"Shut up," says Maimonides, anguished, "I haven't even started . . ." "There's nothing that can be done," Saladin cuts him short, his voice now weak and sorrowful. "And even if you could cure me, they would kill me. My ministers, my generals. I know all about the conspiracy, Musa Ibn Maimun. I know everything."

Exhausted, he stops talking. They remain silent for a few moments. Then reaching out his hand, Saladin lays it on Maimonides's arm. "But you, physician," he says with a smile, "you can benefit from my death. All you have to do is to convince them that you caused it."

"Never!" Maimonides rises to his feet, upset. "I would never do such a thing!"

He bursts into tears. He cries helplessly for a long time. Saladin looks on in silence. Finally, Maimonides wipes his eyes, and sighs. Then something crosses his mind, and he bursts into laughter: "Remember that epidemic, Saladin? That mysterious disease? Well, I traced its cause to the water from the well. The water, imagine!"

"Who would have guessed," murmurs Saladin, sighing. He looks at the physician with entreating eyes: "Could it be cholera what I have, Musa Ibn Maimun? There's a well here too. Could it be cholera?"

"Who knows," replies Maimonides.

They fall silent again. They hear the distant barking of dogs, the mournful singing of a soldier.

"The water," says Saladin, "who would have guessed."

He bursts into laughter. Into uncontrollable laughter, which shakes his body. Astonished, Maimonides stares at him. Then he, too, begins to laugh. The two of them laugh and laugh, delightedly, unrestrainedly; Maimonides laughs so hard that he rolls about on the couch; and there he remains, panting, lying alongside Saladin; finally, tired out, he falls asleep.

When Maimonides wakes up, Saladin is dead. He then flings the doors wide open, and asks Saladin's aides to come in and take the body away. And he leaves, walking past noblemen and soldiers, slaves and professional mourners.

Years later, Moses ben Maimon—Maimonides—died; his descendants returned to Cordoba; they lived in peace, begetting children, rocking them to sleep with lullabies sung in Ladino, the Judeo-Spanish dialect:

> *Duerme, duerme, mi angelico*
> *Hijico chico de tu nación . . .*
> *Creatura de Sión,*
> *No conoces la dolor.*

Later they went to Portugal. The name of the family kept changing: Maimonides, Maimendes, Memendes, Mendes.

The Mendeses settled in the mountainous region of Trancoso, in northern Portugal. A wealthy, God-fearing family, they hadn't forgotten Sion, where they hoped to return one day.

At one time they had in their employ a poet-shoemaker called Bandarra, whose visions were expressed in lyric verses that moved and impressed everybody. But it was of his shoemaking skills that Bandarra was particularly proud. An exacting craftsman, he insisted on personally selecting the leather for the sandals and boots that he made; as time went by, however, he was no longer satisfied with this—he had to inspect the cows from which the leather would come while they were still alive. He would carefully palpate them and listen to their mooing. To the chosen ones, he would then deliver a brief panegyric: Your leather will protect the feet of men of goodwill from the asperity of the paths of life; distinguished toes will be grateful to you for having spared them calluses. You will be evoked with tenderness: A good animal, people will say of you, a creature of God that gave us its own skin. After his speech, Bandarra would then kill the animal with blows delivered by a maul made from the solid wood of trees that grew in the Holy Land.

At the age of fifty, suspecting that death would not be long in arriving, Bandarra decided he would produce the masterpiece of his life—the best pair of boots in the world. For a long time he had been getting ready for it: He had raised a calf of excellent pedigree, had grazed it on the best available grassland, had massaged it daily with premium beer. The animal was now at the right stage; a little while longer, and age would affect the pliability of the leather. Therefore, Bandarra couldn't—shouldn't—wait any longer. Before killing the calf, however, he retreated to the mountains, where he spent three days praying and feeding on nothing but milk and herbs. Weakened in body but strengthened in faith, he returned to the village. He took the calf to the main square and, in front of the assembled villagers, delivered his usual panegyric. Then he spat into his hands, grabbed the maul and delivered a powerful blow. He missed; perhaps it was the fasting that made him miss. Instead of killing the calf, he broke the stake to which it was tied. The animal ran away.

Bandarra chased after it, cursing. The calf climbed up mountain trails—with Bandarra, huffing and puffing, in pursuit. Finally the calf came to the edge of a cliff; it was cornered.

Slowly, Bandarra advanced. As he raised the maul, the calf gazed at him in such a way that he shuddered: it was the look of a human being, the look of someone sentenced to death. Bandarra wavered, but only for a second; then he struck a blow, a terrible blow. The animal staggered, but was still on its feet; it kept stepping farther back until it tumbled down the abyss. Bandarra couldn't help uttering an imprecation. What would remain of the animal after a drop from this height? Nothing, certainly. With great difficulty he clambered down to the bottom of the precipice, clinging precariously to rocks and bushes. As he had feared, the animal was all mangled, the skin bloodied and torn by the rocks and the sharp pointed ends of broken bones; he wouldn't even get a pair of slippers out of it. One of its eyes, however, was still intact, and was gazing at him ironically, with the same expression that had disturbed him earlier. Pulling out his knife, Bandarra cut that eye out of its socket. He examined it intently; there was something strange there . . . Impelled by an unconquerable urge, he peered into the dilated pupil. He then had visions that deeply affected him. Unknown lands; a beautiful landscape. A bay, a blue sea, waves breaking upon the white, very white sand of a beach. Coconut trees. Exotic, brightly colored birds in wheeling flight against the magnificent blue of an uncharted sky. On this beach strange creatures suddenly appear—men, women, and children with bronze-colored skin, their faces painted in gaudy colors, their long hair ornamented with feathers; they kneel down—before whom? The Messiah? A king yet to be born? One of the Mendeses? Bandarra couldn't tell. Slowly the vision faded, and the eye became again what it had been before, the eyeball of a dead calf.

Disturbed, Bandarra went back to the village. He didn't know what to tell his masters, the Mendeses. How to explain what had happened to the calf? And the visions he'd had? Strictly speaking, the visions belonged to the Mendeses, for the animal was theirs, and consequently, the magic eye into which he had peered was theirs, too; but would they believe his story? Probably not. However, there was something he knew: he knew there were distant lands, seemingly fertile, bountiful lands—the place, if not of the Gold Tree, at least of a future kingdom. And it wouldn't be fair to keep this secret to himself. So he began to exhort the young Mendeses to become navigators. "Study the art of sailing," he would advise them. "Learn how to read nautical charts; one day these skills will come in handy."

Whether as a result of this advice or not—it's hard to tell—the fact is that the Mendes family produced a cartographer.

His name was Rafael. He had been given this name (from the Hebrew *rapha*, physician, and *el*, God; physician of God) as a tribute to his illustrious ancestor, the great Moses ben Maimon, who could well have been the physician of God. As a matter of fact, this name would be transmitted from generation to generation. Why, when Jews do not name their sons after their fathers? Quite simple: As a shrewd disguise, as a way of deceiving the Inquisition.

At that point in time the stage for the performance of the Iberian Holy Office had been set. In Spain, Torquemada kept demanding from Ferdinand and Isabella the expulsion of the

Jews; in Portugal, where one fifth of the population was of Jewish origin, there were similar and no less insistent demands. The Jews aroused jealousy and fear, for they were the physicians and the poets, the astronomers and the philosophers; but above all, they were the merchants and the financiers.

Throughout the Middle Ages, the Jews were the only commercial link between the West and the East. They spoke all the important languages: Persian, Latin, Arabic, French, Spanish, the Slavic languages. From Spain and France they would take furs, swords, and eunuchs to India and China; they would return with musk, aloes, camphor; clove and cinnamon; Oriental fabrics. In order to buy such valuable goods, however—as well as mount their frequent military expeditions—the feudal lords needed money. Since the lending of money at interest was forbidden to Christians, such activity was reserved to Jews—a situation that suited the feudal lords wonderfully well: If unable to pay back their loans, all they had to do was to trigger a massacre.

In England this process was simplified by the existence of the *saccarium judaeorum*, a place for the registration of Jewish vouchers, on which a ten-percent tax, collected for the royal treasury, was levied. In case of breach of contract, all the aristocracy had to do was to solemnly burn the vouchers deposited therein.

At the time of the voyages of discovery, money became necessary to finance the oceanic expeditions. This situation placed the Jewish financiers in a dilemma: On the one hand, the rise of the bourgeoisie heralded freedom of speech and of religion, as well as the destruction of the barriers that separated peoples and regions; on the other hand, this greater freedom also permitted new bankers, such as the Fuggers and the Medicis, to enter the money business. Money lending at interest was no longer a sin; on the contrary, accumulation of capital was soon to become a Christian virtue. A critical time: The old era was dying, the new one not yet born; and standing at this historical crossroads were the Jews. Standing there too were their enemies, determined to seize the Jews' wealth or to prevent them from using it to destroy the feudal world. Heresy must be checked, Torquemada maintained. The world is not round, there are no new sea routes, maps are messages from the devil.

Rafael Mendes, cartographer, had frequent arguments with his father, a calligrapher by profession. The old man wanted to persuade his son to take up calligraphy, an art highly valued in the fifteenth century. "Letters," the old man would say, "are well-defined, codified symbols, they have the exactness of logic. Moreover, they allow for flights of the imagination: In a curlicue, for instance, you can see everything, from the dance of the flames to the image of a serpent; or, if you prefer, the sinuous roads of fate. Fate is often contained in one single letter. When drawing an A, for example, you go up, then you go down; with one single stroke, you cut across it; and there you have, in three movements, a summary account of life. How could we ever appreciate the written word if it weren't for calligraphy? Calligraphy makes the writer responsible for every single letter he traces; the effort, the concentration, the dedication necessary to accomplish this task compel him to be wise, prudent, and restrained in his writing. Calligraphy effectively holds whatever is vulgar in check; it reserves books and their beautiful illuminations for the few who are able to appreciate them. As for maps," he would go on, "what are maps? Nothing but winding lines traced at random; even when accurately traced, these lines merely reproduce geographical accidents, which don't follow any human design. But I," he would say, irritated, "I don't put my trust in maps at all. When someone shows me an irregular figure, telling me it's Terceira Island—I don't believe him. Who can assure me that it is indeed Terceira Island? Now, a *B* is a *B*, an *R* is an *R*."

Rafael Mendes, cartographer, would not argue with his father. Out of respect? No. It was because he wasn't even listening. He was floating in space, so to speak; and what he saw from those heights were far-off landscapes, mysterious and fascinating. It was the vision of a bay; waves breaking upon the white, very white sands of a beach. Coconut trees. Exotic, brightly colored birds. The magnificent blue of an uncharted sky.

How to reach such places without maps? It wasn't that the young cartographer undervalued calligraphy; he, too, would draw letters fancifully—but he would draw them on maps, or on the globes which his client, Christopher Columbus, imagined the world to resemble.

A strange man, this Columbus. Little was known about him; it was said that he was a Jew, but he didn't identify himself as one. Anyhow, he had a reputation as a skillful navigator. Rafael had met him through the master cartographer Abraão Zacuto, whom the Genovese had commissioned to chart an expedition that he was preparing; unable to do the job on his own, Zacuto had asked the young Mendes to help him out. Officially, Columbus would be searching for a new sea route to India; however, it was rumored that the voyage had some other purpose. Perhaps the discovery of new lands . . . Anyway, there was an aura of mystery in the whole story. Despite the high price charged, Columbus always paid promptly, in cold cash, for cartographic work. Where did he get the money? Who was financing his expensive and hazardous expedition?

"The people from the nation," the elder Rafael would say, gloomily. "The people from our own Hebrew nation." He disliked this Columbus, but recognized that he was an insinuating person, capable of fascinating the rich Jewish financiers with his schemes of finding territories inhabited by the descendants of Israel's lost tribes: Jews of a strange physical appearance, tall and strong, with copper-colored skin, who lived—and this would fire the imagination and arouse the cupidity of his listeners—in cities paved with precious stones: Eldorado! The country of the Gold Tree!

With this fantastic country could be established a profitable commercial intercourse: manufactures from the mother country would be exchanged for precious metals and spices. In addition, this country would be a safe haven for Jews in case of persecutions. The elder Mendes didn't want to hear about such folly. "A haven? What for? If all Jews minded their own business, the way I mind my art," he would say, "nobody would bother us." His son would then remind him of the massacres at the time of the Crusades led by Richard the Lion-Hearted, among others. "Crusades, my foot!" the old man would shout. "That's all in the past. And don't you talk to me about Columbus. Columbus, Columbus! It's all I hear, Columbus. I'm sick and tired of this Columbus! Who asked him to come to Portugal to upset us? Why didn't he stay in his own country? Damn Columbus! I hope he dies in a shipwreck! Yes, I hope he does. And that the fish will devour his eyes, and that the crustaceans will crawl in through his nostrils. I hope a sea serpent will devour him! And that Neptune will tear him to shreds with his trident! And that he'll go to hell! I hope he'll suffer throughout eternity, this man who has turned my son's head."

Dona Ana would calm her husband and ask him not to hurt the feelings of Rafael, who was a sensible young man of good character—his only flaw being this passion of his for cartography. At the word cartography, not wanting to miss the opportunity, the old man would lash out at maps:

"Maps will destroy your youth, my son. Consider for a moment: Peninsulas keep you awake, archipelagos disturb your good sense, bays turn your head. As for this unknown land... It's like a beautiful woman, my son, who lures you by flinging away her transparent tunic. As soon as you get closer, however, like a siren, she'll vanish into the sea. Give it all up, take up calligraphy, which won't bring you any sorrows and will last for centuries. Nothwithstanding," he said with almost imperceptible disquiet, "these experiments now being undertaken in Mainz, where people are printing texts with movable types made from wood. Something only visionaries would dream up; friends of this Columbus, no doubt. Like those other people who want to measure time with mechanical gadgets—what do they have against the sandglass, the clepsydra? Can't they see that the passing of the hours can only be estimated by the slow trickling of sand or water, by a candle that the flames consume, by the shadow that the sun casts? No, they must resort to weights that fall down, or to coiled metal springs, which, forcibly restrained, angrily unwind; and if they could, they would make crystal vibrate in order to measure minute fractions of time in its nervous, tortured quivering. But they won't succeed, my son, I assure you. No machine will ever replace a man's hand—least of all a calligrapher's hand. Try to find peace within yourself, not on maps or in exotic countries."

All this haranguing ended up undermining the young man's convictions. "Why don't you travel across the Mediterranean like all the prudent navigators?" he once asked Columbus, who had come to pick up his maps. The Genovese didn't reply; he smiled and paid cold cash as usual. He was about to leave when an idea occurred to him. He took from his pouch an ivory box. "This is a game I've invented," he said. "I propose that we play a game. If I win, you give me back the money I've just given you; if you win, I'll pay you three times as much; is it a deal?"

"I don't know," replied Rafael, timidly. "I'm not in the habit of betting."

"Well, then you're not in the habit of living," said Columbus; "in life, dear Rafael, as in business and in navigation, we have to take risks."

"Well, then, I'll give it a try," said Rafael.

It was some kind of a chess game; instead of rooks, however, there were miniature caravels, which, after the king and the queen, were the most important pieces. Rafael was quick to learn the rules. They played, he lost. Columbus pocketed the money and predicting better luck for the cartographer, he took his leave.

That very night Columbus left the city of Oporto to see their majesties Ferdinand and Isabella. Some weeks later, an emissary brought a letter to Rafael Mendes: Columbus's expedition had the approval of the sovereigns. He invited Rafael Mendes to accompany him as the official cartographer.

"Madness," said the calligrapher Mendes when his son talked about going. "You're crazy, young man, completely crazy. But I'll take care of you."

The old man didn't take him to a physician because he had no confidence in them. "After our ancestor Maimonides there hasn't been a decent physician in our nation." He took Rafael to a rabbi. "My son is possessed," he declared. "A wandering soul has entered his body and won't leave him alone. He wants to roam the world. Is it a curse, rabbi? If it is a curse, I ask you to free him from it."

The rabbi asked to be left alone with the young man. And to this quiet man, with gentle eyes and a long white beard, Rafael poured out his soul. He talked of his love for maps; and he talked of journeys, venturesome journeys. He mentioned Eldad Ha-Dani, the mysterious Jew who appeared in Spain in the ninth century, saying that he was a surviving member of the Dan tribe, one of Israel's lost tribes. And he related the travels of Rabbi Benjamin de Tudela, who, having left Navarra in 1159, went to Babylon, to the cities of Tema and Teumira, inhabited by Rehavita Jews; to Basra and to Shushan; to Shiraz and to Samarkand. Like these dauntless people, Rafael Mendes wanted to discover new places; but mostly, he wanted to reproduce on maps the contours of unknown continents—Atlantida, among others. In short, he wanted to accompany Christopher Columbus.

The rabbi has heard about the Genovese. He knows that funds are being secretly raised to finance his expedition; that a company is even being established in order to explore the riches to be found. And as in Isaiah's prophecy: "The islands will be waiting for me; and the ships of Tarshish will transport your children; and also gold and silver to honor the Everlasting." (Tarshish, the rabbi knows, is Tartessus, in Spain.)

It is undoubtedly a new era that is being heralded. What can one say of the alchemists' amazing discoveries? And of the new mechanisms, such as the clock, so much abhorred by the calligrapher Mendes? To the rabbi, it seems at once marvellous and terrible that a mechanical device can register the inexorable flow of time. It won't be long before the small, closed guilds and associations are replaced by establishments with hundreds or thousands of workers. This will require substantial funds, so the financiers are counting on the gold and silver from the unknown lands. The rabbi also knows that the feudal lords watch such movements with mistrust; the Inquisition is well-informed, and the Jews live in fear of mass arrests, of executions.

Such are the thoughts that go through his mind as he observes the young man's lit up face and wild eyes. Yes, the calligrapher is right: He is possessed.

Rafael stops talking, the two men remain silent. Finally, the rabbi begins to speak. Cautiously choosing his words, he offers his advice to Rafael Mendes: No, he should not accompany Christopher Columbus. It would be better for him to stay with his family in Oporto. He can draw as many maps as he wants, the rabbi will have a word with his father concerning this matter, and ask him to be more tolerant; but as for this voyage, no. It's fraught with dangers. The storms, the sea serpents, the savages in the unknown countries . . . It would be better for Rafael to stay home.

The young man says nothing. He remains silent, his head lowered, as the rabbi invites the elder Mendes, the calligrapher, to come in, saying that everything is all right.

"He's not possessed. A bit restive, that's all. But it will pass, it's a phase that youth goes through. I've given him some advice."

He's Gog, the young man says to himself as he stares at his father with hatred. He's Gog, the tyrant, wanting to oppress him. Only Columbus can free him. Columbus is his Messiah.

In January 1492, the young Rafael Mendes runs away from home. Traveling during the night, hiding by day, he finally arrives in Castela and goes straight to the La Rábida monastery to see Columbus. An emotional moment: Rafael, in tears, pleads with the Genovese to let him join the expedition. Columbus hesitates. He has already hired all the men he needs, including a cartographer, whom he engaged when he didn't hear from Rafael Mendes again. Besides, he knows how the young man's father feels about this voyage, and he doesn't want any complications. Finally, he proposes that Rafael and he decide the issue on the chessboard.

After a few moves, the young man is trapped. Enraged, he flings the miniature caravels away. Soon afterward, however, he smiles: He took a risk, he lost, now he must willingly accept the designs of fate. So, saying goodbye to Christopher Columbus, he returns home.

On August 2, 1492, Ferdinand and Isabella issue a decree: Becoming effective at midnight that day, no Jew is allowed to remain on Spanish soil. At eleven o'clock that night, the last of the crewmen went on board Christopher Columbus's three caravels, at anchor in the Port of Palos. Among them were Jews who hoped to find freedom and wealth in a New World. . . .

In 1497, King Manuel of Portugal issues a decree: All Jews must convert to Christianity.

In 1536, the Tribunal of the Holy Office of the Inquisition is established, with the purpose of spying on the New Christians so as to ensure that they are practicing the Christian faith. People are carefully investigated in order to weed out those of Jewish ancestry; only "noblemen of pure blood" can hold positions in the civil service. The denunciation of Judaistic practices, which can be made anonymously, is encouraged. Confession is obtained by torturing the accused. For this purpose the rack is used—it resembles a bed, to which the prisoner is tied with ropes, which are then gradually tightened until they cut into the flesh—and other such instruments of torture. The trial is conducted according to the precepts of secret rules known only to the Grand Inquisitor and a few functionaries of the Holy Office; the solemn pronouncement of judgment takes place in a public square—this ceremony is the auto-da-fé, the first of which was held in Lisbon in 1540.

Sometimes the defendants are acquitted; sometimes they are sentenced to wearing the sanbenito, a sackcloth garment to be worn by the penitents; as for the impenitents, the flames see to their purification.

Two New Christians, Rafael Mendes, the son of the cartographer of the same name, and his friend Afonso Sanches, are arrested by the Inquisition, and accused of Judaistic practices. Due to lack of space in the dungeon, they are thrown into the same cell. Daily, they are submitted to interrogations: Rafael first and then Afonso; or Afonso first and then Rafael; the order in which they are called is unpredictable, as unpredictable as the designs of the Holy Office.

Through dismal corridors, Rafael is taken to a hall with a domed ceiling, where the interrogations take place. Seated behind a huge table, under a colossal crucifix, three inquisitors wait for his arrival. He must stand in the center of a red circle ("the mouth of hell") painted on the floor. His eyes move apprehensively from the faces of the inquisitors to a side door, and from there to the crucifix.

This heavy side door of solid wood has a peephole through which his denouncers can peer. They don't have to say anything. When they want to confirm an accusation, they manipulate a pulley so that the head of the crucified Christ nods. At the sight of the head with a crown of thorns nodding with a rigid, mechanical movement, Rafael's terror is doubled. It's as if Christ himself were accusing him. But even so he refuses to answer their questions. Afonso and he have sworn that they won't reveal anything. And they won't. At least not while their strength holds out.

They do their utmost to keep up their morale. They have devised an intensive program of activities. After waking up early in the morning, they pray fervently. Then they hold a debate on such topics as: Did Jonah commit a sin by refusing to fulfill the mission the Lord had entrusted to him? Was Maimonides really a perplexed man? The discussion, although heated, is always marked by courtesy and held in a low voice to prevent the guards from overhearing them. As for the verdict, it is reached by mutual agreement: The loser should frankly acknowledge defeat.

After the debate, another praying session; as they stand on their feet, facing east, the direction of the distant and beloved Jerusalem, they sway their bodies imperceptibly as they murmur the holy words: *Baruch ata Adonai*... Blessed art thou, oh Lord....

This is followed by other, more joyful activities—games. They play chess, a game they both enjoy very much. There isn't, of course, a chessboard, nor chess pieces, which, however, doesn't prevent them from having chess tournaments: They use their imagination. "Queen on the bishop's fifth square," says Afonso, grimacing with displeasure at the word *bishop*; Rafael, engrossed in the game, looks at him carefully: What is his opponent plotting? "Castle on the king's fourth square," he announces. "But did you still have a castle?" asks Afonso, suspicious. "And would I lie to you if I didn't?" retorts Rafael. "Remember, my friend: between us, nothing but the truth." Accepting Rafael's well-reasoned argument, Afonso admits defeat.

On the other hand, aware that muscle atrophy precedes moral decay, they are careful not to neglect the physical activities. With rags, they have improvised a ball; in the confinement of their dungeon cell—two meters by two meters—they compete against each other in a game: One of them is supposed to kick the ball against the wall, while the other is supposed to prevent him from doing so. Rafael has named this game *ludopédio,* meaning foot game. For thirty to sixty minutes they kick the ball furiously while the guards, amused, look on: "Strange creatures, these Jews," they say. When the game is over, they sit down, exhausted.

Then it's time for some melancholy moments: They reminisce about their families, their friends; they weep together; and then, the interrogation starts again.

The inquisitors are particularly interested in Rafael. They know about his father's connection with Columbus; they want to get to the bottom of this matter. They want the names of the Jews who financed the Genovese's expedition. They want to know about the gold and the jewels. And they also want the names of the alchemists, of the cabalists, of the inventors who have designed diabolical mechanical contraptions that can spin and weave thread, print books. They want to know about those vehicles that can move under the sea like fish of steel. The crafty Grand Inquisitor, trying to persuade Rafael to disclose willingly everything he knows, promises him full acquittal and even a commission on the holdings and properties that are confiscated. Since Rafael persists in his stubborn silence, the interrogation session ends, logically, in torture.

For this, there is a special room equipped with contrivances designed by one of the inquisitors, a very inventive man (he looks Jewish, remark the others, full of suspicion). The prisoner is made to lie naked on the rack. The torturer then begins to tighten the ropes. The poor devil screams out with pain. The screams startle a canary kept in a cage (A), making it flutter about wildly. A cat placed on a point (B) below the cage, leaps up, trying to catch the canary. Then a dog tries to chase the cat, but it can't because it is held on a leash; the action of its paws make a conveyor belt (C) move, and this motion is transmitted by a system of pulleys to a small wooden mallet (D), which then begins to hit the prisoner on the head. In fact, as the Grand Inquisitor remarks to visitors, it is the prisoner himself who inflicts punishment on himself: the guiltier he is, the more he screams, the more the canary flutters about, the more the cat jumps, the more the dog runs, the more the conveyor belt moves, the more the small mallet delivers blows. Were the accused man fortified by his alleged innocence, the punishment inflicted would be less severe.

The inquisitor makes an analogy between this instrument of torture and the Jewish conspiracy. In both instances, he explains, we have a system that operates by chain reaction, their goals being Goodness in the first instance, Evil in the second. By setting off one system against the other, we can turn the sorcery against the sorcerer; the cabala against the cabalist; the philosopher's stone against the alchemist. It's the victory, magnificent albeit sanguinary, of Goodness over Evil, of Godliness over diabolism.

Rafael Mendes and Afonso Sanches come out of the torture room in a wretched condition. They cannot even stand on their feet; the guards have to carry them to their cell, where they spend the night moaning. Only at daybreak do they sometimes get some sleep.

One day Rafael Mendes is brutally awakened from one of those meager scraps of sleep he manages to get. It's Afonso shaking him awake. Rafael sits up: His friend is staring at him in a strange way. "What is it?" he asks, startled.

"You were laughing," says Afonso, gloomily.

"Laughing?" asks Rafael, surprised. "Me, laughing, Afonso?"

"Yes. You."

"But I can't even laugh, Afonso, not with my face hurting so badly, you know. Not with my lips split open like this."

"But you were laughing," Afonso persists. "You were roaring with laughter. You were laughing your head off. You were splitting your sides with laughter. You even woke me up with your laughter."

"Strange," murmurs Rafael. "What could I be laughing at? Is there anything to laugh at? Not under these circumstances. Laugh at what?"

"That's what I'd like to know," says Afonso, and his tone of voice is now openly suspicious. "What were you laughing at? Because I can see no reason to laugh."

Rafael puts forth a conjecture: Maybe it was a dream that made him laugh. Upon hearing this, Afonso rises to his feet, incensed.

"A dream? I've never heard of anyone laughing in their sleep, Rafael Mendes. I know there are people who talk, even walk, in their sleep—but laugh? No. And what kind of mirthful dreams can you possibly have in this place? Do tell me. Because I, Rafael, have nothing but nightmares: Even in my dreams the inquisitors keep torturing me. But even so I value this sleep, it restores my energies, so that I can resist my torturers. Whereas you, you waste in laughter precious moments of rest. And what's worse, you prevent me from getting any."

"I'm awfully sorry," says Rafael with contrition. And he promises: "It won't happen again, Afonso, I assure you."

The other man, however, continues to glare at him, full of mistrust:

"You still haven't told me what made you laugh."

"I don't remember," says Rafael. "Honestly, Afonso, I don't."

The arrival of the guards interrupts this conversation. And for the rest of the day neither of them brings up this subject again.

That night Afonso once more rouses Rafael from his sleep.

"You were laughing again, Rafael!" he shouts. "You did it again! You were laughing happily, like a pleased child."

Rafael sits up. And now he's the one who is angry:

"Stop it, Afonso, stop it! You've gone too far, do you hear?"

"Me, gone too far?" says Afonso, upset. "You're the one who has gone too far. Who do you think you are, anyway?"

Puzzled, Rafael stares at him. An idea crosses his mind: He must be insane, poor Afonso. All this suffering, and the blows from the mallet, no wonder he has a screw loose. Rafael is overcome by a great feeling of compassion. Drawing closer to Afonso, he puts a hand on his shoulder: "All right, I did laugh, but it won't happen again, I promise."

Afonso rebuffs him:

"Take your filthy hand off me, you traitor! Go away, you Christian asslicker, you pig!"

He's crazy all right, concludes Rafael, horrified. It's not the first case: Many have lost their minds in the dungeons of the Inquisition. That was what happened to the prisoner who previously occupied their cell. Sentenced to death, he was taken to the stake to burn. It was a cold day, and upon seeing the flames crackling, he turned to the judges:

"Kindly Christians, I thank you for having lit this fire to warm me up. That's what I really needed. I have arthritis, the cold is bad for me. . . ."

He drew closer to the fire and whistling softly, he warmed his hands. Then, pleased, he greeted the judges and walked toward the exit. He was seized and thrown into the flames.

Crouched down in a corner of the fetid cell, Rafael watches Afonso, who paces back and forth, muttering:

"He has joined the enemy, this dog. They are in cahoots to break my spirit, to make me kneel down before their deity. But if they think that I'll surrender, they are wrong. I'll fight to the very end. They don't know who they're dealing with."

"Enough of that!" Rafael leaps to his feet. "That's enough, Afonso!" He's distraught over the seriousness of the situation: They mustn't fight against each other, not now, not when the inquisitors are watching out for the slightest signs of weakness in them. It's important to bring Afonso to his senses: "You're crazy, my friend. Raving mad! What you're saying is insane. I'm Rafael Mendes, I'm from your nation, too, we're brothers!"

On an impulse he produces his penis, shows him that it's circumcised.

"See? I, too, bear on my flesh the sign of the Divine Covenant, Afonso. Like you."

Impassive, Afonso looks at him steadily.

"Please," Rafael pleads, "believe me, Afonso! I admit I laughed but I have no idea why. Perhaps it's weakness or . . . madness."

He moves a step forward:

"That's it, Afonso. I must be losing my mind. And if I am, I need your help. We can't afford to antagonize each other, Afonso. More than ever we must join forces. We owe it to our elders, Afonso. To our nation, to our God, the God of Abraham, of Isaac, of Jacob."

In silence, Afonso turns this matter over in his mind. The words in the Book of Daniel occur to Rafael: You've been weighed in the balances. . . . Afonso is weighing him, for sure. And what will he find in his deranged gauge?

"All right," Afonso finally says. "Here's what I'll do: If you laugh again, I'll call the guards. I'll tell them that you've been laughing at the Inquisition, that you've been jeering at the wounds of Christ, that you have secrets you haven't told them. And then we'll see: If you are in cahoots with them, they won't harm you, but then I'll kill you. And if you are not on their side, they'll burn you at the stake. So, you'd better control yourself and not laugh."

The day is breaking. And throughout that day Rafael is tortured by anxiety: He fears that Afonso might suddenly do something crazy, that he might call the guards. At nightfall, he makes a decision: He won't sleep. He will resist sleep as much as he resists his interrogators. After dinner—watery soup, a few rotten potatoes—Afonso lies down on his pallet, and is soon snoring, but Rafael knows that he is not asleep: He pretends he is. Although knowing he is being watched by the other man, Rafael finds sleep invincible, and has to fight hard to keep it at bay. He resorts to tricks: He opens his eyes wide, pinches himself, thinks up problems such as, three shepherds are tending one thousand and three hundred sheep. The oldest shepherd is tending twice as many sheep as the second shepherd—in vain, for he drifts off into sleep.

From which he is abruptly aroused: Somebody is shaking him. He rubs his eyes: He is surrounded by guards. Terror-stricken, he scrambles to his feet. Afonso looks at him with a sinister expression on his face.

"Afonso!" he shouts, desperate. "Afonso, my friend, my brother—what have you done? You've called the guards, Afonso!"

"I warned you," says Afonso.

By order of the Grand Inquisitor, Rafael is taken to the torture room. He won't leave it for two weeks: he's tortured night and day: The canary is tired of fluttering wildly about, the cat can barely leap up, the dog, exhausted, lies collapsed on the conveyor belt. The Grand Inquisitor himself undertakes the task of hitting the prisoner on the head with the small mallet, which now displays a cleft.

"What were you laughing at? Answer me!"

But Rafael says nothing. The Grand Inquisitor is finally convinced: It's a hopeless case. This Jew is possessed by Satan, he'll resist to the very end. He sentences him to burn at the stake, as a warning to others.

That same night, however, somebody opens the cell door. It's one of the guards. He signals to Afonso to keep quiet: "The people of the nation have sent me," he whispers. And he opens his hand to reveal a Star of David, in gold, which Afonso immediately recognizes as his brother's amulet.

Picking up the unconscious Rafael, they carry him down the corridors to a secret passage that opens onto the river, where a boat is waiting. On board, Rafael regains consciousness; Afonso then explains to him what is happening. Rafael opens his burst lips into a painful smile. Afonso smiles back, then Rafael begins to laugh, Afonso laughs too, and the two of them laugh and laugh; every once in a while Rafael stops laughing and moans with pain; but soon they are taken with another fit of laughing, and the boatman begs them to be quiet, for God's sake. Finally, Afonso manages to control himself; wiping his eyes, he says, still gasping for breath, that there is something he must tell Rafael:

"During the days I was alone in the cell, I made a very important discovery, Rafael: You had told me the truth. You weren't laughing."

He hesitates, then goes on:

"It was me, dreaming that you were laughing. This happened several times: I would fall asleep and then wake up with your laughter. But it was a dream, Rafael. A dream."

"Everything is a dream, brother," murmurs Rafael. "Everything is a dream. Possibly this place we're heading for, this distant country, is nothing but a dream."

Of the caravel that carried him to Brazil, Rafael Mendes was to remember the creaking of its timbers, the wind whining in the ship's rigging, the shouts of the sailors, the darkness and the stench in the hold of the ship, where, as fugitives, they were confined. And the rats. Huge rats that kept attacking them and that they kept driving back with kicks. This ordeal lasted for weeks. It was not until they were near the coast of Brazil that the captain allowed them to go up on deck. Gaunt, bearded, in tatters, their pathetic grins exposing gums swollen by scurvy, the two men emerged into the light.

The sailors were suspicious of the two strangers, the officers sneered at them. *Sta fermo, Moise!* shouted the first mate, a Genovese who claimed to be related to Christopher Columbus; he was alluding perhaps to the biblical Moses, or perhaps to that other Moses, Ben Mainon. Neither Afonso nor Rafael would say anything in reply; leaning on the gunwale, they would stare out at the greenish sea. Thus they spent their days.

All of a sudden, the weather changed. The wind, until then favorable, died away, and an eerie wind-lull immobilized the vessel. Black birds kept fluttering over the caravel and a huge fish swam around it, at times revealing its dark back, which resembled a rock. "Divine punishment has befallen us," muttered the sailors, "for we are harboring two heretics, two descendants of Christ's killers." Tension kept mounting, and one night Rafael and Afonso woke up with shouts and the clangor of swords. It was a mutiny! Officers and sailors were fighting like demons against one another; an officer lay on deck, with blood spouting out of his slit throat. "Save yourselves," the captain shouted at them, "jump into the sea." Without hesitation, Rafael and Afonso jumped over the gunwale and plunged into the ocean. They swam all night, occasionally letting themselves float in order to rest. "Hanging on, are you?" Rafael would shout in the darkness. "Yes," Afonso would reply, "and what about you?" "Me too," Rafael would say. "Then, keep swimming," Afonso would encourage him, "don't give up." Afraid of drowning, afraid of dying, afraid of having his eyes devoured by fish and his nostrils invaded by crustaceans, Rafael kept swimming. He swam and swam.

The day was dawning, a beautiful day it was; they sighted birds— which lifted their spirits: Land must be near. And indeed, soon afterward, with the help of the current, they came ashore to a white, sandy beach dotted with coconut trees. They stretched out on the sand and fell asleep. Theirs was a sound, dreamless sleep. Upon waking up, they found themselves surrounded by Indians.

About thirty of them. Naked, their bodies painted with annato, they stood staring impassively at the two men. Frightened, Rafael and Afonso scrambled to their feet. Rafael was trembling so much that his teeth chattered; it was Afonso who showed presence of mind. He took out of his pocket a mirror which he, being rather vain, always carried on him. Their curiosity aroused, the Indians drew closer. Upon seeing their painted faces with wide-open eyes reflected on the polished surface, they began to laugh. They laughed delightedly, like children. Any murderous rage that they might have been harboring dissolved at that moment. "Friends!" Afonso kept saying and the Indians would repeat: "Friends, friends!"

Friends, and yet they couldn't make themselves understood. Not even through mime. The Indians eventually got bored and headed for their settlement. Rafael and Afonso followed them.

The tribespeople were eating. With gestures, Rafael and Afonso tried to tell them that they were hungry; but it wasn't until Afonso offered them his belt buckle that they were given food: fish, corn, manioc, fruit. A copious meal, hinting at the ease with which food could be obtained there. "I think that anything you plant in this land will bear fruit," said Afonso.

(Later Rafael was to recall the glitter in Afonso's eyes as he spoke those words. At that moment, however, he was more interested in the food itself.)

In the evening they were taken to the *oca*, the communal dwelling of the Indians. Men, women and children slept there in hammocks or on the dirt floor. Rafael and Afonso stretched themselves out on the floor and were soon fast asleep.

Soon afterward—but was this going to be the norm in Rafael's trouble-ridden life?—they were wakened. Four Indians were shaking them; they signaled to Rafael and Afonso to follow them.

They left the communal dwelling and got into the bushes. After walking for a long time along a rough-hewn trail cut through the jungle, they arrived at a clearing. At the door of a shack, they saw a very old Indian squatting before a fire. When the Portuguese drew closer, he got to his feet and inspected them with his small blinking eyes. Then, at a sign from him, the Indians who had escorted them withdrew. The old man opened his arms:

"Bruchim habaim," he said, smiling.

"Did you hear that?" said Rafael, astonished. "He spoke in Hebrew!"

"In Hebrew?" asked Afonso, who was not well-versed in the language of the nation. "And what did he say?"

"That we're welcome. But how does he know our language?" Rafael couldn't get over his astonishment.

"Ask him," said Afonso.

Rafael addressed the old man in Hebrew. And he heard an interesting story.

"Many, many moons ago," the old man said, "one of King Solomon's sons had a misunderstanding with his father. He wanted to have access to the harem. The king didn't consent to his son's request, claiming that one of the women there, he didn't know which one, was the young man's mother; if he had sexual relations with her, he would be committing incest, a very serious sin. Feeling resentful, the young man then began to conspire against his father and he succeeded in stirring up revolt in some of the palace guards. Just as he was about to be killed, Solomon was changed into a multicolored bird, which flew away. Later on he came back in his human form, accompanied by many soldiers. The rebels were overcome and the king himself passed sentence on them. Solomon ordered that they be put, together with their wives and children, in a rudderless ship so that they would drift aimlessly: a befitting punishment for people who had gone astray.

"After a long time, their ship came to these shores. We are the descendants of those Hebrews. Because we gazed into the sun, our eyes narrowed like this, and our skin turned bronze-colored. Many of us no longer speak Hebrew; but in each generation, there is always one person in charge of taking care of the Torah, which our ancestors brought with them from Jerusalem."

He signaled to them to enter his shack. And there, by the weak light of an oil lamp, they saw the scrolls of the Law.

With devotion, Rafael stroked the parchment, which was rather damaged by the effects of time, of humidity; the letters were almost completely faded, but even so he was able to read a few sentences of the holy text.

They talked for a long time because the old man was curious to know how the descendants of the Hebrews fared in Europe. At daybreak, he put out the light and said: "Let's go outside and take a leak."

As they urinated, Rafael watched the old man stealthily. He was indeed circumcised, but his member was deformed. "Here we have to use a conch to perform the *brit mila,*" he explained self-consciously. "We lost the ritualistic blade. Besides, we lack the ancient skills. . . ."

Squatting by the almost-extinguished fire, he closed his eyes, and softly began to intone a tuneless chant, no longer in Hebrew but in the language of the Indians: He was again just an old aborigine, ugly and toothless. Rafael and Afonso returned to the Indian settlement.

Afonso ended up marrying the cacique's daughter, a great beauty, whom he affectionately called Little Dove because, as he explained to Rafael, of her small breasts, which were round and firm. As for Rafael, he remained faithful to the wife he had left behind in Portugal. He cultivated the land and prayed together with the old Indian patriarch.

Afonso learned the language of the Indians. Although he liked them, their laziness irritated him: "We have to put these people to work," he would say to Rafael. He had a plan: to grow sugarcane. "In Europe sugar is worth its weight in gold." "Yes," Rafael would argue, "but who's going to buy the crops?" Afonso didn't have an answer to this question. He would fall silent, but it was obvious that he wasn't going to give up his plan.

As good luck would have it, a Portuguese ship sailed into the bay. Rafael, afraid of the Inquisition, wanted them to go into hiding; Afonso, however, went to the ship in a pirogue. He came back bursting with excitement: He had struck a bargain with the captain. He and Rafael would plant sugarcane; in the next voyage, the ship would bring them a sugar mill, dismantled; they would start producing sugar right there. They would strike it rich!

It wasn't an unreasonable expectation.

As a matter of fact, according to historian Cá da Mosto, ever since the fifteenth century, sugar had been "a luxury item used in the kitchens of the wealthy." Pounding or pressing the sugarcane released a dense, foamy juice, which after going through a boiling process for three or four times, turned into crystallized sugar. Such sweetness! And what a pot of money it was! However, sugarmaking was an industry that required substantial capital, an industry that would be of interest to the Genovese and the Florentines, people like Cesaro, Spinola, Lomeltini, and Paolo di Nigra, a friend of Columbus's (the same Columbus who had taken cuttings of sugarcane to Hispaniola, where it thrived, as he informed the Castilian monarchs in a letter sent in 1494, its quality leaving nothing to be desired when compared to the sugarcane grown in the Old World); and of interest, too, to the New Christians, who, through their connections, would be able to raise the necessary capital. Through the captain, Afonso sent a letter to Fernão de Noronha, the father-in-law of Admiral Pedro Álvares Cabral, requesting that, "in the interests of the nation," he arrange for the shipment of all parts needed to assemble a sugar mill, and that he also arrange for the financing of the project because "the sugar to be produced here will soon become even more valuable than the highly renowned brazilwood."

"Why go in search of the Gold Tree, which nobody knows where it is?" he would cry out. "We'll make a fortune with sugarcane!"

The Indians, however, were loath to do any planting—except for their own consumption. In vain Afonso tried to explain to them that their efforts would be rewarded with many mirrors, glass beads, and belt buckles. The Indians would laugh at him. Enraged, Afonso resorted to cruelty, becoming the scourge of the tribe. Armed with a whip, he would chase after the savages, trying to force them to work. Terror was rampant in the village, especially because Afonso had become—after the cacique died, of a broken heart, undoubtedly—the sovereign ruler. One day the old man of the Torah sent for him. Afonso went, hoping that the elder would support him in his endeavors to get the Indians to work. He came back foaming at the mouth with rage. Not only had the old man refused to back him but he had also warned him not to mistreat the Indians: "Mistreatment is not sanctioned by our faith," he had said. "Our faith!" vociferated Afonso. "As if I and this old savage belonged to the same faith!"

He took to beating his wife. One night, as Rafael lay asleep in his straw-thatched hut, he felt a warm body next to his. It was Little Dove; the poor thing, in tears, snuggled up against him. Rafael tried to persuade her to leave, but with no success. The young woman spent the whole night there, with Rafael fighting off desire—he didn't want to betray his friend.

At dawn, he woke up with the yells of Afonso:

"Come out here! Come out here, you cur!"

Rafael crawled out of the hut. Afonso stood naked in the yard, with a cudgel in his hand; like an Indian, he had painted himself with annato.

"Come here, I want to kill you, traitor!"

The Indians, motionless, looked on. A child was crying. "For God's sake," said Rafael, "don't do anything foolish, Afonso. I—"

"Come and fight, you bastard!"

A shudder passed over Rafael; Afonso's words made his blood boil. He went into the hut and came out with a cudgel.

"Are you ready?" bellowed Afonso.

Rafael was ready. The cudgels clashed in the air. The fight didn't last long: Livid with rage, Afonso kept missing his target and stumbling over his own feet. He ended up by falling on the ground. Rafael then bashed his head in.

The Indians ate the body of the Jew Afonso Sanches, a fugitive from the Inquisition. On the following morning, as a caravel appeared on the horizon and the Indians were getting ready to set out on a warpath, Rafael left the village after saying farewell to Little Dove and to the old man of the Torah, who presented him with a fragment of the holy book. Taking with him enough food for a journey of many days, he headed south.

He finally arrived at a village inhabited by his countrymen, the Portuguese, who received him with suspicion. He told them about the shipwreck and the long period of captivity among the Indians. He was allowed to stay. He devoted himself to commerce and he even prospered. Later on he sent for his wife in Portugal; the couple then settled in Olinda. In that town, Rafael made friends with Bento Teixeira. Bento, a New Christian, believed that the knowledge of Latin and arithmetic, disciplines that he taught, was indispensable to the Hebrew nation:

"It was through Latin, friend Rafael," he would explain, "that the Christians controlled the world. They transformed the language of their former torturers into a weapon of victory. Besides, Latin is the language of the Holy Office of the Inquisition, so it's a code into which we must initiate ourselves for our own good. As for arithmetic, it's fundamental: The four operations are as important as the four elements—air, water, fire, and earth. Arithmetic is the idiom of finances, an idiom as universal as Latin, my brother. We need both to defend our nation—until the day when we can resurrect our former grandeur, the grandeur of Solomon. As a matter of fact, I'm making a prophecy, a prophecy of peace: Like the phoenix, we, too, shall rise from our own ashes."

The phoenix? Rafael Mendes didn't care for such comparisons. The phoenix was an invention of the Greeks, the same Greeks who had kept the Jewish people subjugated until the advent of the Maccabees. Good-humoredly, Bento Teixeira would explain that it was merely a simile, poetic license.

Bento Teixeira was the first poet of Brazil. His masterpiece, in his own opinion, was a long poem called *Prosopopoeia*, dedicated to Captain Jorge de Albuquerque Coelho, the governor of the captaincy of Pernambuco. By singing the glories of the Albuquerque family, he intended not only to pay homage to Brazil, "beautiful, warmhearting country, a daughter of Sion," but also to enlist the sympathies of the governor, which could undoubtedly prove extremely useful to the people of the nation. His purpose was to sensitize Jorge de Albuquerque Coelho to the sufferings of the chosen people. He gave a copy of the poem to Rafael Mendes, who didn't think that poetry writing was a very good idea; in his opinion, the people of the nation should remain quiet; they should move about silently, like the fish in the depths of the ocean. However, he promised that he would read the poem and give his opinion.

On the night of September 20, 1593, when he was already in bed, he called his wife, to read aloud to her a few lines from *Prosopopoeia*:

> *Oh, cruel, fickle Fate,*
> *Always usurping the rights of the good.*
> *Always favoring what is most abominable*
> *Always berating and loathing what is perfect.*
> *Always favoring the least deserving*
> *While spurning the most deserving.*
> *Oh fragile, fickle, brittle Fate,*
> *Forever robbing us of possessions and justice!*

Then he said:

"Tell me, does this rigmarole make any sense to you? Do you have any idea what these lines mean?"

She didn't reply.

"A certain poet," Rafael Mendes went on, "claims that these lines describe the sufferings of the nation. Do you think so?"

His wife remained silent.

"That's it," said Rafael Mendes, sighing. "We are condemned to perplexity, wife. Good night."

He fell asleep and never woke up. He died that very night, silently, without disturbing anyone.

On the following day, Heitor Furtado de Mendonça, an emissary of the Holy Office, arrived in Pernambuco. And thus began an investigation aimed at rooting out suspected heretics. In 1595 Bento Teixeira was arrested and sent to Lisbon. After being tried, he was then forced to repudiate his heresy publicly in an auto-da-fé. He died of consumption in 1600.

In 1601, the editor Antonio Álvares publishes Bento Teixeira's *Prosopopoeia* in Lisbon, with the imprimatur of the Holy Inquisition (undoubtedly obtained by the Albuquerques). On the front page, the coat of arms of the Albuquerque family; at the end of the poem, a quotation in Latin, but taken from Solomon's *Song of Songs*, *Fortis est ut mors dilectio*, love is as strong as death; and an emblem: the phoenix rising from its own ashes. It was at that time, too, that the phoenix appeared as an emblem elsewhere: in the Judeo-Portuguese synagogue of Amsterdam, the *Neveh Shalom* (*The Prophets of Peace*), built by the marranos who had escaped from the Inquisition.

Fearful of the Inquisition, Rafael Mendes's mother, who had been born in 1591, had her son baptized a Christian. But Rafael Mendes knew that he was from the nation. And he knew that he had to keep his identity secret. What had happened to that imprudent New Christian, Branca Dias? In church, at the moment of the consecration of the Host, Branca Dias would murmur: *There are dogs kept in chains.* She was arrested, tried, and sentenced by the Holy Office. Rafael Mendes wasn't going to let words betray him. He hardly spoke, and then only when necessary, which earned him the nickname "Tight-Lips." He would attend church, kneel down, pray, receive communion. Not that he believed in any of it. But he didn't want to be harassed.

On the other hand, his quick-tempered wife, Ana, also a New Christian but in her heart a fervent Jew, made him secretly practice the Hebrew faith. On Fridays she made him bathe and put on a clean shirt; and on Yom Kippur she made him fast. As soon as the servants brought the meal, Ana would dismiss them, then pour the contents of the serving dishes into leather haversacks, which were later burned. So as not to arouse suspicions, she would leave scraps of food on the dishes and flatware; on that day they wouldn't touch food, much to the displeasure of Rafael Mendes, who was very partial to roasted meat. However, he would follow his wife's wishes without arguing, he didn't want any hassles of any kind. He minded his store, played chess with his friend Vicente Nunes, went fishing once in a while: He caught small fish only. And didn't want much more from life.

Vicente Nunes, also a New Christian, had a different way of thinking. He was an ambitious man; a sugar mill and plantation complex wasn't enough for him. Big business, that's what he had in mind; he wanted to make it to the top. He had good contacts; among them, Diogo Dias Querido, of Amsterdam; a Jewish merchant born in the city of Oporto, Querido had lived in Brazil until the arrival of the Holy Office of the Inquisition, when he fled to Holland. There, Querido established an import-export business. He was one of the staunchest supporters of the idea of sending the West Indies Company of Holland on an expedition to Brazil.

In December 1629 Vicente Nunes let Rafael Mendes in on an extraordinary plan: He knew from reliable sources that the Dutchmen would soon be disembarking in Pernambuco. They wouldn't have to fear the Inquisition anymore; the Batavians, known for their tolerance, would allow freedom of religion. Besides, Vicente was sure that the Dutch were going to invest heavily in Brazil, especially in the sugar industry. Allied to the Dutch, it would be possible for them to take over the European markets. Recife would become the New Amsterdam: A prosperous city, with beautiful streets along which the well-dressed and well-nourished burghers would stroll with their families.

Some measures would have to be taken, and for this purpose, Vicente Nunes needed the cooperation of "Tight-Lips." First of all, Rafael Mendes was to send two of his most trusted employees to meet the Dutchmen and show them around. In addition, he was to hire the services of one Calabar, a shrewd man, very familiar with the region, who sometimes came to Rafael's store.

"But," said Rafael Mendes, perplexed, "you're asking me to collaborate with the invaders!"

"Why not," retorted Vicente Nunes, "we'll eventually reap benefits from this collaboration."

Rafael Mendes turned this idea over in his mind for a few minutes.

"All right," he said finally, "let's decide this issue in a game of chess."

He called a man servant, asked him to bring them wine, told him they were not to be disturbed, then closed the door. He got the chessboard.

"I see," said Vicente Nunes, "if I win, you'll side with me."

Rafael Mendes smiled:

"Every game," he said, "has one unknown factor. This one has two: its outcome and my decision. The perplexed are entitled to an enigma."

Vicente Nunes lost the game. Rafael Mendes rose to his feet:

"I'm with you, come what may."

Despite putting up a fierce resistance, Recife fell to the Dutch. Vicente Nunes was bursting with pride. He had himself circumcised in public; during the operation he howled like a madman; soon afterward, still enveloped in bloodied bandages, he showed the brethren of the nation his prepuce, which he later buried in the soil of New Amsterdam. Exhorting them to return to the faith of their ancestors, he then announced that he and his wife Philipina were changing their names: From then on they would be Abraão and Sara—the patriarch and the mother of the people.

Rafael watched the scene. Calabar was also present, with his enigmatic smile.

At Ana's insistence, Rafael Mendes had his son, already a grown boy, circumcised. However, as a precaution, he decided not to change the boy's name, which remained Rafael Mendes. "But this is a paradox," protested Ana. "The perplexed are entitled to paradoxes," retorted her husband. And "Tight-Lips" made no other pronouncements. Years later he died, as quietly as he had lived.

Two friends, Rafael Mendes (the son of the merchant of the same name) and Joseph de Castro lived in the city of Recife, the New Amsterdam—or, as Rafael would say, the Jerusalem of the New World, a city where the splendors of the Mosaic faith could be celebrated in a magnificent synagogue entirely decorated with jacaranda and gold.

They were partners in business. Lens grinders by trade, they had learned their craft from a Dutch master and they were among the first such craftsmen in Brazil. Of the two, Joseph was the more dedicated to his work: He would arrive at their workshop before sunrise, and wouldn't leave until very late at night, often working by the light of candles. Rafael kept remonstrating with his friend about his imprudence: "You're damaging your eyes," he would say, "the most precious gift that God has endowed us with." Joseph, however, didn't take heed of what Rafael said. He was a stubborn, quick-tempered man.

Joseph had few friends. And he couldn't find a woman willing to put up with him, despite all the efforts of Rafael's wife, an active matchmaker. He never went out, he didn't go to parties; and even during joyful celebrations—such as Purim, the feast in honor of Queen Esther—he would not join in the general merriment as people recalled the punishment the king had inflicted on his cruel minister Haman, the persecutor of the Jews living in Persia, and in a way, the forerunner of the inquisitors.

Joseph read extensively. He admired the works of the nation's philosophers; he knew the entire corpus of Michel Eyquem de Montaigne, whom he often quoted: "I hold on to freedom to such an extent that were I denied access to even one of the remotest corners of the West Indies, this would be enough to make me rather discontented with life," and he particularly respected the defiant Uriel da Costa, who preached a Judaism freely interpreted. He corresponded in Dutch with Baruch Spinoza, who was then living in Amsterdam. While studying at the school *The Tree of Life* and at the *Academy of the Crown of the Law*, Spinoza had become familiar with the works of Maimonides and so, he was quite delighted to learn that Joseph's partner was a descendant of the author of *The Guide for the Perplexed*. In their letters they discussed everything, from the original sin to the grinding of lenses, which was also Spinoza's occupation; the philosopher was proud of the eyeglasses he made, but, he would say, it's absurd to talk about the imperfection of the blind, because in essence every human being can see. It was from Spinoza that Joseph acquired a passion for freedom and an abhorrence of superstition. They continued to correspond even after the philosopher, a free thinker, was excommunicated by the Jewish community of Amsterdam, following a lengthy and scabrous trial; in passing sentence, his judges said in part: "By decision of the angels and the judgment of the saints, we excommunicate, expel, execrate, and curse Baruch Spinoza . . . May he be cursed by day and cursed by night; cursed when he lies down and cursed when he gets up; cursed when he leaves home and cursed when he returns home. No one is to have any spoken or written communication with him; no one is to do him a favor, or remain under the same roof with him, or be within four yards of him; no one is to read anything written or transcribed by him." In a letter to Joseph, Spinoza transcribed the text of his excommunication; commenting upon the letter, Joseph said with a sneer: "Here I am, Rafael, reading something written and transcribed by Spinoza; I'm committing a serious sin, but if it weren't for his letter, how would I know I was committing a sin?"

Such paradoxes, such tricks of reason, delighted Joseph. His father being a descendant of the famous Isaac, the Blind, Joseph was familiar with the works of the ancient cabalists of Languedoc. As for other esoteric subjects, Joseph had read not only Jean Bodin's *The Demonomania of the Sorcerers*, a treatise on the efficacy of numbers and the power of the stars but also the prophecies of Michel de Nostre-dame, known as Nostradamus; both these writers were from the nation. In addition, Joseph had contacts with the Gnostics, the Rosicrucians, and the Freemasons.

He knew about the existence of the Gold Tree. He claimed he would be able to find it at any time he wanted. However, he didn't think that it was right for anyone to obtain gold by means that he considered predatory. Now, alchemy was different. He thought it would be more appropriate for a person to obtain this precious metal by dealing with the hidden nature of quicksilver, by laboriously manipulating kilns and retorts. Although he had never tried, he thought he would succeed in such an experiment; he also thought that he could make a homunculus or a giant from mud, and that a righteous man could breathe life into it. By assembling lenses, he had manufactured an apparatus which enabled him to see tiny creatures of various shapes living in the least expected places: in stagnant water, in feces, in the entrails of fish; even in his own semen, which he collected in a phial with the help of fantasies—a sin for which Onan had been severely punished, and to which he had added the sin of heresy: "To the best of my knowledge," he would say with a snigger, "these tiny creatures were never counted in the Garden of Eden, or in Noah's Ark."

Like Galileo Galilei, he, too, would arrange lenses together in order to make telescopes. On starry nights he would climb to the roof terrace of his house, and from there he would scan the Brazilian skies with his complex tubular contraption. He would search for the planet to which the prophet Elijah had fled in a chariot of fire. He knew that from time to time Elijah returned to earth in search of righteous men and women. Out there in space, a community, similar to Francis Bacon's New Atlantis, had been established. In that place, lost somewhere in the firmament, people had rosy skin and eyes moist with emotion. Nobody ever starved or froze. And no baby, he would add sarcastically, was ever circumcised there: Any kind of pain was forbidden. People could address God directly; all they had to do was to close their eyes, and presto, they were in direct communication with the Lord. They communicated among themselves without speaking—through telepathy, a principle that Joseph planned to use later in his efforts at finding a better system to replace the unreliable postal system of the time.

The inhabitants of that enchanted kingdom used glittering metal vehicles to move in space, and steel fish to travel in the depths of the water. They didn't have to work. Machines did everything; they even cultivated the land, which yielded watermelons over a meter in diameter, and ears of wheat with grains as big as the eyes of a calf. "And the slaves, what do they do?" Rafael would ask. "Slaves?" Joseph would say, irritated. "There aren't any. Nobody enslaves anybody, nobody mistreats anybody. Love reigns on Elijah's planet."

How strange that Joseph, such a lonely, sour man, should speak of love, Rafael would say to himself. One day, as if guessing at Rafael's thought, Joseph confided to him that he was sure that the woman of his dreams lived in that remote planet. He hadn't seen her yet through his telescope, although he suspected that a hazy face glimpsed amid a group of young people singing in a choir. . . From such a distance, it was impossible to tell.

Nobody could figure out why Joseph, who wasn't an astronomer, would spend so many hours gazing at the sky through a telescope. "Why do you have to find beauty in other worlds?" the Dutch painter Frans Post, one of Joseph's few friends, would ask. The painter was forever marvelling at the Brazilian landscape, so serene and at the same time so exuberant. "Even if I were blind, I'd still be able to paint here," he would say, carried away by the success his paintings were enjoying. "Why can't you be content with Brazil?" "You don't understand me," the embittered Joseph would say. "There's but one place in the universe where I could be happy. . . And this place is out of my reach. There's nothing I can do but wait for the prophet Elijah to take me there in his chariot of fire."

Then, impassioned, he would wonder: "But, will the prophet ever come here? Intrigue and corruption reign in Recife. And the people of the nation have sold out to sugar!"

Although Rafael smiled at such remarks, he worried about the rebellious tone in Joseph's voice, and particularly about the implications of such statements, clearly heretic. He tried to persuade his friend to give up his extravagant ideas. Why couldn't Joseph be content with being a lens grinder, with doing his work to the best of his abilities? "There are so many people out there in need of our expertise," Rafael would say, "so many short-sighted and cross-eyed people, so many old people who are almost blind. And they pay well, too." But Joseph ignored his words. He despised material possessions, he wanted neither palaces with purling fountains nor concubines wrapped in silk. He wanted no rings, no bracelets, no necklaces, no gold, no diamonds. "The only thing he wants," Rafael's wife would remark sarcastically, "is to sow hatred; he wants to bring us nothing but pain and misfortune, as if we didn't suffer enough at the hands of the Inquisition."

She kept nagging at her husband to break with his business partner. But Rafael wouldn't. First of all, he considered Joseph a competent optician. Besides, Rafael liked him, and didn't want to desert him—which would probably amount to hurling this man, already weird, headlong into the depths of a well of insanity, there to sink into its putrid waters. And finally, he recognized some truth in Joseph's words, although it was an annoying truth. When it came to truth, Rafael would much rather have the biblical truth, the truth that the rabbi of Recife proclaimed in a stentorian voice in the sermons he delivered every Friday. Yes, that was a good truth, at times bitter, at times sweet, but always nourishing, always comforting. Around this kind of truth the Jewish community could gather, without having to break off relations with the Dutch, who respected the ethics of the Old Testament and who were, like the Jews, a nation of merchants. It was from this truth that Rafael Mendes derived the strength he needed to face the sneering laughter of the malevolent Joseph.

Joseph was also eyed with suspicion by the Dutch administration because of a disagreement between him and the Batavian commander, who had heard marvellous things about his telescope. It was said that with such an instrument, even a rather careless observer would be able to spot a Portuguese sailing ship still at anchor in the harbor of the city of Oporto. When invited to clarify this matter,

Joseph refused to either confirm or deny the alleged qualities of his invention; neither was he willing to give a demonstration to the military authorities. The commander was furious. He knew that there were New Christians who continued to maintain contact with the Portuguese, which puzzled him: Why would the Jews want to have anything to do with their former persecutors? Why were they in league with the Portuguese? What kind of interests were at stake? Lands? Concessions to export sugar? "What perfidious creatures, willing to sell themselves for thirty coins," the Dutchman concluded; if it weren't for their traditional skills—in business, in finances, in the art of cutting diamonds and grinding lenses—it would be better to crucify them, just as they had done to Christ. From then on, Joseph de Castro became the number one suspect on the Batavian government list of suspected people.

The latent conflict between the Jewish community and Joseph came to a head when he published a booklet titled *The Tiny Creatures of the Sugar Business*, whose opening paragraph read:

"The price of sugar is high in Europe, where it is a luxury item: eighteen grams of gold for one *arroba*, or fifteen kilograms, of sugar. Since their lives are so insipid, sugar is necessary to sweeten their mouths, to make them merry, and to help them grow fat. Fat is beautiful. The Dutch, for instance, love chubby, rosy faces, prosperous bellies, ample buttocks; that's how they are portrayed by Rembrandt and Hals. On the Batavian tables, which cave in with the weight of various delectable delicacies, there is a succession of assorted meats and fish topped with rich sauces, followed by syrups, baked meringues, pastries and cakes, candied fruit. Sugar gives them the energy they need to conquer lands where more sugarcane will be planted so that they will have more sugar, which will increase their strength so that they. . . A spiral leading to the domination of the world. But you, dreamer, you are not concerned with such matters. You despise material possessions. That is why I ask you to gaze at a crystal of sugar. Observe how it glitters! Like a diamond. Keep gazing. Observe how the crystal grows before your eyes, how it expands and becomes round until it is transformed into a ball, into a big crystal globe. Inside this globe you will see enrapturing scenes." In the globe the reader would then be able to see strange tiny creatures; with the help of a magnifying glass he would be able to recognize them as "miniature human beings who feed exclusively on sugar. They are Jews; Jeovah has punished them for their pride, reducing them to insignificant proportions."

In another passage Joseph told of a nobleman who had an entire city built of sugar: sugar houses, a sugar castle with sugar turrets; the windowpanes were thin, translucent blades of sugar. If a guest in this castle wanted to have a better view of the scenery, all he had to do was to lick a windowpane until it dissolved; he would then see rolling sugar hills, on which grazed tiny sugar cows. The city even had a lake of sweetened milk; a breed of carp, especially adapted, was developed for this lake. Very tame, these fish let themselves be caught by even the most inexperienced of fishermen, because they could be lured by an ancient Spanish song *Si la mar era de leche*, if the sea were of milk; upon dressing the fish, its flesh showed itself whitish, and pale and sweet was its blood.

What the nobleman feared the most was a heavy rainfall (like the one in the Deluge: Jeovah's punishment for his whimsy) which would dissolve this enchantment, washing away tons of sugar, which would end in muddy rivers and stormy green seas. To ward off this danger, a gigantic white umbrella was kept permanently open over the city.

This lampoon caused indignation throughout Recife's Jewish community. Several hundred copies of the booklet were burned in a public square; an enraged group of people threw stones at Joseph's house, forcing him to seek refuge in the home of a priest whose eyeglasses he had once fixed. From then on he was insulted on the streets, and spat at by children as he walked by. Rafael's wife threatened to leave him if he didn't break with this lunatic. Rafael decided it was time for him to take action.

He sought out the prominent members of the Jewish community and pleaded with them to forgive Joseph. "He doesn't know what he's saying," Rafael would reason with them, "but deep down he's a good man, he needs compassion and help." The prominent people then met with the rabbi to talk this matter over. After meeting behind closed doors for several hours, they called Rafael to announce their decision: They were willing to absolve Joseph from his wickedness provided that he submit himself to public humiliation. He was to come to the synagogue wearing sackcloth and holding a black candle in his hand. Before the community assembled there, he was to declare that he had truly repented. Upon which he was to receive thirty-nine lashes from a whip; then he was to remain lying at the door of the temple so that people could step on him as they went out.

Appalled, Rafael listened to them. He couldn't refrain himself from falling on his knees before those men to beg them to be less severe. In vain: the sentence had already been drawn up.

In a daze, Rafael left the synagogue. He didn't know what to do. He would have to talk to Joseph, but he wasn't up to it. I'll have to pull myself together, he kept murmuring to himself. I'll have to talk to him calmly, as if nothing had happened.

As the day drew to its close, Rafael went to their workshop. Joseph, whistling softly, was busy grinding a lens. Distressed, Rafael stammered an account of what had happened; he told Joseph about the proposal of the religious leaders:

"Do accept it, Joseph! Please, accept it! Do it for your friend!" The other man said nothing. He continued to grind the lens, and when he was finished, he put it into a small box lined with velvet. Only then did he look at Rafael. He smiled. Without a word, he got up and left.

On the following day he didn't show up for work. Alarmed, Rafael went to his house. The door was open. He went in: nobody. In his room, as usual, books and sheets of paper scattered all over. But no sign of Joseph.

He went back to the workshop. He worried all day, unable to concentrate on his work. He didn't know what to make of Joseph's disappearance. Deep in his heart, he hoped that Joseph had run away; that, fearing the community, he had fled to Bahia or to Rio de

Janeiro. Which would solve Joseph's problems; Joseph's as well as Rafael's.

At night he went back to Joseph's house. Empty. He climbed up to the roof terrace. No, Joseph wasn't there. The telescope, however, was in place, the metallic structure pointing to the sky. An absurd idea crossed Rafael's mind: Could it be that the prophet Elijah . . . ? He looked through the telescope. He saw nothing. Not even the moon, which enormous, was shining in the sky.

Two days later Joseph's body was washed up on a beach, his eyes had been eaten up by the fish, crustaceans were sidling off his nostrils. He was buried in the Jewish cemetery of Recife, but next to the wall, as a suicide.

Rafael became the only optician in town. He charged high prices, and if a customer remonstrated, he would retort with scoffs: "Don't make me cry, I'm made of sugar and I dissolve easily."

For a long time his wife kept bugging him to sell Joseph's telescope to the Dutch commander. The sale would bring in quite a bit of money and it would give them distinction. Rafael would say nothing. One day in a fit of rage he threw the apparatus out of the window, threatening his wife with the same fate. She stopped nagging him and from then on he was relatively happy. His son, Rafael Mendes, wasn't as lucky: After the Dutch were defeated, the persecution of the Jews was resumed, and he was indicted in a judicial inquiry for allegedly having in his possession books on witchcraft that had belonged to Joseph de Castro. Hard times were those. In less than a decade, the price of sugar had dropped by thirty-three percent; on top of religious skepticism there was also financial uncertainty. Rafael Mendes decided to run away.

Two New Christians, Felipe Royz and Rafael Mendes, are on the lam, heading for Maranhão. Now that the Dutch have been expelled from Pernambuco, they are afraid of the reprisals with which the people of the nation are threatened. In addition, Felipe Royz has a goal: He wants to kill André Vidal de Negreiros, who was appointed governor of Maranhão as a reward for his bravery in the fight against the Batavians. Vidal de Negreiros insulted him: In front of everybody he accused Royz of having collaborated with the Dutch; he called Royz a treacherous dog and a filthy marrano. His plan of revenge, however, is forgotten as soon as they arrive at their destination. That's because, once in Maranhão, Felipe Royz, with the help of the people from the nation, becomes a settler. As he grows tobacco and sugarcane, he no longer thirsts for revenge, especially because Vidal de Negreiros's sojourn in Maranhão is brief; having arrived in 1654, in the following year he was already leaving for Minas Gerais in search of gold.

The learned Rafael Mendes takes up teaching; as a teacher, he makes friends with Father Antonio Vieira. He suspects that this Jesuit priest is from the nation, too, not only because of the worried and rather wild expression in his eyes, but mostly because he is a passionate defender of the Jews, whose enterprising spirit he keeps extolling. As early as 1649 this priest had backed the formation of a Trade Company, with bankers of the nation as shareholders. He's at sixes and sevens with the Holy Office; and he is looked upon with suspicion because he defends the Indians: "In the State of Maranhão there is no gold nor silver more valuable than the blood and the sweat of the Indians. Their blood is sold to their enslavers and their sweat is transformed into tobacco, into sugar." Royz keeps criticizing Rafael for his friendship with the Jesuit; in the priest's references to tobacco and sugar Royz sees an allusion to his own cultivated lands, where he uses Indian labor:

"And why not? What else are Indians good for, if not for work? Or would you rather see them wandering about, with their bodies all painted with annatto, killing people and eating human flesh?"

Rafael Mendes doesn't reply. He doesn't want to get into a polemic; he agrees with Father Vieira, the enslavement of Indians is not part of the ethics of the nation, but he knows what Royz will say in reply—that in their Indian settlements the Jesuits also make use of Indian labor; and if Mendes then reasons with him, saying that the priests act in accordance with their religious purposes, the embittered Royz will sneer at him: "The salvation of souls? It's rather the salvation of their purses." No, Mendes doesn't want to argue about such controversial matters. On the other hand, Father Vieira has enemies far more powerful than the harmless Royz. The long arm of the Inquisition reaches him; in 1661, due to the intervention of the Holy Office, the priest is forced to return to Europe. Two years later, Father João Felipe Bettendorf, a commissary of the Holy Office, arrives in Maranhão; his mission is to root out bigamists and sodomists, witches and crypto-Jews. The holdings of the Jesuits are extended; the number of Indians under the priests' custody increases, and the clashes with the settlers escalate. One settler is particularly angry: He is Manoel Beckman, nicknamed Bequimão, the owner of a sugar mill and plantation complex, and an alderman. A New Christian? Possibly. His uncle João Nunes de Santarém, a wealthy Lisbon merchant, who had acted as mediator between the Portuguese and the Dutch, was known as being a New Christian; and it was quite possible that his father-in-law, João Pereira de Cáceres, was from the nation. A New Christian for sure. Whenever a steer was slaughtered on his farm, Bequimão would tie the animal to a cross; and he referred to the corral as the *sacrarium*.

It was stories like these that helped create an image of Bequimão surrounded by an aura of mystery, an image that fascinated many people, among them Maria de Freitas, the *Maria-of-the-Blazing-Ass*.

This woman (whose nickname was due to her real or alleged preference for anal copulation) was known as a witch, and was even given to boasting about it. "I'm a sorcerer, a witch, and everything else that they say I am," she would state with pride. Fake pride it was, though: In fact, she was a frustrated witch. To start with, there was the problem of her name: It had fourteen letters. Why fourteen? Had it thirteen letters, people would utter the name Maria de Freitas with awe and fear. But no. At birth she had been given a name with fourteen letters and she was stuck with those fourteen letters until the day she died. Once she went as far as to ask the governor permission to change her name to Maria d' Freitas. Vidal de Negreiros had laughed: "How can you eliminate the *e* and then put an apostrophe before a name that begins with a consonant?" Besides, the change would be less than satisfactory, for the apostrophe could always be construed as a letter; skeptics would no doubt take advantage of the situation: "A witch? But only if it's with an apostrophe!"

An ignorant woman, Maria de Freitas had never really been initiated into the arts of magic, whether black or white. Everything she knew was from hearsay. She resolutely applied herself to her work; however, she never succeeded in achieving anything practical or useful. She would make a wax effigy of a hated neighbor and stick into it a hundred long pins, some of gold; instead of pining away to nothing, the neighbor would even put on weight. Likewise, the evil eye she cast upon the plantations of the wealthy merely made the sugarcane and the tobacco plants grow more luxuriantly. Levitation? A flop. Flying across the skies on a broom? Another flop. She would gallop on a broom, and confidently propelling herself skyward, she would leap up in the air—here I go!—only to come crashing down wretchedly. She would try to foretell the future by examining the viscera of animals; where others saw the weather forecast, victorious armies advancing, the price of sugar on the London or Amsterdam markets, she merely saw the giblets of a rooster; a black rooster it was, a good game bird, killed in accordance with the ritualistic precepts; but still, giblets, pure and simple. What else could she do except eat the giblets? Which she did, cooked.

She was never invited to the Sabbaths of the witches; her attempts to communicate with the dead always ended in failure, nothwithstanding her frequent visits to the cemeteries on Friday nights. She would have gladly submitted herself to incubi and other demons; as a matter of fact, she lusted after their grotesque penises, which she pictured as big and reddish. Rolling about in bed, she would murmur, passionately: "Come, demons, come and take me. I have a delicious ass." They wouldn't come: least of all the Devil, whose asshole she longed to kiss, the *osculum obscenum* being the great dream of her life. She would invoke him, but with no success: "Eko, eko, Azarak! Eko, eko, Zamelak! Eko, eko, eko." Nothing would happen; what she most desired—to have the mark of the devil branded on her flesh—she never got. Sometimes she would notice something, a blotch, a swelling; but no, it was just a boil, or a sore. The mark of the devil? No.

She blamed Maranhão for her failures; this place here is a backwater, how can anyone do a good job when conditions are so unfavorable, nobody takes anything seriously; and she would quote Father Antonio Vieira, to whom Maranhão meant: *muttering, mockery, malevolence, misinformation, meddling, mendacity.*

On the other hand, her own slave Grácia Tapanhuna, a scatter-brained young Negro girl, succeeded—and without any effort—in everything that she, Maria, aspired to achieve. Grácia would predict rain; the sky being blue, people would make fun of her; soon after, however, dark clouds would gather, and not long afterward, there would be a rain shower. She brought luck to gamblers, she made barren women pregnant merely by laying her hand on their bellies, and she could wither the leg of a fat man by merely looking at it sidelong. She could levitate at will, rising a span or more in the air, and she had sexual intercourse with demons at least twice a week, on Saturdays and Sundays, and also on all holy days of obligation. "Ah, Dona Maria, you can't imagine how good it is, ma'am," she would say about her experiences, rolling her eyes.

Such resounding success deeply mortified *Maria-of-the-Blazing-Ass.* She would have liked to ask Grácia Tapanhuna for advice, but it wouldn't do to diminish herself; after all, Grácia was a slave. If she had to associate with anyone, it would be with Manoel Beckman, Bequimão. She believed that the New Christian had secret powers; otherwise, how to account for his ascendancy over the people of Maranhão? He must know the cabala, for sure; the secret of the

Essenes; the works of Michel de Nostradame and of Jean Bodin. If Beckman wanted to, he could turn her into a first-class witch, into a really malevolent sorcerer. Maria de Freitas would be the reincarnation of Lilith, Adam's first wife, an insatiable female, a magician of extraordinary powers.

But Bequimão simply ignored her existence. Deep in thought, he would walk past her on the street, barely greeting her, notwithstanding the ardent glances she kept casting at him. Maria de Freitas wanted the Jew not only as a mentor but also as a lover; she wanted to surrender herself to him, not only to derive magical powers from the carnal union but also to reach peaks of orgasm time after time. However, how could she hope to have him when the love potions that she prepared were nothing but malodorous concoctions containing the blood and parts of repulsive animals? It just didn't work.

One night, driven by lust, she became bold enough to knock on the door of Bequimão's house. "I must talk to you," she whispered when he came to the door; "in private." Beckman, embarrassed, said that it wasn't the right time, but she insisted. They went then to the corral, where letting her robe fall to the ground, she embraced him, quivering:

"I'm yours, magus. Take me!"

At once thunderstruck and outraged, Bequimão stood staring at her; then he coldly ordered her to put on her clothes and never to come to him again.

Humiliated, Maria swore she would take revenge on him. For this purpose, she used the naive Grácia Tapanhuna; at Maria's request, the slave girl denounced Bequimão to the Holy Office of the Inquisition. What she told them was already common knowledge: That Manoel referred to the corral as the *sacrarium,* that before slaughtering a steer he always tied it to a cross, but to this she added that she had seen him perform on his slaves the ceremonial washing of the feet.

"Did he wash the feet of his Negroes?" João Felipe Bettendorf, who was taking testimony from Grácia, asked in disbelief.

"Of his Negroes, yes, sir," she confirmed.

The commissary of the Holy Office closed his face: To wash the feet of Negroes, in imitation of Christ, who had washed the feet of the apostles! A serious breach, an affront to religion, something only a heretic or a Jew would be capable of doing. Beckman was indicted.

The investigation of Beckman by the Holy Office went on for two years, from 1678 to 1680. In charge of the investigation was Father Antonio de Affonseca, who, incidentally, at one time had owned the slave Grácia Tapanhuna.

The accusations were serious and involved the entire Beckman family. Then the process was suspended by order of the king of Portugal, who considered Manoel an honorable man. However, from then on, Manoel began to openly contest the government policies of governor Sá e Menezes and of the Portuguese Crown. He would say that the settlers were suffering hardships, that there was a shortage of hand labor; that freightage was costly, that foodstuffs were in short supply, that taxes were high. Meanwhile, the Jesuits were exempt from export taxes; and the Trade Company of Maranhão and of Grão-Pará had a monopoly on imports and on the slave trade, as well as special privileges and exemption from taxes. "They're sucking our blood," Bequimão would vociferate at anyone who cared to listen to him. "These foreigners are sucking our blood." Rafael Mendes listened, perplexed: foreigners? But Beckman himself wasn't a Brazilian, he had been born in Portugal. And what did he hope to accomplish with all this clamor? Wasn't being a New Christian troublesome enough? Wasn't it bad enough to have the Inquisition at his heels?

Rafael tried to calm him down by reasoning that things could be settled amicably. "You're just a coward," Bequimão would say, "you're good at giving advice, but I don't need any advisors, I need supporters." And he did get them: He could count on the support of at least sixty of the most influential individuals in Maranhão. His brother Thomaz, a poet and minstrel like the shoemaker Bandarra, was an enthusiastic propagator of his ideas.

On February 24, 1684, there broke out an insurgency led by Manoel and Thomaz Beckman. The governor was ordered not to put up any resistance; a junta, called "The Junta of the Three Estates"—the nobility, the clergy, and the people—was established. The laws restricting trade were abolished; the Society of Jesus was ordered to leave Maranhão.

Beckman himself read the decision aloud to Bettendorf, the rector of the College of the Society of Jesus: "I, Manoel Beckman, as the elected procurator of the people, justly angered by the vexations they have suffered due to the fact that Your Excellencies hold temporal power over the Indians in our villages."

Father Bettendorf listened to him in silence. Deep in his heart he liked Beckman; there was between the two men mutual admiration. After assuring the priest that the holdings of the Society of Jesus would be safe, Beckman then ordered that the Jesuits leave for Pernambuco immediately. The priest didn't argue. "We'll see how things turn out," he said with a faint smile.

The revolutionary government lasted fifteen months; and from the very beginning, it became clear that it wouldn't get the support of the neighboring provinces. The Senate of Pará, whose concurrence would be vital, decided to remain loyal to the Crown, and so did the captaincy of Santo Antonio de Alcântara.

Put under a blockade, Maranhão was isolated. The Junta exhorted the people to prepare themselves for a long siege and for the hardships they would have to suffer: The final victory will be ours! Full power to the Junta!

Beckman is a believer; he firmly believes in the Revolution, in a glorious future. As he paces the floor back and forth in a state of agitation, he outlines his ideas to Rafael. He foresees a better world, a world of justice and brotherliness. A world where nobody will starve or freeze. The cultivated lands, the sugar mills, the ships will belong to everybody; from each according to his abilities, to each according to his needs. Science will make progress; the ideas of Copernicus, of Galileo will be developed. Machines will do all the work; people will move in space in flying vehicles. "And what about the nation, what will happen to it?" Rafael ventures to ask.

"But it's about the nation that I'm talking!" bellows Bequimão, impatient. "I'm also talking about the nation! These ideas come from the nation, from its prophets, from Isaiah, and others. The nation? Everybody will belong to the nation!"

Making no reply, Rafael Mendes goes home. His wife and children complain: "We're suffering many privations. With the blockade, even food is hard to come by."

One day Maria de Freitas comes to see Rafael on the sly; she wants to talk to him about a very important matter. They go to the corral, where Maria de Freitas discloses that someone has put a jinx on Bequimão. He is under the spell of Úrsula Albernaz, a bad-tempered hussy whom Maria knows well: They were together in exile before they came to Maranhão.

"A witch. A witch of many powers. She has turned his head, I'm sure."

She can well guess at what lies behind this scheme. Úrsula wants a job with the Administrative Council. Her intention is to get official sanction for her witchcraft practices; if possible, she will even create a Ministry of Witchcraft to be headed by some magician of her choice.

"But," adds Maria de Freitas, "I can undo the hex. All I need is to sleep one night with him."

Rafael stares at her, in disbelief.

"Bequimão won't be able to resist my charms," the woman insists; and to prove it, she sheds her clothes.

Rafael looks her over. She's no longer young; a wrinkled face, sagging breasts, flabby buttocks. The signs of any former beauty are dissolved. What is left is a bag of loose, pendulous skin. If Beckman's return to sanity depends on this . . . He heaves a sigh. He, too, is old; he has a twenty-year-old son, a nineteen-year-old daughter. And Beckman is pushing seventy. Rafael promises Maria de Freitas that he will talk to his friend and arrange for a clandestine rendezvous.

"Let me know, then, will you?" says Maria de Freitas, taking her leave. "But don't breathe a word of this to Grácia Tapanhuna. I don't trust her. And watch out for Úrsula Albernaz."

She walks away but then turns back. An idea has occurred to her: "If I win Beckman's love," she says with a foxy smile, "and if I become the Grand Witch of the captaincy of Maranhão, you'll be rewarded, Rafael Mendes. At the very least I'll get you an aldermanship, you can count on it."

The constrained Rafael, trying to keep his promise, tells Beckman that Maria de Freitas wants to sleep with him. Beckman casts such a reprimanding look at him that Rafael is almost frightened: He realizes that he is now dealing with a man driven by fixed ideas, a fanatic.

As Beckman's power increases, so does his wrath, his holy wrath, as he puts it. He wants to completely eliminate all vestiges of corruption, and do away with luxury, with ostentation; he wants the people of Maranhão to live like the Indians used to, a simple, pure, innocent life. And so he proposes to the Junta that all superfluous expenses be cut, that women in general be forbidden to wear ribbons, and that the *mamelucos*—the women of European and Indian descent—be forbidden to wear silk mantles. The *mamelucos* are outraged: "What? Why can't we wear silk anymore? What are we supposed to wear? Bird feathers, like the squaws?" Beckman is booed on the streets: "Let's burn this infamous Jewish dog," people shout at him. Widespread discord has now replaced the initial enthusiasm of the supporters of the movement. The only member of the Junta Beckman can trust is the Negro Francisco Dias Deiró, the people's representative. The situation is serious: The blockade has created difficulties for the merchants, and for the owners of the sugar plantations and mills. Besides, Bequimão's outlandish ideas raise eyebrows; it is rumored that the Jew is crazy, stark crazy. As if all of this weren't enough, a grave incident is about to stir up feelings even more.

A ship of the Trade Company has just arrived from Guinea with two hundred Negroes, and this event precipitates a riot. Due to the shortage of hand labor caused by the blockade, people start fighting over the slaves; in the middle of the street, two merchants cross swords with each other over a young Negro, and end up by killing the poor devil. To prevent such excesses, the Junta decides to raffle off the slaves. On the raffle tickets, some people write down witty remarks, risqué statements, insults—which triggers new arguments, new fights.

Then the new governor, Gomes Freire de Andrade, arrives in the province. Taking office, he promises to restore law and order. The Jesuits return; the trade monopoly is reestablished. Manoel Beckman is in hiding; his godson Lázaro de Melo discloses his whereabouts to the authorities. Beckman is arrested, together with several other leaders. And so is Rafael Mendes, for being a sympathizer. He is taken to the same dungeon where Bequimão is imprisoned.

And there they are, the two friends, Rafael Mendes and Manoel Beckman, waiting in a dark dungeon cell to be interrogated. Rafael Mendes hesitates; for a long time he has wanted to clarify a suspicion regarding Beckman, but he isn't sure if now is the right moment. Finally, he decides he'll ask, anyway:

"Are you really from the nation, Beckman?"

Taken aback, the other man stares at him, wary. He, too, hesitates before replying:

"From the nation? No way. I'm a Christian by the grace of God."

"But," says Rafael, "when the emissaries of the Holy Office accused you of being a Jew, you didn't deny it."

"True," says Beckman, "I didn't deny being a Jew."

"And why not?" insists Rafael. "Why didn't you, if I may know?"

Beckman remains silent; finally, he says that he can't give a reply right away; he needs time to think it over.

"How much time?" asks Rafael Mendes.

"Some time."

"A lot of time?"

"No. Not a lot of time."

"But, as you know, we might not have much time left," warns Rafael.

"Yes. We might not have much time left," says Bequimão with a sigh. "But don't rush me. I need time."

Rafael looks around. They are in a dark, damp cell; water drips from the ceiling. Rafael points upward:

"See that leak? The water keeps dripping with a regular rhythm. So—"

"How do you know it's a regular rhythm?" Bequimão cuts him short.

"By correlating it with the beats of my heart. It's one drop for every two heartbeats."

"And who says that your heartbeats are regular?"

"I'm the one who's asking the questions," retorts Rafael.

"Are you from the Inquisition?" asks Bequimão, irritated.

"No. But I'm a Jew. And you?"

"Give me time," says Bequimão.

"How much time?"

"Some time."

"After twenty-four thousand drops," says Rafael, rising to his feet, "I'll return to this question."

And he begins to count: *one, two, three, four* . . . His voice trails off; at ten thousand he merely murmurs; and at fifteen thousand, he can no longer speak, he counts in silence. As he comes to drop number 18,412, Beckman says:

"Now. I'm ready now."

"So?" says Rafael, exhausted. "Why didn't you deny it when they accused you of being a Jew?"

"Because to them I am a Jew," replies Beckman; "in their eyes I want to be a Jew."

Laughing, Rafael Mendes lets himself fall upon the pallet. "So you're a Jew," he cries out, joyfully. "Of course you are a Jew."

"Am I a Jew?" asks Beckman, perplexed.

"You are a Jew."

"It's true!" shouts Beckman. "It's true! I'm perplexed: I'm a Jew! I'm a Jew, Rafael Mendes. I'm a Jew by the grace of God. A Jew like Jacob, who struggled with the angel, a Jew like Jonah."

But Rafael is no longer listening; tired out, he has fallen asleep.

The day of the execution arrives. The entire population of the city heads for the main square to watch the hanging; among them is Rafael Mendes, who has been set free so that he, too, can watch. Standing by his side is Maria de Freitas, who ceaselessly invokes all the demons to save the man she loves. But to no avail, no chariot of fire descends from the sky to whisk away Beckman; the earth doesn't split open, night doesn't suddenly fall, winds don't rise, whales don't get out of the sea. In despair, she appeals to Úrsula Albernaz, to

Grácia Tapanhuna: "Do something, save him!" Úrsula Albernaz smiles; she has lost interest in Bequimão, she'll be investing heavily on Gomes Freire. Grácia Tapanhuna doesn't want to jeopardize herself, either; she doesn't like Beckman, he has never washed her feet.

As for Rafael Mendes, he watches the events, perplexed. Why didn't Bequimão flee? The populace would have helped him, even Father Bettendorf had openly repudiated the denunciation. Does he want to die, then, this man? Like Christ? But if he is from the nation, why die like Christ? If he wants to change the world, why surrender himself to the executioners?

The drums roll. The ceremony is about to begin. The hangman proceeds to hang a black dummy dressed in tatters; it symbolizes Francisco Dias Deiró, who being a fugitive, has escaped hanging. The crowd laughs as the grotesque figure sways from the rope. It is now Beckman's turn. He refuses to be blindfolded; he also requests that his hands be left free. He removes the dummy from the hangman's noose, kisses it, then carefully lays it on the floor of the gallows. He places the noose around his own neck; turning to the crowd, he announces that he is happy to die for Maranhão. For Maranhão? wonders Rafael Mendes, perplexed. Why not die for the nation? Or for humanity? Beckman is no longer able to supply answers to these questions: The trap door is opened, he drops abruptly; dexterously, the hangman then steps on Beckman's shoulders so as to speed up asphyxiation. At this moment, Maria de Freitas lets out a scream; casting aside her clothes, she throws herself upon the ground, and there she remains, screaming and rolling. When Rafael Mendes comes to her aid, he notices on one of her buttocks a reddish blotch in the shape of a flower: *Maria-of-the-Blazing-Ass* has finally succeeded in getting the devil's mark.

A few days later she died, but not before letting Rafael Mendes in on a secret: The Gold Tree existed, and it was to be found in Brazil.

"It's in the south, Rafael. Go south."

Rafael didn't go in search of the Gold Tree, but for many years the idea haunted him like an obsession. An old man, the arduous journey was not for him. So, he called his son and told him about what had happened.

"I have no riches to bequeath you," he said. "I'm passing this secret on to you, use it in whatever way you see fit."

The younger Rafael was rather skeptical about what his father told him; but the story roused the ambition of his friend Álvaro de Mesquita.

"Let's go south, friend Rafael," he said, his eyes glittering with cupidity. "Let's go in search of fortune."

They penetrated deep into the jungles of Bahia. They trudged across dense vegetation, a pistol in one hand, a machete in the other, their hearts pounding: they feared the wildcats, they feared the snakes, they feared the Indians, the demons, the ghosts, the agents of the Holy Office. While one of them slept, the other kept vigil: On the 34th day of their journey, however, exhaustion won out and they both fell asleep at the same time in a clearing carpeted with leaves of cacao trees.

Upon waking up, they found themselves surrounded by Negroes. About thirty of them, wearing loincloths, and armed with spears and cudgels. Still dazed, Rafael and Álvaro scrambled to their feet—and soon realized that any attempts at resistance would be futile: They had fallen into the hands of run-away slaves.

"You're our prisoners," said the one who seemed to be the leader, in excellent Portuguese.

Their captors were not going to stand for any foolishness: They tied their hands with bast, then prodding them with their spears, they made the prisoners walk. After a forced march lasting several hours along a narrow, rough-hewn trail cut through the jungle, they came to a large clearing as the day was drawing in. There, surrounded by a high stockade made of wattle, was the *quilombo*, the village of the run-away Negroes. Rafael and Álvaro were taken straight to the presence of Zambi.

Zambi of Palmares. A hefty Negro, with gloomy eyes. Seated on a crude chair made from trunks of trees and decorated with the teeth of animals and the feathers of exotic birds, he awaited their arrival. A man of kingly bearing; and haughty like a king he addressed them. He wanted to know what they were doing in the jungle. Rafael and Álvaro hesitated, they exchanged glances. Finally, Rafael decided he would tell the truth: They were Jews, they were escaping from the Inquisition.

Wary, Zambi considers them. Clearly, he is making conjectures, assessing the situation. Two white men? They could well be traitors. On the other hand, if they are running away from the Inquisition, from the Portuguese, then they could become two allies, two soldiers. Two workers. At the very least, two hostages to be used, should the need arise. A shrewd man, he doesn't disclose his thoughts. "Burn them alive," he orders his men in Portuguese. And he adds, "If the Inquisition can burn white people, so can we, and for stronger reasons." On hearing the verdict, Rafael and Álvaro throw themselves upon the ground, weeping. Álvaro invokes his mother, Rafael remonstrates with his God, saying it's not fair—they've escaped from the Inquisition, they've faced the wild beasts of the jungle, and now they're about to die an inglorious death—and for what crime? For no crime, for no wrongdoing. It's not fair, it's not fair!

Zambi watches them with ill-concealed satisfaction: he's not loath to humiliate the white men.

"Get up!" he orders sternly.

They try to stand up but can't, despair weighs them down. Grabbing them by the arm, the warriors force them to rise to their feet. And on their feet they stand, wailing, leaning against each other.

Zambi keeps staring at them. Strange creatures, Jews. He had met a few before, including—this happened back in Africa—a black Jew, a wayfarer, who, having been condemned by some obscure curse to wander the earth, had left the east coast of Africa and walked across the entire continent. His haughty bearing had made quite an impression on the young Zambi; and so had the story the man told him:

"I'm a descendant of Menelik, the son of King Solomon and Queen Shebah. My illustrious ancestor, an African born Negro, lived in King Solomon's court from the age of thirteen—when he was *bar-mitzvahed* and initiated into the Jewish faith—until the age of twenty-five, when his father sent him back to Africa. As a parting gift, Solomon gave his son a copy of the Tables of the Law; however, by means of an artful ruse, Menelik succeeded in exchanging them for the real Tables of the Law, which he then took with him to Africa. Thus, we Negroes became the true keepers of the divine word."

He said in conclusion:

"We have rights, my brother. And we must assert our rights—if not by force, then by shrewdness."

It was a lesson that made a deep impression on the young Zambi and filled him with admiration for the Jews. Paradoxical admiration, though, for among them are slave traders, whom Zambi, naturally, abhors; but he is deeply impressed by the strength, the perseverance, the finely tuned instinct of survival of these people, traits that propel them to permeate every nook and cranny of society, however small, so that once inside the social structure, they can fill up the gaps, thus making themselves indispensable and progressively irksome, until they are finally expelled and the cycle starts all over again somewhere else.

No, Zambi won't kill his prisoners. Partly because he sees them as brothers in misfortune; partly because he is loath to shed the blood of defenseless men—whether or not they are white, whether or not they are Jews. While he decides on a course of action, the prisoners will be kept under strict surveillance. And in order to deserve the food that they will receive, they will work in the building of fortifications— from sunrise to sunset, like the rest of the inhabitants of the *quilombo,* the village of the run-away slaves.

Backbreaking work it is. To fell trees in the jungle, to lop off branches, to haul logs along muddy trails; to set up the stockade, to shore up the logs; to dig trenches, to build stone walls— three days of this, and Álvaro and Rafael are exhausted, their hands covered with blisters. At night, Rafael collapses on his hard pallet and falls sound asleep, much to the amusement of his guard: "No need to worry about this one, he's too pooped out to run away."

But not Álvaro. Even though he feels tired, he doesn't go to sleep. Accompanied by his guard, he strolls about the *quilombo,* greets the occasional person, strikes up a conversation with them. Suspicious at first, the Negroes eventually get used to him. And thus he makes friends with M'bonga, one of Zambi's chief advisers. Into the mind of this kindly but unsophisticated man, Álvaro begins to instill certain ideas. . . .

Quilombos, he says, shouldn't be conceived as mere hideouts for fugitives but as true republics in embryo, potentially strong and well-organized. Of course, something along these lines is already at work here in the *quilombo* of Palmares; there is division of labor, some people being in charge of planting, others of manufacturing wooden and clay utensils. However, it is possible to move further; it is possible to *progress.* For instance, it will be possible to build *machines.* Machines capable of replacing the human arm in the heavy work of felling and hauling trees, of digging holes in the ground. Machines that will manufacture cloth, domestic utensils, and also—and this is very important—weapons. Machines that will move in the air or in the depths of the ocean, like big steel fish. Machines that will build buildings; and machines inside these buildings that will transport people from the lower to the higher floors, and vice-versa. The machines will do everything; the people of the *quilombos* will spend their time singing and dancing to the sound of drums and of percussion instruments. Pleasure will be the word of command. "Really?" interjects M'bonga, his eyes glittering. "Really," Álvaro assures him. But, he cautions, it won't be easy to make this dream come true. Fortifications and good warriors are not enough. What is needed is a government capable of maintaining interchange—especially commercial interchange—with the other republics. A republic must integrate itself into the worldwide financial system. And for this to happen, it will need coin.

"Coin?" M'bonga creases his forehead. Surely, he knows what it is; however, he hasn't thought of it as being important; at least not important in Palmares, where money is unknown, for everything belongs to everybody, and nothing is bought.

Coin, yes. Carried away by excitement, Álvaro begins to describe the coin unit he envisions for Palmares, a beautiful gold piece having its value on one side, and the effigies of the heroes of Palmares on the other: Zambi and his Finance Minister.

"Me, Finance Minister?" M'bonga is getting more and more astonished, he has never dreamed of such glories, he doesn't even know what a Finance Minister is supposed to do. "Ah, yes," says Álvaro, "no self-respecting country can do without a Ministry of Finance. And who would be better suited to fill the post than M'bonga, the creator of the coin of Palmares?"

(M'bonga: a name adopted by the runaway slave João de Deus upon joining the *quilombo* of Palmares; a name of African origin; a name its bearer utters with religious fervor. M'bonga!)

A coin that will pass into History. A coin that will be exhibited in museums, together with the cruzado, the doubloon, the escudo. "And what do we have to do in order to have it?" asks M'bonga, waxing enthusiastic. "Quite a lot," cautions Álvaro. A financial system: a government mint, banks. But men with a great deal of experience in finances, such as Álvaro himself, would look after such matters. However, all of this will be useless if there is no gold reserve; that's what gives coin validity and substance. Gold.

"Gold?"

"Gold. Without gold, nothing done. No coin, no banks... No Minister."

"Hm..." says M'bonga. "Gold." He falls silent, turning this matter over in his mind. Cautiously and skillfully, Álvaro begins to question him. "Was there, by any chance, gold in the surrounding areas? A few nuggets, maybe, in some purling creek? Or on a tree?" M'bonga roars with laughter. "Gold? Where would us poor Negroes get gold? And what's this about gold on trees? Lunacy."

No, there is no gold. But this idea of Álvaro's, this coin system, has bewitched him. He'll see what can be done. He'll speak to Zambi, the chief trusts him, M'bonga has saved his life more than once.

He accompanies Álvaro back to the small straw-thatched hut that has been assigned to the prisoners and says good night. Álvaro goes in. "We are on the brink of some sensational events, friend!" he announces glowing with joy, but Rafael doesn't want to hear about it: He wants to sleep.

167

On the following day, M'bonga, radiant with joy, wakes them up. He has already spoken to Zambi. Although reluctantly, the chief has approved of the idea. M'bonga is now the Finance Minister (his appointment, though, is to remain secret for the time being—Zambi fears infighting for the control of power). Álvaro is given permission to go ahead with his project of devising a financial system.

"As for gold," says M'bonga after hesitating for a moment, "Zambi hasn't said anything about it. But we'll take steps to get it. We'll do so in good time."

After he leaves, Rafael turns to his friend:

"What's this all about?" he asks, intrigued. "What's going on?"

Álvaro quickly briefs him on the matter.

"But this is madness," protests Rafael.

"Shut up," snarls Álvaro, "it's our chance of saving our skins. And of getting rich!" His eyes are glittering. "Rich, Rafael!"

Álvaro is convinced that M'bonga is not telling him the truth, that he is playing dumb; that there must be gold somewhere in this area, perhaps a mine, perhaps the Gold Tree. Otherwise, why did the Negroes run away from their masters, leaving behind their homes (even if they were only plantation slave quarters) and guaranteed meals (even if they consisted of plain portions of food) and go into the jungle? There must be something behind all of this. Like gold.

Before Rafael can say anything, M'bonga is back. He comes in with stationery, booty taken from the Portuguese troops.

"There you are!" he says, triumphant. "You can start working."

Rafael has no other alternative, for however crackbrained Álvaro is, he can't now abandon him to his own fate.

They embark upon their assignment. At first, they apply themselves to the task of drafting fiscal laws and regulations; soon, however, they realize that there are far more pressing matters that have to be dealt with first. It's pointless to have legislation if there is no government, no structuring of the powers. As Rafael Mendes gets more deeply involved in his work, he undergoes a disturbing transformation. It dawns on him that the *quilombo* is not a mere agglomerate of runaway slaves but possibly an incipient nation, and by some mysterious design, he has been given the honor of witnessing the birth of a nation. Will he measure up to this historical role? Álvaro sneers at his anxieties: The idea is to hoodwink the Negroes, bilk them out of their gold, and then get the hell out of there.

"But what gold?" asks Rafael, perplexed.

"The gold they're going to get."

"How?"

"By selling primary products, that's how."

"But what kind of primary products?" Rafael is more and more puzzled. "The inhabitants of the *quilombo* live hand to mouth, what they plant and hunt is barely enough to feed them."

Álvaro laughs: That's not the kind of primary products he has in mind.

"*They* are the primary product."

"They who?"

"They. The Negroes. The slaves."

He explains: There's no shortage of Negroes in this village of runaway slaves, and there won't be any—he has already noticed the high fertility rate among the women; maybe because feeling free, the Negroes copulate more often. So, it's only a matter of making connections with the slave traders (he happens to know one from the Antilles, a New Christian like them, and like them, a fugitive from the Inquisition), of delivering a certain number of Negroes, preferably young, and of receiving payment in gold, some of which will go to the ministers, as their commission, and some will be set aside as gold reserve to give stability to the coin system to be created.

Rafael's astonishment turns into indignation: "You mean you want to send these poor people back to slavery? You want them to sell their own children for gold, is that so? But when they don't even need gold! They're happy the way they live!" "Don't yell at me," says Álvaro, coldly. "Yes, they need gold. If M'bonga, their leader, says that they need gold, and that they need coin, it's because they need gold, and they need coin. And if that's the case, they must sacrifice one generation so that the other can reap the benefits of a sound financial structure."

And he concludes by saying: "It's a question of options."

Distressed, Rafael looks at him. They've known each other since they were children; they played together; they had their *bar mitzvah* together; Rafael always thought of him as being kind; somewhat roisterous, perhaps, but basically honest and hard-working. And now he has cooked up a plan for selling the Negroes who have harbored them. That's villainy, to say the least. An idea crosses his mind: Could it be that Álvaro is insane? That he has lost his mind, due to the hardships they've been through? No. He doesn't act crazy. He is self-possessed, he expresses himself clearly, he knows what he is talking about. No, he's not crazy. Unfortunately not. Maybe his true nature is finally showing through, maybe he's giving vent to his feelings by casting aside the chaste mantle of virtue to reveal the furry beast of prey that he really is.

"I can't accept something like this," says Rafael, rising to his feet. He begins to pace back and forth. Álvaro watches him. It's obvious that his mind is already made up. That's what he says:

"I've made up my mind, friend Rafael. I'm going to present this suggestion to Zambi, with or without your approval. We can mention our differences of opinion to him. It will then be up to him to decide which of us he will choose as his advisor."

Then rising to his feet, he leaves the hut. Rafael hesitates; finally, he follows him, cursing. Álvaro stops to wait for him; then taking his friend by the arm, he says:

"Hold on! I've just had a bright idea. An idea that reconciles my plans with your qualms."

He explains: They won't actually sell the Negroes, but just go through the motions of a real sale. They'll get the money from the slave trader, but when he comes to collect the slaves, he'll be in for a surprise; he'll be met by well-armed warriors, ready to put up resistance. And he'll have no choice but to beat a retreat and go back to the Antilles.

"So? What do you think?"

Rafael thinks that it is a viable alternative. They'll be cheating one of their own—but after all, he is a slave trader, a sinner; it will be stealing from a thief.

They present their proposal to M'bonga. At first, he has some reservations about it; he considers it dangerous to deceive a white man. However, he acknowledges that the strength of the lion is worthless without the cunning of the fox; if deception is necessary to give his people a future, then he will deceive. And he'll persuade Zambi to do likewise.

That night there is a festive celebration in honor of a black deity. They eat roasted kid goat, corn, summer squash, and they drink the powerful firewater that is distilled in the *quilombo*. Soon everybody is singing and dancing merrily. Álvaro chases after the young Negro women, pinches their bottoms. M'bonga averts his eyes, pretending not to have noticed.

Suddenly, there is a blast of cannons. They are being attacked! Under an intense fusillade, the Negroes scatter every which way. Zambi yells out orders, vainly trying to set up a defense. Rafael grabs Álvaro by the arm, he wants them to take cover. Shaking his friend off, Álvaro runs toward the gates of the *quilombo*, and opens them wide:

"Stop it!" he yells. "Stop it, you white shit asses! Don't damage my goods!"

A bullet hits him on the chest, he throws his arms open and sinks to the ground, dead.

There's nothing Rafael can do, except flee, and he flees.

He arrives in Cachoeira, a town located in the vast and fertile coastal region of the state of Bahia known as the *Recôncavo*. There, in 1705, he meets Bartolomeu Lourenço de Gusmão, who is finishing his studies at the Seminary of the Jesuits, in Belém. They become friends; the young seminarist often comes to see him to talk. Which doesn't surprise Rafael: the young man is a future Jesuit, yes, but didn't that other Jesuit, Father Vieira, also befriend the Jews? All priests are not alike; besides, Rafael has heard that Bartolomeu is from the nation, too. Which, again, doesn't come as a surprise. The same used to be said about Father Vieira.

Bartolomeu is an enthusiastic young man with the gift of gab. He is keen on learning; he has read—secretly—the works of Bacon, Copernicus, Galileo, and Thomas More's *Utopia*; he is well-versed in the art of magic; he has some knowledge of alchemy; he can fix clocks; he has built a manual printing press; he has plans to improve the sugar mills. But his greatest dream, the great ambition of his life, is to fly. To fly like the Brazilian birds: the brightly colored macaw, the garrulous parakeet, the freakish black vulture. But—how will he be able to fly? By means of a balloon, naturally, a balloon big enough to carry people and cargo. He has made sketches and even a prototype of this balloon, which he has named Big Bird. And he ends up disclosing his reason for having sought out Rafael Mendes: He wants to donate his Big Bird to the nation, to the New Christians. He envisions a safe sanctuary for the persecuted: it's the *New Zion*, to be located on a gigantic wooden platform, five leagues long by five leagues wide. On this platform, houses, schools, workshops, a synagogue will be built; there will be reservoirs to collect rain water. In big containers filled with soil, potherbs and trees will be planted. There will be space to raise animals and even a small lake for fish culture. One hundred and twenty Big Birds will raise this monumental structure about a league and a half high up in the air; then, at the whim of the air currents, they will crisscross Brazil, from north to south, from east to west. At that height, the Jews will be closer to God; they will be able to pray, with nothing intervening between them and heaven. And, as they lean over the rail, they will be able to admire far below the magnificent Brazilian landscape, with its verdant forests, mighty rivers, vast meadows; they will hover over cities, towns, and villages, well above hatred and intrigue, deceit and corruption. And, should they so desire, one day they will land on the central plateau and there, in that immense wilderness, they will found a city, which they will govern as they see fit. And it is even possible that the winds will carry them across the seas; it's possible that they will arrive in Palestine, and descend upon the mountain of the Essenes, or upon Jerusalem, the Golden, the millennial dream finally come true, thus making the *New Zion* no longer necessary.

"So?" he asks, eagerly. "What do you think?"

Rafael gazes at him, perplexed.

"Are you from the nation?" he finally asks.

Gusmão hesitates.

"Yes. Let's say I'm from the nation. Yes, I'm from the nation."

He grabs Rafael by the arm.

"I need your help. Convince your friends of this possibility. Tell them it's a unique opportunity."

But Rafael is rather reluctant; deep down, the whole story strikes him as absurd—and couldn't it be a trap set up by the Holy Office to catch crypto-Jews? Could it be that Bartolomeu Lourenço de Gusmão is a useful innocent, or even a spy? He promises to think about it. Then a few days later Pedro Telles pays him a visit.

It is common knowledge that this Pedro is a real scoundrel: ex-slave trader, ex-hawker, ex-jewelry dealer, ex-mercenary soldier. He is always mixed up in some swindle or other, and although he is from the nation, the New Christians shun him as much as possible, but even so, they feel compelled to invite him to their secretly held religious ceremonies, during which he displays unusual fervor (pretense, according to some; a guilt-ridden conscience, according to others).

Pedro Telles has heard about the Big Bird, and he is interested. He has plans of his own for this invention: He wants to use it to capture Indians and Negroes:

"Have you ever thought of it? It's bound to be a success, Rafael!"

He would fly on the Big Bird over a village, capture—with a lasso, if need be—the most able-bodied of the Indians and then flee, as quick as the wind (exactly: as quick as the wind). With the Big Bird he would be able to smuggle slaves, transport riches, relay information (say, on the price of sugar) from Portugal to the colonies.

"And speaking of gold, we might even succeed in finding the Gold Tree. All we have to do is to keep flying over the forests until we spot the metal glittering on the top of a tree."

Stunned, Rafael Mendes stares at him. Such possibilities have never occurred to him; the truth of the matter is that Pedro Telles's ideas are indeed bright. Of course, Rafael is loath to enter into partnership with a person with such a bad reputation; on the other hand, wouldn't it be an opportunity for him to make lots of money? Rafael Mendes is a poor man, with a wife and children to support. He promises Pedro that he will speak to the inventor. The talk has to be postponed because Gusmão is being ordained priest; however, a few days later, Rafael has the opportunity to meet with the Jesuit alone and he then discloses Telles's ideas to him.

Gusmão is incensed: "To use my invention to capture Indians? Never!" It grieves him to see Rafael as the bearer of such an indecorous proposal.

"You're right," says Rafael, embarrassed. "It's indeed indecorous."

And he tells Pedro Telles that Gusmão refuses point-blank to accept his proposal.

Telles, however, is not a man to give up easily. If not through Rafael Mendes, then he'll find other means to achieve his goal. . . .

Weeks later a beautiful young woman arrives in town. She seeks out Father Bartolomeu Lourenço de Gusmão, and introduces herself as Bárbara Santos. She would like to talk to him in private—about certain sins, which are so terrible that it's impossible for her to even mention them in the holy sanctuary of the church. Would he receive her in his own private quarters? Naively, Bartolomeu assents, without suspecting that this Bárbara is a courtesan from Recife, whom Pedro Telles had sent for. The priest is even proud: He'll be hearing confession for the very first time. The harlot doesn't have the slightest difficulty in seducing him; afterward, while Gusmão sleeps off his drunkenness, she absconds with the sketches of the Big Bird, which she promptly hands over to Pedro Telles. The New Christian then hires a foreman—and workers—and the construction of the balloon begins.

Shameless as he is, Pedro Telles is not in the least anxious about keeping the project under wraps; on the contrary, he even promotes the balloon in leaflets, claiming that it is suitable for warring expeditions, the transportation of goods, recreational trips, and naturally, the capture of Indians or fugitive Negroes.

Upon reading one of the leaflets, Bartolomeu Lourenço de Gusmão lets out a yell and collapses on the floor as if struck by lightning. For three days he lies unconscious, without eating or drinking.

Rafael Mendes, being a devoted friend, nurses him, never leaving the room, not even for a minute.

Little by little, Gusmão recovers. However, he is now a much changed man; he has become quiet, taciturn. Only once does he speak to Rafael Mendes; he wants to know when the inaugural flight of the balloon being built by Telles is scheduled to take place.

"Later this week," says Rafael, worried. What could the priest be plotting? He soon finds out: On that very day Bartolomeu Lourenço de Gusmão goes to the emissary of the Holy Office of the Inquisition and denounces Pedro Telles as being a crypto-Jew and a warlock. Telles is arrested and sent to Lisbon, where after a brief trial he is put to death by the Inquisition.

Bartolomeu Lourenço de Gusmão recovers his sketches and then he gets ready to travel to Lisbon. Before going aboard the ship, he shows Rafael a letter that he will personally deliver to the king of Portugal. In it he extols the commercial and military advantages of the Big Bird, which could also be used in the supervision of the colonies: "By preventing the maladministration of the Conquests, Your Majesty could then reap the riches they produce."

Jews continued to be hunted down. Rafael Mendes had no other alternative but leave Bahia for Rio de Janeiro.

There he established himself in business. Two routes: the Old Road, via Paraty, and the New Road, which was shorter, linked Rio de Janeiro to Minas Gerais, the region of the general mines, thus turning the city into a commercial and import center that traded in all kinds of goods imported from Lisbon: salt, olive oil, wine, silk, damask, plush, weapons, gunpowder, mirrors, glassware. All of this was resold in Minas Gerais at a fabulous profit. One *arroba*, or fifteen kilograms of fresh meat, which cost 200 *réis* in Rio, would fetch 6,000 *réis* in Minas; a horse priced at 10,000 *réis* could be resold there for 120,000 *réis*.

It wasn't long before Rafael became a rich man. "The Gold Tree?" he wrote in his journal. "What for? What I have here is better than any Gold Tree." He and the people from the nation continued to practice their religion in secret, of course, but nobody bothered them. His only disappointment was his son, Rafael Mendes, who didn't have the slightest aptitude for business. He contemplated a career in the theater. As if this weren't unfortunate enough, there was also the young man's friendship with one Diogo Henriques, a rebellious, fanatical individual, feared by the Jewish community of Rio de Janeiro because of his reckless statements. Diogo Henriques believed that only through the theater would the Jews be able to act their role of the conscience of the nations, and he would say things that although seemingly silly, were in fact profound and powerful veracities. "But for this to happen," he would say, "the theater will have to go to the people, rather than the people go to the theater." He had a plan: The city would have to be entirely rebuilt around a central public square, where the theater would stand, a small theater, incidentally, consisting only of an enclosed stage on which the actors would perform. A system of tubes would spread out from the stage, connecting it to every single house in the city, and by means of a complex play of mirrors in this tubular contraption, images would be carried to each residence. Thus, without leaving home, people would be able to watch the performance through this kind of periscope.

When Rafael Mendes ventured to reason that such an undertaking would cost a lot of money, Diogo, irritated, would retort: "I want none of this Jewish way of thinking." Diogo, however, ended up settling for the building of a conventional theater. For this project, Rafael Mendes had to ask his father for money; the entire fortune of the elder Mendes was spent on this undertaking.

In 1738 the theater is ready to be inaugurated. The opening play will be *Hijinks in the General Mines*, a comedy satirizing the gold rush in Minas Gerais, written by Diogo himself. The coming performance hasn't roused much interest—nobody takes Dioguinho Screwball seriously. Rafael Mendes and Diogo's wife, Isabel, will play the leading roles.

Beautiful, this woman. Beautiful, sensual, provocative.

Right from the start Rafael feels uneasy with her; and when, according to the script, he has to embrace her, he feels that she responds with an unexpected intensity. What could it mean? Rafael soon finds out. One night the two of them are rehearsing. Diogo watches them; more irritable and critical than usual, he gets angry at everything they do, saying that what they're doing is not theater, it's syrupy idiocy; finally, he gets up and leaves. Isabel shrugs, laughing. "Let him go," she says, "we're better off without him—aren't we, Rafael?"

She goes to her dressing room. She returns naked, her body glowing in the candlelit stage. Rafael takes her right then and there. And from then on, a series of clandestine trysts take place; they even make love on the beach as they lie on the damp sand.

The entire city knows about this affair; Diogo, however, remains silent. One day he calls Rafael and Isabel to announce that there will be a change in the program. He will present a play based on texts written by Antonio José da Silva, the Jew. A playwright born in Rio de Janeiro, he was taken to Lisbon as a child, together with his father, a prisoner of the Holy Office. At hearing the news, Rafael winces; it's that Antonio José da Silva himself is being tried in Lisbon by the Inquisition and chances are he will be convicted. Rafael tries to reason with Diogo, who remains, however, adamant; he has made a decision and he will stick to it. Isabel asks what role she will be playing. Diogo smiles:

"None. It's a monologue. I'll be the only actor."

Something in his tone of voice makes Rafael Mendes uneasy. What is Diogo up to?

The news about the change in the theater program excites vivid interest, which is undoubtedly heightened by the rumors about the backstage goings-on. As a result, all the tickets are sold out; the monologue is a success in advance.

The opening night has arrived. It's a full house; on every face, an air of expectancy; matrons and young ladies whisper behind their fans.

Rafael Mendes is visibly worried; nervous, he keeps fidgeting on his seat. Diogo wanted Isabel and Rafael to sit in the orchestra: "Then you'll be able not only to watch the performance but also feel the audience's reactions." Isabel looks relaxed; she hums softly, and greets the occasional person.

The curtains rise. Half-naked, Diogo lies tied to a rack, the bed on which the Holy Office tortures its victims.

"Friends!" he shouts. "Do you know what ropes are these that bind me? The ropes of treachery! The same ropes that at this very moment are cutting into the flesh of Antonio José da Silva, the great Brazilian playwright, a prisoner of the Holy Office! Do you think it is fair, my fellow Brazilians? Do you consider perfidy fair? Rebel, my fellow Brazilians. Down with the Inquisition! Down with the Portuguese tyranny! Down with immorality! Down with adulterers!"

There is widespread commotion: booing and catcalls from one side; applause from another. In the ensuing uproar the theater is left in shambles, and many people are hurt.

Diogo Henriques is arrested. Rafael Mendes has to leave Rio. He feels very guilty about deserting his father, now old, sick and bankrupt. And like many others who *got a sniff of the mines, and had to go there in the hope of making it big,* as Dom Luís da Cunha wrote, Rafael, too, heads for Minas Gerais. It's not that he really believes in the existence of the Gold Tree; he doesn't. However, he is indebted to his father and wants to pay him back—in gold, if possible. Which he will never succeed in doing.

In 1773, José de Carvalho e Melo—the Count of Oeiros and the Marquis of Pombal—finally succeeded in having the king of Portugal issue a decree that was to abolish the distinction between New Christians and Christians of long standing. Rafael Mendes, however, distrusted laws generally. Fearing that the Holy Office of the Inquisition would be back with a vengeance, he decided to keep his true identity secret.

In Minas Gerais he dealt in gold, and he prospered. He settled down and started a family; he had many children and grandchildren. Toward the end of the eighteenth century one of them, named—naturally—Rafael Mendes, settled in Vila Rica. It was there that he met the Second Lieutenant Joaquim José da Silva Xavier, nicknamed Tiradentes, the tooth-puller. Rafael met the second lieutenant in his capacity as dentist. Having some tooth cavities and abscesses, Rafael went to see him.

The lieutenant made him sit on a hard armchair, and then tied him to it. "What are you doing?" Rafael Mendes asked, startled, but Tiradentes reassured him: "Don't be afraid, friend. It's for your own good."

He examined Rafael's mouth:

"Hm...Bad breath...Gums in pretty bad shape. Cavities. There's at least one tooth that will have to come out. One of the molars. Completely rotten. Down to the roots."

Opening a box lined with red velvet, he took out the forceps.

"Are you ready?"

Rafael was ready. Or so he thought: The extraction proved extremely difficult, the tooth seemed to be cemented to the jaw bone. Tiradentes kept pulling as hard as he could, his face apoplectic with the effort, his black beard bespattered with blood:

"Out with you! Come out, you dog!"

One final vigorous yank, and a moment later Tiradentes was showing Rafael the extracted molar caught in the tip of the forceps:

"Crooked roots," he explained, "that's why it was so hard to pull the tooth out."

He fixed his eyes on poor Rafael Mendes who, pale and shaky, was wiping the sweat off his forehead.

"Anything with crooked roots should be pulled out. Wouldn't you agree?"

"Yes," said Rafael, spitting out saliva red with blood. He had no idea what the man was talking about, but he was in no condition to argue. Whistling softly, Tiradentes was washing his hands. After drying them carefully, he went up to Rafael, who was still tied to the armchair. Again, he fixed his piercing eyes on Rafael:

"Are you from the nation?" he asked in a low voice.

Rafael's heart jumped. "I don't know what you're talking about," he stammered. Tiradentes smiled:

"Oh yes, you're from the nation all right. But fear not: I'm a friend. And I have something to tell you—something very important."

Then raising his voice:

"I have a beautiful collection of molar teeth at home, friend Rafael. Teeth that I've pulled out. Would you like to see my collection?"

That night, disguised in a cloak, Rafael Mendes, still feeling dizzy, went to Tiradentes's house. He plodded through the narrow alleys, and kept sliding on the cobblestones made slippery by a cold drizzle. He knocked on the door, as agreed upon: four raps in quick succession. Tiradentes himself opened the door. He had been waiting for Rafael, whom he then took to a room at the back of the house. The molar teeth were in little boxes lined with velvet and in soapstone containers, which were kept in a cabinet.

"This one here is yours," said Tiradentes, showing a tooth to Rafael. "The molar. One of the most interesting teeth, Rafael Mendes. The *molar*, a millstone, the tooth that grinds. It lacks the sharp cutting edges of the incisor, and it is unlike the canine, the tooth of the dog. The molar is a self-respecting tooth that does its job properly and unhurriedly, working in the deepest recesses of the mouth. Do you follow me, Rafael Mendes?"

There was a knock on the door. Tiradentes opened it: It was his servant, an old woman with a sinister aspect. She brought in a bottle of wine and two glasses, which she placed on the table. The lieutenant remained silent while she was in the room. As soon as she left, he grabbed Rafael and whispered in his ear:

"She's a spy. I have no doubt about it."

Then, raising his voice:

"As for the canines, you have to watch out. They're apt to betray you when you least expect."

He tiptoed to the door, then threw it open: nobody.

"Ah."

He asked Rafael to sit down, then he sat down opposite.

"There's something I'd like to disclose," he said, his eyes glittering. "I'm with the nation."

He poured out the wine, then raising his glass:

"Cheers!"

Then, hit by a sudden suspicion:

"This wine tastes funny, don't you think?"

Then, resuming what he had been saying before: "Yes, indeed, I'm with the nation. And some members of our family even say that we are New Christians. That we're Jews whom the Inquisition forced to convert."

Musing, he takes another sip of wine. "I've often wondered . . . if there's any truth in it. Well, it doesn't matter. Even if I'm not from the nation, it's as if I were. It's as if I indeed were, Rafael Mendes!" Then suddenly impassionate: "Because of all the humiliations, of all the mockery we've suffered! They treat us like dogs, those people from the mother country! They take away our gold, our silver, our precious stones."

Quivering with indignation, he rises to his feet.

"Enough is enough, Rafael Mendes! It's time we put an end to this situation!"

Agitated, he paces the floor back and forth as he discloses his plan. He wants a free country, a republic in which everyone has rights, and he goes even further: He envisions a better world, a world of equality, liberty and fraternity. A world in which nobody will starve or freeze.

Science will make progress. The ideas of Copernicus, of Galileo will be developed; the existence of other worlds will be proved. Man will no longer be the center of the universe, nor will he be the king of creation; after all, man is nothing more than a good savage, a mammal, an ape that acquired speech, true, but at a price: a set of weak jaws and terrible teeth:

"You have no idea how widespread is tooth decay, friend Rafael!"

(Even tooth decay, however, will be treated by ingenious apparatuses.)

There will be no slaves. Machines will do all the work. People will move in space in metallic birds and they will travel across the depths of the ocean in the wombs of steel fish—an invention for which the future generations will be indebted to the prophet Jonah. It will no longer be necessary to prospect creeks or the entrails of the earth for gold; botanists will create in their laboratories that legendary—or is it merely rare?—tree, whose roots have the ability to seek out the precious metal, which once found, is then solubilized, absorbed and carried in the sap, and finally deposited in the tree's fruits or pods. The same can be done to obtain silver, tin, mercury, lead.

"I'm a dentist, Rafael Mendes. I work in a limited space. The mouth often seems to me a dark, damp cave very much like the caves so common in our region. The teeth correspond to the stalactites and stalagmites; as for the tongue, it is the blind, viscous, slow-moving monster that many people claim to have seen in the underground gangways. All day long I toil inside mouths: the exhalations, far from pleasant, I can assure you. At night, however, when I lift up my eyes to the skies, the stars speak to me of a radiant future. . . . So, what do you think of all this?"

"Interesting," mumbles Rafael Mendes, irritated: His jaw hurts badly, and the sight of all those molars has upset him.

"It's not a mere utopian dream," goes on Tiradentes. "We've been actively working to make it come true. . . . We, my friends and I. We're a united, disciplined group, yet capable of daring flights of the imagination. We're patriots, and should it become necessary, we're willing to shed our blood in order to free this land from Portuguese bondage. We call ourselves the *Inconfidentes*, the 'disloyal ones.'"

He interrupts himself in order to assess the effect of his words.

Rafael dabs at his mouth with a handkerchief, which he then inspects: It's blood-stained.

"I'm sorry—this bleeding—"

"Mallow," says Tiradentes, with a certain impatience. "Rinse your mouth with a tisane of mallow. But you still haven't told me what you think of my plan."

Without waiting for Rafael's reply, he goes on talking about the conspiracy. Some important people are involved: the poets Thomás Antonio Gonzaga and Cláudio Manuel da Costa, and also Colonel Joaquim Silvério dos Reis. They've even devised a password: *On such and such a day I'll be baptized.*

"Baptism," he explains, "can include circumcision. The victory of our movement will mean total freedom of worship. Times have changed. Look at what is happening in France, look at what has already happened in North America. Read the works of Locke, Rousseau, Voltaire. It's the end of oppression! Every person should have the right to do as he pleases. If you decide to be circumcised— in public, if you want—it's nobody's business."

A pause, then he goes on:

"Rights, they include the right to own property. Our gold belongs to us. We need it—to maintain ourselves independently, to improve ourselves. But let me tell you: We can't succeed unless we have the support of many people. We must be united. Look at what happened to Bequimão, so shamelessly betrayed. Look at what happened during the War of the *Emboabas*, when those outside adventurers, the *emboabas*, flocked to Minas Gerais in search of gold: people of the nation fighting against people of the nation, killing one another for the vile metal. Do you think it's right? No, it's not right, and it's not right either to smuggle slaves into this region, using the Paraty Road for this purpose. Justice must be above profits, Mendes. So, I ask: Can I count on you?"

Rafael Mendes has hardly listened, so great is the pain afflicting him. He mutters something by way of reply—he'll think about it, he'll let Tiradentes know in three or four days—then, excusing himself, he takes his leave.

For the next several days Rafael Mendes is in intense pain. The inflammation caused by the tooth extraction has spread to his entire face; he runs a high fever. The family doctor, who has been sent for, examines him and is puzzled: He doesn't know what's wrong with the patient. There's lethargy, tremors; there's weakening of the muscles, the eyes are sunken. The fever suggests blood poisoning, but the patient doesn't show any signs of improvement after the application of cupping glasses.

In his delirium Rafael Mendes sees Tiradentes arrested and brought to trial. The Tribunal is in a huge hall with a domed ceiling. Behind a heavy door with a peephole stands the informer—who is he? Every time he wants to confirm an accusation, he manipulates a system of ropes and pulleys so that the head of the crucified Christ nods. Suddenly, this head falls down, then rolls on the floor until it stops at Rafael's feet. He picks it up; it's no longer a wooden head, it's no longer the head of Christ, it's the gory head of Tiradentes. Horrified, Rafael drops it. In his delirium, he flounders about in bed: He wants to warn the lieutenant that someone is betraying him, he wants to get up, but he is restrained from jumping out of bed. *"Save Tiradentes!"* he screams in despair. But nobody knows what he's talking about.

For almost two weeks Rafael Mendes hovered between life and death. Then the fever broke and was replaced by salutary sweating; he began to get better. The day came when, although still feeling weak, he went for a walk. On the main square he stopped short, aghast at the sight: Stuck on a pole was the decapitated head of José Joaquim da Silva Xavier. Rafael moaned with grief. So, it hadn't been a delirious hallucination. So, it hadn't been a dream.

Distressed by what happened to Tiradentes, Rafael Mendes leaves Minas: He doesn't want anything more to do with gold, with caves, with trials. He heads southward, to São Paulo.

It wasn't a random choice. In São Paulo the people of the nation had always enjoyed great prestige, ever since the days of bailiff João

Ramalho, whose duty it was to supervise all commercial activities with the Spanish colonies. The people of the nation owned sugarcane plantations, sugar mills, and ships; they regulated the Customhouse and had a monopoly on the collection of taxes. And they were the physicians and the astronomers, the apothecaries and the merchants; and they operated a commercial network that spread throughout the continent. The New Christians also financed, among other ventures, expeditions that were sent out to capture Indians for manual labor, of which there was a shortage, or to prospect for gold and precious stones. However, by the time of Rafael Mendes's arrival in São Paulo, such undertakings are already in decline. He can't even find anyone from the nation.

One night in a dismal tavern, Rafael meets a garrulous old man called Bento Seixas, who offers him a drink. They drink together and get drunk. Rafael Mendes talks about his life and ends up disclosing the fact that he is from the nation. Upon hearing this, the old man breaks into a grin:

"My brother!"

He, too, has Hebrew blood; he, too, is a descendant of prophets: of Jeremiah, to be specific. And being of noble ancestry, he has a dream: He wants to restore the temple of Jerusalem and make it even more splendorous than it was during the glorious reign of King Solomon. For this purpose, Bento Seixas, who is also a descendant of the *bandeirantes*, those flag-bearing pioneers who joined the armed expeditions to the interior in search of Indian slaves, gold, and emeralds, intends to organize an exploratory expedition similar to the ones of his ancestors.

"To capture Indians?" Rafael is puzzled and rightly so; nobody enslaves Indians anymore, nowadays everybody wants Negroes as slaves.

"To capture Indians?" repeats Bento Seixas, impatient. "Of course not!"

He has moral reservations about this infamous trade: How can the Chosen People be involved in slavery?

No, it's not to capture Indians; nor is it to search for the delusive emeralds that lured his ancestors; what he is after—and Rafael quivers when he hears the words—is the legendary Gold Tree. The secret of how to find it was revealed to him by his uncle on his deathbed. Despite the fact that this uncle was a weird man, a loner who shunned everybody, including his own family—or perhaps for this very reason—Bento Seixas is convinced that the secret itinerary, which he has engraved on his mind, will lead him to the magic tree for sure. There's one problem, though: his blindness. In that poorly lit environment, Rafael didn't notice the expressionless eyes; however, as soon as the old man mentions this fact, Rafael realizes that he is indeed blind.

He is blind and until he met Rafael, there was no one he could trust. With enthusiasm, the blind man now makes a proposal to Rafael: "Let's find the Gold Tree, brother. Let's give the grandeur of the past back to our people!"

Despite being drunk, Rafael Mendes is reluctant to accept the proposal, which strikes him as being rather crazy. But he ends up by agreeing: To stay in São Paulo, or to penetrate into the jungle, what difference does it make? Yes, he'll be Bento Seixas's guide.

With mules and provisions, they set out in secret, just the two of them. At first, they travel in a cheerful frame of mind, they sing songs from the nation: *Si la mar era de leche.* . . . After a few days on the road, the first problems arise; there is a sullen animosity, mostly Rafael's, against Seixas (this old coot, he thinks he knows everything, he doesn't know a thing, how could I have been so stupid), an animosity revealed in the rude replies:

"Is there a hill to our left, Rafael Mendes?"

"No. There's no hill to our left. Why should there be a hill to our left? What a stupid thing, a hill to our left."

"But aren't there any hills in sight?"

"It depends on what you mean by hill, Your Grace. In front of us there is an elevation of land, some might call it a knoll, others might call it a hill, it all depends on the eyesight of the observer. But since you're sightless, Your Grace . . ."

"It's a hill! It's the hill!" Strangely enough, the old man didn't seem to notice the sarcasm; and how could he expect sarcasm from a partner, a brother from the nation? He didn't know about Rafael's misgivings about this undertaking; neither did he know about Rafael's secret spites, some of them the result of recent disillusionment (the trial, execution, and quartering of Tiradentes); others, the result of ancient traumas (premature weaning by his mother; then an impatient wet nurse; and ever since, a permanent feeling that he will never come upon any hidden treasure). "Now tell me, dear Rafael, is it a relatively high hill with a rock on the top suggesting a prophet with raised arms?"

"It's a relatively high hill," says Rafael dryly. "Since Your Excellency used the word *relatively*, I can concur with you. And there is a rock on the top. I don't know if it suggests a prophet with raised arms. Let's suppose it does. Which prophet do you have in mind, Your Excellency? Is it the admirable Jonah, or is it that despicable whiner, Jeremiah? As a matter of fact, however—do you really want to know, Your Excellency?—it suggests nothing at all to me."

"Nothing, Rafael Mendes?"

"Nothing."

"Nothing at all?"

"Nothing at all."

"Not even a tiny little bit?"

"No. Nothing. Zilch."

Strange, murmurs the old man. It suggests nothing. Gradually it dawns on him that something is amiss; Rafael Mendes is not being cooperative, that's it, he's not being cooperative at all.

"Is there any scrub growth to our right?"

"I have no idea," he replies with a shrug, and now old Seixas realizes—by his partner's tone of voice—that Rafael Mendes is shrugging.

"Wait a moment, Rafael! You're shrugging!"

"Since when can a blind man tell someone is shrugging?" retorts Rafael.

"I can feel, you wretched person! I can feel that you're shrugging. You're mocking me, you frivolous rascal! Watch out, I'll get you!"

Drawing his sword, he begins to brandish it every which way. From a safe distance, Rafael looks on:

"A bit farther to the right! Still farther! Oh, you're nowhere near! Move forward! A bit more!"

A few minutes later, the old man, exhausted, lets himself fall on the ground. Then Rafael—whether impelled by a flash of lucidity, or by remorse, or by a mere desire to prolong the old man's suffering for a few more days, whatever the reason—walks up to him:

"Let's go, brother. Don't get all steamed up over this. Let's proceed with our journey. Think of Solomon's temple."

Despondent, Bento Seixas lets himself be led away. Soon, however, the bickering starts all over again:

"Is there a creek in front of us?"

"There's a small river."

"A small river! What's the difference between a creek and a small river?"

"In Minas Gerais we'd call this a small river. But you *paulistas,* you folks from São Paulo—"

"In Minas Gerais! What do you people from Minas Gerais know? That lieutenant, that poor fool . . ."

"Don't disparage him, Bento Seixas!" It's Rafael who is angry now. "Don't disparage that man, do you hear me?"

"I'll disparage him if I want to, him or anyone else."

In retaliation, Rafael Mendes hides himself behind a tree. The old man keeps searching for him:

"Rafael Mendes! Don't do this to me! Don't play games with me, brother! It's cruel! Come on, Rafael Mendes, it's getting dark, I can feel the coldness of the night in my flesh, if I get lost, you won't be able to find me, Rafael. Help! Oh, Lord, have mercy on me!"

Rafael Mendes walks up to the old man, who embraces him, in tears: "Forgive me, brother, if I hurt your feelings by disparaging Tiradentes. I'll never do it again. I'll respect your feelings!"

They become reconciled. On the following day, however, they are at it again:

"Is there a coconut tree with a somewhat crooked trunk standing in front of us?"

"There is a coconut tree all right, but it's not just *somewhat* crooked. It's *quite* crooked."

"You idiot!"

"I've never seen such a crooked coconut tree in my entire life!"

"You pervert!"

"Jeovah himself, even if He wanted to, wouldn't be able to come up with a coconut tree this crooked."

"You heretic!"

"Extremely crooked."

It begins to rain. And as in the biblical times, it rains for forty days and forty nights. Mud, mosquitoes, and swollen rivers to cross. The mules, struck by a mysterious disease, die one after the other. Bento Seixas is so weak that Rafael Mendes has to carry him. However, as they advance, their friendship is rekindled; and when they are 400 leagues away from São Paulo, they enter into a solemn pact, promising each other to remain brothers forever. Rafael no longer has any doubts about their mission: He firmly believes that they will find the Gold Tree. And that they will rebuild the temple. Then one day:

"Is there a small waterfall to our left?"

"Yes, there's a small waterfall to our left."

"And is there a rocky hill to our right?"

"Yes, there's a rocky hill to our right."

"Are there six black birds fluttering over our heads?"

"Yes, six black birds are fluttering over our heads."

"And have we left a long road behind us? And all bitterness?"

"Yes." Tears roll down Rafael Mendes's face. They have indeed left a long road behind them. But all bitterness?

"Brother!" cries out Bento Seixas, his face radiating joy. "Brother, we have arrived! The Gold Tree must be in front of us. Isn't there a tree in front of us?"

"Well . . ." Rafael Mendes doesn't know how to put it. "There is a tree. But not just one. There are many trees, Bento Seixas. Scores of thousands of trees, in rows, as if they were warriors standing in formation. And they aren't exactly trees, they look more like shrubs, and they are covered with berries."

Now it's Bento Seixas who is perplexed:

"No. According to the itinerary, there should be a clearing here, and at the center, the small gold tree. Thousands of shrubs, did you say?"

Then it occurs to him:

"Coffee!"

"What?" says Rafael Mendes, surprised.

"Coffee!" It is heart-rending to see Bento Seixas's despair. "That's what they plant nowadays, this tropical poison! What else could it be?"

He hurls himself upon the ground, rips his clothes to shreds, tears at his hair.

"Ah, my God, such an injustice! Ah, Lord, why do you treat your children like this? Why have you forsaken us?"

All of a sudden, he leaps to his feet.

"It's probably all right!" he shouts, suddenly excited. "It's quite possible, Rafael, that the Gold Tree is somewhere here in the middle of this coffee plantation!"

Rafael takes him by the arm.

"Let's go back, Bento Seixas," he says softly. "Let's go back, brother."

The old man extricates himself.

"No! I won't go back without the gold! I'd rather die here, Rafael."

Groping about, he advances until he comes to the coffee shrubs, then he begins to touch them with his trembling hands:

"It's not this one . . . And it's not this one either. . . ."

Rafael Mendes sets out on his return journey. He looks back just once and there is the old man, in the middle of the huge coffee plantation:

"It's not this one . . . And it's not this one either. . . ."

Rafael Mendes continues to journey southward. What he wants now is virgin land, a place with no gold or coffee shrubs, but also a place free from intrigue and betrayal. Thus, after journeying for months, he arrives at the territory that was later to become the State of Rio Grande do Sul. In the vastness of the pampas, across which the pampero, this purifying wind, blows freely, an idea begins to take shape in his mind. He will head for the Missões, the region of the former mission settlements of the Jesuits;

he will look for the people who stayed in the settlements, and he will reunite them so that together they can establish a new Guarani Republic, and thus redress a flagrant historical injustice. He is not afraid that this undertaking will end in failure; he can count on the support of the nation. Yes, because—and this is an important detail—he will convert the Indians to Judaism; and he will name the city to be founded there, New Jerusalem. In the middle of a forest, strong men with bronze-colored skin will rebuild Solomon's temple; and workshops, laboratories and universities will be created in order to foster, in addition to religious belief, a love for the sciences and the arts. That's what goes on in Rafael's mind as he walks along the roads that cross the pampas, shivering with cold in the pampero wind that penetrates his very bones. It doesn't matter: The coldness of freedom is preferable to the bonfires of the Inquisition. It's a good coldness, this one. And the wind seems to purify him; finally, he can still count on the warmth of the ideals that inspire him.

He ends up in the lands that belong to Colonel Picucha, who is notorious for beheading his enemies and using their heads as balls to play *ludopédio*, a foot game.

Eyes watch him from amid the trees; suspected of being a cattle thief, he is captured by the Colonel's men and taken to his presence. The caudillo, however, takes a liking to Rafael; perhaps it is Rafael's air of impoverished nobility, or his circumspect arrogance; perhaps the Colonel, remotely related to the nation, can hear the voice of the blood whispering in his ears. Whatever the reason, he sets Rafael free and engages him as tutor for his daughter. When the girl grows into an elegant young woman, Rafael falls in love with her. His love is returned. The young woman becomes pregnant. Fearing the Colonel's wrath, they elope. They roam the pampas in a big wagon, similar to the ones used by the gypsies: a veritable house on wheels, with doors, lace curtains on the windows, and smoke always curling out of the chimney. Children are born to them, times goes by. The family eventually settles down in Viamão, near the Mato Grosso Road, which links their village to Porto Alegre. There they buy land. . . .

By the time the War of the *Farrapos,* or the Ragamuffins, as the insurrectionists were called, breaks out, Rafael Mendes is already a teenager. His father leaves home, saying he will join the war. It is not known if he really will, or if he is lying; the fact is, he never returns home.

Little is known about this father. He seems to have been a kindly man, quiet but friendly. He had worries he never talked about, he didn't sleep well, he often dreamed about warriors and prophets. He used to tell stories: about the Gold Tree, among others. The image that Rafael will keep of his father shows him as a strange yet affectionate man who would take him in his arms, and lull him to sleep with a lullaby sung in Ladino, the language of their remote ancestors:

> *Duerme, duerme mi angelico.*
> *Hijico chico de tu nación . . .*
> *Criatura de Sión,*
> *no conoces la dolor.*

Yes, Rafael Mendes knows that he is from the nation; however, he hardly knows anything about Judaism: a few prayers, the rudiments of Hebrew, and that's about all.

He longs for his father, whom he can barely remember. He longs for the sea, which he has never seen. He wants to see his father again, he wants to listen to the stories he used to tell; and he wants to be a sailor, and sail to faraway, mysterious places, Angola, Egypt, Palestine: He wants to see white sandy beaches, coconut trees, exotic birds. To this strange man, to his father, he wants to say, come back home, mother is waiting for you.

In this two-fold objective he is helped by chance. David Canabarro, the leader of the *Farrapos,* is preparing an expedition to the town of Laguna; he is enlisting volunteers for the fleet of the Rio Grandense Republic. Rafael Mendes asks his mother for permission to join the warriors; she is unwilling to let him go, she has already lost her husband and fears she will lose her son, too, in a shipwreck or in the battlefield. But Rafael insists, threatens to enlist anyway; sighing, the poor woman ends up by giving her son permission to carry out what she considers a crazy plan.

A haversack slung over the shoulder, a knife at the waist, Rafael Mendes sets out southward. He heads for a region near the Capivarí River, where, he has been told, the *Farrapos* are camped.

On a densely foggy morning he comes to a meadow, turned soggy because of the recent rains. Spotting a few trees in the distance, Rafael Mendes walks toward them. It's a weird-looking thicket: Some of the trees are very short, others very tall. As he approaches, he is surprised to see that the tall ones aren't trees at all. Although covered with foliage, they aren't trees: They are the masts of the ships lying at anchor in the Capivarí River.

"Stop!"

From amid the trees emerge heavily bearded men dressed in tatters, wielding weapons. Frightened, Rafael Mendes raises his arms; he's shaking so badly that his teeth rattle. "I'm a friend!" he says. "A friend!" His captors, however, are not taking any chances; they tie his hands and take him to Garibaldi.

There stands the legendary rebel everybody talks about, the hero who came from Italy to help out the *Farrapos,* the Ragamuffins, against the imperial government. A bearded man looks at Rafael with his pale blue eyes, in which mistrust and amusement are mingled. Then he orders that the prisoner be set free. Moved by gratitude, Rafael tries to kiss his hands; Garibaldi rebuffs him rudely:

"*Fermo! Sta fermo!*"

Startled, Rafael freezes.

"Who are you, anyway?" asks Garibaldi. Rafael tells him his story, to which the rebel leader listens, his eyes fixed on the boy.

"He's a fool," he says at last. "Send him away."

But Rafael doesn't want to go: "Please, general, allow me to stay with you, sir. I have good reasons, I must find my father. He left us, me and my mother, to join the *Farrapos*. I want to fight side by side with him, I want to take him home after the war is over."

After hesitating for a moment, he adds: "Besides, I want to be a sailor."

"A sailor?" Garibaldi laughs. "We don't even know if we'll ever be able to sail, son. The loyalists are the top dogs."

The boy doesn't give up: "I'm strong, I can make myself quite useful; give me a chance, general."

Garibaldi is reluctant, and even more so when he learns that the youth doesn't have any sea experience. Then an idea occurs to him: "Do you play chess?" he asks. "Yes, sir," replies Rafael, surprised.

"Well, let's then play a game of chess," says Garibaldi. "If you win, you can join us; if you lose, you'll be given thirty-nine lashes and be sent away."

Garibaldi may well be a skillful strategist, but when it comes to chess, he is not so at all. Despite being a mediocre player, Rafael has no difficulty defeating him. And so he gets what he wants: Rising to his feet, Garibaldi declares in a solemn tone of voice that from now on Rafael Mendes is a sailor in the fleet of the Rio Grandense Republic. The men fraternize with him, offer him white rum and unsweetened maté.

However, disappointment follows this cheerfulness: Rafael Mendes's father is not among the men under Garibaldi's command. And no one there has ever heard of him. A man given to singing *duerme, duerme mi angelico*? Nobody knows of any such man. But, they would add, it's possible that his father is with some other detachment. Perhaps Rafael will run into him in the course of the long march ahead of them. Because they won't be sailing in the near future. In order to outsmart the vigilant loyalists, Garibaldi has devised a fantastic plan: They will transport the fleet's two ships—the Seival and the Farroupilha—overland as far as the town of Tramandaí, located many miles to the north; from there, they will go by sea to the town of Laguna, in the state of Santa Catarina, where they will attack the imperial forces, caught off-guard.

It is an undertaking of extraordinary complexity. The Seival is a ten-ton boat, the Farroupilha even bigger. Therefore, first of all, they take the cannons, the ammunition, and anything heavy out of the two ships; meanwhile, the head-carpenter Joaquim de Abreu and his assistants make twelve gigantic wheels of solid wood rimmed with iron bands that turn on axles made of huge logs. The wheels are then taken down a slope to the Capivarí River. Waiting in the water are Garibaldi's men, including Rafael Mendes. Six men take hold of each wheel and at a signal, they all dive together into the water, trying to place the axles underneath the hull of the boats. Finally, the operation is successfully completed and the large barges are ready to leave the water. Sixteen yokes of oxen are hitched to each of the two boats; the air is filled with the shouts of the cowboys: Come on, Pet! Forward, Piebaldy! Let's go now, Half-Boot! Come on, Slobberer! The oxen pull steadily, their hooves sinking into the mud of the river bank; slowly, the boat Farroupilha, its wooden framework squeaking and creaking, its mast tilting dangerously, begins to come out of the water and onto the bank. The men fling their hats up into the air, Garibaldi dances a tarantella with Rafael Mendes, who by now has been adopted as the mascot of the troops.

They are on their way. Pulled by the long-suffering oxen, the boats make a slow advance across the pampas of Rio Grande do Sul. The men walk ahead of them, watching out for bogs; Rafael Mendes is the only person given the privilege of traveling aboard the boats, his mission being to ensure that everything is all right, that there are no breakages or cracks. Standing at the helm, he sings cheerfully. Mornings, when everything is shrouded in a dense fog, he has the feeling that he is sailing across a tranquil sea, the backs of the oxen being gentle furry waves. As soon as the sun rises, he clambers up a mast to unfurl the flag of the Republic of Piratiní. He has but one worry: When will he find his father? The *Farrapos* try to cheer him up: "Maybe when we get farther up north, boy."

Nights, when the boats are at rest and the *Farrapos*, tired out, lie asleep by the campfires, their ponchos wrapped about them, Rafael climbs to the crow's nest, where he remains gazing at the stars; he misses his mother, he sings the songs that she and his father used to sing together:

> *Si la mar era de leche*
> *yo seria un pescador*
> *pescaria mis dolores*
> *con palabritas de amor.*

The days go by. The barges keep advancing. Here and there in the underbrush, there are now patches of white sand. And straw-thatched huts, with the natives of the region standing at the door, small, thin men with rotten teeth, women with sagging breasts, sallow-skinned children with distended bellies. Upon seeing fishnets hanging from poles, Rafael, excited, concludes that the sea cannot be far away. In fact, one night he hears the roar of the waves. In the morning, from the crow's nest, he sights the sands of Tramandaí.

"Sea in sight!" he cries out, his hair ruffled by the wind. The *Farrapos,* who are making coffee, laugh. Rafael slides down the mast, dashes to a nearby brook, washes up, and is back, huffing and puffing, shaking off water. Someone gives him a piece of jerked beef and a mug of hot coffee; and now, it's time to work, shouts Garibaldi, but Rafael pays no heed to his command; he is busy talking to the fishermen who have gathered curiously around the boats, asking them if they've seen such and such a man, a quiet but friendly man given to singing a song about a sea of milk. "No," say the fishermen. And they laugh: "A sea of milk, that's funny. If the sea were made of milk, our children wouldn't have to starve," they say.

When Rafael returns to his post, he is severely reprimanded. "Who ever heard of a warrior that fails to obey orders?" roars the general. "I was trying to locate my father," murmurs Rafael, close to tears.

"Your father!" shouts Garibaldi, irritated. "The future of the world is at stake and you are looking for your father!"

Indignant, he falls silent. Then, cooling down, he touches the sheepish-looking Rafael on the shoulder.

"All right, son. We're going to find your father. It's a promise."

That night, when everybody is seated around the campfires, Garibaldi and Rafael have a long talk. The revolutionary speaks of a better world; a world in which people will have ruddy complexions and eyes misty with emotion. Machines will do everything, there won't be any slaves, people will spend their time singing and dancing: Pleasure will be the word of command. The realm of poverty will give way to the realm of freedom.

Rafael Mendes listens, but in fact he is thinking of something else. Taking advantage of a pause in Garibaldi's speech, he shoots the question which he has had in readiness for a long time:

"Are you from the nation, general?"

"What?" says Garibaldi, astonished.

"I asked you," says Rafael, now haltingly, "if you are from the nation. If you are a Hebrew."

"A Hebrew?" Garibaldi bursts out laughing. "No. Me, a Hebrew, son? Of course not. What makes you think I'm a Hebrew?"

What made Rafael think that Garibaldi was from the nation? He has no idea. The fact is that he has thought of this possibility; and on his list, he has also included David Canabarro, because of the biblical name. And Bento Gonçalves—the name Bento could well be the Portuguese version of the Hebrew name Ben Tov, meaning a good son, a term of endearment used by Rafael's father; or a version of *baruch*, blessed.

But no, none of them are Hebrews. Perhaps the Azorians who live in Porto dos Casais are Hebrews, but none of the leaders of the *Farrapos* are.

Laguna was captured without offering any resistance, which rather disappointed Rafael Mendes for he had anticipated a bloody battle. Windows and doors were flung open and people took to the streets to fraternize with the revolutionaries.

The Juliana Republic is proclaimed.

Garibaldi takes up administrative functions. During the day he works at the Town Hall, rendering decisions on official matters; in the evening, as a measure of precaution, he goes aboard the Seival, which is berthed in the harbor. At dawn, before going on land, he carefully scrutinizes the town through a telescope.

This telescope is a powerful instrument, built in accordance with the ideas of Galileo Galilei. It consists of a complex tubular structure through which Garibaldi can gaze at the stars in the nighttime and spy on his enemies in the daytime.

It is through this telescope that he first sees Anita. A beautiful, haughty woman. She is in her living quarters, getting ready for her bath; she takes off her silk gown. On seeing her naked, Garibaldi heaves a sigh. Rafael Mendes, who is always hanging around, overhears him murmur: *Tu deve essere mia!*

Ever since that day Garibaldi has changed completely. Later, having enticed Anita away from her husband, he strolls with her in the streets of Laguna, unconcerned about the reproachful eyes of its inhabitants.

Rafael Mendes grieves. He wants to ask Garibaldi when they will start searching for his father, but the general won't even see him, enthralled as he is by his Anita. Rafael considers going home; however, he is a disciplined warrior, he won't desert his post.

One night, while wandering sleeplessly about the outskirts of Laguna, he seems to hear the words of a very familiar lullaby brought by the wind: *Duerme, duerme, mi angelico.* . . .

He runs in the direction of the words. It's not his father that he finds there, but a group of loyalist soldiers on patrol.

After being arrested, Rafael Mendes undergoes interrogations, which are followed by various forms of torture. Unable to endure the ordeal, he discloses everything that the loyalists want to know. With this information in hand, they prepare a successful attack: The town is recaptured, the *Farrapos* beat a retreat. Garibaldi and Anita go to Italy. There, in the country of Galileo Galilei they will continue to fight.

Set free by the loyalists, Rafael Mendes returns home. He will never sail again. He will never find his father.

Rafael Mendes set up shop as a leather exporter, and he was somewhat successful. He married and fathered a son on whom he lavished affection; however, even though he used to lull his child to sleep with the song *duerme, duerme mi angelico*, Rafael never told him that he was from the nation, partly because he had a spite against his own father, and partly because he believed that this secret belonged to the past and in the past it should remain; he hoped that his son would enjoy life, with no guilt and no need for dissimulation. He provided his son with all the comforts of home and a sound education. Rafael Mendes, one of the very first engineers to have graduated in Rio Grande do Sul, went in for railroad construction. For a while he worked for the Rothschilds of France, who were then investing in railroads. It wasn't a pleasant experience; Rafael Mendes, a distrustful man whose sleep was haunted by nightmares, hated those financiers, even though he had never met them because he conducted business exclusively with the Brazilian agents of his employers. Somehow, this experience left him with a deep resentment against Jews. And yet, when his own son was born, how did he lull him to sleep? Well, by singing *duerme mi angelico*; he couldn't resist the pull: Because that's how ancient things are: powerful and mysterious.

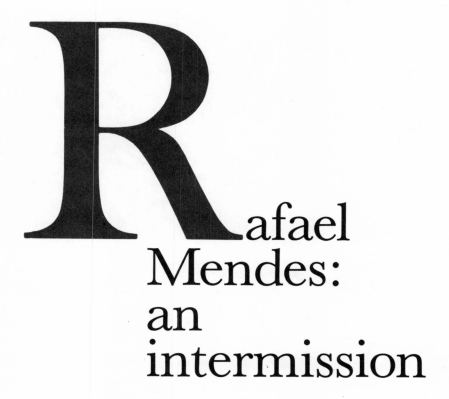

Rafael Mendes: an intermission

J ust before midnight Rafael Mendes finishes reading the first notebook. Setting it aside, he sits motionless for a moment. Then he rises to his feet, opens the door of his study.

The apartment is quiet. Helena is asleep; Suzana, as usual, isn't yet home. He goes to the living room, opens the balcony door, stands gazing at the city, at the lights twinkling in the distance. They twinkle because of the alternating current. Rafael knows this: The electric current changes direction at regular intervals. It's one of the few certainties he has. As for the stories he has just read, he doesn't know what to make of them, and even less so of the man who wrote them. What's the significance of all this succession of historical characters, Jonah and Habacuc ben Tov and Maimonides and all the Mendeses?

What good is it to him to know that one of his ancestors—if he really existed—talked to Tiradentes—if he indeed talked to him? Rafael doesn't know. Neither does he know whether what he has read is true, or false, or a mixture of half-truths and lies. He remains just as perplexed as before; he has merely found out—and cold comfort it is—that this perplexity of his is of long standing. Centuries-old.

The telephone rings. Startled, he makes a dash for the phone.

"Well, Senhor Rafael, have you read them yet?" The genealogist, naturally.

Rafael can barely contain a sigh of irritation.

"I've read the first notebook."

"And what do you think?"

Rafael hesitates:

"Fiction, isn't it? Fiction. Plenty of made-up stuff."

"It's like I said." The man sounds somewhat disappointed; but what did he expect, that Rafael would burst into tears over the telephone? "Your father had a fertile imagination . . . but you'll get to know him better in the second notebook. It's through a series of forward moves that we come to the genealogical truth, Senhor Rafael."

Philosophy at this hour of the night? Rafael is losing his patience, but the little man doesn't beat about the bush:

"I'm phoning to know if I could get the money."

"At this hour?"

"It's that . . ." the other man wavers, "I didn't want this day to end without . . . But it doesn't matter, I can wait until the morning. It's even possible that the dollar will go up during these hours, isn't it?"

"Yeah," replies Rafael dryly.

"So, I'll be there first thing in the morning. Good night."

"Good night," mutters Rafael and he hangs up.

"Still up, Senhor Rafael?" It's one of the maids, the little mulatto with the pert face. Heading for the fridge, no doubt, always eating, these creatures. For a moment Rafael stands staring at the girl as she walks away. A nice piece of tail. If she weren't his servant, and if it weren't for all the hassle . . . Rafael heaves a sigh. He goes back to his study, locks the door, picks up the second notebook and sinks into the armchair.

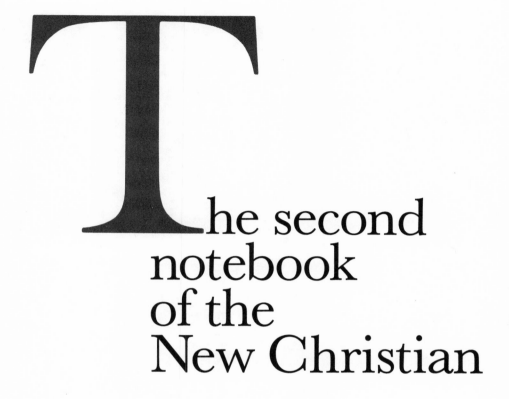

The second notebook of the New Christian

The Mendeses put down roots in Rio Grande do Sul; as time went by, they became a traditional family, although they didn't belong to the so-called rural aristocracy. Among my ancestors who settled down in Rio Grande do Sul one was a farmer, another was a merchant, my father was an engineer; but the name Mendes was held in high respect, at least in my circle of friends. As for the distant roots, nobody had ever talked to me about the New Christians, or the Inquisition, or the Essenes, or the prophets—or the Gold Tree.

And yet there was *something*. A certain attraction for the exotic, the mysterious, the secret; a certain fascination for paradoxes; a certain perturbation whenever walking past a synagogue; a feeling of dissimulation and perplexity. Not the wide-eyed, open-mouthed, speechless kind of bewilderment; a lesser confusion, embryonic but nonetheless disturbing. So disturbing that it necessitated the help of a guide for the perplexed, if available. But it wasn't.

Like Maimonides I too turned to medicine. Like any other physician, my foremost desire was to heal myself. I was a sickly boy; the measles, rubella, fevers, chicken pox, the croup, you name it, I had them all in due course. Maybe I attributed my anxieties to my sickly body, I don't know. All I know is that I wanted to become a physician. As soon as I finished high school, I began to prepare myself for medical school.

The year was 1929. In New York, there was the stock-market crash; desperate financiers were jumping off high-rises, but, they didn't fall into my arms, which were as a matter of fact far from strong. The economic depression was something very remote from me; my really pressing problem was admission to medical school. I used to study together with a childhood friend, Cuvier de Souza, named after the French naturalist Cuvier. The son of a physician, he had handled his father's microscope ever since he was a child, and was passionately interested in fungi, protozoans, bacteria. Later he was to become an outstanding bacteriologist; even in those days he was already known as Microbe—partly because of his small size and restlessness.

It was from Microbe that I first heard about Débora. A few days before the university entrance exams he came running into my house in a state of agitation: "There's a girl sitting for the entrance exams," he said. "She's Jewish, imagine! And they say she's a brain."

A woman, and Jewish to boot, in the Faculty of Medicine? Amazing. Medicine was for men, as everybody knew. "I'll bet she's a dyke." Microbe was indignant. "A witch, at the very least."

No, she wasn't a witch. She was rather beautiful, as I had the opportunity to ascertain a few days later, as we sat side by side to write the first exam, which happened to be on the Natural Sciences. A Hebrew type of beauty, of course, the nose somewhat hooked, and the legs somewhat thick. But she had beautiful greenish eyes and nice brown hair and a well-shaped mouth. She looked at me; I can't say I wasn't disturbed; yes, I was disturbed by the sight of this Hebrew girl—what did I know about Jews, whether male or female? Very little. I didn't associate with them, I hardly ever went to Bom Fim. But the expression of her eyes stirred me. . . .

The examination topics were announced; she leaned over the desk and began to scribble away at an incredible speed, covering pages and pages. Microbe was right, she seemed to know everything. Later, however, when the list of the successful candidates was published, we saw that she came out 24th in the exams, a rather modest placement; she wasn't, as we would soon find out, the genius we had supposed her to be. Intelligent, yes, but not brilliant. Anyway, she did better than I did—I came out second last, and better than Microbe, who came out 25th.

She was the only girl in the class, but not the first woman ever to attend the Faculty of Medicine; there had been others before her.

Anyhow, her presence created perplexity. And irritation. Irritation that translated itself into disguised hostility or wisecracks—the disguised hostility easily turning into open aggression, the wisecracks into coarse jokes. Trying to forestall problems, the Dean of the Faculty of Medicine invited her to a meeting of the Faculty Association. He started by asking her to let them know about any discourtesy on the part of the students, "As you know, the presence of young ladies in this Establishment is unusual," and then he asked her how she would like to be treated. "Like everybody else," she said. A proud reply. She was haughty—a haughty Jewish girl. From her father, a shoemaker, already deceased, she had inherited a sense of dignity—which was somewhat strange, but touching. This man had always dreamed of his daughter becoming a physician; and he had also advised her to hold her head high, no matter what. That's what she was doing now: holding her head high.

The faculty members listened to her in polite silence. At the end of the meeting, a professor of Clinical Practice of Medicine went up to her; his name was Brito, and he came from a traditional family and had a reputation for being arrogant. "Welcome, young lady," he said, "but let me warn you: This isn't a profession for women, nor is it a profession for upstarts. As you'll soon find out for yourself."

Débora made no reply; she turned her back to him and walked away. On the following day she was invited to meet with the executive of the Students' Association; they wanted to know if she would submit herself to hazing. "I will, like all my fellow students," she said, with a touch of contempt: She considered hazing a silly, infantile activity, unworthy of university students. But even so, she went to Praça da Alfândega, stepped into the public fountain there, and put up with the railleries of the idle onlookers. She came out of the fountain shivering with cold, it was an exceptionally cool day in March. I offered her my coat; after a brief hesitation, she accepted it, and thus we struck up a friendship. The three of us—she, Microbe, and I—would study anatomy together, dissecting the same cadaver.

The morgue was a cold, gloomy, poorly lit place; the air, saturated with vapors of formalin, stung our eyes. Such things didn't bother Débora; scalpel in hand, she would dissect the thorax and interpret the anatomical findings.

I couldn't keep my eyes off her. "Here's the upper chest cavity," she would say, but my eyes weren't on the cavity, they were fixed on her—did I love her? I didn't know. And yet I kept staring at her. Which, incidentally, she seemed not to notice; she took things seriously, was conscientious to a fault, and worked hard, ignoring all banter. There were some who wouldn't forgive her for being so bold as to be there among men, wielding a scalpel—which, like knives and daggers, is a male's prerogative. Thus the sniggering, the wisecracks, the practical jokes—which once went way too far.

It was a rainy winter morning. Débora arrived, wearing a smart checkered coat; it was a new coat, and some of our fellow students made flattering remarks about it, although in my opinion, the coat looked more grotesque than elegant, but that's beside the point. She took off her coat, hung it on a hanger, put on her lab smock and set to work. Just before noon we completed that morning's assignment, which was the dissection of a foot; she went to the hanger, put her coat on. Suddenly, she noticed something; putting her hand into the pocket, she took out something that had been placed there.

A penis.

A huge penis from a cadaver, a good-sized rod, a stupendous prick; a tremendous chink stopper, a fine pecker, a magnificent pestle, a gigantic cock.

A silence fell upon the morgue, a tense silence. Her head bowed, she stood staring at the penis in her hand. Without a word, she laid it on the table; and then she looked at each one of us in turn. There was no anger in her gaze; sadness, yes; hurt feelings, maybe; but anger, no.

(I was angry; I was fuming. I should have leaped to her side: You cowards, aren't you ashamed, how can you do such a thing to a girl, whoever did this, step outside if you're man enough. But I didn't; why not? Perhaps because of an unwillingness to get involved in a quarrel that didn't—didn't it really?—concern me; perhaps because of fear; perhaps because of a sense of solidarity with the males in the class. Medicine, as everybody knew, wasn't for girls; why did she have to butt in where she was unwanted? Why didn't she stay in Bom Fim and marry a Jewish merchant? Why didn't she devote herself to raising children, like all other women? Anyhow, what those jerks did was vicious, wicked, loathsome.) When I came to my senses again, I realized that she was gone—and there I stood, perplexed, not knowing what to do next. Should I go after her? I didn't know. The fact is that I didn't go after her; I dithered, I took my time taking off my lab coat. Meanwhile I joined in the laughter, but unlike the others, I wasn't roaring with laughter, I wasn't laughing my head off, I wasn't splitting my sides with laughter; still, I was laughing at least a little, enough not to draw attention to myself, enough not to be excluded; and as soon as the others went back to their cadavers, I dashed out into the street, hoping against hope that I'd catch up with her. But she was nowhere to be seen, she was gone. I went back to the morgue and we—Microbe and I—began to dissect the lower chest cavity of a cadaver. "It serves her right," Microbe kept muttering, "a meddler, that's what she is." "Shut up," I said, and that was all: On that day, at least, that was the only thing I did to side with her.

During the following week preparations for the Freshmen's Ball were under way. Débora wasn't going: "She doesn't have a date," said Microbe with a little laugh of derision—he *really* disliked her. On an impulse I decided I would be Débora's escort; I would proffer her my arm; together we would enter the brightly lit ballrooms of the Commerce Club. . . .

I spoke to her about it. "A ball?" She opened her eyes wide. And she blushed; for the first time I realized that deep down, this Jewish girl was shy, and I felt a rush of tenderness. But she soon reacted, said she wouldn't go—a ball, well, no, that was something for the smart set only. Noticing my annoyance, she amended herself, she didn't mean it, it hadn't been her intention to offend me; finally, resting her hand on my arm (a gesture that made me quiver; did I love her?), she said that yes, she would be delighted to go with me.

I prepared myself carefully for that ball. Like a general preparing himself for a major battle, like a politician preparing himself for a major pronouncement, but also like a lover preparing himself for a major conquest. I rented a tuxedo; I made arrangements for a taxi, a black Oldsmobile with glittering chrome work, an impressive automobile it was; I reserved a table at a restaurant, where we would dine after the ball. I had orchids delivered to her house. And so, on a balmy evening in April I went to pick her up. She lived on Avenida Cauduro, a side street with rows of dinky little houses, each one with a door and a window at the front. I had to wait for her under the suspicious gaze of her mother, a fat old Jewish woman, and her brothers, of whom there were quite a few, all of them snivelling. Finally, she appeared.

She didn't look dazzling, not by a long shot. She was wearing an unattractive dress, the orchids weren't pinned quite right, she hadn't had her hair done. And yet, she looked beautiful; she was smiling, and I couldn't help feeling moved (did I love her?). "I'm afraid we're late," I said rather awkwardly; we were indeed late, but the car took us in no time to the Commerce Club and a moment later we made our entrance into the ballroom, already packed with people.

On the eyes fixed on us I could detect: curiosity, sympathy, scorn, and perplexity, sometimes in combination: curiosity and sympathy, sympathy and perplexity. I couldn't care less whether or not they stared; let them stare and whisper. At least, that's what I kept repeating to myself as we slowly made our way across the hall: I couldn't care less. But did I really feel that I didn't give a damn? Probably not: I wasn't feeling absolutely self-confident, my mouth was dry, and the smile that I was determined to keep on my face at any cost had become a grimace. Anyhow, the orchestra started to play and we were soon dancing amid scores of other couples, and so we no longer drew attention to ourselves. Débora wasn't a good dancer: She kept treading on my toes and apologizing: "I'm not used to dancing." To make her less self-conscious, I steered the conversation into a different subject, medical school. And right away she began talking enthusiastically. "Medicine means everything to me," she declared, and proceeded to explain what she expected from a career in medicine—not wealth, as many of our fellow students did, nor higher social status; what she really wanted was to tread the road of science; she wanted the joy of a new medical breakthrough, and she wanted fame, too, but well-deserved fame. I was listening to her, but just barely, because her body pressed against mine had given me a hard-on; fellow student or not, Jewish or not, she was a woman, a beautiful woman, and I was falling in love, I was on the verge of falling in love, I was only a few centimeters, a few millimeters away from passion; I tried to hold her closer to me...Abruptly, she withdrew. "I don't like this sort of thing, Rafael," she said dryly, on her face an aggrieved expression. Self-consciously, I mumbled a vague apology and we continued to dance—apart—but I was then feeling irritated. Very well, so she doesn't like this sort of thing. And what is it that she likes then? Hm? What does this Jewess like? Not a good prick, one could see that. She must be a dyke all right, as Microbe had so aptly diagnosed. Or frigid. At the very least, frigid.

On the way back to her home neither of us spoke; on the following day, a Sunday, we didn't see each other; on Monday, however, when we ran into each other at the door of the morgue, she said she had to talk to me, so we went to a snack bar on Avenida Osvaldo Aranha for a cup of coffee. She started off by apologizing; it hadn't been her intention to hurt my feelings at the ball; however, she really had no intentions of having a boyfriend, at least not while she was attending medical school. She wanted to devote herself exclusively to her studies, to research work, and she hoped I would understand. I said that I understood, that everything was all right. That's what I said that morning while I stared, with my head lowered, at the tiny iridescent bubbles of coffee. I didn't want to raise my head; I didn't want to look at her; I was afraid to look at her; afraid I would find out that I *loved her**; afraid I would plead with her; afraid I would cry. To cry right there, in front of her, in front of the bar owner, a fat Portuguese man wearing a torn T-shirt? Never. From my father, who had worked hard all his life, and who had died of tuberculosis, I had learned to be tough; stoic, at least. No, I wouldn't dissolve in tears.

She went on talking, seemingly unaware of my perturbation; as for myself, I was no longer listening. Finally, she said: "So, Rafael, will we remain friends?" And I got my wits about me and said that sure, we would remain friends.

*Did I love her? (R.M.)

And friends we remained. Ours was a cordial relationship, we would study together, take in a movie once in a while. On such occasions my arm sometimes brushed against hers; whether accidentally or not, it did, and the effect was electrifying—a thrill I both feared and desired; however, to her it was nothing, seemingly nothing. She would merely move her arm away. She wouldn't cringe or stiffen up, just move her arm away, without taking her eyes off the movie: "What a great actress, this Greta Garbo, isn't she, Rafael?" She would leave the movie theater sighing: "I hope I'll find fulfillment in medicine just as this woman has found self-fulfillment in the cinema." Débora had no other ambition, no other interest; she barely took notice of what went on around her. One day we were downtown, when all of a sudden there was some unusual commotion, people began scurrying about, and groups of citizens were arguing at the top of their voices; and a moment later, the whole thing coalesced into a political rally: "Down with the oligarchies!" an inflamed orator was shouting. The Revolution of 1930 had just broken out. That's what I told Débora on the following day: "We have witnessed the outbreak of a revolution," I said. She shrugged: "I'm not interested, I've no use for revolutions; all I want is to become a great physician."

However, as time went by, it became harder and harder for her to make this burning desire materialize. Débora was not at all a brilliant student. Others were already beginning to stand out— Microbe, for instance, had already been invited by his professor of bacteriology to work with him after his graduation—whereas Débora wasn't even doing well in her coursework. Once she entered a competition to win a prize that a pharmaceutical laboratory was offering to medical students; her paper, a monography entitled *Calcium and Phosphorus: Some Considerations on their Role in the Metabolism of Human Beings*, was placed second last. On the front page of the monograph, the chairman of the evaluation committee had remarked in his own handwriting: *The A.'s considerations are inadequate, inopportune, impertinent, inconsequential, irrelevant, and to a certain degree, immoral.* Débora didn't let such opinions, such failures, weigh her down; she attributed them to her being both female and Jewish. And she would soon come up with another idea, another project. During her first years in medical school, she had considered going into laboratory research; however, when we began our courses in clinical practice of medicine, a whole new horizon opened up for her, a horizon represented by patients—hundreds of them—scattered in the wards of a gloomy hospital. Such a wealth of pathological cases! Such an abundance of research material! What exotic diseases could explain the unrestrained moans, the emaciated faces, the edematous limbs? She would rush from one ward to the next, from one bed to the next, in search of the complex, of the transcendent; of the extraordinary, of the astonishing. Forever in search of rare cases, of peculiar syndromes, of freakish anomalies. Like Hellwig and Didonaeus, she, too, was in search of women who menstruated through their eyes; or through their ears (Spindler, Paullini, Alibert); or through their mouths (Meimobius, Rhodius); or through their scars (McGraw). Cases of false pregnancies, like the ones documented by Weir Mitchell, fascinated her: A woman wanting very much to become pregnant sees her womb grow. . . and grow. . . and grow until "that great student of semiology—Time—rectifies the illusion" (Weir Mitchell). There is no baby! There is no pregnancy! The womb became distended for nothing, for nonsense! Queen Mary of England had been one such case.

Ah, if only she would come across an enormous ovarian cyst, like the one mentioned by Morand, from which 425 pounds of liquid were extracted over a period of ten months. And what about bodies that burst into flames? Taylor talked about spontaneous combustion in human beings: People catching fire while asleep, and then burning, without ever waking up, until finally they are reduced to cinders. Lord Bacon himself, a great humanist, had also made references to such facts.

Great, too, was her interest in teratology: Ah, if only she would come across a bifid or supernumerary tongue; teeth growing on a lower eyelid, like those mentioned by Carver; eyes with multiple pupils. In the absence of such things, she would be satisfied with interesting signs, such as the pulse of the water hammer, the dance of the arteries, Medusa's head, a sardonic smile, a leonine face, the hand of an obstetrician, some fingers holding a drumstick about to beat a drum, an equine foot, the flick of a fillip, the puff of breath in the peep of a seagull, the rhythm of galloping; a joint in a cogwheel, a geographical tongue, the bridge of a nose. Nothing.

Did I love her? One day—we were in our fourth year—as I watched her auscultate a patient, I came to the painful conclusion that I loved her. Because of a strand of hair falling over her face, because of her lips, which were parted and slightly more moist than circumstances warranted, because of the graceful curve of her neck . . . Whatever the reason. The fact is that I was still fond of her, indeed I was, notwithstanding the succession of girlfriends and lovers I had had. I remember heaving a deep sigh in that autumn afternoon; I remember an almost comatose patient opening his eyes wide, surprised at this sigh; I remember my embarrassment. But I also remember how much I loved her at that moment, and how much it hurt to love a woman who was not interested in me or in anyone else, a woman whose only desire was to devote herself to medicine and through it seek a fame that would certainly remain beyond her reach.

"Why do you have to ask such stupid questions, doctor?"

Brito, professor of Clinical Practice of Medicine, disliked Débora and he made no bones about letting her know.

"If you were to put greater effort into learning how to percuss instead of being interested in whatever is out of the ordinary, you'd do much better."

She would be furious; and when furious, even more beautiful. At least I thought so. Microbe thought she was ugly: A dyke. What other woman but a dyke would want to puncture, to cut, to sew up people; always trying to come up with some fancy diagnosis. *Professor Brito, we have here a case of Basedow-Graves's disease. Not at all, lady doctor, it's not a case of Basedow-Graves's disease, it's a case of simple colloid goiter; you know nothing, young lady, your place is at home, looking after domestic affairs.* She would storm out of the room in tears, slamming the door behind her. Some would laugh, others would glower, annoyed at the professor's rudeness (some of our fellow students were finally beginning to like her; besides, everybody in the class hated Brito). As for myself, I neither laughed nor glowered; I didn't know what to do; I loved her; I thought I did; but since my love was not returned, why should I stick my neck out to defend her? Maybe one day I would leap from my chair, yelling: *Take back your insulting remarks, you scoundrel*; maybe I would. But I always wavered for one second, or half a second, and then she was no longer in the room. One day it occurred to me that this minute fraction of time in fact stood for an insurmountable barrier, an abysmal moat between my loving her and my not loving her. I didn't love her, I concluded, or wanted to conclude. I didn't love her because I vacillated, because I wanted to reconcile love with convenience. I knew what convenience was, but love? What was love? In the fourth year I had made up my mind: I'd go into surgery. Thus I opted for objectivity, for asepsis, for incisions made with a steady hand, and for dispassionate assessment. In the fifth year I changed my mind slightly: Orthopedics. Bones: hard and white, I liked the idea. Besides, wars and accidents had given a tremendous impetus to this specialization. Microbe, naturally, would devote himself to bacteriology, Frog wanted to become a neurologist, Afrânio would certainly work with his father, a famous general practitioner, Medonho would inherit his father's professorial chair, Veloso planned to practice surgery in Rio de Janeiro, Ambrósio had already been offered an administrative position with a hospital—in short, in the fifth year everybody already knew what he was going to do, that is, everybody except Débora, who still didn't know because of that terrible need of hers for self-assertion, a need that made her scramble frantically from ward to ward: A case of Fallot's disease! A case of a kidney shaped like a horseshoe! A case of this, a case of that; research this, research that; and everybody laughing at her. The intensity of her obsession would even frighten her: "Am I crazy, Rafael? Tell me, do you think I'm crazy?" I didn't know what to say, but Microbe had no doubts about it: "She's daffy, Rafael, nutty as a fruitcake."

We graduated and she still didn't know what she would be doing. She didn't want to set herself up as a practitioner; she couldn't go to another country because of her mother; neither the interior nor the suburbs appealed to her. And she wouldn't give up her aspirations to engage in research, to have her work published. Then, without pay, she started to work in a hospital ward, whose director had ambitions similar to hers. Right away, they decided to experiment with a new drug, imported from Argentina, to treat high blood pressure. Thirty-five patients were selected for the experiment, and the initial results showed that the medication was effective; however, this drug—a hormone by-product—had a disturbing side effect: feminization. Old cowboys began to develop large breasts and voluptuous curves. After the attempted suicide of one of the patients, the experiment had to be interrupted, which didn't really disappoint Débora: A preliminary report that she had presented at a meeting of the ward's medical staff had been well received. Her other experiments, however, weren't successful. At one time she worked with a doctor who tried to extract diuretic substances from aquatic plants— without success. Then she worked together with another colleague, who envisioned lighting up the human body with searchlights of the kind used in the war and making a diagnosis by examining the shadows projected by the organs. This experiment ended in failure. As did all the others: Using intra-abdominal balloons, whose insufflation could be regulated, to lift sagging organs: a flop. A chamber of rarified air for the treatment of tuberculosis: a flop. Severely burned patients kept afloat by means of balloons filled with hydrogen: a flop. Injections of extract of the cartilage of small rodents to treat arthritic conditions: a flop. Nothing worked, nothing succeeded; nothing, nothing. Each failure plunged her into deeper depression. It was then that she met Kurt Schnitzel.

German by birth, Kurt had emigrated to Brazil in the early thirties. He set up a repair shop in Porto Alegre for medical equipment: sphygmomanometers, spirometers, electrocardiographs. A big hunk of a man, almost two meters tall, with a booming, stentorian voice and a Pantagruelian appetite, Kurt had an unusual talent for working with electric and mechanical gadgets. Not only could he fix, adapt, or improve any machine, he could also invent gadgets for the most disparate purposes. He had devised and built a mechanical heart, a complex machine to treat cardiac insufficiency.

It worked like this: The beats of the diseased heart, collected by the chest piece of a stethoscope (A) applied to the patient's chest, would alter the pressure inside a system of rubber tubes (B), thereby activating an accelerator of high precision (C), which would then inject the right amount of gasoline into the internal combustion engine (D), which in turn would set in motion the pistons of the pump. The blood of the patient, which had been initially diverted to a flask (E), was then reinjected into the patient by means of the pump (F).

Débora watched as the machine was being put to the test. She saw a dog, which had suffered sudden and acute cardiac insufficiency after being injected with an almost lethal amount of quinidine, recover quickly; soon the dog was barking cheerfully. There was no longer any doubt in her mind: It was an invention that would revolutionize medicine. She decided to use the mechanical heart on a twelve-year-old boy who suffered from a serious form of rheumatic cardiopathy; the boy had been given up as incurable by various physicians, including professor Brito, who had sent him home to die. Débora hoped she would at least be able to keep him alive. The experiment, however, ended in disaster, due to an unfortunate circumstance. On the appointed day, Kurt fell ill; the assistant who replaced him got mixed up, he confused the rubber tubes of the gas tank with the tubes of the flask of blood. So, instead of blood, the machine pumped about three liters of gasoline into the boy, who died instantly. In his attempt to stop the apparatus, the young man struck it with a small iron sledgehammer; the sparks caused a fire that razed the entire ward and charred the corpse. Débora managed to clear herself in the inquiry that was held—the young man declared that the patient was already dead when he was hooked to the machine— but she became so depressed that she had to be hospitalized in a psychiatric clinic. "This will put an end to her crazy ideas," Microbe assured me. He was wrong. When Débora was discharged from the hospital, she had a new project, which was the direct result of her being in contact with the mental patients: "The future of medicine lies in psychiatry," she assured me with confidence. Having read extensively on the subject, she now intended to devote herself to psychoanalysis, still a novelty in that year, 1935. She was eager to go to Buenos Aires, where she would look up a Dr. Ernesto Finkel- man—a Jew, naturally; everybody was then saying that psychoanal- ysis had to do with Jews—in order to initiate herself into the secrets of his specialty. Her mother, who had never lost faith in her daughter, sold the few jewels she owned, and so, one day in November 1935, Débora left for Buenos Aires.

I t was with a certain anxiety that I saw Débora off at the railroad station. In what kind of a muddle would she find herself next? This psychoanalysis thing reminded me of cabala, of magic. And it stirred something inside me. Why? Cabala—what did I have to do with cabala? I didn't know, then. But I was disturbed.

In Buenos Aires, Débora looked up Dr. Finkelman. He received her coldly; when Débora said that she would like to get professional training in psychoanalysis, he told her that there was no such thing, that there were no courses or anything like that that people could take. If Débora wanted to become a psychoanalyst, she would have to undergo analysis herself, a long, difficult process. His words felt like a cold shower, but Débora didn't let herself feel disheartened; right away, she decided:

"Then I would like to be analyzed by you."

Finkelman smiled, with a superior air:

"By me? Impossible. I'm booked solid for the next three years."

She couldn't believe what she heard:

"Have I then come all the way from Porto Alegre for nothing?"

"Buenos Aires is a city with plenty of attractions. I'm sure you'll find ways of amusing yourself."

He wanted to put an end to this interview—they were at the headquarters of the Medical Association, where he was scheduled to give a lecture—but Débora wasn't going to give up. She took him by the arm:

"Will you refer me then to someone else?"

He extricated himself free:

"I know of no one who could help you: There aren't many analysts here in Buenos Aires. Why don't you try New York? Many European analysts have been heading for that city, fleeing from the Nazis."

"New York?" said Débora, desperate. "But I don't know any English, doctor!"

The man shrugged:

"I'm very sorry. I'm afraid there's nothing else I can say."

Anyone else would have given up and returned to Porto Alegre; not Débora, though. On the following day there she was, seated on a bench in a public square, right in front of the building where Finkelman had his office. She wasn't quite sure why she was there, but she hoped that an idea would strike her. Resentfully she sat looking at the ugly, gray façade extravagantly decorated. Caryatids, griffins, sphinxes—but what were they supposed to be, anyway? What did those figures with their clearly threatening expressions represent? She shrank in her overcoat, lit a cigarette. In Porto Alegre she never smoked in public; but in Buenos Aires and under the circumstances, she didn't give a damn.

A black limousine pulled up in front of the building. The chauffeur leaped out and rushed to open the back door. Finkelman hurried into the building. A moment later lights went on on the fourth floor, where he had his office. All she could see from the public square was a bowl-shaped lighting fixture made of chrome-plated metal. She couldn't see Finkelman, or what he was doing with his patients. It was indeed a mystery, psychoanalysis. Débora sighed.

It was then that she noticed the For Rent sign on the fifth floor. Which gave her an idea. She went to the real estate agency, and after ascertaining that the empty suite was located exactly above Finkelman's office, she rented it. Then she went to a hardware store to buy a flashlight, a hammer, a chisel; at nightfall, she went into the building. There were no lights on in Finkelman's office—he had already left, which suited her just fine.

Shunning the elevator, she climbed up the old stairway; as she stealthily opened the door, her heart was pounding, not just from exertion but also from emotion. Switching on the flashlight, she looked around. Two adjoining rooms, empty: completely bare of furniture. Nothing but old newspapers and cardboard boxes.

Sitting down on the dusty floor, Débora unfolded the floorplan with which the real estate agency had provided her, and it showed not only her floor but Finkelman's as well. With the help of a tape measure, she determined the exact location of the lighing fixture in Finkelman's office. And then she set to work. With the hammer and the chisel she managed to pry off a few parquet blocks, and then she proceeded to bore a hole in the floor. The cement slab wasn't very thick and soon she succeeded. She wasn't worried about the debris, they dropped into the bowl of the ugly lighting fixture. Finkelman's taste in decoration was terrible, but quite providential under these circumstances.

When the hole was ready, she carefully rounded its edges and then obliterated it with a bung painted in white. Unless the psychoanalyst was in the habit of studying the ceiling, he would never notice a thing. Satisfied with her work, she returned to her hotel.

Quite early next morning she was already at her post, peeping through the hole. Finkelman was late; she was chainsmoking, and getting impatient: Why didn't he keep to his schedule, this distinguished gentleman? Could he afford the luxury of sleeping in? At long last the door opened: Finkelman walked in. Crooning softly to himself, he took off his overcoat, hung it in the closet, sat down in an armchair, and began to read the newspaper. Fifteen minutes later the doorbell rang. He got up and answered the door. It was a patient; obviously a patient; a young man, very agitated. He came in, barely greeted Finkelman, and lay down on the couch. There he remained, with his mouth half open, staring at the ceiling. For a moment Débora was afraid that he would notice the hole—but no, the young man was looking at nothing; glassy-eyed, he stared vacantly. And he was silent. Once in a while he sighed but didn't say a word.

A quarter of an hour went by like this. Débora was growing more and more intrigued: What kind of treatment is this? They don't speak, they don't do anything—where is this great scientific novelty? She was beginning to feel anxious, not just for the patient, who was unable to speak, but also for the doctor (what a waste of time), when the young man finally stirred on the couch:

"I smell," he said in a strangled voice, "something burning."
Finkelman remained silent.

"I smell something burning," the patient repeated.
Finkelman still silent.

"Quite pronounced, this smell," persisted the young man.
Finkelman cleared his throat:

"Last week," he finally said, "it was a rotten taste in your mouth. Now, a smell of something burning. Rotten, burned; burned, rotten. Let's consider the implications, Juan. What is turning rotten? What is burning?"

The young man, restless, was squirming on the couch like an eel. All of a sudden, Finkelman leaped to his feet:

"By golly, there is indeed a smell of something burning!"

Only then did Débora notice: Engrossed in the psychoanalytical session, she had forgotten about the lit cigarette, and it had set the old newspapers on fire! Jumping to her feet, she quickly extinguished the flames with her coat, then tore down the stairs—one second before Finkelman came out of his office, shouting for help.

The incident had its beneficial aspect. Débora (enough of hair-raising experiences! enough of fires!) felt it was high time she developed some common sense; which she did. Upon returning to Porto Alegre she began, like any other physician, to frequent the wards of the Public Charity Hospital, where she would discuss cases, assist in operations, deliver babies. For she had made up her mind: She would move to the interior, together with her mother. The old woman didn't like the idea; she even came to see me, requesting that I have a word with Débora, that I try to talk her out of this idea. But there was nothing I could do. Besides, I didn't want to get involved. My life seemed to be on the right track; I was engaged to Alzira, a good girl from a traditional family: Her father was an influential person in state politics, a personal friend of Getúlio Vargas, the President of the Republic. Weli, in a small, provincial town such as Porto Alegre was in those days, my friendship with Débora was looked upon with spiteful suspicion. I always made a point of saying that we were nothing but colleagues. And that's what I said to Débora's mother: "We're just colleagues, ma'am, I cannot interfere in your daughter's life."

Débora came to my wedding. When she appeared at the door of the reception hall, alone, with that forlorn expression of hers, anxiously glancing around her, I felt a lump in my throat: It was now too late for hesitations—or for hopes, which might or might not be fulfilled; our paths had now definitely diverged. I hoped from the bottom of my heart that she would look at me mockingly so that I could hate her; so that I could compare her Semitic features, her wishy-washy appearance, with the aristocratic bearing of my bride Alzira; so that I could say, without any remorse, without any of that sour grapes feeling, go away, you Jewess, make yourself scarce, you dyke, disappear from my life once and for all, you worthless creature. But she didn't; with a disarming expression, she wished us happiness and said goodbye: She was leaving for the interior that same night. Keep in touch, I said, my voice sounding so strangled and strange that Alzira stared at me, wondering. Saying that of course she would keep in touch, Débora left.

Upon returning from my honeymoon there was a letter from her already waiting. She was living in a small town located in the region of the former mission settlements: " . . . Mother and I live in a small house on the top of a hill. A beautiful panorama unfolds before my bedroom window, at which I now sit writing—there's a meadow, where cows graze placidly, and in the background, the ruins of São Tolentino's Church, which belonged to the mission settlements built by the Jesuits. A beautiful view, but I must tell you, a tranquil landscape is not what I was after. What I'd really like to do is to frequent hospitals; to study, do research, publish papers, attend conferences. But here, I don't even have anyone I can talk to. My friends are the pharmacist, the school principal, and the priest, who is an intelligent, learned man. But there's plenty of work to keep me busy. My waiting room is always full of patients, and I handle everything: general practice, surgery, obstetrics. The people here really like me. At first they would look at me askance; to them, a doctor, particularly a doctor practicing in the interior, had to be a man. A woman, and Jewish to boot, was inadmissible! Then they got used to me, and now they won't take a step without first consulting with me. Even the mayor, who doesn't like women, respects me. And Mother is happy. . . . "

After the wedding, my life settled into a pleasant routine: In the morning I operated; in the afternoon I saw patients at my office. Two or three times a week I went to my club to play cards with friends, but this was not a matter of discord between me and the sweet Alzira. On Saturdays, a party or a dance.

So everything was fine—and yet, there was this strange feeling: a certain emptiness, a certain anguish. All of a sudden I was struck by the urge to study—history, philosophy—and I would spend hours shut up in my study, leafing through books written by obscure authors. Until then I had never been much of a reader; my friends were amused. "You're turning into a doddering old man before your time," Microbe would say.

But life was peaceful. We celebrated our first wedding anniversary with an intimate dinner attended by relatives and friends. Before taking his leave, my father-in-law took me aside; then, after hesitating for a moment—he was by nature reserved, this typical frontier gaucho—he announced that he was very pleased with me:

"You're making my daughter happy, Rafael. I admit that there was a time when I had some misgivings about this marriage. What with all that gossip about you and that colleague of yours, that Jewish woman . . . Nonsense, but it did upset me. If you had made Alzira miserable, I would have killed you, Rafael. Upon my word, I would have, Rafael. But now I'm no longer worried. And I have a present for you."

He handed me a thick envelope. It contained an advance copy of the government's Gazette, which would be in circulation on the following day. And listed there was my appointment as Head of the Department of Communicable Diseases of the state of Rio Grande do Sul. Puzzled, I looked at him.

"It was Doutor Getúlio himself who authorized the appointment," he said, pleased. "I've been pulling strings for quite some time . . . But I never said anything to you. I wanted it to be a surprise."

I didn't know what to say. Choosing my words carefully, trying to be as tactful as possible so as not to hurt his feelings, I said that this position wasn't suited to an orthopedist; also, I was already very busy; besides, I didn't need a job, I was making good money with my own practice. With a gesture, he dismissed my reasoning:

"I know how busy you are, but you won't even have to go there, everything has been taken care of: There's someone there who will be looking after things. It's an important position; besides, it will provide security for a rainy day."

"But—"

He closed his face.

"Let's not discuss it anymore, Rafael. Tomorrow you go there and take office, they'll be waiting for you." Alzira came up to them, he smiled at her: "I was telling your husband some good news, my daughter."

He took his leave. I told Alzira the news; she listened without being impressed, for she was quite used to her father's impulsive acts of generosity:

"He's a very kind man. People like him are a rarity nowadays."

The following morning I went to the Department of Communicable Diseases, which was located in an old mansion on Rua Duque de Caxias, near Praça da Matriz, not too far from my own office. All the government functionaries were waiting for my arrival; as I came in, they broke into applause, which rather embarrassed me; however, I was also pleasantly surprised—I had never been applauded before. I greeted them one by one, the old bureaucrats and the smiling secretaries, as well as the two physicians—Artêmio, an elderly man nearing retirement; and Raul Castellar, a well-known bon vivant who spent his days playing snooker and had no other job on the side. After I was shown into my office, they brought me some papers to sign—nothing of any consequence; when I was through with signing, the administrative officer said:

"That's all, doctor. You're free now."

On the following day it was the same thing; and so it was on all the succeeding days. My father-in-law was right: The job was no sweat and it made no demands on my time. And it gave me prestige: During Getúlio Vargas's next visit to our state, I was one of the officials that had been invited to welcome him, and my photograph appeared on the front page of the newspapers. As for the communicable diseases—well, they were taken care of by old Dr. Artêmio, a taciturn, cantankerous man but a highly competent sanitarian, totally devoted to his work in the department. He attended to everything: He investigated all cases of contagious diseases, visited hospitals and health clinics, traveled to the interior whenever necessary, often driving his own jalopy. It was rumored that he was a communist. I didn't care what he was. As long as he found solutions to problems, I saw nothing wrong with him. Besides, I had no intentions of getting embroiled in politics.

Everything was fine. On January 1, 1936 my little Rafael was born. We were at my father-in-law's farm, where we had gone to spend New Year's Day. Soon after midnight, Alzira began to feel pains. Fortunately a physician who practiced in that region, a competent obstetrician, was a guest at the farmhouse; labor progressed with no incidents, and at sunrise there was the boy, howling. What a joy! To celebrate the birth, my father-in-law invited four hundred people to a *churrasco,* an outdoor barbecue party; we even got a telegram of congratulations from Getúlio Vargas.

Everything was fine. Was it? In Spain a civil war was raging, and people were saying it was a prelude to a world war. In Brazil, after the failure of the communist uprising of 1935, Getúlio Vargas began to consolidate his position, but in many states—including his native Rio Grande do Sul—people were conspiring to overthrow his government. None of these things concerned me, of course, and everything could indeed be fine—however, not everything was. There were sensations, forebodings, strange happenings. "What's this song you keep singing to lull little Rafael to sleep?" Alzira asked me one day. I didn't know what to say, I didn't know where it came from: *Duerme, duerme, mi angelico / hijico chico de tu nación.* I was then reading voraciously; reading and working. Performing operations provided me with a diversion; there was something comforting, soothing, about a white bone emerging from the gory flesh.

One night I came home to find Alzira worried.

"Dad phoned. He wants you to go to his house right away. He has some urgent business to discuss with you."

I was tired and hungry; my first reaction was to send the old man to the devil; but I couldn't, obviously. I took the car and drove to his house.

The silent manservant showed me into my father-in-law's study. There I found him, not seated in his favorite armchair but standing on his feet, talking to his friend Doutor Saturnino, a wealthy rancher from the region of the former mission settlements, a great-grandson of the notorious Picucha, the Cutthroat; upon seeing me, the worried expression on my father-in-law's face cleared up somewhat:

"Ah, there you are. I'm glad you came, Rafael. Sit down, do sit down. It's Saturnino here who's having a problem."

Without a word, the rancher handed me a newspaper clipping. SQUATTERS VOW TO PUT UP A FIGHT, read the headline: A group of Indians—men, women, and children—led by a white man were squatting on Doutor Saturnino's lands and they refused to budge.

"And what is it that they want?" I asked.

"The land," replied my father-in-law. "They claim it's theirs, that it's been theirs ever since the days of the Jesuits. That they've been expelled, and that they're now back to reclaim their land. And that they'll only leave dead."

"This is what they say?"

"What this white man says. He's their spokesman."

"And who is he?"

"Well, that's the point. Nobody knows. Probably a rabble-rouser; a communist, for sure. They haven't yet learned their lesson from the recent communist revolt."

"The problem, Dr. Rafael," Saturnino cut in, "is that it wasn't the Indians themselves who started all this. This is a snake that someone has deliberately planted, my dear doctor. It's not just me that they want to hurt; they are after Doutor Getúlio, who is a personal friend of mine. And they know he is."

"They who?" I asked. I didn't like this at all; it boded no good, it looked like a real imbroglio, and I wanted no part in it, I didn't want to get entangled at all.

"*They.* Those people, here, in Rio, in São Paulo, who are conspiring to overthrow Getúlio." Saturnino, a short-tempered man, could barely control himself.

"But I don't see . . ."

"Where you come in?" It was my father-in-law. "Simple, Rafael: According to the latest reports that we've received, some of these people are ill. And it's apparently something contagious. All you have to do is to order that they be sent to the Isolation Hospital, and then you make the hospital off limits to the press."

Which would require that the Brigade be called in, of course. No, I didn't like this at all. I tried to find a way out:

"But are they really ill? Rumors sometimes—"

"That's the information we've received. Of course, you'll have to go there in order to find out for sure."

"Me?"

That was all I needed: To leave my patients, the hospital. However, it wasn't the right time to argue about such details. "Leave it to me," I said. I already knew how to solve this problem. I would dispatch the discreet and efficient Dr. Artêmio to the scene.

On the following day, I sent for him as soon as I arrived at the Department. The secretary looked up at me, surprised:

"But didn't you know, sir? Dr. Artêmio doesn't come in anymore. He has retired."

"What?"

"That's right: He has retired. You yourself okayed his application for retirement, don't you remember?"

Well, this came as a total surprise. What should I do? I couldn't entrust the irresponsible Raul with this mission. I made a decision. I sent for the chauffeur:

"Do you know where Dr. Artêmio lives?"

"Yes, sir."

"Then let's go there."

It was a modest house near Ponta da Cadeia. Dr. Artêmio, in his pajamas, was sitting in the verandah, reading a newspaper—exactly what one would expect a retired person to do. He didn't give me a chance to address him first:

"I know what brings you here: those squatters."

"Yes, I'd like you . . ."

"I won't go there."

"Listen, Artêmio—"

"*Doctor* Artêmio," he said dryly. "Retirement doesn't invalidate my degree."

Why this sudden aggressiveness in a man usually courteous? I tried to appeal to his noble sentiments:

"But some of those people there are sick. We're in a desperate situation. . . ."

"You are. I'm not. I'm sitting here in my pajamas, relaxing like any other pensioner."

"But . . ."

He folded the newspaper. "Well, I can see I won't be able to read in peace." Taking off his glasses, he fixed his eyes on me:

"Listen, young man. I'm going to tell you something: I've been in this business of public health ever since my graduation in nineteen fifteen. I've crisscrossed this country. I worked with Oswaldo Cruz on his campaign to eliminate yellow fever and bubonic plague. I was one of the very first doctors ever to go to the Amazon Region to fight malaria. I devised a plan to control the disease caused by tropical parasitic flatworms, and another plan to control Chagas's disease. I've received awards for my work in Public Health, I ended up here in Rio Grande do Sul; you know—or should know—that I worked hard until my very last day. Well, during all those thirty years I was never promoted to department head. I was always pushed aside because of political protegés like yourself. But now I no longer have to put up with this sort of thing, understand? I've had it. Therefore, do me a favor, will you, get the hell out of here so that I can read my newspaper in peace."

"Well, there's no need to fly off the handle." I was trying to take it as a joke. "After all, this is not something that—"

He leaped to his feet. He was shaking:

"Get out!"

"But, doctor—"

"Get out, do you hear me? Get the hell out of here or I'll set my dog on you!"

I left.

"The little man sure flew into a temper," remarked the chauffeur, who had witnessed the incident. But I barely listened, worried as I was about how to get out of this tangle. At the hospital I got a phone call from my father-in-law:

"I thought you were already on your way, Rafael."

"Take it easy. This thing can't be too—"

"It *is*, Rafael. A very serious thing! I was downtown a while ago. The squatters are the talk of the town. The matter has now become a political issue, Rafael."

I hung up. I had an operation scheduled for that morning but I cancelled it. There was no other way: I would have to go to Doutor Saturnino's ranch. On my way home, though, a news item I heard on the car radio was to change the course of events. *Drastically,* as I was to find out later. According to the news, the squatters had entrenched themselves in the ruins of the old São Tolentino's Church, which was located on Saturnino's land. I was immediately reminded of Débora's letter, the one in which she said she could see the ruins from her house; and it occurred to me that I could ask her to investigate the situation there. So, I drove to the Governmental Palace, where I found the Director of the State Health Department and several aides of the *interventor,* the temporary state governor appointed by the President of the Republic as his direct agent—they were all worried: Getúlio Vargas himself had phoned from Rio, wanting to know what was going on. I reassured them: I already had the situation under control.

Communications with the region of the mission settlements were difficult, but using the radio transmitter of the Governmental Palace, I succeeded in getting hold of Débora through the garrison of the Brigade. Yes, of course, she had heard about the situation. No, she hadn't been there; nobody had sent for her. If she could go there and examine the sick people? Sure. She would do so right away and then report back on the situation.

"But be careful," I warned. "I understand they're armed."

She laughed: "A woman still commands respect in Rio Grande do Sul," she said, "and even more so if she happens to be a doctor too."

Then I went to my office; in my state of worry, indeed of anxiety, I didn't attend to my patients properly. At six P.M. the phone rang; it was from the Governmental Palace: There was a message for me from the lady doctor. So I went there, and read the message that a captain had written down: "Among the ruins, she came upon a makeshift tent—inside, on the floor, seventeen corpses of Indians, men, women, and children—some still warm, suggesting sudden death—bluish and yellow blotches on their faces, chests, arms—one person, a white man, is alive—"

Soon afterward the radiotelegraph operator reestablished contact with the garrison at São Tolentino. Débora wanted to speak to me. Her voice sounded very excited over the earphones: She would be driving to Porto Alegre, and she would bring the patient, the white man, with her—she wanted to study this case carefully, it was certainly an exceedingly rare situation, possibly a new disease, something worthy of being published:

"It could well bring us fame, Rafael!"

Fame. Well, now, things were really getting complicated. How stupid of me to have brought Débora into this case. As if I didn't know that something unpredictable or crazy was bound to happen whenever she was involved. Sighing, I removed the earphones. They were all looking at me: my father-in-law, Saturnino, the politicians, the top military men. "The situation is like this," I began, then stopped short. How to tell friends from enemies in that room? I didn't know; all I knew was that I was treading on a minefield, I would have to watch my step. I put the message into my pocket: "Everything is under control," I said. Then they began to leave; finally, only the ones I could really trust remained: my father-in-law, Saturnino, and a couple of other people. To them I relayed Débora's message.

"But isn't she that Jewish doctor?" My father-in-law creased his forehead. "Did you entrust her with this task?"

"Débora practices medicine there," I retorted. "And as for her ability to handle this situation, I have no doubts whatsoever."

Suspicious, he stared at me, but said nothing. We then began to discuss the situation. We all agreed that it was indeed a serious matter and that it should be kept secret. I ordered that an entire ward of the Isolation Hospital be blocked off; the patient—we only knew his nickname, Redhead—would stay there, watched round the clock by soldiers from the Brigade. And then we waited.

It wasn't until the following night that Débora finally arrived. The trip had been ghastly: the car had stalled several times on the flooded roads; the patient, in a state of agitation, had to be tied; even so, he had bitten her in the hand, and the bite, fairly serious, had almost prevented her from driving. Fortunately, a soldier from the Brigade had come with her, which had been a blessing.

She had driven straight to the Isolation Hospital, from where I got a phone call informing me of her arrival. I went to the hospital; I found her exhausted, disheveled, but radiant with joy: "A really beautiful case, Rafael, a great scientific opportunity."

I hugged her. We hugged each other. Colleagues, finally; and friends. But I tried to press her tightly against me; or I think I did; and she resisted slightly; or I think she did; yes, she did; there were people watching us, the soldier from the Brigade. But maybe that wasn't the reason why she extricated herself from my arms; maybe it was something in herself (a dyke? a potential dyke?). Maybe the reason was the patient, who was still on the back seat of the car, tied and apparently unconscious; a stocky young man, who looked German. I ordered that he be taken to the ward right away. Débora had requests of her own:

"I want the best possible care for him. And all the tests that are necessary."

She, in charge of this patient? It struck me as rather inconvenient. But it was not the right moment to argue, so I decided I would talk about something else. I asked her where she would like to stay:

"I could find you a room in a hotel."

She looked at me in disbelief:

"A hotel, Rafael? You must be kidding. I'm staying right here at the hospital. I want to follow this case minute by minute."

I was taken aback. Upset, I tried to reason with her, pointing out the lack of comfort at the hospital, a rundown old building, where only the destitute ever went. But she brushed off my arguments. She would stay there:

"Ask them to place a cot by his bed, will you?"

"But, Débora, a cot by a patient's bed, whoever heard of such a thing? What if his illness is contagious?"

She shrugged, smiling:

"It *is* contagious, Rafael. There's no doubt in my mind. But if I'm destined to catch it, I must already have caught it. Don't forget, he has even bitten me."

She held up her bandaged hand. She was absolutely unconcerned about the danger; she was like a little girl playing with her favorite toy.

"But, Débora—"

She was pushing me away:

"Go, now, Rafael. Go home. Leave it to me, I'll look after the patient."

There was no other way. So I instructed that the man be taken to his sickroom and that the hospital staff comply with the lady doctor's requests. Right away she gave them some instructions and ordered some tests.

The following morning I returned to the hospital rather worried. The first news broadcast of the day had reported on the disappearance of the Indians; there was speculation that they had either left the place or hidden themselves in the nearby woods; no mention was made of either the deaths or Redhead. The matter was, of course, an open secret; but I was hoping that time would be on my side, and that the whole thing would deflate on its own.

The difficulty was holding Débora back. She wanted medical examinations; she wanted the opinion of other physicians; she wanted to discuss the case the way we used to in medical school. Tactfully, I tried to make her see that we weren't faced with an academic situation, that there were certain connotations. . . . Impatiently, she cut me short:

"I'm not interested in connotations, Rafael. You've promised to help me, and you're going to keep your promise."

We went to have a look at the patient. There he was, strapped to the bed, apparently in a deep coma, receiving serum and oxygen.

"I don't know if we have much time left," she said. "In all the other cases death came quickly. I'd like to come up with a diagnosis while he's still alive. And I'd like to cure him, if possible."

I sighed:

"So, what is it that you need?"

She handed me a sheet of paper with a new and long list of tests. I looked at her, then sighed again: None of them could be carried out at the hospital. Outside technicians and radiologists would have to be called in: more people to learn about the case. No, there was no way I could keep this case under wraps.

"All right. I'll make the necessary arrangements. By the way, Débora, you know, don't you, this hospital has its own medical staff. . . ."

"I'm not interested, Rafael. It's my case, I'll see it through. If you want to help me, fine. If not, I'll continue on my own."

"Listen, Débora . . ."

I explained the situation to her, all the events of the last few hours; I ended up by saying that she would have to shoulder the responsibility for whatever happened. She smiled:

"Trust me, Rafael. I can't make head or tail of these political things, but if they depend on a diagnosis, leave it to me. Poisoning, well, that's a good one. If Renard were here, he would be tickled to death. Poisoning, indeed!"

There was a knock on the door. It was the man from the laboratory with the results of the tests that had been carried out in the hospital. She skimmed through the results:

"Everything normal."

Disappointed? No. The results didn't contradict her assumptions. On the contrary, they reinforced her theory that she was dealing with a new disease:

"If it were something known, these routine tests would have told us. Wouldn't you say so, Rafael?"

I didn't want to express an opinion; as a matter of fact, what I wanted was the presence of some other colleagues, of people who were more experienced, and particularly more levelheaded. Débora, however, wouldn't budge on the stand she had initially taken:

"I'll discuss this case with the professors at the Faculty of Medicine. As soon as I have gathered all the facts. I'll be spending the rest of the morning in the library, looking up things to update the bibliography. And I'll write up the material this afternoon."

I had a scheduled operation, but I decided I would stop home first. Alzira was waiting for me, peeved:

"Where have you been? I was getting worried."

Then I realized: I had forgotten to let her know.

"I'm sorry, Alzira. I worked all night."

"With that lady doctor?" she asked, cross.

That was all I needed: jealousy.

"For heavens' sake, Alzira—"

Just then the phone rang. I answered it: It was Doutor Saturnino. An idea had just occurred to him: Why not have the patient transferred to São Paulo or Rio, on the pretext of providing him with better medical facilities? It was a good suggestion, but Débora would never agree to it. And the reporter from that newspaper *Alerta* would raise a squawk. Saturnino was displeased:

"If it were up to me, I'd take this devil out of here," he said, ill-tempered.

Calmly yet firmly, I stated that it was my prerogative to decide on this matter, which irritated him even further. Well, let him be irritated: I couldn't care less.

Anyhow, it would be better to share this responsibility with someone else. Knowing that Débora would be away from the hospital the following morning, I decided to take advantage of this opportunity to bring in Brito—physician to the big shots—to examine the patient. I phoned him; he agreed right away. We decided on ten o'clock next morning. At ten I was already at the hospital. Brito, however, was late as usual; when he finally showed up, he couldn't examine the patient. Débora, who had just then returned from the Faculty of Medicine, burst into the sickroom in a fury:

"May I ask what you're doing here, sir?"

"Me?" asked Brito, no less irritated. "I'm here at the request of Dr. Rafael Mendes, head of the Department of Communicable Diseases, to which this hospital is related. And you, madam, may I ask you what you're doing here?"

"I'm the physician in charge of this case. Didn't Rafael inform you, professor?"

No, I hadn't, and now there was this muddle. To my surprise, however, Débora controlled herself: She said that she was ready to

236

report on the case at the next session on clinical practice at the Faculty of Medicine, and that she had thought of talking to Professor Brito about this matter; therefore, it would be wonderful if he were willing to examine her patient—she would be delighted. But no, there was no way Brito was going to examine the patient now. Glancing at me reproachfully, he picked up his hat and left, but not before fixing on a day for Débora's presentation: the following morning.

I was getting increasingly worried, but Débora was jubilant—just what she had been waiting for, a meeting with the professors of the Faculty of Medicine, with the cream of the medical practitioners in Rio Grande do Sul:

"I've read everything I could find on the subject, Rafael, and I'm now absolutely convinced: It's a new disease, no doubt about it."

Defiant, she stood smiling, her eyes fixed on me. Such was the degree of my desire for her at that moment that I quivered. But what was it, anyway? Love? Once more I shrank away from this disturbing question.

"All right, Débora. Go ahead. But I don't want to hear any complaints later."

I was about to leave, but she held me by the arm:

"Don't you want to examine the patient?"

As a matter of fact, I didn't. It wasn't my specialty, he wasn't my patient; why should I get even more involved than I already was? Besides, there was that nagging suspicion that it was a contagious disease, and I was in a hurry. But with Débora's hand on my arm . . . It wasn't an affectionate press of the hand: I wished it were, but it wasn't; perhaps there was an affectionate component in the way she pressed my arm, but it was mostly a forceful, commanding gesture: Examine him!

I examined the patient. Quickly and reluctantly. I found nothing.

"I don't know what's wrong with him."

She smiled:

"That was rather quick."

I felt like saying something cruel in reply: That she could spare me her opinions, that I knew how to examine a patient, that I was experienced in examining patients, and in many other things which she knew only from hearsay, like screwing, for instance. But I controlled myself and even managed to smile:

"You're right. But as a matter of fact . . ."

I interrupted myself: My eyes were on her cot, still unmade, where she had slept—fully dressed? in a nightgown? naked?—next to a stranger. I didn't see any generosity in her behavior; what I did see was shamelessness, something one would expect of a hooker or a dyke.

"As a matter of fact, I'm in a hurry," I said dryly. "Is there anything else that you need?"

She asked me to inform her mother that she was fine, and that her patients should see the doctor in the neighboring town: It was an arrangement that had worked well on previous occasions.

I left. At the entrance to the hospital I was accosted by a shabby young man with a little mustache and a cheeky air.

"Dr. Rafael? I'm a reporter. . . ."

Well, it had started then. "I'm in a hurry," I said and got into the car. He hung on to the door, preventing me from closing it.

"If I were you, sir, I wouldn't be in such a big hurry to get away. My newspaper, the *Alerta*, has received some interesting information. . . ."

The *Alerta*. My father-in-law was right: They were on top of the situation. The *Alerta* had been on an insidious drive against Getúlio Vargas. It was a satirical, sensationalistic rag, still tolerated because of its small circulation, which, however, was already on the increase. I hesitated; should I appease him?

"Later, maybe," I said. "Now you must excuse me, my friend, I have an operation to perform."

And I told the chauffeur to drive away. In the rearview mirror I saw him standing on the sidewalk, his eyes following the car: Trouble in the offing, for sure. I went to the hospital but never got anywhere near the operating room. Doutor Saturnino had phoned, asking me to attend a meeting at his hotel. This situation was beginning to get under my skin, but I saw no way out of it. When I arrived at the hotel, several people were already assembled there: Saturnino, my father-in-law, two aides from the Governmental Palace, and a hefty, fashionably dressed mulatto, who introduced himself as an agent of the Department of Press and Propaganda. Saturnino apologized for having disrupted my work schedule:

"But it's an important matter, doctor. Early this morning I received a telegram from Getúlio. According to their sources there in Rio, the newspapers are going to milk every drop out of this story about these sick Injuns. They'll want to know what has befallen them. And above all, they'll be demanding news about this fellow that is now at the hospital."

The mulatto listened, smiling enigmatically. I told them there was nothing I could state beforehand; I didn't even know what was wrong with the man.

"What about this lady doctor?" asked my father-in-law. "Can she be trusted?"

I replied that I couldn't vouch for her, but neither could I take the case away from her. And I rose to my feet:

"I have a patient waiting in the operating room. An exposed fracture, a serious case, so if you'll excuse me . . ."

The mulatto from the Department of Press and Propaganda accompanied me as far as the corridor in order to tell me that he would handle the press. I didn't want to enter into an argument: I merely thanked him, got into the car, and went back to the hospital. I couldn't operate well: all that commotion had upset me. At the end of the operation, which lasted five hours, I was exhausted. Even so, I decided I would go to the Isolation Hospital. I found Débora quivering with excitement:

"I spent the morning at the medical school library, Rafael. And I dug up some very interesting things."

She handed me a sheet of paper.

"There you are. A copy of my notes."

I read: "In the *Annales de l'Académie de Medicine* of 1898, Renard mentions five cases of a disease characterized by fever and multicolored skin blotches that occurred in the Belgian Congo, but all his patients were black. In 1902, V. Kranz, in a memo to the Institute of Tropical Diseases at the University of Berlin, refers to a disease characterized by fever and yellowish and bluish blotches—but in his patients there was also the occurrence of alopecia in patches as well as gangrene of the extremities—the sputum was fetid, which suggested a pulmonary abscess—the urine was dark, murky. In 1912, in an editorial in the *Journal of Tropical Diseases*, Allen and Dunswick remark upon the *Riu-riu*, a curious disease that strikes the aborigines of Polynesia, a disease which they attributed to a curse from the sacred serpent. Multicolored blotches...fever...mystic delirium. In 1925, in the same *Journal of Tropical Diseases*, Tate and his collaborators analyze an epidemic outbreak among the natives who were building an American railroad in Panama. In all those cases, however, the ganglions were swollen to a very large size...In 1932, Merrill, an Englishman, gathered data on eight cases in Malaysia ...Multicolored blotches, but also paralysis of the lower limbs...In 1935, Bengstrom described twenty cases of a communicable disease characterized by multicolored blotches that struck the members of a safari..."

But what the hell was all this about? Renard and *Riu-riu*? Merrill, safari? Perplexed, I stood staring at Débora.

"But can't you see, Rafael?" she asked, elated. "There are no references to a disease similar to this one here. Which means: We're dealing with a new disease, Rafael! Just as I had suspected, Rafael!"

And she began rattling off a list of what had to be done; there was one thing she considered particularly important:

"An autopsy of the deceased. The bodies are probably still there in the ruins of the church—I hope they aren't badly decomposed. Have them brought here, Rafael. Send for them urgently and request that the Faculty of Medicine perform the autopsy."

I assented, or rather pretended to assent. In fact, I was thinking of how I could extricate myself from this tangle—there seemed no way out at the moment. I looked at my watch; I was already late for the office.

"All right, Débora. I'll see what I can do."

I went to my office. The waiting-room was crowded as usual, and I saw one patient after the other until ten o'clock in the evening. When I thought I had seen the last of my patients, my secretary announced:

"There's one more. A young man who didn't want to give his name. He says he's here on a personal matter."

"Tell him to come back tomorrow."

But he was already standing in the doorway; it was, naturally, the reporter from the *Alerta*.

"Go away, please," I said, gruffly.

He smiled:

"I'd like you to peruse this material, Dr. Mendes. You might find it of interest."

They were proof sheets. I hesitated, but ended up by sitting down to read them. It was a report on the deaths at São Tolentino. Saturnino was mentioned by name; there was some reference made to his friendship with Getúlio. And the possibility of poisoning, possibly due to the water from a nearby well, was raised.

Poisoning? Where had they gotten this idea?

"Where did you people get this idea?"

"If you're willing to deny it, we'll print your statement," the reporter said.

I didn't know what to say. "If I decide to make a statement, I'll phone you," I said. Then he left. Bewildered, I plopped myself on a chair. And now, what should I do?

All of a sudden it occurred to me: the D.P.P., the Department of Press and Propaganda. I loathed the idea, but it could well be the solution. I would have to locate that mulatto without delay, before the newspaper went to press. Rather than wait for the elevator, I tore down the stairs. I ran all the way along Rua da Praia, deserted at that hour, then went up Rua Ladeira, arrived at the Palace—the sentry at the door already knew me—and burst into Moreira's office. Fortunately Moreira, who was the aide assigned to this case, was still there; an industrious man, he often worked far into the night. After briefing him quickly on the situation, I asked if he could locate the D.P.P. agent for me. We phoned his hotel. He wasn't there, obviously—it was not for nothing that he looked like a skirt chaser.

"Let's go to Marlene's."

The place was nearby, on Rua Sete de Setembro. Marlene herself welcomed us:

"To what do I owe the honor?"

Yes, the D.P.P. man was there. Without further delay, we burst into a bedroom, where we found him with a woman. She immediately started to scream, while he made a dash for a revolver lying on the night table. Then recognizing us, he relaxed; we gave him a quick account of the situation, and he felt that under these circumstances the newspaper should indeed be prevented from circulating; however, he would have to ask Rio for authorization:

"Unfortunately, it's not going to be easy."

We returned to the Palace. The phone connections were slow, there were delays; and it was always someone else we would have to speak to, so it wasn't until six o'clock in the morning when we finally had an official decision, which came from Getúlio himself: The newspaper was to remain in circulation. We could reply to the accusations, but the newspaper was not to be prevented from circulating. The D.P.P. man was annoyed:

"That's stupid! Real stupid!"

Anyway, by then the paper had already hit the streets: From the Palace we could hear the newsboys hollering out the headlines. Moreira turned around to say:

"The ball is in your court now, doctor."

Was it? Yes, but everything would now depend on Débora. But—how could I make them understand my predicament? Indeed, the ball was now in my court.

I left for the Isolation Hospital, went into the sickroom. Débora was still asleep on the cot that had been placed next to Redhead's bed. I stood gazing at her. What could have been the significance of the fact that I stood gazing at her in spite of the urgency of the situation? Was it love? Some love? How much love? How to evaluate the dosage of love? By measuring the duration of the stationary fascination? By converting this duration into equivalent units (which units?) of passion?

But a moment later she woke up; she was a light sleeper, like many other physicians, who leap out of bed even before an anguished voice begins to cry "wake up, doctor." On seeing me there, she smiled—a sweet smile, or at least I thought so, and how could I evaluate the fact that it had seemed sweet to me?—but she soon turned her attention to her patient, who was still in a coma. A tragic face, that man's: deep-set eyes, a sharp-pointed nose, high cheekbones, a sparse, red stubble. Débora jumped out of her bed—she had slept in her labcoat, as I could now ascertain—and proceeded to examine him.

"There's no change." She looked disappointed. "No new signs, no blotches whatsoever."

Suddenly she remembered:

"What about the autopsy, Rafael?" she asked, turning around. "Have you arranged for the post-mortem?"

I just couldn't bring myself to tell her that there wasn't going to be any autopsy; that as soon as she had left São Tolentino, the soldiers, terrified, had requested over the radio permission to cremate the bodies, which I granted. It was foolish of me, as I now recognized, but at the time it had seemed the best solution to prevent the disease from spreading; besides, Doutor Saturnino didn't want any graves or crosses on his lands.

"It's been arranged," I lied, "but it will take a few more days, our pathologist is away on leave, but don't worry, the bodies are safely stored in the morgue's refrigerators." And before she could ask me any further questions, I left.

When I got home, I found a note from Alzira saying she had left for the farm, where she would be spending a few days with her mother, and that she had taken little Rafael with her. I was not pleased at all; this would soon set tongues wagging. Anyway, it was one more burden I would have to bear. I had lunch by myself, then went to my office. I couldn't keep my mind on my work, so I went back home, stayed up reading until the small hours, but still couldn't fall asleep. It was with both relief and renewed worry that I saw the day dawning.

I arrived at the Faculty of Medicine at the time appointed for Débora's presentation. The auditorium was packed with people; everyone was aware of the importance of this case. There was an air of anticipation. Brito came up and invited me to join them at the table. Débora was sorting her papers. She looked calm; she smiled at me with self-confidence.

Brito rang a bell and declared the session open. He started by thanking everybody for coming. He said that this meeting would be particularly interesting because the subject matter was the outbreak of a contagious disease that had occurred in Rio Grande do Sul. And then he gave the floor to Débora. She rose to her feet and was now visibly nervous:

"Gentlemen: professors, physicians . . ."

Then she stopped. There was an oppressive silence, interrupted only by the noise of traffic and the shouts of the newsboys outside. Holding my breath, I sat watching her, ready to intervene if necessary. But it wasn't necessary. Taking a deep breath, she went on:

"I'd like to present a report on cases of a disease, as yet unknown, that have occurred in the region of the mission settlements."

She began to shuffle her papers, and was again showing signs of nervousness; when she finally resumed her exposition, it was with a faltering voice; stammering, she described the circumstances under which she had found the bodies, and the condition of the man now hospitalized. I looked around; the expressions I saw on the faces showed perplexity, suspicion, irritation. They shot questions at her, which she fielded to the best of her abilities, apologizing for her inexperience and lack of resources; when asked whether autopsies had been performed, she looked at me as if to ask for help. But I said nothing, there was nothing I could say, and then she announced that she hoped to have the data from the autopsies in the near future.

I was feeling ill at ease, terribly ill at ease, the scene reminded me—naturally—of the Inquisition: a helpless Hebrew woman before her unyielding judges. And what was I doing? Merely nodding my head mechanically. Was my behavior honorable? No, it wasn't. I should be doing something, but what? As I wavered, Brito rose to his feet. For a few moments he stood looking at the audience, saying nothing. Then he began in an ominous tone of voice:

"Present at this meeting are the luminaries of medicine in our state. Your presence here, gentlemen, attests to our interest in the medical science."

A pause. A tense pause.

"Regrettably, however, this meeting has been a waste of time. Dr. Feinstein talked about an outbreak of a new disease. But there has been no outbreak, the existence of a new disease has not been substantiated. And I don't even know if there is a disease."

"But there must be something!" shouted somebody from the back of the auditorium.

It was the old Dr. Artêmio. He stood on his feet, shaking with indignation.

244

"There *is* something, Professor Brito. Go to the Isolation Hospital, and see for yourself, there's a patient there, lying in a coma. There is something!"

"I didn't say there isn't anything," Brito replied coldly. "What I did say was that I don't know if the coma of this patient, whom incidentally I saw but briefly—because our lady doctor here wouldn't let me examine him—can be attributed to a disease."

"To what can it then be attributed?" Artêmio was now advancing up the aisle. "To poisoning, as the *Alerta* claims?"

Brito hesitated—for a second, half a second—but when he tried to give an answer, it was already too late. Facing the audience, his back turned to Brito, Artêmio had already launched forth into a speech:

"Because if it is poisoning, gentlemen, we'll have to clear up this matter. We're no longer living in an age when crime could go unpunished in our country. Nowadays the world clamors for justice, gentlemen. Right now in Spain there is a bloody fight going on for democracy, a fight in which we too are engaged. It is our duty to find out what is behind this incident!"

"Ah, you bastard," shouted Doutor Saturnino, advancing upon Artêmio. With difficulty, the two men were separated; Artêmio was dragged out of the auditorium, shouting. Two soldiers then took him away.

Brito tried to bring the situation under control, but it was impossible: the melee was now widespread, students had invaded the auditorium with clenched fists raised in the air, shouting *down with the dictatorship*. "Things are getting grim, doctor," somebody whispered in my ear; it was, naturally, the mulatto from the D.P.P. I was trying to reach Débora, who looked frightened, to take her away from this place, but my father-in-law was pulling me away by one arm and Moreira by another, and from the door—was he, too, involved in this brawl?—Kurt Schnitzel, holding a sheet of paper in his hand, was signaling to me. Standing on a chair a young doctor, applauded by some, booed by others, had launched into a diatribe against Getúlio. Brito kept ringing the bell, but nobody paid any attention. The situation was finally brought under control by a slightly built university beadle: One by one, he kept pushing people out of the auditorium until only Brito, my father-in-law, Saturnino,

Moreira, Débora and I remained. Irritated, Brito, whose jacket had been torn, put on his hat.

"I suppose we can now declare the session closed, right?" he said. Then, turning to Débora: "Congratulations, doctor. If it was an affray you were after, you surely succeeded, no doubt about it." Doutor Saturnino and Moreira wanted to call an urgent meeting, but I was not up to it; taking Débora by the arm, under my father-in-law's suspicious eyes, I left. At the door of the building, that reporter from the *Alerta* stood waiting. "I have nothing to say—" I said, but he cut me short:

"Okay, doctor, this time I'm the one who has something for you. Your friend Kurt Schnitzel was trying to give you this," and he showed me a handwritten sheet of paper, "but that beadle pushed him out of the auditorium, so I offered to deliver it to you. I took the liberty of reading it—after all I am a newsman, right?—and I found the contents most interesting. And let me tip you off: This material will appear in tomorrow's edition of the newspaper."

Schnitzel's note was long:

"I have every reason to believe that the man known as Redhead, now at the Isolation Hospital, is a militant Trotskyite whom I met in Berlin in nineteen thirty. Although he was then only a young student, he was already under surveillance by the authorities. He was considering fleeing to Latin America, for he was particularly fascinated by the Indians, whom he intended—to use his own words—'to set free from the bondage of the white man.' He went to Mexico, where he lived in seclusion for a long time. He wrote several books under the pen name B. Traven. He made a lot of money from his writing, and he could have led a comfortable life; but, on the one hand, the Nazis kept harassing him, they wanted to do him in; on the other hand, he was obsessed by the idea of inciting the Aztecs to rise up and usurp power. For this reason he had to flee the country. He went to Peru, with the intention of rebuilding the Inca empire, but on socialistic foundations. He was arrested and after two years in jail, he was set free. Then he crossed the border and came to Brazil. Here he ran into a group of his fellow countrymen, who had been expelled from the lands they owned in the state of Santa Catarina. He talked them into accompanying him to Rio Grande do Sul,

246

where in the ruins of the mission settlements they would found a new republic; for this he believed they could count on the concurrence of the local Indians. But somebody tipped off the police in an anonymous letter, undoubtedly written by members of the Nazi movement in Rio Grande do Sul. He then threatened to reveal everything he knew about Nazism in Latin America, including the names of important individuals in the government and in the business sector. . . ."

This, of course, complicated things even further, and I was about to say to the newsman, "Don't you dare make any of this public," but when I lifted my eyes from the letter, he was gone. Débora, her eyes fixed, was still standing there motionless, utterly devastated. I considered taking her to lunch at the Palace of Commerce, but it wasn't a good idea; she wouldn't accept the invitation, and anyhow, it wouldn't be pleasant to have lunch with prying eyes fixed on us. I made her get into the car and we drove to the Isolation Hospital. We went to the director's office, which was empty at that hour; she let herself fall into an armchair, and there she sat, in silence. I was at a loss for words and didn't have the courage to look at her. She burst into tears: She wept convulsively, her entire body shook with her sobbing; it was painful to watch. Suddenly she raised her head and looked at me, haughtily:

"No, Rafael. We're not going to give up so easily." She began to cheer up. "I can prove, Rafael, that it is a new disease, which hasn't been described yet. When the data from the autopsies come in—"

She stopped short, intrigued:

"By the way, Rafael, have they finished the autopsies yet?"

Now is the time, I thought, now is the time to clear the air, right now. I took a deep breath:

"There hasn't been any autopsy, Débora."

And I told her that the bodies had been cremated. She couldn't believe her ears:

"But how could you have allowed something like that, Rafael? How could you have been so foolish?" Desperately she asked, "But why, Rafael? Can't you see that this is our undoing? Now there's no way we can prove anything, Rafael!"

I couldn't even look at her. "I've hurt myself, too," I mumbled, but she was no longer listening. She rose to her feet, walked up to the window, stood there motionless, looking out. Without turning around, she said in a clear, steady voice:

"I'll see it through, Rafael. I don't know how, but I'll see it through. This man has a disease which is yet unknown, and I'm going to prove that it is so."

"Don't do anything rash," I cautioned, but she had stopped listening to me. She left and went to the sickroom.

I looked at my watch. It was time to leave for my office. When I got there, the phone was ringing. "It's for you, sir," said my secretary. "It's Senhor Moreira." I thought I wouldn't take the call, but it would be futile; he would keep trying until he got hold of me.

"Hallo!"

"The situation is bad, Rafael."

"I know."

"The *Alerta* is already printing an extra edition with a report on the melee at the Faculty of Medicine. They're going to say there's a political dispute behind this incident."

"What about this D.P.P. guy?"

"I don't even know where he is, probably in a brothel somewhere. What are we going to do, Rafael? Tell me something, is this Redhead still in a coma? Because if he were to regain consciousness and say that he hadn't been poisoned . . ."

"Yeah, sure, but he *is* in a coma. So long, Moreira."

I asked that the first patient be sent in, but a moment later the phone rang again. It was my father-in-law:

"Saturnino is furious, he says he'll set fire to the editorial room of that newspaper. . . And the worst is that Getúlio doesn't even want to speak to him, he sent him a message saying that he doesn't want to get involved in this tangle, and that Saturnino must fend for himself. Is there anything we can do, Rafael?"

"Nothing," I said.

"Nothing." His voice sounded sarcastic. "We're now in the hands of this little lady friend of yours, this lady doctor. While the two of you are having a good time, we are here, eaten up by anxiety. She, I can understand: She comes from a rootless family, they have no self-respect, no dignity, nothing. But you, Rafael, you come from a good family. How disgraceful, Rafael."

"Listen—"

"*You* listen to me now!" He was shouting furiously. "*You* listen to me! You'll rue the day if you involve my daughter in a scandal, Rafael, do you hear me? You'll rue the day!"

I hung up. The patient sitting before me, an elderly man, was staring at me in astonishment.

"You may go," I said.

"But you haven't examined me yet."

"And I'm not going to. Not today, I can't. Come back some other day. Go now, will you?"

I called my secretary and said I wouldn't see anyone else. I closed the door, took a bottle of cognac and a glass out of the cabinet. I intended to get drunk; I wouldn't go back home, I'd stay right there in my office, and would sleep on the examination table; but all of a sudden I missed Alzira and my little Rafael, my dear son. Maybe they were home waiting for me. . . .

But the house was dark when I got there. Swaying, I was trying to insert the key into the keyhole when somebody touched me on the shoulder. I jumped in alarm and swiped at the shadowy form, which staggered and fell to the ground.

"What's the matter, Rafael? That's no way to treat a friend."

It was Microbe, my colleague Microbe. He knew about the case at the Isolation Hospital and he wanted to talk about it. I invited him in. He sat down, and with shining eyes proceeded to say that he could cure the patient with a new drug he had just discovered:

"It will make us famous, Rafael!"

I sighed: here we go again, fame: I sighed. But Microbe, enthusiastic, had already launched into an explanation: For some time now he had been studying how fungi and bacteria reacted to each other; even before Fleming, he had succeeded in isolating a substance found in the moulds of the genus *Penicillium*, a substance which he called—before Fleming, mind you, and such a coincidence, isn't it?—penicillin. He knew that the Americans were already manufacturing it on an experimental basis and that they would soon be dumping it into the Brazilian market; however, he wasn't discouraged by this fact. He was convinced that his own penicillin was better, and he had been waiting for an opportunity to prove—dramatically—that it was so. And now the opportunity came with this patient, Redhead. The situation struck him as ideal: a difficult case, a guarded prognosis, a great deal of curiosity about the evolution of this disease not only in the medical circles but also among the general public. After hesitating for a moment, he went on:

"Besides, if by any chance this doesn't work out all right—well, he's a transient and nobody knows who he is . . ."

Then, with growing animation:

"But it's going to work out all right, Rafael. It has to. You should see the guinea pigs getting over an infection . . . As if by magic. Yes, it will work out all right. Penicillin is the drug of the future. I'll establish an industry, I'll supply the entire country with penicillin. We mustn't let the gringos take over, Rafael."

I hesitated. A new drug . . . Maybe it would work out all right, but quite frankly, I didn't have much faith in Microbe. Also, how could anybody be sure that we were really dealing with an infectious disease? What if it were a case of poisoning? Then I asked him: "How do you know it's not a case of poisoning?" He looked at me astonished. "Poisoning? You're talking nonsense, Rafael. Everybody knows it's an infection. There have been outbreaks in the region of the mission settlements, and in Argentina the disease is rare but not unheard of. There are even historial references to it."

Opening his briefcase, he took out an old, yellowing, moth-eaten booklet. The title: *Recollections of São Tolentino's Church;* the author, Father João de Buarque, S.J. Astonished, I read its few pages.

In the first part, Father João gave an account of how he had been entrusted with a mission, which he called divine. Born in the city of Oporto, he had been steered into the priesthood at an early age.

Being exceptionally gifted, he seemed destined to rise quickly in the ecclesiastical hierarchy. One day, however, worn out by fatigue, he fell asleep in the chapel and had a dream that was to change his life. He dreamed that Saint Tolentino appeared to him, surrounded by Indians; the saint asked him to abandon everything and leave for America, where he was to build a church and devote himself to converting the Indians.

It was a revelation. On that same day he asked his superiors' permission to follow the saint's edicts. All attempts on their part to make him change his mind were in vain. "God inspired my tongue and I refuted their arguments calmly, firmly, and self-assuredly."

In the second part of the booklet, Father João gave an account of his voyage to Brazil; of his long journey across the pampas; of his meeting with the Guarani Indians, "so pure and innocent that when I saw them my heart burst with joy"; of his peregrinations on foot across the rolling hills of the region until "coming upon a certain pleasant place, I heard Saint Tolentino's voice saying that was the place where he wanted to be venerated." So, without delay, the Indians built a settlement there; the construction of the church, however, took many years because "Saint Tolentino kept appearing to me in dreams to say that he wasn't pleased with the temple, there was always something wrong: the door, too big or not big enough; or the churchyard, too large or not large enough; or the right foot of his statue, placed too high or not high enough"—and so on and so forth until the priest, disheartened, began to think of giving up the idea.

It was then that a young Indian arrived at the settlement. He was known as Sepé Tiarajú; and right from the beginning, it became clear that he was a man of strong character, a Guarani ready to challenge everything. He would enter into discussions with the priest, arguing that what the Indians needed were spears, not crucifixes; fortresses, not churches.

"A church is a fortress," the priest would retort. "A fortress of faith."

"But can it withstand cannons?" the Indian would ask, ironic.

"You know everything," the priest would say, baffled and irritated. "You're like Adam after he ate of the fruit of the Tree of the Knowledge of Good and Evil; but don't forget, the only thing he discovered was his own nakedness."

"And quite a discovery it was," Sepé would reply. "It's good to be aware of our own nakedness, don't you think? Except that, had I been Adam, I would have stayed naked. As a matter of fact, that's how we Indians were before you priests arrived. We were happier then."

"But we brought you the Divine Word," the priest would object. Sepé would laugh. "The Divine Word? We already had the Divine Word, Father. Don't forget—you yourself have said so—that we are one of Israel's lost tribes, that we're the descendants of King Solomon."

The Divine Word? No, that was not what he was after. Nor had he any desire to eat of the fruit of the Tree of Life, which would give him eternal salvation; what he was after was the Gold Tree:

"I know that it exists, and I'm going to find it, Father, you can bet on it."

With the gold he intended to buy cannons. But that was not all, he also wanted to build foundries, to import machinery. "Progress, Father, our salvation lies in progress," he would state, his eyes glittering with defiance.

Conversations like these disturbed Father João, who didn't know how to refute Sepé's statements. *Inspire my tongue, Saint Tolentino*, he would beseech the saint in his prayers. His patron saint didn't accede to his request; on the other hand, he stopped appearing in the priest's dreams, and so the construction of the church was finally completed. The first mass was held there in an atmosphere of jubilation, attended by hundreds of Indians as well as by priests from the other Indian settlements. Sepé Tiarajú looked on, smiling ironically. Father João wasn't upset. He decided he would ignore him. He had ascertained himself that the rest of the Indians didn't share the ideas of this rebel. On the contrary: They worked, attended the religious ceremonies, kept up their morale, practiced good habits. Thus Father João had accomplished his mission and now, being an old man, he was preparing himself to die in peace when tragedy struck: They were attacked by the Spaniards. The Indian settlement was quickly wiped out amid a real carnage: "Streams of blood flowed down the streets." The survivors sought refuge in the church, determined to resist until the very end. Father João related at length how his conscience was assaulted by conflicting ideas: Could he desecrate a temple in order to save human lives—the lives of Indians? (Yes—suddenly he felt disgusted with those savages: disgusted and angry with the whole situation—what keeps me here? Why don't I fling the doors open and join the white people, who are, after all, my own kind? Why don't I go back to Portugal, there to spend the rest of my life in peace?) But then Saint Tolentino appeared to him once more in a dream; the saint showed him the sword he held in his hand, a sword of fire; the priest understood the message. He announced to the Indians that he would fight together with them.

The siege continued. Although the defenders of the temple disposed of only a meager amount of weapons, they had stored there much food, as well as water, which was piped in from an underground cistern located nearby; they were in good spirits; but then a sudden event occurred: "On the 32nd. day of this heroic siege, Sepé Tiarajú, the Indian leader, the dauntless warrior whose courage inspired everyone, woke up sick . . . He complained of pains in his legs and arms . . . He vomited a large amount of black bile . . . His body was very hot . . . And upon examining him more closely, I noticed on his forehead a red blotch, which looked like a beauty spot."

The blotches spread quickly, "acquiring different colors, some looked yellow, some blue." These symptoms then appeared in other Indians. The priest's consternation turned into panic two days later when the first Indian died—his death soon followed by another, then another, and yet another. At first he suspected that the enemy, having discovered the hidden cistern, had poisoned it; but later, when he noticed that the animals—dogs, cats, goats—drank of the same water with no ill effects, he concluded that it must be a plague hitherto unknown. And then "a great fury rose in my soul against Saint Tolentino: *You put the wrong people to the sword,* I cried out, *you struck down your own votaries instead of your enemies, you stupid saint!*" At that moment "the wrath of heavens descended upon me; my eyes became dim, my legs felt weak, and I fell to the ground; I don't know for how long I lay there unconscious; my guess is hours, or days, for when I came to I saw the Indians, all dead, piled on top of each other. Sepé

Tiarajú had disappeared." Peering through a window, the priest still caught a glimpse of him riding away at a gallop, brandishing his spear. "Thank God," he said with a sigh, "thank God and Saint Tolentino, one of them managed to escape."

Even though being extremely debilitated, with his body burning with fever, the priest was determined not to surrender; he would die with his Indians, and with them ascend into heaven. But then the Spaniards, tearing down doors and windows, burst into the church. What they saw "horrified them to such an extent that they fell on their knees, and weeping, begged for forgiveness."

The priest's condition worsened and for weeks he was "between life and death, beseeching death to take me . . . God, however, chose not to bestow his mercy on me." The priest recovered and returned to Portugal, where he spent the remaining years of his life writing and rewriting his *Recollections of São Tolentino's Church.* . . .

I finished reading; perplexed, I looked at Microbe. Suddenly it dawned on me: Here was the very proof I needed! It was History's own voice speaking through the priest's narrative, a voice more powerful than the headlines of any filthy sensationalistic rag. Jumping to my feet I ran from the room. "Hey, where are you going?" Microbe, astonished, shouted. "We still haven't fixed on a date for the test." But I wasn't interested, all I wanted now was to show Father João's booklet to Débora, it proved that the disease was real, that it wasn't a figment of her imagination, that it wasn't poisoning; Doutor Saturnino's reputation was safe, and so was Getúlio Vargas's, the government wouldn't fall—everything was all right, at last everything all right!

I arrived at the Isolation Hospital and as I was running into the building, I was stopped by the head nurse, who grabbed me by the arm.

"One moment, doctor. May I have a word with you before you go to the sickroom, sir?"

What's the matter, I was about to say, but she was already handing me a letter which an orderly had written to her. I read it, aghast: "Dona Marta, I'm writing this to let you know about something I saw, something that got me worried, when I was on duty last night, I went to the sickroom and saw Dr. Débora with a syringe, she was taking blood out of the patient, I didn't want to interfere, so I said nothing and just stood there watching, and her back was turned to me, so she didn't see me, but I saw her inject the patient's blood into her own vein, I couldn't understand why, so I decided to ask, what's that for, doctor, what are you doing, and then she said it was nothing, just an experiment and that I was not to mention it to anyone but it's a great responsibility for me to shoulder and for this reason I'm relating this incident to you. Yours truly."

"Well, doctor?" She could barely conceal her glee, the bitch. "What should I do? It's a very serious matter. As the head nurse, I—"

"Shut up!"

"But—"

I grabbed her by the arm, and shook her.

"Not a word about this, do you hear me? Or else you'll be fired."

"Is this a threat, doctor?" she asked, defiant.

"You bet it is. And now leave me, will you?"

Muttering, she walked away. I stood there in the hall, not knowing what to do. Then I realized I was still holding the letter in my hand; quickly, I put it into my pocket. As if it would solve the problem. As if it would.

No, it couldn't be true. Débora couldn't have done such a crazy thing; not even a person like Débora would have gone so far.

I went to the sickroom. She was examining the patient. I waited for her to finish, and then I showed her the letter. After skimming through it, she handed it back to me:

"That's right, Rafael." Just like that: As if its contents were of no consequence.

"But why, Débora?" I was aghast. "Why in the world did you do such a thing?"

"To prove to them . . ." she said softly.

"To prove what?"

"You know what: That it's a new disease, and that it's contagious. That it's a disease that can spread from one person to another."

It was frightening, it was a nightmare; it even made me feel sick, my mind was reeling.

"And what's going to happen?" I asked, anguished.

"I suppose," she began in the same calm, controlled voice, "that the first symptoms will be indefinite: fever, an achy body, indisposition, nausea, vomiting. Then blotches will appear. If I'm unconscious, someone should follow the evolution of these blotches on a daily basis, and if possible, photograph them. If ganglions appear, a biopsy should be carried out."

Shocked, I stood staring at her. But it was about herself that she was talking, as if she were some indigent patient or a guinea pig!

"But Débora, listen, we've got to do something!"

She smiled sadly.

"Like what, Rafael? There's nothing to be done."

"But your life is at stake, Débora!"

"That's right." Her eyes, blank, were staring into space. "Yes, my life is at stake. I know."

Suddenly Microbe and his penicillin crossed my mind. And if we were to try? First, on Redhead and afterward—if the drug worked out well—on Débora. I phoned him at home and asked him to come over right away. Fifteen minutes later he arrived with his penicillin— a white powder stored in vials. He diluted it in sterilized water. Before injecting the solution into the sick man's vein—I hadn't told him anything about Débora—he made a dramatic pause:

"An historical moment!"

Then he injected the patient with the penicillin. "Now we'll have to wait, he should improve within hours or days," Microbe said. And he left, requesting that we keep him informed about any unforeseen difficulties.

I stood staring at Débora. I still couldn't believe what she had done; and her air of tranquil resignation filled me with despair. "Ah, Débora, Débora," I groaned. She laid a hand on my arm.

"Go home, Rafael, go home."

I was reluctant to leave her. She assured me that she was all right—so far—and that I could go. The day was already breaking when I got home and the phone was ringing. It was Alzira, with a tearful voice:

"I've been trying to get hold of you for hours, Rafael, the long distance operator said that your phone kept ringing but nobody

256

answered. My God, Rafael, what's been going on? What kind of mess is this woman dragging you into?"

I tried my best to reassure her; then, worn out, I collapsed on the bed. I woke up with the phone ringing again, but it was now nine o'clock in the morning.

Moreira, the aide from the Palace, wanted to talk to me:

"It's that crazy old Dr. Artêmio. He's been circulating a petition requesting that our patient be removed from the Isolation Hospital. He claims that this fellow is in jeopardy there, that Saturnino's thugs are quite capable of snuffing out the patient right there in the hospital."

"That's ridiculous," I muttered, still muddle-headed with sleep.

"Exactly what I said, too: ridiculous. But it would be good if this patient were to last for at least one more week. Couldn't we perhaps send for some drugs from the United States?"

I informed him that we were already using a new drug and that the patient's condition was bound to improve. Then I phoned the Isolation Hospital and asked to speak to Débora.

"She's taking a shower at the moment," a nurse's aide said, "but she asked me to tell you that everything's fine."

"And the patient in the sickroom?"

"The same, doctor."

"Hasn't he improved?"

"No, doctor."

"Not at all?"

"No."

"Not even a little bit?"

"No, he's just the same."

No improvement: and the penicillin? I got into the car and drove to the hospital. I went straight to the sickroom, where I found Débora. She was well; seemingly well, which was a great relief. Soon afterward Microbe came to give the patient another dose of his penicillin. "He's much better," said Microbe, pleased. Better? I didn't think so, but chose not to say anything. Microbe was peering at the patient. "Just like the cases described by Father João," he remarked.

"By the way, have you shown the booklet to Débora yet?"

The booklet: No, I didn't want to show her anything with sickness or death in it. I promised him I'd let her have it later, after this whole business had settled down. I saw him to the front door of the hospital; and then I asked him if this disease could be transmitted by blood—say, by a blood transfusion.

"Certainly." He stared at me, surprised. "Why? Has there been a blood transfusion?"

I dissembled: "Nothing, just curiosity." Then an orderly came to say there was a phone call for me. It was Moreira again:

"The city is seething with rumors because of this petition. Lots of people are subscribing their names to it, it's already been reported in the *Alerta*, and the medical students are going to have a rally in front of the hospital. Saturnino thinks it's time we called in the Brigade. What do you think?"

"I'm sick and tired of all this baloney. I have plenty of other things to worry about. If they want to have a rally, let them."

I hung up, surprised at the way I had given vent to my feelings, and went back to the sickroom. Débora was lying down. "What's the matter?" I asked, alarmed. "Nothing," she replied, "I feel a bit dizzy." I felt her pulse: fast. Not too fast, yet fast enough to worry me.

She was staring at me. And suddenly we found ourselves holding hands, gazing at each other, overcome by tenderness—and love? But all of a sudden she shuddered and withdrew her hands from mine. The arrogant head nurse had just walked in to check the patient's temperature, or on some other pretext.

"And how is our lady patient?" The tone of mockery made me lose my cool. I grabbed her by the arm: "Get out! Out!" I pushed her away and closed the door.

Débora was crying softly. I helped her back to the bed and wrapped a blanket around her; we remained there together, talking and reminiscing about our days as medical students until she fell asleep. It was a restless sleep, which filled me with anxiety: Could it be a symptom of the disease? I sat watching her for a long time; when I left the sickroom, it was almost two o'clock in the afternoon.

Waiting for me at the entrance to the hospital was, naturally, the reporter from the *Alerta*. "What is it this time?" I said, gruffly. He grinned.

"You're not exactly full of goodwill, are you, doctor? Can't blame you. You're getting hopelessly entangled in this mess, aren't you? But tell me something: What's wrong with this lady doctor in charge of the case? Why has she been hospitalized?"

Stunned, I stared at him: How could he already know? And immediately I realized: the head nurse, of course. The bitch: As soon as I had kicked her out of the sickroom, she must have hurried to the nearest phone. As if guessing at my thought, the reporter said:

"We have our sources, doctor. There are lots of people siding with us. I would advise you to follow the example of your old colleague Artêmio and join us. As for this lady doctor Débora—"

I grabbed him by the collar and shook him:

"Leave the doctor out of this, do you hear me? Leave her out of this or you'll regret it!"

I let go of him. Livid, he composed himself; the glance he cast at me was full of hatred, but he said nothing. Then he got into his car, an old Packard, and drove away.

I went to my office. The waiting room was full, but after seeing the first two patients, I felt I couldn't go on; I told my secretary to inform the patients I wasn't feeling well and that all appointments were cancelled. Then I stood at the window watching the groups of people that had gathered on Rua da Praia. Raised fingers, turgid jugular veins, angry voices—the reporter was right, the case aroused controversy, public opinion was divided on the matter.

My secretary came in to say that my father-in-law was on the phone.

"I want to inform you," he said dryly, "that I'm on my way to the farm. Alzira wants to see me. You must know what about, isn't that right, Rafael?"

I said nothing; he went on, barely containing his anger:

"Have you considered the consequences, Rafael? Of a legal separation? To Alzira, to your son? To my family's reputation? To your own reputation, which I doubt is still worth anything?"

I remained silent.

"Rafael! Are you listening? You'd better listen carefully, you'd better heed my words: I told you once that I would kill you if you ever made my daughter miserable. I'm warning you, Rafael, my promise still stands."

He hung up.

Motionless, I stood there holding the phone.

But why didn't I go with him? Why didn't I drop everything, this damned patient, the Isolation Hospital, the Department of Communicable Diseases, the *Alerta,* Microbe, the sickroom, Kurt, Brito, and all the rest of it? Why didn't I leave Débora and join my family at the farm? Why didn't I?

I didn't know why. But I knew I would stay. Oh shit, I groaned, putting the phone back in the cradle, and it immediately began ringing again. It was an orderly from the Isolation Hospital, sounding extremely upset.

"Doctor, there are some men here, they want to take the patient away..."

"What?" I was mystified.

"Some men! They are here to take the patient away! They say they're acting on your orders. They're in the sickroom arguing with Dr. Débora. The poor lady is not well at all, she asked me to phone you."

"Don't let them! I'll be right there!"

I tore down the stairs, and on the way out, I grabbed the superintendent, a huge mulatto who on occasion helped me out, and dragged him behind me. We got into the car and ten minutes later, after a reckless drive, we were at the hospital; I burst into the sickroom, and indeed, there they were, Saturnino's thugs—so he had decided to have the patient removed by hook or by crook—four men, one of them holding Débora by the wrist as the others wrapped Redhead in a blanket.

"Stop it! Let go of the patient, you bastards!"

They hesitated, but obviously their orders were to take Redhead away, no matter what. Pulling out a club hidden under his shirt, the mulatto advanced upon them, while I was trying to free Débora. There was a brief scrimmage: the thugs were strong but they were not in their own territory, and the mulatto, in a fury, succeeded in making them flee. Then we carefully picked up the patient, who had rolled across the floor, and we laid him on the bed. Then I turned to Débora. She was pale and shaking. I laid her on her cot and covered her with a blanket, and all the time, her eyes were staring wildly at me. Suddenly she hung on to me:

260

"Save me, Rafael, don't let me die! Save me! You're a doctor, save me!"

It was awful to watch. It wasn't easy to control myself and keep calm: "Well, now, Débora, that's nonsense, you're not going to die."

"Yes, I'm going to die, Rafael, I know. Oh God, why did I do it? Tell me, Rafael, why in the world did I do such a thing?"

Hiding her face in the blanket, she began to cry convulsively. Just then Microbe came in. "What's the matter?" he asked, alarmed. Quickly, I gave him an account of what had happened; he dashed to the sick man's bed.

"This man is dying, Rafael! What an atrocity!"

It was then that he noticed Débora, and his eyes opened wide:

"But what's wrong with her?"

"I'm afraid she has caught this disease," I said, my voice cracking; I could barely hold back my tears. I asked that he send for Brito urgently. He went to the phone and was soon back:

"He's now at the Portuguese Beneficent Hospital, looking after a patient who's seriously ill. He'll come as soon as possible."

Microbe gave the sick man another injection of penicillin. "Just for conscience's sake, really, I don't think it will do him any good." Then he asked if there was anything I needed. I said there wasn't, and he left. I pulled up a chair and sat by Débora, holding her hand. She shuddered. "It's me, Rafael," I whispered. "Don't leave me, Rafael," she murmured. "I won't leave you," I promised. She didn't say anything else; with her eyes wide open, she lay motionless; she made no reply to any of my questions.

At dawn Brito arrived. He examined Débora and was hesitant about saying anything; at my request, he examined Redhead too.

"It's not the same disease," he said. "Definitely not. In her case, we shouldn't exclude the possibility of a psychiatric problem. She has a history of. . . I'd like a second opinion. With your permission, I'll bring in someone, a specialist."

"Of course, of course," I hastened to say. He left and I sat by Débora, who remained motionless, her eyes closed.

I dozed off. I woke up with a start, with the impression that Débora was looking at me; but no, she wasn't, her eyes were closed; and yet there was something—the expression she wore on her face was strange, an expression at once serene and droll; happy and resigned. What caused it? Delirium? What kind of delirium? All of a sudden, her eyes still closed, she stretched forth her arms and pulled me toward her. I tried to hold back, I think I did, she was a patient and I couldn't, but she was also a woman and I could, I should, I wanted—and did I love her? I had always thought that perhaps I did—and what I had never imagined possible, not even in dreams or in moments of delusion, was now happening, she was embracing me, pulling me down toward her, her warm arms around my neck, and then with her breasts already against my chest, her mouth began searching for mine, and I was overcome by panic, what if she is sick with heaven knows what kind of disease or plague, it could be something contagious, and I had always been afraid of contagion, whenever I was in the ward for tropical diseases I avoided getting close to the typhoid and smallpox patients; but even greater than my fear was my desire, an overwhelming desire, and I began kissing her furiously, and I had a hard-on and I began pushing the bedclothes aside, oh God, I'm going to screw her right here on a hospital bed, next to a sick man, something unheard of, and she's a virgin, I know she is, I'll have to deflower her and the sheets will be stained and the orderlies will no doubt conjecture, no, not the orderlies, but that loathsome nurse will, hell, let her conjecture, let her gossip, ah, these breasts, Débora, my love. . . .

But is Rafael still in there?"

It was Microbe's voice outside in the corridor: he had come—of course—to give the patient yet another damn injection. Jumping out of bed, I tidied myself as well as I could, he walked in, went straight to the sick man's bed without noticing my agitation, gave him a shot of penicillin, then turned dejectedly to me:

"There are only two doses left, Rafael. Let's pray that he'll pull through."

Only two more doses? What if Débora were to need the drug? No, she wouldn't need it. I was now sure she would pull through. And yet, she remained motionless, her eyes closed. Why? What did it mean?

I went to the office of the hospital's director, stretched out on the couch, and tired out, fell asleep. In the morning Brito phoned to say that he would be coming with a psychiatrist.

"An Argentinean who's teaching a course here. An authority. He was reluctant at first, but I succeeded in persuading him, I explained that a colleague was involved, that the case had implications, that it would be better for us if we could get an outsider's opinion. We're leaving now. His name is Finkelman."

Finkelman, of course. Who else? They arrived soon after. He was a short, ugly man, who looked at us with an air of superiority. At Brito's request, I briefed him quickly on the situation. He said he would like to see the woman patient.

"Actually, you've met her before," I ventured to say cautiously.

"I know."

He asked to be left alone with Débora. He went into the sickroom and closed the door. Minutes went by; Brito, impatient, kept looking at his watch. Finally Finkelman appeared:

"You may come in," he said.

Débora was sitting up in bed, looking at us.

"She's all right now," said Finkelman. "Aren't you, Débora?"

She nodded in reply.

"Incredible," said Brito. "How did you . . . ?"

"Well, my friend," replied a smiling Finkelman, "we doctors have our little tricks, don't we?"

He looked at his watch: He had to teach a class, there were people waiting for him; Brito would give him a ride. He took his leave, then before getting into the car, he looked at me intently but without saying a word. I never saw him again.

I went back to the sickroom. I hesitated at the door, but I went in. I had to force myself to look Débora in the eye. Her eyes met mine in a steady gaze, her face empty of emotion. With an effort, I spoke.

"So, what happened, Débora? What happened?"

"Nothing, Rafael."

Nothing? What the hell was that supposed to mean? Was she

dissimulating, was she crazy, or what? Nothing? How come, nothing?

"Nothing, Débora?"

"Nothing, Rafael."

"Nothing at all?"

"Nothing at all."

"Do you know what I'm talking about, Débora?"

"I think so. But nothing happened."

Calmly, and with a somewhat curious expression in her eyes, she stood staring at me. Which should distress me but didn't; I was feeling rather benumbed, maybe because I was so tired.

"Nothing."

"That's right. Nothing."

And didn't we embrace each other? I could have asked. And didn't we kiss and caress each other? Questions I could have asked, but chose not to; once again, I opted for perplexity.

Redhead died that morning. In the afternoon the *Alerta* published an extra edition: Among other things, the newspaper claimed that the patient had been used as a guinea pig to test an imported drug, and it raised again the theory of murder, laying the blame point-blank on Saturnino.

Surprisingly, this *fazendeiro*, this owner of ranches and farmlands, decided to take up the challenge. The patient had been killed, yes, but the killing had been perpetrated by people interested in upholding the theory of poisoning. Saturnino discredited the *Alerta* reporter in the news media, saying he had been carrying on with one of the nurses that worked at the Isolation Hospital, a fact that could be corroborated by several of the hospital workers. And he also pointed out that the *Alerta* had connections with certain groups that were conspiring to overthrow Getúlio.

An autopsy, which could have thrown light upon this issue, was never performed. That very night, the body was stolen from the morgue where the post-mortem was to be carried out on the following day; the guard claimed that he had seen nothing. Saturnino and the *Alerta* reporter continued to hurl accusations at each other but the issue finally died down. Anyway, it was a mere drop in the ocean, for political unrest kept growing at an alarming rate, culminating in the coup d'état of November, which gave rise to the *Estado Novo*, the New State.

A week later Débora left for Spain via Uruguay. In Spain she enlisted in the International Brigades as a medical doctor. Why? When she was neither a communist nor a radical; she hadn't even been interested in politics. So why Spain? Why the Civil War? What did she have to do with them? And what about me, didn't I deserve at least an explanation? She left without even saying goodbye to me. Well, I've had enough, that's what I thought.

I was studying History, I was really into History. I had a growing desire to know the past—in the hope of understanding the present. And from the study of History I moved on to genealogy—who am I? Who were my ancestors? By studying their lives I hoped in fact to find out who I was; I wanted answers to the questions that kept tormenting me; I wanted to know what had happened, what was happening, what would happen. I wanted to trade perplexity for wisdom—not for passion.

In this undertaking I was helped by a good friend, a genealogist whom I had met by chance, and who became not only an advisor but also a real spiritual guide. With the utmost equanimity, this man revealed to me astonishing things. That I am a descendant of the prophet Jonah—I would never have imagined. And yet, from which other prophet but the bewildered Jonah could I be descended? From which other physician but the perplexed Maimonides? I developed a liking for them; about them I wrote pages and pages of real or imaginary facts, I was thrilled by their adventures, distressed by their tribulations. While trying all the time to understand their perplexity. My perplexity:

Did I love her? Débora: Did I love her? Oh God, was I ever haunted by her. Haunted by her defiant eyes, her sad smile; haunted by her mouth, her breasts, her body. Oh God, I wanted her; I *had* to find out if I loved her. I decided to leave for Spain.

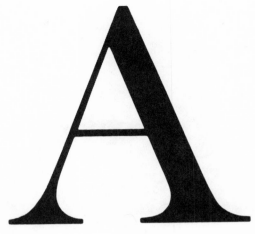

A genealogical note

At the end of this narrative, there is a note written by the genealogist:

Dr. Rafael Mendes never got to Spain. He died on board the freighter in which he was traveling, victim, according to the ship's doctor, of a mysterious fever whose prodromes had manifested themselves before he set off on his voyage. Throughout his illness Dr. Rafael Mendes was often delirious, when he would talk about things that made no sense to the bystanders, such as: the eyes of the prophet, the Inquisition, caravels, the head of Tiradentes. During a brief moment of lucidity he announced that he would be dying soon; he asked that his body be cast into the sea so that *like Jonah* (to use his own words) he could reach his destination. He didn't clarify which destination he had in mind. His wishes were carried out: his body, wrapped in the Brazilian flag, sank into the sea while two Brazilian crew members sang the National Anthem—not all of it, just the parts they knew.

Two people were notified of the death of Dr. Rafael Mendes: Dona Alzira Mendes, his wife; and myself, his genealogist. In accordance with Dr. Rafael's wishes, the ship's captain sent me the two notebooks that he had in his possession, and these I have kept together with the other personal effects he had left at my house.

Whenever people asked Dona Alzira about him, she would

reply, quite understandably, that her husband, impelled by his magnanimity, had gone to Spain to fight for democracy and that he had died there and that he was buried in a common grave on the outskirts of Madrid.

As for myself, I remained silent. And unless there are any new developments, the period at the end of this sentence marks the end of the story of Dr. Rafael Mendes and of all the perplexed Mendeses.

Thе notebook slips out of Rafael's hands; he falls asleep. The day is dawning.

Rafael Mendes: the race

H

e wakes up with someone pounding violently on the door.

"Rafael! Open the door, Rafael!" It's Helena.

He leaps to his feet, looks at the watch: eight o'clock. How in the world—

"Open the door, Rafael! Open the door, for heavens' sake!"

He opens the door, Helena walks in, dishevelled, wild-eyed, upset:

"What's the matter?" he shouts, alarmed. "What's the matter, Helena?"

Weeping, she flings herself into his arms.

"Ah, Rafael, what a misfortune! What a misfortune!"

"Come on, tell me, Helena! What happened?"

"It's Suzana. She's gone, Rafael."

"Where did she go? When?"

"Early this morning, Rafael..." Sobbing her heart out, she can barely speak. "She came home early this morning, packed a suitcase with clothes, and left. She said we shouldn't worry, she was going away for a while, she would be soon in touch..."

"But why, Helena? Why didn't you stop her?"

"I begged, Rafael... I begged her to stay. But she said it would be better this way, better for everybody. She said you'd understand...."

"Me?"

"Yes, you. And that's not all, Rafael. The radio, since early in the morning, has been reporting on the finance company. They say it went bankrupt, that there are crowds of people in front of the building, wanting to withdraw their money."

Oh no, moans Rafael, that's the last straw.

"And Boris?" he asks.

"He phoned a while ago, he wanted to speak to you. I said I'd wake you up but he said he couldn't wait, he had to catch a plane. . . ."

"A plane?"

Ah, the bastard: the rat running away, abandoning ship. And all of a sudden it dawns on him: Suzana and Boris . . .

"They're leaving together, Helena! The two of them! Tell the doorman to get the car going, hurry!"

He dashes out of the apartment: The elevator won't come, it's stuck somewhere, he bangs on the door, then giving up, tears down the stairway, two steps at a time, and panting, reaches the ground floor. As he goes out the front door, he almost crashes into a little man who's just coming in—it's the genealogist.

"Wait a minute!" shouts the little man. "Where are you going? We have to settle our accounts!"

"I can't just now," Rafael shouts back. "I must hurry to the airport, it's urgent. We'll talk when I'm back."

"The airport?" The little man sounds astonished. "Are you running away? Wait, there! I want my money, my ten thousand dollars!"

But Rafael is no longer listening—he gets into his car, drives off in great haste, making the tires screech, and races to the airport.

Leaving the car at the entrance, he dashes into the building. The lobby is crowded. He runs to and fro, searching for Boris, he can't find him, is he gone already? Suddenly Rafael spots him in a corner, there he is, in a hat and dark glasses, cloaked in a raincoat. But there's no sign of Suzana. That's something: Suzana is not with Boris, they are not travelling together, what a relief! Controlling himself—he mustn't make a scene—he walks up to Boris, touches him on the arm. Startled, Boris flinches.

"Relax, Boris. It's me."

"You startled me." Boris heaves a sigh. Glancing around him, he explains that he's fleeing to Montevideo: There's a warrant to arrest him.

"And do you know who obtained it?" With a bitter smile, he says: "Celina. Our friend Celina Cordeiro."

Rafael sighs.

"But why did you let things get this far, Boris? With your social position you could have saved the finance company..."

"No, Rafael." His smile was sad; sad and at the same time ironic, a smile typical of Boris. "I couldn't. I just couldn't hack it anymore. Incredible as it may sound, I couldn't anymore. I was tired, you understand, don't you, Rafael? Sick and tired of everything. Sick and tired of the dinners with the fat cats, of the formal interviews with the ministers, of the under the counter transactions, of political collusion. Sick and tired of all the lies, of all the crookedness. And do you know why, Rafael? Because I discovered something that really matters...."

He stops speaking: Rafael is not listening.

His eyes are fixed on Suzana, who appeared out of the blue. She is dressed for a trip; with her arms around Boris, she is telling him something—I phoned Mother, or something like that—and she is kissing Boris on the face; and now she is looking at Rafael and there is no defiance in her eyes, just a firm and calm determination.

So, here's the confirmation. The nights his daughter spent away from home, and Boris's conduct, and now this escape—everything has fallen into place. They are lovers. They are lovers and they are fleeing the country together. Boris continues to talk but to Rafael his voice sounds distant, although what he is saying is important (he is talking about how their love for each other started: suddenly; he is explaining why they are leaving together: Because they want to start a new life far away—Montevideo is just a stopover—in a place with an idyllic landscape, a bay, and the sea breaking against a white, sandy beach full of coconut trees, of multicolored birds fluttering against the sky; and they are through with finances or mansions or anything else; all they want is to love each other); and Rafael isn't listening because he is thinking of the little girl Suzana, whom he used to rock to sleep with a lullaby (*duerme, duerme mi angelico*) and of the young girl Suzana and of the young woman....

Over the public address system, passengers are asked to board the plane for Montevideo. Suzana embraces her father, kisses him on the face: "Goodbye, Dad, take care of mother; and don't worry, we know what we're doing, Boris and I. We're after our happiness." And Boris says:

"So long, Rafael, old chap." The sad smile. Sad and sly? "Goodbye, my friend." Ironic? Ironic and affectionate?

Hand in hand, they walk toward the departure lounge as Rafael looks on. Perplexed; above all, perplexed. And suddenly he shouts out:

"Wait!"

They turn around: Boris, Suzana, the people in the airport.

"Wait!"

Alarmed, Boris takes hold of Suzana's hand but before they can reach the departure lounge, Rafael tackles him, then drags him toward the lobby. Boris struggles, desperately trying to pull himself free. The two men end up on the floor and then the whole scene turns topsy-turvy, Helena, oh God, Helena is here, she shouldn't have come, Helena screaming like a madwoman, and the old genealogist comes running into the airport lobby.

The old man at the airport

Running like this despite my age and the pain in my chest, and yet run I must, for Rafael Mendes intends to abscond, he and Boris together, notwithstanding the steps taken by my friend Celina Cordeiro, who has denounced them to the police; and if they succeed in escaping, that will be kissing my ten thousand dollars goodbye, so I must catch up with Rafael Mendes, make him cough up the money before he boards his plane; however, before I can reach them, the secret agents nab them, and in no time, Boris Goldbaum and Rafael Mendes are handcuffed; too late, there goes my money.

And all of a sudden I'm overcome by an intense desire to laugh, and I begin to laugh my head off, and everybody, astonished, turns to stare at me, even the agents, everybody thinking I must be an investor who has been cheated out of his money and is now avenged, but I'm not an investor, just a foolish old man. Taking advantage of the opportunity, I walk up to Rafael:

"Your debt is cancelled," I say.

But he is not listening. His eyes, naturally, are riveted on his wife and his daughter. The wife is in tears, but the daughter supports her while looking proudly at her father, who is now being taken away.

It's over. All I can do now is return home, go back to bed, and write.

The third and last notebook of the New Christian

A Jew and a Christian, or a Jew and a New Christian, or in fact, two Jews—in short, two men, are arrested. The charge is embezzlement.

Antecedents. Three days before this incident, Senhora Celina Cordeiro went to see an old friend of hers, an elderly man who practiced, without success, as a genealogist—and also as an astrologer, a chiromancer, a diviner, and other such—a man whom she had been helping out with a small sum of money for many years. She had reasons to believe, she told him, that Boris intended to flee the country. And there was more: "He's taking that girl Suzana, Rafael Mendes's daughter, with him; he and the girl are lovers. I've been entertaining the idea of denouncing him. What do you think?" The genealogist approved of the idea; he had reasons to dislike Boris, whom he held responsible for the death of his only son, Julio, a broker with Pecúnia S.A, the finance company headed by this same Boris. However, he asked that Celina give him twenty-four hours, the time he needed "to pull off a deal of my own," as he put it. On the night of November 17, 1975, as they had previously agreed, Celina Cordeiro denounced Boris to the police. On the following morning, right in the middle of the airport, Boris Goldbaum and Rafael Mendes were arrested and taken to a special jail—a house in a distant neighborhood of Porto Alegre, especially converted for this purpose. Allegedly for security reasons, this arrangement was in fact the result of some string-pulling on the part of Celina Cordeiro. Although she loathed Boris Goldbaum, she had a soft spot in her heart for Rafael Mendes, and wanted him to be at least in comfortable surroundings.

A rather spacious room was set aside in the prison-house for Boris Goldbaum and Rafael Mendes; it is furnished with two beds with foam mattresses and chenille bedspreads, two bedside tables with lamps, a wardrobe, a chest of drawers, a rug with an Oriental design, and, on the wall, the reproduction of a painting: a bay, the sea breaking against a beach with pure white sand, and birds—one, two, three, four, five, six—six multicolored birds against a bright blue sky. But the birds seem to be frozen; the painter lacked the skill to create the illusion of flight. Still, they're nice to look at. Anyway, for scenes of greater motion, there is a TV, although it's only a sixteen-inch black-and-white without cable, made in the free zone of Manaus, in the distant Amazon region, a mysterious place where Indians and melodious birds with brightly colored plumage are still to be found. To sum up then, this room even has a bathroom ensuite, and it could well be a bedroom in a two-star or maybe even a three-star hotel (depending on the whim of the inspector from Embratur, the Brazilian Tourism Authority).

But there are bars on the windows. Which Rafael notices as soon as he walks into the room. Not the kind of bars usually seen in prisons; less conspicuous, but still bars, iron bars, of good quality iron. There are also bars on the small window on the door (made of solid wood), and when the door closes behind them, which happens as soon as the two men are pushed into the room (perhaps not pushed; shown in; however, shown in with firmness, with determination, and perhaps even with a touch of brutality, let's say, ninety percent firmness/determination; ten percent brutality) it does so with a loud noise (not too loud, though; a noise maybe about twenty decibels; loud enough, though, for someone accustomed to nothing louder than Musak and the whirring of the air-conditioners). Rafael

Mendes—he realizes with an anguished heart—is imprisoned.

He sits down on one of the beds, which by tacit agreement, as usually happens under such circumstances, will be his from then on. Boris sits down on the other, his face still bloodied by Rafael's blows. Boris smiles; despite everything, he smiles enigmatically. By acting on the same impulse that overcame him only half an hour ago, Rafael could fall upon Boris and punch him on the face until he erased that smirk off his face. However, Rafael is so depressed now that the idea doesn't even occur to him.

The door opens. In comes the chief of police. There's nothing belligerent about his manner; on the contrary, he seems an affable man, with something of a math professor about him, but one of those easygoing professors, the type that refers tenderly to the logarithm tables. He goes over the situation: Yes, Boris and Rafael are under arrest and they will remain imprisoned until their case goes to court, or until some other solution is found (through Celina Cordeiro? But does Celina Cordeiro still have any clout—and supposing that she is willing to use it to protect the prisoners, which is a moot point—or did she use up all the clout she had to get them into this special prison? It remains to be seen). Anyhow, they will be well-treated, as the meal about to be served will prove. The chief leaves, and indeed, a moment later in comes a man bringing them dinner. Roast beef, summer squash, pasta with sauce, sago pudding. There is plenty of food and it is pretty edible. Although Rafael Mendes hasn't eaten much during the last several days, he is not hungry. Unlike Boris, who eats, in that avidly ill-mannered way which has always made a bad impression on Rafael and on the high society people; it's his lack of table manners that most clearly identify him as an arriviste.

They don't speak. At times Rafael stares at Boris, who, however, meets his eyes in a steady gaze. There is no hatred in Boris's expression, not even insolence or defiance. Generally speaking, he seems calm, even resigned. One could say that during the short period of time between his arrest and his imprisonment Boris has matured. Artificial maturation? Yes, but maturation nonetheless.

Dinner over, and certainly having come to the conclusion that any attempts at striking up a conversation with his cellmate would be doomed to a self-conscious failure, Boris turns on the television.

They watch a soap opera, soon followed by the news. Franco remains in a coma, naturally, but no mention is made of their arrest. Which is odd and rather disturbing. Their arrest is important enough to be one of the lead stories not only in the local but also in the national news. So why was it never mentioned? Hell, they're not political prisoners. Or are they? No, they couldn't be: They've been arrested for embezzlement, which is, after all, a common enough crime, as the chief of police himself said. True, his supervisors might think otherwise. But then . . .

They'd rather not think. Although not speaking to each other, one thing is clear: Both of them would rather not think about this matter. Each one knows that the other would rather not think about it; they know because there was a time when communication between them was so perfect that they could guess what was on each other's mind, and it wasn't just in the case of interest rates.

After the news, Boris asks if Rafael would mind if he turns off the television. He asks just for the sake of asking, he knows Rafael won't reply; but in such matters he is always courteous, his courtesy to others on a par with his rotten table manners. After waiting for a few seconds—ten seconds, which might be considered a reasonable length of time—Boris gets up and turns off the television. A bright spot lingers on the screen: a reminder of that day's news; a reminder of that day and of all the other days. It's an historical synthesis of exceptional brightness. As for the bedside lamps: each man switches off his own; they undress in the dark. Out of modesty? Maybe. Enemies probably don't like to be seen naked. Boris, of course, doesn't consider Rafael an enemy, and even if he did, he wouldn't mind undressing in front of his former partner. If he has turned off the light, it's because Rafael did so first. Rather tactful of Boris.

It's Rafael who wouldn't be able to bear to see the other man's nakedness. The sight of the hairy chest, of the long ape-like arms, of the big circumcised penis—especially the penis, the size, the circumcision—would unleash an uncontrollable loathing, a murderous fury (this bastard used to sit my daughter in his lap, I bet he was already fondling her when she was a three-year-old kid, this pervert, this heel). Which is quite understandable—after all, Boris is his daughter's lover. But without this aspect, Rafael's hatred cannot be

286

justified. Yes, Boris was irresponsible in the way he handled the affairs of the Pecúnia; flighty even. But Rafael was aware of this fact, and even so he didn't take any drastic steps. If in the past he could accept Boris as a friend, as a boss—why can't he now accept him as a son-in-law or what amounts to one? Why did Boris keep him in the dark about his relationship with Suzana? Maybe to spare his feelings.

Maybe Boris had been waiting for the right opportunity to disclose it. Even though Boris is considered an enemy, Rafael must give him the benefit of the doubt. Such cogitations, however, do nothing to mitigate Rafael's hatred. For it's not just this matter between Boris and Suzana; it is this, plus Celina's betrayal (even though attenuated by the special privileges), plus this humiliating imprisonment. Besides hatred, there's anguish and anxiety over everything that has happened to him ever since he came upon that box containing his father's belongings—a succession of mind-blowing revelations. He wasn't a Jew, but now he's a Jew, or a half-Jew, or a descendant of Jews, or a Judaizer, or a New Christian, or a member of the nation— it doesn't matter: What is certain is that now there is something Jewish about him, nothing to do with circumcision, something else, which wasn't there before, something which is at the very least unpleasant, depressing even. Like finding a cavity in a tooth. Or a leak in a drainpipe in the apartment. Or an ugly birthmark on the buttocks of a beloved woman. The genealogist had tried to convince him that it was something good—of course he would, with ten thousand dollars at stake—but what is the good of being the descendant of a prophet, of an illustrious physician? Actually, judging from his father's description of them, they were weirdos; perplexed creatures. They didn't pass on to him any values, whether material or moral; nor the secret—well, the legend, yes—of the Gold Tree; nor any ennobling instances that he in turn could pass on to his daughter (and would Suzana be impressed by ennobling instances?) or to his grandchildren (he'd better not even think of this possibility, it's far too painful).

He wasn't a Jew, now he's a Jew. He had a good position or at least it looked good; he had a high-paying job, people looked up to him. Now he is unemployed and in prison. If before he knew nothing about his father, at least he had an idealized and somewhat comforting image of him; now he knows that his father was an eccentric who cheated on his wife, walked out on his family and gave up his medical practice because of a woman doctor just as eccentric as he was—bequeathing to his only son nothing save some old clothes, books and notebooks with stories about the nation. The nation. What a strange nation it is, a nation that includes rebellious prophets as well as blind *bandeirantes,* flag-bearing pioneers; illustrious physicians as well as senile Indians; great financiers as well as swindlers like Boris Goldbaum. Who, incidentally, doesn't torture himself with such issues: he lies sound asleep, and is even snoring. Scoundrels have no problem falling asleep, Rafael observes with bitterness. He gets up and walks to the window. From between the bars he can see a small tiled patio bathed in moonlight; its boundaries are the house itself and a high, moss-covered wall. What lies beyond this wall? An empty lot? A house? Who lives in that house? And what are they doing right now? Eating dinner? Watching TV? Discussing the latest events? Neighbors, can you tell me what happened? Can you tell me what's going to happen?

Rafael goes back to bed and lies down; he tosses about until, exhausted, he falls asleep on a bed that isn't his, in a house that isn't his: It's as if he were in a capsule adrift in outer space.

His dreams, however, don't forsake him. What is this room if not a stronghold of nightmares? Before the day dawns, the medieval knight steps out of the mists of a restless sleep. He walks toward Rafael, who waits for him, trembling; the knight then devotes himself to his habitual task of encircling his victim's throat with his iron gauntlets. And his grip, now stronger than ever, leads Rafael to believe that this time the knight is in real earnest, that this time he will indeed put an end to the long—long according to the genealogist, but who is to say if everything is not just lies, nothing

but the fabrications of a senile and/or unscrupulous old man?—
Mendes lineage.

To his rescue comes—who? God? No: Boris. Boris Goldbaum.
There he stands, shaking Rafael awake, looking at him with that
faunlike face of his, a worried face, true, but still like a faun.

"You were moaning."

Dazed, Rafael stares at him. Then he realizes: He was dreaming,
having his recurrent nightmare; then Boris woke him up. He should
feel grateful, and for a moment (to what length of time does this
moment correspond? To one single pulsation of a quartz crystal
oscillator in a Japanese wristwatch, this electronic marvel developed
in the country that created the bonsai? To one tenth of a pulsation?
To two tenths?) he feels grateful because he is not wide awake yet;
but once he is, and on his guard, hatred is back. And the look he
throws at his former partner is so rancorous that Boris, caught by
surprise, steps back, his feelings certainly hurt, for it was only
reasonable to have expected a shred of gratitude for his role as
exterminator of nightmares. But is this hatred strong enough? Had it
been as strong as Rafael believed it was, shouldn't it have sent Boris
flying against the opposite wall as if he had been hit by an electric
discharge or by the rays of a cosmic pistol? Rafael wonders. He
wonders, but at least for the time being, he would rather not delve
into this matter. Anyway, a man (obviously a plainclothesman)
comes in with breakfast on a tray:

"Good morning," he says pleasantly.

Irony in his greeting? Probably not. It seems unlikely that this
man—stocky, bronze-colored, with Indian features—should have the
degree of sophistication needed for early morning ironies. It looks as
if the man is merely carrying out a task; and as he learned in the
public relations course (duration: twenty-eight hours) he has just
completed, any task should be carried out as joyfully and willingly as
possible. Thus: good morning!

Bread, butter, jam, salami, coffee with milk: a copious meal, as on
the previous day. And, as on the previous day, Boris eats with relish.
In silence Rafael bites on a slice of bread and takes a few sips of black
coffee with no sugar.

The chief of police comes in. He wants to know if they rested comfortably. Yes, says Boris, it's not like home, but . . . The chief of police laughs; the news he then imparts to them, though, is not encouraging: They are to remain in this "house" for a while; they are not allowed any visitors, be they relatives or lawyers. Solicitous, he concludes by saying, "Should you need anything, just let us know."

As soon as he leaves—it looks as if they are taking turns, but it's just a coincidence, or who knows, maybe they are indeed taking turns yet making it look like a coincidence—in comes the Indian-looking individual. It becomes increasingly more obvious (an obviousness that will probably grow in geometric progression with each appearance of this man) that he is a plainclothesman, despite the fact that he is here—the real reason or a pretext?—to bring them the newspapers. He puts them on the table:

"The newspapers."

Unnecessary words. Or maybe necessary for this man to act the role of the host rather than the jailer; or if he is indeed a jailer, then he must be a special jailer for special prisoners. Or maybe necessary for the peace of mind of this man who perhaps only reluctantly plays the role of the jailer, his dream being getting a job as a receptionist at a three- or four-star hotel. Or maybe the man is overawed by the presence of prisoners connected with the financial world, to him a mythical, magical world; or maybe he is a sensitive man who doesn't mind stating the obvious if by doing so he can break a silence which, he has already noticed (as sensitive people are apt), has become awkward. The fact that he looks stupid doesn't invalidate the last hypothesis. He may well be stupid on the outside and sensitive on the inside.

He leaves.

He leaves, leaving behind a problem.

There are three newspapers—two tabloids, one full-sized paper. Who will read them first, Boris Goldbaum or Rafael Mendes? Rafael Mendes or Boris Goldbaum? Perhaps this is a pointless question. Rafael Mendes wants to read the newspapers, or at least he *thinks* he does; it's quite possible that he doesn't, but it is certain that if Boris reaches out for the papers, Rafael will want to read them. Therefore, it is wise to assume that Rafael does want to read them. It's *possible* that Boris isn't interested in reading them, but assuming both men want to read the newspapers at the same time—how are they going to divide the three newspapers between them? Especially when the newspapers are of different kinds? The possibilities are endless, practically endless. The two tabloids for Boris and the big newspaper for Rafael—that's one possibility. Or vice-versa. Or they could total the number of pages, then divide them by two—but then there's the problem of the various sections: who will get the sports pages, the crime pages, the business news? Besides, who will establish the criteria and make the final decision? Boris? Why should he? At the Pecúnia he was at the top, he was the boss. But now both of them are in jail. On an equal footing. Actually, no: It's Boris who is now in the doghouse, his reputation sullied. (Is that so? Isn't it possible that Rafael, who knew about the embezzlement, is just as guilty?) But is this relevant to the matter of deciding who will read what? Does the guiltier person have a greater or a lesser right to choose than the less guilty? Generally speaking, the guiltier a person is, the fewer the privileges to which he's entitled; however, if one takes into account the fact that the guiltier person will serve more time for his crime, perhaps it's only fair, or at least humane, to allow him to read more. Then again, will reading do him any good?

Boris picks up one of the newspapers. He does so seemingly at random—seemingly, for it is impossible to know for sure. The atmosphere is not suitable for a discussion; they could come to blows. Rafael picks up one of the remaining newspapers and flips through it. Franco remains in a coma; not a word, however, about their arrest. In the business section, a brief news item informs that Pecúnia S.A. Credit and Investment is operating normally, any other reports notwithstanding. Which strikes Rafael as being very strange. How could it be operating normally with the President-Director and his top advisor in jail? Something is up. Could it be that Boris has pulled off yet another sting? Rafael gives him a sidelong look, a perplexed yet spiteful look; fearing however that his perplexity might undermine his hatred, Rafael gives up this silent questioning and returns to the newspaper. Boris seems oblivious to everything. Maybe he is not even interested in any news about the Pecúnia. Maybe he's reading the social column. The scoundrel.

Lunch is brought in by the jailer; just as copious as the dinner on the previous day. Great, says Boris, sitting down at his table. He looks at the tray with a puzzled expression, as if something were missing. Nothing to drink? he asks. Only water, says the man.

"Water!" Boris breaks into laughter. "Water is poison. Wouldn't you agree, my friend?"

Constrained, the man joins in the laughter.

"I agree, Doutor, but . . ."

Boris puts his hand into his pocket, takes out a green bill, crackles it in his hand. It's a twenty-dollar bill. (How many such bills does he carry on him? Quite a few, for sure, considering that he was—they were—about to board a plane, never to return. That he still has this money on him is yet another mystery.) Even though the cop might be unfamiliar with American money, even though he might not know what the current rate of exchange is, he probably realizes that it is enough to buy a great deal of beer. He hesitates: On the one hand, his position, his honesty, his fear that it might get him into hot water; on the other hand . . . But the dollar bill, after being weighed on these quickly assembled scales, is found to be heavy enough; pocketing it, the man leaves, but not before asking if Rafael would like some beer too. No, he wouldn't. Minutes later the man returns carrying under his arm a rolled-up newspaper, inside which is a bottle of beer. The man also supplies a bottle opener and then he leaves, saying—his solicitousness more and more obvious—that he is at their disposal.

Boris pours himself some beer. Before he starts drinking, he silently proffers the glass to Rafael, who ignores the gesture; he would like a beer, but acceptance would amount to surrender. Besides, another thought is now nagging him: After this beer, then what? What is Boris up to? Maybe nothing. Maybe he is just ensuring the future supply of beer. However, knowing Boris as he does . . .

The door opens. It's the chief of police. "A visitor," he announces. "From Brasilia," he adds, with ill-concealed satisfaction. He's enjoying one of the highlights of his life, the chief of police is.

He shows in a man, still young; his cropped hair and thick eyeglasses give him an earnest appearance, very much like that of a well-behaved schoolboy. He wears a striped suit, which hangs loosely from his body, and a gaudy necktie; and he carries the inevitable attaché case.

"How are you, Toledo?" asks Boris, without getting up.

"What?" The chief of police is surprised. "You know each other?"

"Toledo and I are old friends," says Boris. "Rafael here hasn't met him yet. Rafael, let me introduce you to Doutor Toledo, from the Ministry of Finance."

Rafael cannot ignore the man just because it's Boris who is introducing him. Rising to his feet, he greets him; Rafael is courteous rather than effusive; constrained rather than crestfallen (or almost crestfallen). After all, he is in jail, not in his own office. Anyway, the visitor hasn't come to see him, of course. He is there to see Boris, who asks, as he lights a cigarette:

"So, Toledo? Did you have a nice trip?" The usual small talk.

"Pretty much so, Goldbaum." The man is constrained but cordial. "A bit rough-going as we flew over the state of Santa Catarina; otherwise, it was fine. May I sit down?"

"By all means, make yourself at home. It's your house." Boris laughs. "I'm just a guest here."

Toledo chooses to ignore the insolence. He sits down. The chief of police takes his leave, he has other things to do:

"So, make yourselves at home. Anything you need, just give us a shout."

He leaves, closing the door behind him noiselessly. Boris turns to his visitor:

"Well, then, Toledo? What brings you here?"

"Guess, Goldbaum," replies Toledo with what could be a grimace or a nervous tick; it is probably a grimace, a mixture of irritation and fatigue (brought about by the flight? or by something else?), with the addition of a certain amount of glee verging on sadism. This complex grimace, and other grimaces like it, surely would account for the wrinkles and the tortured expression on Toledo's face. "Can't you guess that it is the situation of your finance company? This time you went too far, Boris. People in Brasilia have had it with you."

Then he realizes that Rafael is in the room:

"I don't know if—"

"You can talk freely," Boris cuts him short. "Rafael works with me, he can be trusted."

"Good. So, let's get down to business, I haven't got much time, I'm flying back to São Paulo tonight. My mission is not exactly official, Goldbaum . . . But it's just as important. If not more."

Opening his attaché case, he removes a stack of papers, which he peruses.

"Let me see . . . Yes. Your situation is really pretty bad, Goldbaum. You're in hot water. We have the names of your agents in the United States, in Europe, in South Africa, we know the numbers of your bank accounts, the total amount of the embezzlement. We know enough to make you rot in jail; not in this one, somewhere worse. But . . ."

A smile. A wan smile. A wan and ominous smile.

"You've got powerful friends in high places, Goldbaum. Somebody has intervened . . . It's to nobody's advantage to let you sink. Or to strike you down. Any intervention now would cause alarm . . . Particularly at this point in time. We're expecting the arrival of an international delegation, Goldbaum. Major investors. The message I have for you is, find a way out of this mess."

"Find a way . . ." Boris grins, amused. "What way? Any suggestions?"

"Don't play the fool," says Toledo. Angry; the anger of the timid man. It is clear that he normally contains rather than displays his anger, which accounts for the insomnia, the eczema of nervous origin, the duodenal ulcer. In addition, like his wife and his little daughter, he suffers from asthmatic bronchitis, which is the reason why he accepted this post in Brasilia, with its high altitude, dry climate, unpolluted air. Brasilia is good, Brasilia is safe. Toledo dislikes having to travel to the other states; the hotels, even though they are four- or five-star hotels, the restaurant meals, and mostly the missions entrusted to him, are detrimental to his health; his consumption of antacids and tranquilizers rises sharply when he is on the road. And when, on top of everything else, an already difficult and delicate situation involves dealing with Boris Goldbaum, then . . .

"You know far more about such things than I do, Goldbaum. Far more than anybody else. It's your problem. Talk to your friends abroad, or to your own people. They wouldn't let you down."

"My own people, Toledo?" says Boris with mockery. "My own people have disowned me." The mocking tone in Boris's voice increases in proportion to the other man's visible signs of insecurity. On a graph, Line 1 (corresponding to Boris's levels of mockery), and Line 2 (corresponding to Toledo's levels of insecurity) are almost parallel and sharply ascending. "Do you know that I am reputed to be anti-Semitic?"

Toledo now frowns, and it looks as if he has closed this subject for good:

"You've got to be joking, Goldbaum. But you're playing with fire. I'm laying my cards on the table: You've got some friends in the Ministry, but you've also got enemies who would like to see you dead. Mostly because you are a Jew, and to some people the idea of having a Jew as a scapegoat is rather appealing. You think it's passé, Goldbaum? Well, so it is. But it has happened before, you know. Can you picture, Boris, an enraged mob invading neighborhoods like Bom Retiro? Or Bom Fim? Beating up your people, setting stores on fire—wrecking your home?"

"I don't live in Bom Fim," says Boris, stubbing out his cigarette.

"Don't you want to do anything to save your finance company?"

"I'm not interested. At least not now."

"You're out of your mind, Boris. Completely off your rocker." Toledo is uneasy and despondent: It looks as if his return trip will be soured by a mission that ended in failure. And he hates failures. As much as he hates such missions. He considers himself a technocrat, not a politician; this kind of scheming strikes him as dishonest, absurd. He is loyal, however, to the Minister of Finance, whose ideas he endorses, particularly the Minister's ideas about the workings of the stock market. As a matter of fact, Toledo's master's thesis— written under the guidance of the Minister himself, who at the time was a professor at the University—dealt with this very subject, the mechanism of the stock markets. However, figuring out the workings, the mechanism, is one thing; shenanigans are something else; just as a financier like Rothschild is one thing and a financial adventurer like this Boris is something else. However, the fact is that

Brazilian capitalism, if such a thing really exists, is full of the likes of him. Yes, capitalism thrives in São Paulo, and to a lesser degree in Rio, but here in Porto Alegre—the capital city of a state which is not among the poorest and most backward—things already begin to deteriorate; so, what is to be expected from regions like the North, the Northeast? The hinterland? An economy based on bartering, Indian style: You give me a little mirror, I'll give you brazilwood. Absolutely no accumulation and no investment of capital. And nothing that is calculable: let people sleep to the sound of the war drums. Sighing, he puts the papers back into his attaché case:

"What do I say to the Minister?"

"That I appreciate his concern. But there's nothing I can do. Tell him I'm into something else now. Did you get it, Toledo? I'm into something else!"

"What the fuck are you talking about?" asks Toledo, perplexed. "You're in jail, Boris! You're up to your neck in shit!"

"Maybe," says Boris, smiling. "But I'm now into something else. Rafael here knows about it."

Toledo gives Rafael a look. It's a half-entreating look, as if he were asking for help; he even opens his mouth to say something, then changes his mind:

"All right." Rising to his feet, he makes for the door. Something occurs to him, he turns around, and in one last—and it's definitely *last*—attempt, he says:

"And what about the tree, Goldbaum?"

"What tree?"

"Your tree. The one everybody talks about. The one with the gold nuggets."

Boris makes no reply. He keeps smiling.

"Fake, aren't they?" There is weariness in the voice of the economist Toledo. "They're fake, aren't they? I've always thought they were. Everything about people like you is fake, nothing but a front. Buildings with marble façades and tinted windowpanes, full-page ads in the magazines with nationwide circulation, trips to other countries in chartered jet planes. Everything a façade, everything designed to impress people. Statues with clay feet, that's what the likes of you are. You, Goldbaum, you don't have the slightest notion of what makes for a sound economy, neither you nor people of your ilk. You and your kind creep into the interstices of the economic structure. You are the termites undermining the economy. But the DDT of austerity is in store for you, you can bet on it. We'll squelch you, Goldbaum. We'll ruin you, with or without your Gold Tree. We'll destroy the Pecúnia, just like the wolf destroyed the piglet's house in that fairy tale—with one single puff. We'll seal everything with wax, we'll go through your files with a fine comb. We'll probe your life. We'll interrogate your employees, your friends, your relatives, your lovers. We'll ferret out your international connections, and everything and everyone that is behind you—subversive activities? A possibility, isn't it, Goldbaum? Terrorism, maybe? It wouldn't surprise me in the least. In short, we'll do a complete cleanup, something that will be a lesson to all the Goldbaums of the world."

Panting, he falls silent; with the back of his hand he wipes the froth off his lips. He motions to the guard to open the door. He leaves. His footsteps reverberate in the corridor; there is the sound of another door opening and closing, and then there is silence.

I n silence they watch TV. In silence one of them gets up and turns off the set. In silence they undress and lie down.

Rafael Mendes is unable to sleep. Of what is Rafael the Insomniac thinking? What all insomniacs think of: mother, father. Wife. Daughter. But mostly, this sleepless man, this Rafael Mendes, is thinking of Suzana. Resentment gradually gives way to a nostalgic, melancholy tenderness. He recalls now the good moments; the joyful, tender scenes of his family life: the parties, the picnics, the trips.

Suddenly Boris begins to talk.

It's about himself that he talks. He goes back to his childhood, he tells the story of a poor boy, the son of a communist tailor. He says that this boy was raised in deprivation; he was often absent from school because he had no shoes to wear. And being poor, he had to earn a living at an early age, first peddling clotheshangers, then lottery tickets, and finally books.

"I enjoyed selling books, Rafael. I felt that in this way I was making a contribution to mankind, that I was being faithful to my father's ideas."

But it was a constant source of irritation. Some customers wouldn't pay; others would keep the books for a few days and then return them soiled and damaged (and even with pages ripped out!). And there were also those that would criticize him for selling socialist books at capitalistic prices.

"I grew more and more disillusioned, Rafael. Finally, the pinch of poverty became unbearable and I decided that I would make money. And then . . ."

Boris talks and talks. And suddenly he changes the subject. Now he talks about Suzana. And Rafael doesn't jump out of bed, doesn't strike out at him with punches and kicks; maybe he would like to, but he does nothing. He listens in silence. For many reasons, the main one probably being that Boris now talks about a Suzana that Rafael doesn't—but *wants* to, *has* to—know. "As you know, Rafael, I was like a second father to her," Boris is saying. (It's true: he was a second father.) "She started coming to see me because she was filled with concern; she needed help and I did what I could to help her. I did so not just on her account, or on yours, Rafael, but on my own account too. Helping her made me feel good. Made me feel worthy, do you understand? And it wasn't difficult for me to come up with solutions to her adolescent anxieties.

"Things became complicated when she started university. That's when her political activism began. Up to then she hadn't been interested in politics, but as soon as she became so she turned into a radical. She joined a small but belligerent group of irate leftists, a split group within a dissident group. She began talking about seizing power by violent means, about rivers of blood streaming down the streets. Once she showed me a weapon—a revolver, true, it was old and had no bullets; but I was alarmed and wasn't reassured by the fact that she burst into laughter, saying that she was afraid of weapons and only carried one to impress her friends. But it wasn't just the weapon: She handed out leaflets and edited an underground publication that attacked the multinationals and evoked Tiradentes as the model to be emulated.

"She would often ask me for money—for the cause. Whenever I objected half seriously, half jokingly, that by helping her cause I was in fact digging my own grave, she would reply that my helping out was my only hope, my alibi before the People's Tribunal. 'But will you,' I would then ask, 'testify on my behalf at this Tribunal?' Yes, she would; in fact, she didn't consider me an oppressor, my case being one of opportunism, of speculation, rather than of oppression. 'You're not like the big industrialists or the latifundium owners,' she would say; 'they're the ones who exploit the people directly, and they'll pay with their blood.'

"Just as abruptly as it had started, this political phase ended. Suddenly Tiradentes was a wimp and Trotsky an idiot. She became depressed; she was smoking too much, drinking, doing drugs. And just as suddenly as she had fallen into this pit of depression she came out of it—and joined the sect of the New Essenes. With glittering eyes and a radiant smile, she would say she had found the right road; she took to wearing the long white tunic that was the trademark of the followers of the sect; she became actively engaged in proselytizing, and would approach people on the street. Naturally, I became the favorite target of her tirades. She made me read the leaflets, she tried to prove to me that Jesus was the true Messiah I had been waiting for. 'But I'm not waiting for any Messiah,' I would retort. To which she would say, 'You Jews are full of bitterness, which is only natural, for you haven't tasted the sweetness of the love for Jesus.' One evening she invited me to visit their temple, which was located on the top of a hill, near Belém Novo. We climbed up the hill on foot, as was required by the sect; anyway, there was no road leading to the place. After a two-hour walk—with me on the verge of giving up— we arrived at the temple. A building made of rough stones, with no windows and no furniture, except for a few rustic wooden benches. It was empty; the worship was over.

"Asking me to wait there, she disappeared through a side door. I stood in the stuffy premises, lit only by a single candle. A few minutes later she was back, smiling, with flowers in her hair. Naked."

Boris stops talking. In the ensuing silence his breathing is quite audible; he is panting slightly.

"Naked, Rafael. She walked up to me, embraced me. I returned the embrace. We kissed. And that was all, Rafael. I swear, that was all. Nothing else happened, Rafael. And do you know why not, Rafael? Do you?"

He explains: At that very moment he began to realize that he loved Suzana, just as she too—all of a sudden—was making the same discovery. And what a joy it was to learn that they loved each other! Afterward Suzana left the sect and they became indeed lovers. They were happy, very happy. There were problems, of course: She would fly into a temper, she was jealous even of the secretaries that worked at the Pecúnia. On the other hand, Boris wanted them to get married as soon as possible; he disliked the furtiveness, the dissimulation, especially because of Rafael. She would reply that she didn't want to get married, that marriage was a drag; however, she ended up by agreeing to marry him on condition that they leave for somewhere distant, some peaceful place by the seaside, preferably in another country. There they would lead an idyllic existence—they would stroll about naked, or practically so; they would sleep in the open air or in caves; they would live on wild fruit, and her body would always be adorned with flowers. With the local Indians they would maintain a relationship of amiable respect, expressed only through friendly gestures; they would never speak to the natives, so as to avoid resorting to the corrupting power of words, even of the spoken word. And they would never give those Indians any gifts, little mirrors being particularly perilous. For the moment they did so, or even worse, the moment they accepted something, for example, brazil-wood, in return for their gifts, commerce would be introduced, with the resulting loss of the innocence that she and Boris had so painfully regained.

At first such an idea struck Boris as absurd, but gradually he became more and more enthralled by it: a new life, why not? Innocence, why not?

"When things started looking grim at the Pecúnia, Rafael, I felt that the right moment had come. Unfortunately, they caught me— *us*. But I'm going back to Suzana, Rafael, that's a fact, there's no question about it. And I'd like you to accept this fact, Rafael. Nothing is going to keep us apart. Nothing."

He falls silent.

In the darkness, Rafael gets up. He takes a few steps toward Boris's bed. Not many steps; three, to be precise. Considering that the distance between their beds measures two meters and twenty centimeters, and that each of Rafael's steps is sixty centimeters long, it would be possible for him to reach the other man's bed in four steps—but this is not to happen: He suddenly wavers, raises his hand to his forehead, utters a strange sound, a cross between a moan and a grunt, though more like a grunt than a moan, and falls, but not forward, which would allow him to hit his target. Supposing, that is, that Boris's bed *was* the target, supposing that Boris *himself* was the target, which are both—whatever the emotions, hatred or a rush of affection, that prompted this nocturnal wanderer to move—perfectly reasonable suppositions. He falls slightly sideways, more backward than sideways; he falls.

Boris's face is the first thing Rafael sees upon waking up. And Suzana's anxious face—have they sent for her then? is it serious then?—and there's also the face of an old man wearing glasses, a stethoscope dangling from his neck—the doctor.

"Well, then, Senhor Rafael, feeling better?" It's the doctor who asks the question.

With difficulty, Rafael tries to lift himself up.

"Lie back," cautions the doctor. "You mustn't get out of bed. Your blood pressure went way up."

Rafael lets himself collapse on the bed. Suzana kneels by his side:

"Take it easy, Dad. Everything is all right now."

"And your mother, how is she?" Rafael murmurs.

"She's fine," says Suzana, attempting a smile. "She really is,

Dad, believe me. She was a bit shaken up at first . . . But she soon rallied, she's taken on the responsibilities of running the house, of looking after your affairs, she's coping well, and she even stopped taking those tranquilizers. The two of us—"

Unable to contain herself, she bursts into tears. And there she is, the girl Suzana, kneeling by her father, who strokes her hair with tremulous fingers. And Boris stands gazing at them, without saying a word.

Boris makes Suzana get to her feet, he helps her to a chair. Then he draws near Rafael, looks him steadily in the eye.

"Rafael, I've got to talk to you. It's important. Are you well enough to listen?"

Rafael closes his eyes; Boris persists: "Open your eyes, listen to me." Oh God, Rafael thinks to himself, why doesn't this accursed man leave me alone? Why doesn't he disappear? Boris is about to speak, hesitates, turns to the doctor:

"Will you excuse us, doctor?"

"Certainly," the man hastens to say. He makes for the door:

"I'll be standing just outside. Call me when you're through."

Boris leans over Rafael.

"We'll cut and run, Rafael. Today. In a little while."

Quickly he explains that the doctor will facilitate their getaway. He needs money: His wife is ill, his son a drug addict. It was the doctor himself who put the idea to Boris and Suzana: For ten thousand dollars he will help them escape. It's simple: Boris will pretend that he, too, doesn't feel well. Saying that they might be suffering from food poisoning, the doctor will then have them transferred to a friend's clinic. From there it will be easy for them to escape, especially because interest in them is already on the wane now that the Pecúnia is under intervention. The press doesn't even mention them anymore; Toledo will only be too glad to see them gone.

"Well? What do you think?"

"Well, Father?" says Suzana, anxious.

Rafael looks at her: There she is, embracing Boris, just as at the airport.

"Well?" says Boris again.

Rafael makes no reply; he closes his eyes. With his eyes closed, he hears Suzana and Boris finalizing the details of their escape. They'll go first to the state of Paraná, and from there to Paraguay, where Helena is to join them. Boris then asks the doctor to come in. They settle on eleven o'clock that night, when Boris will ask the guard to send for the doctor, who will be on the alert. The doctor moves closer to Rafael:

"Everything will turn out all right," he murmurs. "Don't worry, Senhor Rafael."

Rafael stares at him; for a moment, the doctor lowers his eyes, ashamed of what he is doing—this man, this old Brazilian, is ashamed of lying, of cheating; if he didn't need the money, he wouldn't be doing it, not even for ten thousand dollars. However, this embarrassment, this painful embarrassment, is short-lived. A moment later the old man is again looking Rafael in the eye; and in the expression on his face there is no longer any constraint; there is sadness, there is bitterness, there is even—just as in Boris's face a short while ago—a certain dignity. Pulling up a chair, he sits at the bedside.

"I know what you're thinking, Senhor Rafael. Strictly speaking, I shouldn't give a damn about what you think, but I'd like to tell you something: You know, I'm not doing this just for the money. Sure, I need the ten thousand dollars, I need them badly, it's something urgent, desperate. But there's another reason why I want to help you. I knew your father, Senhor Rafael. My name is Castellar, Raul Castellar, maybe you've heard about me."

Castellar? Raul? At first the name doesn't ring a bell; but that's because Rafael feels dopey, his mind is sluggish—what kind of drug did this charlatan inject into him? Then it dawns on him: Ah yes, in the *Second Notebook*, he's the doctor who used to work in the Department of Communicable Diseases; the one who only wanted to play snooker.

"Your father was a gentleman of refinement," the old man went on. "As a matter of fact, all the Mendeses were refined people, such an illustrious, traditional family, but Rafael Mendes, my friend Rafael Mendes, he was like a father to me. When he first met me I was going through one of the worst phases of my life: I was a loafer then, interested only in having a good time and in playing snooker;

the seven-ball was all that mattered to me. Well, Rafael was very patient and tolerant, he never humiliated me in front of the government employees, unlike the other physician who worked there, a certain Dr. Artêmio, a communist he was. One day Rafael sent for me to announce that he was going to Spain and he asked me to be the acting department head for a while. I was surprised, Senhor Rafael, genuinely surprised, and moved too; nobody trusted me then, nobody believed in me, my wife had just left me after calling me a good-for-nothing, a shameless person, and other such names. And here was your father placing his trust in me! I had never received such an honor before. During my three-month term as department head, I regained my male pride; I was a strict but sensitive boss; dynamic without being chaotic. People liked the way I ran the Department, I can assure you, and they missed me after I was gone. I was replaced for political reasons, and I never held another position of trust, but I achieved something that really mattered to me. I proved to myself that I wasn't a useless creature, a parasite . . . as my wife had claimed. Actually she came back to me, admitted she'd been wrong, and asked me for forgiveness. I was a reformed man, Senhor Rafael. With the small number of patients I had in my neighborhood practice, we were happy and comfortably off until my younger son turned to drugs. This wrecked our lives, Senhor Rafael. I've done everything to get money. Abortions, everything."

Taking a handkerchief out of his pocket, he wipes his eyes; he remains silent for a moment before he continues:

"During all these years I've never forgotten that last talk I had with your father—that was when he told me he was leaving for Spain. I thought it was a beautiful thing to do, Senhor Rafael. Nowadays there's no idealism, everybody wants to do his own thing, it's a rat race, a jungle where the bigger animals devour the smaller ones. But your father was a gentleman who lived in an age of gentlemen, Senhor Rafael, a man capable of dying for a passion."

"By the way," Rafael murmurs in a faint voice, "did he die, Franco?"

"Who?" The old man wonders if he has heard it right.

"Franco. General Franco."

"Ah!" The doctor sounds surprised. "Oh, yes, he died. But why do you ask?"

Then it dawns on him.

"Why, of course, because of your father. It would have been a great moment to him, Senhor Rafael. And it will be a great moment to you, too, when you escape from this place."

The guard puts his head around the door:

"Well, doc? Everything okay?" A warning rather than a question, as if to say: Look, doctor, don't encourage the likes of him to talk. They are important prisoners, yes, but still prisoners, we have to watch out for them. "I'd better be going," says the doctor. He puts the stethoscope into his old, battered valise: "It's a keepsake I've been carrying since my days in the Department," and before rising to his feet he whispers to Rafael: "Don't forget—at eleven o'clock." And turning to Boris: "Complain of pains, Senhor Boris. Moan to your heart's content."

"I'm leaving with you," says Suzana in a firm, assertive voice— now that she's involved in this, she probably wants to make the final arrangements with the doctor and be assured that everything will turn out all right. Before leaving she turns around and throws one final look at her father; a look full of tenderness, naturally; a look of grateful reconciliation. She is about to say something, but at that moment the guard closes the door (without banging it: it's a sick-room now, he can be considerate).

The two of them alone again.

Boris looks at his watch: "Five P.M.," he says. As if talking to himself. He lies down, clasps his hands under his neck. Music from the guard's battery radio filters through the door. A plaintive little waltz in which a pair of country singers bemoan the fact that they've left behind their beloved pampas and their darling mestizas.

In the room the shadows grow denser. Gradually the numbness in Rafael's body recedes and he can move an arm, a leg; he feels better. He sits up on the bed, and right away Boris gets to his feet, concerned:

"No, Rafael, you shouldn't—"

"Leave me alone."

Rafael gets out of bed. Walking with difficulty, he enters the bathroom. He closes the door, turns on the light. The raw brightness of the bulb reveals his face in the mirror. A discomposed face, naturally; but besides being discomposed it looks strange, too. So strange that he is impressed; he has never seen himself looking so *weird* before. It's not just perplexity—or rather, it's perplexity, but of a different kind. A grievous perplexity; what he sees in the mirror is the face of a person undergoing torture. Where does it come from, this startling expression? Could it be caused by something that the doctor injected into him? By the conversation they had before? By everything else? He doesn't know and he doesn't care. What is important now is to react, to not give himself up. *Come on now, Rafael. Make an effort, Rafael.*

It lasts for several minutes, this titanic battle of his will, this conflict of antagonistic muscles; minutes when Rafael sees himself as the loser, defeated by a superior power; but, as he is about to give up, he makes one last effort—and he succeeds. His face undergoes a slow transformation. The corners of his mouth lift, the lips begin to part. The skin beneath his lower eyelids crinkles—he is *smiling*, smiling at his own image. Good, he thinks, relieved, rewarded. Leaning forward, he rests his forehead on the mirror; the coldness of the smooth surface on his damp forehead feels good—and it amuses him, this image he now has of himself, an image distorted by the droll strabismus. He then closes his eyes and remains alone with himself, in peace and quiet. For how long? For a while; when he leaves the bathroom he notices that the guard has already brought their dinner; the tray, untouched, lies on one of the tables. "How are you feeling?" asks Boris. Rafael doesn't make a reply; he lies down. He feels fine; now he feels fine. His head light, his forehead cool; fine. And thus he drifts off into drowsiness; and in this twilight between sleep and wakefulness, it seems to him that all of them are there, standing around the bed—Jonah and Habacuc, Maimonides and Rafael Mendes, all the ones named Rafael Mendes. In silence they look at him. Suddenly he realizes: All of them have the face he saw in the mirror a while ago; all of them are him, he is all of them. Now he understands the *Notebooks of the New Christian;* they are his father's legacy to him—Rafael is no longer beset by doubts. Instead of solutions, fantasies; instead of answers, imaginary possibilities. The perfect message from a perplexed individual, concludes Rafael—and then the figures begin to vanish, and he falls asleep.

He wakes up startled. Boris is shaking him: "It's time," he whispers, "I'll start moaning now."

He lies down, and indeed, he starts moaning. But his performance is so poor and so unconvincing that Rafael can't contain himself; he bursts into laughter, quietly at first, but soon he's roaring with laughter, and a moment later he's laughing his head off, and laughing he rolls on the bed; at times he stops for a moment, his eyes brimming with tears, in order to catch his breath but soon he starts all over again, while Boris, frightened, asks him to stop, for he'll ruin everything, but Rafael, unable to control himself, can't stop laughing, and he laughs and laughs and then Boris begins to laugh too, that's insane, Rafael, we're doomed, this will be the end of us, but he, too, can't control himself, and he laughs and laughs until finally he manages to pull himself together, and he sobers down. Rising to his feet, he draws near Rafael, who has stopped laughing and he, too, gets up. For a moment the two of them stand motionless, their eyes fixed on each other. And then Boris says in a restrained but forceful voice:

"Punch me now, Rafael. Punch me in the belly."

But who are you to be ordering me about?—or so Rafael must be asking himself.

"Come on, punch me," Boris repeats.

"Ah, you dog," moans Rafael. Closing his hand into a fist, he punches Boris in the belly—but not hard enough, Boris barely feels the blow:

"Again. Harder."

Rafael musters all his energy and this time the blow is so heavy that Boris, reeling, steps back and collapses on the bed, moaning. And now he moans properly, and unrestrainedly, as he writhes like a worm—and all of a sudden he winks at Rafael. What a scoundrel, what a royal scoundrel; once again the winner, this crook gets what he wants, and he's now moaning to the letter, thanks to Rafael, thanks to Rafael's fist, and Rafael just stands there, not knowing what to say, what to do.

The door opens; it's the guard.

"What is it, Senhor Boris, what happened?"

"A pain," moans Boris, shrewd Boris. "An unbearable pain."

"You, too?" asks the guard, worried. "Where does it hurt?"

"Here, in my diaphragm," whimpers Boris.

"It couldn't be the food I brought you, could it?" The guard sounds alarmed, afraid that the chief of police will lay the blame on him.

"I don't know," says Boris. "Call the doctor, please, call the doctor."

The guard leaves; a few minutes later Dr. Castellar comes in:

"Wait outside," he tells the guard.

He closes the door behind him.

"Are you ready?" he asks Boris and Rafael, then Rafael and Boris. Boris says he is; but Rafael remains lying motionless.

"I'm not going," he says.

"What?" asks the doctor, surprised.

"I'm not going," Rafael repeats. "I'm staying here."

"But you're going to ruin everything!" The old man is now truly astounded. "What am I going to tell them?"

Boris looks at the doctor; he can't help being amused by the flabbergasted expression on his face. Poor fellow, he is completely floored by what's going on, all he wanted was to make a few dollars and pay a debt of gratitude, or vice-versa, but now he won't be able to do either, in whatever order, the story won't unfold the way he thought it would; it will be a different story, it's already different, and he's unable to make head or tail of it, he doesn't know what's happening, he can't imagine what might happen.

"What are you going to tell the men?" the doctor asks, confused and frightened.

Rafael smiles. He deserves the Gold Tree, this man, this old doctor; instead, what has befallen him is perplexity, the perplexity of generations, from which Rafael has finally freed himself:

"What am I going to tell them?" Rafael shrugs. "Well, my dear fellow. That I was asleep."

"Let's go, doctor," Boris commands. Supported by the doctor, he makes for the door; before leaving, he turns for the last time, gazes at Rafael and it seems that he is about to say something, but refraining, he says nothing. They leave; the door closes.

Rafael Mendes lies down and closes his eyes. He waits for sleep, which will come—and for the dreams . . . Not the eyes of the Prophet, nor the bonfires of the Inquisition, nor the decapitated head of Tiradentes, nor the medieval knight, nor the priestess of Astarte, nor Habacuc, nor Eliezer, nor Naomi, nor any of the Essenes, be they Old or New; nor Maimonides, nor Saladin, nor Bandarra, nor Columbus, nor the Grand-Inquisitor, nor Afonso Sanches; nor the cacique, nor Little Dove, nor the Indians; nor Bento Teixeira, nor Vicente Nunes, nor Joseph de Castro; nor Frans Post; nor Felipe Royz; nor Manoel Beckman, nor João Felipe Bettendorf, nor Maria de Freitas, nor Grácia Tapanhuna; nor Álvaro Mesquita, nor Zambi, nor M'bonga, nor the people of the *quilombos*; nor Bartolomeu Lourenço de Gusmão, nor Bárbara Santos, nor Pedro Telles; nor Diogo Henriques, nor Isabel Henriques; nor the blind *bandeirante*; nor Garibaldi, nor Anita; nor Dr. Débora, nor Microbe, nor Doutor Saturnino, nor the reporter from the *Alerta*, nor Father João de Buarque, nor Sepé Tiarajú; nor any of the many Rafael Mendeses that lie under the earth, bones and dust, dust and bones; none of them will he see; what he will see is a smiling boy in a sailor suit peering at him from amid the branches of the Tree of Life.

DATE DUE

NOV 1 9 1979			
FEB 2 7 1980			
FEB 2 5 198			
3-17-82			
FEB 1 6 1983			
APR 1 6 1986			
APR 2 3 1991			
NOV 0 5 2003			
NOV 0 8 2001			
GAYLORD			PRINTED IN U.S.A.

SOCIAL DEVIANCE
A SUBSTANTIVE ANALYSIS

THE DORSEY SERIES IN ANTHROPOLOGY
AND SOCIOLOGY

EDITOR   ROBIN M. WILLIAMS, JR.   *Cornell University*

SOCIAL DEVIANCE
A SUBSTANTIVE ANALYSIS

ROBERT R. BELL
Professor of Sociology
Temple University

1971
THE DORSEY PRESS Homewood, Illinois 60430
Irwin-Dorsey Limited, Georgetown, Ontario

Library of Congress Catalog Card No. 70–153169
Printed in the United States of America

To my wife, Phyllis,
who is my partner in all that matters

PREFACE

IN A BOOK of this kind there is a great variation in what may be included and how the substantive areas may be analyzed. Therefore, the purpose of this preface is to briefly explain some of the reasons the book has taken the direction it has.

I have been very much interested and influenced by the development of the deviance approach in sociology over the past decade. I wanted to develop my analysis around that approach—even though it does have limitations. Probably the greatest limitation is that the approach is in a rapidly changing stage of development. However, it does provide a method to study deviance both from within and from outside. At the same time, I have also attempted to relate a more traditional social-problems approach to those cases where it seemed appropriate. In the same manner, the concept of subculture has been developed to help the analysis in some of the deviant areas. But I would like to stress that the theoretical approach was developed as an analytic tool and not as a theoretical system.

What may puzzle some readers is the choice of substantive areas that have been included as well as those that have not. Some areas have not been included primarily because they were felt to be too complex to deal with in a single chapter; i.e., minorities, crime, poverty, etc. I also tried to include some areas of deviance that are "relevant"—that are a part of the current scene. This is particularly true of the last three chapters. The relevance factor also in part explains the large number of chapters that

vii

deal with various aspects of sexual deviance. Yet it should be quickly added that my own interests and competencies have influenced my choice in many substantive areas. In other words, this book on deviance is based in part on one sociologist's views as to what are the relevant areas of deviance and which are those he feels the most qualified to write about.

There are several other factors that have influenced the direction this book has taken. For example, it is a book about deviance in the United States; and references to cross-cultural materials are for the most part to help point up the nature of American deviance. I have also developed a brief historical background in many of the areas of deviance. This has been done because I believed that historical perspective is often basic to any understanding of deviance in today's society.

Finally, it should be mentioned that my dealing with many areas of deviance now undergoing rapid change means that some points in the book may be obsolete very quickly. For example, in such areas as abortion or drug use the laws may change before this book even reaches the reader. Therefore, in many respects this book refers to deviance at a given point in time.

I would like to thank Michael Gordon, University of Connecticut, for his critical reading of the manuscript. I would also like to thank Barbara Bendzynska and Tanya Johnson for their work in typing the manuscript. My greatest appreciation as always goes to my wife for her many hours of critical reading and editing of this book.

February, 1971   Robert R. Bell

CONTENTS

CHAPTER 1

THE CONCEPTUAL
APPROACH

A MAJOR INTEREST in the early days of American sociology centered around the social problems of those days. The American sociologists looked around in the rapidly developing urban areas and saw what they felt were many undesirable patterns of behavior. Often their interest was not in why the problems existed, but rather in attempts to eliminate the problems. It was common for many early sociologists actually to be involved in various types of social reform, frequently with little knowledge about what they wanted to reform.

Around the beginning of the 20th century, as American sociology developed, most early sociologists came from rural backgrounds and were concerned with the new urban influences and their new patterns of social behavior. As Mills has pointed out, most early social problems arose because of urban deterioration of certain traditional values. Those were values that could only really flourish in a relatively homogeneous and primarily rural environment. Therefore the early "problems" discussed typically concerned urban behavior, and even when rural problems were discussed, they were seen as the result of urban encroachment. So the early view of the disorganizational characteristic of social problems was quite often "merely the absence of that *type* of organization associated with the stuff of primary-group communities having Christian and Jeffer-

1

sonian legitimations."[1] In general it may be said that the traditional idea of a social problem emerged initially as an attitude of middle-class reformers around the end of the 18th and the beginning of the 19th centuries. This idea resulted not only from the stresses created by the new urban industrial order but also because of the new scientific ideology and a growing humanitarianism.[2]

In the early part of the twentieth century sociological interest started to shift away from social reform. More and more sociologists began to study social problems as sociological problems. This meant they were studied with increasing objectivity and less concern with directed social change.

During the 1930's the interest of sociologists shifted increasingly away from the study of social problems and social movements. The interest began to lie in a systematic approach to the analysis of social and cultural sources of deviant behavior. It was argued that "the sociological task was to explain variations in rates of deviant behavior, not its incidence, and functional theory emerged as a means of explanation."[3] Even where the interest in social problems continued over the years, not only did the approach change, but also the substantive areas that were considered to be social problems. Any substantive area can only be seen as a social problem when related to a given society at a given point in time. "A look through the textbooks in the field over so short a period as the last 25 or 30 years would be enough to demonstrate that there is no necessary continuation in any of the subjects covered. Several decades ago poverty was the dominant theme, and today it is discussed briefly or disappeared all together."[4] The above statement was written in 1963 and itself shows how rapidly what is of interest as a social problem changes, because today poverty is once again a social problem area of high importance to sociologists.

Often in the past there was no theoretical perspective developed and used in the study of social problems. This was especially true in the writing of textbooks where the author would present an introductory chapter that would define social problems, their alleged causes and cures, their extent, and so forth. The rest of the book would then be a series of distinct chapters dealing with social problems but not conceptually related to one another in any fashion. Whenever a theoretical approach was

[1] Mills, C. Wright, "The Professional Ideology of Social Pathologists," in Mark Lefton, James K. Skipper Jr., and Charles H. McCaghy, *Approaches to Deviance* (New York: Appleton-Century-Crofts, 1968), p. 15.

[2] Bernard, Jessie, *Social Problems at Mid-Century* (New York: The Dryden Press, 1957), pp. 90–91.

[3] Reiss, Albert J., "The Study of Deviant Behavior: Where the Action Is," in Lefton, Skipper and McCaghy, *op. cit.*, pp. 56–7.

[4] Petersen, William and David Matza, *Social Controversy* (Belmont, California: Wadsworth Publishing Co., Inc., 1963), p. 3.

developed it tended to be related to a social disorganization model. The social disorganizational approach looked at the harmonious and inharmonious aspects of the structure of society. It looked at the ways in which basic activities in the organization of a society were either mutually reinforcing or mutually contradictory. "Social disorganization may then be conceptualized in terms of some conflicts among norms and values in a society. Social disorganization deals with ways in which activities which are in some sense the product of, and legitimized by the social structure conflict with one another."[5]

One of the problems with the disorganizational approach is that when it is applied to deviant behavior it tends to overvalue conformity, implicitly if not explicitly. "There is a kind of halo around conformity and almost any kind of nonconformity tends to be viewed as a problem."[6] Of course, given certain values in a society, disorganization might be seen in a desirable goal. For social organization, as well as for social disorganization, stress may be generated. For example, the stress in social organization "may be exploitive, characterized by gross inequities that create the stresses of poverty and illness in a disenfranchised class."[7]

Whatever the theoretical explanation given to social problems, a social problem is in part the result of a discrepancy between the values of a society and the actual state of that society. Therefore, a primary motive for the study of social problems has been to look for ways to prevent, control, and ameliorate. Basically, social problems can be said to exist when they are so defined as such by members of a society. Initially, this may be by intellectuals, social scientists, or policymakers, but eventually the definition must be accepted by at least one broad stratum of society. This clearly implies that underlying each social problem is generally a difference of opinion or a clash of values.[8]

Jessie Bernard has suggested that three types of criteria have been used in the past to determine whether or not a given stress situation was judged to be a social problem.[9] The three criteria were:

1. *Humanitarian-sentimental.* Does the situation cause pain or suffering? This is intrinsically bad and therefore anything which produces this should be changed, reformed, or done away with. However, the absence of suffering does not necesarily imply the absence of a social problem.

2. *Utilitarian.* The situation is a social problem because it imposes costs on the rest of society, either official in the form of taxes or unofficial in the form of voluntary contributions. Often in the past anything was

---

[5] Turner, Ralph H., "Value-Conflict in Social Disorganization," in Lefton, Skipper and McCaghy, *op. cit.*, p. 24.

[6] Bernard, *op. cit.*, p. 139.

[7] *Ibid.*

[8] Petersen and Matza, *op. cit.*, p. 2.

[9] Bernard, *op. cit.*, pp. 105–6.

viewed as a social problem which was defined as interfering with business or disturbing the peace. Within this context sickness would be considered a social problem, not because it caused pain or suffering, but because it slowed down production or because it cost the taxpayer money.

3. *Dysfunctionality.* Anything that threatens a group, a nation, a society, or a culture constitutes a social problem. The threat that constitutes the social problem exists within the group and is not something outside it.

It is clear that these criteria have a limited application to what might be defined as social problems today. In one respect they represent a simplified cause and effect view of social problems that often existed in the past.

By the 1950's the concern with social problems as traditionally studied had lost prestige and interest among most American sociologists. To a great extent this was due to the scientific view of sociology that emerged in the 1930's and reached its peak following the end of World War II. Jessie Bernard represents the approach of the scientific sociologist toward the traditional study of social problems. She writes that so long as those who studied social problems "substituted moralistic judgments for careful observations and interpretations they could not be scientific. So long as they assumed answers instead of looking for them, they were not scientific. So long as their terminology reflected a condemnatory attitude toward people, they were not scientific."[10]

Many of the areas that historically have been treated as social problems have come to represent a number of the important substantive areas of sociological specialization today. For example, delinquency, criminology, minority groups, problem areas of the family, and so forth. In the broadest sense social problems came to be distinguished from other types of problems by their close connection with moral values and social institutions. Merton points out that "they are social in the sense that they pertain to human relationships and to the normative contexts in which all human relationships exist. They are problems in the sense that they represent interruptions in the expected or desired scheme of things; violations of the right or the proper as a society defines these qualities; dislocations in the social patterns and relationships that a society cherishes."[11] The modern argument has been that social problems should be studied in the same way that other forms of human behavior are studied by sociologists. "As a scientist, the sociologist has a professional responsibility to deal with such matters as crime, suicide, narcotics, and ethnic tensions" in the same way as he approaches the rest of society.[12]

---

[10] *Ibid.*, p. 117.

[11] Merton, Robert K. and Robert A. Nishet, *Contemporary Social Problems* (New York: Harcourt, Brace & World, Inc., 1961), p. 4.

[12] *Ibid.*, p. 9.

The belief also developed that social problems should be studied not only for what they shed in the way of insight on themselves, but also for what they may contribute to the better understanding of the rest of society. This is based on.the assumption that social problems, even the worst of them, generally have a functional relationship to the rest of society. For example, many have suggested that even prostitution exists only as a reflection of the value that is placed on the monogamous family and the sanctity of marriage. In fact it may be argued that all social problems have some value to society even if it is nothing more than providing careers for those who deal with or attempt to eliminate the social problems. This suggests an irony in that those who supposedly work the hardest to eliminate a social problem often have the most to lose if they are successful. For example, what would happen to the Federal Narcotics Bureau if there were no more illegal narcotic users?

Ultimately any study of social problems can be understood only in light of what a society holds to be right and proper. "At bottom, social problems are problems of moral value, they are problems because the behavior involved in these breakdowns and deviations is widely regarded as immoral, illegal, or potentially destructive of some established institution."[13] But basically the social problem approach has lost its utility in sociology because it has not provided a theoretical framework for understanding what constitutes social deviancy and what the interrelationships are of the areas of social deviancy with the rest of society. Because of the inabilities of the traditional social problem approach a new perspective has emerged since the 1950's—although its roots go much further back.

THE SOCIAL DEVIANCY APPROACH

In the 1950's and 1960's there developed in American sociology a rapidly increasing interest in the study of deviancy.[14] To a great extent

[13] Merton and Nisbet, op. cit., p. 11.

[14] See: Becker, Howard S., Outsiders: Studies in the Sociology of Deviance (New York: Macmillan, 1963); Becker, Howard S., The Other Side: Perspectives on Deviance (New York: Free Press, 1964); Clinard, Marshall B., ed., Anomie and Deviant Behavior (New York: Free Press, 1964); Cohen, Albert K., Deviance and Control (Englewood Cliffs, N.J.: Prentice-Hall, 1966); Dentler, Robert A. and Kai T. Erikson, "The Functions of Deviance in Groups," Social Problems, 7 (Fall, 1959), pp. 98–107; Erikson, Kai T., Wayward Puritans: A Study in the Sociology of Deviance (New York: Wiley, 1966); Gibbs, Jack P., "Conception of Deviant Behavior: The Old and the New," Pacific Sociological Review, Spring, 1966; Lemert, Edwin Jr., Human Deviance, Social Problems and Social Control (Englewood Cliffs, N.J.: Prentice-Hall, Inc., 1967); Matza, David, Delinquency and Drift (New York: Wiley, 1964); Matza, David, Becoming Deviant (New York: Prentice-Hall, Inc., 1969); Rodman, Hyman, "The Lower-Class Value Stretch," Social Forces, 42 (1960), pp. 205–15; Rubington, Earl and Martin S. Weinberg, Deviance: The Interactionist Perspective (New York: Macmillan Co., 1968); and, Wilkens, Leslie T., Social Deviance (Englewood Cliffs, N.J.: Prentice-Hall, 1964).

this new interest was due to a dissatisfaction with the previous definitions of social problems and the attempts to explain those phenomena. Social deviance has been defined as "behavior which violates institutionalized expectations, that is, expectations which are shared and recognized as legitimate within the social system."[15] This definition suggests that deviant behavior is a reflection of how persons perform and the structure of the group within which they perform. In other words deviance has both an individual and a group perspective, although the usual pattern for analysis is to look at the interaction of deviants within a social setting. A somewhat different way of defining deviance is that it refers to behavior by an individual where the group responds with the feeling of danger, embarrassment, or irritation and where "they bring special sanctions to bear against the person who exhibits it."[16] Erickson goes on to make the important point that "deviance is not a property *inherent* in any particular kind of behavior, it is a property *conferred upon* that behavior by the people who come into direct contact with it."[17] For example, if one uses a narcotic he is not a deviant simply because he has taken the drug. If the drug is given to him in the hospital for medical treatment it is not defined as deviance, but if it is given to him by an illegal "pusher" it is.

The notion of deviance is implicit in the very idea of society. This point was made many years ago by Durkheim and has been accepted by sociologists ever since. Durkheim wrote "Imagine a society of saints, a perfect cloister of exemplary individuals. Crimes, properly so called, will there be unknown; but faults which appear venial to the layman will create there the same scandal that the ordinary offense does in the ordinary consciousness."[18] As David Matza points out, the moral improvement of a society will not in itself diminish deviation since the very fact of moral uplift will suggest new and more demanding standards of conduct.[19] For example, in Victorian England social morality reached new levels of "purity"—but that simply meant one was defined as "impure" for doing much less than during an earlier or later period.

There are several major contributions that sociology has made to the study of deviancy. One is that "persistent deviancy typically is not an individual or group innovation, it has a history in particular locales."[20] This means that many areas responsible for deviance have existed for some time, and attempts to adapt have contributed to a history and to certain

---

[15] Dentler and Erikson, *op. cit.*, p. 98.

[16] Erikson, *op. cit.*, p. 6.

[17] *Ibid.*

[18] Durkheim, Emile, *The Rules of Sociological Method* (Chicago: The University of Chicago Press, 1938), pp. 68–69.

[19] Matza, *Becoming Deviant, op. cit.*, p. 13.

[20] Matza, *Delinquency and Drift, op. cit.*, p. 63.

systems of behavior. The point of time is important to social deviance because when deviance persists it often becomes patterned (although not all deviance is systematic nor is all systematic deviance socially organized). There may be systematic individual deviance where there is no interaction between the participants. That is, many deviants practice in private or as solitary individuals. For example, transvestites follow similar patterns but do not usually interact with one another.

Another major contribution to the study of deviancy by sociologists has been suggested by Howard Becker. He argues that the new approach to the study of deviance always involves an interactional process between at least two kinds of people. "Those who commit (or are said to have committed) a deviant act and the rest of society, perhaps divided into several groups itself. The two groups are seen in complementary relationship. One cannot exist without the other; indeed, they are functions of one another in the strict mathematical sense."[21] This definition clearly suggests the possible development of subcultures, a concept which will be discussed later in the chapter. The new approach differs from the earlier sociological concern with social pathology where deviance was seen as direct evidence of social disorganization.

The new approach to deviancy generally follows the model of the scientific approach, rather than that of the earlier value commitment or directed social change. David Matza defines this approach in terms of neutrality. Matza writes that "neutrality, buttressed as it is by the philosophy of science, is the sentiment toward deviant phenomena commended by most contemporary sociologists. We are to empathize with neither the correctional enterprise nor its deviant subjects."[22]

The new approach to the study of deviancy has in it several research implications. First, the researcher is dependent to a high degree on what those of deviant groups give him in the way of information and insight. Because the deviant is often in an activity that is illegal he must be careful in terms of his own protection. Therefore the misleading of the researcher may be a real problem in the study of deviant phenomena. As Matza points out, since "authority may frequently intervene to counteract or arrest the deviant tendency, deviant persons must frequently be devious."[23] In other words, deviousness is a part of the pattern of much deviancy, and being devious in the presence of outsiders may be seen as a normal feature of persons participating in deviant phenomena.[24]

Secondly, the new stress on deviancy means that at least some new questions are being asked in research. In the past, whenever it was possible

---

[21] Becker, *op. cit.*, p. 2.
[22] Matza, *Becoming Deviant, op. cit.*, p. 37.
[23] *Ibid.*, p. 39.
[24] *Ibid.*

to identify the deviant individuals making up a social problem area the research tended to concentrate on the question of cause. For example, in the areas of criminal behavior the overwhelming concern in the past has been to try to find out why some people become criminals while others do not. With attention "almost exclusively focused on the underlying forces pushing individuals into deviance there is relatively little consideration of just *what* the deviance itself is. Indeed, various specific forms of deviance are often viewed as being caused by the same underlying forces."[25] It will be seen in the presentation of most of the research in the chapters ahead that the focus of study in deviancy has been much less concerned with the study of *causes* and much more with the analysis of *consequences* of deviancy for both deviants and for the broader society.

In the discussion to follow much of what will be said is drawn from the thinking of those who represent the new approach to the study of deviancy that has developed since the mid-1950's. The interest will be in looking at the meaning of deviance, its relationships with the rest of society, some legal aspects of deviancy and the concept of deviant subcultures.

MEANINGS OF DEVIANCE

First of all a distinction must be made between deviant behavior on the level of social interaction and deviant behavior of basically an individual or psychological nature. One illustration of this distinction would be where a person believes he is being injured by the magical practices of his associates, and as a result would be diagnosed as a psychotic and paranoiac if he lived in a university community. However, if he were a member of a group which generally believed in magical practices the belief in magic might be entirely expected and normal. In fact, if he did not share the general belief in magic he might be thought of as deviant by his associates.[26] The above illustrates the cultural relativity of social vs. individual deviancy. Of course, there are some forms of deviancy that are almost always deviant and almost always individual in all societies, for example, the committing of incest.

There may also be statistical groupings of individual deviants who do not socially interact with one another. For example, most transvestites have in common a particular sexual orientation and may have similar behavior patterns, but unless they socially interact with one another in some symbolic ways they are not social group deviants. It does not appear to be common for transvestites to have any great influence on one another

[25] Schur, Edwin M., *Crimes without Victims: Deviant Behavior and Public Policy* (Englewood Cliffs, N.J.: Prentice-Hall, 1965), p. 2.

[26] Lindesmith, Alfred R. and Anselm L. Strauss, *Social Psychology* (New York: Dryden Press, 1956), p. 665.

through social interaction. Therefore, they would most accurately be defined as individual deviants who make up a statistical category called transvestites.

What does the term deviance imply? It probably suggests a number of different meanings depending on the respondent. Possibly the simplest and most common definition of deviance is a statistical one, that is, defining anything as deviant that varies too far from the average in society. Put another way, that which is defined as "normal" is frequently that which is statistically average. As Simmons points out "this is the basis of most psychological tests. If you fall near the average you're okay; if you fall too far from it you're not."[27]

Thus, basically, deviance implies some straying on the part of persons from certain patterns or norms. People may therefore be classified as straying on the basis of a number of criteria. For example, "the clarity of the path, the distance from the path, the auspices under which the path is constructed or commended, whether one strays from the path in isolation or in company, the penalty, the motives, commonly imputed for straying and so forth."[28] Yet, given the complexities in defining paths of deviancy when all is said and done, "we inevitably return to the wise observation that there are many kinds of deviance and that deviance is in some measure a matter of degree."[29]

As previously suggested it is important to keep in mind that there is always some deviance in society. Complete deviancy or complete conformity represent "ideal" types at either end of a continuum and in no society is either extreme ever achieved. Somewhere between the extremes in a society is the range of tolerance acceptable to the society. This allows for some deviancy's being acceptable to society but sets up limits beyond which social and often legal punishments are the consequence of deviance. For example, the drinking of alcoholic beverages is accepted in society so long as the drinking does not go beyond a certain point—a point seen as threatening in some way to society.

It might also be added that not only does society define some deviancy as acceptable, but it may even take some satisfaction in the deviance it tolerates. Sagarin has suggested that in the United States there is often pride in tolerating nonconformity. Providing that the nonconformist "operates within certain socially stipulated limits, the nonconformist is almost glorified; however, when he goes outside these limits, he is pilloried."[30] Given this kind of acceptance Sagarin suggests that when some kinds of deviance are glorified by society this may arouse in other deviants

[27] Simmons, J. L., *Deviants* (Berkeley, Calif.: The Glendessary Press, 1969), p. 21.

[28] Matza, *op. cit.*, p. 10.

[29] *Ibid.*

[30] Sagarin, Edward, *Odd Man In: Societies of Deviants in America* (Chicago: Quadrangle Books, 1969), p. 240.

the hope that they too may become a part of the mainstream of society "if not by becoming conformists themselves, then by forcing a redefinition of their deviant characteristics as acceptable conformity."[31]

Often the extent and the nature of society's reactions towards deviants will be determined by how the deviant presents himself to society. That is, often among any given group of deviants there is a range of possibilities as to how a given deviant may present himself. This will be reflected in the particular patterns of behavior he follows in his deviance. For example, a homosexual male may live with one partner for several years, circulate with other discrete homosexuals in a circumscribed way, and not fill the stereotype of homosexual social "traits." By contrast another homosexual may center his life in the public places of homosexuality, aggressively seek out new sex partners, and make it known to the broader society that he is a homosexual. In these two cases it is how one presents his homosexual "self" to the broader society that determines how he will be seen. The amount of interaction and the number of others involved in a deviant activity is not simply a uniform function of a type of deviancy. So in many types of deviancy the individual has some choice in selecting behavior patterns that will determine the extent to which the broader society knows of his deviancy.

Some deviants bring attention to their behavior by renouncing themselves to the broader society. This is usually done when the deviant shouts out that he has sinned and wants to repent. This serves the important function of reaffirming the validity and "rightness" of the norms of society. For example, contrast the social reactions to two unmarried, pregnant girls: one of them says she has done wrong and is sorry she is pregnant; the other girl says she is glad she is pregnant, will have her baby, and has no intention of getting married. In the first case the girl is saying the social values were right and she is wrong and regrets her action. The second girl is saying that the social values are not right for her and she is not sorry for what she did. As another illustration, society can accept deviant acts that are seen as those of sick people because they leave the values and norms intact—they are seen as not responsible for their actions and the assumption is that if they were not sick they would abide by the values and norms. In general, a society will accept deviancy when it does not threaten the norms and values held to be important.

It would also appear that for many people some deviancy has a mysterious quality—a quality of the unknown, the strange, and sometimes the exotic. For example, even though most Americans have been saturated by the mass media with the marijuana phenomenon they still know little about it factually, but rather respond within the context of the unknown and mysterious. This means that often a relatively few persons are func-

---

[31] *Ibid.*

tionally able to define what is deviance, and when the mass media go along with their definitions then the few often become the unquestioned definer for the majority. It would appear that some forms of deviance as they get to be better known and understood in society become less defined as deviance. As a result the behavior or attitudes may shift from being defined as deviant to being defined as an irregularity. "This is why pre-marital sex is no longer considered deviant in most quarters and why the acceptance of marijuana as a mild intoxicant is becoming wide spread. But as long as something remains deviant most people will know little of it, and as long as people don't know, it is likely to remain deviant."[32]

Frequently what is defined as deviance, as well as the kind of definitions that go with the behavior, is a result of social class or power differences in society. For example, it is often the welfare worker who defines for the poor, the physician who defines for the woman wanting an abortion, or the priest for the woman seeking birth control help. Inherent in the thinking about many areas of deviance is the assumption that some persons are better able to decide for others than those persons are for themselves. This is a kind of "playing God" syndrome which is not always based on fact but very often on subjective evaluation and the power to control or influence the deviant. This also helps to explain why the deviant is very often hostile to those in power—he is being treated like a child and told what would be better for him.

Because there is never universal agreement on what is deviance there is always the potential for conflict. People look at the world from angles influenced by slightly different value systems, and often what becomes the prevailing value system of what is right is not determined by any evaluation of "rightness," but rather is based on the power to impose re-wards and punishments related to what one defines as right. Even when there is no conflict, people vary by different reference groups and there-fore deviance is generally something that is relative and subjective. As a result, different judges often react very differently to the same behavior. As Simmons points out, "everyone, square or hip, straight or criminal, is outraged by something."[33]

Basically the ultimate measurement of whether or not an act is de-viant depends on how others who are socially significant in power and influence define the act. One could commit any act, but it is not deviant in its social consequences if no elements of society react to it. And in any given society there is always a problematic element in what the response will be. Those who commit deviancy must be in a social setting where their behavior will be defined as such for there to be real social conse-quences to their behavior.

---

[32] Simmons, *op. cit.*, pp. 8–9.

[33] *Ibid.*, p. 19.

It is clear that there is a high level of relativity to what will be defined as deviancy and the sanctions that will go with the definitions. It is always important to keep in mind that what will be defined as deviant will vary by time and place. One reason for differences in response to deviance over time is that a society will for various reasons on some occasions direct their attention at some forms of deviancy at a given time, but not at another. This is seen in the various attentions over time directed at gambling, drug use, homosexuality, and so forth. Another reason for different responses to deviance may be determined by who commits the act and who has been defined as being harmed. For example, this is often the case for the middle class defining as juvenile delinquents lower-class boys but not middle-class boys, although the behavior may be the same. Still another variation in defining deviancy may be due to the consequences of an act. A girl is generally not strongly condemned for having premarital sexual experiences; however, if she gets pregnant she may be subjected to strong punishment.

From the discussion and example it is clear that deviancy is a "naming process." That is, regardless of the act the behavior must be defined as deviant by some important or significant elements of society. However, the person who is defined as a deviant may or may not define himself in the same way. The relationship between deviance and the broader society is a basic one. It has sometimes been assumed that if the broader society defines persons as deviants then they are deviants. While this may be true for the broader society it is not necessarily so from the perspective of those defined as deviants. The deviants may not accept the definitions applied to them or they may define themselves as deviant for different reasons.

From the point of view of the broader society deviance is what it defines as such and not something inherent in particular values and patterns. Erikson has pointed out that at any given time "the 'worse' people in the community are considered its criminals, the 'sickest' its patients, no matter how serious these conditions may appear according to some universal standard."[34] Therefore it is not the forms of behavior *per se* that distinguish deviants from non-deviants; "it is the response of the conventional and conforming members of the society who identify and interpret behavior as deviant which sociologically transforms persons into deviants."[35] The deviant is one to whom that label has successfully been applied; deviant behavior that people so label.[36] Erikson writes:

From a sociological standpoint, deviance can be defined as conduct which is generally thought to require the attention of social control agencies—that

---

[34] Erikson, *op. cit.*, p. 26.

[35] Kitsuse, John I., "Societal Reaction to Deviant Behavior: Problems of Theory and Method," in Becker, *op. cit.*, p. 88.

[36] Becker, *Outsiders, op. cit.*, p. 9.

is conduct about which "something should be done." Deviance is not a property *inherent* in certain forms of behavior; it is the property conferred upon these forms by the audiences which directly or indirectly witness them. Sociologically, then, the critical variable in the study of deviance is the social audience rather than individual person, since it is the audience which eventually decides whether or not any given action or actions will become a visible case of deviation.[37]

Closely related to the definitions of deviancy, and often even implied in the definitions, is an attempt to define the alleged causes. In the Western world the oldest and most common view of the causes of deviancy has been one of individual pathology. That is, the something wrong exists in the individual. In an early day the deviant was thought to be possessed of devils, while later on he was believed to have genetic defects. Because his "problem" was seen as inside of him the belief was that generally there was little that could be done for him. He was either punished, destroyed, or removed from the rest of society. Under the biological or genetic interpretation of deviancy there was something believed inherent in the deviant that set him apart from the non-deviant. For example, from Lombroso to the present, criminals have been defined as biologically distinctive in one way or another. However, in recent decades the definitions of the causes of deviance have for the most part shifted from genetic to ones of illness. That is, the view of the deviant moves from his being seen as morally or biologically defective to being seen as having psychological incapacities. This has meant that often society has shifted its views of how deviants should be dealt with from punishment to treatment.

It would seem clear that deviance cannot be explained on any simple cause and effect basis, because it represents a diverse phenomenon with complex causes. "Sometimes there is a biological anomaly, sometimes a disrupted home, sometimes bad companions, sometimes too little legitimate opportunity, sometimes too much pressure, and so on."[38] In discussing the various areas of deviance in the chapters ahead an attempt will be made to look at some of the causal suggestions, and in general it will be seen that for some areas of deviancy there are a number of causal explanations given.

Before leaving the discussion about causes of deviancy it is necessary to indicate the possible effects of mass media. It seems clear that the amount of exposure that the mass media, and especially television, give to almost any activity influences how it will be viewed and the importance that will be attached to it. For example, in recent years the hippies were undoubtedly made to be socially "important" to a great extent by the mass media. By 1967 there was not a major magazine or newspaper in the United States that had not devoted space to the hippie phenomenon. This was

---

[37] Erikson, Kai T., "Notes on the Sociology of Deviance," in Becker, *The Other Side, op. cit.*, pp. 10–11.

[38] Simmons, *op. cit.*, p. 51.

also true of radio and television. The possible influences of mass media coverage on the many different kinds of social deviance will be discussed with some of the specific deviances.

As there are many theories attempting to explain the causes of social deviance there are also many attempts to suggest what might be done to cure social deviance. It is almost always the case that when cures are suggested the assumption has been made that a cure is needed. That is, one might assume that the first level of consideration would be to see if a cure in an area is needed—but this is rarely ever a serious consideration. Often the deviant also assumes a "cure" is needed without serious question. When the deviant agrees to the cure recommended for him he is agreeing with the definer who has designated him as a deviant needing help. For example, when a homosexual seeks out psychiatric help to rid himself of his homosexuality he is in effect agreeing with those who have defined him as a deviant. "There is a consensus between the designator and the deviant; his dependence confirms the norm."[39]

As suggested earlier most views of the causes of deviance are on the personal rather than the social level. Therefore, most suggestions for cures are aimed at individual alteration rather than at social change. As Wilkens points out, "if one takes the view that crime is identical with sin it is likely that one will restrict one's thinking to remedial measures affecting only the individual."[40] Therefore, most curative theories follow the lines of trying to affect the individual, either through force, medical treatment, or education.

A common view of individual responsibility for deviance is that the person is willfully aggressive against the norms of society or is too weak to follow the norms that most people do. If the deviant is willfully aggressive, for example commits criminal acts, his treatment will generally be punishment and imprisonment. On the other hand if he is a drug addict, which is often defined as his being a weak-willed individual, he will be treated in a repressive manner. He is therefore not allowed to have legal drugs and he must then seek them out through illegal sources. So one possible consequence of this "cure" of not allowing him to get legal drugs is to intensify his deviance. He is placed in a position where it will probably be necessary to resort to deceit and crime in order to support his drug habit. His drug behavior "is a consequence of the public reaction to the deviance rather than a consequence of the inherent qualities of the deviant act."[41]

It is often very hard for many Americans to accept the fact that for

---

[39] Gusfield, Joseph R., "On Legislating Morals: The Symbolic Process of Designating Deviance," *California Law Review*, January, 1968, p. 60.

[40] Wilkens, Leslie T., *Social Deviance* (Englewood Cliffs, N.J.: Prentice-Hall, 1964), p. 73.

[41] Becker, *op. cit.*, pp. 34–5.

many social problems there are no real cures. This is in part due to the exaggerated belief that American "know-how" can find a solution to almost anything. This belief explains why many Americans willingly turn to all sorts of "quacks"—because many believe that those who say they have a solution must have because there "should" be one. People are often attracted to a simplistic view of how to resolve problems. This is reflected in such things as *Reader's Digest* articles, "Dear Abby" columns, or in television commercials. People are constantly told about new "miracle drugs" that never reach the market, to stand firm and your children will respect you, or that all your dating problems can be solved by using a new deodorant. But cures to social problems may be nonexistent or very complex; rarely are they simple. It may also be that some cures work only for some people; for example, Alcoholics Anonymous works for some alcoholics but not for all. In actual fact it may be that the passage of time cures more deviancy than any psychological or social programs.

Generally, the assumption is made that if a cure can be found, and can be applied successfully, then the problem will be solved. However, it sometimes happens that when one problem is alleviated or cured, that very success may contribute to the emergence of a new problem. For example, in the past one problem in the United States was the second-class status of the woman. And as this changed and she achieved greater rights as a human being they were not always in an area she would define as desirable. That is, not only did she achieve greater opportunities for education and occupation closer to those of the man, but she also achieved a greater opportunity to become a drug addict or an alcoholic. Therefore, one important question in looking at the cures of social problems or deviance is what the consequences of success are. It may be that the cure is not always worth the consequences.

DEVIANCE AND THE COMMUNITY

It has been stressed that deviance is common to all societies, but that what is acceptable is not inherent in the activity but rather dependent on how the society views the activity. Deviant behavior is therefore common and natural to a society and is a "normal and inevitable part of social life, as is its denunciation, regulation, and prohibition. Deviation is implicit in the moral character of society." Sartre wrote that "to give oneself laws and to create the possibility of disobeying them come to the same thing."[42] In deviancy, then, there is always the relationship between individuals engaging in particular patterns of behavior and the community which defines that behavior. As pointed out, different societies may define the same thing in different ways. For example, norms about pre-

---

[42] Quoted in Matza, *ob. cit.*, p. 13.

marital chastity for the female may fall anywhere along a continuum from high permissiveness to high authoritarian control. As another illustration Wilkens points out that a property-owning society will define deviance with respect to property-owning concepts, beyond which action will not be allowed. And if the deviance is carried out the action will be defined as illegitimate or illegal. By contrast, a nomadic society will not have any such concept of property deviance.[43]

In the past when the power of the community was directed at defining an activity as a social problem or as unacceptable deviance there was little that the deviants could or did do in any organized or systematic way. However, this is changing because of an increasing tendency for deviants to organize both defensively and offensively. A few years ago when deviants sought each other out it was usually for mutual support and protection. For example, male homosexuals would go to their own vacation spots to escape critical treatment from the broader society. But now some homosexuals are not attempting to escape but rather are taking the offensive and aggressively attacking the dominant society by insisting on their rights to do what they want sexually. Many other persons who have been defined as deviants are being provided with advice and guidance on how to avoid moral and often legal restrictions placed on their behavior. For example, one can now get advice on how to avoid the military draft, how to avoid narcotics agents, how to get an abortion, or even how to give oneself an abortion. This would seem to be a logical extension of the old American tradition on how to avoid moral and legal restrictions. For many years there has been a great body of information on how to avoid paying income tax or how to pursue "sharp" business practices—some legal, some illegal, and some highly questionable.

It is also important to look at the deviant in relation to the broader society as well as the broader society with reference to deviancy. One important question with regard to the deviant in society is how much choice he has in his deviancy. Very often people become deviants because they have little or no control over the situation. The person may be a part of a deviant social group because he has been socialized to it, or because he was in a particular social setting at a given time. An illustration of the first might be a child growing up in the black lower class, and an illustration of the second a teen-ager as a part of an adolescent subculture. However, there are also in most societies some people who "choose" a deviant career *because* they know it offends an important value of the broader society or because they have a need to challenge some dominant values. The rebellious or militant college student would in some cases be an illustration of this type.

In the late 1960's it became increasingly common for persons deliber-

---

[43] Wilkens, *op. cit.*, p. 49.

ately to turn against some of the values of society and sometimes deliberately to become deviants. When they did, they very often sought each other out and became part of deviant social groups, for example, "hippies," draft resisters, the "new left," and so forth. Of course, with time the new deviant groups frequently threw forth their own deviant sub-groups; for example, the splinter groups that have emerged from the "new left." Often in this situation the conflict between splinter groups becomes greater and more intense than that between the sub-groups and the larger society. So in terms of values and behavior patterns there may be a number of different levels of social deviancy with each being deviant relative to the others.

It is obvious that for most deviants there are some problems encountered in filling their deviant role demands. For example, the woman engaged in extramarital "swinging" has to reconcile her new sexual role with the monogamous sex life role she was socialized to. It is clear that certain kinds of deviants have a great deal of difficulty maintaining their deviant roles. For many, the strain of fitting statuses, roles, and selves together is too great or not worth the effort. "In the first case, certification seems unattainable, and the person experiences no interior peace, no real self-acceptance. In the second case, his certification is no blessing, but actually a curse."[44] These writers go on to point out that the neurotic homosexual is a good example of the first case and the drug addict an illustration of the second. "Failure or success in certification comes to the same end. The homosexual wishes to resolve his unconscious conflicts whereas the addict wants to give up his addiction."[45] The high strain for the individual practicing deviancy is also often reflected in his steady practice of duplicity in trying to explain his behavior to the broader society. There are two possible consequences to duplicity for the deviant. "It may make it possible to knit together one's repertory of statuses, roles, and selves into a plausible whole, in which case the person comes to believe the story himself he has invented and told to other people. Or the strain of duplicity is so great that he must ultimately give it up."[46] Furthermore, the deviant is often caught in a position of filling unsupported statuses that are also sometimes illegal. Therefore, one would generally expect that the deviant, in contrast with the non-deviant, would have more problems with his self identity.

However, to point out that deviants often have role problems and confusion is not to say that all deviants are unhappy and would like to change their style of life. The ideology of the broader society generally

---

[44] Rubington and Weinberg, *op. cit.*, p. 322.
[45] *Ibid.*
[46] *Ibid.*, p. 319.

SOCIAL DEVIANCE

assumes this to be true, but the facts suggest otherwise. The deviant's degree of frustration or unhappiness will often be determined by the kind of deviance he is involved in. For example, as Lemert points out, persons who deviate because of such things as stuttering, systemative check forgery, alcoholism, and drug addiction are marked by the almost total absence of any durable pleasure. "Instead their lot is one of gnawing anxiety, pain, unhappiness and despair, in some cases ending with deterioration or suicide."[47] But by contrast may other deviants appear, by any reliable measure, to be just as happy as the non-deviant population. Very often to the deviant, his behavior can be quite reasonable and rational and from where he sits, with his needs and attitudes, what he does is quite logical. It is possible that many homosexuals are as happy or happier than many heterosexuals. Deviance and happiness or role satisfaction is not an either/or proposition; that is, some deviants are unhappy and some happy, as are non-deviants. Yet, statistically there is probably more unhappiness and role frustration for deviants than for non-deviants.

It may be that most of the problems the deviant encounters in his deviant role are due to social reactions and definitions of his situation rather than to his having personal problems and inadequacies. That is, personal disturbance is the result of reactions from society toward the deviant. Simmons writes that "the free-floating paranoia and defensiveness so commonly seen among pot-smokers, homosexuals, Puerto Rican gangs, and other deviant groups is easily traceable to the everpresent threat of retribution from the surrounding society, not to an earlier personality syndrome nor to anything in the deviant activity itself."[48]

Wilkens has made the important point that all societies reject many types of deviants. That is "both saints and criminals have been excluded from the cultures into which they were born, and the majority of saints have suffered exactly similar fates to the deviant sinners."[49] The societies recognized deviance, but not the direction that the deviance took. So what gets stigmatized in a society is not always easy to determine or anticipate. For example, Schur points out that because of the importance of sex to questions of personal identity, confirmed homosexuality (if recognized) appears to carry a built-in stigma. "But not all kinds of 'differentness' or deviating behavior are equally stigmatizable, nor is being easily stigmatizable the same as actually being stigmatized."[50]

Wilkens has also pointed out that it is usual to think of deviant behavior as almost automatically implying bad or undesirable behavior.

[47] Lemert, *op. cit.*, p. 55.
[48] Simmons, *op. cit.*, p. 15.
[49] Wilkens, *op. cit.*, p. 71.
[50] Schur, *op. cit.*, p. 5.

However, there is deviant behavior that is "good" or functional for society. For example, the genius, the reformer, the religious leader, and many others are "deviant from the norms of society as much as is the criminal."[51] Therefore, deviance is not a sufficient condition for behavior to be seen as undesirable, but rather it must be morally or legally defined as "bad" deviant behavior. It is also true that a society does not always define conformity as desirable, and the person who unquestioningly conforms may be seen as a problem. This might be true of the child in school although not true of the enlisted man in the army. So one may think of deviance as falling on a continuum of human acts ranging from the most sinful to the most saintly. In reality there are very few social acts in our society which are regarded as extremely saintly or extremely valuable to the society, and there are very few acts which are regarded as extremely sinful or seriously criminal.[52] Most activities, whether deviating or conforming, fall somewhere between the two extremes.

The discussion has centered on the defining of deviancy as coming from the broader society. Actually the defining might range from high social agreement to agreement among relatively few individuals. But deviance is not going to be very significant if the few who define it that way have no real influence on others or on the deviant. The same thing is also true in how people react to a particular deviance. If most people define something as deviant but irrelevant, then that deviancy is not very important. However, even when most people respond to someone's deviance with tolerance but a few do not, this may make the deviant somewhat wary. And if the few have any influence then it doesn't take much in the way of negative reactions to create problems for the deviant. Even when the few do not seek to "expose" the deviant to the community they may still attempt to have a strong influence on the deviant. For example, they may attempt to reform him and bring him back into the fold.

The deviant often finds that even if he accepts the definition of his deviancy and leaves that role he doesn't always leave behind the stigma of his former deviancy. For example, frequently when a person has been in prison or in a mental institution his status as an inmate and patient may be reactivated in the community long after he has left the institution. Often when it is found out that a person was institutionalized this is given more weight in determining how one will respond to him than are face-to-face experiences. "Once he knows of the person's 'past,' the layman quite naturally withdraws the benefit of the doubt that he automatically accords to people in most ordinary social contacts."[53] There is sometimes a legal requirement that the person report his previous deviant status, for

---

[51] Wilkens, *op. cit.*, p. 45.

[52] *Ibid.*, pp. 46–7.

[53] Rubington and Weinberg, *op. cit.*, p. 115.

example, the ex-convict in applying for particular jobs. In certain attempts to treat various types of deviance the individual is constantly required to think of his past status. In fact in some cases he is never allowed to leave his previous deviant status. This is true in Alcoholics Anonymous, where a man may not have had a drink in years but is constantly told that he is still an alcoholic. Also the past deviant status of an individual may go with him because it is seen as significant or as something one should know about the person. For example, references to Senator Harold Hughes of Iowa often characterize him as an ex-alcoholic. It is difficult to determine if this reference is intended as a compliment because he was able to overcome a problem or as a warning of a past weakness that might come out in the future.

From the point of view of the larger society deviance sometimes provides a positive function. This may be true when the deviant violates rules which the dominant society holds in high respect that bring the society together to express its outrage over the offense, and in bearing "witness against the offender, they develop a tighter bond of solidarity than existed earlier."[54] Therefore deviance cannot always be treated as disrupting to the broader society but may actually contribute to preserving stability. This helps to explain why on some occasions a pattern of behavior may be defined as deviant, but not at another time. That is, the broader society defines it as deviant and subject to social outrage because a scapegoat is needed to help bring together members in the broader society. Furthermore, it is known that deviant activities often appear to get support from the very agencies that have been developed to suppress them. One obvious factor is that often the controlling agency needs the deviance to maintain its own existence. As suggested earlier, if there were no illicit drug trade there would be no need for the Federal Narcotics Bureau. But even beyond this many institutions gather deviant types (and people marginal to the deviancy) into tightly segregated groups and provide them with the setting in which to teach one another the values and skills of a deviant career. As a result members of society often push individuals "into employing these skills and attitudes of a deviant career, and often provoke them into employing these skills by reinforcing their sense of alienation from the rest of the society."[55]

Erikson has pointed out that many cultures develop patterns that provide for deviancy expression. First, there are some societies which have special days or occasions which allow for periods of general license and where the members are allowed to violate the usual rules, for example, during the Mardi Gras in New Orleans and similar pre-Lent activities in the Caribbean and some South American countries. Second, there are

---

[54] Erikson, *op. cit.*, p. 4.
[55] *Ibid.*, pp. 15–16.

societies where deviance is seen as a natural form of behavior for some groups, for example, the special behavior tolerated among adolescents and young people. Third, there are societies where special clubs are allowed to deviate from the ordinary rules of the society. An example would be a nudist colony in the United States.[56]

THE LAW AND DEVIANCE

Next, in this chapter it is necessary to say something about the function of laws with reference to deviance. The concept of law implies rules characterized by regularity. "A *law* may be defined as a rule of human conduct that the bulk of the members of a given political community recognize as binding upon all its members."[57] However, the extent to which a law is binding varies greatly and the sanctions against deviating may range from none to very severe. It is important to keep in mind that a law is one kind of rule. When a rule is enacted into law it then has the police power of the state behind it, whereas rules are dependent upon informal sanctions. So laws always imply a formal governmental context of power and authority, although it doesn't necessarily mean the power will be used. A society may feel strongly about something and yet feel that social ends may be better met by having the controls remain informal and general rather than becoming formal laws with a more precise application. This is because many rules (like the Ten Commandments) function primarily as ideals, "as positive models toward which the population should strive, in addition to being negative limits. By making the rules more realistic the institution would hence lower the ideal standard of 'good.' "[58]

The law makes an important distinction in defining what is illegal. That is, in most cases it may not be for the being of something but rather it is for the possessing or doing of something. For example, it is not illegal to be a drug addict, homosexual, or alcoholic. For the drug addict, what is illegal is "the illegal procurement, possession, or use of illegal drugs; for the homosexual (with the exception at this time of Illinois), it is homosexual acts of almost any nature; and for the alcoholic it is public intoxication."[59]

There is no necessary relationship between the importance of an area of behavior and whether or not it will be controlled by law. For example, the use of marijuana is probably much less dangerous than the use of alcohol or cigarettes, but the laws about marijuana use are very severe

---

[56] See *ibid.*, p. 28.

[57] Gould, Julius and William J. Kolb, eds., A *Dictionary of the Social Sciences* (New York: The Free Press of Glencoe, 1964), p. 378.

[58] Simmons, *op. cit.*, p. 117.

[59] Pittman, David, *Alcoholism* (New York: Harper and Row, 1967), p. 112.

while the laws about alcohol use or cigarette smoking are few and weak. Often a society exaggerates the danger of those things it wants to control. Once again a good illustration is the overstated dangers of marijuana. It is quite possible that the exaggerated stereotypes about hazards arise from a universal bias. "Every society seems to grossly exaggerate the terror and risks of what is disapproved of and to minimize the risks of approval and encouraged behavior."[60]

The important point is that something doesn't have to be dangerous to society to be against the laws. Some acts may be criminal or deviant not because they are dangerous, but because they are legally proscribed as such. In fact the law may be irrational in that the members of the society cannot explain it, but the law is real nevertheless. Or a law may be "arbitrary" because "it is imposed by a powerful minority and, as a consequence, lacks popular support and is actively opposed."[61] Therefore laws do not always reflect the dominant values of society, as for example the old "blue laws." And some laws may represent the consensus or perhaps a majority, but are opposed by a large number of the population, for example, the gambling laws in many states. What often happens is that the enforcers of policies where there is high social disagreement become ambivalent in their enforcement because the public is for the most part indifferent towards the particular forms of deviance.[62] However, there are some who argue that even though a law does not prevent certain acts from occurring it is still effective. Schur says that while some laws may not deter they still have strong influence "through their influence in the social meanings read into various acts or behavior patterns, and through their role in structuring total problem situations."[63]

However, it seems clear that with a few possible exceptions the more intense the enforcement of laws the greater the effect the laws will have on deviance. Pittman points out that this can be seen in the treatment of drug addicts in America. Even though addicts may never encounter personally any law enforcement agency, they cannot help but be constantly aware of the law's presence. "The secret manner in which they must purchase drugs is the product of law enforcement. Many of their associates have had personal contact with the law. Finally, the high price and low quality of the black market drugs are a result of social policies. The stringent enforcement of narcotic laws produces secondary deviance among drug addicts. The addict must resort to illegal behavior to support his habit, usually petty larceny and prostitution."[64]

---

[60] Simmons, op. cit., p. 70.

[61] Gibbs, Jack P., "Conceptions of Deviant Behavior: The Old and the New," in Lefton, op. cit., p. 46–7.

[62] Pittman, op. cit., p. 109.

[63] Schur, op. cit., p. 7.

[64] Pittman, op cit., pp. 110–11.

The processing and handling of the legally defined deviant has become the work of complex social agencies set up to perform these functions. Their function of controlling deviance is performed within the context of an elaborate and often precise set of official rules. There may also be private agencies dealing with the deviant, but they differ in several important ways from the legal agencies. "In power, in legitimacy, and in routine, public regulation and private regulation are at opposite poles. Generally, the power of the political state stands behind officials who take action against the deviant; they have the principle of legality supporting them, and their work with deviants is efficient and routine, i.e., carried out in accordance with a stock, official plan. In the operation of private regulation power is frequently distributed equitably between the deviant and others, the rule of law is irrelevant when people may be strongly committed to opposing norms, and action against the deviant need not take place according to any plan at all."[65]

It seems possible that in the near future laws will be increasingly influenced by a new and emerging view about deviance. That is the view that people should be legally punished only for acts that are socially dangerous, independent of their moral character. This point of view makes a distinction between public and private morality, as well as between illegality and immorality. Here the law would be restricted to those acts which offend against public order and decency or subject the ordinary citizen to what would be offensive or injurious. This argument does not believe that laws build character.[66] This point of view can be illustrated in the area of sexual behavior. Such sexual activities as rape, exhibitionism, solicitation, and so forth would continue to be against the law. However, sexual activity in private between consenting adults would no longer be subject to legal control. There is some evidence that this kind of distinction is being made in the planning of new legislation in several different states.

SUBCULTURES

In the last part of this chapter the purpose is to briefly discuss a more complex level of social deviance—that of subcultures. "The term *subculture*, though not the concept, did not become common in social science literature until after the Second World War."[67] The variables used to distinguish subcultures have been many and varied. As a result there have been so-called subcultures of longshoremen, professional baseball players,

---

[65] Rubington and Weinberg, *op. cit.*, p. 109.

[66] Johnson, Elmer H., "Abortion: A Sociological Critique," in Jeffrey K. Hadden and Marie L. Borgotta, *Marriage and the Family* (Itasca, Ill.: F. E. Peacock, 1969), p. 333.

[67] Wolfgang, Marvin E. and Franco Fernacuti, *The Subculture of Violence*, (London: Tavistock Publications, 1967), p. 97.

university professors, hippies, prison inmates, Texas oilmen, gangs, both delinquent and nondelinquent, the world of fashion, musicians, behavioral scientists, homosexuals, adolescents, and so forth. The term subculture has ranged in application from two persons in a family unit all the way to the suggestion that men and women each constitute a separate subculture. The term frequently has been used as an *ad hoc* concept when a writer wanted to emphasize the normative aspects of behavior that were different from the general social norms.

However, the usage most valuable to our purposes concerns itself with groups in some conflict with the broader society. Within this usage the "norms" of a delinquent gang or the standards of an adolescent peer group have often been designated subcultural.[68] It is useful to look more specifically at how the concept of subculture has been defined and particularly how the definitions relate it to the "conflict" point of view.

It should be remembered that whenever the stress is on the subculture it always implies a close relationship, often both positive and negative, to the larger society. In this broad context, when subculture is used it refers to a subdivison within society that forms a functioning unity of values and behavior patterns that have an integrated impact on the participating individuals. The concept of subculture implies that all groups in society share many factors in common, but that the *areas of difference* peculiar to a given subculture are the focus of major interest at a given time. And the areas of difference may shift over time.

A simple operational definition of culture and subculture has been provided by Sebald. He suggests that "since for sociological purposes *culture* refers to a blueprint for behavior of a total society, the largest human grouping, *subculture* refers to the blueprint for behavior of a smaller group within the society."[69] He goes on to point out that it is a "special blueprint of the society."[70] However, the formal definitions are only the starting point for analyzing a concept. One must move to the interrelated statuses, norms, and functions subsumed in the concept and also examine how the concept is related to other major social concepts.

In the discussion that follows it is assumed that *all* subcultures are deviant. This appears logical given the "conflict" level in which the concept is to be used. To say that all subcultures are deviant is not necessarily to say that from the point of view of the broader society they are all "bad." The larger society may see the deviance as something it cannot control and must simply accept. For example, adolescent subcultures may be seen as acceptable deviant behavior resulting from "growing up" but

---

[68] Yinger, J. Melton, "Contraculture and Subculture," *American Sociological Review*, October, 1960, p. 627.

[69] Sebald, Hans, *Adolescence: A Sociological Analysis* (New York: Appleton, Century, Crofts, 1968), p. 205.

[70] *Ibid.*

still defined negatively with regard to the ideal values of the broader society. Actually, from the perspective of the broader society, many subcultures are seen as falling along a continuum of "badness" and what is "bad" varies over time. So while subculture implies deviancy it does not follow that deviancy necessarily implies "badness."

Subcultures often emerge as a response to a problem faced in common by a group of people. Many people who engage in certain kinds of deviant behavior feel that what they believe is not shared by other members of the society. It is assumed that often the person wants to share his deviancy and will seek out others like himself. However, there are many deviants who perform their behavior in private and have no desire or opportunity to develop their behavior with others and therefore have no desire or opportunity to develop a subculture. An example, as previously mentioned, would be many transvestites—they are individual deviants, but they do not constitute a subculture.

For a subculture to emerge, far more is needed than simply individuals suffering a common fate. Obviously it is necessary for the individuals to be in contact with one another and to find out through communication that they actually do have common values and interests. When the subcultures develop they present "a common understanding and prescribed ways of thinking, feeling, and acting when in the company of one's own deviant peers and when dealing with representatives of the conventional world. Once these deviant subcultures come into being and flourish, they have consequences for their bearers and conventional outsiders as well."[71]

It is difficult to determine the amount of time which makes participation in a subculture significant for the individual. What is more important than the simple measurement of time is the amount of "significant involvement." Take for example a homosexual who spends his work week in contact with the broader heterosexual society and has no involvement with his homosexual subculture during that time. But on the weekend his life becomes totally immersed in his homosexual subculture. While most of his life is spent in the heterosexual world, his "significant involvement" is with the homosexual subculture. In fact the work week may be very insignificant to him, something he has to do, and many of his thoughts during the week may be directed at his way of life in the weekend.

There is one type of deviant subculture where individuals spend all their time. This has been defined by Goffman as a "total institution" and refers to a place where people live and work with a large number of like-situated persons, where they are cut off from the broader society for significant periods of time and together lead an enclosed, formally administered life.[72] In a total institution all aspects of life are carried out in the

---

[71] Rubington and Weinberg, *op. cit.*, p. 203.

[72] Goffman, Erving, *Asylums* (New York: Anchor Books, 1961), p. xiii.

same location under the same general authority. Each member's daily activity is performed in the close company of other members, all of whom are treated alike and required to do the same things together. All aspects of the day's activities are closely scheduled and the whole sequence of activities is imposed from above through a system of explicit rules with a group of designated leaders. "The various enforced activities are brought together into a single rational plan purportedly designed to fulfill the official aims of the institution."[73]

Goffman suggests that total institutions in American society may be divided into five general groupings. First are those institutions set up for the care of persons felt to be both helpless and harmless, for example the blind, the aged, and so forth. Second are those institutions set up to care for those defined as incapable of taking care of themselves, as well as being a threat to the community, even though their threat is defined as unintentional, for example, TB sanitariums or mental hospitals. A third type is where institutions are set up to protect the community against persons who are believed to represent intentional dangers. Here the primary interest is to remove the individuals; their welfare and rehabilitation is secondary. An illustration would be a jail or penitentiary. A fourth type of total institution is purportedly set up to more effectively pursue some worklike task. They justify themselves on instrumental grounds, for example, army barracks, ships, boarding schools, work camps, etc. And finally are total institutions set up as retreats from the world while also serving as training stations for the religious, i.e., abbeys, monastaries, convents, and so forth.[74]

For the person in a "total institution" the subculture becomes in effect his entire life, and there is no broader culture in terms of his actually participating in it. Even persons who come in from the outside to work have their behavior altered by their working in the closed institution. From the extreme of the "total institution," persons with subcultural involvement taper off and increasingly participate in the broader culture. It seems reasonable to suggest that almost all Americans have some involvement with subcultures, at least at various stages during their life cycle, but that most of their involvement is in the broader culture.

There are also some people who engage in behavior that is not acceptable to the broader society or to a subculture the person might be thought of as belonging to. A "marginal deviant" has been defined as one who has been excluded from the conventional world and at the same time has been denied admission and certification in a deviant subculture.[75] One example of a marginal deviant would be a "reformed drunk," a social type that is recognizable among certain types of alcoholics. The reformed drunk is at

---

[73] *Ibid.*, p. 6.

[74] *Ibid.*, pp. 4–5.

[75] Rubington and Weinberg, *op. cit.*, p. 320.

the time sober and intolerant of drinking and generally believes that his sobriety is due only to himself. "These attitudes are not shared by conventional people or by most alcoholics. He is out of both worlds. When he comes into contact with either of these worlds the signs and symbols he puts forth are not accepted."[76]

While some subcultures may get their members through no real choice on the part of the individuals, as for example in prisons or mental hospitals, other deviant subcultures may be entered through the choice of the individual, as is true for many homosexuals, sexual "swingers," marijuana users, and so forth. The motive for persons who choose to become a part of a subculture is usually the belief that there is something for them to gain. For example, the homosexual does so to be with people of similar sexual interests, as well as for many other reasons. Sometimes after joining the group the deviant may want to hide his subculture involvement from the broader society. This often means that the deviant will present to the broader society signs and symbols that will give him a social identity quite distinct from his personal identity. Frequently, "secret homosexuals working in all-male groups find it necessary to join in conversations that ridicule or condemn homosexuality; in so doing, they obtain, at least in this group, a social identification as heterosexual."[77]

SOCIALIZATION TO SUBCULTURES

While we have pointed out that it is difficult to measure the significant involvement in a subculture in terms of hours, there is another aspect of time which is important, and that is the continued involvement in the subculture over a period of time. This suggests that varying amounts of time are needed for the individual to become socialized to the subculture. And once he is socialized he must actively participate so that the subculture will be maintained. Therefore the emergence and maintenance of a subculture has something to do with the continuing nature of the behavior's being deviant. Simply because deviance is ongoing it is not sufficient to say that a subculture will necessarily emerge and continue. For example, the physician-addict is continuously addicted but he does not show subcultural involvement. It is not then merely the continuing nature of the basic deviant act that establishes the basis for a subculture but, again, the *need for continuous contact with other like individuals in order for the basic deviant acts to be carried out.*[78]

Basically it appears that for a subculture to emerge the *necessary condition* is that there be a number of persons in the society who seek a solution to common problems and who are able to interact effectively with one an-

---

[76] *Ibid.*

[77] *Ibid.*, p. 318.

[78] Schur, *op. cit.*, pp. 172–73.

other. "The *sufficient conditions* for the establishment of a subculture lies in the acceptance of common norms and values specifying the 'proper' and 'right' way of doing things."[79]

Once a subculture is in operation one of its important functions is the recruiting and socializing of new members. It sometimes happens that people want to be members of a subculture but are not accepted. For example, the child who is too young to be accepted into the adolescent subculture, the delinquent who is seen as too dangerous to the delinquent gang, and so forth. One writer suggests that subcultures, much like colleges, can be rated on how hard they are to get into and how hard they are to stay in.[80] Once the individual is admitted he may be put through a period of apprenticeship before he is fully accepted. "He must learn a stock of beliefs, values, norms, and ways of acting that will guarantee continued participation in the group and, at the same time, provide some of the gratifications for being deviant."[81] He may over time stay or leave, but whether or not "he becomes fully committed to the deviant way of life depends partly on the mode of entry, content, and instruction as well as the nature of the deviant acts practiced."[82] Rubington and Weinberg go on to point out that the deviant who wants to sustain his new identity must make the signs and symbols of the subculture his own. He must be able to present deviant behavior when it is required of him or when he wishes to. His actions must be certified first by the subculture and then by himself. "Put another way, if he fails to learn from his teachers he is in jeopardy of being called inauthentic."[83]

One further point about the time aspect of subcultures is that a person may spend varying lengths of his life in a subculture. For example, the adolescent in a delinquent subculture can only be there for a specific period of his life. That is true because by definition that subculture requires a person to be within definite age limits to be a member. But there may also be subcultures in which the person spends his total lifetime. This is often the case in the black lower-class subculture. In subcultures that run during the lifetime of the individual it often means that those persons in them have not been presented with the contrasting values of the dominant society. This is true because the background of many deviants shows that they were never originally socialized into the broader conventional society. In those cases early socialization occurred in the deviant subculture and was explicitly in terms of the deviant norms and values.[84]

---

[79] Sebald, *op. cit.*, p. 207.

[80] Rubington and Weinberg, *op. cit.*, p. 206.

[81] *Ibid.*, p. 235.

[82] *Ibid.*

[83] *Ibid.*, pp. 320–21.

[84] DeLamater, John, "On the Nature of Deviance," *Social Forces*, June, 1968, p. 447.

Whatever the reason for the person's being in the subculture, he must rationalize in some meaningful way to himself the relationship and differences of the values and norms in the broader society with those in his subculture. This is especially true when the subculture provides the means for sanctioning behavior that is not acceptable in the broader society. "The acquisition of status within the new group is accompanied by a loss of status outside the group. To the extent that the esteem of outsiders is a value to the members of the group a new problem is engendered. To this problem the typical solution is to devalue the good will and respect of those whose good will and respect are forfeit anyway."[85] But what is of overriding importance is the relative value of what had been left behind to what has been acquired by moving into the subculture. As Cohen points out, over time the main ideas "of any particular individual are derived from the subculture to which he is most exposed and with which he most strongly identifies."[86]

Whenever a deviant examines what he feels he may gain from his participation in a subculture he must also look at the possible costs for him with regard to the broader society. That is, very often the patterns of behavior expected in the broader society will in turn involve a clash of values for the deviant. For example, homosexuals may have problems in the social activities of society where heterosexual feelings and inclinations for marriage are taken for granted. In many businesses there are stages in a man's career where it is almost required that he marry if he wants to move ahead. The homosexual who wants to succeed in his occupation may be faced with a real personal dilemma.

Ultimately the measurement of successful indoctrination into a subculture is the same as in the broader society—the individual has been effectively socialized. "Individuals commit deviant acts because they have learned the supporting beliefs and values, from subcultures in which they have participated, in the same way people learn conventional beliefs and values from *their* subcultures, and they are sustained in this behavior by the agreement and approval of their reference groups. Social organization determines the distinction of deviant behavior and conformity by structuring the networks of social interaction in which reference groups are acquired and cultural learning occurs."[87]

Always implied is that the broader society has the greater power which allows it to define the subculture as deviant and to subject it to some forms of criticism or punishment. Also, as previously indicated, it is often the factor of power that creates a deviant subculture, that is, the power to punish, to withhold, that is important to the subculture. And while this is

---

[85] Cohen, Albert K., *Delinquent Boys* (Glencoe, Ill.: The Free Press, 1955), p. 68.

[86] Cohen, *Deviance and Control, op. cit.*, p. 85.

[87] *Ibid.*

usually the case, it is not always true. The subculture must "recognize" the power of the broader society. For example, they could be indifferent as is often the case when "respectability" is withheld and where a subculture doesn't really care. In other words, knowing the relative power of the broader culture to the subculture is not enough. One must also know how each defines the power and what significance the power has for each.

Another problem related to power distribution is that generally the broader society sees deviant subcultures as behaving the way they do because they are negatively willful or are victims of circumstances. This implies the belief by the broader society that if the negative hostility can be removed or the circumstances can be altered to give subcultures a chance they will choose the values of the dominant culture. However, a subculture may reject the values of the broader culture because it does not believe they are worth pursuing *under any conditions*. When the broader culture becomes aware of this assessment, the need to make the subculture conform often becomes even greater. The broader culture then has the need to reaffirm the worth of its values to itself, and to do this it must change the thinking of the subculture or in some way discredit its "subversive" beliefs.

A problem which any social organization has to resolve is how much deviance it can accept before it feels it is seriously threatened. This is true of the society in general, as well as for subcultures. In the broader society, because of its size and complexity, the problem of accepted deviance is generally a group one. That is, any threats will normally come from deviant groups rather than essentially unrelated deviant individuals. In the subculture any internal threat may be from a group, or in some cases there may be a threat internally by a few deviant individuals. But because the subculture deviates from the broader society in some significant ways it must often insist on a high level of conformity to those values which makes it different from the larger society. If it doesn't the sharpness of difference and the basic reasons for its existence become blurred and less significant. So within the subculture conformity to value differentiation becomes increasingly important for all individuals. Also important for both the broader society and its subcultures are the significance of the values from which deviation is occurring. "Even a subculture can tolerate values outside its value system so long as they do not disturb allegiance to its own existence, or the existence of its leaders and opinion-makers is not menaced."[88]

An important part of the value sharing in the subculture is related to the need for a rationale for the members, and this is especially true when the subculture is in conflict with the broader society. The historical di-

---

[88] Wolfgang and Ferracuti, *op. cit.*, p. 101.

mension of the subculture is important in providing a rationale for the members. This often gives the members a sense of belonging to something with some permanence and stability. Certain events and incidents become the special histories of distinct subcultures. For example, "the subculture of delinquency possesses a rich folklore in which tales of injustice hold a prominent place. Thus, the subcultural adherent is not fully dependent on personal experience."[89]

One other important characteristic of the subculture is the development of specialized languages. Some specialized language is a characteristic of most groups, deviant and otherwise, in American society. Specialized argots may develop because of the need for more precise communication between members. This is often the case in specialized occupational jargons. Other groups may develop specialized language forms because they don't want others to understand them or because this gives a special quality to things they hold to be important. Maurer suggests that "argots are more than specialized forms of language; they reflect the way of life in each of the numerous criminal cultures and subcultures; they are keys to attitudes, to evaluation of men and society, to modes of thinking, to social organization and to technology."[90]

The argots of a group may be very extensive or quite limited. For example, one writer talks about the relatively limited argot of the stock-market subculture.[91] But an illustration of a much more elaborate and complex argot would be that of the black lower-class subculture. Here is the specialized language of a group which is ongoing and which has a history of a special argot's being valuable and necessary in most areas of life. Hammond suggests that the use of a specialized jargon exists to a very substantial extent throughout the lower-class Negro subcultures of the United States. He further suggests that "while it may be true that each ghetto has its own local vocabulary, it is still tied in with the larger based subcultural system."[92]

The function of language appears often to be more than simply communication in the subculture. It also helps to set the subculture apart from the broader society. "Subculture segmentation is well reflected in the special languages, peculiar jargon, and secret symbolic accouterments that go with membership in one or more of these groups. They are 'badges of belonging' that make for solidarity, social cohesive and *esprit de corps*.

[89] Matza, *op. cit.*, p. 102.

[90] Maurer, David W., "The Argot of the Dice Gambler," *The Annals*, May, 1950, p. 119.

[91] Lerman, Paul, "Individual Values, Peer Values, and Subcultural Delinquency," *American Sociological Review*, April, 1968, p. 210.

[92] Hammond, Boone, "Jargon: The Language of the Ghetto," Occasional Paper #42, Washington University, May, 1967, p. 10.

Communication among members is greatly facilitated, but the more cohesive their group becomes, the more difficult it is to maintain easy communication with outsiders."[93]

It also appears that in some areas of deviance a specialized argot serves the important purpose of allowing strangers to give and receive cues as to their similar deviant inclinations. One way in which this is done is through a casual kidding verbal exchange. Teasing or kidding provides an out where one can say he was only fooling if things appear to get touchy. Simmons further points out that such verbal exchange provides freedom to explore others and to make suggestions without fear of great consequences. "In such encounters deviants often employ language innocuous to conventional people but with signal meanings for fellow deviants or the recruitable. You're saying several different things in the same breath and watching to see who picks up what."[94] In some cases the communication may be more subtle than language—it may be an inflection or intonation or even a gesture.

As suggested earlier, one important characteristic of deviancy in recent years has been the increasing tendency for some deviant groups to fight back in various ways. This may be through strikes and riots, as in prisons, or through the development of formal organizations. It is the development of organizations that is recent and of particular interest. It appears that the common model for these organizations to pattern themselves after has been that of the Civil Rights movement. For example, out of that movement came the tactics of passive resistance as well as confrontation now used by many protesting organizations.

As deviants interact with one another they mutually influence the thoughts of one another and develop positions of rationalization with regard to their behavior. In some cases they may develop an extensive historical, legal, and psychological justification for their deviant activities. One good illustration of this has been the development of formal organizations in the homosexual subculture. The organizations have "magazines and books by homosexuals and for homosexuals that include historical articles about famous homosexuals in history. They contain articles on the biology and physiology of sex, designed to show that homosexuality is a 'normal' sexual response."[95] Recently there has emerged among some homosexuals an aggressive movement toward achieving greater civil liberties.

Today there are organizations representing such deviant subcultures as male and female homosexuality and extra-marital "swapping," and for the practice of birth control and abortion, as well as for those who have left

---

[93] Bensman, Joseph and Bernard Rosenberg, *Mass, Class, and Bureaucracy* (Englewood Cliffs, N.J.: Prentice-Hall, Inc., 1963), pp. 36–7.

[94] Simmons, *op. cit.*, p. 81.

[95] Becker, *op. cit.*, p. 38.

deviant activities, for example, ex-alcoholics, criminals, mental patients, and drug users. How many deviants the various organizations represent and how much influence they have is not known. Many of the organizations put forward exaggerated claims as to their following—which is a characteristic of almost all political, social, and special interest groups in the United States. Sagarin suggests that organized deviants generally speak for only a small percentage and that "the organizations' rates of success, as judged by the numbers of people who have, through them, either overcome a stigmatizing problem or adapted to it, are to be considered self-serving declarations never subject to verification."[96]

There is a risk for the deviant who becomes a part of an organized group. Public exposure can result in either greater understanding or ridicule or the same program may result in both. Sagarin feels, after his study of deviant group organizations, that often the organizations have sought publicity for their own sakes rather than for any goal they are working toward. But "whatever good or harm publicity brings to the deviants themselves, it almost invariably strengthens their organizations."[97] Furthermore, one of the dangers of organizations is that they can cause a greater split between the dominant and deviant groups. There is some evidence that this has been true because of some of the militancy of homosexual groups. But some deviants may feel that this is a price they are ready to pay.

CONCLUSIONS

In this introductory chapter the primary concern has been to present a broad conceptual approach for the study of social problems, social deviancy, and subcultures. As suggested, these three concepts overlap one another and in the chapters ahead these different views will be used in various ways wherever they seem appropriate. Part I, which includes most of the chapters in the book, consists of substantive areas that would generally be defined as areas of social deviance. Part II examines deviance areas that appear to be in the process of developing as subcultures. They are of particular interest because they may develop increasing strength or even go the other way and become less important in society.

Drawing from the discussion in this chapter, there are six major themes that will be applied to the areas of deviance discussed in each of the following chapters. Not all of them will always be appropriate and there will be themes discussed other than the following six. But the intent is that these themes provide in general for a systematic application of the theoretical considerations discussed in this chapter. The themes also serve as a guide for the organization of each chapter.

---

[96] Sagarin, *op. cit.*, p. 235.
[97] *Ibid.*, p. 238.

1. *Historical Background.* How long had this been an area of deviancy and why? Are there variations in different cultures? Have the views of the deviance varied in a given culture over time?

2. *Legal Aspects.* What is the legal nature of the deviancy and how important are the legal definitions for society? What are the relationships between the legal systems and the social values and norms?

3. *Causes and Cures.* What are the various theories and what does the evidence suggest about their utility and effectiveness? These are considered only when they are a major part of the discussion that centers on the substantive area, that is, when they are an intrinsic part of the deviance itself.

4. *Self Images.* How do deviants see themselves in relationship to one another and to the broader society? Are they concerned with their deviancy and with those who define them as such?

5. *Social Organization.* To what extent have the deviants established values, norms, and roles that function for them in their relationships to one another and to the rest of society? Do they constitute a subculture, and if so to what extent?

6. *Specialized Language.* Has one been developed? How is it different from the broader society and what functions does it perform?

Along with the above themes there are also three social patterns that are common to many of the areas of deviance discussed. One is a rebellion against the institutional defining of personal behavior. That is, the increasing belief that one's behavior should be defined by oneself and not the traditional social agencies of morality. This is seen in all areas of sexual behavior, abortion, and drug use. Second, in many areas of deviance the major sources of conflict are generational and social class based. It is not only the old against the young, but even more strongly the educated young against the less educated, lower middle-class, older generation. This conflict is also reflected in all areas of sexual expression, abortion, and drug use, as well as among militant women and students. The third pattern is the increasing push for equality of women in the United States with the belief and insistence on the same rights as men have. This is also seen in sexual expression, abortion, and drug use, and is discussed specifically in Chapter 14.

BIBLIOGRAPHY

BECKER, HOWARD S., *Outsiders: Studies in the Sociology of Deviance* (New York: Macmillan, 1963).

BECKER, HOWARD S., *The Other Side: Perspectives on Deviance* (New York: Free Press, 1964).

COHEN, ALBERT K., *Deviance and Control* (Englewood Cliffs, N.J.: Prentice-Hall, 1966).

ERIKSON, KAI T., *Wayward Puritans: A Study in the Sociology of Deviance* (New York: Wiley, 1966).

LEMERT, EDWIN M., *Human Deviance, Social Problems and Social Control* (Englewood Cliffs, N.J.: Prentice-Hall, 1967).

MATZA, DAVID, *Becoming Deviant* (New York: Prentice-Hall, Inc., 1969).

SAGARIN, EDWARD, *Odd Man In: Societies of Deviants in America* (Chicago: Quadrangle Books, 1969).

SCHUR, EDWIN M., *Crimes without Victims: Deviant Behavior and Public Policy* (Englewood Cliffs, N.J.: Prentice-Hall, 1965).

SIMMONS, J. L., *Deviants* (Berkeley, Calif.: The Glendessary Press, 1969).

WILKINS, LESLIE T., *Social Deviance* (Englewood Cliffs, N.J.: Prentice-Hall, 1964).

PART I

GROUP AND SUBCULTURAL DEVIANCE

CHAPTER 2

PREMARITAL SEX

TRADITIONALLY in the United States premarital sex has been defined as an undesirable social problem from which the society must protect itself and its members. Like so many social problems it has been defined within a strong moral context and therefore seen as something inherently bad and destructive. Premarital sex has been treated within the broader context of sexual values held to be important in American society. Man has developed a variety of means for satisfying his sexual needs, and all of these means are found among both the unmarried and the married population. The actual sexual behavior of the unmarried and married do not differ nearly so widely as do the social and psychological definitions and interpretations. For the married population, some forms of sexual outlet are approved, but for the unmarried *no* outlets are given explicit social approval. Yet the sexual needs of the unmarried individual do not lie dormant until the wedding day and then for the first time suddenly burst forth. Rather, the sexual needs of the unmarried exist with some change over time and with wide variation during the unmarried years. Often it is assumed that the sexual needs of the unmarried individual can be ignored, conditioned, or transferred, but in reality, they usually find some form of expression.

It must be kept in mind that sexual intimacy between males and females is approved within the socially defined role relationship of monogamous marriage, and in all other role relationships sexual intimacy goes against the commonly stated and approved social values. When premarital sex is discussed it is almost always applied to attitudes and behavior related to the adolescent and young adult. The word "premarriage" clearly implies a stage in life assumed to be *prior* to marriage, even though 6 or 7 percent of the American population never marries. However, the sexual behavior of those who never marry is generally subject to premarital values, regardless of their age or any reasons that may be related to their never marrying. This chapter will be limited to a discussion of the young and their premarital sexual activity as deviant behavior.

While it has been common to define premarital sexual behavior as a social problem it has not been examined within the context of social deviancy. That is, there have been no attempts to look at it within the context of some of the concepts of deviancy presented in Chapter 1. If, on the most general level, deviant behavior is defined as behavior which is seen by a large number of people in society as bad and as going beyond the limits of tolerance then premarital coitus qualifies as deviance. Reiss points out that in the eyes of most adults (77 percent in a national sample of adults, 21 years and older) premarital coitus is viewed as a violation of a norm, "and many people hold this view with sufficient intensity to place such behavior outside their tolerance limits."[1] Reiss goes on to suggest that the study of premarital coitus as deviancy might contribute to a better understanding of related deviant behavior such as prostitution, illegitimacy, and abortion. "The relation of these other substantive areas of sex deviancy is clear since one must often engage in premarital coitus before the possibility of illegitimacy, prostitution, or premarital abortion is present."[2]

The study of premarital sex as deviance is important in a broad sociological sense. That is, the present American society is characterized by rapid social change and problems frequently develop around what is believed to be right and proper by the older generation but is not adhered to by many in the younger generation. Two major social variables related to the understanding of deviance in this chapter and in many of the subject areas covered in chapters ahead are generational conflict and differential expectations for males and females in society. Therefore, the discussion of those two variables as crucial to the study of premarital sex are important in themselves, but are also important in many other areas of deviancy.

HISTORICAL BACKGROUND

To better understand the nature of deviancy with regard to premarital sex it is necessary to look at how this behavior has been perceived and defined in the past. Views about premarital sex have been closely linked to values about sex in general, love, and the family. If one looks back at early

---

[1] Reiss, Ira L., "Premarital Sex as Deviant Behavior: An Application of Current Approaches to Deviance," *American Sociological Review*, February, 1970, p. 78.

[2] *Ibid.*, p. 85.

Greek society it can be seen that love and sex were often closely linked together. While love among the Greeks stressed physical beauty the Greek male did not often feel that beauty could be found in the female, and certainly not in the wife. In fact the prestige of the female was so low that she was often seen as being unworthy of idealistic love; and, as a female, she was believed to be incapable of returning the male's love. The ideal Greek love was often homosexual, between a younger boy and an older man. That love was based on the belief that the essence of beauty, and therefore the realization of love, could be found by the male in the male. It is an ironic and sometimes disconcerting historical fact for many people that love and sexual expression as it is viewed today, with the exchange of deep emotional commitment between members of the opposite sex, had some roots in male homosexuality.[3]

Restrictions against various forms of sexual expression have long been linked with religious beliefs and controls. However, nowhere in the Old Testament is there any prohibition of noncommercial unpremeditated fornication—apart from rape. "Once a girl had reached the age of twelve-and-a-half years, she was free to engage in sexual activity unless her father specifically forbade it. Prostitution, though frowned upon, was common and in Jerusalem the whores were so numerous that they had their own market place."[4] The religious taboos against sex in general did not become strong until the development of Christianity. For the early Christians, the highest form of achievement that man could reach was as complete a rejection of his body as possible while still retaining life. Among early Christians sex was seen as carnal, sinful, and inferior to all things of the spirit.

In early Christianity the root of all evil was woman. Woman was believed, simply by the fact of being woman, to possess evilness and therefore to be distrusted, watched, and controlled. "Woman was believed to inherit from Eve the natural propensity to lure man to his undoing. The sin in the Garden of Eden, St. Augustine maintained, had caused the sex organs to become the seat of lust. Thus, even with the sanction of marriage the sex act became a deed of shame."[5] The highest possible state for the woman was to be in the glory of everlasting virginity. Early Christianity was characterized by severe ascetic attacks against the inherent sinfulness and implied witchery of woman. This view of woman was a basic part of early Christian beliefs, and celibacy (the taboo against woman) was the way that man could be saved from corruption.

The inferior status of the woman continued for many centuries. Isabel

[3] Hunt, Morton M., *The Natural History of Love* (New York: Alfred A. Knopf, Inc., 1959), p. 8.

[4] Taylor, G. Rattray, *Sex in History* (New York: The Vanguard Press, 1954), p. 241.

[5] Drummond, Isabel, *The Sex Paradox* (New York: G. P. Putnam's Sons, 1953), p. 8.

Drummond suggests that "the period of hatred and contempt of woman pervaded the Crusades, the age of Chivalry, and lasted well into the Renaissance."[6] She writes that one of the most degrading examples of the low value of women was the use of the "chastity belt" and that "it was during this dark age of women that the doctrine of the Immaculate Conception arose."[7] Hunt suggests that by the end of the fifteenth century the concept of the woman had developed as completely dualistic: "She was not woman—she was either Lady or Witch, Blessed Virgin or sinful Eve, object of adoration or vessel of abominable lust."[8] During the period of the Middle Ages and the Renaissance the influence of romantic love and sexual expression varied. Morton Hunt argues that three general influences emerged over time: (1) a greater emotional relationship between men and women, which led to the eventual uplifting of woman's status; (2) sexual fidelity to a single partner; and (3) the belief that love must be mutual, which ultimately contributed greatly to the improvement of the woman's status.[9]

Many values basic to American society today have their origins with the early Puritans who settled New England. Unlike many other patriarchal systems, the Puritans believed in the premarital chastity of *both* the male and the female. In Puritan theology, premarital sexual behavior was interpreted as succumbing to the temptations of the flesh—behavior not found among the "chosen." The strength of the premarital chastity norms was derived from, and supported by, economic as well as religious values. But, even with the strongly supported norms against premarital sexual experience, a number of Puritans deviated from those norms. The records of Groton Church show that of 200 persons owning the baptismal covenant there from 1760 to 1775, 66 confessed to fornication before marriage.[10] Unlike many patriarchal societies, the Puritans did not protect the sexual purity of their women by providing a special group of prostitutes to meet the sexual needs of a number of men. And finally it should be stressed that not only were the restrictions against premarital sexual experience strong, but there were also strong restrictions against any pleasure derived from sex. The sexual asceticism of the Puritans was different only in degree from monasticism.

It may also be suggested that in some peasant societies of Europe couples do not marry until the girl gets pregnant. This may have centered around the high importance of fertility and maintaining the family lines. The records above from Groton Church may be reflecting the same consideration. Even the highly moral society may get caught in a dilemma

---

[6] *Ibid.*

[7] *Ibid.*

[8] Hunt, *op. cit.*, p. 175.

[9] *Ibid.*, p. 171.

[10] *Ibid.*, p. 133.

where they must be "immoral" to insure the perpetuation of their basic values.

During roughly the first two-thirds of the 19th century almost all aspects of sex were taboo when associated with "good" women. During that period it was commonly believed that for good women the sexual relations of marriage were an unspeakable and unpleasant duty necessary for reproduction and on some occasions to satisfy the "animal' sexual needs of their husbands. Women were not expected to experience sexual pleasure, and to do so often led to suspicion by the husbands and guilt by the wives. The view that good women had no sexual interest was strongly supported by the males in the patriarchal society. The patriarchal male could conveniently seek out sexual partners before marriage and outside of marriage. To meet the male sexual need, prostitution emerged as an important social institution. It was believed that only the prostitute as a woman felt any sexual desire and enjoyed sexual relations. The patriarchal male could turn to "bad" women not only to satisfy his animal needs, but also to protect his good women from his uncontrollable sexuality. The dichotomy of good and bad women seems to have been accepted by most of the women. So the period between the Revolution and the Civil War was the most restrictive period in American history on the freedom of women.

World War I probably triggered the developing social forces that resulted in the new social patterns of the 1920's. In the area of sexual behavior a decrease in the "sinful" view of sex, along with the new arguments for sexual expression provided by science, brought about important changes. Also during that period, the increasing use of contraceptive methods led to an increasing acceptance of the view that sexual intercourse could be an end in itself rather than only a means to a procreative end.

The 1920's saw an increasingly important social force emerge in the United States—the intellectual community. During the period the intellectual community was engaged in psychological and moral revolt from the Puritan values, Main Street mores, and the complacency of a cold business culture. The intellectual movement with the greatest importance for values of sexual behavior centered around the Freudian view of human behavior. While during the early stages of science Social Darwinism was used to support the traditional views of male dominance and morality, in the 1920's many of the interpretations of Freudianism seemed "to provide scientific sanction of conventional standards and morals."[11] In the 1920's among many intellectuals, as Baltzell puts it, "the Social Gospel was replaced by the gospel according to Freud."[12]

Those who represented and supported the traditional morality were

---

[11] Curti, Merle, *The Growth of American Thought* (New York: Harper and Row, Publishers, 1951), p. 706.

[12] Baltzell, E. Digby, *The Protestant Establishment* (New York: Random House, 1964), p. 218.

shocked by the revolt of the younger generation during the 1920's. In part the shocked reaction can be viewed within a social class context. With rebellion often strong among those of middle-class background the traditionalists saw the rebels as not just accepting different values but also as rejecting the old values. It is easier for the dogmatic moralist to "understand" those who are different because their whole life pattern has been different than to understand those who have had all the "advantages" and then rejected them. (These points of generational confusion and hostility are just as appropriate today as they were in the 1920's.)

The period of the 1920's also saw a basic change in the traditional role of the American woman. The superiority of the male was no longer an accepted belief for many women as well as men. The "sexual rights" of the woman were held to be very important and there was an increasing belief that her sexual drives both existed and needed to be satisfied.

Before ending this discussion on the historical background to premarital sex it is important to say something about the institutional influences of religion and the law. Religion has been the major social agency for the defining of American morality. The religious institution has been especially significant with reference to sexual behavior. In the United States every type of sexual activity *in and of itself* is a crime or a sin. "Marriage removes the stigma of criminality from vaginal heterosexual congress, but many Christians believe that it does not mitigate its sinful quality, unless engaged in for the sole purpose of procreation."[13] The most general values in the American society hold that premarital sex is sinful, and in many cases it is also illegal.

In general, the religious taboos against sex continue to be strong in the American society. The religious values about premarital sex are a part of the broader values that see lawful monogamous marriage as the only acceptable means for sexual pleasure and procreation. Therefore, all other forms of sexual behavior are defined as wrong. The male-female sexual relationship is given approval or disapproval according to the social role relationships of the two individuals when it occurred. If the couple is married then it is approved at least as a means to procreation; however, if the couple is not married the act is condemned. American moral values probably define more negatively those sexual relationships where one or both of the individuals are married, but not to each other, than those where neither of the individuals is married. There is rarely any stated belief by religious groups that premarital sex is less sinful than is extramarital sex. Yet, as Reiss points out "premarital coitus is not adultery and thus is not part of the Ten Commandments."[14]

---

[13] Drummond, *op. cit.*, p. 3.

[14] Reiss, Ira L., *Premarital Sexual Standards in America* (New York: The Free Press of Glencoe), 1960, pp. 162–63.

It is very possible that the strong positions by many religions against sexual behavior outside of marriage are given lip service in the abstract but have decreasing influence as significant determinants of behavior. This is not to argue that traditional religious values are unimportant, for many individuals have incorporated the moral values into their personality structures, and often do have feelings of shame or guilt when their behavior is contrary. The important difference is that in the past the strong sense of guilt was a result of a strong feeling of sin, and faith in God was almost the only relief. However, today there are accepted alternative explanations, especially psychological ones, by which the individual can deal with his guilt feelings. The use of such explanations for guilt feelings is so common today that even the minister often acts in accord with psychological explanations rather than traditional theological principles.[15]

The influence of religious beliefs on sexual laws has been very strong in the United States. These influences have been a part of the development of the state. Drummond points out that in common law "all the sexual transgressions other than adultery were at first merely torts, or civil wrongs, whatever the punishment inflicted. They were classified as "sins" and "wrongs," the former being offenses against God, the latter against one's neighbor. She further suggests that it was "only when the state became an entity that sins took on the aspect of crimes against the state and became indictable offenses."[16] One consequence has been that sexual laws have been altered little over time. "Today, in twentieth-century America, formal sex restrictions are—in their general outlines—much the same as they were in the times of Tertullian, St. Augustine, Martin Luther, or John Wesley."[17]

Premarital sexual relations are at present forbidden by more than two-thirds of the States. However, the laws are rarely applied. That premarital virginity for the female is not of great legal importance is reflected in the fact that in only one state, Maryland, is female unchastity before marriage a grounds for divorce. In summary it may be said that attempts to legislate controls over sexual morality in the United States have not been successful. Morris Plascowe points out that legislators have failed to recognize two factors that are necessary for effective legal sanctions: "(1) the support of public opinion; and (2) the ability of law enforcement agencies to get at the behavior involved. Neither element is present for much of the sexual behavior prohibited by the criminal law."[18]

---

[15] Gustufson, James M., "The Clergy in the United States," *Daedalus*, Fall, 1963, p. 733.

[16] Drummond, *op. cit.*, p. 9.

[17] Stephens, William N., *The Family in Cross-Cultural Perspective* (New York: Holt, Rinehart & Winston, Inc., 1963), p. 259.

[18] Plascowe, Morris, "Sex and the Law," in Edwin M. Schur, ed., *The Family and the Sexual Revolution* (Bloomington, Indiana: Indiana University Press, 1964), p. 195.

SOME CROSS-CULTURAL COMPARISONS

While the basis of the sexual drive is physiological, there is no known society where the frequency or form of sexual behavior is determined completely by physiological factors. In all cultures some degree of social control is exerted over sexual expression. Premarital sexual activity is one area of sexual outlet that is less restricted in many cultures. For example, most cultures place far more severe restrictions on extramarital and homosexual activities. Murdock found in his analysis of 148 cultures that premarital license prevailed in 70 percent and that, in the rest, the taboo fell mainly on the females and appeared to be largely a precaution against childbearing out of wedlock rather than a moral requirement.[19]

When a society does approve certain forms of adolescent sexual activity, it does not leave matters of behavior to chance. There are usually special social institutions that provide the facilities for the young people to meet and spend time together. However, it is rare in the history of man to find a society like the American, in which premarital sexual activity is prohibited and, at the same time, wide opportunity is allowed for private interaction to occur. Ford and Beach point out that in most restrictive societies there is a public conspiracy against the acquisition of any sexual knowledge by children. In restrictive societies the methods used during adolescence "include segregation of the sexes, strict chaperonage of girls, and threats of severe disgrace or physical punishment."[20] But, as Ford and Beach further point out, "there are probably no societies in which methods of control are completely effective in preventing coitus among young unmarried couples."[21]

In the discussion ahead premarital sexual attitudes and behavior will be discussed for two historical periods. First, the period of highly stabilized sexual behavior extending from about the 1920's until the mid-1960's. Second, evidence will be presented for the argument that premarital sexual behavior has been changing, at least among a number of college girls, since the mid-1960's.

PREMARITAL SEXUAL BEHAVIOR: 1920'S TO MID-1960'S

Before looking at the rates of actual behavior during this period there will be an examination of some attitudes about premarital sex. The major contribution to the scientific study of premarital sexual standards in the

---

[19] Murdock, George P., *Social Structure* (New York: The Macmillan Co., 1949), p. 265.

[20] Ford, Clellan S. and Frank A. Beach, *Patterns of Sexual Behavior* (New York: Harper and Row, Publishers, 1952), pp. 180–82.

[21] *Ibid.*, p. 182.

United States has been made by Ira L. Reiss.[22] Reiss has suggested that in the United States there are two basic types of premarital sexual behavior, with their related attitudes, that may be seen as extremes on a continuum: (1) *body-centered*, with the emphasis on the physical nature of sex, and (2) *person-centered*, with the emphasis on the emotional relationship to a given individual. Premarital attitudes may be usually classified in one of four categories falling along a continuum:

1. *Abstinence*—premarital intercourse is wrong for both the man and the woman, regardless of circumstances.
2. *Permissiveness-with-affection*—premarital intercourse is right for both men and women under certain conditions when a stable relationship with engagement, love, or strong affection is present.
3. *Permissiveness-without-affection*—premarital intercourse is right for both men and women regardless of the amount of affection or stability present, providing there is physical attraction.
4. *Double standard*—premarital intercourse is acceptable for men, but is wrong and unacceptable for women.[23]

The traditional belief in the double standard continues to be accepted by many Americans of both sexes. And the attitude of abstinence is often found going along with the double standard. In the past in the United States the double standard was often applied to the male and the abstinence standard applied to the female. Permissiveness-without-affection places value primarily on the sheer physical satisfaction derived from sex, although it is assumed that individuals will be sophisticated enough to control their pleasure in a careful way.[24] This standard tends to define sex as an end in itself, and while it has been accepted by only a minority in the past there is some evidence that in recent years it has been increasing. Permissiveness-with-affection appeals to many for several reasons. The feeling of love or affection justifies sexual intercourse for many individuals, and while for many love must be within the context of marriage, for others the emotional commitment has been sufficient. "Permissiveness-with-affection is an equalitarian standard, allowing premarital coitus for both men and women."[25]

In an earlier book the writer examined in detail many values that influence premarital sexual attitudes and behavior, but here only a few of the major variables will be examined.[26] Historically, the family has been the most powerful source of socializing the offspring. The family can transmit

[22] Reiss, *op. cit.*, p. 80.
[23] *Ibid.*, pp. 83–84.
[24] *Ibid.*, pp. 118–23.
[25] *Ibid.*, p. 144.
[26] Bell, Robert R., *Premarital Sex in a Changing Society* (Englewood Cliffs, N.J.: Prentice-Hall, Inc., 1966).

values to the child during the most impressionable years. Whatever values the family draws upon—religious, ethical, legal, or practical—the children, and especially the daughters, are almost always taught restrictions against premarital sexual intercourse. But it is clear that other forces of great strength are also in operation because many young people during their adolescence and early adult years reject those restrictive values about premarital sexual expression. If the conservative force is the family the liberal force can be described as the peer group.

The adolescent, being neither child nor adult, and having no clearly defined role made available to him by the overall culture, often turns within to his peers for self definitions. Frequently, the adolescent desires some decisiveness and precision in role definitions and tries to create his own. When he does, he often demands a high degree of conformity by other adolescents as "proof" of the rightness of his definitions. One consequence is that while the adolescent peer group deviates in some ways from the adult world the requirements for conformity within the group are very strong. It seems clear that most peer groups take a more liberal view about premarital sex than do the adults, and because this is true they are important to each other in giving psychological support in this area. The values about premarital sexual expression may be the most functionally significant values the peer groups of the young are actually involved with.

Many of the activities engaged in by young people in their peer group activities contribute to increased premarital sexual possibilities. Some of the values are "high exposure to temptation via privacy, dancing, and drinking; youth culture approval of adventure and hedonism; and approval of youth culture for the importance of affection as a basis for sexual relationships."[27] How persons perform according to the values of the group determines how the group defines them. That is, the peer group can give status and take it away. And sometimes how an individual is labelled within the group will have a strong influence on his future behavior. For example, labelling may affect premarital sexual permissiveness. "It is possible that a girl who is labelled by the boys or others in her school as an easy mark may react to this label and decide to continue or increase her sexual activities because of such a group label."[28]

It is clear that even within peer groups there may be differences in defining appropriate behavior. It would be a mistake to assume that within the peer group setting there is no conflict over sexual behavior. The most important source of conflict is between males and females. Studies have shown that even among college students strong male sexual aggression is quite common. One study found that over half of the coeds studied had been offended at least once during the prior academic year

---

[27] Reiss (February, 1970), *op. cit.*, p. 80.
[28] *Ibid.*, p. 81.

at some level of sexual intimacy. Of those coeds, 21 percent were offended by forceful attempts at intercourse and 6 percent by aggressively forceful attempts at sexual intercourse in which menacing threats or coercive infliction of physical pain were employed.[29]

In general the various studies during the period from 1920 to the mid-1960's indicated that there were no significant changes in the rates of girls' having premarital coitus. During that period the most reliable and best known statistics came from the Kinsey research. The Kinsey findings showed about one-half of all the women they studied who had ever married reported having premarital coitus. The data showed that for 44 percent of those with premarital coital experience, the entire experience had been confined to one year or less. For almost one-third, the coitus had covered a period of two or three years, and for 26 percent it had extended over four or more years. But only a very few women had premarital sexual intercourse with any continuity over such periods of time.[30]

The Kinsey findings showed the great importance of education to the probabilities of premarital coitus. There was a strong inverse relationship, by education, between male and female frequency of premarital coitus. By education level, the percentages for the females were: grade school, 30; high school, 47; and college, 60.[31] The percentages for the males were: grade school, 98; high school, 85; and college, 68.[32] Frequency of premarital coitus for the girl goes up with increased education because of the later age at marriage, more petting, and a less rigid view of the importance of virginity. The rates by the education of the boy go down because of less coital opportunity and the use of other sexual outlets.

The Kinsey findings indicated that while there continued to be important differences between males and females with reference to premarital sexual relations, the double standard had undergone change. The important difference between the unmarried female and male, at least for some groups, was no longer the virgin-nonvirgin double standard, but rather a double standard in which nonvirginity was found for both sexes, with the male often sexually promiscuous and the female generally restricted in number of sexual partners. Of those persons who were not virgins at the time of marriage 53 percent of the females, as contrasted with 27 percent of the males, had premarital coitus with only one partner; however, only 12 percent of the females, as contrasted with 40 percent of the males had premarital coitus with six or more partners.[33]

---

[29] Kirkpatrick, Clifford and Eugene Kanin, "Male Sex Aggression on a University Campus," *American Sociological Review*, February, 1957, p. 53.

[30] Kinsey, Alfred C. *et al.*, *Sexual Behavior in the Human Female* (Philadelphia: W. S. Saunders Co., 1953), p. 291.

[31] *Ibid.*, p. 293.

[32] *Ibid.*, p. 330.

[33] *Ibid.*, p. 292.

There are several general points that may be summarized from the various premarital sex studies made during the period up to the mid-1960's. First, while the major studies dealt with quite different samples the findings were in high agreement. In general the studies showed that of those women born after 1900 about half of them were not virgins when they married. And when women born after 1900 were compared by decades of birth there was no evidence to suggest any significant differences in their rates of premarital coitus. Second, the studies indicated that being nonvirgin at the time of marriage was not an indication of extensive premarital experience with a variety of partners. For the female, premarital coitus usually depended on strong emotional commitments and plans for marriage. Third, if the assumption of a temporary stabilization of premarital sexual coitus was true in the United States it meant that young people had been engaging in essentially the same types of behavior for three or four decades. It is the contention of the next section that these summary findings have been undergoing change in the last few years.

PREMARITAL SEX SINCE THE MID-1960'S

It is suggested that there has been a change in the sexual experiences of unmarried college girls since the mid-1960's.[34] In recent years, even more than ever, the group primarily responsible for rebellion among the young has been the college students. While there has always been rebellion by the younger generation toward their elders, it probably never has been as great in the United States as it has been since the mid-1960's. In recent years youths have not only rebelled, but have also rejected many aspects of the major institutions in American society. The mid-1960's have produced an action generation and their *modus vivendi* has been to experience, to confront, to participate, and sometimes to destroy. Since the mid-1960's a small but highly influential proportion of college students has been deeply involved in the civil rights movement and then in the protest over the Vietnam War. What may be most important about that generation of college students was that many were not just alienated as others have been in the past, but they were *actively* alienated.

Many college students believed that many of the norms of adult institutions were not only wrong but were also immoral. That view has been held by many college students toward the treatment of the black, toward the war in Vietnam, toward American political procedures, and so forth. It therefore seems logical that if many of the norms of those institutions are viewed as wrong and immoral by large numbers of the younger generation, they are also going to be suspicious and critical of other norms

---

[34] Bell, Robert R. and Jay B. Chaskes, "Premarital Sexual Experience among Coeds, 1958 and 1968," *Journal of Marriage and the Family*, February, 1970, pp. 81–84.

in various adult controlled institutions. Certainly a social institution that one would expect the younger generation to view with skepticism would be that concerned with marriage and sexual behavior. There are several other social factors that appear to be related to change in premarital sexual experiences.

One important factor of the 1960's was the development, distribution, and general acceptance of the birth control pill. On many large university campuses the pill is available to the coed, or it is not difficult for her to find out where to get it in the local community. While studies have shown that fear of pregnancy has not been a very important deterrent to premarital coitus for a number of years, it now seems to have been largely removed for most college girls. Another influence since the mid-1960's was the legitimization of sexual candor. In part the new sexual candor has been legitimized by one of the most venerable of American institutions—the Supreme Court. (This point is further discussed in the chapter on pornography.) In recent years the young person has had access to a level of sexual expression far greater than just ten years ago. The new sexual candor, whatever its original cause, is often seen by the rebelling younger generation as "theirs" in that it too critically subverts the traditional institutions. As a result the sexual candor of the late 1960's was often both a manifesto and a guidebook for many in the younger generation.

Finally, it should also be recognized that the rebellion of the younger generation has been given both implicit and explicit approval by many in the older generation. Many adults like to think of themselves as a part of the younger generation and its youth culture. For example, this is seen in the music and fashion of the youth culture which has had a tremendous impact on adults. It would seem that if many adults take on the values of the youth culture, that would raise questions as to the significance of many of their adult values for the youth world. In other words, the very identification of many adults with youth culture contributes to adult values having less impact on college youths.

Reiss has suggested that in the past the groups that developed a tradition of sexual permissiveness were often groups that had the least to lose. "Men and Negroes would be examples, for men cannot get pregnant and Negroes have less social standing to lose."[35] But he goes on to say that the present movement toward permissiveness among many is based differently than it used to be. This may be occurring within a context of general liberality. "It may be that liberalism emphasizes the types of social forces that maintain high permissiveness, for example, low religious orthodoxy, low value on tradition, high value on autonomy. The stronger the amount of general liberality in a group, the greater the like-

---

[35] Reiss, Ira L., *The Social Context of Premarital Sexual Permissiveness* (New York: Holt, Rinehart and Winston, Inc., 1967), p. 54.

lihood that social forces will maintain high levels of sexual permissiveness."[36] Reiss's statement very clearly describes the type of college student considered here. It is being argued that the social forces developing since the mid-1960's have led to a rapid increase in rejecting many traditional values and developing important patterns of behavior common to a general youth culture. And out of this has come an increased rate of premarital coitus among many college girls, along with less feelings of guilt about their experiences.

It must be stressed that the change in premarital sexual behavior being suggested is far from total. Rather, the contention is that a degree of change has occurred and that the minority has increased in size and in significance. But what may be most important is that there is a trend, however small, where one did not exist before. The nature and the degree of change can be examined in several different areas. One possible indication of change is suggested by the rates of virginity found in several recent coed populations that have been studied. One study, by Luckey and Ness, was carried out on a number of campuses around the United States. They asked their respondents if it would trouble them to marry a person who had experienced coitus with someone else before they became involved with them. To that question 61 percent of the females and 30 percent of the males answered no.[37] In another recent study done at the University of Colorado 45 percent of the males felt virginity in a prospective mate was an important consideration although only 17 percent of the males felt it was important for themselves to be virginal.[38] Luckey and Ness also asked: "Do you feel a person can have numerous sexual affairs and still bring a deep, enduring emotional commitment to the person he or she marries?" A little more than half of both males and females answered yes.[39]

The evidence for the argument of greater sexual experience for a significant minority of coeds can be examined by looking at virginity rates, the number of premarital sexual partners, and the feelings of guilt after experiencing premarital coitus. During the period from 1945 to 1965 the various studies of coital rates among coeds of all ages and class standings was about 25 to 30 percent. This percentage refers to the estimated rate at a given point in time if a sample of college girls could be drawn. Obviously the rates were much higher among college educated women when they married because in many cases several years elapsed from the time

[36] *Ibid.*, p. 73.

[37] Luckey, Eleanore B. and Gilbert D. Ness, "A Comparison of Sexual Attitudes and Behavior in an International Sample," *Journal of Marriage and the Family*, May, 1969, p. 369. Data from the same study are also found in Vance Packard, *The Sexual Wilderness* (New York: David McKay, 1968).

[38] Kaats, Gilbert R. and Keith E. Davis, "The Dynamics of Sexual Behavior of College Students," *Mimeograph* (University of Colorado, 1968), p. 14.

[39] Luckey and Ness, *op. cit.*, p. 369.

they would have been studied until when they married. The study done by Kaats and Davis in the spring of 1967 reported a coital rate of 41 percent for the females studied. However, those females were all 19 and 20 year old sophomores.[40] Therefore, if the rate were projected to the total coed population in that school it was probably well over 50 percent. In a study done by *Playboy* magazine in 1969 five very different types of colleges were investigated. They found the rate of about 50 percent for the three liberal colleges that they studied. The lowest rate was 19 percent of the coeds in a southern university.[41]

The writer had done a study of premarital sexual behavior and attitudes among a sample of coeds in a large urban university in 1958.[42] In 1968 the same questionnaire was used with a sample of coeds in the same university. A careful effort was made to match the two samples by age and by class standings. In those studied the rates of coitus were determined for the different levels of the dating relationship. The coeds were asked about the highest level of intimacy ever engaged in while dating, going steady, and engaged. The number of girls having premarital coitus while in a dating relationship went from 10 percent in 1958 to 23 percent in 1968, and the coitus rates while going steady went from 15 percent in 1958 to 28 percent in 1968. The rates of premarital intercourse during engagement went from 31 percent in 1958 to 39 percent in 1968. "Further examination of the data suggests that in 1958, the relationship of engagement was very often the prerequisite to a girl having premarital sexual intercourse. Engagement often provided her with a high level of emotional and future commitment which she often felt justified having coitus. However, in 1968 it appeared that the need to be engaged and all it implied was much less a condition the coed thought necessary before sexual intercourse. Therefore, the data suggest that the decision to have intercourse in 1968 was much less dependent on the commitment of engagement and more a question of individual decision regardless of the level of the relationship. To put it another way, if, in 1958, the coed had premarital coitus, it most often occurred while she was engaged. But in 1968, girls were more apt to have their first sexual experience while dating or going steady."[43]

NUMBER OF PARTNERS

As pointed out earlier the Kinsey findings indicated that most girls who had premarital coitus had limited that activity to one person. It was mentioned that of all the females who had premarital coitus 12 percent had

[40] Kaats and Davis, *op. cit.*, p. 1.
[41] "Close-Up:5 Schools," *Playboy*, September, 1969, p. 198.
[42] Bell and Chaskas, *op. cit.*, pp. 81–84.
[43] *Ibid.*, pp. 82–83.

had coitus with six or more partners.[44] The recent studies seem to indicate that of the girls who have premarital coitus it is still about one-half who have the experience with only one partner.[45] The change may be that many girls who do have more than one sexual partner are apt to have more partners than was the case in the past. For example, in the Luckey and Ness samples 34 percent of the coeds reported having coitus with several or many partners.[46] Similar evidence was also suggested in the recent study by the writer. "There is some evidence that girls having premarital coitus are having this experience with more different individuals. For example, of all those girls who had premarital coitus while in a dating relationship 56 percent had more than one partner—in fact, 22 percent had coitus in a dating relationship with five or more partners."[47]

Age at First Coitus

In the past, the Kinsey data showed that age was an important factor in understanding the higher probability of college-educated females' having premarital coitus. Many of them did not have their first sexual experiences until they were at an age when the lower-educated girl was already married. The Kinsey data showed that of those girls who had premarital coitus, 18 percent of the grade school group were having premarital coitus by age fifteen, as compared with 1 percent of the college-educated girls, while between the ages of sixteen and twenty, 38 percent had it as compared with 18 percent. After age twenty, the figures are about the same for all educational levels.[48] That 81 percent of the college-educated females who have premarital coitus have it past the age of twenty suggests that premarital coitus is not usually an event of their adolescence, but rather of their young adult years.

Reiss has suggested that informal patterns of behavior related to sexual behavior among the young have developed. He suggests that petting is accepted around the sixteenth birthday by the average girl who will eventually accept premarital coitus, and shortly before her eighteenth birthday by the average female who is not going to accept premarital coitus.[49] Reiss goes on to suggest that around the age of eighteen or nineteen a major change in sexual standards occurs for many females. This is because that is the time when they leave high school and go on to college, and in that process they change peer groups and increase their

---

[44] Kinsey, *op. cit.*, p. 292.

[45] Luckey and Ness, *op. cit.*, p. 376.

[46] *Ibid.*

[47] Bell and Chaskas, *op. cit.*, p. 84.

[48] Kinsey, *op. cit.*, p. 295.

[49] Reiss, *op. cit.*, p. 110.

autonomy. There may also be another period of increased permissiveness for many of those young women, "around the ages of twenty-two or twenty-three—when they move into the world of business and of the professions."[50]

The available data indicate that the age of first coitus for the college girl has not sharply decreased. For example, in the study of the five different colleges the mean age for first coitus for the male was 17.9 years and for the female 18.7 years of age.[51] The *Playboy* study offers similar evidence. In the most radical college population, where two-thirds of the coeds sampled were not virgins, only 17 percent had had their first coital experience at age 17 or younger. In that same sample 57 percent were age 20 or older when they had their first sexual intercourse.[52] So there is no evidence that coeds are having their first coital experience at younger ages than in the past.

Nowhere in the research literature on premarital sexual behavior in the past has there been any information as to participation in certain types of sexual expression. That is, studies have asked about necking, various types of petting, and coitus, but not about oral-genital contact. Yet, the Kinsey study showed that oral-genital sexual experience was common to many married couples and that area of sexual expression has gained increasing acceptance by many in recent years (although it is almost completely ignored in the research literature about the means for sexual fulfillment, even among the married). The only evidence available at present as to its frequency comes from the *Playboy* samples. In that study the respondents were asked if they had engaged in oral-genital contacts during the past school year. In the more radical colleges it was an experience for about four out of ten girls and for about one-half of the men. In the southern colleges it was admitted to by less than one in ten of the coeds but by almost one-half of the males.[53] It is suggested that oral-genital sexual experiences have contributed to the wider repertoire of sexual behavior for college students and that not only do they often participate more in coitus but also in these activities. If this is true it would make them even more sexually experienced than what just the findings on coital experience would indicate.

As has been suggested, what is important to understanding rates of coitus is their occurrence by the level of the dating relationship. In the spring of 1970 the writer did a study related to attitudes about various types of sexual expression. In that study a sample of 178 coeds filled out questionnaires about a variety of sexual attitudes. The respondents were

---

[50] *Ibid.*, p. 111.
[51] *Playboy, op. cit.*, p. 196.
[52] *Ibid.*, p. 198.
[53] *Ibid.*, p. 220.

also asked some behavioral questions about themselves. In that sample, of the girls who had never had any interpersonal relationship with a boy beyond dating, 96 percent were virgins. Many of these girls represented a highly select subsample: they were young, highly restricted in their interpersonal activities, or often quite unattractive. Of the girls in the sample whose highest level of relationship was going steady, 46 percent were virgins. Where the highest level of relationship had been engagement, 24 percent were virgins; and of those girls who were married, 27 percent were virgins at the time of their marriage.

The coeds in the above sample were also asked how they felt about certain sexual activities. For example, in casual dating 15 percent of them said that coitus was "always acceptable," 49 percent that it was "sometimes acceptable," and 36 percent that it was "never acceptable." During engagement the responses were 40 percent "always acceptable," 47 percent "sometimes acceptable," and 13 percent "never acceptable."

The recent studies contribute to the general observation that engagement is less important as the stage for justifying premarital coitus than it was in the past. As previously mentioned, the studies in the past have consistently shown that for the coed who had premarital coitus it was usually limited to one partner and then only during engagement. However, in the Bell and Chaskes study, when all girls in the 1968 sample who were ever engaged and who had ever had premarital coitus were analyzed, it was found that only 19 percent had limited their coital experience just to the period of engagement. "Expressing it another way, of all girls who were ever engaged and ever had premarital coital experience, 75 percent had their first experience while dating, 6 percent while going steady, and 19 percent during engagement. For all coeds with premarital coital sexual experience, 60 percent had coitus while dating, going steady, and engagement."[54]

Closely related to the past condition of engagement before a coed had premarital coitus was the condition of love. It seems clear that this condition has changed, and while coeds do not usually have coitus with males they know only in a casual way they no longer demand that there be a strong emotional commitment on the part of both. The *Playboy* sample indicated that in the three liberal schools over one-third of the coed respondents felt that it was permissible for a girl to have intercourse with someone she did not love.[55] It may also be that the younger generation defines love in a less complex and overwhelming way than it was defined in the past. While many of them may say love is important, what they mean by love may be quite different from what was meant in the past.

[54] Bell and Chaskes, *op. cit.*, p. 84.
[55] *Playboy, op. cit.*, p. 220.

RELIGIOUS INFLUENCES

As suggested, historically in the United States religion has been the force defining appropriate sexual behavior. However, the influence of religious beliefs on premarital sexual activity has steadily been decreasing. In the Bell and Chaskes study it was found that both in 1958 and 1968 the rates of coitus among coeds was lowest for the Catholics, next for the Jews, and highest for the Protestants. But what is of particular interest is that the rates went up proportionately about the same for all three religious groups over the ten year period.[56]

Whatever measurements are used as to religious intensity, regardless of the denomination, they appear to show higher rates of virginity among the more devout. For example, just taking the type of educational institution coeds attend, Packard found that of the coeds in public institutions 49 percent were not virgins, and this was true of 42 percent in private institutions, but only 12 percent of church related colleges.[57] There is a strong selection process taking place, with the most conservative girls going to the most conservative colleges. Another measurement of religious intensity is that of religious attendance. In the 1970 study by the writer it was found that 67 percent of the non-virgins had not attended any religious ceremony during the past month while non-attendance was true of 51 percent of the virgins.

The various studies indicate another social variable related to premarital sexual experience for coeds and that is geographical region—especially if the coed is from the south. The south has the highest rural population and it is also the most conservative in general moral values and religiously, all of which contribute to conservative sexual behavior. Also as would be expected, the south has the highest proportion of double standard adherents to premarital sexual behavior. For example, in the Packard study it was found that in the eastern colleges studied 57 percent of the females and 64 percent of the males had coital experience. By contrast, in the south the rates were 32 percent for the females and 69 percent for the males.[58]

When one examines the various social variables related to present rates of premarital coitus some of the old and reliable variables are no longer the absolute indicators they once were. For example, it used to be found in whatever group one studied that the rates of premarital coitus for the male would be higher than for the female. Yet when different types of college populations today are compared, this distinction doesn't always

---

[56] Bell and Chaskes, *op. cit.*, p. 83.
[57] Packard, *op. cit.*, p. 507.
[58] *Ibid.*, p. 188.

hold up. Packard writes that at six of the nineteen schools attended by males, *"fewer* than 50 percent of the males reported that they had ever experienced coitus. And at 6 of 19 schools attended by females, *more* than 50 percent of the females responded that they had at some time experienced coitus."[59] Packard goes on to point out that for the girls the lowest rates of coitus were reported at a Catholic university where less than one-fifth reported coital experience. "The highest reported incidence for females was at the eastern woman's college with liberal rules, where more than three-quarters of them reported coital experience."[60]

GUILT FEELINGS

Given the argument that many coeds are engaged in premarital sex in less emotionally demanding situations today than they were in the past, what are the consequences of that behavior? If the norms of society are incorporated into the personality structure of the individual and are felt by him to be important, any deviation from those norms will usually lead to guilt feelings. Certainly, those who hold to the norms expect that to be true and assume that even when young people go "wrong" they will feel bad about it. And what particularly bothers an older and more conservative generation is not only that the younger generation goes against the norms, but that it does not indicate that it is sorry. For the young person to have premarital intercourse *and* to be little influenced by the norms of the older generation is really the crux of the generational conflict pertaining to premarital sexual matters.

What evidence is there of feelings of guilt? In the Bell and Chaskes study the respondents were asked at each stage of the dating relationship if they had ever felt they had gone "too far" in their level of intimacy. Of coeds who had coitus, by the level of dating relationship the rates for those saying they "went too far" were: "while dating, in 1958, 65 percent and in 1968, 36 percent; while going steady, in 1958, 61 percent and in 1968, 30 percent; and while engaged, 1958, 41 percent and in 1968, 20 percent. In general, when the data of 1958 are compared with 1968 the coeds were more apt to have had intercourse at all levels of the dating relationship and at the same time felt less guilty than did their counterparts in 1958."[61]

There is also some related evidence from the *Playboy* samples. The coeds were asked if they thought a girl would lose the respect of a boy with whom she went to bed before she married him. Over 80 percent of the coeds in all the schools except the one in the south answered "no."

---

[59] *Ibid.*, p. 186.
[60] *Ibid.*, p. 187.
[61] Bell and Chaskes, *op. cit.*, p. 83.

Eighty percent of the coeds who had engaged in premarital coitus during the previous school year described their emotional state as one of "contentment."[62]

Regardless of the limitations the available evidence seems to indicate a change in the premarital sexual activity of an important minority of college students since the mid-1960's. From the point of view held by the older members of society there has been no easing up of the traditional restrictive values about premarital coitus. Therefore, the differences by generation contribute to greater potential conflict. This chapter is concluded by looking at the nature of generational conflict as it is reflected in the beliefs about premarital sexual behavior held by parents and their young adult offspring.

GENERATIONAL CONFLICT

Given their different stages in the life cycle, parents and children are almost always going to show variations in how they define appropriate behavior for a given role. Values as to "proper" premarital sexual-role behavior from the perspective of the parents are greatly influenced by the strong emotional involvement of the parent with his child. But by contrast, the child is going through a life-cycle stage in which the actual behavior occurs, and must try to relate his parents' values to what he is doing or may do. There is a basic difference between defining appropriate role conduct for others to follow and defining proper role conduct to be followed by oneself. What is important is that there is often more than one significant group of role definers that the young person may turn to as guides for his sex-role behavior. From his perspective, what his parents think about how he should behave may be much less important than what his peers see as the best mode of behavior. There are some studies that show the contrast in attitudes about premarital sex by the younger generation when compared with the values of parents and other adults.

One study compared the attitudes of over 200 coeds and those of their mothers. Both mothers and daughters were asked to respond to the question, "How important do you think it is that a girl be a virgin when she marries?" Of the mothers, 88 percent said they thought it was "very wrong" not to be a virgin, while the remaining 12 percent thought it "generally wrong." Fifty-five percent of the daughters thought it "very wrong," 34 percent "generally wrong," and 13 percent "right in many situations."[63] The responses show sharp differences between the attitudes of mothers and daughters toward premarital chastity. It is probable that many of the

---

[62] *Playboy, op. cit.*, p. 220.

[63] Bell, Robert R. and Jack V. Buerkle, "Mother and Daughter Attitudes to Premarital Sexual Behavior," *Marriage and Family Living*, November, 1961, p. 391.

mothers were influenced by having a daughter in the age setting where the questions had an immediate and highly emotional application. Even so, the sharp differences between mother and daughter responses indicate that the area of premarital sexual behavior is one of potentially great conflict.

Probably the most common technique for minimizing of conflict used by the daughter is to avoid discussing her sexual attitudes or behavior with her mother. In the above study it was found that only 37 percent of the daughters in contrast with 83 percent of the mothers felt that daughters should freely answer questions from their mothers about attitudes toward sexual intimacy.[64] The entire area of sexual attitudes is highly influenced by emotion, especially for the mother as it concerns her daughter. The emotional reactions of some mothers may also be influenced by recollections of their own premarital sexual experiences. The Kinsey study, which provides data on the mothers' generation in their younger years, indicates that the mothers were actually no more conservative in their premarital sexual behavior than are many of their daughters.

There is a question as to whether the liberal sexual attitudes of coeds will continue for long as they get older. In the study discussed above it was found that differences in the educational background of the mothers did not produce differences in attitudes toward premarital virginity. It is quite possible that later in her life the college-educated daughter may be as conservative as her mother, when her attitudinal rationales are not related to herself or her age-peers, but rather to a daughter of her own. It is possible that the "sexual emancipation" of many college girls exists only for a short time in their life span—the time when they are personally involved in premarital sexual behavior.

In the mid-1960's Ira Reiss did research with several large samples of adults, high school and college students. In that study the respondents were asked to express their beliefs about different combinations of intimacy and degree of interpersonal commitment for both unmarried males and females. They were asked if they believed that petting during engagement was acceptable for the engaged male and female. In the adult sample, the belief that petting during engagement was acceptable for the engaged male was the response of 61 percent, and for the engaged female it was the response of 56 percent. Of the student respondents, 85 percent approved for the engaged male and 82 percent for the engaged female.[65] Thus, not only were the adult attitudes about petting during engagement more conservative than those of the student population, but for both the adult and student groups there is a single standard—that is, the acceptance rates are roughly the same for both males and females.

---

[64] *Ibid.*, p. 392.

[65] Reiss, Ira L., "The Scaling of Premarital Sexual Permissiveness," *Journal of Marriage and the Family*, May, 1964, pp. 190–91.

Reiss also asked his respondents if they believed that premarital petting was acceptable when the individual felt no particular affection toward his partner. To this question, "yes" was the response of 29 percent of the adult group with reference to the male, and of 20 percent for the female. In the sudent sample, "yes" was the response for 34 percent of the males and 18 percent of the females.[66] These responses offer some evidence for a number of persons fitting into Reiss's category of "permissiveness-without-affection." The adult responses suggest a single standard of rejecting this kind of behavior, however, while the student sample gives some indication of a double standard—a higher proportion suggesting approval for this behavior pattern for males than for females.

Reiss asked his respondents if they believed full sexual relations to be acceptable if the male or female is engaged. Approval was the response given by 20 percent of the adult group for males and 17 percent for females. In the student group, acceptance was given by 52 percent for the male and 44 percent for the female.[67] Finally, Reiss's respondents were asked if they believed it acceptable for both males and females to have premarital coitus even if they felt no particular affection toward their partner. In the adult sample, 12 percent stated approval for the male and 7 percent for the female. In the student group, 21 percent approved for the male, 11 percent for the female.[68] It should be remembered that these samples were taken in the mid-1960's and it seems very likely that the rates of acceptance among the college students would be higher today.

The values of parents and the adult community in general may in time become more liberal and the conflict between the generations reduced. (There seems little possibility that the younger generation will become more conservative and reduce generational conflict in that way.) It appears most likely that parents and their children will continue to live with somewhat different value systems with regard to premarital sexual attitudes and related behavior. Many parents will probably continue to hold to traditional values and assume that their child is conforming to those values unless his actions force them to admit otherwise. The younger generation will probably continue to develop their own modified value systems and keep those values pretty much to themselves, implicitly allowing their parents to believe they are behaving according to the traditional values.

In summary, it has been argued that premarital sexual involvement has increased in recent years and represents an important area of social deviancy as defined by older, more conservative elements of society. As suggested in Chapter 1, deviancy often exists primarily in the eyes of

---

[66] *Ibid.*
[67] *Ibid.*
[68] *Ibid.*

the beholder and therefore there are strong generational differences in defining whether or not premarital sex is deviance, and if so, to what extent it actually exists. Related values held by different generations are important in understanding many other defined areas of deviancy and social problems, and this will be seen in a number of the substantive areas to be discussed in the chapters ahead.

BIBLIOGRAPHY

BELL, ROBERT R., *Premarital Sex in a Changing Society* (Englewood Cliffs, N.J.: Prentice-Hall, Inc., 1966).

BELL, ROBERT R., "Parent-Child Conflict in Sexual Values," *Journal of Social Issues*, April, 1966, pp. 34–44.

BELL, ROBERT R. and JAY B. CHASKES, "Premarital Sexual Experience among Coeds, 1958 and 1968," *Journal of Marriage and the Family*, February, 1970, pp. 81–84.

LUCKEY, ELEANORE B. and GILBERT D. NESS, "A Comparison of Sexual Attitudes and Behavior in an International Sample," *Journal of Marriage and the Family*, May, 1969, pp. 364–79.

PACKARD, VANCE, *The Sexual Wilderness* (New York: David McKay, 1968).

REISS, IRA L., *Premarital Sexual Standards in America* (New York: The Free Press of Glencoe, 1960).

REISS, IRA L., *The Social Context of Premarital Sexual Permissiveness* (New York: Holt, Rinehart and Winston, Inc., 1967).

REISS, IRA L., "Premarital Sex as Deviant Behavior: An Application of Current Approaches to Deviance," *American Sociological Review*, February, 1970, pp. 78–87.

CHAPTER 3

EXTRAMARITAL SEXUAL
BEHAVIOR

In the United States, while all sexual relations outside of marriage are morally condemned, the negative views towards extramarital coitus are generally even stronger than those directed at premarital sexual intercourse. This is the result of two beliefs: first, that with marriage there is an approved sexual partner and therefore the individual has the opportunity of having his sexual needs met; and second, that any extramarital sexual involvement threatens the highly valued relationship of marriage. In the past, the American male could often discreetly indulge in sexual relations outside of marriage, but under no circumstances was the wife allowed any such sexual outlet. For many Americans the traditional double-standard values have been altered to the extent that both partners are expected to restrict their sexual needs to marriage; and, if the husband has any extramarital "rights," then it is believed that the same "rights" should also exist for the woman. In this chapter the interest first is in examining extramarital sexual activity as it has traditionally been viewed, and second, to look at a fairly new and emerging type of sexual behavior outside of marriage that involves the husband and wife together with other married couples—called "swinging."

Under American law the specific legal restrictions placed on extramarital coitus fall under the heading of adultery.

63

ADULTERY

In the United States adultery is legally punishable, but actual prosecution is rare and in most states the penalties are mild. Adultery has its greatest importance as legal grounds for divorce, since it is the only legal grounds for divorce recognized by all legal jurisdictions of the United States. It is useful to look first at views of extramarital coitus from a cross-cultural perspective.

All known societies have placed some limitations on extramarital coitus as well as developed some means for enforcing the restrictions. However, the nature of the restrictions and the means to effectively control them vary widely between societies, and often within a given society over time. The reason for the restrictions in most preliterate groups, ancient societies, and even recent civilizations has not been because of sexual restrictions *per se* or even because of morality. Rather, "adultery has most often been considered a threat to the economic stability of society; most specifically, male property rights."[1]

As suggested, when one actually examines the many cultures, past and present, it is seen that the taboos against extramarital involvement are widespread—although sometimes more honored in the breach than in actual practice. Murdock found in his sample of 148 societies that taboos against adultery appeared in 120 (81 percent). "In 4 of the remaining 28, adultery is socially disapproved though it is not strictly forbidden; it is conditionally permitted in 19 and freely allowed in 5. It should be pointed out, however, that these figures apply only to sexual relations with unrelated or distantly related persons. A substantial majority of all societies permit extramarital relations with certain affinal relatives."[2]

Many societies reflect a double standard with regard to extramarital rights. Ford and Beach in their study of various societies found that 60 percent of them forbid a married woman to engage in extramarital relationships. They point out that in some societies the married man is also restricted, although most societies are much more concerned with the behavior of the wife. Yet, in those societies, very often any man who seduces a married woman will be punished.[3] They go on to point out that "although in theory many societies accept a double standard of restrictions on extra-mateship liaisons, it is only in a few cases that the mated man can take advantage of his theoretical liberties."[4]

---

[1] Harper, Robert A. "Extramarital Sex Relations" in Albert Ellis and Albert Abarbanel, *Encyclopedia of Sexual Behavior* (New York: Hawthorne Books, Inc., 1961), p. 384.

[2] Murdock, George P., *Social Structure* (New York: The Macmillan Company, 1949), p. 265.

[3] Ford, Clellan S. and Frank A. Beach, *Patterns of Sexual Behavior* (New York: Harper and Bros., 1952), p. 115.

[4] *Ibid.*

When it is seen that in most societies women have fewer opportunities for extramarital sex, and even where the opportunity exists they have lower incidences and frequencies, it must be recognized that this is due to cultural differences rather than biological ones. That is, the evidence clearly indicates that if women are given the opportunity without strong social and psychological restrictions many find extramarital sexual involvement attractive and enjoyable. As Harper points out, in those countries where strong progress has been made toward social equality of the sexes, "such evidence as exists indicates increased incidences among married women of extramarital sex behavior that approximates the male pattern."[5] This appears to be a pattern for an increasing number of American women—especially among the higher educated.

Some cultures have made special adaptations to the question of extramarital sexual involvement in allowing it to take place under special circumstances. Often a society will be very restrictive about many areas of activity, but at special times of the year will lift those restrictions. For example, there are some societies which have special days or occasions which allow for periods of general license and where the members are allowed to violate the usual rules. This is seen during the Mardi Gras in New Orleans and similar pre-Lent activities in the Caribbean and South America. Ford and Beach write "sexual liaisons may be generally prohibited, but on certain special occasions the prohibitions are lifted for a short time and everyone is expected to have sexual intercourse with someone other than the spouse. The occasions for sexual license usually appear to have religious significance and may range from harvest festivals to mortuary feasts."[6]

It is also found that in some societies extramarital sexual relationships take place as a specific form. This is because with few exceptions every society that approves of extramarital liaisons limits them in some way. For example, some societies forbid extramarital relationships except where the persons are siblings-in-law.[7] And in some societies extramarital sex takes the form of "wife lending" or "wife exchange." "Generally, the situation is one in which a man is granted sexual access to the mate of another only on special occasions. If the pattern is reciprocal an exchange of wives occurs. Both wife lending and wife exchange may be involved in patterns of hospitality."[8]

Given the exceptions and variations against the absolute control over extramarital sexual relationships, nevertheless the strengths of these controls have been very powerful, especially in the Western world. This raises the question of why extramarital sexual behavior should have been

---

[5] Harper, *op. cit.*, p. 386.

[6] Ford and Beach, *op. cit.*, p. 115.

[7] *Ibid.*, p. 114.

[8] *Ibid.*

so strongly controlled. Probably the most important reason has been the great influence of religion over sexual behavior in terms of creating norms of sexual morality. The only sexual restriction in the Ten Commandments is against adultery. But Biblically adultery referred to an offense against property and meant the infringing on the rights of another man. And it did not necessarily mean that a man must restrict his sexual attentions to his wife. In fact if his wife did not bear children she often gave one of her handmaidens to her husband. "Moreover, as the Bible often reminds us, men were free to maintain mistresses ('concubines') in addition to their wives; and on the number of wives a man might have there was no restriction."[9]

However, over time and with the emergence of Protestantism, the church gained increasing influence over sexual behavior.

In the United States the religious restrictions against extramarital sex have had a great influence on the laws. The relationship between these two institutions in strongly controlling American behavior from the beginning is seen in the attempt to repress all sexual matters among the Puritans. For adultery the death penalty was instituted by the Puritans, although for ordinary fornication the penalty was the relatively mild one of three months' imprisonment. The death sentence was actually imposed as there is on record a man of 89 who was executed for adultery in 1653.[10]

Down through the years the institutions of religion and law have worked together. In theory, most laws about adultery are based on the assumption that adultery is a cardinal sin. But there has often been a wide disparity between the legal punishments in principle and in practice. This has been especially true for men because exceptions have constantly been made. The study of the "historical, anthropological, and sociological data fails to reveal a society that has consistently suppressed and severely punished extramarital sex relations for its males."[11] This was true even among the early Puritans where even though the punishment was very severe and conformity was high there is still evidence of some sexual deviancy. An anthropologist writes on this point that however much moralists push the obligations of chastity in marriage "this obligation has never been even approximately regarded: and in all nations, ages, and religions a vast mass of irregular indulgence has appeared, which has probably contributed more than any other single cause to the misery and degradation of man."[12]

There are many complex reasons for the breakdown of the traditional

---

[9] Taylor, G. Rattray, *Sex in History* (New York: The Vanguard Press, 1954), p. 241.

[10] *Ibid.*, p. 173.

[11] Harper, *op. cit.*, pp. 384–85.

[12] Stephens, William N. *The Family in Cross Cultural Perspective* (New York: Holt, Rinehart and Winston, Inc., 1963), p. 241.

means of control over sexual morality. Certainly the decreasing influence of religion in defining behavior for many people is a major change. But on the broadest level the decrease in control has been because the American society is modern, industrialized, and urbanized. As a specialized society it has developed to the point where the traditional institutions of marriage and the family are of much less significance for survival and physical well-being. "Adultery has, therefore, ceased to be a serious threat to the economy of these societies."[13] With this in mind it is possible to examine the contemporary scene in the United States with regard to extramarital sexual attitudes and behavior.

Like all areas of deviancy it is impossible to know with any accuracy how common extramarital sexual experience is in the United States today. The best empirical evidence we still have is from the Kinsey studies. Kinsey found that by age forty, 26 percent of the married women and 50 percent of the married men had had an extramarital coital experience.[14] (It would appear possible that today, twenty-five years after the Kinsey studies, that by age 40 about a third of all married women and possibly 60 percent of all married men have had an extramarital coital experience.) Kinsey discovered important age differences for men and women; for the men, the highest percentage was in the very young married group and then gradually decreased with increasing age. For the women, the highest percentage was in the age group thirty-six to forty, but was low for the very young and older women.[15] The peak rates for extramarital coitus correspond to the different stages of greatest sexual interest and drive in the male and female. The increase for women as they grow older may be because often the husband's sexual activity declines as he gets older and she seeks out other sexual outlets. Not only do many older women have a high sexual interest, but some may have their sexual desires increased because fear of pregnancy has been removed by reaching their menopause. "There is also some evidence that older women are more skeptical of the validity of the moral taboos against extramarital sex relations that seriously impressed them in their earlier years."[16]

The Kinsey studies also provided information as to the number of different partners had by those with extramarital coital experience. For the females Kinsey found that at the time of the study 41 percent of the women had limited their extramarital coitus to one partner; another 40 percent had had sexual relations with from two to five partners. This left 19 percent of the women having had more than five partners in their extramarital

---

[13] Harper, *op. cit.*, p. 388.

[14] Kinsey, Alfred C., Wardell B. Pomeroy, Clyde E. Martin, and Paul H. Gebhard, *Sexual Behavior in the Human Female* (Philadelphia: W. B. Saunders Co., 1953), p. 437.

[15] *Ibid.*, p. 416.

[16] Harper, *op. cit.*, pp. 386–87.

activities.[17] There are no corresponding figures in the Kinsey studies for the male. Kinsey also provides information on other variables related to frequency of extramarital coitus. For the female, the Kinsey data show no relationship between frequency of extramarital coitus and educational level; however, for the male, the rates were significantly higher among the less-educated.[18] By religion for women, the active incidence of extramarital experience was higher among the less devout, and this finding was true of Protestants, Jews, and Catholics alike. The same general relationship to devoutness of religion was also found for the male.[19]

The available data clearly indicate that a large number of both husbands and wives find some sexual experience outside of marriage. It also suggests that this behavior cannot be attributed in all cases to chance circumstances or "momentary weakness." While there are no socially approved changes in the values about extramarital coitus, it is clear that the traditional values and norms no longer exert effective control over the behavior of many husbands and wives. Of greatest significance may be the indicated behavioral change in the sexual activity of many wives. The philandering husband has often had latent social acceptance in the United States but the philandering wife has not, either in the past or the present. As suggested, the involvement in extramarital sexual acivity is a result of many factors. The following are some suggestions as to possible reasons for becoming involved in extramarital coitus. It should be kept in mind that, for any given individual, the suggested influences may operate in various degrees of intensity.[20]

1. *Variation of Sexual Partners.* The monogamous sexual relationship of man and woman is a result of cultural conditioning, which may not be as strong for some individuals as for others. In some cases, the sexual relationship of marriage becomes routinized and boring, and the idea of another sexual partner seems different, new, and exciting. In other cases, the person may feel his spouse is no longer able to meet his sexual needs and, consequently, he seeks out a person he believes will be a better sexual partner than the spouse. Within this setting, the basic motivation appears to be the desire for the new experience of a different sexual partner.

2. *Retaliation.* If one partner in a marriage finds out that his partner has had an extramarital affair, his reaction may be "If he can, so can I." Reiss suggests that this reaction is most commonly found among double-standard men and women.[21] In the case of an affair by a husband whose

---

[17] Kinsey, *op. cit.*, p. 425.

[18] *Ibid.*, p. 437.

[19] *Ibid.*, pp. 424, 437.

[20] See Kinsey *op. cit.*, pp. 432–35. The following are partially drawn from this source.

[21] Reiss, Ira L., *Premarital Sexual Standards in America* (New York: The Free Press of Glencoe, 1960), p. 170.

wife believes in sexual equality, the wife may respond by thinking she should have an affair to show her sexual equality. Retaliation indicates that getting even may be more important than the sexual interest in another partner.

3. *Rebellion.* Some people feel that the monogamous nature of marriage places an unnecessary restriction on them, and through extramarital coitus they can show their independence. The rebellion sometimes may be aimed at the spouse, who they feel restricts their sexual "rights." In other cases, the person may feel that the social norms of monogamy are unreasonable and he shows his objection to and contempt of the norms by entering a sexual liaison. The motivating force often appears not to be so much a desire for the extramarital sex partner, but rather to "show" the spouse or society in general.

4. *Emotional Involvements.* Some individuals do not feel their personal needs are being met in the marriage relationship and as a result they may seek satisfaction (not always sexual) from a partner outside the marriage. But if a woman feels that the extramarital partner is satisfying some of her emotional needs, sexual activity may enter the relationship. Here the motive appears to be the need for an emotional relationship outside of marriage, which may then lead to the inclusion of sexual intimacy.

5. *Emerging from Friendship.* In American society cross-sexual friendships among adults are often difficult because of the possibility of having the friendship shift to a romantic or sexual one. In some cases men and women who are friends may, in spending time together, find themselves developing an emotional and sexual interest in each other. In this setting there may be no explicitly conscious motive moving them toward sexual relationships, but rather the sexual interest may develop along with increased mutual interest and feeling.

6. *Spouse Encouragement.* Kinsey found that in some cases the husbands had encouraged their wives to have extramarital affairs. The motive of a number of husbands was the desire to find an excuse for their own extramarital activity.[22] Yet one of the striking findings by Kinsey was that "most of the husbands who attempted or encouraged their wives' extramarital activity had done so in an honest attempt to give them the opportunity for additional sexual satisfaction."[23]

7. *The Influence of Aging.* It was pointed out that the highest frequency of extramarital coitus for women occurred in the age group from thirty-six to forty. Several influences may operate on women in this general age classification. First, the woman's sexual desires and interests are often high as a result of a strong sex drive and the loss of many sexual inhibitions that influenced her when she was younger. During the same

---

[22] Kinsey, *op. cit.*, p. 435.
[23] *Ibid.*

age period many of the husbands have a decrease in sexual drive and interest. Second, the woman in entering middle age may see herself as leaving her youth behind and find this aspect of aging very upsetting. She may want to prove to herself (and sometimes others) that she is still a desirable female, and an extramarital affair may be seen as one way of doing so.

8. *Hedonism.* One final category centers around the fact that while sex is usually highly enjoyable, most people will often forego the pleasure because of various types of social conditioning. If the moral restrictions are not meaningful for the individual then the individual may take an amoral, hedonistic view toward sex. So some people may have extramarital sexual intimacy simply because new sexual relationships are pleasurable and they do so with no negative consequences. Of course, in this day and age of belief in deep-seated and hidden motives (many of which are never empirically proven), a simple hedonistic approach to extramarital sex is denied. Yet we would suggest that some people may enter "illicit" sexual activity not to prove a thing—but simply because sex is pleasurable and they are not subject to many of the usual social restrictions.

It is now possible to examine some of the effects of extramarital experience on the spouse who is left at home. Undoubtedly the most common reaction of the innocent spouse is one of jealousy. Stephens points out that while the urge to philander is strong nevertheless in many cultures it collides with feelings of possessiveness and sexual jealousy. "When one spouse 'cheats,' the other spouse—if he or she knows about it—often suffers."[24] Stephens goes on to point out that even in those societies which allow adultery the problem of jealousy still exists. "Some people are still hurt when their spouses engage in perfectly proper and virtuous adultery."[25]

Given the strong social restrictions against extramarital coitus, the sexual satisfactions and reactions of those who deviate are of interest. Kinsey found in his sample about 85 percent of all those females engaging in extramarital activity were responding, at least on occasion, to orgasm. But Kinsey points out that selective factors were probably involved, and that the most responsive females may have been the ones who had most often engaged in extramarital coitus.[26] Kinsey also provides some information on the significance of extramarital coitus for divorce. In general, females rated extramarital coitus as a less important factor in divorce than did men, and both sexes assessed the extramarital coitus of the spouse as more significant than their own extramarital activity. Fourteen percent of the females and 18 percent of the males saw their own extramarital

---

[24] Stephens, *op. cit.*, p. 254.

[25] *Ibid.*, pp. 251–52.

[26] Kinsey, *op. cit.*, p. 418.

experience as a major factor in their divorce; however, when the extra-marital activity was that of the spouse, 27 percent of the females and 51 percent of the males rated it as a major factor in their divorce.[27] Finally, pregnancy attributed to extramarital coitus appears to be quite rare. "Of our 2,221 ever-married women, 26 reported a total of 32 pregnancies known or believed to have been the result of extramarital coitus."[28]

Of great significance are the psychological reactions of women to their experiences in extramarital coitus. If the norms and values of society were fully accepted and integrated into the personality structures of individuals, then one would expect strong feelings of remorse and guilt by women who had extramarital experiences. Kinsey found that "among the married women in the sample who had not had extramarital experience, some 83 percent indicated that they did not intend to have it, but in a sample of those who had extramarital experiences, only 44 percent indicated they did not intend to renew their experiences."[29] These findings suggest that a number of women did not have severe enough negative feelings about their past experiences to deter them from anticipating the same experiences in the future.

With the traditional importance attached to the husband's exclusive sexual rights to his wife, it would seem that if a husband found his wife guilty of adultery he would either divorce her or drastically alter the nature of the marriage; yet Kinsey found that, of the females who had extra-marital coitus, about 49 percent believed that the husband knew or suspected. In those marriages where the husband suspected or learned of the wife's extramarital activities, 42 percent of the women reported no difficulty with their husbands.[30] While some of the women may have been interpreting their husbands' reactions inaccurately, it is also possible that many were not. If they were not, it indicates a great change for some husbands from the traditional view of their wives' sexual exclusiveness for them.

Implied in the discussion thus far is that extramarital sex may follow many different patterns. One writer has suggested that today the two extremes are the new open and accepted affair and the old secret and guilt ridden one.[31] The variation as well as the changing nature of extramarital sex is reflected in what they are called. Not too many years ago it was *cheating*, but now it's an *affair*. In fact it is increasingly getting to be that

[27] *Ibid.*, p. 438.

[28] Gebhard, Paul H., Wardell B. Pomeroy, Clyde E. Martin, and Cornelia V. Christenson, *Pregnancy, Birth and Abortion* (New York: Harper & Row, Publishers, 1958), p. 85.

[29] Kinsey, *op. cit.*, p. 431.

[30] *Ibid.*, p. 434.

[31] Love, Nancy, "The '70's Woman and the Now Marriage," *Philadelphia Magazine*, February, 1970, p. 56.

only the lower middle and lower classes call it cheating. In fact, adultery is getting to sound old fashioned and almost quaint.[32]

One type of extramarital sexual involvement that has always existed but has changed a great deal in recent years is the mistress relationship to the married man. This is an intimate relationship that involves far more than sex. It usually lasts for some period of time and there are generally no real expectations that marriage will ever occur. By contrast an "affair" is much more sexually oriented and has much less interpersonal commitment between the two individuals. Cuber has described the mistress relationship in some detail. He found that the mistress was just as apt to be married as unmarried. When two married people move into a mistress relationship it is usually because they feel their respective marriages are lacking in interpersonal or sexual fulfillment. "However, for one reason or another they do not wish to terminate their marriages legally and so find their fulfillment in what is really a *de facto* marriage, without any legal or moral sanction by the community."[33]

Cuber found no simple configuration of attitudes and life style which distinguished the wife from the mistress. Just as with a wife a mistress may fit a wide variety of attitudes, life styles, fulfillments, and frustrations.[34] Also, the importance of sex to the mistress relationship can be overdone. "Some mistresses are primarily intellectual companions, women who share some intellectual pursuit with their men, some important hobby, some political or ethical commitment in a way which neither has had or is not able to have with anyone else."[35] He goes on to point out that the stereotype of the young mistress and the aging man does not fit the fact. In fact he found that a number of men even in their later middle ages had mistresses who were about the same age. Cuber suggests that perhaps the most startling finding of his study was that a considerable number of the mistress relationships endured for long periods of time.[36]

As suggested, in Cuber's discussion of the "mistress" affair sex may not always be important and in some cases may not occur. There may be some nonsexual affairs that are based upon fairly strong emotional attachments. In fact an emotional attachment that is nonsexual may be a far greater threat to a marriage than a brief sexual nonemotional relationship. This distinction is very important to the "swingers" that will be examined later in the chapter.

The stress has been on the patterns of extramarital sexual experience but it should always be remembered that many Americans probably never have any sexual experiences outside their marriages. For most of these

---

[32] *Ibid.*

[33] Cuber, John F. "The Mistress in American Society," *Medical Aspects of Human Sexuality*, September, 1969, p. 86.

[34] *Ibid.*, p. 85.

[35] *Ibid.*, p. 86.

[36] *Ibid.*, p. 87.

people the traditional controls over sexual morality will continue to be strong. But for more and more, especially among the young, the views about sexual morality are changing. In fact today many people who engage in extramarital sexual relationships suffer little or no social criticism if their behavior is discrete. Generally, extramarital sex is seen by many as a personal concern unless it becomes general knowledge. "Even then no legal action is likely unless the adultery, left unpunished, is thought to set a bad moral example for youth or otherwise to encourage wrongdoing."[37]

As in so many areas of deviance, many persons who are involved moved from a defensive to an offensive point of view. Put another way, they have often shifted from rationalizing their behavior to proselytizing it. For example, the Sexual Freedom League believes "that sexual expression, in whatever form agreed between consenting persons of either sex, should be considered an inalienable right. . . . Sex without guilt and restriction is good, pleasurable, relaxing, and promotes a spirit of human closeness, compassion and good will. We believe that sexual activity . . . has a wealth of potential for making life more livable and enjoyable."[38]

In the past the belief existed that extramarital sexual involvement would destroy a marriage, which it often did because the belief was so strong, even though there may have been no other logical reason for ending the marriage. However, there is no reason to believe that man, if he chooses, cannot invent ways to reduce or remove the social conditions that make extramarital coitus hazardous for happily married people.

Whatever changes do occur will be a part of the new sexual morality that argues for equal rights of sexual expression for both men and women. This means that women will increasingly demand the same sexual rights for themselves as do men, whether in or out of marriage. As Love points out, "No matter what the outcome of the academic and ethical debates, women are going to continue to demand equal time and equal rights to erotic pleasure, to self-realization, to self-respect—and if they can't find these qualities within marriage, they will quietly go on seeking them elsewhere."[39]

It is also of interest to see that the new sexual morality places great importance on the woman's achieving sexual satisfaction. It is believed by many that she has greater freedom to enjoy sex in the same way that men have always enjoyed it. But the irony of this liberation is that a woman may have greater apprehension if she doesn't fully enjoy the sexual experience. She knows she has a right to orgasm and if she is not getting it with the frequency or intensity she believes she should she may begin to

---

[37] Harper, op. cit., p. 387.

[38] Lind, Jack, "The Sexual Freedom League," in Walt Anderson, The Age of Protest (Pacific Palisades, Calif.: Goodyear Publishing Co., Inc., 1969), p. 184.

[39] Love, op. cit., p. 93.

wonder what is wrong. At the same time the man who also accepts the new morality may wonder what is wrong with himself if his mate doesn't reach full sexual fulfillment. These kinds of concerns are important whether in or out of marriage. But in one sense they may be most important outside of marriage where the affair is essentially sexual and any sexual failure undermines the limited tie of the relationship. In the next section we will consider an essentially avant garde type of sex outside of marriage—"swinging"—the sexual exchange of marriage partners.

SWINGING

For years stories have been told about "wife-swapping" and "key clubs." When the tellers of the stories were pushed for evidence it was almost always found that the stories were third or fourth hand and their origins lost in the foggy past of rumor. One story which it was possible to track down was based on one married woman having sexual intercourse with a number of neighborhood men. But this was not "wife-swapping" or "swinging." However, in recent years many stories about swinging have been heard and it has been possible to trace them down and find that many are based on fact. There has probably always been some swinging, but not to the extent that it has developed in recent years. Furthermore, swinging does not seem to be limited to any one part of the United States, although it is probably less common in the south.

"Swinging" as it is used here refers to the sexual exchange of partners between married couples. And their sexual activities with one another are viewed as primarily recreational and an end in themselves. Swinging is a single standard of sex which insists that what is sexually right for the husband is also right for the wife. This is in contrast with an affair, which usually involves guilt and dishonesty and often does not include any notion of fun and recreation. There are also unmarried swingers who interact with each other. And sometimes single people swing with married couples either as singles or as unmarried couples. However, the primary interest here is to examine swinging among married couples. The following sections draw on a study done by the author and a colleague.

The study is based upon extensive interviews with about 25 swingers, sometimes as couples, but most often separately. Each interview lasted between two and five hours. While a number of different topics were consistently explored with all respondents the interviews were for the most part unstructured and carried out as free and open discussions. Observations were also made at "socials" and "open parties." The purpose here will be to describe and analyze some of the general social characteristics of swinging. The analysis must be general and it is recognized that swinging may vary greatly in some situations from what is described here.

There may be two married couples who on occasion exchange sex partners, but never do this with any other couple. There are probably many couples who have had this experience but they would not usually be thought of as swingers either by themselves or by others. In the broadest sense swinging can describe a wide range of events. A brief description of two extreme types will illustrate the range. One way of describing the variation is to see swinging as ranging from some interpersonal interaction and commitment to an almost totally impersonal relationship. This range is represented by "closet swinging" at one extreme to "open swinging" or "orgies" at the other extreme. A brief discussion of each follows.

CLOSET SWINGING

This occurs when two or more couples get together, usually at someone's home. Often the couples do not know each other and the initial arrangements for getting together are made by telephone. Sometimes they will agree that the evening is to be "social," which means that there may or may not be sex, depending on how they feel about each other. The first part of the evening often involves a few drinks, talking, and sometimes dancing. The smoothness of the evening is often determined by the experience of the couples with swinging. If the couples decide to swing that evening a pair will usually leave and go to a bedroom. If a couple go into a bedroom and close the door they are truly "closet swingers" because the closed door means that no one else is to come into that room. However, if the door is left open that means that others may join them and watch, participate alongside of, or participate with. If there are more than two couples they will often go off with different sexual partners before the evening is over. Often between sexual experiences people will return to the living room either nude or partly dressed and talk and drink as at any party.

OPEN PARTIES OR ORGIES

In this setting the interaction may be almost completely physical with little or no verbal communication. For example, after a "social" six or seven couples may go to a hotel suite and most of them may not know each other. After a few minutes one couple may simply say "let's get started," strip, and within five minutes almost all are involved in various sexual activities. This can go on for several hours with almost no verbal exchange until people get tired, dress, and go home. There are many occasions when two people will have long, complex sexual exchanges with each other and never say a word to one another. This extreme represents the almost ultimate sexual experience.

Between the two extreme types described there are many combinations and permutations. For example, a party may start out as closet swinging and turn into an orgy. Or at one party there may be one couple in one room swinging privately while in another room a number of couples are swinging together. Many swingers will not engage in all types of behavior, and that is often the factor that determines what direction the sexual activities will take at a given party.

RECRUITMENT

In some types of deviance many persons are recruited against their wills. For example, many homosexuals don't really make a choice as to the direction of their sexual expression. In other types of deviance some persons are recruited even though they are not sure they want to enter, as for example, in some delinquent gangs. But recruitment into swinging appears always to imply that at least one partner wants to enter and the other is willing at least to the extent that he knows that is what his partner wants. Most often it is the husband who initially wants to try swinging and then persuades his wife. Many times the couple will enter swinging but the wife resists and the couple drop out somewhere along the way. When couples stay for a relatively long period of time, that may be the result of two different responses by the wife. After wives enter swinging they may continue for a while because their husbands want them to stay. The wives may keep thinking their husbands will want to drop out. But after a while when they realize the husband has no intention of stopping they may begin to convince themselves they are in it because they (the wives) want to be. On the other hand it appears that when many couples stay with swinging for a period of time the wife does develop an enthusiasm for it that may become even greater than that of her husband. This pattern is similar to one sometimes found with regard to husband and wife views about sex in marriage. Often the husband enters marriage with great enthusiasm about having a sexual partner always available. The wife frequently enters marriage with some inhibitions and anxieties as to her sexual participation. But as the newness of the sexual availability wears off the husband's interests often decrease. But at the same time the wife's inhibitions are often removed and her sexual interests become greater.

How many swingers there are in the United States there is no way of knowing. This activity, like all areas of "hidden" deviancy, is impossible to measure. Any attempt to estimate how many swingers there are would be like trying to estimate how many men and women are homosexuals. The estimates that are given have no empirical basis. About all that can be said is that there are more swingers than non-swingers believe, but not as many as swingers think. There are three general ways in which recruitment into swinging takes place. The three paths may be followed separately or in combination by different persons entering swinging.

MAGAZINES

There have emerged several profit making organizations directed at swingers, and one of the things they do is publish magazines. The main function of the magazines is to run personal ads. The ads have code numbers and anyone who wants to respond must do so through the publisher. This offers some protection to the persons who place the ads and contributes to the profit of the organization. It may cost ten dollars to join a club and about five dollars to place an ad. (A single woman can usually place an ad free because they are in great demand.) The clubs may charge a dollar to forward a letter. Often the ads are accompanied by a picture which often has only a remote resemblance to the real person. The ads are usually quite short and the following are actual illustrations:

S-115
Married couple, attractive, both late twenties. Wife 36–25–35, Husband, 5'10", 170 lbs. New York City. Desire to meet other marrieds and single women. Both enjoy French culture, photography and erotic movies.

S-225
Married couple, middle thirties. Wife 37–25–36, husband muscular. Los Angeles area. Willing to try anything. Interested in French, Greek, and Arab culture. No single men.

While some of what is said in the ads would be understandable to most people, some phrases are not commonly understood. For example, French culture means the couple like oral sex, Greek that they like anal intercourse, while Arab refers to an interest in some sadistic-masochistic practices. Many of the ads are not genuine. For example, single men often place ads as if they were a part of a married couple and this can create problems for couples who respond to those ads. But most swingers do not use ads for making their contacts.

SOCIALS

The same clubs that publish the magazines also sponsor parties or "socials." These are parties held in hotel or motel ballrooms where a buffet dinner and a dance band can be presented. The socials are publicized through the magazines and are very well attended even though the price for the evening may run to $25.00 per couple. The parties are presented as opportunities for couples to get together, meet each other, and exchange phone numbers if they choose. And that is what happens—although there is often much more.

Many people go to socials out of curiosity and will never participate in swinging. However, for many who see socials as a major source for making sexual contacts it is in effect a "flesh market." This is an accurate description because the giving and receiving of phone numbers and party invitations is primarily based on physical appearance. This means that the youngest or most attractive couples are the most in demand on the flesh market. This is also reflected in the unadvertised function of the social, which is to provide contacts for swinging that night after the party ends.

Some couples go to a social and rent rooms, or if they live near plan on having a party at the end of the evening. Those who are most attractive are the ones who get the most invitations. For some people, as the evening draws to a close, not to have an invitation to a party leads to a sense of panic at the fear of being a reject. In some cases, almost out of desperation, the rejects may seek each other out and have their own party.

NETWORKS

Once people get into the swinging scene the most common way of making new contacts is through a network system. Initially, their contacts are made through the advertisements, socials, or through some couple they have met. Through their first contact they are often told of other couples to call, or that third couple may be asked to call them. This process continues and contacts increase and are in turn passed on to others. There are some networks that at times may involve 25 or 30 couples who each know some of the others and where they get together as two couples or with a number of couples. In the networks there are always some people coming in and others dropping out. But once a couple has successfully engaged in swinging with one or two couples it is not difficult to meet others.

VALUE SYSTEM OF SWINGING

Some swingers are very ideological and believe that they have found the answer to a good and happy life. As with any ideological commitment there are some who believe with a religious fervor and want to proselytize their faith. Many who are not so ideological nevertheless believe that it leads to the best possible sex life. And as suggested, swinging does mean a single standard of sex for both the husband and wife. This single standard of participating sex implies important value changes for the wife and husband who accept it. For the wife it means that she has to separate sex from love, which she has been socialized to believe must go together. And her very ability to make this distinction may be the best indicator of her being able to swing without serious personal problems. For the husband it means that he must undo the socialization process that has conditioned him to believe that a wife is exclusively the sexual property of the husband. Not only are many swing husbands able to do this, but some are even able to find that seeing their wives in sexual contact with others is a highly erotic experience. The ways in which wives and husbands are able to effectively alter their socialization away from the monogamous view of sex is an area worthy of future research.

While there are some exceptions, basically swingers define sex as recreational and as an end in itself. Not only do they believe that swinging sex has nothing to do with love, but they develop strong sanctions to keep the two separate. What may be the most important value among swingers is that sex with others must be kept as physical and as impersonal as possible. Most swingers realize that if any interpersonal commitment develops this may constitute a real threat to the marriage. Swingers feel that sex between two people doesn't threaten their respective marriages but a developing emotional commitment between them could.

This taboo against interpersonal involvement is seen in the fact that if two couples swing together five or six times one of two things usually happens. Either they stop seeing each other completely, or if the two couples develop a friendship and continue to see each other they drop the sex. And if they don't end or change their relationship their other swinging friends may remind them about their "going steady." The interpersonal restriction is also seen if any pair spends a good deal of time together and alone at a party and is *not* involved in sex—they are viewed with suspicion. Even in sexual activity there may be interpersonal limitations. That is, when a couple gets together foreplay is viewed as leading directly to possible orgastic experience. Couples do not usually spend a lot of time necking and petting interspersed with romantic conversation with one another.

While the above types of detached relationships are the common pattern there are some exceptions among swingers. For example, there are some couples who are able to maintain close friendships over time and still have sexual activities. These people will often say they love and care about each other. What appears to happen is that the friendships are close but there is not a strong emotional involvement. They are like any good friends who feel close but are not emotionally interdependent. This relationship does have the potential of developing into a deep emotional one because they already have the strong ties of sex and friendship. It is our observation that a few couples have been able to maintain this type of relationship for several years.

If a man and woman want to see each other outside of swinging this is to be done only with the full knowledge of their respective spouses. "Single dating" is not very common, but if a man visits a woman both their respective spouses should know about it and the couple would be together only for sexual purposes and not for interpersonal ones. This would be acceptable behavior to all so long as the sex is open and single standard. Not to tell one's spouse would be double standard, or from the sincere swingers point of view dishonest and hypocritical.

ORGANIZATION

Because we have no idea of how many swingers there are we can't say with any accuracy who they are. About all that can be discussed are the visible swingers, the ones that researchers have encountered. A few studies have found them to be quite conventional in their political views and essentially middle class, with swinging their only significant deviation from middle-class norms. This also appears to be true of what we have found in the Philadelphia area. The swingers we have met have generally been in their twenties and thirties with at least some college education and in business or the professions. They drink moderately and rarely use any kinds of drugs. (We know there exists, but have not encountered, lower middle-class as well as middle-age swinging groups.)

The swingers do have some fears. For some there is the concern that their children will find out, and those couples will never swing at home. Because the woman places a high reliability on birth control methods pregnancy generally is not a great fear. Some are quite nervous about public exposure or even blackmail, although there is no evidence that these fears are well grounded. Probably most swingers do not consider themselves to be either immoral or law breakers. They usually feel the laws are wrong because there should not be legislation against personal morality. In fact many swingers feel superior because they believe they have gotten rid of many of the sexual "hangups" that plague most American adults.

Oftentimes swingers will say there are no rules governing their behavior, but in many ways and some cases already suggested this is not true. The most important rules are the sanctions against the development of interpersonal involvement. There are also rules on who may participate in swinging. As suggested, physical attractiveness is important, and this means that one must be up to at least minimal standards. For example, if people are too heavy they are usually excluded. Also the rules tend to restrict people to similar ages. The fact that many parties involve nudity means that weight and age may be stigmata hard to hide.

Probably the more important rules center around the actual sexual selection and interaction among swingers. It is almost always true that no one is forced into any kind of sexual behavior if he lets it be known he doesn't want to participate. The man usually initiates by asking the woman, and if she doesn't want to participate he is expected not to be overly insistent. And if he is turned down by most or all of the women he will probably not be invited back. Sometimes a woman may feel sorry for a rejected male and feel an obligation to him and take him on what is called a "charity" case. However, if a woman keeps refusing men then she and her husband will not be invited back. But the basic rule is that the wife does have the right to refuse any person, and if this happens when there is only one other couple it ends the evening, at least sexually. And there are many evenings that end this way. It appears to be a general rule that if the women take a dislike to each other there will be no swinging.

There is often greater pressure on the woman to sexually participate when there is only one other couple than at an open party or orgy. This is because she knows if she does not participate with the other husband the evening is over sexually. However, at an orgy where there are a number of other women she can say no and not be pressured. This is because there are enough women to take care of all the men sexually. It is common at orgies to find some women who enjoy having sex with two or three men at the same time. Of course, any attempt to force a woman goes contrary to the basic belief of sincere swingers that sex must be voluntary and pleasurable for both partners.

SEXUAL BEHAVIOR

Basic to the swinging movement and the desire to participate is what persons believe they will get from the experiences. It is clear that both men and women have many motives for entering swinging. For men there is often a great excitement because they see the experiences as giving reality to the sexual fantasies they have enjoyed for years. It is also a chance for the man to fulfill the highly important male role of sexual activist. And, of course, it is seen as a highly exciting and pleasurable experience. When women are asked what they get out of the swinging experience there are a variety of answers. For many of them the factor of pleasure is highly important, but it generally has nothing to do with fulfilling sexual fantasies or of meeting basic feminine needs for sexual expression. For some women the most satisfying aspect is to be desirable and attractive to men. In some cases they say this makes them feel young again. Others have suggested that it is satisfying to be wanted by someone other than the husband and to be able to respond to that want. They feel not only that are they wanted but that they can control the situation in terms of their giving to the man who wants them.

Rarely does a swinger criticize in any moral way any kind of sexual behavior. They may say that something is not "their thing" but will make no moral judgments against any persons who want that behavior. Among swingers coitus is always acceptable, unless there is some reason on a given occasion for not indulging. Also oral genital sex contact between men and women is practiced most of the time. Anal intercourse is accepted, although probably not practiced by most swingers. Many have tried it but choose not to indulge because they find it too painful.

As suggested, oral sex is very popular among swingers, both the man and the woman. Oral sex may be used both as foreplay or as a sexual end in itself. Often oral sex by the man is used when he is temporarily not able to get an erection for coitus. This is common when the men and women over the course of the evening have more than one orgastic experience. Visual sex is also a very common practice among swingers. There is frequently a highly erotic influence on both men and women in seeing the others have sexual relations. Often both husbands and wives find it very sexually exciting to see each other having sex with other partners.

One important area of sexual behavior among swingers is homosexuality. It is rare to find male homosexuality among swingers, but very common to find female homosexuality practiced. This difference is due to several important reasons. First, for most men a homosexual experience would be very threatening to one's sense of masculinity. This sexual activity carries with it a potentially severe threat to the basic sex role image. But this same sex role concern is not true for women. Generally women have no strong fears about homosexuality and do not see it as threatening to their sense of femininity. Second, most men find the idea of two women having sexual contact highly erotic, but most women do not find the notion of two men having sexual relations at all sexually exciting. Therefore, men often encourage the women to have sexual experiences with one another in the swinging situation. Because men do find it erotic they often find that while they rest from a previous orgastic experience it is exciting and sexually stimulating to watch the women having sex with each other.

Among many swingers there is competition among the men as to being the top sexual performers. The man is generally expected to have at least one erection to orgasm in an evening. But frequently the man feels he has to have sex with as many women as possible. If in the situation there are half a dozen women present he may feel a strong need to have some kind of sexual experience with each one of them. For some men it is like being a boy with a box of candy who feels he must sample every piece—even if it gives him a stomach ache.

The women are also interested in satisfactory sexual experiences during the evening but this doesn't always mean that they feel their orgasm is necessary. It appears that among the more experienced swinging women orgasm is often not a measurement of their sexual satisfaction. That the woman always reach orgasm with each partner is often far more important to the man than to the woman. The man often sees her orgasm as a measurement of his ability as a sexual "artist." It is common to hear a woman tell how she has mentioned to a man not to worry about her orgasm because it is hard for her to make it. And the man interprets this as a challenge and may try for hours to bring the woman to a climax. This effort doesn't always mean that the man is interested in his partner's sexual welfare as much as that he sees it as a measurement of his sexual ability.

To most Americans swinging seems so morally deviant and abhorrent that they immediately feel that people who do it are mentally sick and must have terrible marriages. By contrast, many swingers believe that the rest of the world is hung up on a hypocritical sexual monogamy and that rarely do they have good marriages. As is often the case the truth probably falls somewhere between the two extreme points of view. Among the ideological swingers, those who are philosophically committed to it as a way of life, there is the belief that swinging is no solution for a marriage in trouble. They believe that swinging would probably intensify the problem and should be avoided. But there are also many swingers who use it for their own psychological needs and hangups.

When swinging works for a couple, it appears to be when the couple are able to separate sex with other partners from their relationships to one another. This means that sex with other partners is seen by both partners as a recreational end, and therefore the constant concern that swinging not develop into any interpersonal involvement. So those who believe they are successful swingers argue that sex with others is recreational and *different* from the emotional sex they have with their spouse. Sex in swinging is physical, while in marriage sex is physical *and* emotional. Because they see sex as different in the two settings some argue that swinging sex helps marital sex because it makes each partner more sexually sophisticated and aware of the other as a desirable sex object.

Sociologically, the emergence of swinging in the United States is a logical extension of increased sexual freedom. This is a part of a value pattern, how large nobody knows, that believes that sex can be an end in itself and participation is to be determined by the individuals themselves and not by moral norms or legislated controls. This same pattern has been shown in recent years in studies of premarital sex where the girl is less concerned with sex's being a part of any interpersonal commitment than was true in the past. That is, sex is becoming viewed by more and more females on at least some occasions outside of mariage as a recreational end in itself. Given this change one may speculate that in the future the recreational nature of sex will continue to increase.

Many in the younger generation are growing up with a philosophy that sex can be recreational and privately decided upon. It is logical to predict that as they marry more and more will have swinging experiences. In fact, it is striking that many swingers today are in their early twenties and many have been married only a few years. It may also be that many people have not tried swinging because they have not been aware of it as a possible activity.

Most Americans will continue to be monogamous in their married sexual experiences and find the idea of swinging immoral, indecent, and generally reprehensible. Yet, for many people today there are no real moral forces that control their behavior. For many people, the traditional arguments of religion with a stress on sin or the psychological arguments with a stress on "guilt" are ignored or seen as irrelevant. So the swinging phenomenon appears inevitable in a society where norms are rapidly losing their strength and where values centered on individual moral decisions are becoming increasingly powerful, especially among the younger generation.

POSTMARITAL SEX

Before concluding this chapter we will discuss briefly sexual behavior for persons who were once married. This is appropriate because premarital and extramarital values extend to postmarital sexual behavior in defining appropriate behavior. This is true whatever the reasons for ending the marital interaction, i.e., by death, divorce, separation or desertion. While it is generally assumed that the postmarital are sexually experienced because of their previous marriage, once their marriage ends they are expected to conform once again to the sexual values that operated for them when they were young and unmarried.

Regardless of the reason their marriages ended, the postmarital constitute a group of sexually experienced individuals. The American society, in effect, says that even though an active, socially approved involvement was a part of their lives for many years, and even though their sexual needs and interests may continue to be very strong, once they are no longer legally married they must give up all personal interest and involvement in sex. In reality, the postmarried, especially the women, are treated in somewhat different fashions according to how their marriages ended. The widow is assumed to have had a satisfactory sexual relationship with her deceased husband, and if she shows an interest in sex she may be viewed as being disloyal to the memory of her husband. Frequently implied for the widow, if she does not remarry, is that she can and should live with her memories.

Toward the divorced woman there is often a different view—she is frequently viewed by men as sexually exploitable. After divorce, the assumption is that the marriage was a failure and that the sexual aspect had also been unsatisfactory. The divorced woman is often seen as sexually experienced, but without "good" sexual memories of her past marriage, so many men define the divorcee as sexually experienced and in "need" of a good sexual partner—a role that the man sees himself as eminently capable of filling. Jessie Bernard points out that in theory the mores of chastity apply to the divorced woman as to all unmarried women, but that in reality the divorced woman is considered fair game.[40]

Kinsey found that for males who were ever married, but whose marriages had ended through death, separation, or divorce, the sexual frequency was considerably higher than for single males of the same age, and nearly as high as for married males of the same age. In his postmarital years the male tends to follow sexual patterns similar to those of the married man. This appears to be true even though he no longer has marriage to provide the physically convenient and legally approved sexual partner. Kinskey found that among the postmarried males, between the ages of 16 and 30, total sexual outlet was 85 to 95 percent as high as among married men, and this rate was 40 to 50 percent higher than for single men. However, after age 30 the rates of total sexual outlet for the postmarital males were about three-fourths the married male rates, and "this actually places them below the rates of even the single groups after age 30."[41] The

---

[40] Bernard, Jessie, *Remarriage* (New York: Dryden Press, Inc., 1956), p. 155.

[41] Kinsey, Alfred, *et. al. Sexual Behavior in the Human Male* (Philadelphia: W. B. Saunders Co., 1948), p. 262.

above statement refers to total sexual outlets; if only coitus is compared between the postmarried and single males then the previously married group has the higher frequency.

In the Kinsey study the rates of sexual involvement for postmarital women were lower compared to married women than was the case for postmarital males in comparison with married males. For previously married women between the ages of 26 and 50, Kinsey found that from 80 to 86 percent had some sexual outlet.[42] Of the women between the ages of 36 and 40, 95 percent of the married, 96 percent of the previously married, and 71 percent of the single had some sexual activity. As to weekly frequency for this age group, the rates were 1.2 for the married, 0.7 for the postmarried, and 0.5 for the single.[43] These data suggest that the incidence rate for the postmarried woman places them closer to the married than the single, but that with regard to weekly frequency of sexual activity they are closer to the single.

It is also useful to look at some comparisons of various sexual outlets of the never-married, postmarried, and married. "The most notable aspect of the histories of these previously married females was the fact that their frequencies of activity had not dropped to the levels which they had known as single females, before they had married."[44] In types of sexual outlets the general sexual patterns for the single, postmarital, and marital females was the same as found for the males. For women between the ages of 36 and 40 heterosexual coitus accounted for 88 percent of the sexual outlet of the married women, 70 percent of the postmarried, and 43 percent of the single. By contrast, masturbation accounted for 13 percent of the sexual outlet of the married, 28 percent of the postmarried and 39 percent of the single. Homosexual outlets accounted for 0 percent for the married, 2 percent for the postmarried and 19 percent for the single women.[45]

Kinsey's data clearly show that sexual involvement of some type is a common experience for many postmarried men and women. For most of them the decision is an individual one and they must cope with any guilt feelings by themselves. However, for some postmarried, particularly the divorced, there emerges a subculture that helps them in their adjustment to their deviant status. Morton Hunt has provided a picture of the subcultural world of the divorced and how it helps provide a setting for many decisions and activities with regard to sexual behavior. Hunt suggests that divorced people, while they are a part of the overall American culture and interact with it, "elsewhere have a private and special set of norms that guide them in their interactions with each other, and from which they de-

---

[42] Kinsey, Alfred, et. al., Sexual Behavior in the Human Female (Philadelphia: W. B. Saunders Co., 1953), p. 394.

[43] Ibid., p. 533.

[44] Ibid.

[45] Ibid., p. 562.

rive their own customs, moral values, rules of fair play, and devices for coping with the problems special to their condition."[46] Hunt goes on to suggest that many of their life patterns are quite different from those of the inhabitants of the wider culture.[47]

The subculture of the divorced is not highly restrictive, in fact in most respects it is quite permissive. The individual can arrange the details of his new dating life to suit his personal needs. "No one need consent to any suggestion he or she dislikes, but it is not impossible for the other to have made it."[48] This value of permissiveness without force is very similar to that found among the swingers.

The divorced people that Hunt studied were predominately urban and highly educated. Therefore, their behavior was no doubt much different from many other divorced persons in the United States. This limitation should be kept in mind. In his sample he found that almost none of the men and only about 20 percent of the women had no sexual experiences since their marriages had ended. Hunt found that about 80 percent of the "formerly married" started having sexual intercourse during the first year after their divorces, and most of them with more than one partner. Nearly all of the men and a fairly large number of the women found their sex lives more intense, less inhibited, and more satisfying than it had been during their marriages.[49] Hunt suggests that those divorced persons who did not have sexual relations typically had problems. He writes that a common type of divorced woman without sexual experience had been characterized by a limited amount of sexual excitement in the past in what was an unhappy marriage. "Her innate negative feelings about sex gradually gained the upper hand and anesthetized her sexual feeling or even caused her to find the act somewhat repellent."[50] Hunt goes on to point out that the common male abstainer was generally of normal sexuality, "who lost potency or desire in the course of a deteriorating marriage and avoids sex afterward out of fear of failure."[51]

Many of the divorced enter into their first sexual encounters with a great deal of fear and anxiety. They were faced not only with the general moral restrictions but with the fact that their previous sexual experience had been in a relationship that had failed. Therefore the anxiety was often both sexual and interpersonal. As would be expected, the anxiety about entering a sexual affair was greater for the woman than the man and

---

[46] Hunt, Morton M., *The World of the Formerly Married* (New York: McGraw-Hill, 1966), p. 4.

[47] *Ibid.*, p. 5.

[48] *Ibid.*, pp. 112–13.

[49] *Ibid.*, p. 144.

[50] *Ibid.*, p. 146.

[51] *Ibid.*, p. 147.

greater for those married a long while than those married only briefly.[52] But except for those with real neurotic problems about sex, the great majority did have successful sexual experiences, most only after some initial failures, the fortunate few at once.[53]

The subcultural world of the divorced is like other areas of deviancy in that many members often feel it necessary to hide some of their subcultural activities from the broader society. Even when the divorced woman is able to successfully adjust to her extramarital activities she often feels it necessary to hide them from her friends, her parents, and especially her children. If she has older children she usually says in effect that there is one set of values to govern her nonmarital sexual behavior and a different one for her unmarried children. Hunt says that divorced women are caught between two cultures; "while they permit themselves their present conduct and justify it, they also have a nagging residual feeling that it is not really proper, and do not want their children to emulate them."[54]

The contrast between the generally stated values controlling all aspects of sex outside of marriage and the actual behavior of many postmarried persons points up the conflict in the United States. Because the general values do not change, the individual must adapt to them. He can accept them, he can deviate as an individual with no support from others, or he can deviate and seek support from others who share his position. That more and more people follow the third choice is not surprising because it provides some adaptation to a situation of values they find intolerable for their life patterns.

BIBLIOGRAPHY

BELL, ROBERT R., *Premarital Sex in a Changing Society* (Englewood Cliffs, N.J.: Prentice-Hall, Inc., 1966).

BREEDLOVE, WILLIAM and JERRYL, *Swap Clubs* (Los Angeles: Sherbourne Press, 1964).

CUBER, JOHN F., "The Mistress in American Society," *Medical Aspects of Human Sexuality*, September, 1969, pp. 81–91.

HARPER, ROBERT A., "Extramarital Sex Relations," in Albert Ellis and Albert Abarbanel, *The Enclyclopedia of Sexual Behavior* (New York: Hawthorne Books Inc., 1961), pp. 384–91.

HUNT, MORTON M., *The World of the Formerly Married* (New York: McGraw-Hill, 1966).

LOVE, NANCY, "The '70's Woman and the Now Marriage," *Philadelphia Magazine*, February, 1970, pp. 55–58, 84–88, 90–93.

---

[52] *Ibid.*, p. 154.

[53] *Ibid.*, p. 155.

[54] *Ibid.*, p. 163.

CHAPTER 4

FACTORS RELATED TO
BIRTH CONTROL

THIS CHAPTER concerns two separate, but closely related problem areas. One at its broadest is on the national and even international level—that of population size and composition. The basic problem for many countries is with their economic development and their abilities to meet the needs of their populations. The second problem area is with regard to the various birth control measures used by individuals. At this level the problem is usually with the inability of some individuals to control the number of children they have to accord with their desires. This level is clearly related to the first but involves problems in a number of different ways.

Discussion of these problem areas starts with a brief look at the historical development of birth control methods, then an examination of the "population explosion," followed by some social variables related to birth control success, and finally the various methods of birth control, their usage, and their reliability.

The conceptual approach used in this chapter to examine the data is more from a social problem than a social deviance view. Population limits are a social problem because large numbers in society define them as such. Also many who contribute to the overall problem by having large numbers of children also see themselves as having a difficulty. "In this country we know that poor people often do not have access to adequate birth control information and techniques and therefore have more children than they want or can afford."[1] So from the perspective of the individual deviant there is often a strong desire to correct that which is the problem—having a large number of children. There was a time when using birth control methods was defined as eccentric or deviant behavior. For most of mankind's history the general value has been that having large families was desirable and usually inevitable. And anyone who tried to change this "natural" process was sometimes seen as being deviant. While this viewpoint is still held by some groups of people it is no longer a major belief in most societies, including that of the United States.

HISTORY OF BIRTH CONTROL

While most societies, preliterate and literate, past and present, have accepted large birth rates as natural and inevitable it is also probably true that in many of those societies at various times there have been some people who have attempted to control conception. To the problems of birth control there have always been two general approaches. The first has been a mystical formula, and practices stimulating emotional responses.[2] The second general approach has been one based on rationality. This approach has centered around whatever had been believed in a given society to be the processes whereby procreation occurred on the one hand, and the powers of the substances used to stimulate or defeat them on the other.[3] These approaches were not only used among primitive tribes but also among the civilized nations of antiquity. The Egyptians, the Jews, the Greeks, and the Romans all possessed beliefs about the reproductive process and some knowledge of contraceptive devices.

In most societies of the past there was no knowledge of how conception occurred and therefore no awareness of a process that could be halted by some contraceptive measure. The rational development of birth control methods assumes the knowledge that conception occurs as a result of sexual intercourse. When this knowledge did not exist societies had to wait to try to do something about birth control until pregnancy could be seen or the infant was born. Therefore, in primitive societies the chief method of birth control was abortion, and in many societies infanticide was also used. These were much more common than any contraceptive methods. A study of anthropological monographs shows that there were other practices also used by some preliterate groups, for example, "delayed marriage and celibacy, both almost negligible among primitive peoples; sex taboos limiting the time and frequency of connection, pre-puberty

[1] Rainwater, Lee, "Family Planning in Cross-National Perspective," *The Journal of Social Issues,* October, 1967, pp. 2–3.

[2] Draper, Elizabeth, *Birth Control in the Modern World* (Baltimore: Penguin Books, 1965), p. 53.

[3] *Ibid.*

coition, sex perversions (more or less neglected by most writers), prolonged lactation, and conception control, both magical and rational."[4]

Because preliterate societies often developed magical systems to cope
with many aspects of their lives it is logical that they would seek in that
way to attempt to control births. Among primitive groups there has often
existed the belief in a panacea or elixir—something could be taken and resolve a given area of difficulty. This might be a potion that would give all
men great strength, make all women beautiful, make all men great hunt-
ers, and so forth. And it was common for many preliterates to believe that
some magical potion existed that would prevent conception. Those beliefs
took many directions. For example, a symbolic kind of contraceptive potion was the drinking of water used for the washing of a dead person. A
more medical kind of potion has been the infusions of the bark of different trees, especially the willow, the yoke of the egg, and so forth.

The anthropological data show that thousands of materials have been
used in primitive societies in attempts to control conception. Because so
many methods were tried, some on the basis of chance had to be successful. For example, women in Guiana and Martinique used a douche solution containing lemon juice mixed with a decoction of the husks of the
mahogany nut which worked fairly well. This is because lemon juice is an
effective spermicide. Another related and more ingenious approach is reported to have been used in the eighteenth century. "This consisted of
cutting a lemon in half, extracting most of the juice, the disk being used
as a cervical cap."[5] Another illustration is that among the Djukas the
women inserted into the vagina an okra-like seed pod about five inches
long from which one end was cut off. "The intact end probably lies against
the cervix, or in the posterior fornix, the open end receiving the penis.
This is, therefore, a kind of vegetable condom held in place by the vagina."[6]

The above illustrations of contraceptive developments in preliterate
societies that had some practical reasons for success should not be over-
stressed. They were due to chance and not based on knowledge. It should
be remembered that it was in the late 1600's that we first knew that contact between the sperm and the egg had to occur for fertilization to take
place. And it was not until 1850 that it was understood that the spermatozoa had to penetrate the egg for fertilization to take place. Himes, after
his extensive research into birth control methods, writes: "It cannot be
too strongly emphasized, therefore, that whatever primitive peoples may
have known about contraception, they hit upon by trial and error, by trial-

---

[4] Himes, Norman E., *Medical History of Contraception* (New York: Gamut Press,
Inc., 1963), p. 4.

[5] *Ibid.*, p. 18.

[6] *Ibid.*, pp. 18–19.

success-and-survival processes, not as a consequence of a thorough understanding of the physiology of conception."[7]

The societies of the Western world have used a variety of means to influence their overall birth rates at least on some occasions. However, this was not true for the majority of persons in most countries in the past. With the high death rate in societies of the past, a high birth rate was needed to meet the economic and military demands of most societies. The concern for developing the means of birth control was among the wealthier and upper class levels of society. There was generally little concern about the "inevitably" high birth rates of the lower classes. This social class distinction has continued over the centuries and still is true in many parts of the world.

Probably the first significant breakthrough in the development of a reliable means of mechanical birth control was the invention of the condom. A treatise published in 1564 by Gabriele Fallopio contained the first written account of the condom or sheath which Fallopio claimed to have invented. This was not initially seen as a contraceptive device and over the years gained popularity as a measure against venereal infection. The condom was used during the 18th century, both in England and the Continent, mainly in brothels, but was also sold in London and in other cities. "At the end of the century, contraceptives were still associated exclusively with immorality and vice, but by the close of the nineteenth century, this position had been deeply undermined and the way prepared for the general acceptance of contraceptives which has been so marked a feature of our time."[8] During the 18th century, the use of the condom being associated with protecting the male from possible diseases from prostitutes meant that man did not consider using the same method to protect his wife from pregnancy. In a patriarchal society where pleasurable sex was associated with prostitutes and the danger of disease the condom seemed appropriate, while in marriage where sex was often chaste and a means to the procreative end the condom did not seem appropriate.

It was not until the 19th century in the Western world, especially in England, Germany, and France that contraceptive practices started to spread rapidly. In brief, the major reasons for this development were growing industrialization, urbanization, lessened church authority, and greater freedom for women. Himes points out that any concern with the social and economic desirability of birth control was a characteristic of the 19th century and had not existed to any extent before that time. "Medical discussion is old; the economic and social justification, the body of doctrine

---

[7] *Ibid.*, p. 53.

[8] St. John-Stevas, Norman, "History and Legal Status of Birth Control," in Edwin M. Schur, *The Family and the Sexual Revolution* (Bloomington, Indiana: Indiana University Press, 1964), pp. 333–34.

known as Neo-Malthusianism, is new."[9] In the 1820's in England there developed a fairly extensive amount of birth control propaganda. This was led by Francis Place (1771–1854) who appears to have been the first individual to venture alone upon an organized attempt to educate the masses on techniques of contraception. "Place holds, therefore, the same position in social education on contraception that Malthus holds in the history of general population theory."[10] The pamphlet written by Place presented in clear language to poor women some ways in which they might avoid having more children than they wanted. The reliability of the pamphlet was limited by the knowledge of effective means of birth control that existed at that time. But what is most important is that that publication launched the birth control movement.

During the early years of the birth control movement it had little support. And in the first century of its history the birth control movement was more opposed than supported by the medical profession. The leading activists were not physicians. For example, Francis Place started his career as a maker of leather breeches, Marie Stokes was a botanist, and Margaret Sanger was a nurse. Organized religion was also indifferent or opposed to the birth control movement for much of its history. No major religion advocated the use of contraception prior to its popular adoption. "The common people took it over in the face of almost universal ecclesiastical opposition."[11]

But the greatest resistance to the birth control movement probably came from the belief that having children was inevitable and natural. This belief assumed that nothing could be done or should be done—it was the natural order of things. Most of mankind has seen attempts to tamper with births like attempts to influence death—trying to alter what is believed to be beyond the power of man. This belief in the inevitability of birth was further supported by the fact that most of mankind has lived in patriarchal societies. Therefore, in male controlled societies the having of babies was the woman's problem. The fact that women often had problems associated with their giving birth was taken as a reflection of their "inferior" status. Men in most societies have seen the question of controlling the birth rate as one for the woman to worry about. The patriarchal male has traditionally seen sexual intercourse with his wife as his right and her getting pregnant as a measurement of his masculinity. Therefore, to ask him to influence his sexual activity in some way that might influence his wife's frequency of pregnancy was to try to influence his basic belief about his masculine rights as a husband. So birth control problems

---

[9] Himes, *op. cit.*, p. 211.

[10] *Ibid.*, p. 212.

[11] Davis, Kingsley, "Values, Population, and the Supernatural: A Critique," in William Petersen and David Matza, *Social Controversy* (Belmont, California: Wadsworth Publishing Co., Inc., 1963), p. 30.

have traditionally been seen as problems for women to deal with if anything was to be done.

The values that existed with regard to birth control among the early settlers in the United States was the same as that found in Europe and especially in England. There is some evidence that during the colonial days fertility was among the world's highest, with the average woman having about eight children. "In those days, high infant and general mortality rates claimed perhaps half of these children before they reached marriageable ages. Nevertheless, despite this higher mortality, the size of families was much greater than now."[12] But during the 19th and 20th centuries there was an almost consistently decreasing birth rate that reached its all time low in the 1930's.

During the 1800's in the United States the birth control movement slowly developed in strength and influence. However, the movement was drastically restricted in 1873 with the passage of the Comstock Law. This was a statute enacted by Congress which excluded contraceptives and contraceptive information from the mails by defining them as being obscene. Many states followed along and also passed statutes banning the sale and distribution of contraceptives. At that time there were no major social institutions supporting the birth control movement. It was not until 1888 that the first medical symposium was presented in an American medical journal on the subject of the prevention of conception. That symposium came about as a result of an editorial in the *Medical and Surgical Reporter* that declared that while the subject demanded "discretion" for its discussion, "even so delicate a subject may be regarded with too much timidity. . . ." It added that "no medical man of any experience can fail to know that the propriety and feasibility of preventing conception engages, at some time or other, the attention of a large proportion of married people in civilized lands." The editorial went on to say that "the woman who lives in dread of her husband's sexual appetite cannot satisfy him as a wife, and, with this poison in her life, must find it hard to be a kind and wholesome mother to her children."[13]

The most influential person in the American birth control movement was Margaret Sanger. She did more than any other American to make birth control known to the public through her educational or propaganda campaigns. Margaret Sanger was a woman of extreme vision, personal courage, and organizing ability and gave unity to the American birth control movement. She published a monthly magazine, *The Woman Rebel*, and was later arrested and indicted under the Comstock Law. She escaped to Europe but returned to the United States and in 1916 opened the first

---

[12] Westoff, Charles F., "The Fertility of the American Population," in Ronald Freedman, *Population: The Vital Revolution* (New York: Anchor Books, 1964), pp. 110–11.

[13] Himes, *op. cit.*, p. 289.

birth control clinic in the United States. The clinic was raided by the police and Margaret Sanger and her sister were both sentenced to thirty days in jail. Over the years she continued her work and propaganda, basing her appeal on the suffering caused women by unlimited childbearing rather than on any theoretical Malthusian arguments.[14]

It was not until the 1930's in the United States that the birth control movement began to take on influence through some of the institutional forces of society. This came about through the influences of the religious, legal, and medical institutions. For example, in 1931 the Federal Council of the Churches of Christ was the first religious group to publish a report favoring birth control. During the same year support also came from the American Neurological Association, the Eugenics Society, and Central Conference of Rabbis. In the middle 1930's there were also some important legal breakthroughs. The Court of Appeals upheld a ruling of the District Court in 1936 that contraceptives imported for a lawful purpose did not come within the restrictions of federal law. And in 1937 the American Medical Association unanimously agreed to accept birth control "as an integral part of medical practice and education."[15]

There also have been legal and governmental influences on birth control in a variety of more subtle and indirect ways than through direct intervention. Draper has argued that "the influence of government upon population size is immense and is by no means confined to legislation directly concerned with birth control."[16] For example, birth control is affected by government influence in many countries through the provision of family allowances and maternity benefits. Or as in the United States income tax allowances for children give financial encouragement or ease the burden on the family budget. Also such factors as free education, vocational training, and in many countries free medical services provide for the cultural and occupational rewards and general "physical and mental well being which makes it good to live and worth having children to share."[17] Other indirect legal influences are laws providing minimum ages for marriages. In the United States these are four to six years after the female is capable of reproducing. Because most women do not have their children until after marriage the early years of child bearing are usually eliminated. Probably no society encourages reproduction up to the limits of the biological capacity in the female. Some limits, if not in the laws then in the values of the society, are imposed on the reproductive potential of the woman.

There are still some states that have legal restrictions on the use and

---

[14] St. John-Stevas, *op. cit.*, pp. 337–38.

[15] *Ibid.*, p. 338.

[16] Draper, *op. cit.*, p. 179.

[17] *Ibid.*

sale of contraception but it seems likely that these will be eliminated in the near future. This would seem logical from a legal point of view which increasingly argues that the right to control pregnancy and have children should be the right of the individual woman. The legal implications of this view are discussed in some detail in Chapter 5 in dealing with changing legal views with regard to abortion.

Even when governments have been concerned with birth control problems they have generally restricted themselves to policy statements and have not advocated contraceptive rights for the individual. However, in some countries explicit population policies attempting to influence birth rates first became important before World War I, when many European countries appointed population commissions to investigate their declining birth rates and to develop policies they thought would reverse those trends. It has been in recent decades that first mortality and then fertility became subjects of government policy, "not only to further the health and welfare of the individual citizens, but also to influence the rate of growth, size, and age structure of populations."[18]

All in all, by the 1930's in the United States, there was an acceptance of birth control by many in the general population. For example, a poll in 1936 asked, "Do you believe in the teaching and practice of birth control?" and 63 percent of the respondents answered "yes." In 1943 another poll asked a group of women ages 21 to 35: "Do you believe that knowledge about birth control should be available to all married women?" and 85 percent of them answered "yes." By 1965 when a national sample of women was asked: "Do you think birth control knowledge should be available to anyone who wants it?" about 80 percent of *both* Protestant and Catholic women answered "yes."[19]

The view that control can and should be directed at family size is one accepted today in many parts of the world besides the United States. In fact, Ryder suggests that there is now a remarkable demographic consensus throughout the modern world. That is, that marriage occurs at a rather young age and the couple have a small number of children at regulated intervals. He further states that celibacy and voluntary infertility are highly improbable, and at the other extreme the large family is becoming an anachronism. "The range of fertility differences among modern nations depends essentially on the question of whether the proportion of couples who have three children is greater or less than the proportion who have two children."[20] Many persons feel that the most threatening problem facing the world today is the question of a "population explosion."

---

[18] Freedman, *op. cit.*, p. 8.

[19] *Trans-Action*, April, 1967, p. 3.

[20] Ryder, Norman B., "The Character of Modern Fertility," in Jeffery K. Hadden and Marie L. Borgatta, *Marriage and the Family* (Itasca, Ill.: F. E. Peacock Publishing Co., 1969), p. 344.

THE POPULATION EXPLOSION

The concern with this problem became very great during the 1960's and many saw the problem of population growth as potentially more dangerous to the world than even atomic warfare. Before examining the problem of recent population growth it is of interest to look at the way in which the world's population expanded in the past. It has been estimated that the population of the world at the end of the Neolithic Period (8000–7000 B.C.) was somewhere between five and ten million. By the beginning of the Christian era the world's population probably numbered between 200 and 300 million. At the start of the Modern Era (1650) world population had reached about 500 million. The present world population is about three and a half billion. "In the course of man's inhabitation of this globe, then, his rate of population growth has increased from about 2 percent per millennium to 2 percent per year, a thousandfold increase in growth rate."[21] Put another way, of all persons who have ever lived it is estimated that about 4 percent of them are alive today.

The population explosion was a result of a high birth rate and a somewhat lower death rate. The population of the world can only increase for a given period of time when the number of births is greater than the number of deaths. During the initial population explosion the death rate was high but the birth rate was even higher. For example, the expectation of life at the time of birth was about 30 years at the beginning of the Christian Era and remained at that level until well through the 19th century. By 1900 the death rates had decreased to the point where life expectancy in western Europe and the United States was 45 to 50 years. And by 1960 another 20 years of life had been gained, with life expectancy having reached about 70 years.[22]

If the present rate of population growth continues there will be well over six billion people in the world by the start of the year 2000. This potential growth is seen by many experts as leading to severe problems. It is argued that with a world population today of about three and a half billion, more than two-thirds of the people in the world are undernourished or starving. As a result, birth control is seen by many as a major weapon of civilization and an essential part of any satisfactory solution to population problems, from the personal to the international.[23]

The population explosion may be examined in several ways. On the practical level the *modus operandi* for the reduction of fertility must take one of three forms. First, the reduction of the probability of intercourse; second, the reduction of the probability of conception if intercourse oc-

---

[21] Freedman, *op. cit.*, p. 16.
[22] *Ibid.*, p. 20.
[23] Draper, *op. cit.*, p. 15.

curs; and third the reduction of the probability of birth if conception occurs. "The first of these is control through nuptiality, the latter two constitute control of marital fertility."[24] The control of marriage has existed for centuries so the stress when it does occur is on marital fertility. In most societies of the world abortion has been used as a supplement or an alternative to contraception. Historically, abortion has probably been the most important influence in holding population expansion below what it could have been. But the extent to which it has influenced population growth in time and space is not known and probably never will be. "Nevertheless, the more we learn of the ineffectuality of most efforts at contraception, the more we are inclined to suspect a major covert role for abortion as a second line of defense against the unwanted birth."[25]

In recent decades abortion has been used in many countries as a major means for controlling the birth rate. First Japan, then Russia, and subsequently all the countries of eastern Europe, with the exceptions of East Germany and Albania, have permitted abortion on socioeconomic grounds. As a result of legal abortion the birth rates dropped rapidly and the lowest fertility rates in the world today are found in those countries. "Controls associated with legalization have reduced the health risks appreciably. Nevertheless, and entirely apart from moral considerations, abortion is an expensive alternative to contraception. Consequently, we may expect a persistent effort to induce a shift from abortion to contraception."[26] But it is increasingly clear throughout the world today that no society can remain indifferent to reproduction and therefore every society maintains some fertility norms. "The society indoctrinates its members into conformity with these norms, by explicit and implicit rewards and punishments."[27]

The problems of population vary with different societies and even in the same society over time. For example, many of the poorer countries appear to be condemning themselves to continued poverty if they don't control their population growth. The technologically advanced societies often find that they, too, have population problems. They may be able to control size but still find that the distribution of population at a given time creates problems for them. For example, in a technological society fewer are needed in the labor force, and therefore one problem is what to do with the young and the old that are not occupationally needed. It would seem safe to suggest that while a society may cut down on many of its population problems it never gets to a point where all problems are eliminated.

---

[24] Ryder, *op. cit.*, p. 340.
[25] *Ibid.*, p. 341.
[26] *Ibid.*
[27] *Ibid.*, p. 342.

There is some evidence in recent years that the population explosion in the world may be slowing down and becoming somewhat less of a problem, although this is still an area of great disagreement. One reputable spokesman for this interpretation is the demographer Donald Bogue. He argues that the trend of the movement around the world toward fertility control has reached the point where declines in death rates are being surpassed by declines in birth rates. Because possible new developments of controls over death are slackening and the means for controlling births are rapidly increasing the world has entered a stage where population growth has begun to slow down. Bogue has suggested that this switch occurred in about 1965 and from that time on the rate of world population growth has declined each year. "The rate of growth will slacken at such a pace that it will be zero or near zero at about the year 2000, so that population growth will not be regarded as a major social problem except in isolated and small 'retarded' areas."[28]

Bogue points out that all over the world where studies of attitudes of the public on family size have been taken the majority of couples with three living children do not want any more. Of the populations studied, a large proportion approve of family planning and would like to have more information about it, and they also approve of nationwide health service that includes family planning. In other words, objection among the great masses of people on cultural, moral, or religious grounds to birth control is becoming increasingly minor. "This is true in Asia and Latin America, and seems to be developing in Africa. Thus, at the 'grass roots' level, the attitudinal and cultural conditions are highly favorable."[29] Bogue also finds that in nations with population problems the national leadership openly accepts family planning as a moral and rational solution. "Heads of state in India, Pakistan, Korea, China, Egypt, Chile, Turkey, and Columbia, for example, have made fertility control an integral part of the national plan for economic development. The national ministers of health and welfare not only are permitted but are expected to provide family planning services."[30]

Bogue's arguments for a leveling off of the "population explosion" may be summarized as follows. Wherever one looks in the underdeveloped segments of the world there is evidence of established and functioning family planning activities. It is clear that a large share of the populations are using modern contraceptives and this has had an inhibiting effect on their birth rates. "Even conservative evaluation of the prospects suggests that *instead of a 'population explosion' the world is on the threshold of a 'contraception adoption explosion.'* Because of lack of adequate vital sta-

---

[28] Bogue, Donald J., "The End of the Population Explosion," in C. H. Anderson, *Sociological Essays and Research* (Homewood, Ill.: Dorsey, 1970), p. 333.

[29] *Ibid.*, p. 327.

[30] *Ibid.*, p. 328.

tistics, the effects of this 'new explosion' will not be readily measurable for a few years, but they will start to manifest themselves in the census of 1970 and will be most unmistakable in 1980."[31]

However, there are many experts who are not nearly so optimistic about the future. For example, while Bogue's arguments make sense if one assumes he is right about the uses of birth control methods, the world's population nevertheless could be drastically increased in another way—through the extension of life. While life expectancy in industrial countries like the United States has changed very little in recent decades there is great potential for change in the near future. If (and it is a big if) there are significant breakthroughs in heart research, cancer control, and other major killers in the United States, and if safety devices in automobiles, factories, and the home are developed, then it can be expected that people will live longer. It is very possible that by the end of the 20th century there will be the means of replacing defective human organs with artificial ones. All in all there is a strong possibility that by the end of the century life expectancy could be increased by ten or even twenty years. If this happens the population explosion will be great even though birth control methods are highly effective.

At the present time it is highly important that as births become increasingly under control, greater social value is attached to the small family. In fact, contrary to a popular belief, the increase in the average number of children per couple has not been the main reason for the high fertility levels of the past two decades. More important has been an increase in the proportion marrying, as well as a trend toward marrying at younger ages.[32] In the United States increasing social pressure is developing among some groups against having large families. It used to be that couples who had large numbers of children, if they were middle or upper class, were applauded. (The lower classes were seen as "irresponsible".) Invariably the "mother of the year," one of our many commercialized honors, was a woman with six or seven children. Yet, in 1970 one United States senator suggested that it might be more sensible to give the "mother of the year" award to a woman who had her tubes tied and adopted two children. This symbolizes dramatically the changes with regard to family size among some social groups.

For many years there also was a belief that children were better off being reared in large families. But that may have been an exaggeration. As Guttmacher points out, children that were raised in large families, when they grow up and marry, tend to have small families—in fact, smaller than average.[33] It would seem that the large family in the United States is on

---

[31] *Ibid.*, p. 332.

[32] Westoff, *op. cit.*, p. 113.

[33] Guttmacher, Alan F., *The Complete Book of Birth Control* (New York: Ballantine Books, 1963), p. 22.

its way out; and studies indicate that the vast majority of couples believe that the control of fertility is desirable and the ideal number of children is two or three.

USING BIRTH CONTROL METHODS

In this section the discussion moves more directly to questions of who uses what birth control methods and under what social conditions. More specifically, the interest is in some of the social variables that are related to people using birth control methods. In any society where birth control methods are available there will be many variations between groups of people who use them as against those who do not.

RELIGION

In the United States certain religious values have been the greatest overall negative force against the use of birth control. This religious interest in birth control has not been common to most religions of the world. The major religions of the Eastern world do not have explicit ideologies with regard to birth control. Some aspects of some religious beliefs do encourage large families but they do not have objections to family planning. So religious beliefs in the Eastern world have not been a major factor in resistance to population control. However, in many parts of the Western world, and specifically in the United States, religious values *have* had a major impact on population control.

Among Protestant groups, beliefs are now almost unanimous in giving strong endorsement to birth control. This was strongly demonstrated in a statement adopted in 1961 by the General Board of the National Council of Churches of Christ in the United States. This is a federation of 25 major Protestant denominations with about 40 million members in the United States. The Protestants' point of view is based on their notion of the basic purposes of marriage. Those purposes include not only parenthood, but just as important the development of the mutual love and companionship of the husband and wife, and their service to society.[34] The Protestant position is illustrated by that of the Methodist Church, the largest single Protestant denomination. In 1960 they adopted the unequivocal position that "planned parenthood, practiced in Christian conscience, fulfills rather than violates the will of God."[35] It should be stressed that among almost all Protestant groups birth control methods are not just accepted, but are encouraged.

The support for birth control methods among Jews has paralleled the

[34] *Ibid.*, p. 108.
[35] *Ibid.*, p. 109.

developments among the Protestants. The initial endorsements among Jews first appeared in 1931. Now all Jewish groups, except for the most extreme Orthodox group, endorse birth control. And even the extreme group sanctions female contraceptive methods under special health circumstances.[36] Not only do Jews accept the use of contraceptives but all the available evidence indicates that they use the methods most effectively. For example, Westoff in his studies found that Jews had the highest rates of any religious groups in using contraceptive methods and chose to use the most effective methods that were available.[37] It is clear that whatever problems exist in birth control methods among Protestants and Jews, they are not due to ideological acceptance but rather to the availability and efficiency in using the methods. However, by contrast, the primary problem for Roman Catholics is the ideological position of the Church, and secondarily for many, the choice and effective use of the various methods. It is therefore important to devote some attention to the Catholic position with regard to birth control.

CATHOLICS

The basic theological difference in Catholic doctrine from that of Protestants and Jews relates to the basic purpose of marriage. The Catholic Church believes that procreation is the primary reason for marriage, with companionship and vocation being secondary. Therefore, according to the Catholic Church, birth control by any chemical or mechanical means would frustrate the primary purpose of marriage and as a result violate natural law. The position of the Catholic Church can be seen more clearly by looking briefly at its position with regard to several different means of birth control.

For whatever purpose it might be used, *sterilization* is outside the moral pale insofar as Catholics are concerned. "The Catholic Church conceives of direct sterilization as an unwarranted attack upon the dignity of the human person."[38] Because it goes against the natural manner of sexual intercourse, *coitus interruptus* is also ruled out if used in any way to influence birth control.

The Catholic Church opposes *artificial birth control,* which means the use of any mechanical, chemical, or other procedures that are used for the purpose of keeping the sperm from entering the uterus and/or from reaching the Fallopian tubes. "The precise type of contraception is not the important issue; neither is the fact that there are different rates of effective-

---

[36] *Ibid.,* p. 111.

[37] Westoff, Charles F., *et. al., Family Growth in Metropolitan America* (Princeton, N.J.: Princeton University Press, 1961), p. 79.

[38] Gibbons, William J. (S.J.) "The Catholic Value System and Human Fertility," in Petersen and Matza, *op. cit.,* p. 21.

ness. Rendering the sperm nonviable, or impeding its normal motility, is included under the general heading."[39] The fact that conception will not be the result of a particular coital act does not make that act unnatural or illicit in the eyes of the Catholic Church. "The governing principle enunciated by moralists is that the act of intercourse must be performed in a natural manner and without the interposition of any positive obstacle to conception."[40]

There is also confusion by many on the Catholic Church's position with regard to the rhythm system. Approval of the rhythm method was given by Pope Pius XI in his 1930 encyclical, *Casti Connubii* (*On Christian Marriage*). However Gibbons, a Catholic spokesman, states that the advocacy of periodic continence must never be such as to obscure or ignore the purpose for which marriage exists according to Catholic doctrine. "Such would be the case were the impression left that rhythm is the Catholic answer to the query of the selfish: how to achieve the gratification of marriage, while avoiding its major responsibility."[41] Gibbons goes on to say that the precarious health of a mother, or the well based fear that another child cannot be cared for properly are valid reasons for having recourse to continence. Nor, he continues, should the motivation of those who look ahead and try to foresee how they will care for future offspring be condemned. "Such an approach to fertility is rational and legitimate, provided of course the parents avoid the opposite error of thinking the fewer the children the better."[42]

The contention of Catholic spokesmen is that Catholicism does not tell married people that they must have a high birth rate, but it does warn them about the abuse of marriage and the dangers of undersized families. "It opposes selfishness and excessive individualism, whether it be in the use of sex or in the utilization of material wealth."[43] It may be argued that while Catholicism does not tell its members that they must have large families it usually makes that result occur if the members follow the church's restrictions with regard to birth control. It seems safe to say that if all Catholics followed the restrictions of their Church with regard to birth control most of them would have very large families. In fact, they would have far larger families than they do in actual fact. This raises the question: Is the restrictive view of the Catholic Church on birth control being accepted and used by its members? In other words, how successful are the restrictions against birth control methods on the actual lives of Catholics?

[39] *Ibid.*, p. 23.
[40] *Ibid.*
[41] *Ibid.*, p. 24.
[42] *Ibid.*
[43] *Ibid.*, p. 28.

On the broadest level it would seem that many Catholics are not too different from non-Catholics in controlling their family size. For example, the annual birth rate is 18.1 per 1,000 for all the Catholic countries of Europe. The corresponding figure for the non-Catholic countries of Europe is 18.0 per 1,000. In the United States somewhere around a third of all Catholics restrict themselves to abstinence or the rhythm method as a means of birth control. One study found that 46 percent of lower middle-class Catholics practiced withdrawal, condom, diaphragm and jelly, or combined uses of these methods. As Westoff points out, "one assumes that these couples must be highly anxious about their child-spacing in order to use methods disapproved by their church. To practice efficient methods of contraception, Protestants do not have to overcome the same religious inhibitions."[44] It seems possible that guilt would make the Catholic less effective in his use of birth control methods. It is also possible that many Catholics do not feel any guilt about using birth control. Some of them may feel that birth control is really not the Church's business. That is, simply because the Catholic Church defines areas of behavior it has jurisdiction over does not always mean that its members accept those jurisdictional imperatives.

There are variations among American Catholics in their acceptance and use of birth control methods. Religious education is related to whether or not Catholic women follow the dictates of the Church. The factor of education in religious schools has been one of the strongest single predictors in the study of differentials in Catholic fertility. "Catholics who did not go to Catholic schools behave more like Protestants with respect to fertility—than like the more indoctrinated members of their own faith."[45] Other studies have shown that Catholic women who are highly devout and highly educated are most effective in using the rhythm method. This was because they had the knowledge and sophistication to use the method most efficiently as well as the strong religious motivation to do so. Another study indicates that fertility is closely related to the frequency with which the person receives the sacraments. "The average most likely expected total number of births rises from 3.2 for Catholic wives who never received the sacraments to 4.4 for those who received them once a week or more."[46]

All of the evidence indicates that there is a wide gulf between the position of the Catholic Church on birth control and what a majority of Catholics actually do. One of the basic measurements of the strength of any social institution is the extent to which its stated value system with

---

[44] Westoff, *op. cit.*, p. 94.

[45] *Ibid.*, p. 201.

[46] Whelpton, Pascal K., *et. al.*, *Fertility and Family Planning in the United States* (Princeton, N.J.: Princeton University Press, 1966), p. 83.

proscribed behavior patterns are followed by its members. For example, the military institution states as a basic value assumption that there must be unquestioning obedience by those in subservient positions to those in superior positions. On occasions the military elite finds that this is not occurring. They immediately institute various means for punishing deviants and force behavior back in line with the values of obedience. This is roughly analogous to the situation the Catholic Church is confronted with. Basically, the leadership of the Church has two possibilities. One, it can attempt through various methods to bring the behavior of the membership into line with the values of the leadership. Hypothetically, the Catholic Church could impose strong sanctions on its members to abide by the values of birth control, and if necessary, excommunicate those who will not conform. If all members who did not go along with the values of the Church on birth control were excommunicated there then would be congruence between the stated values and the actual behavior of the members. The second possibility could be that the Church modify its values with regard to birth control methods to fit more closely the actual behavior of its members. For example, many have argued that if the Church would allow the use of some chemical means of birth control, then its members would have something reliable to turn to. At the present time there seems to be little chance of this occurring. Yet, it is also clear that there are great pressures from within the Catholic Church to bring about changes with regard to birth control. This is one of the major issues around which the liberal and conservative forces of the Catholic Church are struggling.

In the United States there is great opposition to the Catholic Church's position on birth control and abortion by many non-Catholics. This is because the Catholic Church's concern with individual obligations for procreation and parental responsibility presents the only major theological obstacle to population control. The Catholic Church contributes to this conflict when it opposes legislative change to more liberal laws on birth control methods or abortion wanted by many Protestants. In other words, the Catholic power groups find themselves arguing on their religious grounds for restrictions that affect a population that is overwhelmingly non-Catholic. One of the dangers of the Catholic position on birth control and abortion in the United States is that of stimulating increasing anti-Catholicism.

Next is a brief examination of some other social variables related to the use of birth control methods. Education is one important variable. It is highly correlated with the most effective use of birth control methods, although not necessarily families with the smallest number of children. That is, highly educated women often have large families, but when they do it is most often from planning rather than chance. By contrast, studies show that women who have a low level of education not only expect to have larger families but do, in actual fact. In general, the higher educated woman knows more about available means of birth control and knows how to most effectively use whatever methods she does choose. Closely related to the difference by education is the variation by social class. The lower the social class of the women the greater the average number of children she has. One exception to this is the upper upper class in the United States, who often have large families. One major reason is that they can afford to have all the help they need in taking care of their children and home.

There is a common belief that one reason many women in the lower social classes have more children is that they have a higher level of sexual frequency. In other words, they have large families because they have greater sexual frequency leading to greater chance of pregnancy. There are several misconceptions in this assumption. First, there is no evidence that a high rate of sexual coitus increases fertility. In fact, there is a counter argument that it cuts down on fertility because the sperm count is less in a given act of coitus. Second, there is no reason to believe that the lower class actually has a higher rate of coitus than the higher social classes. And in fact it may be that because of hard physical labor and malnutrition their coital rates are even lower. However, studies show they are less informed and least effective in their use of birth control methods. This could be the major reason for the large families.

The birth rates among blacks have been higher than among whites. But the higher birth rate among blacks is not due to any greater fertility capacity. The differences in birth rates between blacks and whites can be explained primarily by their differences in education, income, and occupation. In general, educated women, and wives of educated husbands, have fewer children. Because a small number of blacks are highly educated and most of them are unskilled workers with low incomes it is to be expected that their fertility is high. Well-educated blacks in white-collar occupations with high incomes are somewhat less fertile than whites of the same general status. It is quite possible that the relationship between race and high fertility is a spurious one and that other variables are the important causal ones.

WORKING WOMEN

One of the most important consequences of the birth control development over recent decades has been the large number of married women in the work force. The development of birth control methods has been the single most important factor in the emancipation of the American woman. For almost the entire history of mankind most women have been locked in the home because of their having large numbers of children. Birth control methods have allowed women to have fewer children and have them when they want them. At the same time women have developed the willingness to turn their children over to schools and other agencies for care while they work. In general, when a woman decides to work she has fewer children. Whelpton found that those wives who worked after their marriage not only had fewer births than those who had not worked but also anticipated a significantly smaller total number of children. Furthermore, the longer the wife worked the fewer the births she had or expected to have in contrast to those women who worked for short periods of time.[47] However, the causal relationship between women working and their fertility is a complex one. "Many wives are probably motivated to limit the size of their families because of their desire to work, and many wives who cannot have as many children as they want as a result of fecundity impairments probably work primarily because they have comparatively few responsibilities at home."[48] Whelpton also found that those wives who said they worked primarily because their families needed the income had and expected significantly more children than did those women who worked because they like to. This suggests that some wives work because of the economic needs that arise from the fact that they have or expect to have a fairly large number of children.[49]

Birth control use is also related to certain views that are held about the sexual nature of marriage. Historically, in the vast majority of cultures, sex in marriage has been important in two ways. First, as the means of reproduction, and second, as a means of satisfying the sexual needs of the husband. In the past, with few effective means for controlling conception, pregnancy frequently resulted from marital coitus. This resulted in large numbers of children, high rates of maternal and infant mortality, and a short life span for the reproductive wife. Also in the past, while women could and did receive personal satisfaction from the sexual aspect of marriage it was not usually an expected right. In the patriarchal system, sexual need was generally assumed to be a need of the man. The woman who also received sexual satisfaction was sometimes viewed by her husband (and herself) as somewhat "unnatural." "Good women," at least in terms of accepted sexual values, did not usually derive pleasure from the sexual act. Their role as sexual partner was one of duty to the husband. However, all of this has changed for many American women in that they now see their own sexual satisfaction as their right and to be achieved separately from any decision with regard to reproduction. That is, a woman may enter marital coitus relatively few times in her life where the primary aim is conception, but will enter coitus hundreds of times where the aim is sexual satisfaction.

---

[47] *Ibid.*, p. 108.
[48] *Ibid.*
[49] *Ibid.*

Views about birth control methods also enter into the thinking about many aspects of premarital sexual intercourse. Initially when the birth control movement was emerging one of the common arguments against it was that contraceptive methods would lead to greater sexual promiscuity among the unmarried. The argument went that if the fear of pregnancy were removed through the use of contraception the unmarried would become highly active sexually. There is some indication that new contraceptive devices did contribute to greater premarital sexual activity, although it probably has not been a major force. The difficulty with this argument is that even if there are possibilities of greater premarital intercourse among the unmarried, is that sufficient reason for restricting the overall use of contraceptive devices? In reality the only way in which one could be sure that no unmarried persons used contraception would be to make them unavailable to all persons. This would, of course, infringe on the rights of the married to use these methods for important and accepted reasons.

At the present time there is general acceptance in the United States that the young and unmarried should learn about birth control methods. For them to learn may mean of course that some will use the knowledge before they are married. In a Gallup Poll in 1969, 71 percent of a national sample said they approved of schools giving courses in sex education. And of those who approved, over half of them said they approved of courses that included the discussion of birth control methods. However, most people do not approve of providing birth control pills to the unmarried girl. For example, a national sample was asked if they approved of giving birth control pills to unmarried girls in college. Seventy percent of the men and 77 percent of the women answered "no."[50]

It is generally overlooked that the sale of birth control devices is a fairly large business. Most contraceptives, whatever the type, are manufactured, distributed, and sold by private business. The sales in the United States run into the hundreds of millions of dollars every year. The attitudes associated with the sale of contraceptives are of interest because contraceptives are usually defined as either a medical concern or a public health issue. Governments usually classify contraceptives as pharmaceuticals. However, many consumers see contraceptives as personal rather than medical products. "In England barber shops are popular sources of supply; in Jamaica rum shops and groceries serve the same purposes, as do peddlers in India, and vending machines and fraternity brothers in this country."[51] There tends to be an implicit standard in the United States against encouraging the private sales of contraceptives for profit, except

[50] *Trans-Action, op. cit.,* p. 3.

[51] Farley, John U. and Harold J. Leavitt, "Population Control and the Private Sector," *Journal of Social Issues,* October, 1967, pp. 136–37.

through drug stores. "Surprisingly, this standard seems to be shared by a composite of some clubwomen, contraceptive manufacturers, physicians, churchmen, public health officials, foundation executives, and social scientists. While many favor population control in general and many of these, contraception in particular, they either ignore or abhor broad distribution of contraceptives."[52] This is to a great extent a result of a lack of respectability associated with contraceptive devices that exists in the minds of many. This is illustrated in the sale of some types of contraceptives, especially of condoms. About half of all condom sales in the United States take place in semiprivate settings like men's rooms (and ladies' rooms) and often through vending machines. They are sold "for the prevention of disease," and many are bought for nonmarital sexual intercourse.[53] Condoms also tend to be associated with the lower class and are probably most often used in that group, especially in nonmarital coitus. Among the higher educated it is common for the female to provide the contraception through the use of a diaphragm or the pill. This indicates that in the middle class the woman commonly takes the responsibility for not getting pregnant.

CONCEPTION PROBLEMS

The great interest in birth control methods often clouds over an opposite problem that exists for many couples. That is the problem of having children. It is estimated that about 10 percent of all married couples will be childless, but only 1 to 3 percent are personally satisfied with their childlessness. So about one out of every 12 couples is childless even though the couple desires children. Draper points out that the reverse of the birth control penny is the side concerned with greater help for couples unable to have children. As science finds ways of reducing the percentage of couples unable to have children it will contribute to the overall birth expansion number. And medically the problems of fertility and infertility are closely linked and often represent medical problems and processes that apply to each other in reverse.[54]

METHODS OF BIRTH CONTROL

Birth control methods, in the broadest sense, refer to the various ways used to stop either pregnancy or live births. Sometimes the concept of birth control applies to "positive" aspects of controlling family size through the spacing of children over time. Ultimately this means not

---

[52] *Ibid.*, p. 143.
[53] *Ibid.*, p. 136.
[54] Draper, *op. cit.*, p. 22.

having children except when desired. There are a variety of birth control methods that may be applied in a number of ways. First, *destruction* after conception; this may range from destroying the fetus by induced abortion or by giving birth to the child and then ending its life. Second, through *sterilization*, a process by which a person is made biologically incapable of producing or transmitting the ovum or the sperm. Third, the *processual* ways of controlling pregnancy. This may be through the withdrawal of the penis prior to ejaculation of sperm, or through a system where the sperm is present but no ovum is available for fertilization. Last are the various contraceptive methods. The term contraception is generally applied to "mechanical or chemical barriers that prevent the access of spermatozoa to the uterus and Fallopian tubes at times when fertilizable ova are present."[55]

The arguments for the means and ends in using birth control methods fall into two groupings; one is generally medical and the other social. When birth control methods are proscribed by physicians in the United States today it is mainly to achieve the goals of better maternal health, improved child care, financial stability, and family happiness.[56] Several related reasons have been suggested by McCary. They are: (1) to aid in early sexual adjustment in marriage, (2) to space pregnancies, (3) to limit the number of children, (4) to avoid aggravation of any existing illnesses or diseases, and (5) to prevent the perpetuation of inherited diseases.[57] We now examine some of the different types of birth control methods and give some attention to their reliability.

ABSTINENCE

This is obviously the most reliable method of birth control, but it is also the most extreme. It represents the total linking of coitus with reproduction because coitus would never be engaged in unless the intention was pregnancy. This method has been used by many individuals or groups of individuals in various cultures. Of course if it were used completely by a social group that group would never replace itself unless it did so by bringing in new members from the outside.

THE RHYTHM METHOD

This method is based on refraining from sexual intercourse during the

---

[55] Gordon, Edgar S. "Taking Physical Factors into Account," in Howard Becker and Reuben Hill, *Family, Marriage and Parenthood* (Boston: D. C. Heath & Co., 1955), p. 337.

[56] Guttmacher, *op. cit.*, p. 17.

[57] McCary, James L., *Human Sexuality* (New York: D. Van Nostrand Co., 1967), pp. 131–32.

period when the female ovum is at the stage in the menstrual cycle when conception is possible. The most difficult problem with making this method work is that extreme care must be used in the calculation of dates so that sexual abstinence will occur during the mid-stage of the menstrual cycle when conception can occur. In general, the more irregular the menstrual cycle, the less dependable is the rhythm system. About 15 percent of all women have such irregular menstrual periods that they cannot safely use this method. And after childbirth, the first few menstrual cycles are often so irregular that the rhythm method is unreliable at that time.[58] So this is not a highly dependable method, although the unplanned pregnancies are often the result of the woman's not being careful in following the basic requirements of the method.

WITHDRAWAL (COITUS INTERRUPTUS)

Like the rhythm method, withdrawal is a "processual" means of controlling conception in that it does not involve artificial impediments. Sexual intercourse is interrupted immediately before the male orgasm by withdrawal of the penis and ejaculation outside the vagina. This is one of the least used methods in the United States today. A number of problems are associated with this method. First, it calls for strong will power on the part of the male. He must be willing to give up the final and often most satisfying stage of sexual intercourse. Another problem involves the ability of the male to anticipate accurately when he is ready to ejaculate. Still another difficulty is that even if the male withdraws ahead of ejaculation, some possibility of pregnancy continues to exist. The danger rests with the "sperm cells in the few drops of seminal fluid which often escapes from the penis before the orgasm is reached."[59] The reliability of this method, like that of the rhythm system, depends to a great extent on the user. This is a major disadvantage of the method.

DOUCHE

This is the cleaning of the vagina with a mild acid sperm-killing solution after sexual intercourse. It is often also used as a supplement to other methods, for example, it may be used with the diaphragm. The assumption of this approach is that the semen will be flushed from the vagina before it has a chance to enter the mouth of the womb. "Actually, however, sperm move so quickly that the douche often fails to reach them."[60] This is probably the least reliable of all the methods and really serves better as a means to cleanse the vagina than to prevent pregnancy.

---

[58] *Ibid.*, p. 143.

[59] Gordon, *op. cit.*, p. 354.

[60] McCary, *op. cit.*, p. 140.

STERILIZATION

Sterilization prevents parenthood without destroying the sexual abilities of the individual. The usual methods are the cutting of the *vas deferens* (vasectomy) of the male and the Fallopian tubes (salpingectomy) of the female. The vasectomy removes no organs (nor does salpingectomy) and is relatively simple surgery which interrupts the seminal duct so that the male fluid that reaches the female no longer contains sperm cells. The operation is safe and only takes about twenty minutes. This operation is totally reliable and is the most effective means for making sure that pregnancy does not occur. However, it does have one major disadvantage for some who use it, and that is that the effects of the operation are often permanent. If at a later date a man wants to undergo an operation that reverses the effects of the vasectomy there is only about a 50 percent chance of success. The female operation costs far more and requires about ten days in the hospital. It is estimated that in the United States about two million couples have had surgical birth control. For most of them there is probably no great concern about changing the operation at some later date because they do not want children or already have all the children they want.

Sterilization has often been involved in governmental policy decisions where there has been a desire to control pregnancy potentials. Sterilization for eugenic reasons has been sanctioned in some states, particularly in state supported institutions. There the physician can perform the operation on mentally deficient patients without fear of legal consequences. There appears to be approval of sterilization in the United States at least under certain conditions. In the mid-1960's in a national sample 67 percent of the respondents approved of sterilization when persons have mental or physical afflictions and ask to be sterilized. In the same sample 78 percent approved of sterilization when the health of the mother would be endangered by having more children.[61] In 1970 in Great Britain male sterilization operations were made free under the National Health Service Law if both the husband and wife agreed.

CONDOM

As indicated, this may be the oldest of the artificial or mechanical methods of contraception. It is the most widely used method of contraception in the United States because it is commonly used more in nonmarital than marital coitus. When the condom is used correctly it is a highly reliable method of contraception. While there is some danger of breakage this has been controlled to a great extent because the manufacture

---

[61] *Trans-Action, op. cit.,* p. 3.

of condoms is now under government supervision and there are fewer failures due to tearing and to defects than in the past. Some men object to the condom because it somewhat dulls pleasurable sensations. "Also, its use may interfere with the natural progress of mounting sexual tensions because sexual play must be interrupted in order to put it on."[62] Historically the condom has been linked with venereal diseases, giving it a bad "image" and some people do not like to use it for that reason. The condom is unique in another way—of all the mechanical or chemical means for controlling pregnancy now in use this is the only one that is the responsibility of the man to use.

DIAPHRAGM

This is a flexible rubber disk that is coated with a spermicidal jelly and covers the cervix, thereby preventing the sperm from reaching the ovum. It must be left in place for 8 to 12 hours after coitus. This device can be obtained only by prescription from a physician and must be fitted by him the first time. Prior to the pill this was the method used by the highest educated women in the United States and was used with a high level of reliability.

INTRAUTERINE CONTRACEPTIVE DEVICES (IUCD)

These are small plastic or metal devices of various sizes and shapes. They are designed to fit into the womb and may act as an irritant to prevent implantation of the fertilized ovum in the uterine wall. The process is simple and usually painless. The placement can be made without danger by any physician or other trained medical technician. Once in place the device can remain for years and be removed if the woman wants a baby. However, there are some women who cannot tolerate the device because it causes bleeding and pain. A recent study of 24,000 women found that about two-thirds of them can use the device satisfactorily.[63] These devices may come to play an important part in controlling population in many parts of the world because not only are they medically simple to insert but they can also be manufactured for as little as two cents apiece.

ORAL CONTRACEPTIVES (THE PILL)

The pill works through: (1) the suppression of ovulation or spermatogenesis; (2) prevention of fertilization; or (3) preventing the implanting

---

[62] McCary, op. cit., p. 39.

[63] Havemann, Ernest, Birth Control (New York: Time, Inc., 1967), p. 37.

of the fertilized ovum in the uterus.[64] The so-called "steroids," pills that contain synthetic hormones, have been the most effective of the oral contraceptives. When they are taken daily from the 5th to the 25th day of the menstrual cycle, they halt conception by halting ovulation. The Federal Food and Drug Administration in 1959 approved for public sale the first pill to be used for purposes of birth control. Its advantages over older methods are that it offers a high degree of reliability—not only biologically but also psychologically, in that the human errors often found with the use of the condom or the diaphragm are minimized. Oral contraception can also contribute to greater spontaneity in the sexual act because the pill can be taken prior to sexual intercourse. Because of its great simplicity of use, it can also be taken by many not willing or able to correctly use the condom or diaphragm. If the pill is taken as prescribed it is virtually 100 percent effective and its success is unequaled by any other means of contraception.

It has been recognized that there are side effects from the pill for some women. "The most common symptoms reported are mild gastrointestinal disturbance, nausea and bloated feeling, increase in weight, and spotting and irregular bleeding. Other occasional negative side effects are persistent menstrual-like cramping and painful swelling of the breasts."[65] By 1969 the use of the pill had reached an estimated 7,000,000 women in the United States. This meant that approximately one seventh of all women in the child bearing years were using the pill. It was estimated that the wholesale value of domestic sales was about $100,000,000 per year and export sales about equal to that. All indications were that the pill would increasingly be used by a greater proportion of women, but in 1969 came the "pill scare."

The pill scare came about as a result of congressional hearings on oral contraception. At that time testimony was heard that the pill was dangerous and had not been adequately tested as to side effects and possible dangers for the user. The hearings received a great deal of publicity and panic set in among many users. By the winter of 1970 it was clear that many users of the pill had stopped. A Harris poll found that 50 percent of a national sample of women said they had stopped the pill because they thought it to be injurious to their health. The same poll asked: "From what you have heard or read, do you feel the birth control pill is dangerous to use or not?" To this question 60 percent of the respondents felt the pill was dangerous. However, most of the respondents do not feel that the pill should be outlawed.

There are other indications of the panic related to the pill. A number

---

[64] Lehfeldt, Hans, "Contraception," in Albert Ellis and Albert Abarbanel, eds., *The Encyclopedia of Sexual Behavior* (New York: Hawthorne Books, Inc., 1961), p. 297.

[65] McCary, *op. cit.*, p. 136.

of New York city obstetricians say they have been approached to perform abortions on women who stopped using the pill. Also, birth control clinics in New York funded by the Office of Economic Opportunity reported that before Senator Nelson's congressional hearings on the pill about eight out of every ten women asked for the pill, but after the hearings only about 60 percent chose oral contraception.[66]

Some counter support for the pill has developed, but it has received much less publicity. Most of the congressional testimony emphasized the hazards of the pill and did not pay much attention to it as the most effective means of family birth control. Guttmacher has argued that blood-clotting problems, some of which can be fatal, are the only proven risks associated with oral contraceptives. Death from clot complications occurs in about three out of every 100,000 women on the pill, but for women who become pregnant the risk is fifteen times greater.[67] Guttmacher further points out that if all the women who quit the pill turn to the next most effective method, the intrauterine device, almost 50,000 will become pregnant because of the higher failure rate of that method.[68] There is need for a careful and objective study of the pill with a clear statement on the dangers and the advantages from that method.

The discussion of birth control methods may be summarized in terms of their relative effectiveness. The most effective methods are oral contraception, IUCD, diaphragm and jelly, condom, and withdrawal: the least effective are the rhythm system and the douche. Many times the failure of contraception is attributed to the method, rather than the person using it. The fact is that the most reliable methods used by careful individuals can and do effectively control pregnancy.

There is a constant attempt by experts in the area of birth control methods to discover new or better procedures. Some physiologists argue that the present methods are crude with various problems that can be worked out. They also believe that superior methods are close to being developed that can be produced cheaply and will be free of the human error in using. Actually huge sums of money are being poured into research in this area both through the public and private sector. "The giants of the drug industry know that huge markets can be gained by improving upon present contraceptive technology—and that huge markets will be lost if a competitor discovers and markets a superior product."[69] The ideal contraceptive they all seek would be harmless, reliable, free of unpleasant side effects, cheap, and simple to use. It would also have to be easy to reverse so that a woman could become pregnant if she desired. "And,

---

[66] *Newsweek*, March 9, 1970, p. 46.

[67] *Ibid.*

[68] *Ibid.*

[69] Bogue, *op. cit.*, p. 330.

finally, one should be able to apply it at a time completely removed from the sexual act, so that the couple does not have to bother about birth control whenever they have intercourse."[70]

One interesting possibility for a future contraceptive pill would be the morning after type—taken sometime after having coitus. This type has been tested on animals and it prevents the fertilized egg from being implanted on the wall of the womb. This method would have interesting implications for nonmarital coital protection from pregnancy. All present methods must be used beforehand and this means that the female must plan on coitus or at least think there is a possibility. Some single women may not be willing to plan ahead and use contraception, and refuse to have coitus for that reason. However, if there were a pill to be taken after coitus women could have protection from pregnancy without premeditation. Hypothetically, this could contribute to an increase in nonmarital coitus.

Yet, with all the attempts to develop new and better methods of contraception it should not be assumed that any method will ever be developed that will reduce the frequency of unwanted pregnancies to zero. This is true because unwanted pregnancies most often occur among the underaged, the overaged, and the psychologically disturbed. "The underaged become pregnant because they cross the sexual threshold before they think they are going to, and do so unprepared. The overaged, entering the menopause, neglect contraceptive precautions because they *think* they are sterile. The psychologically disturbed, typically a neurotic woman involved in a marriage that is going on the rocks, behave impulsively and sometimes with destructive intent."[71]

Of all the areas of social problems and deviancy discussed in this book there is the greatest irony with regard to birth control. That is, since the beginning of mankind the having of children has been seen as inevitable, natural, and in most cases highly desirable. For a man to marry and not have children was in most societies a loss of face as well as an economic deprivation. When this occurred the blame was usually placed on the woman, and in many societies barrenness in marriage was grounds for the man to divorce his wife. However, in recent years the problem has come to be associated with just the opposite—those who will not control the number of children they have. Today, there are often dominant values that say a small family is desirable and possible in the very same society where many individuals continue to believe that having large numbers of children is highly desirable. So in many parts of the world the technological knowledge of highly effective birth control and the broad social

---

[70] Guttmacher, *op. cit.*, p. 55.

[71] Hardin, Garrett, "The History and Future of Birth Control," *Perspectives in Biology and Medicine*, Autumn, 1966, p. 10.

and governmental encouragement often exists while the value of the large family of the past is still basic to many persons in those societies.

BIBLIOGRAPHY

DRAPER, ELIZABETH, *Birth Control in the Modern World* (Baltimore, Maryland: Penguin Books, 1965).

FARLEY, JOHN U. and HAROLD J. LEAVITT, "Population Control and the Private Sector," *Journal of Social Issues*, October, 1967, pp. 135–43.

FREEDMAN, RONALD, *Population: The Vital Revolution* (New York: Anchor Books, 1964).

GUTTMACHER, ALAN F., *The Complete Book of Birth Control* (New York: Ballantine Books, 1963).

HARDIN, GARRETT, "The History and Future of Birth Control," *Perspectives in Biology and Medicine*, Autumn, 1966, pp. 1–18.

HAVEMANN, ERNEST, *Birth Control* (New York: Time, Inc., 1967).

HIMES, NORMAN E., *Medical History of Contraception* (New York: Gamut Press, Inc., 1963).

MCCARY, JAMES L., *Human Sexuality* (New York: D. Van Nostrand Co., 1967).

CHAPTER 5

ABORTION

IN ONE SENSE this chapter can be read as a logical continuation of the previous chapter on birth control. This is true because many of the variables of acceptance and rejection related to birth control are also important to abortion. However, the major difference is that public feelings about abortion are generally stronger and more intense than about birth control. For example, there are a number of people who approve of birth control methods but who disapprove of abortion. Basically this distinction appears to center around views of the developing life cycle and when life begins. For many it is believed to be all right to stop the sperm from entering the ovum but not all right to stop the development of the ovum once fertilization has taken place. It is the belief by many that abortion ends a "life" that has started that makes it such a highly charged and emotional area. It is for this basic reason that abortion is defined as deviant behavior by a large majority of Americans—at least under most circumstances.

Abortion refers to the termination of pregnancy before the unborn child or fetus attains viability, i.e., the capacity for life outside the womb. Abortions are divided into three categories. *Spontaneous abortion* is caused by uncontrolled internal conditions in the woman and represents the termination of about 10 percent of all pregnancies. *Therapeutic* abortion is the legal ending of pregnancy by artificial means before the fetus is viable. It usually occurs for medical reasons where it is decided that some physical or mental complications may threaten the woman's health or life.

117

Illegal abortion is the unlawful termination of pregnancy. The individual woman may seek illegal abortion when, for many and varied reasons, she feels strongly against carrying the fetus full term and giving live birth. The types of abortion and their social and personal implications will be discussed in some detail later in the chapter.

The view of abortion as social deviancy comes about from two related, but somewhat different, value perspectives. One, as suggested, is the view that abortion ends a life, and the second perspective is the setting that brought the life about in many cases—premarital coitus. Looking a little more at the first perspective, concerned with the ending of life, it does go against existing legal and social norms and therefore may be considered a form of deviant behavior. Yet, many times abortion is undertaken to *prevent* the social problems of family disorganization and economic hardship or to cope with major threats to the pregnant woman's physical or psychological health. "Thus although its legal status as deviance may be established, abortion must also be viewed as a mechanism of social control."[1]

When abortion is linked to the unmarried female it often takes on strong moral overtones. The fact that a large number of women engage in premarital coitus is never openly brought to the attention of most Americans. That is, they may hear about premarital sexual permissiveness but they are not directly confronted with it. However, when the unwed girl gets pregnant she confronts them with her pregnancy as proof of her sexual "immorality." And in the minds of many to allow her to have a socially approved abortion would appear to condone her immoral sexual behavior. Therefore, the fact of her pregnancy makes the single woman a social deviant. She may enter into the abortion-seeking process with bitterness and desperation. "This is particularly so because society has sanctioned, even encouraged, behavior of which premarital pregnancy is a foreseeable result."[2]

The question of premarital pregnancy and its resolution may be one that faces almost one million women every year. This estimate is suggested because it is believed that each year about 300,000 brides are pregnant at the time of marriage, about an equal number of single women have abortions, and an equal number become unwed mothers. There are methods available that could be used to halt a large amount of this deviancy if society so desired. That is, the contraceptive techniques are available that would make possible the reduction of that number of pregnancies to a minimum. But as Reiss points out, many of the very same people who strongly oppose premarital pregnancy just as strongly oppose contraceptive knowledge for young people. "Instead, verbal persuasion,

---

[1] Schur, Edwin M., *Crimes without Victims: Deviant Behavior and Public Policy* (Englewood Cliffs, N.J.: Prentice-Hall, 1965), p. 12.

[2] *Ibid.*, p. 46.

curfews, and other pressures are used to control premarital pregnancy. Such methods may work for special segments of the population, but these are typically conservative segments with very low rates of premarital pregnancy anyhow."[3]

In effect the unmarried pregnant girl is told get married or have the illegitimate offspring. If she gets married she may suffer some embarrassment about her "premature" baby and the marriage may have difficulties. If she has the baby and keeps it she will often suffer strong moral stigma if she is in the middle class—in fact, probably more stigma than if it were found that she had had an abortion. Of if she can afford it she can leave her local community and have the baby where she is not known. If she has the baby the common pattern is to place it out for adoption. The relationship between the two social problems of illegitimacy and childlessness is an interesting one. Illegitimacy is viewed as a social problem that should be eliminated; however, a significant decrease in illegitimacy would result in an increase in the number of marriages that would have to remain childless because of lack of adoption opportunities. A marriage which is without children when they are desired is also viewed as a significant social problem. So one social problem (illegitimacy) helps to resolve another (childlessness), but there is a social class difference in the two solutions. The higher the social-class level, as measured by education, the less the belief that the unwed mother should raise her child and the greater the belief that the child will be better off reared by adoptive parents.

How premarital pregnancy is treated by society is seen as a means of punishing the individual for his deviance and deterring him from doing the same in the future. One measure of the effectiveness of the punishment is what the future premarital sexual activity will be like for unmarried girls who had babies or abortions. For example, there is no evidence that women who become unwed mothers alter their sexual activity afterwards. It has also been found in one sample that 90 percent of the females who had premarital induced abortions continued to have premarital intercourse after the abortion.[4] The same study also concluded that "there is no evidence in these data to suggest that a premarital induced abortion is sufficiently traumatic to the woman to lead to the breakup of a subsequent marriage."[5]

Closely related to the "punishment" view of not allowing abortion to the unmarried is the argument that the liberalization of abortion laws would somehow constitute the sanctioning of "immorality." The assumption seems to be that proscription of abortion acts as a deterrent to pre-

---

[3] Reiss, Ira L., "The Sexual Renaissance," *The Journal of Social Issues*, April, 1966, p. 128.

[4] Gebhard, Paul H., *et al.*, *Pregnancy, Birth and Abortion* (New York: Harper and Brothers, 1958), p. 210.

[5] *Ibid.*, p. 211.

marital and extramarital relations. However, as suggested, there is no evidence that such is the case. This is also the same kind of argument used against the public availability of birth control methods—that if they are made available they will contribute to an increase in immorality.

The arguments against abortion also become tied up with considerations about children. One general argument goes that more permissive abortion laws would diminish our reverence for life and our concern that all forms of life receive protection. In other words, legalized abortion would be a step in the direction of callousness toward human life. However, in a country with liberal abortion laws such as Sweden there is no evidence of any less concern and feeling for human life than in America. There is also a certain irony in the fact that generally there is far greater legal, medical, and moral concern with the unborn fetus than with controls over how children are treated once they are born. That is, parents may mistreat their children to a great degree before there is moral censure or legal authorities intervene. Parents are allowed a great deal of latitude in how they can treat or mistreat their children. When the treatment of children is compared with the restrictive views toward abortion the child is more closely guarded in the abstract than he is when real and alive.

Another reason for the restrictive concerns with abortion is the assumption by society that having and wanting children is "natural, right and inevitable" for women. However, the majority of women who seek abortions do so because they find themselves with unwelcome or unwanted pregnancies. "It is the situation *of not wanting a child* that covers the main rather than the exceptional abortion situation." Alice Rossi goes on to point out that "many people are unwilling to confront this fact because it goes counter to the expectation that women are nurturant, loving creatures who welcome every possibility of adding a member of the human race."[6] Many believe that for a woman to willingly have an abortion is for her to go against her basic womanness—that of bearing children.

As indicated, abortion as a form of social deviance is linked with other areas of social deviance and social problems. One consequence of this is that often abortion is responded to as it affects other problems either in a negative or positive light. People respond in various ways when abortion is linked with illegitimate children, broken families, poverty, premarital sex, and so forth. This means that the intensity of concern for making abortion easier or more difficult to get becomes confused with the other problems. In other words, when a person is strongly for stricter controls against abortion it may really be because he believes that that is the best way to control premarital sex, the deviance that really bothers him. Or the person who wants easier abortion laws wants that because he sees abortion as a right that the individual should have. Therefore, his basic

---

[6] Rossi, Alice S., "Abortion Laws and Their Victims," *Trans-Action*, September, 1966, p. 7.

concern is really for what he feels should be overall human rights, one of which is the right of abortion. With this general introduction to abortion as social deviancy, the next section looks at the historical background to abortion and how it has been defined and applied in society.

HISTORICAL BACKGROUND

There have been few, if any, societies that have not on some occasions practiced abortion. For example, in an ancient Chinese work estimated to have been written almost 5,000 years ago, a method is described for bringing about abortion through the use of mercury. The Assyrian Law, about 1500 B.C., punished with death any woman who deliberately aborted. Early Jewish law penalized abortion according to the rule "thou shall give life for life."[7] In ancient Greece, Aristotle and Plato advocated abortion to limit the size of the population and maintain an economically healthy society.[8] In Greece, abortion was seen as the logical choice if birth control failed.

Historically neither the early Romans, Greeks, nor Jews had opposed abortion. However, Tertullian, following an inaccurate translation of Exodus XXI, 22, which refers to punishing a man who injures a pregnant woman, "but which appeared to prescribe punishment for injuring the fetus, gave currency to the idea that the Bible held abortion to be a crime."[9] Tertullian devoted a great deal of energy and ingenuity to determining when the fetus became animate, and came to the conclusion that it was after forty days in the case of males and eighty in the case of females. Although this error has long been exposed, the "Church still maintains this position, and it has become incorporated in the law of the state, which beautifully demonstrates that moral laws are not really derived from Biblical authority, but that Biblical authority is sought to justify regulations which, because of unconscious prejudices, seem 'natural' and 'right'."[10]

While at the time of early Christianity it was unlawful for a man to take away with intent his own life, was it also unlawful to destroy life in the womb? The gospels never mention this question, and the natural deduction is that the first Christians simply accepted the old Mosaic laws which forbade abortion. "In both Greece and Rome the interruption of pregnancy was sanctioned by law, advocated by the leading philosophers and moralists, and generally practiced by the people. Yet even Paul, who

---

[7] Neumann, Gothfried, "Abortion," in Albert Ellis and Albert Abarbanel, *Encyclopedia of Sexual Behavior* (New York: Hawthorne, Publishing Co., 1964), p. 38.

[8] Tietze, Christopher and Sarah Lewit, "Abortion," *Scientific American*, January, 1969, p. 3.

[9] Taylor, G. Rattray, *Sex in History* (New York: The Vanguard Press, 1954), p. 58.

[10] *Ibid.*

devoted so much attention to the problems of sex life, found it prudent not to endanger the success of his missionary work by broaching this delicate question. It was only much later and in quite different circumstances that St. Augustine expressly renewed the old Jewish ban on abortion and condemned all forms of contraception."[11]

In the late 18th century, at the time the United States became a nation, the states and the colonial assemblies left to the individual the choice of action directed at the fetus before quickening. So the early United States law on abortion followed the common-law tradition that forbade abortions after quickening (which was defined as about the sixteenth week of pregnancy, where fetal motion is felt). However, the laws were silent on the question of abortion before the quickening. During the middle of the nineteenth century in both England and throughout the United States, laws were passed prohibiting abortions completely, with a few exceptions regarding the life and sometimes the health of the mother.

In general, before the Civil War, based on English common law, abortion was not a statutory crime but was considered the right of women prior to quickening. But after the 1830's there was a developing atmosphere of asceticism which resulted in many states passing restrictive controls changing what had been a private matter into one of social control. This meant that the moral assumption that abortion was wrong held by some persons became legislature and forced on all. This assumption was based on religious concepts of original sin and the attributing of life to an embryo immediately after conception. This was simply a part of the overall highly restrictive legislature that developed around all sexual matters during the latter half of the 19th century. However, along with the moral restrictions that developed with regard to abortion laws in the 19th century there were also medical and legal considerations. Some laws had to be adopted to protect women from the crude surgery of that period.

CROSS-CULTURAL APPROACHES

As suggested, all known cultures have shown some interest and concern with abortion. This has been both in developing methods of abortion and in controlling those methods. The search for simple and effective methods of abortion has been going on for centuries. For example, many kinds of internal medications have been tried, "ranging from the bush tea of preliterate tribes to white phosphorus to hormones; almost invariably these treatments fail to induce abortion. It does not seem likely that a safe and reliable 'abortion pill' will be realized in the near future."[12]

At the present time it is estimated that about 25 million abortions oc-

---

[11] Lewinsohn, Richard, A *History of Sexual Customs* (New York: Harper and Brothers, 1958), p. 84.

[12] Tietze and Lewit, *op. cit.*, p. 4.

cur throughout the world as compared to roughly 120 million live births. These rates are distributed in countries in part according to their policy about legal abortion. The views about abortion held by countries range from the restrictive to the liberal. This range is illustrated in the statistics which show that in the northern European countries there are about three to seven legal abortions for about every one hundred live births. By contrast in eastern Europe and Japan the number of legal abortions ranges from about 30 per 100 live births to 140 per 100 live births in Hungary. It seems clear that the worldwide trend is toward the liberalization of laws controlling access to medical abortions. This is especially true in the socialist countries which have made abortion a national policy available upon the request of patients.

The liberal countries now have policies that in effect permit abortion simply upon the request of the mother. This is now the case in the Soviet Union, Bulgaria, and Hungary. The Soviet position is stated in the decree that the intent is the limitation of the harm caused to the health of women by abortions carried out outside of hospitals, as well as to give the woman the choice of deciding upon her own motherhood. Japan also permits abortions under a broad set of circumstances related to the health of the mother, which in effect amounts to abortion on request.

By contrast with the liberal views about abortion, the United States is one of the most highly restrictive nations. Actually there are only a few countries, particularly in western Europe, where the laws against abortion are even more restrictive—virtually forbidding any abortions—than they are in the United States. The countries of northern Europe, Norway, Denmark, Sweden and Finland, occupy about the middle ground between restrictive and liberal abortion laws.

It is often assumed that those countries characterized as Catholic have the most restrictive conditions with regard to abortion. However, this is often not the case. In a number of Catholic countries the church's stand on birth control is widely ignored and there are high rates of abortion. For example, in France illegal abortions are roughly equal to the number of live births. In South America, induced abortion is the number one cause of death for women in the childbearing years. In the United States Catholic women are less apt to have abortions than are their non-Catholic counterparts. However, the Catholicism of the United States is much more conservative and influential on the lives of its members than it is in many other countries.

Given the fact that a number of countries have taken on more liberal policies about abortion, what have been the consequences of that change? One important consequence is that the birth rate declines more rapidly following the liberalization of abortion than any other means of developing a contraceptive campaign. That is, introducing and making available birth control methods do not have the results that making abortion available does. It may be that abortion replaced contraception as the means of birth control in many countries. Some women stop using the birth control methods and relied entirely on abortion.

The medical risks associated with legal abortion are not great, and with time the risks have decreased. For example, in Sweden, as legal abortions increased, the death rate associated with the operation declined. Mortality fell from 257 per 100,000 legal abortions in the period 1946–48 to 39 per 100,000 in the period 1960–66.[13] Furthermore, the data from studies indicate that when abortions are performed legally and in hospitals "at least in countries where a nunpunitive attitude toward abortion is widespread and even official, no serious adverse psychic consequences need be anticipated."[14]

When a country legalizes abortion it doesn't mean that illegal abortions disappear. It is difficult to determine the degree to which legalization of abortion in the various countries has reduced the incidence of criminal abortions. That they are not eliminated entirely is evidenced by the fact that a number of women with difficulties arising from illegal abortions turn up at hospitals for treatment. "This stubborn survival of illegal abortion can probably be attributed to the fact that, for one reason or another, women sometimes want to conceal their pregnancy and therefore avoid the procedure of formal application and official approval."[15] In the northern European countries women must get official approval for abortion, and some women have illegal abortions who do not receive permission or because of bureaucratic delays in receiving official permission. Basically, a legal abortion involves a lack of privacy and that appears to be a problem for some women, especially those who do not live in the larger cities.

THE LEGAL DIMENSIONS OF ABORTION

It must be recognized that a woman has absolute control over her personal reproductive capacities so long as she can successfully utilize contraceptive or birth control methods, but she forfeits that right if her method of birth control fails and she gets pregnant. It has been suggested that if the logic "behind present abortion laws were rigorously followed, abortion would be treated as murder punishable by death or life imprisonment.[16] Basically the legal system says that the woman has the right of

---

[13] *Ibid.*, p. 6.

[14] Schur, *op. cit.*, p. 43.

[15] Tietze and Lewit, *op. cit.*, p. 9.

[16] Lucas, Roy, "Federal Constitutional Limitations on the Enforcement and Administration of State Abortion Statutes," *The North Carolina Law Review*, June, 1968, p. 759.

control over her reproductive capacity until she gets pregnant, and then she loses that right to determine whether or not she will be a mother.

There are no standard figures on the number of induced abortions in the United States but the rate is figured to be at least 200,000 per year, and may be as high as 1.2 million. Most of those abortions are illegal ones. It has been reported that police consider criminal abortion to be the third largest illegal endeavor in the United States, surpassed only by gambling and narcotics.[17]

Up until recent years it has been estimated that approximately 10,000 women per year have been able to receive legal abortions performed in hospitals. If it is estimated that a total of 700,000 induced abortions occur each year and 10,000 are legal, then only about three out of every 200 abortions are legal. And even today after the recent legal reforms of abortion there are still probably no more than 10,000 legal abortions in the United States each year as compared to 700,000 illegal ones and the 3.6 million live births.

Abortion is one of the areas of deviance, like nonmarital sex or homosexuality, where the number of illegal acts are very great in proportion to the number of deviants apprehended and prosecuted by the legal authorities. In general the only time that abortion cases come to the attention of law enforcement authorities is when death or hospitalization results. But the possible threat means that many medical practitioners, although very sympathetic to the abortion needs of the woman, are usually reluctant to take a chance on being discovered and facing possible legal prosecution. So while the number of legal prosecutions is small, the threat is often a powerful deterrent against most medical men's performing an abortion, regardless of how much they may think it should be done. One common way for them to get out of their dilemma is to pass on the responsibility for deciding whether or not an abortion should be performed to a hospital board, "thus demonstrating to the patient a desire to help but running no personal risk."[18]

In those cases where an individual is arrested for performing abortions it is difficult in some states to get a conviction. "The state must usually prove not only that the operation was performed but also that it was not necessary to preserve the mother's life. However, lenient rules regarding evidence in abortion cases considerably lessens the state's burden."[19] In most states it is enough to show that the woman was healthy at the time of the operation and "in a normal condition prior to the operation to raise the inference that the operation was not necessary to preserve her life."[20]

[17] Schur, op. cit., p. 25.

[18] Ibid., p. 21.

[19] Ibid., p. 20.

[20] Ibid.

It is generally recognized that the laws against abortion are highly difficult to enforce. Over the years, in all of the states, the number of prosecutions and convictions has been very small. As a result the practical function of abortion laws has been limited to the control of abortion rather than to its elimination. It should also be mentioned that there are some states that make it a crime for a woman to submit to an abortion. "There is no record of reported American cases involving conviction of a woman for submitting to an abortion. Hospitals, which contravene the abortion laws from time to time, also are—within broad limits—free from prosecution."[21]

It is clear that until recently the legal restrictions against abortion were accepted by most social institutions and most Americans as right and proper. However, in the 1960's a changing view developed about the legal and social definitions of abortion control. What sometimes happens is that a single, highly dramatic situation will bring to the attention of many the nature of legal restrictions they had never thought about before. This is what happened to the highly publicized case of Mrs. Sherri Finkbine in 1962. Mrs. Finkbine tried to get an abortion when she discovered she had taken thalidomide, a sedative that had been linked to the birth of thousands of deformed babies in Europe. She was refused a legal abortion in the United States and finally, after a widely publicized trip, she was aborted in Sweden and her unborn fetus was found to be deformed. Public interest in abortion restrictions was further developed by the German measles epidemic of 1963–64, blamed for the birth of some 30,000 infants with congenital defects. Out of these and other influences there has emerged a view held by many that the laws with regard to abortion should be changed. This has up until now been focused almost completely on the state level, but strong pressure is developing to bring about new legislative rights to abortion on the federal level.

During the period from 1967 to 1970 fourteen states adopted more liberal laws that permit interruption of pregnancy for reasons other than to save the life of the mother. However, the trend is not entirely liberal. For example, while in 1970 New York passed a liberal abortion law the governor of Maryland vetoed one. Very often the consideration for new laws on abortion are not examined on their merit, but rather in terms of their believed political gains or losses. The main political consideration is usually: Will a liberal abortion law antagonize the Catholic vote?

The new laws are primarily based on medical assumptions. That is, the right to abortion is *not* usually a decision given to the individual woman but in most states a decision that must be made by and for medical reasons. The laws in most states permit only medical factors to be taken into account in determining whether legal abortion shall be per-

---

[21] *Ibid.*, p. 36.

mitted, "although the medical health clause of the laws of some states is used as an elastic provision to include some cases which primarily involve social factors."[22] The laws in the various states differ in the language used and whether the focus is on the mother alone or the mother and the child. In about 60 percent of the states abortions are unlawful unless they are necessary to save or preserve the life of the mother. In nine states the preservation of life covers the mother or her child.

Of the states that did bring about change in their abortion laws during the 1960's, the first was Colorado in 1966. It set the pattern that has been commonly followed by legalizing abortion on three principal medical grounds. That statute authorizes abortion whenever pregnancy: (1) threatens grave damage to the woman's physical or mental health, (2) results from rape or incest, or (3) is likely to produce a child with a severe mental or physical defect. North Carolina enacted a similar law as did California, except that it bars abortion of potentially defective children.

What has been the consequence in these states that have brought about legal changes in their abortion laws? In general they have not changed two major characteristics of the past. Namely, they do not make abortions much easier to get, and they discriminate in favor of the wealthier. In fact after Colorado and California reformed their abortion statutes it was found that New York, where the law only permitted it to save the mother's life, was performing more abortions.

There is other evidence that abortion reform has not led to any great change in abortion rates. For example, it appears that abortion reform in Georgia and North Carolina exists in word but not in deed. With 90 percent of the in-hospital abortions in Georgia performed on white women, it seems that the small incidence of abortion in that state is due in part to the relative unavailability of legal abortion to black women. It is also of interest that no abortions have been reported for rape or incest in either Georgia or North Carolina.[23] What this indicates is that new laws must be applied, and if the legal and medical authorities choose to ignore the new abortion rights then the rates are not going to change.

By 1970 abortion laws were changing so rapidly that it is possible to describe only what the situation is at a given time. In 1970, at the time this is written, Hawaii is in the process of passing a liberal abortion law. As with most states, Hawaii has in the past permitted physicians to perform an abortion only to save the mother's life. But Hawaii's new bill would in effect remove all restrictions on the operation and would allow any woman to have an abortion if she does not choose to have a child. The major restriction imposed would be that to obtain an abortion a

---

[22] Lee, Nancy Howell, *The Search for an Abortionist* (Chicago: The University of Chicago Press), 1969, p. 4.

[23] *Association for the Study of Abortion*, Newsletter, Summer, 1969, pp. 2–3.

woman would have to live in the state for at least ninety days. This is to stop women from other states from coming into Hawaii for abortions. However, that restriction may prove to be unconstitutional because of a recent federal court ruling which abolished residency requirements for welfare recipients.

At the time of this writing the most liberal new abortion law to be passed and put into effect has been in New York state. The new law was adopted in April, 1970 and went into effect on July 1, 1970. The new statute permits abortions to be performed at any time up until the 24th week of pregnancy as a matter of discretion between a woman and her doctor. It is estimated that 50,000 to 75,000 abortions will be performed in New York during the first year. There will be many coming in from other states, as the New York law imposes no residency requirements, though initially most hospitals were giving preference to women from New York. The costs of the abortion vary widely, depending on the nature of the operation and where it is performed. Medicare patients in city hospitals are able to get their abortions free. Other patients coming to city hospitals are charged on a sliding scale up to $156 for a simple abortion done on an outpatient basis. Voluntary hospitals are charging from $100 to $300 a day, and some doctors are receiving as high as $400 in addition to the hospital charge. However, health insurance may help. Blue Cross and Blue Shield have said they will pay up to $300 of the cost of an abortion for a woman regardless of marital status.[24] The new law has been criticized because of its high costs and because it is not meeting the great need among poorer women for legal abortions. The success of the new law in New York is impossible to estimate at the present time.

With the exception of the abortion laws in Hawaii and New York the laws are under the control of the medical profession. And even in the two above states the medical adviser that the woman talks to can decide not to give her an abortion. The medical and legal professions have not been at the forefront in bringing about abortion reform. The medical profession has been traditionally conservative in this area. And even at the present time, although the American Medical Association favors liberalization of the law, it has not come out for outright repeal of the present abortion restrictions. However, in June, 1967, the American Medical Association endorsed a proposal by the American Law Institute (ALI) with regard to abortion reform. The ALI defines three instances in which abortions would be justified: one, when there is substantial risk that continuance of the pregnancy would gravely impair the physical or mental health of the mother; two, when there is a substantial risk that the child will be born with severe physical or mental defects; three, when the pregnancy was caused by rape, incest, or other felonious intercourse, including

---

[24] *Newsweek*, "Abortions on Demand," July 13, 1970, p. 60.

statutory rape of girls under sixteen. That proposal goes on to say that the operation must be performed by a licensed physician in a licensed hospital. Also at least two physicians must make a written certification of the justifying circumstances. Finally termination of pregnancy would be justifiable only before viability. This proposal is quite conservative when contrasted with the new law in New York. It is a good illustration of making abortion rights solely a medical matter, because nowhere in the proposal are the desire or rights of the mother recognized.

The right of the mother to determine whether or not she shall have an abortion is increasingly becoming the major question. But there continues to be the belief in the minds of many that basically the woman should not have the right to have an abortion as her own decision. The assumption by most authorities is that they know what is better for the woman than she knows for herself. It is of interest that there is no strong assumption by authorities that women should be counseled and controlled about their using contraceptive methods. That is, the woman is assumed to be capable of making the decision as to whether or not to get pregnant, but once she is pregnant she is not capable of making the decision to end that pregnancy. And it is basically around this point that the appeals for legalized abortion on the federal level are being made. If the Supreme Court should rule that abortion is a right, then what is happening in the various states with regard to abortion reform will become irrelevant in the future.

Up until very recently the idea that an American woman might have a constitutional right to have an abortion was heard among only a very few. However, at the present time there is an increasing number of lawyers and judges predicting that this right will eventually be recognized by the Supreme Court. There are others who believe that the courts will declare the nation's anti-abortion laws unconstitutional on other grounds, but with the same consequence—to leave abortion as a private matter for the woman to decide. This has meant that the tactic of some of the agencies for abortion rights is to demand abolition rather than reform, and they are using litigation rather than legislation to achieve that end. What is emerging is the belief by many that abortion is a fundamental right and should be available to all women—those who are poor and single as well as those who are well-off and married.

More specifically, what are the legal approaches on the federal level? One argument is in terms of the first amendment to the constitution of the United States which states that "Congress shall make no law respecting an establishment of religion." The argument is that the continuance of state abortion laws is a result of religious pressures and values that are not universally subscribed to. And the argument is that this should be found by the Supreme Court to violate the establishment clause. It has also been suggested that the existing abortion laws raise a number of significant constitutional issues. "The statutes sharply curtail a woman's freedom of choice in (1) planning her family size, (2) risking her physical or mental well being in carrying a pregnancy to term, (3) avoiding the birth of a deformed child, and (4) bearing a child who is the product of rape or incest."[25] Furthermore, the argument goes on that the present abortion laws "are (1) largely unenforced, (2) uncertain in their scope, (3) at odds with accepted medical standards, (4) discriminatory in effect, and (5) based upon the imposition of criminal sanction of subjective religious values of questionable social merit upon persons who do not subscribe to those values."[26]

Lucas, in his extensive study of abortion law, states that the right of abortion by consent performed by a licensed physician can be strongly asserted in at least three related forms within the Bill of Rights and fourteenth amendment framework. "First, as a fundamental right of marital privacy, human dignity, and personal autonomy reserved to the pregnant woman acting on the advice of a licensed physician; second, as a right emanating from values embodied in the express provisions of the Bill of Rights themselves; or, third, as a necessary and altogether reasonable application of precedents namely, Groswald v. Connecticut."[27] It may be that with time there will not only be an ending of laws against abortion but the establishment of an affirmative right to an abortion.

RELIGIOUS VALUES AND ABORTION

Laws and religious values have been closely interwoven in the areas of sexual behavior and family values. However, it has also been argued that in many areas of behavior the religious values have lost much of their traditional power and influence and this is the case with religious pressures against abortion. However, before looking at religious views toward abortion it is necessary to say something about the scientific meaning of life, because the view of when life begins is a major point in the arguments of the Catholic Church against abortion.

When the ova is fertilized it is at that time little more than the seed out of which develops a human being. At twelve weeks the fetus is about 3½ inches in length and has bone and cartilage that can be clearly distinguished. Also at that time fetal heart function can be detected through the use of an electrocardiogram. Also at twelve weeks the muscles and nerves have developed sufficiently so that the fetus moves its arms and legs vigorously. Yet, there is no sharp line when life begins. "However, we can draw an arbitrary line, just as we do in the case of legal majority, and

---

[25] Lucas, *op. cit.*, p. 752.
[26] *Ibid.*
[27] *Ibid.*, pp. 755–56.

just as we do in the case of a speed limit. Good medical practice draws such a line at 12 weeks of pregnancy in the United States."[28] The twelve week stage is important to the medical issue of abortion. Before this point, it is possible to perform an abortion by the simple method of dilation and curettage. After twelve weeks, however, doctors can no longer use this procedure with safety. Scientifically the beginning of life is a process and not a specific point in time. Basically the period from conception to birth is where life is in the process of becoming.

At the present time in the United States almost all Protestant and Jewish spokesmen (with the exception of extremely Orthodox Jews) generally uphold the morality of therapeutic or legal abortions. One study found that Jewish women were the most liberal with regard to abortion. That same study found that among Protestants the Episcopalians, Presbyterians, and Congregationalists were the most liberal on the issue of abortion. And at the opposite pole were the members of the fundamentalist sects and the Baptists.[29] In general the more traditional and conservative the religious beliefs, the greater the opposition to abortion. By contrast some liberal Protestant groups have developed programs to help women get abortions. For example, The National Clergy Consultation Service on Abortion, formed in 1967, had in 1970 branches in more than a dozen cities and were referring about 25,000 women a year to physicians in the United States and abroad.

The only large scale, organized opposition to abortions comes from the Catholic Church. The Roman Catholic Church opposes all abortion reform. The Catholic position against abortion was delivered by Pope Pius XI, December 31, 1930, in his *Casti Connubi* (*On Christian Marriage*). He wrote that abortion is against the precept of God and the law of nature: "Thou shalt not kill." The life of each is equally sacred, and no one has the power, not even the public authority, to destroy it." Pius further wrote that "however much we may pity the mother whose health and even life is gravely imperiled in the performance of the duty allotted to her by nature, nevertheless what could ever be sufficient reason for excusing in any way the direct murder of the innocent?" He goes on to state that "those show themselves most unworthy of the noble medical profession who encompass the death of one or the other, through a pretence of practicing medicine or through motives of misguided pity." This formal Catholic position has not been changed over the past forty years.

As suggested, science sees the beginning of life as a process. However, the Catholic Church has settled the question of animation on the grounds that the soul enters the embryo at the moment of conception. Therefore, the Catholic position is that the gravity of the sin of abortion is the same

---

[28] Hardin, Garrett, "Semantic Aspects of Abortion," *Etc.*, Vol. XXIV, 1966, p. 231.

[29] Westoff, Charles, *et. al.*, "The Structure of Attitudes toward Abortion," *Milbank Memorial Fund Quarterly*, January, 1969, p. 19.

regardless of the time when it is committed.[30] At the present time there is no indication that the Catholic Church is planning on modifying its restrictions on abortion. This is true even though many Catholic women are obtaining abortions. As discussed in Chapter 4 on birth control, there are severe problems for the Catholic church when it adheres to a strong position that many of its members refuse to follow.

That many Catholics do practice abortion is well documented. In fact, many countries with predominately Roman Catholic populations show high abortion rates. As suggested earlier, the number of abortions in France is about equal to the number of live births. In a recent survey of Roman Catholic Chile 27 percent of the women reported they had induced abortions.[31] In the United States there are few reliable statistics on the number of Catholic women having abortions but there is no doubt that many of them do. There are many American Catholics who believe that abortion decisions should not be a legal matter. In a Harris survey in 1969, among Roman Catholics, it was found that 60 percent agree with the belief that the decision to have an abortion should not be determined by law.

There are a variety of different ways in which the Catholic opposition to abortion expresses itself. For example, restrictions placed on Catholic doctors and nurses are significant factors in the abortion situation. The Protestant physician can follow his individual conscience and his best medical judgment. By contrast, the Catholic doctor is enjoined to adhere to what the church holds to be theologically sound practice. "Hence arises a lamentable gulf between the practice and attitudes of Catholic and non-Catholic physicians, and the fate of the patient will frequently depend entirely on the religion of her adviser and the denomination of her hospital."[32]

There are also other arguments used by the Catholic Church and by others against abortion. For example, some have said it makes more sense to wait until the child is born and have it killed if it is defective and the parents so desire. It is further argued that this is consistent with the permissive nature of laws demanded by some people in favor of completely free personal choice by the mother with regard to abortion. Whatever the logic of this position it is the case that society would see it as infanticide and murder and not accept the position as a real alternative.

SOCIAL VIEWS RELATED TO ABORTION

It was suggested earlier in the chapter that the married woman who plans her family size and child spacing carefully through the use of contraceptive techniques is in most cases given social approval. However, if

---

[30] Neumann, *op. cit.*, p. 39.

[31] Rossi, *op. cit.*, p. 11.

[32] Schur, *op. cit.*, p. 53.

her methods fail and she gets pregnant her alternatives are to accept a pregnancy she doesn't want or to have to undergo what may be the unsafe and often traumatic experience of an illegal abortion.[33] If the pregnant woman is unmarried she has several alternatives with varying consequences. First, she can marry the man with whom she conceived (if he is single). But the consequence is often a high risk marriage. Second, she can go through with the pregnancy and put the child up for adoption. For many women this may not be a severe personal problem, although it might be very inconvenient to go through the pregnancy. And for a number of women it may lead to extensive therapeutic problems. Third, she can have the child illegitimately and rear it herself. But the costs, especially if she is middle class, both personal and social, are often very great. Fourth, she can have an illegal abortion, with all the problems that go with that.[34] Rarely is there the fifth alternative available to the unmarried woman of having a therapeutic abortion.

One study of unmarried women that had abortions found that not all of the above alternatives actually were in operation. It was found that among the single women who conceived with a serious boyfriend they only really considered two alternatives—abortion or marrying the father. Those single women who conceived in a casual affair considered only abortion, illegitimacy, or adoption.[35] In the total sample of that study only two of the 65 single women had wanted to get married to the man involved and have the baby.[36] Lee, in her study, came to the conclusion that the decision of whether a pregnancy is wanted or unwanted depends upon an interaction between the circumstances of the pregnancy and the values and beliefs of the individuals involved. "Some women, probably a very small proportion of the population, would reject any pregnancy that occurred under any circumstances, while others would require extremely difficult circumstances before rejecting a pregnancy and others would not reject a pregnancy under any circumstances at all."[37]

But for many women, whether single or married, there is the belief that abortion is the right of the woman to decide. That is, abortion is but one phase of the American women's effort to control when they shall bear children. "Legal prohibitions can have the effect of forcing women to bear unwanted children and, in this sense, be means to further women's subservient social status in an age when emancipation of women is a major cultural theme."[38] This perspective about her rights to control her role of

---

[33] Rossi, op. cit., p. 12.

[34] Ibid.

[35] Lee, op. cit., p. 150.

[36] Ibid., p. 48.

[37] Ibid., p. 148.

[38] Johnson, Elmer H., "Abortion: A Sociological Critique," in Jeffrey K. Hadden and Marie L. Borgatta, Marriage and the Family (Itasca, Ill.: F. E. Peacock, 1969), pp. 336–37.

mother is reflected in how she sees abortion and her marriage roles. In recent decades women have been able to exert greater personal control over their marriages through easier divorce opportunities. And now many are seeking greater control over the motherhood role through more liberal abortion laws.

Abortion is still primarily a characteristic of married women. It is estimated that four out of five abortions are performed on married women who already have children, but who want no more. This does not mean that the married pregnant woman is more likely to have an abortion than the nonmarried pregnant women. In fact, the opposite is true. However, since there are many more married than single pregnant women in the United States, four out of five abortions are performed on married women. Even though most abortions are performed on married women and there have been a number of studies about them, there has been little research into their husband's reactions to the abortions. It would appear that in most cases the decision to have an abortion is made primarily by the wife and although she may discuss it with her husband it is primarily her decision to make.

There are a number of social variables related to which women get abortions. Probably the most important predictive variable on who gets a therapeutic abortion is that of social class. A variety of studies show that legal abortions are far more frequent among upper social class and educational level groups. For example, one study in New York City reported that the ratio of therapeutic abortions to live births for private hospitals was five times that reported for municipal hospitals.[39] It has also been found that marital status makes a difference, with unmarried women having much less chance of getting a therapeutic abortion than married women.[40] The racial factor is also an important variable, with therapeutic abortions going most frequently to the white population. "The white ratio is more than five times that among the nonwhites and 26 times that among the Puerto Ricans." (Well over 90 percent of all therapeutic abortions in New York City are performed on white women).[41]

Interpersonal contacts may also be very important in determining whether or not a woman will be able to get a legal abortion. Lee, in her study, found that to get a legal abortion it was usually necessary for the woman to have a long-standing relationship with a doctor as a private patient. Physicians are most apt to help a woman they have known over a number of years, "who is personally and socially the kind of woman they respect, and whom they know to be level-headed and unlikely either to embarrass the doctor by talking about it too much or become hysterical or

---

[39] Gebhard, *op. cit.*, p. 210.
[40] Schur, *op. cit.*, pp. 21–22.
[41] *Ibid.*, p. 142.

resentful afterward."[42] Lee goes on to point out that a woman past age forty is especially apt to gain a sympathetic hearing, "followed by younger mature women who have already had several children."[43]

It is possible to draw a general picture about who gets a legal abortion in the United States. Not only is it the wealthiest who are most likely to get the safest abortion, but it is most likely to be done for alleged psychiatric reasons. The time when the pregnant woman appears before the doctor is also an important factor. The private white patient usually seeks prenatal care early in pregnancy when abortion is still possible. By contrast, nonwhite or ward-service patients usually do not seek prenatal care until after the twelfth week when abortion can no longer be performed through a D and C. As indicated, the kind of hospital that one goes to makes a difference as to the possibility of getting an abortion. The wealthier go to private hospitals where abortions are easier to get. But the poorer women often go to municipal hospitals which are subject to the scrutiny of the public and are much more apt to be strict in their interpretation of the abortion laws. Some hospitals establish abortion quotas, in order to give the impression that it is not easy to get an abortion there.

There has been in the discussion thus far reference to the therapeutic abortion, so it is important to say something of the nature and the medical setting for that type of abortion. A therapeutic abortion is the intentional ending of pregnancy for medical reasons. As suggested earlier, the number performed in the United States has been about 10,000 per year. The annual number of therapeutic abortions has declined considerably in the past few decades. In New York City there were about 700 therapeutic abortions per year in the period 1943–1947, and this declined to about 300 per year in the years 1960–1962. Per 1,000 live birth, the ratio thus fell from 5.1 to 1.8. The general decline in hospital abortions is mainly the result of medical advances in the treatment of conditions that once contributed major threats to pregnancy. "Women with heart disease, hypertensive renal disease, tuberculosis, and other serious conditions are increasingly allowed to fulfill the term of pregnancy."[44] Over the same general period there has been some increase in psychiatric causes, together with the sharp decrease in physical reasons, and this has resulted in the proportion of therapeutic abortions performed for psychiatric reasons to increase a great deal.

The medical operation for abortion is of two types. As indicated, the usual operation is dilation and curettage (D and C). This operation involves widening the cervix, the neck of the womb, and introducing a "currette" (a long semi-sharp spoon-like instrument) to scrape the uterine

---

[42] Lee, *op. cit.*, p. 163.

[43] *Ibid.*

[44] Schur, *op. cit.*, p. 14.

cavity. This operation only takes about twenty minutes and a day's stay in the hospital. A more recent technique is the suction curettage which is a faster and less traumatic procedure used by an increasing number of obstetricians. In this method a tube is inserted into the uterus and the fetus and placenta are extracted by means of a vacuum pump. The D and C operation is generally recognized as a standard medical procedure. Schur points out that at least from that standpoint alone, "it need not more constitute a social problem than does appendectomy, X-ray treatment, or administration of pain-relieving drugs."[45] If the abortion is performed after the third month of pregnancy it is more extensive. After three months abortions are performed by means of a Caesarean type of surgery or by injecting a concentrated salt solution into the uterus that causes the fetus to be expelled in a few days. These procedures call for longer hospitalization of the woman.

The risks of a therapeutic abortion are very small. When it is performed under clinical conditions an abortion is safer than a tonsillectomy, and many times safer than childbirth. It has been found that women who regulate their fertility "exclusively by means of abortions performed in hospitals are exposed to a risk of life of the same order of magnitude as an equal number of women using oral contraception consistently over the same period of time."[46]

There is the common belief that women who have abortions, even therapetic ones, suffer a great deal of guilt and remorse over their actions. This belief seems to be based on the notion that the natural function of women is to bear children and any woman who goes against that natural function has to suffer some feelings of guilt. However, there is no evidence that women who have abortions are typically stricken with guilt or remorse.[47] Therefore, the consequences of legal abortions, both physical and psychological, are not severe and cannot be legitimately used as an argument against legalizing abortion.

It is of value to look at public opinion about abortion. It should be remembered that about twenty years ago legal abortion was approved of by very few persons. In fact, for many the idea of abortion was so reprehensible it was not even seen as a subject for discussion. However, this has changed and a Gallup poll conducted in 1969 showed that half the population opposed legalizing abortion, while 40 percent were in favor and 10 percent had no opinion. However, the population varied in a number of ways. For example, while only 31 percent of the grade school educated favor legalizing abortion, that was the case for 58 percent of the college educated. Also, of those 50 years of age and older 38 percent favored legal-

---

[45] Schur, Edwin M., "Abortion," *The Annals*, March, 1968, p. 137.

[46] Tietze, Christopher, "Mortality with Contraception and Induced Abortion," *Studies in Family Planning*, September, 1969, p. 45.

[47] Rossi, *op. cit.*, p. 11.

izing abortion as contrasted with 46 percent of those between the ages of 21 and 29. As is typical in other areas of social deviancy, the greatest resistance comes from the older and least educated elements of the population.

It has also been found that more liberal attitudes toward abortion are found among working women. The more liberal attitudes are held by women who have worked since their marriage but are not now working as well as by those currently in the labor force, as compared to those women who have never worked since marriage.[48] This fits the fact that women who work are generally less conservative and traditional about family roles than those who do not work. Women who stay at home often have a high commitment to the traditional role of the woman which places its greatest importance on the role of being a mother.

Westoff also found that "white women tend to be more in favor of abortion than are non-white women, a relationship that persists regardless of the amount of education."[49] This may be because the role of mother has been even stronger for the black woman than for the white woman in the United States. In part this has been because the black woman has had a greater responsibility for supporting and rearing her children than has her white counterpart. As a result there is a greater resistance to negatively influence the major, significant role of the adult Negro woman, that of mother.

The Westoff study also found a relationship between the use of oral contraception and attitudes toward abortion. It was assumed that the modern point of view reflected in the choice of the pill as the means of birth control might also imply a more liberal attitude toward abortion. "Results indicated that women currently using the pill, those who had only temporarily interrupted its use and those who never used it but indicated they might, are indeed the most favorable toward abortion. Less favorable are women who have tried but rejected it, and those who never used it and do not intend to try it; least favorable are those who never heard of the pill."[50]

The acceptance or rejection of abortion for many is determined by the circumstances in which pregnancy occurs. A large sample of respondents were asked if they thought it should be possible for a pregnant woman to obtain a legal abortion under a variety of circumstances. The highest agreement was stated by 71 percent in cases where the woman's health was seriously endangered by the pregnancy. But only 56 percent said "yes" if she had become pregnant as a result of rape. And 55 percent said she should be able to obtain a legal abortion if there was a strong chance

---

[48] Westoff, *op. cit.*, p. 23.

[49] *Ibid.*, p. 16.

[50] *Ibid.*, p. 26.

of defects in the baby. However, approval dropped off sharply when it came to more personal reasons. Only 15 percent said "yes" if she was married and did not want any more children. Only 18 percent said "yes" if she was not married and did not want to marry the man. One response of particular interest was that only 21 percent approved legal abortion for women whose family had a very low income and could not afford any more children.[51] While one common criticism in the United States is that many who are poor have large families, there is not the willingness to provide them with the means of controlling the number of children even when they want that help.

There have also been several recent studies as to medical viewpoints about making abortion more available legally. One study shows that about nine out of ten physicians sampled approved abortion for the reasons presented in the 1966 Colorado abortion law. The same study reports that the older physician seemed to be more favorable to abortion reform than was his younger colleague. "For example, 86 percent of the physicians in practice for 25 years or more approved the provision permitting abortion when pregnancy may result in the birth of a baby with permanent physical deformity or mental retardation; 79 percent of the physicians in practice less than ten years approved the provision."[52] Another poll conducted in 1969 found that 63 percent of the doctors responding said that abortion should be available to any woman capable of giving legal consent upon her own request to a competent physician. What is of particular interest is that a large number of medical persons no longer see abortion as something to be decided only by a physician, but rather as a right belonging to the woman, with the implication that she can get a doctor to agree to her decision.

It should also be mentioned that the developing interest in abortions over the past decade has been highly profitable for some physicians. This is a consequence of the fact that only some who have the money can get a legal abortion if they try hard enough. Or they can get an illegal abortion from a competent physician often under a "legal" subterfuge. One illustration of the subterfuge was the method one doctor worked out for performing illegal abortions openly. He would draw some blood from the patient's arm and squirt it into her vagina and send her to the hospital emergency room with instructions to have him summoned as her private physician. On arrival he would diagnose the trouble as a miscarriage, and do a D and C. On examination, the hospital pathologist would find a fetus and confirm the diagnosis. For this operation the doctor's fee was $1,200.[53]

---

[51] Rossi, op. cit., p. 9.

[52] Ortho Panel 4, "Sexual the Law," Ortho Pharmaceutical Corporation, 1969, p. 8.

[53] Newsweek, "Abortion and the Changing Law," April 13, 1970, p. 56.

CRIMINAL ABORTIONS

Schur points out that large numbers of women who are quite respectable and show no other tendencies for deviancy find themselves for a variety of reasons violating the laws against abortions. "Abortion is a private consensual transaction, a willing payment of money for (illicit) services received."[54] In these respects it is a form of deviancy similar to that of buying illicit drugs or sex. Schur goes on to make the point that while some persons may view the aborted woman as the "victim" of the abortionist, the woman herself does not share that definition of the situation. "Even where she has found the experience extremely distasteful or frightening—perhaps especially in such cases—she is most unlikely to wish to bring a complaint against the person who has performed the operation.[55]

There is no way of knowing how many criminal abortions are performed in the United States. For most illegal abortions only the patient and the abortionist know about it. But as suggested earlier, the estimates place the number of illegal abortions as anywhere from 200,000 to 1,200,000 per year. Illegal abortions are performed in two basic ways, either by the individual woman on herself or by some other person.

There has always been some folk knowledge about various ways that may be followed by the individual to induce abortion. Many women in the United States today will try mechanical abortifacients, such as hot baths, steam, hot douches, and so on which are ineffective. Many women still believe that such things as jumping, stretching, traveling on bad roads, lifting, and even hitting and massaging the abdomen work, but they bring about poor results. Some women turn to chemicals taken orally and purgatives, pelvic and intestinal irritants, drugs stimulating contraction of the uterus, as well as poisons, all of which are dangerous if taken in dosages large enough to abort the fetus. "Attempts at laceration with a sharp object, obviously perilous, demonstrate that extreme desperation of some women."[56]

It has been found that most women who claim to have aborted by using drugs or herbs were either not pregnant or would have aborted spontaneously in any case. In fact the evaluation as to the success of self-induced abortion is complicated by the fact that, "according to much medical evidence, the woman who with any real ease induces her own abortion often could have been likely to abort spontaneously anyway."[57]

For women who turn to others for illegal abortions a distinction can be

[54] Schur, *Crimes without Victims*, op. cit., p. 54.

[55] *Ibid.* p. 39.

[56] *Ibid.*, p. 23.

[57] *Ibid.*

made between those abortionists who are medically trained and those who are not. There are many M.D.'s who perform illegal abortions as a means of supplementing their income. In most cases they are never caught and the abortions they perform are usually highly reliable and safe. There are also other trained physicians who perform abortions. This may be the physician who for some reason has lost his license to practice medicine, "and the foreign trained doctor, who experiences difficulty in being admitted to practice in this country, may be especially likely to turn to illegal abortion practice."[58]

There is also the nonmedical abortionist, and this group can cover a range from those who are quite qualified to dangerous uninformed butchers. The methods they use vary. Those with some medical knowledge often perform D and C's. In recent years probably the most common method used by the nonmedical abortionist is the "packing" method. In this method a plastic or rubber tube is inserted into the uterus and the vagina is packed with gauze. The patient is then sent on her way and if she is lucky will a few days later expel the fetus without subsequent infection or hemorrhaging.

There are a variety of risks attached to the illegal abortion as a result of how and where it is done. There are some risks regardless of how conscientious the abortionist is because he must work under imperfect conditions and must for his own safety get the woman to leave his place of work as soon after the operation as possible. Therefore, one of the major risks is the inadequacy of abortion aftercare.[59] However, the use of antibiotics has greatly decreased the likelihod of death from criminal abortion. For example, the statistics on known abortion deaths in New York City show a steady declining trend, from 144 deaths in 1921 to 15 in 1951. "A disproportionate number of the women who died from abortions were Negroes, and although more of the women who underwent abortions were married, there were more deaths from crudely done criminal abortion with severe injury among those who were single."[60]

A survey in New York City has also indicated an increase in the proportion of maternal deaths due to abortion with almost half of all maternal deaths attributed to this cause in the most recent years studied.[61] When it comes to dying from abortion, the discrepancy in the quality of the abortions performed can be seen in the maternal death statistics. Between 1960 and 1962, for every 10,000 live births in New York City, 1.0 white women, 4.7 Puerto Rican women, and 8.0 black women died from abortion. It is likely that the greatest dangers are found for those women

---

[58] *Ibid.*, p. 26.
[59] *Ibid.*, pp. 28–29.
[60] *Ibid.*, p. 28.
[61] Schur, "Abortion," *op. cit.*, p. 141.

who are poorly educated, in the lowest social classes, and who are the most inadequately informed about the likely consequences of "home remedies" and techniques touted by the informal social grapevine.[62]

Of those women who die from abortions the main causes of their deaths are hemorrhage or infection. In 1964 there were a total of 247 known deaths from abortion in the United States and in 1965 the figure was 235 maternal deaths. Those figures include death from spontaneous miscarriages, legal therapeutic abortions, and illegal abortions. The vast majority, however, occur from illegal abortions. Projecting from these figures it is estimated that a total of about 500 abortion deaths occur per year in the United States.[63]

Getting an illegal abortion is not always easy. The recent study by Nancy Lee in Chicago of a sample of middle-class women shows what they had to go through to attain an illegal abortion. One immediate problem with arranging an abortion is the time factor. Most abortionists refuse to accept cases in which the pregnancy is past the twelfth week. So those seeking an abortion usually have less than six weeks to make a decision, locate an abortionist, raise whatever money is necessary, and have the abortion carried out."[64] Lee goes on to point out that one might think that with so much activity associated with abortion it would be a highly visible activity in society; "yet, outside certain small circles, abortion is carried on almost invisibly."[65]

Lee found in her sample of 114 women that only two of them had not discussed the question of an abortion with some other person before making that decision, and a majority of the women talked with three or more persons before deciding on an abortion.[66] Most of the persons suggested that of the alternatives available abortion was the best course of action for the pregnancy, and doctors advised the woman to go through with the pregnancy. Lee writes that "since most Americans are apparently opposed to abortion in general, one must conclude that the women consciously or unconsciously selected those they told about the pregnancy on the basis of whether the person was likely to support their tentative decision that abortion was the best alternative available."[67] It may also be that people are conservative when it is an abstract issue but when it is applied to an individual they know they may become more liberal in their feelings about abortion.

Once the woman had made the choice to have a criminal abortion she had to find the abortionist. This was not easy. The woman, acting jointly

[62] *Ibid.*

[63] Schur, *Crimes without Victims, op. cit.*, p. 43.

[64] Lee, *op. cit.*, pp. 6–7.

[65] *Ibid.*, p. 7.

[66] *Ibid.*, p. 53.

[67] *Ibid.*, p. 58.

with the man involved in the pregnancy in slightly more than half the cases, approached between one and thirty-one persons during her search.

The median number of persons consulted was five.[68] The ability to locate an abortionist, qualified or unqualified, expensive or cheap, nearby or far away is primarily determined by whom one chooses to ask and the recent history of abortion experiences known to the people who are asked. "One finds New York women flying to Puerto Rico to reach the only abortionist they learn about, while Puerto Rican women are flying to New York to follow up the leads they have found."[69]

In the Lee study most of the women had no physical symptoms after their abortions other than a sense of general weakness. She does report that somewhat less than half the women reported depression after their abortions, and 8 percent termed their depression severe.[70] It seems quite possible that many women who feel depressed after an illegal abortion do so because there is something they feel ashamed of in the illegal nature of what they did rather than in the abortion itself. This would seem to be supported by the evidence that women who have therapeutic abortions show no particular tendency toward depression.

Finally something should be said about the financial aspects of the criminal abortion. Estimates indicate that as much as $350,000,000 each year is spent for illegal abortions. It is believed that a large part of that money winds up in the crime syndicates. So illegal abortions not only create economic demands and physical dangers for the pregnant woman, but also account for the third largest criminal racket in the United States. The very nature of illegal abortion practices implies a fairly high degree of organization. To be successful, the abortionist must have adequate equipment, a place in which to work, and some technical or other assistance. The potential customers must learn of his existence and where he is located. Also some means of avoiding police interference must be developed. Schur writes that in New York City there are two types of abortion operations—the "mill" and the "ring." The mill involves one or more abortionists permanently located and aborting about a dozen women daily. The ring consists of a number of interacting abortionists or mills working intermittently at several occasionally changing locations and aborting an even greater number of women daily. "Clients are accommodated at the various locations depending on the pressure of referrals, the availability of operators at the moment of need, and the ability of the client to pay."[71]

What is the future of abortion in the United States? In Chapter 4 there was a discussion of the possibility of developing a birth control pill

---

[68] *Ibid.*, p. 76.
[69] *Ibid.*, p. 13.
[70] *Ibid.*, p. 121.
[71] Schur, *op. cit.*, p. 31.

to be taken after coitus. If the "morning-after" pill is developed the line between contraception and abortion would become quite blurred. The development of an abortifacient pill, to be taken later than the "morning-after" pill would make the practice of abortion more difficult, if not impossible, to regulate. These pills are not yet in general use but may be in the near future. It should be remembered that one of the reasons why abortions are subject to control is because they involve a clinical operation. But if that becomes no longer necessary it removes one more reason for controlling abortion.

In whatever way the abortion is to be performed it seems quite probable that in the future it will become the right of the individual to decide. This seems highly probable because it is part of the increasing drive for the emancipation of the woman and because there is no large scale organized opposition to legal abortion other than the Catholic Church, and the Church is losing a great deal of its influence in this area. It seems that the right to an abortion will become the decision of the individual woman to make. While she can consult her husband, her physician, or anyone else if she so chooses, it will be her ultimate decision to make. This projected trend clearly illustrates the developing resistance to institutional authority over individual morality. The institutions of religion, the law, and medicine have all been stripped of a great deal of their traditional control over abortion in the United States. As a result the individual takes on the right to make decisions about herself. The shift from institutional responsibility toward individual responsibility is a powerful illustration of the breakdown of the traditional defining of morality in the United States. It is also an indication of deviancy's becoming less a social concern and more an individual one.

BIBLIOGRAPHY

GEBHARD, PAUL H., et. al., Pregnancy, Birth and Abortion (New York: Harper and Brothers, 1958).

LEE, NANCY HOWELL, The Search for an Abortionist (Chicago: The University of Chicago Press, 1969).

LUCAS, ROY, "Federal Constitutional Limitation on the Enforcement and Administration of State Abortion Statutes," The North Carolina Law Review, June, 1969, pp. 730–78.

ROSSI, ALICE S., "Abortion Laws and Their Victims," Trans-Action, September, 1966, pp. 7–12.

SCHUR, EDWIN M., Crimes without Victims: Deviant Behavior and Public Policy (Englewood Cliffs, N.J.: Prentice-Hall, 1965).

TIETZE, CHRISTOPHER and SARAH LEWIT, "Abortion," Scientific American, January, 1969, pp. 3–9.

WESTOFF, CHARLES, et. al., "The Structure of Attitudes toward Abortion," Milbank Memorial Fund Quarterly, January, 1969, pp. 110–22.

CHAPTER 6

PORNOGRAPHY

OF ALL THE AREAS of deviancy discussed in this book there is probably none where there is a greater gap between the low significance of the problem and the high social indignation toward it than is found with pornography. The word pornography seems to denote to most Americans something that is obscene, sinful, and childish. As a result almost all Americans are against pornography, and while some are indifferent there are very few who are openly for it. Probably most people who use pornography with any frequency do so surreptitiously and rarely volunteer any indication of their interest. So one of the major purposes of this chapter is to try to analyze the social problem of pornography that leads to so much public indignation about so little in its behavior consequences.

The word pornography is basically a negative one, as is the word obscenity. A more positive term referring to the same thing is erotica. Later in the chapter there will be an examination of the uses of the term pornography. However, at this time pornography may be defined as some appeal to the human senses to bring about the arousal of sexual desire in the respondent. This implies that the creator of pornography has the purpose of sexual arousal in mind and in fact that is the main reason for the product. However, one cannot always know the intent of the producer, and oftentimes what is used as pornographic may not have been intended as such. For example, in the past excerpts were sometimes taken from literary works not considered to be pornographic and were reprinted and sold as pornography. The interest in this chapter is with those things that are

144

deliberately created to be erotically stimulating, i.e., consciously created pornography.

Probably in all societies there have been some types of erotic productions or pornography. Even in the earliest drawings of preliterate man there were pictures that were sexual in nature and probably represented something more than simply a graphic record of that behavior. This fits the fact that man's sexual involvement is something more than just physical drive and release. The records of the development of mankind indicate that he early recognized and used his senses of touch, sight, and smell in his sexual activities. Therefore, it is logical to assume that pornographic uses came about fairly early in the development of mankind.

With the emergence of written language man had a new means for pornographic expression, and as more people were able to read, the potential of this form of expression became greater. Written pornography had its origins in the Western world in the 17th century but it probably did not come into full existence until near the end of the 18th century. In England the growth of written pornography was closely related to the development of the novel. Marcus suggests that those social forces which acted to contribute to the rise of the novel ". . . and to the growth of its audience—acted analogously in contributing to the development of pornography."[1]

In 18th century England there had been little concern with pornography or obscenity, "though it had been ruled in 1729 that an obscene *libel* constituted a common-law misdemeanor."[2] In the latter part of the 18th century there developed a pornography of unprecedented richness. Those products are striking when compared with the Victorian pornography that was later produced in England. Taylor points out that Cleland's *Memoirs of a Woman of Pleasure* is frankly sexual in character, but it also has a human warmth and the characters are convincing by their naturalness and the activities in which they are engaged. He goes on to point out that this is very different from the Victorian pornography, "which is shot through and through with sado-masochism, and which is quite unredeemed by an air of the protagonists even getting any enjoyment from their desperate attempts to stimulate lust. All spontaneity is gone."[3] But it should be recognized that what is depicted in pornography must have some appeal to readers or they won't respond to it. For example, sado-masochistic pornography has never been very popular in the United States. But the sado-masochistic stress in the Victorian pornography was

---

[1] Marcus, Steven, *The Other Victorians* (New York: Basic Books, Inc., 1964), p. 282.

[2] Taylor, G. Rattray, *Sex in History* (New York: The Vanguard Press, 1954), p. 216.

[3] *Ibid.*, p. 217.

appealing to the sexual interests and patterns of sexual expression common to many during that period.

Early in the 20th century a new form of pornographic expression developed—the movie film. These initially appeared and gained notoriety by their use in houses of prostitution. Prostitution has had a long history of using many visual methods to encourage sexual stimulation. For example, many houses of prostitution had murals, tapestries, and pictures that were sexually erotic. The early visual erotica were presented in some cases like the films to serve as an end in themselves. That is, the observer received his sexual pleasure from the viewing. But far more often, the visual approaches were used as a means of encouraging sexual arousal and the use of the prostitutes. This kind of exposure of stag films led to their increased popularity. "By the end of *la belle Epoque*, no self-respecting brothel in any of the large cities on the continent considered its facilities complete without a stock of these films for showing either as an artistic *whore d'oeuvre* or as an entertainment in their own right."[4]

Given the Victorian heritage in Great Britain and the United States it is not surprising that with any public knowledge of pornography there often followed great moral indignation, sometimes leading to attempts to legally restrict or eliminate pornography. With the Victorian view that sex was evil there was the belief in the need to control that evil in the same sense that other varieties of evil should be controlled. The Victorian mode of thinking has never concerned itself with whether or not there are social and personal dangers from pornography—that has always been assumed to be the case. Therefore the problem was always one of how to eliminate what was believed to be very dangerous. In recent decades this belief in the United States has led to a wide and complex variety of legal decisions with regard to pornography.

LEGAL ASPECTS

In most modern societies there have been some restrictions on the public sale of at least some types of pornography. Generally societies are more restrictive about visual than written pornography. In the past pornographic stag films have been shown in most countries only clandestinely. One well known exception was the Shanghai Theater in pre-Castro Cuba, which offered a continuous show of stag films to the general public. Knight and Alpert, in their extensive study of the history of stag films, write that there was evidence that a sizable market for such films "did exist as early as 1904, with Buenos Aires then a principal center of production. Movies of fully detailed sexual activity were shot and shipped to

---

[4] Knight, Arthur and Hollis Alpert, "The History of Sex in Cinema: The Stag Film," *Playboy*, November, 1967, p. 158.

private buyers, mostly in England and France, but also in such distant lands as Russia and the Balkan countries."[5]

There has been a recent trend for many countries to become more liberal in what can legally be sold. This has been the case in the United States, and later in the chapter the limits that continue to prevail on what may be legally sold will be examined. At the present time the best illustration of permissiveness toward all forms of pornography by a society is that of Denmark. In Denmark there are pornography shops that sell all kinds of written and pictorial pornography and one may buy the films or pay for a showing in the shop. In 1969 a great deal of attention was directed at Denmark when the first international pornography fair was held there. In a large convention hall the various manufacturers of different types of pornography displayed their products to prospective buyers in the same way that other types of products are shown at international trade fairs. However, Denmark represents an extreme degree of social acceptance of pornography which is far more permissive than found in the United States.

In recent years some of the major concerns about pornography in the United States have centered around legal questions. This has been because of legal restrictions that have developed around the question of obscenity. As a result many things other than pornography have been lumped together under the general category of obscenity. As pointed out in Chapter 4, the Comstock Law of 1873 excluded the sending of contraceptives and contraceptive information through the mails by defining them as obscene. In recent years the question of control over pornography has become complexly linked with questions of censorship. It is therefore useful to look at two recent decisions made by the United States Supreme Court. A major decision was handed down in 1957 in the case of *Roth v. United States*. The majority opinion declared that "obscenity is not within the area of constitutionally protected speech or press," but that "sex and obscenity are not synonymous. Obscene material is material which deals with sex in a manner appealing to prurient (lustful) interests."[6] This decision said some things about sex are all right and some are not and therefore a part of the *Roth* decision was its definition of obscenity. It was believed that the legal tests must set up standards of judgment that would protect socially important literature. The Court said that literature dealing with sex in a manner not appealing to prurient interest is socially important literature. The court said the authoritative test will be: "Whether to the average person, applying contemporary community standards, the dominant theme of the material taken as a whole appeals to prurient interest."[7]

---

[5] *Ibid.*, p. 156.

[6] Clor, Harry M., *Obscenity and Public Morality* (Chicago: University of Chicago Press, 1969), p. 14.

[7] *Ibid.*, p. 31.

The test is not whether the material would arouse sexual desire in people making up a particular segment of the community, but in the average person. "You judge the circulars, pictures, and publications which have been put in evidence by the present day standards of the community. You may ask yourselves does it offend the common conscience of the community by present day standards."[8] As Clor points out, it is very difficult to determine how the "community standards" test is supposed to function. "Is an obscene publication one which violates the community's current standards of right? Or which offends the average person in the community? Or which arouses the sexual desires of the average person?"[9] But the even more difficult question is how one determines who is the average person in the community.

The second important Supreme Court decision was handed down in the Ginzburg case in 1966. In that case the court did not explicitly hold the defendant's conduct to be "the central issue, but it did pave the way for an increasing interest and stress on the behavior of the purveyor and a decreasing concern with the nature of the materials."[10] The concern with Ginzburg in part centered on the stressing of sexually provocative aspects of his publications and that fact may be decisive in the determination of something's being obscene. To the court, one of the proofs of Ginzburg's motives was his request for second-class mailing privileges through the post offices at both Intercourse and Blue Ball, Pennsylvania. He finally obtained mailing privileges at Middlesex, New Jersey.

Gagnon and Simon have suggested that the Supreme Court's concern with pornography has in recent years had two dimensions. The first dimension has dealt with sexual representations that are held to be offensive to public morality or taste. This was the primary concern in the Ginzburg case. The second dimension centers around the effects of pornography on specific individuals or groups. This is the focal point of most public discussions and prior court decisions on pornography. "This dimension was mentioned only twice in the array of decisions of 1966, but much of the confusion in discussions of pornography reflects a difficulty in distinguishing between these dimensions or a tendency to slip from one to the other without noting the change."[11]

There has been a strong demand on the part of many Americans to put controls on pornography, especially with what are perceived to be obscene materials being sent through the mail. A 1969 Gallup survey asked respondents if they would like to see stricter state and local laws dealing with obscene literature sent through the mails and 81 percent of the men

[8] *Ibid.*, p. 37.

[9] *Ibid.*, pp. 37–8.

[10] *Ibid.*, p. 82.

[11] Gagnon, John H. and William Simon, "Pornography—Raging Menace or Paper Tiger?", *Trans-Action*, July, 1967, p. 42.

and 88 percent of the women answered "yes." The survey also indicated that those who most wanted the stricter laws were the older respondents and the ones with the least amount of education.

There is one other level of interest by the federal government in the question of pornography. In October, 1967, Congress established the Commission on Obscenity and Pornography and the president appointed its members in January, 1968. The commission was assigned four specific tasks. First, with the help of leading constitutional law authorities, to analyze the laws pertaining to the control of obscenity and pornography, and to evaluate and pass on recommendations for defining obscenity and pornography. Second, to determine the means used in distributing obscene and pornographic materials and to study the nature and volume of traffic of such materials. Third, to study the effect of obscenity and pornography upon the public, especially among minors, and its relationship to crime and other antisocial behavior. Fourth, "to recommend such legislative, administrative, or other advisable and appropriate action as the Commission deems necessary to regulate effectively the flow of such traffic without in any way interfering with constitutional rights."[12] This commission reported its findings to the president and the Congress in the early fall of 1970.[13] When the commission report appeared it was met with great indignation and hostility. Basically, the findings of the commission were that there was no established link between exposure to pornography and criminal or anti-social behavior. The report also indicated that pornography should be available to adults if they choose to use it. The report appeared several months before the congressional elections of November, 1970. Therefore, most politicians violently attacked the report and there were few who defended it. The president of the United States refused to accept it. Rarely were the attacks on the report made for methodological reasons or theoretical interpretations. Rather, the critics simply *knew* they were right and the report was wrong. In the discussion ahead some references will be made to the findings of the report.

INTERPRETATIONS OF PORNOGRAPHY

Before examining the various forms of pornography it is important to say something about attempts to understand this kind of deviancy. At the present time there are two different approaches to studying pornography. One is a social science approach and the other is through literary criticism. Rosen and Turner suggest that there have been two major approaches in the social science attempt to define and understand pornography. The first

[12] "Progress Report," *Commission on Obscenity and Pornography* (Washington, D.C., July, 1969), pp. 1–2.

[13] *The Report of the Commission on Obscenity and Pornography* (New York: Bantam Books, 1970).

is a cultural relativist position that sees pornography as anything which a society defines as such. "In other words pornography is that which violates the societal norms of sexual expression."[14] They go on to point out that the second approach tries to discover objective, universalistic characteristics in the material which when presented makes an item pornographic. They suggest that the best illustration of this is the assertion by the Kronhausens in 1964 that "hard core pornography is erotic material which is unrealistic, voyeuristic, and contains infantile sexual fantasies."[15]

Sociologist Ned Polsky has speculated on the relationship of pornography to society. He suggests that pornography and prostitution are at least in modern societies functional alternatives. By that he means they are different roads to the same social end because both provide for the discharge of what society defines as antisocial sex, i.e., "impersonal, nonmarital sex: prostitution provides this via real intercourse with a real sex object, and pornography provides it via masturbation, imagined intercourse with a fantasy object."[16] Gagnon and Simon also suggest that pornography and prostitution are the forms of collective sexual deviance most intermixed with and linked to the conventional social order."[17] Both prostitution and pornography are found in all societies large enough to have a fairly complex division of labor. Polsky writes that although pornography develops in only a rudimentary way in preliterate societies, "whenever a society has a fair degree of literacy and mass-communication technology then pornography becomes a major functional alternative to prostitution."[18]

The sexual needs and desires of individuals cover a wide range. As discussed in Chapter 8, one of the functions of prostitution is to provide the customer with the opportunity to express his sexual deviancy because a woman may not be willing to participate unless she is paid. Pornography is also produced to meet all forms of sexual deviancy. Whatever the reasons, it is clear that although a great deal of pornography presents sexual relations that are not highly deviant a large amount of pornography offers fantasy involvement in sex acts that society proscribes as "unnatural."[19] For many who can't or won't find a prostitute to meet their deviant sexual needs the various forms of pornography may be their only outlet.

Although societies use both prostitution and pornography, the extent to which one is used in preference to the other varies widely from one so-

[14] Rosen, Lawrence and Stanley H. Turner, "Exposure to Pornography: An Exploratory Study," *The Journal of Sex Research*, November, 1969, p. 235.

[15] *Ibid.*

[16] Polsky, Ned, "Pornography," in Edward Sagarin and Donald E. MacNamara, *Problems of Sex Behavior* (New York: Thomas Y. Crawell Co., 1968), p. 271.

[17] Gagnon, John H. and William Simon, "Sexual Deviance in Contemporary America," *The Annals*, March, 1968, p. 117.

[18] Polsky, *op. cit.*, pp. 270–71.

[19] *Ibid.*, pp. 276–77.

ciety to the next. Polsky points out there are also variations within a given society. He suggests that first there may be variations in what is considered appropriate in different social situations. "For example, a group of adolescent boys might collectively visit a prostitute but masturbate to pornography only singly and in private, with group contemplation of pornography serving merely to convey sex information or as the occasion for ribald humor."[20] Another type of variation may be seen as related to broad social variables. For example, the Kinsey data indicated that masturbation to pornographic materials was most common among the higher educated. "At the lower levels of our society, this is generally put down (as is long-term masturbation *per se*), and, conversely, prostitutes are visited much more often."[21]

One functional value of pornography that has generally been overlooked is its use in social situations where heterosexual outlets are highly limited or not available. For example, pornography is commonly found in boys' schools, the military (particularly aboard naval vessels) and so on. But the best illustration of its use is in prisons. Polsky suggests that sociologists have been so concerned with the extent to which homosexuality is used in prisons that they have neglected the use of pornography by prisoners.[22] There is within prisons a great deal of written but unpublished pornography. Polsky points out that here is a major difference between prostitution and pornography. "Hardly any man can, as it were, be his own prostitute (although many try, by attempting autofellation), but every man can be his own pornographer."[23] Some pornography that has been published was originally written to aid the writer in his own masturbation. "For example, Jean Genet indicates this was why he wrote *Our Lady of the Flowers*. And it is apparently to this motivation that we owe the pornography produced by the most noted pornographer of them all, the Marquis de Sade."[24]

The social science approach to the study of pornography is not concerned with it morally, but rather functionally. Because pornography has prevailed for so long and is of interest to many people it is of social relevance. By contrast, the approach of literary criticism is primarily concerned with making moral and aesthetic judgments about pornography. There are some literary critics who believe that it is legitimate for literature to attempt to sexually arouse its readers. Marcus writes that "if it is permissible for works of literature to move us to tears, to arouse our passions against injustice, to make us cringe with horror, and to purge us through pity and terror, then is is equally permissible—it lies within the orbit of literature's

---

[20] *Ibid.*, p. 271.
[21] *Ibid.*
[22] *Ibid.*, p. 273.
[23] *Ibid.*
[24] *Ibid.*, pp. 273–74.

function—for works of literature to excite us sexually."[25] But then Marcus follows this up by saying that pornography is not literature. The argument then is that nothing written as pornography can ever be literature. Yet, there is nothing inherent in pornography, however it is defined, that makes it as written expression incapable of being literature. If written pornography is material designed to sexually arouse the reader, it often achieves that goal. But if a man writes something which he believes to be pornographic and it is read with laughter and no sexual excitement then he has not produced pornography. But as Gebhard points out "there is no reason why in skilled hands pornography could not be an aesthetically legitimate art form."[26] It is with regard to this point that many literary critics disagree. Many believe that there is something inherent in pornography that makes it incapable of true artistic expression.

Literary critics are often highly subjective observers and this means that some can see social worth and significance where others cannot. For example, some critics now see the works of Genet as literature while only a few years ago those writings were dismissed as pornographic. The same may also be said of the Marquis de Sade. For many readers, having something defined as literature allows them to read and be titillated with less guilt than if it were defined as pornography. It is doubtful that the erotic response of the reader changes because a work is called literature instead of pornography. In other words, what is erotic exists however it is labeled —but the label often removes guilt for the reader and may even give him the feeling of being *avant garde* and aesthetically sophisticated.

It also appears that the acceptance of erotic scenes in a book may be determined by the context in which they are presented. That is, does the plot of the book suggest that the sexual scenes are a part of guilt, shame, fear, or frustration? When this happens it is a soul searching book and the sex becomes acceptable. As Loth points out, however, if the book treats sex in a spirit of bravado with everyone capable of intense sexual activity at all times and to a rousing climax on every page it is doomed to be called pornographic.[27]

It is commonly observed that American novels since World War II have presented sex with all its variations, and in highly descriptive detail. Yet, amidst all the frank and open descriptions of sexual behavior in novels, there also continues to be a strong Puritan influence. With few exceptions the sexual life of characters in novels either leads to or results from severe individual problems. Rarely does one find a character in the modern novel who engages in sexual behavior (even in marriage) without prob-

---

[25] Marcus, *op. cit.*, pp. 277–78.

[26] Gebhard, Paul H., *et. al.*, *Sex Offenders* (New York: Harper and Row, 1965), p. 669.

[27] Loth, David, *The Erotic in Literature* (New York: Julian Messner, Inc., 1961), p. 19.

lems. The common theme appears to be that, while one may indulge in all types of sexual experiences, he rarely entered the experience simply for pleasure or leaves it satisfied and free of personal and social problems. The modern novel seems to suggest that sexual involvement is bad, not in the sense of "sin," but in terms of psychological and social problems. Punishment continues to be the overwhelming consequence of sexual behavior—either because it is a manifestation of some deep-seated problem or because it leads to new problems. David Loth in his analysis of the erotic aspect of the modern novel writes that "most of us disapprove (for consumption by others) of fictional characters who enjoy sex or its perversions frankly and heartily without shame or pain. We want them to suffer in mind or body (or both) before the last page."[28]

The sexual motivations of characters in modern novels are very often presented as resulting from a need to "prove" something. Characters may attempt to "prove" their sexual adequacy, that they can cut the umbilical cord, that they are not latent homosexuals and so forth. However, it is striking that in few cases do the characters in modern novels ever successfully "prove" anything by their sexual involvement—except that sex was not the answer. That sex might be entered for its own sake, without complex causes and effects, and simply be a relationship of pleasure is rarely suggested.

In the 1960's in the United States a genre of the modern novel developed that was presented to the public as pornographic. This kind of novel was strongly rejected by critics as not being literature. These novels should also be rejected as not being pornographic because they are not erotically stimulating. The best illustration of this genre of novel has been those written by Jacqueline Susann. She writes novels with characters who are miserable and sad human beings. As one critic points out "the love in *Love Machine* is joyless, violent, and cruel. This is the kind of sex which probably discourages going out and trying it."[29] It is hard to imagine anyone reading a Susann novel and becoming sexually aroused. While literary critics see her books as insulting to the novel it may also be suggested that to call them pornographic is insulting to pornography.

When a person buys something with which he hopes to be sexually aroused he generally doesn't care whether it is literature or not. The user of pornography may get what he wants from the "hard core" pornographic literature or from erotic "art" literature. "So far as he is concerned, the only significance is that in the latter he usually gets less for his money."[30] But it is clear that the literary critic, in contrast with the user of exotic literature, is looking for different things. Therefore, many critics define

---

[28] *Ibid.*, p. 30.

[29] Davidson, Sara, "Jacqueline Susann: The Writing Machine," *Harpers*, October, 1969, p. 66.

[30] Polsky, *op. cit.*, p. 279.

something as pornographic which means they are hostile and contemptuous of that work. Many of the critics are doing more than just making literary judgments about various works—they are also trying to define what is appropriate sexual behavior for mankind. For example, one literary critic states that sex is an obsession in the United States today and this has brought about a new wave of pornographic literature which "approaches the quality of mechanical repetition and unreality," and this new pornography makes sex dull.[31] (It is obviously not dull for many who read it.) The critic goes on to say there is no use for pornography in society today. As a result the purpose of pornography is not fulfilled leaving it to be a useless part of literature. The writer further states that the purpose of sex is serious and sex in literature is to help convey the feeling of meaning of life as it is.[32] What is striking about this type of view is the narrowness with regard to both sex and literature. It is also important that these kinds of social observers make categorical statements but are never troubled with presenting evidence.

Another rather tortured argument of the literary critic is that sex is private and pornography invades that privacy. Elliott writes that "the trouble with pornography in our culture is that it offends the sense of separateness, individuality, and privacy and it intrudes on the rights of others." He goes on to say that one should wish to remove oneself from the presence of man and woman enjoying sexual intercourse. "Not to withdraw is to peep, to pervert looking, so that it becomes a sexual end in itself."[33] This seems a rather silly argument because those who feel their privacy is invaded wouldn't use pornography. And the argument that fantasies about fictional characters invade the privacy of real persons doesn't make sense.

But probably the most common literary argument directed against pornography and its use is that it is adolescent and therefore demeaning to adults. Marcus writes that pornography is, after all, "nothing more than a representation of the fantasies of infantile sexual life, as these fantasies are edited and recognized in the masturbatory daydreams of adolescence. Every man who grows up must pass through such a phase in his existence."[34] The critics never say why it is an adolescent behavior other than that this is when the strong interest in pornography and masturbation first develop. By the same logic one could refer to man's sexual interest in women as adolescent because it is during the same adolescent period that he becomes highly oriented to females and masturbates to all kinds of fantasies about them.

---

[31] "The New Pornography," *Time*, April 16, 1965, p. 29.

[32] *Ibid.*

[33] Elliott, George P., "Against Pornography," *Harper's*, March, 1965, p. 53.

[34] Marcus, *op. cit.*, p. 286.

It has been necessary to say something about the literary critics' view of pornography because they are often the intellectually "respectable" spokesmen who write about the subject. Their expertise is assumed to be based on the fact that they are authorities on literature. But as suggested, the critics very often go beyond that and become authorities on the causes and consequences of pornography. And these are areas where there is very little empirical evidence, and pronouncements from any source should not be taken as statements factually verified.

Implied in the discussion thus far has been that the primary purpose of all types of pornography is to evoke erotic response from the person subjected to it. We may take this a step further and look at what the purposes of pornography are. The Kronhausens state that "pornographic writings are 'meant' to function as psychological aphrodisiacs and are successful only to the extent that they accomplish this particular purpose.[35] Wayland Young goes a step further and says that the purpose of all-out pornography is "a determination that the customer shall have his money's worth, and that the purpose of the whole operation is to provide male consumers with something to masturbate over."[36]

Polsky has pointed out that pornography is not simply limited to its role as an adjunct to masturbation. He suggests that for some persons pornography may sometimes serve as a sex instruction manual. Or it may be used as a form of foreplay in being used to stimulate real coitus, as in, "say, the case of whorehouse murals from Pompeii to the present."[37] But probably most people who read pornography with any regularity on most occasions read the materials for erotic titillation that does not lead to any physical sexual release.

As indicated earlier the public reaction in the United States to all forms of pornography often conveys the notion that it is highly significant and dangerous to society. But as Gagnon and Simon point out, what is most important about pornography is not that it is particularly relevant to sexuality, but that it brings forth special treatment when it confronts the law.[38] They go on to suggest that the danger from pornography itself is minor but that the real danger goes with the thinking in dealing with pornography because it may become "prevalent in controlling the advocacy of other ideas as well."[39] To many the attempts to control the buying and use of pornography by adults is censorship.

The importance of pornography is also linked to what is defined as such.

[35] Kronhausen, Eberhard and Phyllis, "The Psychology of Pornography," in Albert Ellis and Albert Abarbanel, The Encyclopedia of Sexual Behavior (New York: Hawthorne Books, Inc., 1961), p. 849.

[36] Young, Wayland, Eros Denied (New York: Grove Press 1964), p. 88.

[37] Polsky, op. cit., p. 272.

[38] Gagnon and Simon, Trans-Action, op. cit., p. 48.

[39] Ibid.

The 1957 Supreme Court decision makes clear that pornography or obscenity is what the community says it is and these definitions vary over time. As a result the definitions of the past are no longer adequate today. Not very many years ago people smuggled into the United States copies of such books as *Fanny Hill* and Frank Harris' *My Life and Loves* but these can now be bought legally in book stores and drug stores in most parts of the United States.

There is another consequence of the significance of pornography and that is the results that sometimes occur when something is labeled as pornographic. If persons of authority define something as pornographic or obscene then it becomes such in the minds of many people. For example, family-planning pamphlets and pictures of human birth have in the past been defined as pornographic and in some cases have been treated under the obscenity laws. There is an opposite consequence of labeling something as obscene which is to make it sell better to the public. For many years for a movie to be "banned in Boston" was great publicity and helped make the movie financially successful. A recent illustration of millions of dollars being made through the publicity given by moralists to a movie was *I Am Curious (Yellow)*. In the summer of 1970 a road troupe of *Hair* came to Detroit and according to the manager ticket sales were not good until two city councilmen got a lot of mass media coverage on how their fair city was being besmirched by that production. So having something labeled as obscene may be harmful in some cases but in others it may be highly profitable.

TYPES OF PORNOGRAPHY

In this section we will look at various types of pornography. As suggested at the start of the chapter, pornography is defined as something created to bring about sexual arousal in the respondent. The types of pornography to be discussed here share in common the deliberate attempt to bring about sexual arousal in at least some of those who are presented with it. The three types to be discussed are the exposure of the body, movies or films, and the written narrative.

EXPOSURE OF THE BODY

Under the broadest interpretation of the definition of pornography one could argue that any women who deliberately dress to be sexually provocative (and are successful) are pornographic. However, this erotic type can be eliminated by adding one other criterion to the definition of pornography—that the primary motive behind pornography is to make money for the sale of the product. Within the profit context there are certain groups of women engaged in occupations who expose their bodies in what may be defined as a pornographic fashion. The exposure of the nude body for profit is not enough in itself to make that behavior be defined as pornographic—there must also be the conscious intent to bring about sexual arousal. As a result women in nudist colonies are not pornographic because they are not deliberately trying to bring about sexual arousal. By contrast most erotic dancers are concerned with sexual arousal. If the customers have no erotic response to a stripteaser she will be a failure in her occupation. (Some strippers see themselves as artists and get indignant when it is suggested that their function is to sexually stimulate the customers. But few customers will go to see a stripper because they are art connoisseurs.) Because the striptease dancer is the most common type of pornographic body exposure it is useful to look briefly at that occupation.

There has been a long tradition of burlesque theater in the United States and over the years it has come to be more and more centered around the strippers. Even with the general sexual liberalization of today stripping is still considered deviant or at best a marginal occupation. In a recent study of strippers it was found that almost every one of them believed that most people's conception of their occupation was that it was dirty and immoral. "This belief affects their behavior in public; for example, many of the girls avoid identifying themselves in public as strippers, preferring to call themselves dancers, entertainers, and the like."[40]

To achieve success the stripper must have a body that is erotically attractive to many of the male customers. As a group their physiques are larger than average for women of their age, particularly their bust size. That their primary function is their visual erotic appeal is reflected in the fact that most strippers begin with little or no training. It was found that the career sequence for most of the strippers involved three contingencies: "(1) a tendency toward exhibitionistic behavior for gain, (2) an opportunity structure making stripping an accessible occupational alternative, and (3) a sudden awareness of the easy economic rewards in stripping."[41]

The legal definition of what is obscene for strippers varies greatly. This is because the enforcement of obscenity laws in the states where the strippers work is left up to the local officials. Thus the strippers find considerable variation in interpretation of what is obscene among the cities where they work. In some cities performers are allowed to "bare their breasts completely and are permitted to 'flash.' Flashing consists of lowering the G-string so that the pubic area is displayed. Although the G-string may be lowered to the knees or ankles its complete removal is apparently considered obscene."[42] Over all it is estimated that there are about 7,000

[40] Skipper, James K. Jr. and Charles H. McCagny, "Stripteasers: The Anatomy and Career Contingencies of a Deviant Occupation," Social Problems, Winter, 1970, p. 392.

[41] Ibid., p. 402.

[42] Ibid., p. 394.

women in the United States earning their living by removing their clothes in a titillating fashion.

What the successful stripper does is to erotically excite the viewer. She does this by revealing her body within a context, often with "mood" music, of sexual seduction. For example, the traditional bumps and grinds of the stripper are the movements of sexual intercourse. And as with all pornography the stripper sometimes erotically arouses the viewer to the point where he masturbates.

There are other ways in which the body may be used pornographically but they are not common in the United States. One way is where sexual shows are presented for customers. People are hired to perform all types of sexual acts in all kinds of erotic combinations. These performances are roughly to the stag film what the legitimate stage play is to the movie. The viewer sees persons act out pornographic scenes in person rather than on film. However, the legal risks to this are so great that live pornographic sexual shows are quite rare in the United States, although this is not true in some other countries of the world.

MOVIES OR STAG FILMS

Besides the films there are also the pornographic visual aids of cartoons, drawings, and photographs. These are often used along with written pornography or are used by themselves. In the past the cartoon book was a common form of pornography. It was usually a take-off on some well known comic strip characters with exaggerated sex organs engaged in sexual activities and the quality of the drawing was usually very poor. In general, pornographic photographs range from crude to highly sophisticated products and can be highly erotic. In recent years the photograph has become a part of a legally acceptable kind of pornography which is presented within a pseudo-medical context. Brochures are sent through the mail telling one how he can learn to be more successful sexually. One approach is to talk about sexual positions and include photographs to illustrate. It is this kind of literature, often sent indiscriminantly through the mails, that has raised a great deal of indignation among many Americans. Legally it appears to be acceptable because the brochures have "redeeming social qualities." But there continue to be limits on what can be shown legally in these types of photographs. Both the male and female sex organ can be shown, but the penis is not erect. And they are not allowed to show actual pictures of the penis in the vagina. These restrictions appear to be informally imposed by the postal authorities and could ease up or become tighter in the future.

The pornographic movies or stag films have been a part of the American scene for many years. Stag films have in the past been subject to uniquely ambivalent social attitudes. Publicly, stag films have been almost universally condemned but in private they have been endorsed by a large and responsive element of the community. The support of the community is evidenced by the *sub rosa* stag screenings frequently sponsored by "our nation's leading—and most patriotic—civil, social, fraternal and veteran's organizations."[43] Gagnon and Simon point out that stag films are commonly seen by two kinds of male groups. First are those living in group housing in colleges and universities and second are those belonging to upper lower-class and lower middle-class voluntary social groups."[44]

The basic ingredients in stag films are a simple and contrived situation to provide initial motivation. The plot is often "sexual excitation of the female by visual means, comparatively rare in real life but a persistent theme in these films: a direct and rapid seduction—so direct and rapid that in many films it cannot properly be called a seduction at all; and, finally, sexual activity, which of course is the focal point of the film."[45] The world of movie pornography is often a fantasy world. This means that all females are in a state of constant sexual arousal and waiting to be sexually serviced by the first male to come along. As Knight and Alpert point out, the beginning of countless stag films concerns a female who becomes sexually aroused "by reading an erotic book, masturbating, dreaming, watching a nude male, watching horses have sex, sunning herself, doing housework, listening to the radio—or even being hit by a car."[46] All of this fits the fact that stag films are made for male audiences who are presented with highly sexed women that fit their male fantasy of the sexual nature of at least some women.

The sexual activities included in stag films cover the range of both heterosexual and homosexual activities. Included are fellatio, cunnilingus, sodomy, bestiality, and mutual masturbation. But what is included in the films reflects the American males' preferences and prejudices. For example, Knight and Alpert found in their analysis of over 1,000 stag films that male homosexuality was relatively rare while lesbian activities were quite common. Heterosexual oral-genital contact is quite common, especially in recent stag films. "But, once again, the men come out ahead, with 89 percent of the films including fellatio and only 46 percent including cunnilingus."[47] There has been in recent years a number of male homosexual films produced for the male homosexual audience. However, the female homosexual films that have been produced have been for male audiences and not for a lesbian market.

The stag films have traditionally reflected certain social values. While the main function of stag films is sexual stimulation they sometimes also

---

[43] Knight and Alpert, *op. cit.*, p. 155.

[44] Gagnon and Simon, *op. cit.* p. 43.

[45] Knight and Alpert, *op. cit.*, p. 158.

[46] *Ibid.*

[47] *Ibid.*, p. 170.

serve as an outlet for pressures created by social and sexual taboos. "In strongly Catholic countries, for example, there is a significantly anticlerical strain in the local pornography. As a less rigidly religious country, the U.S. has no marked anticlerical feelings of any kind, so that the irreverent themes so common in the stag films of Mexico, Cuba, and France are almost unknown here."[48] American prejudices control what may be seen in American produced stag films. For example, while a black female may be involved in the films it is rare to find a black male.

Knight and Alpert in their extensive study of stag films over the years found a number of changes had occurred. The main difference between the early films produced in the twenties as contrasted with those of the thirties was the increased concentration on sexual activity, with less concern with the narrative development of the story. "Particularly pronounced in the thirties was a pervasive antiwoman theme, with the female treated as a sex object rather than as a sexual partner."[49] In the forties and early fifties, U.S. stag films generally declined in quality, with less attention given not only to humor but to plots, sets, and editing."[50] By the sixties youth and attractiveness had become common rather than the exception for actors in stag films. Most of the females found in present stag films are in their late teens or early twenties. This is about ten years younger than their counterparts of a generation ago. Although most of the females are recruited from the ranks of professional prostitutes, "many films are now being made with semipro and nonprofessional females, who may agree to perform more for erotic and egotistical reasons than for the traditional economic considerations."[51] Whatever their motives the actors in today's films are much less inhibited than their predecessors and have a far greater erotic effect on the viewer.

Other changes have occurred over the years in the nature of the sexual activity shown in stag films. Only about one-third of the films produced in the twenties included fellatio, but in the 1960's this was found in over three-fourths of the stag films. Also the "increasing sexual emancipation of women in the intervening years is reflected clearly in an equally striking increase in the incidence of oral-genital activity performed on the female by her male partner. This was found in only about 10 percent of the films of the twenties but in two-thirds of those produced in the sixties.[52] Also in contrast with the past there is more variety in sexual position and performance with more group activity. The changes over the years in stag films correspond with changing views about the greater sexuality of the woman.

---

[48] *Ibid.*

[49] *Ibid.*, p. 176.

[50] *Ibid.*, p. 178.

[51] *Ibid.*

[52] *Ibid.*, p. 180.

In the late 1960's a kind of legal stag film emerged. This film was found in San Francisco and possibly in a few other large cities. There was in San Francisco in 1969, 22 legitimate movie houses showing pornographic films. These films run between five and ten minutes, and while a few have some dialogue, most of them are accompanied only by music (which has no connection with what is shown on the screen, such as setting the mood). There are some restrictions on what can be shown—the restrictions are the same as those on what can be sent through the mails—no erect penis or the sex organs in coital position. For the most part the photography is expertly done and the females are young and attractive. The theaters are small and the audiences are almost entirely made up of middle-aged and older men. The commission's report suggests that "patrons of adult bookstores and adult movie theatres may be characterized as predominantly white, middle class, middle aged, married males, dressed in business suit or neat casual attire, shopping or attending the movie alone."[53] It is quite possible that with time these legal stag films will drive the illegal films out of business in the same way that legally written pornography has driven the underground, illegal written pornography out of business.

There are also other types of films that are legally shown that are pornographic by definition. These are films that expect to make a profit by sexually arousing their audience. The difference between them and the stag films is that they are much longer and one must watch a lot of plot that is not sexual to see the erotic scenes. These types of films are found in many movie houses around the country and are advertised with an "X" rating, which practically guarantees a large audience. Thanks to the Hollywood rating system people, any persons who want to see movies that are at least partially pornographic don't have to take chances—they can look for "X" ratings in the newspaper movie advertisements.

NOVELS

The deliberately pornographic novel is usually short in length. In the past, when hard-core pornography was illegal, the novels were often no more than twenty or thirty pages in length and cheaply printed with many printing errors. However, this type of pornographic novel is now primarily a collector's item because in many parts of the United States there is no longer a distinction between what can be written legally and illegally. There is nothing that can be said in print about sexual activity that cannot be sent through the mails or sold in various paperback shops in many cities. The new pornography is written with a skill equal to what is usually found in the cheaper types of paperbacks and the quality of book production is about the same. One difference is the higher price. The porno-

---

[53] Commission's Report, *op. cit.*, p. 25.

graphic novels run about 175 to 200 pages of large print and sell for between two and four dollars. The prices vary from one location to another,
and the same book may sell for a dollar more in one city than in another.
These books are generally not sold in drugstores or neighborhood paperback stores. They are most often found in the center of cities in the hotel
and business, but non-residential, areas. And they are usually sold in
stores that sell other kinds of paperbacks although they usually have a
section of the store or even a room to themselves. So that they can be
found easier they may have a sign over them telling the person he must be
twenty-one or older to read them. It is rare to see women looking at the
pornographic books in these types of stores. The commission report states
that a vast majority of "adults only" books are written for heterosexual
males, "although about 10 percent are aimed at the male homosexual
market and a small percentage (less than 5 percent) at fetishists. Virtually
none of these books is intended for a female audience."[54]

The pornographic novel assumes that some plot is necessary if the description of sexual behavior is to take on erotic character for the reader.
In the past the illegal hard core pornography had a minimal plot because
it knew that its readers bought the books for the sexual scenes. But the
more recent, legal pornography appears to be trying to get readers who
want both a story and sexual description. The sexual description is the
main part of the book though the new books appear to be aiming at a
higher educated readership, one that wants some setting of realism to the
sexual scene. This approach seems logical because the evidence indicates
that it is the higher educated male who is most responsive to written pornography.

As earlier indicated, almost all pornography is aimed at the male consumer and as a result women are described by male writers in ways that
they think men want to perceive at least some women to be sexually. For
example, one common scene in pornographic novels is the woman being
described in the privacy of her room looking at her body, caressing herself,
and sometimes masturbating. What is of interest is that the women are
presented as seeing themselves as they look at their bodies in the same
way as would men, and as sexually responding to the thoughts they have
about their own bodies. "Thus, the main sex object is frequently for both
the men and women the female body and the same descriptions are seen
as appropriate for the reactions of both sexes to that stimulus."[55]

The main female character in pornographic novels is almost always one
who is at the start of the story highly inhibited sexually. She is described
as being puritanical and repulsed by sexual relationships even with her

---

[54] *Ibid.*, p. 18.

[55] Gordon, Michael and Robert R. Bell, "Medium and Hard Core Pornography:
A Comparative Analysis," *The Journal of Sex Research*, November, 1969, p. 266.

husband. She is seduced by another man, often while she is under the influence of alcohol or fictitious aphrodisiacs, or while seeing another couple having sexual relations (which is often her husband being willingly seduced by her seducer's wife). She resists mentally, but physically she can't control herself and there always comes a moment when she gives in and tells her seducer to "do it to her." By the end of the novel she has had all kinds of sexual experiences with a variety of persons and she and her husband decide that it is a good life and that they enjoy each other even more sexually. So with their new found sexuality they together and with others sexually live happily ever after.

In written pornography all disturbing elements of life are avoided. One never reads about unwanted pregnancy, abortion, venereal disease, or other unpleasant side-effects that sometimes accompany sexual activity.[56] The novels might be described as presenting a "happy world of pornography," where the characters seek and accept sexual pleasure with no problems. Not only are there no difficulties in that world but the world becomes therapeutic for many problems—for example, frigidity is always solved. Even putting aside the obvious errors and exaggerations of the pornographic novel the notion they convey of sex as simple and uninhibited is one difficult for many Americans to accept. We usually insist that sexual behavior be intricately interwoven into the complex web of human behavior. For example, if a novel deals with sexual behavior within the context of psychological struggles, it is treated seriously and is defined in most communities as acceptable literature. Yet, it is doubtful that the "happy world of pornography" is any more an exaggeration of reality than the presentations in many of the "serious" literary works or psychoanalytic treatises on sexual behavior that are viewed as telling it "like it is."[57]

As suggested, pornographic books are written almost entirely for male audiences. However, the more specific aim of the books may vary. For example, there are many pornographic books written for male homosexuals. The male with homosexual interests is seen as a potential buyer of pornography in the same way as is the heterosexual male—basically all that is varied is the gender of the sex object. By contrast it appears that it is believed there is no market for female readers with either heterosexual or homosexual interests. There does not appear to be any significant number of lesbian oriented books written for female homosexuals. However, there are a large number of books about lesbians written for male readers and sexual experiences between women are common to a majority of pornographic books. This is because many men, especially among the higher educated, find the description of sex between women very erotic.

With the various forms of pornography available to many people in the

---

[56] Kronhausen, *op. cit.*, p. 849.
[57] Gordon and Bell, *op. cit.*, p. 267.

United States it is important to look at how people view this availability. One would assume that of the types of pornography just discussed that the display of the female body would be the least offensive to people. However, the evidence indicates that nudity in any form is offensive to most Americans. One study found that a large percentage of people rate nudity, even without genital exposure, as obscene, and this was especially true in the lower socioeconomic groups.[58] It should be remembered that the display of *any* part of the body was considered obscene during the Victorian period and residues of that thinking continue.

How Americans feel about nudity is shown in a national Gallup survey carried out in 1969. The respondents were asked, "Would you find pictures of nudes in magazines objectionable?" Eighty percent of the women and 66 percent of the men answered "yes." And what is a consistent pattern is that the older and the lower educated were the most apt to object. In the same national survey 87 percent of the women and 63 percent of the men said they would find topless nightclub waitresses objectionable. And 89 percent of the women and 73 percent of the men said that they would find actors and actresses appearing in the nude on Broadway plays objectionable.

In recent years strong public reaction has developed and polarized against all types of sexual materials whether they are shown or written. It seems clear that a large number of Americans believe that their country is suffering from "moral decay" and they are upset and often indignant about it. This reaction tends to be most common among the older and the lower educated and contributes to the great hostility that many of them feel toward the young and the higher educated—the college student. Many of the older people see things they find sexually objectionable in areas that are far from pornographic. For example, the most conservative of the mass media is television, but the Gallup survey of 1969 found 38 percent of the respondents saying they had seen something involving sex on television that was objectionable. The hostility is reflected in the Gallup finding that 50 percent of the respondents said they would be willing to join a neighborhood group to protest the sale of objectionable literature on newsstands.

It is clear that in the United States the legal rights given for sexual expression through all possible outlets is far greater than what is believed to be right by most of the adult population. For many Americans, to be against pornography is like being against sin. That is, there is no rational reason for not being against it, and in fact to be for pornography is almost incomprehensible. It is important to recognize that there are few things that such a large number of Americans so unquestioningly believe to be

---

[58] Katzman, Marshall, "Obscenity and Pornography," *Medical Aspects of Human Sexuality*, July, 1969, p. 82.

wrong. This is even reflected in the fact that many people who buy pornography often do so with some guilt. In "dirty book" stores or the pornographic movies in San Francisco one rarely finds customers talking or even looking at each other. It may be that many customers have the feeling of being a little "sick" or at least being immature. This is also why even those who purchase pornography do not publicly resist those groups trying to halt the sales. To be a supporter of pornography in the local community would be the equivalent in the minds of many of admitting to being a moral degenerate.

THE USERS OF PORNOGRAPHY

It has been stressed throughout this chapter that pornography is for the most part produced and used by men. In the past the use of pornography was best typified by the stag party, which tended to be a group of respectable men in the community. For those men the stag evenings had a kind of ritual and allowed the men to express crude emotions in a masculine context.[59] And in the past when the medium was written pornography it was produced, bought, traded, and exchanged between men. Yet, there may be some change in recent years with some women becoming more interested in pornography and it is therefore useful to look at how women respond to pornography. In a recent study of college student exposure to pornography it was found that males and females had had about equal access.[60] This means that encountering pornography is much less sex segregated than in the past, which is a reflection of the greater display of legitimate pornography.

The commission report found that experience with explicit sexual materials varied according to a number of characteristics in the potential viewer. As suggested the report found that men were more likely to be exposed to erotic materials than were women. "Younger adults are more likely to be exposed than are older adults. People who have more education are most likely to have experience with erotic materials. People who read general books, magazines, and newspapers more, and see general movies more also see more erotic materials. People who are more socially and politically active are more exposed to erotic materials. People who attend religious services more often are less likely to be exposed to erotica."[61]

The Kinsey studies provide some evidence on the difference between male and female responses to various sexual stimuli. In his sample he found that 88 percent of the females and 46 percent of the males said they had never been erotically aroused by observing portrayals of nude

---

[59] Knight and Alpert, *op. cit.*, p. 172.

[60] Rosen and Turner, *op. cit.*, p. 236.

[61] Commission's Report, *op. cit.*, pp. 23–24.

figures.[62] In observing portrayals of sexual action 68 percent of the females and 23 percent of the males said they were never erotically aroused.[63] And as to being stimulated by the reading of erotic stories, 86 percent of the women and 53 percent of the men said they were never aroused.[64]

Masters and Johnson found in their extensive research into physiological sexual respones that none of their study subjects included individuals who could fantasize to orgasm. But they did examine the excitement phase levels of sexual response by providing suggestive literature for their study subjects. "A clinically obvious tumescent reaction of the clitoral glans could be demonstrated in only a few of the women who normally developed this reaction during somatogenic stimulation."[65] They further found that a minimum of a half-hour of exposure to stimulative literature was necessary to produce any observable glans tumescence in any woman. In their same study the response to suggestive literature showed "fewer than one-third of the responding women produced a demonstratable increase in clitoral shaft diameter and no shaft-elongation reaction was observed."[66]

Not only are women much less stimulated by pornography than are men, but they are much less apt to be involved in the writing of it. The Kronhausens state that very rarely do women produce clearly erotic art and writing, despite the fact that often pornographic books are presented as having been written by women. Most of the books were written by men using female pseudonyms. They point out that this pretense is one of the tricks of the trade, "in order to give the illusion that the supposedly female author was as sexually active and lascivious as the male author wished us—or himself—to believe."[67]

While the evidence clearly indicates that men are statistically more responsive and interested in all types of pornography this may be changing, at least to some extent. The women who do show interest are most apt to be among the younger and the higher educated. These are the women who are most apt to be sexually emancipated and who feel they have the same rights to sexual expression as men. The Commission's Report found some link between age and sex in responding to erotic stimuli. Men and women in their early twenties reported a higher frequency of erotic dreams and sexual fantasy after exposure to older people. Thirty-five percent of men in their twenties and 30 percent of women in their

[62] Kinsey, Alfred C., et al., Sexual Behavior in the Human Female (Philadelphia: W. B. Saunders Co., 1953), p. 652.

[63] Ibid., p. 662.

[64] Ibid., p. 671.

[65] Masters, William H. and Virginia E. Johnson, Human Sexual Response (Boston: Little, Brown and Co., 1966, p. 55).

[66] Ibid., p. 55.

[67] Kronhausen, op. cit., p. 856.

twenties report having erotic dreams frequently or occasionally, as against smaller proportions for later ages.[68] Knight and Alpert wrote that not too many years ago, it was understood that no "nice girl" could have anything but a negative reaction to the crudities of a stag film. But they found that the viewing of stag films has become more and more a heterosexual activity in recent years. They believe this to be true because of "the increasing availability of home movie equipment and because of the increasing acceptance of erotica in our more sexually permissive society."[69]

The products of pornography are produced primarily because they are economically profitable. The pornographer is in the business to make money and if he were not successful he would have to change to another occupation. Gagnon and Simon have suggested that there are two different images of the pornographer in the United States. The one image is that he is "self-consciously evil, a representative of the antichrist, the Communist conspiracy, or at the very least, the Mafia. We also tend to see him in terms of the obscenity of ill-gotten wealth as he deals in commodities that are assumed to generate high prices."[70] The other image of the pornographer sees him more as a public nuisance. "Here we find not a sinister villain but a grubby businessman producing a minor commodity for which there is a limited market and a marginal profit and which requires that he live in a marginal world."[71]

Pornographic Consequences

After one states that he is morally and ethically opposed to all pornography his next argument against it is that it "harms" people. One of the difficulties in determining if pornography does harm people is that what is defined as pornography varies so greatly. For example, one study found that there was a "strong, statistically significant relationship between the personality rigidity of the observer as measured by a standard personality test, and the number of works of accepted great art considered to be obscene."[72] So there are variations in who defines what as pornography and what they believe the consequences of exposure to be.

One must make a distinction between how people respond to pornography for others and how they personally respond to it for themselves. That is, one may feel that pornography is very bad for others and yet be erotically stimulated oneself. But probably most people who are exposed

---

[68] Commission's Report, op. cit., p. 228.

[69] Knight and Alpert, op. cit., p. 174.

[70] Gagnon and Simon, op. cit., p. 43.

[71] Ibid.

[72] Stuart, I. R. and W. G. Eliasberg, "Personality Structures which Reject the Human Form in Art; An Exploratory Study of Cross-Cultural Perceptions of the Nude— Cuban vs. The United States," The Journal of Social Psychology, 57 (1962), p. 384.

to pornography for any length of time become satiated and bored. Many persons may be quite sexually aroused by reading their first pornographic novel, but after reading many of them find that their level of arousal sharply decreases. Gebhard and his associates found that the possession of pornography did not differentiate sex offenders from non-sex offenders. "Even the combination of ownership plus strong sexual arousal from the material does not segregate the sex offender from other men of a comparable social level. We have often found that men with large collections of long standing lose much of their sexual response to the materials, and while their interest in collecting may continue unabated, their motivation is no longer primarily sexual."[73]

The most commonly stated concern with pornography is the belief that it corrupts and harms young people. It is believed that pornography will erotically arouse adolescent boys and contribute to their masturbation. And this belief is undoubtedly true because the major users of at least pictorial pornography are adolescent males. For many of those boys the materials are used as an aid to masturbation. Yet, there is no evidence that the availability of pornography increases the rates of masturbation among adolescents. (And there is no evidence that if the rates did increase that that would cause problems of any kind. Adolescence is the period of life for the male when rates of masturbation are highest, particularly among middle-class boys. Given this high sexual interest, when pornography is not available the boys may create their own stimulation from mail-order catalogues, magazine ads, and so on.[74] It should also be kept in mind that the use of erotic literature as an aid to fantasies in masturbation is not limited to adolescence and is often found among adult males. The point is that among adolescents masturbation will occur with or without pornography and there is no evidence that pornography is harmful.

Gebhard, in his extensive study of sexual offenses, examined the possible influences of pornography on all types of sex offenses. He came to the conclusion that all that can be said about a strong response to pornography is that it is associated with imaginativeness, ability to project, and sensitivity, "all of which generally increase as education increases, and with youthfulness, and that these qualities account for the differences we have found between sex offenders, in general, and non-sex offenders. Since the majority of sex-offenders are not well educated nor particularly youthful, their responsiveness to pornography is correspondingly less and cannot be a consequential fact in sex offenses."[75]

The overwhelming reaction of clinicians and researchers who have studied pornography is that it has little or no relation to sex offenses.

---

[73] Gebhard, *op. cit.*, p. 678.

[74] Gagnon and Simon, *op. cit.*, p. 46.

[75] Gebhard, *op. cit.*, p. 673.

The Kronhausens observe that "it is extremely doubtful whether even continued exposure to specific pornographic stimuli will result in behavior changes, unless they are accompanied by actual contacts with individuals who are so predisposed."[76] In a survey of psychiatrists and psychologists in New Jersey it was found that among those who responded 94 percent said they had not had normal patients who were incited to antisocial acts by exposure to sexually stimulating materials. "Further, two-thirds believed that erotic materials might provoke a substitute outlet for some individuals who might otherwise engage in antisocial acts."[77] In another sample of 3,400 clinicians in mental health professions 84 percent said they believed that persons exposed to pornography were no more likely to engage in antisocial sexual acts than persons not exposed. Furthermore, 86 percent of the clinicians said they believed that people who vigorously sought to suppress pornography were motivated by unresolved sexual problems of their own.[78]

However, as with so many areas of deviancy there may be a wide range in who gets defined as an expert and how he defines pornography. For example, when the question was asked, "Do you think that reading obscene books plays a significant role in causing juvenile delinquency?" only 12 percent of a sample of professional workers in the delinquent area answered "yes" in contrast with 58 percent of a sample of police chiefs.[79] The general finding from the commission report that upset so many went as follows: "In sum, empirical research designed to clarify the question has found no evidence to date that exposure to explicit sexual materials plays a significant role in the causation of delinquent or criminal behavior among youth or adults. The commission cannot conclude that exposure to erotic materials is a factor in the causation of sex crime or sex delinquency.[80]

One of the major concerns about those who want to control the sale of pornography is the question of censorship. Many people who have no personal interest in pornography are afraid that restrictions on the sale of that kind of material could lead to restrictions in other areas. In the above study of clinicians two-thirds of them felt that censorship was socially harmful "because it contributed to a climate of oppression and inhibition within which creative individuals cannot express themselves adequately."

It appears that the sale of legal pornography in the United States is fairly well controlled. The young person is not exposed to materials unless he seeks out those stores that sell them and often then he will

---

[76] Kronhausen, op. cit., p. 858.
[77] Katzman, op. cit., p. 83.
[78] Detroit Free Press, August 23, 1969.
[79] Commission's Report, op. cit., p. 194.
[80] Ibid., p. 32.

not be sold the materials. Even if he is not sold pornography he can get it if he wants in the same way he gets cigarettes or alcohol. When written pornography was prohibited it was still available and it may be that with it now legal, and for the most part in a few restricted stores, that its sales will be controlled. What may happen is what appears to be occurring in Denmark—access to pornography often means the user quickly reaches his satiation point. Continued experiences with alcohol or drugs may become increasingly exciting, but such is not the case with continued use of pornography.

It would appear from the discussion in this chapter that pornography constitutes a special type of deviancy. That is, people believe it to be wrong although its uses have no significant negative consequences either personally or socially. This is a deviance of values rather than behavior. It may be that in a changing society where there are so many beliefs that are undergoing questioning and rejection that many people resist the idea that pornography may not be harmful. It is almost as if "if you can't believe that pornography is undesirable and harmful, what is there left that one can believe is evil?" People not only need things to believe in but they also need things to believe against.

BIBLIOGRAPHY

CLOR, HARRY M., *Obscenity and Public Morality* (Chicago: University of Chicago Press, 1969).

GAGNON, JOHN H. and WILLIAM SIMON, "Pornography—Raging Menace or Paper Tiger?," *Trans-Action*, July, 1967, pp. 41–48.

GORDON, MICHAEL and ROBERT R. BELL, "Medium and Hard Core Pornography: A Comparative Analysis," *The Journal of Sex Research*, November, 1969, pp. 260–68.

KATZMAN, MARSHALL, "Obscenity and Pornography," *Medical Aspects of Human Sexuality*, July, 1969, pp. 77, 81–83.

KNIGHT, ARTHUR and HOLLIS ALPERT, "The History of Sex in Cinema: The Stag Film," *Playboy*, November, 1967.

KRONHAUSEN, EBERHARD and PHYLLIS, "The Psychology of Pornography," in Albert Ellis and Albert Abarbanel, *The Encyclopedia of Sexual Behavior* (New York: Hawthorne Books, Inc., 1961), pp. 848–59.

LOTH, DAVID, *The Erotic in Literature* (New York: Julian Messner, Inc., 1961).

POLSKY, NED, "Pornography," in Edward Sagarin and Donald E. MacNamara, *Problems of Sex Behavior* (New York: Thomas Y. Crawell Co., 1968), pp. 268–84.

The Report of the Commission on Obscenity and Pornography (New York: Bantam Books, 1970).

ROSEN, LAWRENCE and STANLEY H. TURNER, "Exposure to Pornography: An Exploratory Study," *The Journal of Sex Research*, November, 1969, pp. 235–46.

CHAPTER 7

ALCOHOL

THE ORIGINS OF ALCOHOL go back into the unknown past of prehistory. For hundreds of years there has been controversy over the value and use of alcoholic beverages. Probably in most societies it has not been a question of whether or not alcohol should be used, but rather a concern with who would use it, where and when, and under what conditions. So in various cultures alcohol has been used as a means of social facilitation, to celebrate or commiserate, as a part of religious ritual, to try to psychologically "escape" and for many other functions.

Alcohol has been used in the United States from the very beginning. In colonial America there was general acceptance of some alcoholic beverages such as rum, beer, wine, and cider. Contrary to what is generally believed the Puritans were not against the use of alcohol—but they did punish drunkenness. Yet, as Blum points out, the first moves toward the condemning of alcohol were found during the early colonial period when Increase and Cotton Mather both preached against "demon rum."[1] But in general during that early period, drinking was common to most adult men and was not usually seen as either a personal or social problem.

Historically, in the United States, it was not until the westward movement that there began to develop a concern with heavy drinking and it came to be defined as a social problem. The new social problem of heavy

---

[1] Blum, Richard H., *Society and Drugs* (San Francisco: Jossey-Bass, Inc., 1969), pp. 36–37.

171

drinking came about as a result of a combination of events. First was the general social disorganization and lawlessness that was a part of the western frontier. Second was the developing industrialization, urbanization, and heavy migration that were expanding and changing the cities. Third was that in the east there was an increasing availability of rum which allowed for increasing numbers of persons to drink large amounts. Finally, there was the production of corn "likker" for the drinkers in the rural areas as well as for the frontiersmen who wanted a strong, cheap, and portable liquor.[2]

The campaign that developed against drinking was based on moral disapproval and sought total prohibition of alcohol. In the early 1800's a new definition of the drinker emerged which pictured him as an object of social shame. There are some observers who argue that after the 1850's American drinking became very extreme and most people were either heavy drinkers or totally abstinent. By the 1870's rural and small town America had developed middle-class morals that included the dry attitude of abstinence and sobriety. Gusfield suggests that "moral persuasion, rather than legislation, has been one persistent theme in the designation of the drinker as deviant and the alcoholic as even further debased."[3] Well into the twentieth century the alcoholic was viewed as a sinner. This definition affected how the family of the alcoholic was viewed. Fifty years ago the members of an alcoholic's family were usually seen as innocent victims of the willful self-indulgence of an irresponsible, weak, and sinful person. The drunkard was seen as someone for the family to hide, the police to control, and the clergy to reform. The family was to be pitied and shown charity.[4]

The anti-drinking view reached its peak of power and influence in January, 1920 when national prohibition was enacted. It may have been that drinking was so much a part of society that it could not be legislated out. During prohibition even many non-drinkers saw drinking as a right for the individual to choose. As a result the society developed a view of ignoring and circumventing prohibition that was increasingly accepted by large numbers of Americans. There were also many powerful pro-alcohol forces, with a vested interest in the sale of alcohol, anxious to have prohibition repealed. In general, since the repeal of prohibition there has developed on the broadest social level in the United States a basic indifference to alcohol. People do become concerned about problems resulting from drinking—alcoholism, drunk driving, adolescent

---

[2] *Ibid.*, p. 38.

[3] Gusfield, Joseph R., "On Legislating Morals: The Symbolic Process of Designating Deviance," *California Law Review*, January, 1968, p. 63.

[4] Jackson, Joan K., "The Adjustment of the Family to the Crisis of Alcoholism," in Earl Rubington and Martin S. Weinberg, *Deviance: The Interactionist Perspective* (New York: Macmillan Co., 1968), p. 50.

drinking and so forth. But there does not appear to be any general strong social concern with the use of alcohol because it is immoral or bad, especially when it is used in moderation.

Before continuing to views of other societies we discuss the meaning of alcohol and its effects on the user. Many people believe that alcohol serves as a stimulant on the drinker. But in fact alcohol is a protoplasmic poison with a depressant effect on the nervous system. If alcohol is taken in large enough quantities it can render a person unconscious, and in the past alcohol was sometimes used medically as an anesthetic. So as alcohol is absorbed into the system it functions as a continuous depressant of the central nervous system. What appears to be stimulation effects are the result of the depression of inhibitory control mechanisms. "Alcohol is thought to exert first its depressing action on the more primitive parts of the brain responsible for integrating the activity of other parts of the central nervous system, thereby releasing the higher centers from control."[5] In general, the drunker a person gets the less control over himself he has physically, psychologically, and socially.

The views toward alcohol cover a wide range among various societies. It has been argued that there is a tendency that may be universal for valuations of alcoholic beverages to become polarized in any given society. "At one extreme liquor, wine, and beer are glorified in song, poetry, and drama as keys to ecstasy and sublimity; at the other extreme, they are viewed as perverters of human morality and the chief causes of the ills of society as well as of the sorrows of individuals."[6] It also has been suggested that there are three general ways in which a society can influence its rates of alcoholism. One is the extent to which a society creates tensions in its members that would lead them to alcohol as a possible source of reducing their tensions. Second are the kinds of attitudes that a society develops in its members toward drinking. Third is the degree to which a society provides other means of tension reduction than alcohol.[7]

The ways in which different cultures use alcohol may be closely related to various social institutions. There may be a variety of social functions, one of which is religion. When alcohol is used in a religious setting this means it centers around ceremonial functions. For example, among Roman Catholics wine is used in Holy Communion. Or alcohol may be used at the celebration of a Bar Mitzvah or at a wedding party. Often alcohol may be used hedonistically—to show solidarity between friends

---

[5] Nowlis, Helen H., *Drugs on the College Campus* (New York: Anchor Books, 1969), pp. 85–86.

[6] Lemert, Edwin M., *Human Deviance: Social Problems and Social Control* (Englewood Cliffs, N.J.: Prentice-Hall, 1967), p. 73.

[7] Bales, Robert F., "Cultural Differences in Rates of Alcoholism," in William A. Rushing, *Deviant Behavior and Social Process* (Chicago: Rand McNally and Co., 1969), p. 283.

and relatives. And in some societies alcohol is used in a utilitarian way —to gain some advantage over another person or sometimes for medicinal purposes.[8]

One may describe social patterns of drinking for societies but it should be recognized that the more complex societies rarely ever follow any single, clear cut pattern. In fact, many societies are unclear and ambivalent about their drinking patterns. It has been suggested that the American culture may be the prototype of ambivalent cultures. The reason is that the cultural attitudes toward drinking are not uniform and, moreover, this "social ambivalence" is reinforced by the conflict between the drinking and abstinent values that co-exist in many communities. On the one hand are those who support alcohol for religious reasons and for it's being a part of a tradition as an expression of hospitality and sociability. And economically there is the liquor industry which is powerful, and influential. "The abstinent groups are characteristically composed of ascetic Protestant groups who believe the use of alcohol is sinful and who therefore see little difference between the occasional social drinker and the chronic inebriate, since the former is the beginning stage for the latter."[9]

There may also be another group emerging in opposition to alcohol and this would be among the more sophisticated young who are usually college students. There has developed in recent years an increasing awareness and concern about things harmful to life. This is true with regard to ecological dangers and sometimes to mental and physical dangers and many young people are aware of the dangers of alcohol to the body and reject it for that reason. Many see drinking as the irrational crutch of the older generation who put them down for using marijuana which they feel is less harmful than alcohol. Generally the more that people use marijuana the less they use alcohol. So marijuana may be replacing alcohol for many in the younger generation.

The amount of drinking and the rates of alcoholism to be found in various countries is not possible to determine. However, it does appear clear that the proportion of alcoholics varies from country to country, "but does not seem to exceed in any country 5 percent or 6 percent of all users of alcoholic beverages."[10] When one examines various cultures there seems little question that in those cultures where there are strong social and religious pressures for proscribing the sale and distribution of alcohol the arrests for drunkenness are quite high. By contrast the rates of arrests for drunkenness are much lower in countries that have per-

---

[8] Pittman, David J., *Alcoholism* (New York: Harper and Row, 1967), p. 14.

[9] *Ibid.*, p. 8.

[10] Jellinek, E. M., "Phases of Alcohol Addiction," in Simon Dinetz, *et al.*, *Deviance* (New York: Oxford University Press, 1969), p. 254.

missive laws with regard to alcohol. "It seems clear that arrests for drunkenness as a reflection of deviant behavior are higher where a background of proscription is greater."[11]

As mentioned earlier there is variation in drinking patterns among various religious groups. Mizruchi argues that among ascetic Protestant and Mormon groups the norms against drinking are proscriptive. Therefore, any deviation from the abstinence pattern, even in what is usually defined as socially approved drinking in the broader society is seen as an almost complete absence of directives. "So if in the ascetic religious groups drinking behavior is adopted variation must be the rule because for those groups there are no norms for drinking but only against. As a result extremes often occur in drinking because the behavior itself represents rejection of social rules."[12] The contrast to this pattern is seen among Jews where there are elaborate norms with regard to drinking. There are directives as to what, when, where, with whom, how much, and why a person is expected to consume alcoholic beverages. "The norm is predominantly *prescriptive* in nature, and deviation from the drinking norms is associated with gradual and predictable patterns of deviant behavior."[13]

LEGAL ASPECTS OF ALCOHOL USE

Probably in all societies there have developed some controls over drinking and in most societies the controls are at least in part built into the legal systems. There are in many societies, including our own, elaborate legal controls over who may sell alcoholic beverages, where they may sell, to whom, and under what circumstances. But our main interest is in the controls over people who are using alcohol. And the legal view of the drinker is closely related to the social view of his use of alcohol and the effects it is believed to have on him. As suggested, the drinking of alcoholic beverages is culturally defined as to whether or not it is deviant behavior. In general, in the United States, the use of alcohol is defined as deviant behavior when the person is defined as an alcoholic, as an excessive and problem drinker, or when he engages in offenses related to his being influenced by alcohol. This last would include such things as driving an automobile while under the influence of alcohol or being drunk and disorderly.

There are large numbers of persons who are arrested for public drunkenness. There are about two million arrests each year on this charge

---

[11] Mizruchi, Ephraim H. and Robert Perrucci, "Prescription, Proscription and Permissiveness: Aspects of Norms and Deviant Drinking Behavior," in Mark Lefton, *et al.*, *Approaches to Deviance* (New York: Appleton-Century-Crofts, 1968), p. 163.

[12] *Ibid.*, p. 157.

[13] *Ibid.*, p. 158.

and this accounts for about one out of every three arrests made in the United States. This places a very heavy burden on the criminal justice system. The laws provide maximum jail sentences ranging from 5 days to 6 months; the most common maximum sentence is 30 days. "There is strong evidence, however, that a large number of those who are arrested have a lengthy history of prior drunkenness arrests, and that a disproportionate number involve poor persons who live in slums."[14]

Drunkenness arrest practices vary greatly from one place to another. And there are some police departments that strongly enforce the laws against drunkenness while others are far more permissive. "In fact, the number of arrests in a city may be related less to the amount of public drunkenness than to police policy."[15] After a drunk is arrested he is usually placed in a barren cell called a "tank" where he is held for at least a few hours. The tanks in various cities may hold anywhere from 1 to 200 people. In the tank one major problem is that medical care is rarely provided and it is difficult to detect or to diagnose serious illness since it often resembles intoxication.[16] Most drunkenness offenders are picked up at night and therefore stay in the tank until the next morning before they are brought before the judge. He usually sees them in groups of 15 or 20 and rarely are the normal procedural or due process safeguards applied to these cases.

It seems clear that the criminal justice system is ineffective in deterring drunkenness or in meeting the problems of the chronic alcoholic offender. What the legal system does in effect is remove the drunk from where he can be publically seen, "detoxify him, and provide him with food, shelter, emergency medical service, and a brief period of forced sobriety."[17] Built into the arrest system is inherent discrimination against the homeless and the poor. "Due process safeguards are often considered unnecessary or futile. The defendant may not be warned of his rights or permitted to make a telephone call. And although coordination, breath, or blood tests to determine intoxication are common practices in driving while intoxicated cases, they are virtually nonexistent in common drunk cases."[18]

THE CAUSES

We next look at some beliefs about the causes of heavy drinking and alcoholism. It should be stressed that the vast majority of those who use alcoholic beverages stay within the limits of the culturally accepted

---

[14] *The Task Force Report,* "Drunkenness Offenses," in Simon Dinitz *et al., Deviance* (New York: Oxford University Press, 1969), p. 244.

[15] *Ibid.,* p. 245.

[16] *Ibid.*

[17] *Ibid.,* p. 246.

[18] *Ibid.,* p. 247.

drinking patterns and drink predominantly as an expression of their socialization. But there are some drinkers who are alcoholics and this may be defined as a complex chronic illness although it is not very well understood. According to the American Medical Association alcoholism is a form of drug dependence characterized by preoccupation with alcohol and loss of control over its consumption, usually leading to intoxication once drinking has started. The alcoholic has a high tendency to relapse and usually suffers physically, emotionally, occupationally, and socially because of his alcoholic addiction. And too, the very size of the problem with the number who are alcoholics makes the question of causes and cures extremely difficult to determine.

Whatever the causes of alcoholism the process of becoming an alcoholic takes time. This is true because repeated ingestion of alcohol results in tolerance and a higher level of alcohol is needed in the blood stream to produce a given level of intoxication. So both physical and psychological dependence may also result from prolonged use. It has been found that alcohol dependence occurs in about 10 percent of all users and that the development of physical dependence requires the consumption of large amounts of alcohol over a period of about three to fifteen years or more, "In the dependent individual, even a few hours of abstinence precipitates the beginning of the alcohol withdrawal syndrome, a syndrome similar to that following withdrawal of the barbituates or other depressant drugs."[19]

As suggested, there are many social factors related to the development of drinking patterns. One study suggests that among persons who drink those who have received few, if any, restrictive guidelines defining appropriate drinking behavior are more likely to become heavy drinkers than those who are given specific directives about their drinking. "In other words, heavy drinking is associated with a *relative* lack of norms regarding the consumption of alcoholic beverages in an environment which does not prohibit drinking."[20]

What makes the problem of drinking difficult to define in the United States is that it is less a question of whether one should drink but more one of *how much* one should drink. Of course, the amount of drinking varies greatly between individuals and groups and what may be defined as appropriate for some may be seen as inappropriate for others. So at certain times and in certain situations drinking meets with at least some degree of social approval. Its positive orientation is based on its usefulness in decreasing feelings of tension and anxiety and in fostering pleasant and sociable moods in most individuals."[21] This is in contrast to the

---

[19] Nowlis, *op. cit.*, p. 87.

[20] Larsen, Donald E. and Baha Abu-Laban, "Norm Qualities and Deviant Drinking Behavior," *Social Problems*, Spring, 1968, p. 449.

[21] Nowles, *op. cit.*, p. 87.

person doing much more drinking who is defined as a heavy drinker or alcoholic and who is often seen as self destructive and socially a detriment.

Yet, society is also mixed in its views concerning drinking that is generally seen as acceptable; drinking that may be seen as reducing tension and contributing to sociability is also seen as lowering sensitivity, efficiency, and caution. It has been argued that in a complex society these influences can be socially dangerous because a complex society puts strong emphasis on self control and on inhibitions and repression of aggression and irresponsibility. Alcohol releases these inhibitions and can wreck regularity of behavior.[22] "The need for imagination and perception, for control over responses, for timing and balance, is greatly increased by the complex culture; just to get things done is a more delicate task, and the penalty for not getting things done has far greater social implications than in the simpler society."[23]

We have indicated the relatively high rate of drinking in the United States and it is necessary to look more specifically at some rates of drinking and alcoholism. It has been estimated that about 70 percent of all American adults have at least one alcoholic drink in a year. There are millions of persons who may be variously classified as light drinkers, moderate drinkers, heavy drinkers, problem drinkers, and alcoholics. The most recent estimate is that there may be as many as nine million adult Americans who are alcoholics and there are millions more on the verge of having serious drinking problems. Alcoholism is estimated to cost industry more than two billion dollars a year and has been found to be a causal factor in half of all traffic fatalities. It is estimated that the damage done while under the influence of alcohol amounts to half a billion dollars a year. When alcoholism is defined as a medical problem it is outranked only by mental illness, heart diseases, and cancer. Furthermore, it is estimated that 20 percent of the people in state mental hospitals are there because of alcoholic brain disease and 50 percent of the people in prisons have committed their crimes in association with alcoholic consumption. Alcohol also generates other enormous costs in marital breakdown and welfare costs. In total, alcoholism is very costly to American society.

The effects of the alcoholic on his family have always been of great concern. Joan Jackson has done extensive research on the relationships between the alcoholic and his family. The impact of the alcoholic on his family is usually a gradual one and how each family member responds to the alcoholic is influenced by different personality structures and the various roles filled within the family. The action that is directed toward

---

[22] Bacon, Seldon D., "Alcohol and Complex Society," in Simon Dinitz, et al., *Deviance* (New York: Oxford University Press, 1969), p. 225.

[23] *Ibid.*

the alcoholic is influenced by the past effectiveness of that particular action. The family members' views of the alcoholic are affected by the broader cultural definitions of alcoholism as evidence of weakness, inadequacy, or sinfulness; "by the cultural prescriptions for the roles of family members; and by the cultural values of family solidarity, sanctity and self-sufficiency. Alcoholism in the family poses a situation defined by the culture as shameful but for the handling of which there are no prescriptions which are effective or which permit direct action not in conflict with other cultural prescriptions."[24] This is in contrast to such family crises as illness or death where there are cultural definitions that family members may draw on.

Jackson suggests there are a number of different stages through which the family goes in its response to the alcoholic father. The first stage is where excessive drinking begins and although at this stage the drinking is sporadic it does place a strain on the husband-wife relationship. The second stage is where social isolation of the family starts as incidents of excessive drinking multiply. Increasingly, behavior and thought become drink-centered and the husband-wife relationship breaks down and tension between them increases. During the third stage the family give up their attempts to control the drinking and start to develop their behavior to relieve tension rather than to achieve long-range ends. At this stage there is no longer any attempt to support the alcoholic in his roles as husband and father. At the fourth stage the wife takes over control of the family and the husband comes to be defined as a recalcitrant child. The family becomes more stable and organized in a way to minimize the disruptive behavior of the husband. The wife begins to rebuild her self confidence. During the fifth stage the wife separates from her husband if she is able to resolve the problems and conflicts that surround that action. So then stage six is one of the wife and children reorganizing the family without the husband-father. Finally stage seven may be when the husband achieves sobriety and the family attempts to reorganize itself to include a sober husband-father. There are often problems in reinstating him to his former roles within the family.[25]

Data on the impact of an alcoholic on the family have been limited to the husband-father. There are no empirical studies of the alcoholic wife's effect on her family. There is some indication that the alcoholic wife is able to hide her drinking from her husband longer than can a male alcoholic hide drinking from his wife. One reason may be that the alcoholic woman is more concerned about hiding her drinking. Also, the man is often in a variety of social situations because of his occupation and it is therefore often difficult for him to hide his alcoholism. The woman

---

[24] Jackson, *op. cit.*, pp. 52–53.
[25] *Ibid.*, pp. 53–54.

who is a housewife follows a workday that permits more frequent drinking, "and most of her tasks can be accomplished despite a state of mild intoxication."[26]

One area of marriage that is affected by the husband's heavy drinking is the sexual one. Often the wife begins to avoid sexual contact with her husband when he is drinking. She may define sex under those circumstances as sex for its own sake rather than an indication of affection by him toward her. "The lack of sexual responsiveness reflects her emotional withdrawal from him in other areas of family life. Her husband, on his part, feels frustrated and rejected; he accuses her of frigidity and this adds to her concern about her adequacy as a woman."[27] The relationship of alcohol usage and sexual impotency in the male is a strong one. Masters and Johnson found that impotency that developed in the male in the late forties and early fifties had a higher incidence of direct association with excessive alcohol consumption than with any other single factor. The truly alcoholic male as he progressively deteriorated physically and mentally saw his sexual tensions and desires simply disappear.[28]

As would be expected, children are more affected than other family members by living with an alcoholic. The personalities of the children are developed in a social setting that is unstable, characterized by conflict and social disapproval. The children must model their behavior on roles being filled in a distorted fashion. "The alcoholic shows little adequate adult behavior. The non-alcoholic parent attempts to play the roles of both father and mother, often failing to do either well."[29] It is somewhat ironic that there was a common tendency among some children to feel more affection for the alcoholic than for the non-alcoholic parent. This was probably because the "alcoholic parent is rewarding when sober, while the non-alcoholic parent tends to be irritable and rejecting under the constant situation pressure."[30]

As suggested, the family with an alcoholic member suffers some shame, knowing that society generally defines the alcoholic as a weak and shameful person. Even though the family may have no responsibility for the alcoholism it still must suffer some stigma because of the member of the family unit. This is basically the same way in which a family gains prestige in the community because of some personal success by the father. But alcoholism is deviancy and in its efforts to handle the problems the family

---

[26] Ibid., p. 57.

[27] Ibid., pp. 57–58.

[28] Masters, William H. and Virginia E. Johnson, Human Sexual Response (Boston: Little, Brown and Co., 1966), p. 268.

[29] Jackson, Joan K., "Alcoholism and the Family," in Jeffrey K. Hadden and Marie L. Borgatta, Marriage and the Family (Itasca, Ill.: F. E. Peacock Publishers, Inc., 1969), p. 277.

[30] Ibid., p. 577.

labors under the reflection of blame. It often feels "guilty, ashamed, inadequate, and, above all, isolated from social support."[31] Often friends contribute to the feeling of shame. Frequently when the wife consults friends about her alcoholic husband the friends discount her concern and tell her it is really not so bad. This may contribute to her tendency to deny that a problem exists and can also add to her guilt by making her think she has disloyal thoughts about her husband.[32]

The problems for the family do not end even when the husband-father stops drinking. It is often the case that he has stopped before and then gone back on alcohol. The wife may often find it very difficult to believe that her husband is sober permanently and she is therefore unwilling to relinquish her control over family affairs even though she knows that is necessary for her husband's continued sobriety. The wife vividly remembers when his failures to handle responsibilities had created severe problems for herself and her children.[33] There is a difficult dilemma for the wife. To turn over more and more responsibilities to him is to increase the risk of problems for herself if he doesn't stay sober. But not to turn some responsibilities over to him may contribute to his sense of failure and inadequacy and push him back toward the use of alcohol.

SOCIAL VARIABLES RELATED TO DRINKING

Other than the family there are a number of social factors that are related to drinking patterns. One area of high concern in most societies is drinking among young people. In most societies the concern is not so much with whether or not they drink but rather whether they drink to a degree defined as socially excessive. For the most part the drinking patterns of the young can be predicted from the drinking patterns of their parents. In most cases in the United States the first drinking experience among the young occurs in the home while under parental supervision. Among various social groups those with the lowest risk of developing alcoholism are those where drinking was learned at an early age in a context of complex social and ceremonial activities supervised by persons who themselves drink safely.[34]

In the United States most adolescents at some time enter social situations in which there is a temptation to experiment with alcoholic beverages. This may be because they are curious, "because their parents include them in their drinking habits, because they wish to imitate adult

---

[31] *Ibid.*, p. 582.
[32] *Ibid.*
[33] *Ibid.*, p. 584.
[34] Blum, op. cit., p. 39.

behavior patterns, or because they find it a means of expressing their rebellion against being classified as less than adults."[35] Because the peer group is very powerful among adolescents and the pressures to conform and thereby achieve one's identity is so great the introduction of drinking as a positive force is very hard for the individual to resist. Also, because drinking is defined as adult behavior and the adolescent often wants to be seen as an adult he will turn to drinking because he thinks it will give him that adult status. The various studies of high school students have found that anywhere from one-third to four-fifths have had some experience with the use of alcohol. The average age of first experience appears to be about fourteen or fifteen.[36]

Only a small percentage of adolescents are alcoholics. This is reflected in the findings that the median age of alcoholics is in the middle forties. A small minority of adolescents who drink will eventually become alcoholics. It has been suggested that involvement with alcohol by adolescents can be seen as a matter of degree and may range from: "(1) relatively harmless, occasional drinking, consisting of nothing more than mere imitation of a permissible adult custom; to (2) peer-associated drinking that has overtones of rebelliousness against and alienation from adult institutions; to (3) heavy "escapist" drinking symptomatic of serious personality problems."[37]

It is also of interest that older people generally drink less than younger adults and middle age people. The reduction in drinking occurs roughly after age 60. It has been suggested that older people drink less because they grew up at a time when drinking was less common, or they may drink less because the process of aging influences them to cut down on their drinking.[38] It may also be that the heaviest drinkers have died or have been institutionalized and those with lower drinking rates represent the "survival of the fittest." Also, older people are more often under the care of a physician at least on some occasions and would therefore often have their drinking patterns subjected to medical control.

MALE-FEMALE DIFFERENCES

Far fewer females than males drink, and when women do drink they consume less than do men. There are also four or five times as many male

---

[35] Sebald, Hans, *Adolescence: A Sociological Analysis* (New York: Appleton-Century-Crofts, 1968), p. 470.

[36] Sterne, Muriel, *et al.*, "Teen Agers, Drinking and the Law: A Study of Arrest Trends for Alcohol-Related Offenses," in Pittman, *op. cit.*, p. 57.

[37] Sebald, *op. cit.*, p. 477.

[38] Knupfer, Genevieve and Robin Room, "Age, Sex, and Social Class as Factors in Amount of Drinking in a Metropolitan Community," *Social Problems*, Fall, 1964, p. 229.

alcoholics as there are female ones. However, one may predict that the rates of drinking and alcoholism among women will become closer to those of men in the future. This is predicated on the fact that women are achieving greater equality in the United States. One consequence of equality is the right and opportunity to acquire the socially undesirable problems of men. For example, if many men drink because of occupational pressures then as women become increasingly involved in these occupations they too will probably turn more and more to alcohol. One measurement of total sexual equality's having been reached will be when there are no differences in alcoholic rates among men and women.

RACE DIFFERENCES

Most studies suggest that male alcoholism rates, whether crude or standardized by age, are usually higher for blacks than for whites. Rates of alcoholism for black females are also uniformly higher than those for white females. Furthermore, the rates of arrest, conviction and incarceration for public intoxication tend to be higher for blacks than for whites.[39] This would be at least in part a reflection of higher arrests for all causes in a black population. Studies have also indicated that the tavern is a major point for public drinking and is often an important institution in the black community. "Although church and tavern represent the extremes of respectable and nonrespectable behavior, they serve analogous functions: Each is an accepted area for seeking individual recognition and for relatively uncircumscribed behavior, provides a mode of relief from problems, attracts a regular clientele to customary, ritual-like attendance, and is run by and for Negroes."[40]

SOCIAL CLASS

Drinking in the middle class is much less visible than in the lower class. This is because there is a high rate of drinking at home and therefore less visibility on the street while under the influence of alcohol. In general the public defines the middle-class drinker in much less harsh terms than it does the lower-class drinker. "On the other hand, the same public considers lower-class alcoholics and excessive drinkers as derelicts, beggers, petty thieves, and worthless drunks unable to support themselves."[41] The middle-class drinker, unless he clearly shows otherwise, is believed to be a good provider and is generally believed to be able to handle his

---

[39] Sterne, Muriel W., "Drinking Patterns and Alcoholism among American Negroes," in Pittman, *op. cit.*, p. 74.

[40] *Ibid.*, pp. 85–86.

[41] Pittman, *op. cit.*, p. 114.

drinking. In effect, the lower-class drinker is condemned as much for being lower class as he is for being a drinker.

In the middle class there has developed a system of norms and behavior patterns related to drinking. Permissive drinking goes with a notion of cosmopolitanism and abstinence is often seen as a negative symbol of a life style. To drink socially is to be cosmopolitan and often carries with it the implication that one is emancipated from traditional Puritan values.[42] The person who doesn't drink is often looked down upon as a "square"—as one who lacks sophistication. Hence, it is often the case that the actual use of alcohol is not important; rather it symbolizes a certain life style. The style is sometimes reflected in what one chooses to drink. A martini (very, very dry) is a sign of sophistication while a rye and coke is "square" or lower middle class.

One of the lowest social class levels is that of the "skid rows" to be found in most large cities. On skid row most of the inhabitants are heavy drinkers or alcoholics. They constitute a crude and relatively simple subculture. There appears to be little interpersonal concern and they cooperate on occasion primarily because it is more effective than not to cooperate. One way in which they cooperate is to get alcohol. When they don't individually have enough money to buy a bottle of wine they may pool their resources as a "bottle gang." Generally they meet, pool their money, get a cheap bottle of wine, drink it, and split up once the bottle is empty.

THE TAVERN OR BAR

How and where one drinks is important in that there are different social patterns for different settings where drinking occurs. For example, the alcoholic will often drink alone and in secrecy. But most people who drink prefer to do so with other people and the drinking becomes social and contributes to what is often enjoyable interaction. This can be done in one's home or in a tavern. It is not known how many taverns there are in the United States but the number is probably somewhere between 200,000 and 300,000. Many people who go to taverns or bars go on a regular basis. One study of persons going to taverns in Dane County, Wisconsin showed that about half the men were regular patrons while only 15 percent of the women who went were regulars. In the neighborhood taverns and bars drinking is often a secondary function because while people go to drink they also go for other reasons. Often when a person says to another "let's have a drink" he actually means "let's talk."[43]

Taverns and bars are often viewed as potential trouble spots both

---

[42] *Ibid.*, p. 18.

[43] Clinard, Marshall B., "The Public Drinking House and Society," in Dinitz, *op. cit.*, p. 235.

legally and socially. "In general, and unlike houses of prostitution and opium dens, bars in America are not, by law, as much deviant settings as they are places of potential deviant activity."[44] But since the end of prohibition the public bar has been seen as a legitimate retail business. However, it is different from other retail business in that special restrictions are placed on where it can be located, when it can open for business, and who may trade there. All of the restrictions serve to define a setting in which, from the point of view of the conventional order, trouble is apt to occur.

As suggested, the tavern or bar is a public meeting place where the individuals may actively participate with one another. The degree and nature of the participation is determined by the type of tavern. In the neighborhood bar the clientele know each other and constitute a kind of subculture. The bar is seen as important by the regulars. For example, the tavern can be very important in a rooming house area, because there it serves as a meeting place for persons who have no other way of meeting people. In this kind of tavern the regular customer often finds a sense of belonging and a place in the community.

There are also some bars that serve quite different functions. There are what Cavan calls marketplace bars and she points out that other than liquor the commodity most frequently handled in public drinking places is sex, either on a commercial or non-commercial basis.[45] There are also bars that market other commodities such as narcotics, gambling, stolen goods, and a variety of illegal products. In general the marketplace bars do not sell to anyone walking in off the street. Generally the buyers and the sellers must be vouched for before they can enter into the activities of the bar. Even in those bars where it is common knowledge that one can get information about prostitutes "patrons walking into the bar cannot always receive such information, since it can be used by the police as evidence of pimping, even though the one giving the information may be getting no fee from any transaction that may take place."[46] There are many other types of bars, but the most common is probably the neighborhood bar and the second most common those that deal in sex either for a fee or free, and both heterosexually and homosexually.

Cures for Alcoholism

For centuries there have been attempts to cure alcoholism. The attempts at cures have been closely linked to what was believed to be the

---

[44] Cavan, Sherri, *Liquor License: An Ethnology of Bar Behavior* (Chicago: Aldine Publishing Co., 1966), p. 37.

[45] *Ibid.*, p. 171.

[46] *Ibid.*, pp. 172–73.

cause. When it was believed that man became an alcoholic because he was possessed of the devil or was committing a sin it was the church that tried to cure him. But the problems of drinking have for the most part been removed from religion and placed more in the hands of medical clinics. So the tendency to handle drinkers through protective and welfare agencies, rather than through the police or clergy, has become more frequent.[47]

There has developed the establishment of detoxification centers. There are many experts who argue that these should be developed and replace the police station as the first detention for drunkards. In this setting the drunkard is brought to a public health facility by the police and kept there until sober. After that the decision to continue treatment would be left to the individual. There has also been some work with "inpatient programs" where the patients are given high protein meals with vitamin and mineral supplements and appropriate medication to help cut down on withdrawal symptoms. In these settings bath and laundry facilities are also available, as are basic clothing and limited recreation facilities. For any continued success "aftercare" programs are also needed. There is little reason to believe that the chronic drinker will change a long term pattern of drinking after a few days of sobriety and care at a public health unit. It has been suggested that a network of aftercare facilities should be expanded to include halfway houses, community shelters, and other forms of public housing.[48]

ALCOHOLICS ANONYMOUS

This approach is by far the best known attempt to help the alcoholic stop his drinking. This group is important not only in itself but also because it has served as a model for many other attempts to deal with problems. Programs to deal with the drug addict, the chronic gambler, and so forth have been modeled after Alcoholics Anonymous. This also means that the public image of the organization is very high and is generally seen as the only really successful way to "cure" alcoholism. Therefore, it is important to look at how it operates and to examine its successes and failures.

Alcoholics Anonymous (AA) was founded by a medical man and a stockbroker through a chance meeting they had in 1935. The stockbroker, through some kind of mystical experience, had stopped his own drinking and wanted to share his new sobriety with others. Initially there was a twelve step program to stop drinking. Some of the steps were: you admit you are licked; you get honest with yourself; you talk it out with

---

[47] Gusfield, op. cit., p. 67.
[48] The Task Force Report, op. cit., p. 250.

someone else; you make restitution to the people you have harmed; you try to give of yourself without stint, with no demands for reward; and you pray to whatever God you think there is, even as an experiment, to help you do these things.[49]

The various Alcoholics Anonymous groups are very powerful and pervasive subcultures. Basically one has been a deviant through his alcoholism and he wants to give up that deviant role. He does so by joining a powerful subculture made up of persons with similar motivations. He is rewarded for making the changes by persons in the same situation and by their confirming his new self-in-transition. "When these conditions are met, transforming a deviant identity is encouraged."[50] One supporter of the AA approach says that the subculture provides a way of life "which is more realistic, which enables the member to get closer to people, which provides one with more emotional security, and which facilitates more productive living. Thus, the AA group becomes an important new reference group—a new point of orientation."[51] The high value and importance to conformity in the subculture is a major value in AA. It is argued that when the alcoholic seeks help it is the great strength of AA that he is interacting with persons who have been through the program and have stopped drinking. So the subculture says come on in, do what we say and you can be like us—people who no longer drink.

A basic belief in AA is that there is no such person as an ex-alcoholic. This is because alcoholism cannot be cured according to AA and the person who has stopped drinking must give constant vigilance to his own urge to drink as well as to the urges of other AA members. For AA members there are only alcoholics in control (for the time being) of their temptations and never ex-alcoholics. In the jargon of the group they are referred to as dry or sober alcoholics.

There are a number of other ways in which the subculture of the AA members develops. For example, a ritualism of behavior develops. Initially all members were called by their first names as a means of protecting their identity but this now continues as a ritual.[52] As is true with all subcultures, the members of AA develop an argot of their own which contributes to their sense of solidarity and exclusiveness. The argot often has meaning in referring to the special experiences that they have in common or have actually shared. For example, such phrases as "nickel

---

[49] Maxwell, Milton A., "Alcoholics Anonymous: An Interpretation," in Pittman, op. cit., p. 216.

[50] Rubington, Earl and Martin S. Weinberg, Deviance: The Interactionist Perspective (New York: Macmillan Co., 1968), p. 323.

[51] Maxwell, op. cit., pp. 218–19.

[52] Sagarin, Edward, Odd Man In: Societies of Deviants in America (Chicago: Quadrangle Books, 1969), p. 51.

therapy" for "phoning another AA member to avert a 'slip' " and "the guy upstairs" for "God as you conceive him."[53]

Alcoholics anonymous sees alcoholism as a disease and the disease is arrested when one stops drinking and erupts again if the person starts to drink. The AA refuses to consider alcoholism as a symptom rather than a disease. Sagarin says that if they did there would be more need for psychotherapy and much less need for AA. As a result, the organization has become almost by nature and in spite of itself, anti-therapy. The AA strongly denounces at its meetings and in its publications all those who argue that alcoholics are psychopathological or that they have behavior disorders in any way similar to those of manic depressives and persons who are possessed of compulsive obsessions.[54]

An important part of the AA subculture is the pressure for honesty about one's self, which is reflected in a strong need to confess. Sagarin suggests that the great need to confess brings about a catharsis, "similar to that produced by religious confessions and psychoanalysis."[55] This contributes to the high sense of personal commitment and spiritual ideology of the highly committed AA member. The subculture not only influences his behavior and interaction with others but more important becomes his reason for being. This appeal to the alcoholic appears often to transcend many social factors. The AA is found in prisons, in hospitals, in small towns and large cities, and among the rich and the poor. In fact there are AA branches in several police departments, and others that cater especially to priests.[56]

There is disagreement about the success of Alcoholics Anonymous. It is quite likely that more contemporary alcoholics have reached sobriety through AA than through all other agencies combined. However, the AA plan, while it works for some does not work for many, and there is no clear understanding of why it works when it does. A critical view is that of Sagarin who states that many of AA's claims and assumptions about their success are unproved, obviously self-serving, and of doubtful validity. "They may be not only wrong but actually harmful. Some of these claims are: that alcoholism is a disease; that it is incurable but can be arrested; that AA has had a 50 percent success rate with its members; and that only an alcoholic can understand—or help—another alcoholic."[57] But another observer has suggested that the major contribution of AA has been not only in the rehabilitation of alcoholics, but also in the

---

[53] *Ibid.*, p. 42.
[54] *Ibid.*, p. 47.
[55] *Ibid.*, p. 37.
[56] *Ibid.*, p. 40.
[57] *Ibid.*, p. 45.

dramatization that alcoholics can be helped. "By virtue of their interest, they have made work with the alcoholic legitimate."[58]

It has been suggested that one possible consequence of arresting or halting deviancy is that the undesirable may be stopped but the consequences may not always be desirable. It is possible that the results of halting a deviance may be worse than the deviance itself. But more often there are negative consequences that tend to be ignored in light of the primary problem's being halted. For example, one consequence for the individual who stops drinking may be loneliness, frustration, and other difficulties.[59] This is especially true if the individual became an alcoholic because of personal problems. When he stops drinking his problems return and he is therefore in the same situation as when he originally developed his alcoholism. And because AA does not accept the approach of psychotherapy the alcoholic usually has not been helped with his original problem.

The alcoholic who goes on the wagon may also create problems for his family. In many cases the woman has been managing the family and with his continuing sobriety he usually wants to return to his former family roles. There is often resistance to the man by both the wife and the children. "Their mother has been both parents for so long that it takes time to get used to the idea of consulting their father on problems and asking for his decision. Often the father tries too hard to manage this change overnight."[60]

Jackson found in her research that if the man's sobriety came about because of AA he very often commits himself so totally to the AA activities that his wife sees little of him and feels neglected. And as she worries less about his drinking, she may push him to cut down on some of his outside activities. But this can be dangerous because AA activity is correlated with success in Alcoholics Anonymous. The wife further learns that even though her husband is off alcohol she is by no means free of alcoholics. "In his Twelfth Step work, he may keep the house filled with men he is helping. In the past her husband has avoided self-searching; and now he may become excessively introspective, and it may be difficult for her to deal with this."[61]

In conclusion it can be said that alcohol in the American society is not the cause of deviancy, but rather deviancy is related to the degree to which alcohol is used. In general social drinking that is personally

---

[58] Chefetz, Morris E. and Harold W. Demone, Jr., "Alcoholics Anonymous," in Dinitz, *op. cit.*, 272.

[59] Sagarin, *op. cit.*, p. 47.

[60] Jackson, "The Adjustment of the Family to the Crisis of Alcoholism," *op. cit.*, p. 60.

[61] *Ibid.*, p. 64.

controlled is not viewed as deviancy and in fact is often given some positive social value. The problem of deviance is with the heavy drinker and the alcoholic. And even when there is an agreement that this is a problem there is little agreement on what to do about it. The conflict is seen by the fact that most medical persons define alcoholism as a psychological problem that should be treated through some form of physical and psychological therapy. By contrast Alcoholics Anonymous defines it as a disease that can never be cured. So alcoholism refers to something most people would agree is a problem but where there is limited knowledge and high disagreement on what should be done about it.

BIBLIOGRAPHY

BACON, SELDON D., "Alcohol and Complex Society," in Simon Dinitz, et al., Deviance (New York: Oxford University Press, 1969), pp. 217–227.

CAVAN, SHERRI, Liquor License: An Ethnology of Bar Behavior (Chicago: Aldine Publishing Co., 1966).

JACKSON, JOAN K, "The Adjustment of the Family to the Crisis of Alcoholism," Quarterly Journal of Studies of Alcohol, December, 1954, pp. 564–86.

KNUPFER, GENEVIEVE and ROBIN ROOM, "Age, Sex, and Social Class as Factors in Amount of Drinking in a Metropolitan Community," Social Problems, Fall, 1964, pp. 224–40.

LARSON, DONALD E. and BAHA ABU-LABAN, "Norm Qualities and Deviant Drinking Behavior," Social Problems, Spring, 1968, pp. 441–50.

MIZRUCHI, EPHRAIM H., and ROBERT PERRUCCI, "Prescription, Proscription and Permissiveness: Aspects of Norms and Deviant Drinking Behavior," in Mark Lefton, et al., Approaches to Deviance (New York: Appleton-Century-Crofts, 1968, pp. 151–167.

PITTMAN, DAVID J., Alcoholism (New York: Harper and Row, 1967).

SAGARIN, EDWARD, Odd Man In: Societies of Deviants in America (Chicago: Quadrangle Books, 1969).

CHAPTER 8

DRUGS

In RECENT YEARS a great interest has developed in the "drug problem." Drug use is often presented as a major social problem that is seen as undermining the morality of society and destroying many of the younger generation. The use of drugs is a form of deviancy that operates within the context of passionate response frequently based on limited knowledge. This is true whether the view is that all drugs are evil and dangerous or that drugs are the way for the individual to find his true identity. In this chapter the interest is in the various types of drugs and their consequences as well as the social settings in which drugs are used.

Drugs have been a part of most cultures in the world. The evidence indicates there have been only a few societies where there were no mind-altering drugs. The American society places great stress on the use of drugs under many circumstances, but our society also makes many strong distinctions between kinds of drugs to be used and the circumstances under which drugs may be used. However, this has not always been true in the United States. For many years many remedies that had narcotic contents of 5 to 10 percent were sold over the counter without any controls. Through the wonder working medications of Mrs. Winslow's Soothing Syrup, Dr. Cole's Catarrh Cure, and Perkin's Diarrhea Mixture large amounts of opium, codeine, and cocaine were fed to children as well as adults. Also, every well equipped home had a rosewood chest, the earlier version of today's medicine cabinet, with its ball of opium and its bottle of paregoric. By 1863 the estimates of addiction in the United

States ran as high as 4 percent of the population.[1] By 1900, there were institutions of different types for the treatment of drug addiction at various locations around the country. Before the attempt to suppress the drug trade started in 1915 the drug addicts were mostly scattered throughout respectable society and did not form a deviant subculture.

There had been some initial concern with the possible dangers of drug use as early as the 1830's. But for the most part during the 19th century the problem of drug dependency was handled through the continued availability and consumption of the drug. The discomforts of abstaining from drugs were seen as just another set of aches and pains that could be eliminated by the use of drugs that were seen as the panacea of all ills.[2] The first law that tried to control the drug addiction situation was the Boylan Law passed by the New York Legislature in 1904. The Harrison Narcotic Law, which became a law in 1914, was modeled on the Boylan law, but it omitted the important measures that were concerned with the physician's role in treating addiction. The Harrison Narcotic Law was designed to control the production, manufacture, and distribution of addictive drugs by making it necessary to register all transactions and it was specified that only physicians could prescribe these drugs.[3] Over the years the Harrison Act has been supplemented by a number of other anti-narcotic statutes under which the unauthorized possession, sale, or transfer of drugs is severely punished. "Rather than constituting a rationally planned program for dealing with the narcotics problem, this legislature has mainly represented an emotional response to periodic crises."[4] During this period the Federal Narcotics Control Board came up with what it saw to be the solution to drug use. That was compulsory treatment and its successor since 1930, the Bureau of Narcotics in the Treasury Department, still considers compulsory treatment the only road to complete cure.[5]

What the laws have meant for the drug addict is that he is stopped from being a respectable member of the community and becomes a common criminal. This is because the law requires the registration of all legitimate drug handlers and the payment of a special tax on drug transactions, resulting in a licensing system for the control of legitimate domestic drug trade. Schur suggests that through a combination of restrictive regulations, attention only to favorable court decisions, and harassment, the

---

[1] Nyswander, Marie, "History of a Nightmare," in Dan Wakefield, *The Addict* (New York: Gold Medal Books, 1963), p. 21.

[2] Clausen, John A., "Drug Addiction," in Robert K. Merton and Robert A. Nisbet, eds., *Contemporary Social Problems* (New York: Harcourt, Brace and World, 1961), p. 185.

[3] Nyswander, *op. cit.*, p. 22.

[4] Schur, Edwin M., *Crimes without Victims: Deviant Behavior and Public Policy* (Englewood Cliffs, N.J.: Prentice-Hall, 1965), p. 133.

[5] Nyswander, *op. cit.*, p. 24.

Narcotics Division of the United States Treasury Department (and its successor, the Federal Bureau of Narcotics) has effectively and severely limited the freedom of medical practitioners to treat addicts as patients. Physicians are not allowed to provide addicts with drugs even when that is believed medically advisable.[6]

It must be recognized that the highly restrictive laws with regard to drug addiction have occurred in a society quite permissive about drugs in general. In fact the American public places a high positive value on the use of "legitimate" drugs. In the United States drugs are acceptable and approved usually when they are seen to relieve some kind of pain, illness, or disability. Or more generally, to help bring a person from some negative state toward a condition seen as "normal."[7] More and more drugs are not only seen as legitimately used in reducing physical pain but also in alleviating mental anguish. In 1966 the United States government estimated that 13 billion amphetamine, barbituate, and tranquilizer pills were being produced. This was roughly six dozen for every man, woman, and child in the country. In fact "every other prescription written in this country is written for a drug that affects the mind."[8] An increasingly rare type of person in the United States is one who takes no drugs of any kind. While the legitimate drugs help many there are dangers of overdependency, and even more serious, there is danger of death. There are, for example, approximately 3,000 deaths per year resulting from overdoses of barbituates.

Another danger from the legitimate use of drugs is that along with the widespread and intense belief in the power of medicine there is often a tendency to ignore the limitations and the side effects of drugs. There is also some indication that with the breakdown of the traditional patient-doctor relationship and an increasing amount of medical specialization, people depend more on medication than on the physician. The patient often sees the physician simply as the one who prescribes the drugs that will take care of his problem. Once the patient has the medication he sometimes uses it excessively or indiscriminately. One writer suggests that there is a kind of patient who "used medication as a kind of magical protector and depends on medication rather than people to handle certain emotional drives and needs."[9]

Adult society, with its use of many kinds of drugs, and not always according to medical prescription, has socialized many of the younger

---

[6] Schur, *op. cit.*, p. 130.

[7] Weakland, John H., "Hippies: What the Scene Means," in Richard Blum, *Society and Drugs* (San Francisco: Jossey-Bass, Inc., 1969), p. 359.

[8] Young, Warren and Joseph Hixson, *LSD on Campus* (New York: Dell Publishing Co., 1966), p. 52.

[9] Nowlis, Helen H., *Drugs on the College Campus* (New York: Anchor Books, 1969), p. 25.

generation to the use of drugs. The generation that is sometimes now looking for new values in a sugar cube with LSD or through a stick of marijuana received its orientation in a society that had been using various pills for adjustment to its psychic imbalances. Over the years, among the adults, barbituates and "bennies" had been finding their way into the hands of many and this had been increasingly reflected in accident and suicide statistics.[10] So in one sense the medicine cabinet in the middle-class home has been a socializing experience that in some ways predisposed children toward experimentation with drugs.

The use of illegal drugs for benefits they are felt to provide for the user covers a wide range. At one extreme, the believers in drug use see the psychedelic compounds like LSD, mescaline, and marijuana as a way of counteracting the "depersonalization," "commercialization," and inhumanity of modern American society. For these people the use of drugs is a modern means equivalent to the old mystical experience and to the great "inward journey of self-exploration and self-discovery."[11] At the other extreme, those who oppose drug use see it as self-indulgent, degenerate, and both psychologically and physiologically damaging. "Drug use is viewed as a 'symptom'—either of profound psychological problems or of some fatal weakness in the moral fiber of American youth. It is a form of moral depravity, and it must be ruthlessly stamped out, its users thoroughly punished, and the young indoctrinated in the 'hazards' of drugs."[12] These two extremes help set the stage for the discussion ahead and indicate that the area of drug use is one that brings forth great passions and doctrinaire points of view in the United States.

Before looking at the various kinds of drugs and their use and consequences it is necessary to define some terms. The word *narcotic* is used to refer to opium and the various pain killing drugs that are made from opium, such as heroin, morphine, paregoric, and codeine. These, as well as other opiates, are taken from the juice of the poppy fruit. There are also several synthetic drugs, such as demerol, and dolophine that are also classified as narcotics. The opiates are widely used in medicine to kill pain. Cocaine, made from cocoa leaves, and marijuana are legally classified as narcotic drugs although they are not narcotic in chemical makeup. Pharmacologically, the term narcotic is applied to a drug which, in most people under most circumstances and at the right level of dosage will produce sleep and relieve pain. However, from the legal point of view the term narcotic has been applied to almost any drug assumed to be habit forming or addictive. The general public has gone even further in its definition of the term narcotic, using it to refer to any drug which is socially disapproved or

---

[10] Young and Hixson, *op. cit.*, p. 52.
[11] Nowlis, *op. cit.*, p. x.
[12] *Ibid.*, p. xi.

associated "with delinquency, crime, and the underworld, as well as any drug which was controlled by the Federal Bureau of Narcotics."[13] The term *drug* is any chemical substance that alters the mood, perception, or consciousness. The social and legal setting define the nature of drugs as they are used. The term *drug addiction* refers to a state of periodic or chronic intoxication brought about by the repeated use of a drug of either a natural or a synthetic nature. The characteristics of drug addiction are:" (1) an overpowering desire or need (compulsion) to continue taking the drug and to obtain it by any means; (2) a tendency to increase the dose; (3) a psychic (psychological) and generally a physical dependence on the effects of the drugs; (4) an effect detrimental to the individual and to society."[14] It has been suggested that the term *drug addiction* has taken on so many different meanings that even the pharmacologist no longer has a specific definition for the term. In 1965 the World Health Organization Expert Committee on Addiction Producing Drugs came to a similar conclusion and suggested using the term *drug dependence* in place of *drug addiction*. The two terms during the rest of the chapter will be used interchangeably.

Before talking about the various categories of drugs it is necessary to say something further about the legal treatment of drugs in the United States as well as in some other countries. The discussion here is general, with the more detailed legal restrictions and punishments as related to specific drug use presented in the next section. A better understanding of the legal view toward drugs in the United States can be seen through a very general cross cultural comparison. The best known drug control system outside of the United States is the one used in Great Britain. The British approach is to treat drug addiction almost completely as a medical matter, but they keep careful control over the possession and supply of opiates (and certain other drugs). The law requires authorized distributors of drugs to keep full records of all drug transactions.[15] The important consquence of the British system is that there are very few drug addicts in that country. Most important is that there is very little illegal traffic in opiates, because the legal provision of low cost drugs has for the most part eliminated the profit motive in pushing illegal drugs. The addict qualifies as a medical patient under the National Health Service and is charged a small amount per drug prescription.[16]

The British pattern is not special because most other Western nations have similar narcotic control systems. None of those nations imposes

---

[13] *Ibid.*, p. 34.

[14] Expert Committee on Addiction-Producing Drugs, *Seventh Report*, World Health Organization Technical Report Series No. 116, (1957). Reprinted in Schur, *op. cit.*, p. 122.

[15] *Ibid.*, p. 153.

[16] *Ibid.*, p. 154.

compulsory cures upon its drug addicts except under special circumstances. These countries have programs designed and controlled by medical people. All of the countries, even taken together, have a combined drug problem that is less serious than in this country. The irony is that these countries are those from which "our peoples, our social and legal institutions, our language and our culture are derived."[17]

As indicated, the major difference between the United States' handling of drug addiction and that of other countries is that this country sees it as a legal matter and the other countries see it as a medical concern. This has not always been true in the United States. Before 1914 the drug addict had little or no involvement in any kind of criminal behavior. He did his job, maintained his home and family life, and for the most part his drug dependence did not inflict injury on anyone other than himself. But, under the controls of the Harrison Act the treatment of the addict was basically ignored and with amendments and various court decisions that approach was expanded. As a result "the addict was gradually forced out of the role of the legitimately ill into the role of the willful criminal."[18] Like so many legal control systems in our society this development was not a result of rational and planned decisions. Rather, as legal agencies developed an increasing vested interest in the handling of drug addicts they helped to bring about the laws that made them more significant and gave them even greater control. In other words once the direction of drug handling was toward the legal approach, rather than the medical, it became a snowballing process.

One of the strongest critics of the present legal handling of drug addiction in the United States is the sociologist Alfred Lindesmith. He argues that the fatal weakness of our present system is that it fails to take into account the basic human situation with which it is supposed to be dealing. By not allowing the physician to relieve the addict's suffering during drug deprivation the idea of sanctity of human life and the desirability of preventing needless suffering is rejected. Lindesmith goes on to say that "the narcotic laws are basically immoral and essentially unjust because of the manner in which they affect the addict, the way in which they distribute punishment, and because they require that the police engage either in immoral or criminal behavior, or both, in enforcement of the laws."[19]

The American system has been severely attacked on a second ground—other than that it should be handled as a medical problem—that is, that the legal approach to drug addiction itself has been a failure. Obviously

[17] Lindesmith, Alfred R., "Beginnings of Wisdom" in Dan Wakefield, *The Addict* (New York: Gold Medal Books, 1963), p. 187.

[18] Nyswander, *op. cit.*, p. 23.

[19] Lindesmith, Alfred R., "Torture by Law," in Dan Wakefield, *The Addict* (New York: Gold Medal Books, 1963), p. 41.

the laws have failed in that they have not eliminated drug addiction. Actually they have contributed to the narcotics problem. The addict, because he is cut off from any legal supply of drugs, must seek out illegal drug sources. The strong demand of addicts for their drug needs to be satisfied means there are huge profits to be made on the illegal market. Because there are great profits to be made the illegal activity is seen as worthwhile by the drug sellers. One indication of the vast profit is an estimate that the retail value of one thousand dollars worth of heroin may surpass three million dollars.[20] The traffic in illegal drugs has been estimated to gross hundreds of millions of dollars per year. So narcotics smuggling and distribution are big business for the criminal syndicates. Yet, as pointed out, at the beginning of the century there was little illegal profit being made from drug sales. Therefore, it seems clear that the illegal view of drugs that has developed since 1914 has been the major cause in creating the highly profitable criminal business of selling illegal drugs.

As indicated, the legal restriction on the medical distribution of drugs places the drug addict in an almost impossible position. As Lindesmith points out the dilemma for the drug addict is that if he does not secure drugs, he is punished by his disease; if he does secure them he is punished by the police. He goes on to point out that drug users or anyone who knows them at first hand knows that drug withdrawal is usually a serious, frightening, and dangerous experience. "To deny him his medical care on the grounds that he should not have acquired the habit in the first place is the moral equivalent of denying medical treatment for gonorrhea on the same grounds."[21]

After suggesting that the legal system with regard to drug treatment in the United States has been a failure both in *not* treating the addict as a medical problem and in *not* controlling the distribution of drugs, one might question why the system continues. One explanation is that using heavy criminal sanctions to control drug addiction rather than treating the addict as a sick person may continue because the drug laws are primarily symbolic rather than instrumental in their effect. The severe treatment of addicts is evidence that policymakers may be more interested in expressing disapproval than in controlling the problem effectively. "The stereotype of the drug addict suggests that this hostility is related to the view of the drug addict as representing a world outside conventional society."[22] In fact the constant publicity given to various drugs by politicians and some of the police have sensationalized many drugs and stimulated curiosity about them. When new laws are developed they have almost always been enacted on the basis of anecdotal, unscientific, and illegal testimony. This often

---

[20] Schur, *op. cit.*, p. 134.

[21] Lindesmith, *op. cit.*, p. 33.

[22] Gusfield, Joseph R., "On Legislating Morals: The Symbolic Process of Designating Deviance," *California Law Review*, January, 1968, p. 71.

occurs in the climate of hysteria which may be consciously developed and reinforced through the mass media. For example, recent laws against the use of LSD were passed with little medical, sociological, or scientific testimony.[23] Often politicians can be against drugs in the same way they can be against sin. That is, it is something safe to be against and in fact may win votes because most people are also against drugs—at least when used by others.

There is a commonly heard argument that there should be drug reforms but the argument almost always takes it for granted that the current policies are still desirable. In other words the legal view of drugs, rather than the medical approach taken in other countries, is rarely questioned by politicians. But some experts, who receive little attention, state that what is needed is an absolute reversal of the present attitudes and laws toward drugs. These experts argue that the addict will get his drugs, no matter how hard the law enforcers try to stop him, "and the only sensible course of action is to try to substitute medical supervision for police persecution."[24]

Another explanation for the continuation of the legal approach to drug addiction is the Federal Narcotics Bureau. A common theme throughout this book has been that the agencies that emerge to deal with deviancy usually develop a vested interest in the maintenance of that deviance. It is not that such vested interests are recognized by the agencies. But if a system similar to that of Great Britain developed in the United States and the drug addict were able to get his drugs cheaply and illegally there would be little need for illegal, expensive criminally organized sources of drugs. Therefore, there would be little need for the Federal Narcotics Bureau. It has been pointed out that the Bureau has constantly attempted to expand its jurisdiction and one way to do this is to add nonaddictive drugs to addictive ones. The stated goal of the Bureau is to prevent drug use, and they therefore attempt to develop arguments which make that policy appear sound. Therefore, anything that contributes to drug use is seen as bad. Thus, the continued attempt to link marijuana and heroin has powerful political as well as Narcotics Bureau implications. So if it is believed and can be argued that there is some property inherent in the substance of marijuana that "leads" to the use of drugs of addiction then the ends of the Bureau are better served.

There is also a certain irony about the drug laws that shows the lack of rationality often found in society, since drug use is often not as harmful as other legally accepted materials. Judged impartially, alcohol is probably more harmful to the user even than heroin, because the use of alcohol over a long term causes physical and nervous deterioration, which heroin does not. In fact, if alcohol were invented today by a re-

---

[23] Fort, Joel, "Social Problems of Drug Use and Drug Policies," *California Law Review*, January, 1968, p. 20.

[24] Schur, *op. cit.*, p. 160.

search chemist it would probably be severely controlled through law.[25] But alcohol has been around for centuries and in the United States it is a part of large, legitimate business enterprise. Therefore, any attempt to control alcohol has met with little success. It is quite possible that, if around 1914 the drugs of addiction had developed as a legitimate business enterprise, they too would be accepted today. Another illustration of this point is the reaction to cigarettes. Since the mid 1960's the evidence has been increasingly overwhelming that the use of cigarettes is dangerous. Yet, cigarettes are not being taken off the market and probably will not be in the foreseeable future.

Society also often reacts in another way toward things that are defined by many as bad. For example, with cigarettes, one argument for their continued manufacture and sales is an economic one. That is, if the sales of cigarettes were drastically reduced many people would be put out of work and the tobacco regions would become depressed areas. It is also common to hear a similar argument about war or the need at least for the continued threat of war, that is, if defense industries were closed down people would be out of jobs. There is something strange in the argument that the killing of people is needed to maintain jobs for other people— but it is, nevertheless.

TYPES OF DRUGS

In this section the interest is in examining some various types of drugs. However, there is one term that cuts across several of the categories of drugs: *hallucinogens*. In this group are included such drugs as LSD, mescaline, psilocybin, and marijuana. These drugs have a hallucinatory effect and influence the user's perception of the world both within and outside of himself. These drugs are not addictive, although under some personality conditions they may become habit forming. This group is also sometimes referred to as the *psychedelic* drugs. The black market for the sale of hallucinogens is loosely organized, often with friends supplying one another and covering their costs, rather than an organized network of pushers. "The non-addictiveness of the drugs makes for a frustration in demand that hardly attracts the established operators, who prefer the stability of the opiate market."[26] Some of these drugs will be further discussed under the five general types of drugs to follow.

BARBITURATES

The first barbiturate appeared in 1903 and was called barbital (veronel), and this group is classified as one of the general depressants. They are not

---

[25] Laurie, Peter, *Drugs: Medical, Psychological, and Social Facts* (Baltimore, Maryland: Penguin Books, 1967), p. 15.

[26] *Ibid.*, p. 123.

specific in the effect they have and are capable of depressing a wide range of functions. Their influence on the central nervous system ranges from a mild sedation to coma, depending on the level of dosage. At moderate dosage levels the barbiturates often produce disinhibition and euphoria much as alcohol does (also a depressant). The drug depresses other functions such as nerves, skeletal muscle, smooth muscles, and cardiac muscles. Addiction to barbiturates differs from that of opiates in several important ways. It appears to be more destructive to personality; "the barbiturate addict tends to dope himself until he is completely intoxicated —his object is oblivion."[27] The barbiturates are estimated to be the cause of about 3,000 deaths per year.

Barbiturates are under the regulation of the Bureau of Narcotics and Dangerous Drugs, Department of Justice. The laws provide for a strict accounting of drug supplies by the manufacturer, distributor, and seller, and they limit the user to five refills of the prescription, at the discretion of the physician. This means that barbiturates can be attained legally only through a physician. The illegal manufacture and dispensing of barbiturates can lead to fines as high as $10,000 and prison sentences of up to 5 years. Those who are convicted of selling the drugs to persons under 21 years of age can be fined $15,000 to $20,000 and receive 10 to 15 years in prison. To be in possession of these drugs illegally can bring a fine of from $1,000 to $10,000 and/or imprisonment of 1 to 3 years. There are also state laws that control the illegal use of barbiturates.

AMPHETAMINES

The amphetamines which were first produced in the 1920's for medical use stimulate the central nervous system and are best known as a means to fight against fatigue and sleepiness. They are also sometimes used to limit appetites in medically controlled weight reduction programs. The most commonly used are amphetamine (benzedrine), dextroamphetamine (dexedrine) and methamphetamine (methedrine). These drugs are also known under the slang terms of "pep pills" and "bennies."

The amphetamines produce effects resembling those resulting from the stimulation of the sympathetic nervous system, that part of the nervous system which has major control over bodily functions. There is a high potential for psychological dependence in some individuals if they use amphetamines regularly over a period of time. It appears that the psychological dependence is a function of the drug's ability to bring forth feelings of energy, initiative, self-confidence, and well being. After a period of usage many people find it very difficult to meet the demands of life without this uplift.

---

[27] *Ibid.*, p. 63.

There is little doubt that amphetamines can improve a person's performance on a wide variety of tasks, especially those involving an element of fatigue or boredom. It is in a way a "superman" drug because it can increase the capacity for simple physical and mental tasks, and increase intelligence by an average of up to eight points, as measured by simple tests. "However, highly coordinated tasks like playing golf or flying an airplane are unaffected in quality, though they can be prolonged beyond the normal duration."[28] One of the most dangerous uses of amphetamines is that of "speeding." This is a series of injections and each one is followed by a general climax of intense feelings and bodily sensations.

Production figures for the United States for 1962 showed that four and a half billion tablets were produced, about twenty-five tablets per citizen. The Food and Drug Administration estimates indicate half of these were consumed without a medical prescription. Continued use can lead to a habit which is reinforced by physiological as well as psychological distress upon withdrawal.

MARIJUANA

Marijuana is a drug found in the flowering tops and the leaves of the Indian hemp plant. The plant grows in mild climates in countries all over the world. The marijuana plant is a relative of European hemp and looks like a scrawny, six foot nettle. The term marijuana has become synonymous with *cannabis* and all of its products and derivatives, including the natural and synthetic tetrahydro-cannabinols. The substance cannabis is derived from the resin exuded by the female hemp plants. This substance has been used by man throughout recorded history. It is the leaves, stems, and flowering tops that are dried and chopped to produce the marijuana common to the United States and Mexico. The chopped up product is usually rolled and smoked in short cigarettes or in pipes, and may be taken in food. The cigarettes are commonly known as "reefers," "joints" and "sticks." The smoke from marijuana is harsh and smells like burnt dried grass, and the rather sweetish aroma is quite easy to identify.

The effects of marijuana vary not only among different individuals but also with a given individual over time. The wide variety of individual differences in responding seems to be more closely related to personality differences and the cultural setting where it is used than to any specific property of the drug itself.[29] The effects of the drug also vary as one learns to smoke in the most effective manner and then becomes sensitized.

---

[28] *Ibid.*, pp. 70–71.

[29] Pet, Donald D. and John C. Ball, "Marijuana Smoking in the United States," *Federal Probation*, September, 1968.

In most individuals, these effects are pleasurable at low dosage levels and unpleasant at higher dosage levels.[30]

More specifically the effects of marijuana commonly include a euphoric state accompanied by motor excitation and mental confusion. These reactions are frequently followed by a period of dreaminess, depression, and sleep. Intellectually, the use of marijuana tends to increase imagination but reduce concentration. For example, intelligence test scores are slightly lower or unchanged, "and if attention is held, say in a game of poker, an expert player can more than hold his own against other good players. Jazz musicians claim that they can play more excitingly under the influence than without; in simple—but musically sterile—laboratory tests of note identification and beat duration, their performance is worse on the drug."[31] What often happens is that the person "thinks" he is better at performing tasks than he is by any objective criterion. This is a result of the psychological lift and optimistic interpretation marijuana generally induces in the user.

Pet and Ball write that there is no evidence that marijuana increases sexual potency. However, no studies have been discovered by the writer that specifically relate the use of marijuana to sexual reactions. Many people who have had sexual activities under the influence of marijuana will argue that it is a more erotic and exciting experience. It may be that the loss of inhibitions makes them feel that such is the case. We have also been told by a number of men and women that they physically feel sexually more responsive. Whether there is a physiological heightening of sexual response, or whether it may be explained entirely on psychological grounds is not known.

In a recent study 302 selected professionals who were involved in research of some kind with psychedelic drugs were asked a series of questions. They were asked to assess the danger to the user's mental health from marijuana. Six percent said "very much," 22 percent "somewhat," 33 percent "only in rare cases," 21 percent "none," and 17 percent said "insufficient evidence." Fifty-nine percent of the researchers felt that marijuana should be at least as available as alcohol. Fifty-seven percent of the researchers regarded marijuana as less likely to cause genetic damage than such commonly used drugs as caffeine and tranquilizers.[32] These experts in general saw the risk level of marijuana as not very great.

There is no evidence that marijuana is a drug of addiction. There is also no evidence that marijuana has a direct causal relationship with criminal behavior in the sense that it leads the user to commit criminal acts. Most authorities have dismissed the lurid charges that have been a

---

[30] Nowlis, *op. cit.*, p. 96.

[31] Laurie, *op. cit.*, p. 85.

[32] Clark, Walter H. and G. Ray Funkhauser, "Physicians and Researchers Disagree on Psychedelic Drugs," *Psychology Today*, April, 1970, p. 50.

part of the traditional "marijuana menace." The current medical thinking is that "tolerance and physical dependence do not develop and withdrawal does not produce any abstinence syndrome."[33] Although the use of
marijuana is not seen as a cause of crime it is often associated with illegal
acts. "First, many persons who are otherwise delinquent or criminal may
also smoke marijuana. Second, marijuana use is often pursued in a hedonistic peer-group setting in which laws are violated. Third, use of more
dangerous drugs is frequently preceded by the use of marijuana."[34] The
link between the use of marijuana and hard drugs can be overdone. It is
obviously true that many addicts started out on marijuana, but many of
them also started out on cigarettes and alcohol.

The failure to link in a causal way the use of marijuana with drugs of
addiction is a fact that many young persons are fully aware of. For them,
the attempt by authorities to present a causal link where none exists makes
them suspicious and skeptical of statements that are true. For example,
when the Federal Bureau of Narcotics writes "that it cannot be too
strongly emphasized that the smoking of marijuana is a dangerous first
step on the road which usually leads to enslavement by heroin" many
persons know that scientific knowledge does not support this kind of
assertion and they often become distrusting.

Under the federal law in the United States, to give or to sell marijuana
is a felony, which is a serious crime. The federal government and most
states deal with marijuana just as severely as if it were a narcotic. The
federal penalty for possessing the drug is 2 to 10 years imprisonment for
the first offense, 5 to 10 years for the second offense, and 10 to 40 years
for further offenses. There may also be fines up to $20,000 for the first or
subsequent offenses. For the transfer or sale of the drug, the first offense
may bring a 5- to 20-year sentence and a fine up to $20,000. If a person
over 18 sells to a minor under 18 years of age, he is subject to a fine of up
to $20,000 and/or 10 to 40 years in prison for the first offense, with no
suspension of sentence, probation, or parole. The various state penalties
are also very severe. In some states sentences are mandatory and probation
and parole are denied. In several states the penalty for the sale of marijuana to a minor is death.[35]

The severity of penalties is considered by many experts to be out of
line considering the effects of marijuana. The degree of danger and the
lethal effects from the use of alcohol and tobacco are as high as or even
higher than from the use of marijuana.[36] Yet, young people are often
picked up for having marijuana and the result is that many of them are

---

[33] Wakefield, Dan, *The Addict* (New York: Gold Medal Books, 1963), p. 18.

[34] Pet and Ball, *op. cit.*

[35] Nowlis, *op. cit.*, p. 33.

[36] Sebald, Hans, *Adolescence: A Sociological Analysis* (New York: Appleton-
Century-Crofts, 1968), p. 490.

legally defined as "narcotic" offenders. This charge goes onto their records and they are lumped together with the users of the far more serious drugs of addiction. This distinction is seen in the alleged increase in narcotics users in the United States. For example, in California, from 1962 to 1966 non-marijuana arrests for narcotics and other dangerous drugs remained about the same, "but marijuana arrests for adults increased from 3,291 to 14,293 and for juveniles from 284 to 3,869. These enormous increases are not spread equally throughout the population but are concentrated among the young and the white."[37] As a result the mass media tend to present a picture of drug addiction as concentrated among members of the young, white middle class. But this is inaccurate because their drug is non-addictive. This is not to say there is not an addiction problem in this group, but rather that it is not of the scope that the figures on narcotic arrests among the young would lead persons to believe. The figures reflect the general error of lumping users of drugs of addiction and those of non-addiction. This fails to distinguish the real drug problem, which is the use of drugs of addiction, rather than the general use of drugs.

LSD (LYSERGIC ACID DIETHYLAMIDE)

LSD is an odorless, colorless, and tasteless drug that is taken in very small amounts. It is a powerful man-made chemical that was first developed in 1938 from one of the ergot alkaloids. Ergot is a fungus that grows as a rust on rye. LSD is so powerful that one ounce is enough to provide 300,000 average doses. It is legally classified as a hallucinogen. The story of LSD in the United States begins in 1949 with the first shipment to a Boston psychiatrist for the possible treatment of mental illness. At first there were no legal controls on LSD, but in 1963 the American Medical Association asked for an editorial on LSD from Harvard University campus physician Dr. Dana L. Farnsworth. He wrote, in effect, that he thought that legal restrictions should be imposed on LSD.[38]

There is a belief that LSD is cheap and easy to produce, but such is not the case. It takes the investment of a lot of time and several thousand dollars to produce even poor grade LSD. Obtaining the lysergic acid is also a problem. As a result, while "LSD is not scarce, it requires considerable skill to make it, considerable financing to set up the lab, and fairly good contacts to get the raw ingredients."[39]

The effects of LSD are important because it is the most powerful mind-affecting substance known. However, the observable effects are slight and

[37] Carey, James T., *The College Drug Scene* (Englewood Cliffs, N.J.: Prentice-Hall, 1968), p. 44.

[38] Young and Hixson, *op. cit.*, p. 11.

[39] Carey, *op. cit.*, p. 34.

it is often not easy to tell that a person is on LSD. The most noticeable effects are usually goose pimples and enlarged irises. Of all the effects, the perceptual changes are probably the most dramatic. Of the senses, vision seems to be the most affected. Objects and patterns appear to come alive and shift or become wavy, colors may seem very vivid, intense, and beautiful. White light may seem much brighter with numerous colors surrounding it. Also a person's smell, taste, hearing, and touch may seem more acute. Even the experience of hearing music may seem more intense than ever before. However, true hallucinations are relatively rare.[40] Other related effects that LSD has on some people may be that walls appear to move or they "see" unusual patterns unfolding in front of their eyes. It may also appear that flat objects become three dimensional. In some instances one sensory impression may pass over into another and sounds appear as colors, or colors may appear to have a taste.

The subjective effects of LSD are what make the use of the drug so attractive to most users. It is therefore useful to list some of the main effects that LSD has on users. First, as suggested, the sense perceptions are perceived more strongly. Second, the mechanism that relates one sense impression to another is altered so that a person touching himself may find it difficult to be sure that it is *his* hand touching *his* leg. Third, the relationship between current sense impressions and past ones is eliminated so that one sees things as if for the first time. Fourth, muscular coordination and pain perception are often reduced. Fifth, personality tests indicate that learned patterns of behavior, logical thinking, and role playing that allow persons to function as social beings may dissolve away. Sixth, emotional repressions are altered and one often behaves more fundamentally. For example, people often become more sensitive to each other's personalities.[41] Yet, with all the descriptions of LSD "trips" it must be recognized that many never "see" what others do. In any listing of LSD "trips" there are those who say it was "the greatest experience of my creative life" or "a living hell I'll never forget," "restoring my vision of the infinite" or "a shattering nightmare."[42]

What are the dangers of LSD? Recently 302 persons who were professionals involved in some kind of research with LSD were asked if they believed there was a danger to the mental health of those taking LSD. Forty percent answered "very much," 32 percent "somewhat," and 20 percent "only in rare cases." This indicates that most experts define LSD as at least potentially dangerous. However, 59 percent of the researchers said the danger of LSD type drugs to chromosomes had been exaggerated.[43]

---

[40] Nowlis, *op. cit.*, p. 104.

[41] Laurie, *op. cit.*, pp. 99–100.

[42] Young and Hixson, *op. cit.*, p. 31.

[43] Clark and Funkhauser, *op. cit.*, p. 50.

There are four rough categories of danger when LSD is used without close medical supervision. First, there may be panic reactions as the user feels he cannot stop the drug's action and he may as a result feel that he is losing his mind. The panic reaction usually subsides after eight to twelve hours. Second, there may be a feeling of paranoia where the user becomes increasingly suspicious and feels that someone is trying to harm him or control his thinking. This feeling often lasts for about three days after the drug has worn off. Third, for days, weeks, and even months after the person has stopped taking LSD there may be recurrences of LSD-type perceptual phenomena for brief moments. Fourth, there are some accidental deaths. For example, the user may feel that he can fly, and jump off a high building to his death. Although this happens, it is not common, and the incidence may range from one in one thousand "trips" to one in ten thousand trips.[44] How many deaths there are from LSD use is unknown because there is no way to distinguish conscious suicides from those deaths where the person thought he could fly. Another danger of LSD is that psychosis following its use has been verified. However, with all the dangers, LSD is not a drug of addiction.

The present legal controls over LSD in the United States are very strong. In 1965 a federal law was passed that gave federal narcotic agents increased power to seek out and arrest pushers of LSD and other hallucinogenic drugs. There are also stronger penalties, including longer jail sentences and heavier fines, for those caught distributing hallucinogenic drugs. In 1968, even stricter federal laws were passed. By 1968 about half of the states had enacted legislation against the possession of LSD. The federal law gives with a conviction a fine of $1,000 to $10,000 and/or imprisonment for up to 5 years. For persons over 18 years of age who sell or give drugs to anyone under 21, the law provides penalties of 10 to 15 years in jail and fines up to $20,000. Merely the illegal possession of LSD can bring a fine of from $1,000 to $10,000 and/or 1 to 3 years in prison. And some of the state laws are even more severe.

DRUGS OF ADDICTION

This group of drugs is also called opiates. They are drugs with pain-killing and euphoria-producing properties and include chemicals derived from or which are the equivalent of opium. The best known are morphine and heroin. The term narcotics is also often used to describe the opiates. The addiction implies a physical dependence that is far more than just habit or some vague emotional craving. The morphine or heroin addict's organism depends on a regular supply of the chemical just as a normal organism depends on the regular supply of important vitamins.[45] In this

---

[44] Fort, *op. cit.*, p. 24.
[45] Sebald, *op. cit.*, p. 459.

section the interest is limited to heroin and morphine. Heroin is one of the opiates, which are derivatives of synthetics of opium, and is classified as a depressant. Heroin can be purchased in the United States only through illegal markets. Therefore, people addicted to it are engaged from the first shot in what they know to be an illegal activity. The second most common drug of addiction is morphine and it is similar in its effects to heroin. But many people who become addicted to morphine develop their addiction unknowingly, often through the medical use of it as a pain killer. In fact a number of physicians become addicted to morphine, a drug which they have access to. Often the morphine addict, with no legitimate sources to get that drug, may get pushed into the illegal drug market to meet his addiction.[46]

Morphine and heroin are depressants and this is contrary to the misconception that an addict is dangerously "hopped up." Actually these drugs produce a general lowering of the level of nervous and other bodily activity.[47] Also there are no known organic diseases associated with chronic opiate addiction as is often found with alcohol addiction, cigarette smoking, and even chronic overeating. "Although opiate use does produce such effects as pupillary constriction, constipation, and sexual impotence, none of these conditions need be fully disabling, nor are they permanent."[48] The great danger with drugs of addiction is not what is done organically but rather the consequences of drug addiction for the person. The extreme physical and psychological need for the drug means that the addict will usually do most anything to meet his needs, and this is often what is most harmful.

The legal controls over the sales of narcotics are very strong. The illegal possession of narcotics is punishable by sentences that can range from 2 to 10 years for the first offense, 5 to 20 years for the second, and 10 to 20 years for further offenses. The illegal sale of narcotics can mean a fine of $20,000 and a jail sentence of 5 to 20 years for the offense, and 10 to 40 years for further offenses. A person who sells narcotics to someone under 18 is refused parole and probation, even for the first offense. If the drug is heroin, he can be sentenced to life imprisonment or to death.

THE "CAUSES" OF DRUG USE

In this section the interest is in the "causes" of drug addiction, not only why one becomes a drug addict but also how it takes place. The first interest is in the process of drug addiction. There is a great difference between using something that is addictive and something that becomes

---

[46] Wakefield, op. cit., pp. 16–17.

[47] Schur, op. cit., p. 120.

[48] Ibid., p. 121.

habit forming. A habit is primarily mental and emotional—the smoker's desire for a cigarette, the drinker's desire for a cocktail. However, addiction is as physical, as urgent, and as implacable as a man's need for water.[49] One study of young addicts suggested that three conditions were necessary for them to emerge as addicts: first, a psychological and predisposing inadequacy on their parts; second, a crisis that occurred in their lives; and third, the timely offer of drugs.[50] Of course, those same conditions might have led the young person to getting drunk for the first time, but what appears to be crucial is a state of readiness and the availability of the drug. When one first takes drugs there may be some positive feelings in one's reactions to the drugs but this seems to last only during the early stages of addiction. "In the later stages, a reversal of effects occurs, in which the drug is no longer taken primarily to obtain positive pleasure but rather to avoid the negative effects of withdrawal."[51]

As suggested, some addicts who get started on morphine without their knowledge may wind up as addicts against their wills. But others do make a conscious move toward addiction. It takes a deliberate act to become addicted to heroin and a first step is taken possibly because of a feeling of uselessness and despair. But the addict must see some positive hope through his involvement in drugs; "to him, if to no one else, they offer some improvement to his present condition."[52] It would seem that few non-addicts could ever anticipate what it means to become an addict. For most who try narcotics there is undoubtedly an exaggerated expectation of what they will gain and an unrealistic anticipation of what the costs will be. It is often only when it is too late that an accurate understanding takes place.

Alfred Lindesmith has explained how drug addiction occurs in part as essentially a "naming process." This is best illustrated by the morphine addict that emerges from medical treatment. A person given morphine while in a hospital to relieve pain will find that when the drug is stopped he will suffer severe withdrawal symptoms. That is, his body will become extremely painful. In this situation the crucial point is whether he defines the pain as caused by his no longer receiving the drug. If he does, he is "naming" his physical distress as being caused by the lack of morphine. He is then hooked and will do everything possible to get the drug to relieve the painful withdrawal symptoms. The person who turns to heroin initially and then stops suffers the same kind of withdrawal pains and "names" the cause in the same way. For Lindesmith the initial causes

---

[49] De Lapp, Robert S., "Torture by Drugs," in Dan Wakefield, *The Addict* (New York: Gold Medal Books, 1963), pp. 43–44.

[50] Laurie, *op. cit.*, pp. 38–39.

[51] Schur, *op. cit.*, p. 122.

[52] Laurie, *op. cit.*, p. 46.

may be many but the motive to maintain the drug habit is the relief of the pain.[53]

The most difficult question is why people consciously turn to the drugs of addiction, especially in light of all the negative publicity about those drugs. There are some persons who see the use of drugs as the means of finding their sense of identity. Laurie suggests that it is unfortunate that "this motive is likely to be most compelling for just those inadequate, unsure, standardless personalities who seem to be particularly susceptible to drug dependence."[54] The availability of drugs does not seem to be too important in the formation of drug addiction. Almost all studies show that people who become drug addicts do so because of personality factors rather than the availability of the drugs. That is, drug addiction is a symptom of some need rather than a disease. A part of the personality training may derive from socialization experiences to the use of drugs. One study pointed out that users of drugs of addiction, in contrast to non-users, had been ill more often as children, had been taken more often to a physician, and had been given more medications.[55]

There is no single cause for becoming an addict, as there is no single type of addict. For example, the physician who becomes an addict is very different from the lower class black subculture member who is a part of a delinquent and addict subculture. "However, individuals in certain socioeconomic categories run a relatively greater risk of encountering and using narcotics than do those in other categories. Also, it seems likely that of those individuals in the high-risk categories it is the more troubled or the more disadvantaged, situationally, who are especially likely to take up drugs."[56] Addiction is not distributed around the United States in a random fashion. Broadly it exists where there is social and economic squalor and the opportunity to get drugs. There is a "southern pattern" which is a survival from the early part of the century. This is found in Alabama, Georgia, and Kentucky where the addicts are about 90 percent white, middle aged, and using old morphine mixtures. By contrast the modern pattern is to use imported heroin and this is found in New York, Puerto Rico, the District of Columbia, and Chicago. There two-thirds of the addicts are black or Puerto Rican and their average age is about 27. There is also a narrower belt of heroin users emerging along the Mexican border in Arizona, New Mexico, and Texas.[57] Almost all of these groups have to resort to illegal ways of getting the money to support their drug habit.

Sociologically the studies clearly show a relationship between poverty

---

[53] Lindesmith, Alfred, *Opiate Addiction* (Bloomington, Indiana: Principia Press), 1947.

[54] Laurie, *op. cit.*, pp. 49–50.

[55] Nowles, *op. cit.*, p. 24.

[56] Schur, *op. cit.*, pp. 128–29.

[57] Laurie, *op. cit.*, p. 30.

and drug addiction. Addiction comes in a setting where many other social problems also exist. The slum areas are also characterized by high rates of delinquency, dropping out of school, truancy, unemployment, family disintegration, poverty, and so forth. But drug addiction is not characteristically filled by the young. In the mid-1960's the number of known drug addicts in the United States was reported to be between 50,000 and 60,000. Of those addicts about 3 or 4 percent were under 21 years of age. So narcotic addiction, especially with reference to the use of heroin, is far more an adult than an adolescent problem.[58]

Drug Addiction "Cures"

The great concern with drug addiction as a social and psychological problem has resulted in many attempts to find solutions. At the same time there is often indifference or even hostility directed at the drug addict. Schur suggests that the American treatment of drug addicts may in part be attributed to the addict's serving as a conventional scapegoat—"one more enemy in the perpetual battle against crime and immorality of which Americans seem so fond."[59] It is probable that most Americans believe that the drug addict could cure himself if he would only put his mind to it. It is believed that for some reason, being lazy, or sinful, or irresponsible, he will not take the responsibility of curing himself. But those persons who work with drug addicts know that addiction is very powerful and strong, and often severe methods are needed if the addict is ever to be cured. When a person stops taking drugs his problem is usually just starting—the problem of staying off drugs.

This problem has been well documented in the research of Ray in the study of the drug abstainer caught between continued abstinence and a relapse back into drug use. Stopping addiction often means major life style changes, the leaving of a way of life. So often in the early phases of an episode of cure, the drug abstainer may show considerable ambivalence about where he stands in the addict and non-addict social situation.[60] The tendency for him to relapse occurs if he develops an image of himself as socially different from non-addicts, and actual relapse occurs when he redefines himself as an addict. "It is at this point, when the old values and old meanings he experienced as an addict are still immediate and the new ordering of his experience without narcotics not well established, that the ex-addict seems most vulnerable to relapse."[61]

---

[58] Sebald, *op. cit.*, p. 465.

[59] Schur, Edwin M., "The British System" in Dan Wakefield, *The Addict* (New York: Gold Medal Books, 1963), p. 158.

[60] Ray, Marsh, "Abstinence Cycles and Heroin Addicts," in Earl Rubington and Martin S. Weinberg, *Deviance: The Interactionist Perspective* (New York: Macmillan Co., 1968), p. 402.

[61] *Ibid.*, p. 403.

One of the problems for the ex-addict is to try to adjust to his new role of how others view him. This is because the addict has established an image of himself in the eyes of others who knew him as an addict—members of his family, social workers, law enforcement officers, physicians, and so forth. Through their gestures the non-addicts indicate suspicion toward the addict as to his right to participate in their worlds. And in his contacts with non-addicts the former addict is highly sensitive to their cues. The non-addicts have their expectations about the abstainer's future conduct. In general they exhibit skepticism concerning his "cure" and success for his future. Often when the abstainer becomes an addict again he has redefined himself as an addict and has as a consequence the actions necessary for relapse. "But it should be noted that the seeds of a new attempt at abstinence are sown, once addiction has been reestablished, in the self-recrimination engaged in upon remembrance of a successful period of abstinence."[62] Ray's study suggests that whatever the approach to a cure for many addicts they have the expectation of failure.

We next look at two social settings where cures are attempted in working with drug addiction. One is in the federal hospitals and the other is the Synanon approach.

FEDERAL HOSPITALS

There are two United States Public Health Service psychiatric hospitals, one at Lexington, Kentucky opened in 1935 and the other at Fort Worth, Texas opened in 1938. The two hospitals treat both voluntary and convict addict populations. About 90 percent of the patients enter voluntarily. The program is one of detoxification in a stable controlled environment with some therapy. The average length of stay is about six weeks and about 10 percent remain free of drugs for the first year after their release.

Over the years there has been a change in some characteristics of the patients. For example, the patients have become increasingly younger. In 1937 less than one male patient in five was under 30, while in 1962 almost half were. Most addicts admitted to the hospitals are using heroin, but many are also on barbituates. Some have become used to barbituates because of police control of heroin. "Occasionally mystified patients at Lexington find that they are not really heroin addicts at all; their suppliers have them fooled—and hooked them on an alien drug of low status."[63]

The rate of long range success in the federal hospital attempts to cure drug addiction is not high. The most favorable estimates suggest a cured rate of around 25 percent, but the less optimistic estimates place success at 5 to 10 percent.[64] These low rates indicate the difficulty of changing,

---

[62] *Ibid.*, p. 407.

[63] Laurie, *op. cit.*, p. 65.

[64] Schur, *Crimes without Victims, op. cit.*, p. 146.

through conventional medical procedures, what to the drug addict is often a way of life. "On his return to the community, the treated addict faces many of the same sorts of difficulties experienced by the former convict; lack of understanding among relatives and nonaddict friends, inability to obtain a decent job, reinvolvement in the very cultural climate and interpersonal associations which may have led him into the deviance in the first place."[65] There is also the problem that when the addict is in Lexington undergoing treatment he is at the same time having experiences that undercut the purpose of the institution. That is, he is interacting with and being influenced by other drug addicts. The conversation of their world is almost completely about narcotics. "Rather than being weaned away from the world of drugs, the patient may thus experience a strengthening and reinforcement of his identification with that world."[66]

The two federal hospitals are limited in the number of patients they can handle, and because for most addicts it is voluntary and short internment, they are often limited to pursuing their remedial treatments. But as suggested, even when they are able to bring about full treatment the rate of success over a period of time is not very great. This approach is probably best viewed as a stop-gap measure, rather than an established treatment pattern which should be applied on a much larger scale. We next look at a second, and very different, approach to "curing" drug addicts.

SYNANON

This approach has received a great deal of publicity through the mass media although it has only been tried on a small number of drug addicts. But as will be seen the methods are dramatic and therefore prone to receive interested response and some sensationalism. Synanon has its origins with AA (Alcoholics Anonymous), of which its founder was a member and ex-alcoholic (but not an ex-drug addict). Not long after its start the organization left the alcoholics and became fully involved with drug addicts, and Synanon was founded in May, 1958. One writer points out that it is ironic that the dominate person in Synanon was never a drug addict, which contradicts the Alcoholics Anonymous type of slogan, "Only an addict can help an addict."[67]

Admission into a Synanon house appears to have two principal functions. First, the newcomer is forced to admit, at least on the verbal level, that he is willing to try to conform to the norms of the group he is entering. He knows that the members will tolerate no liking for drugs nor drug

---

[65] *Ibid.*, p. 146.

[66] *Ibid.*, p. 150.

[67] Sagarin, Edward, *Odd Man in Societies of Deviants in America* (Chicago: Quadrangle Books, 1969), p. 143.

addicts. From the moment he enters the door of the house he is tested as to his willingness to conform to *all* the demands made on him by the members of Synanon. For example, he has to have his hair cut off, give up all of his money, and sever all family ties. The second function is that the admission process seems to weed out those who simply want to rest for a few days, to get a free place to stay, or to keep out of the hands of the police. So the new person is expected to want to completely stop his drug addiction. "This means that he must *say* that he wants to quit using drugs once and for all, in order to realize his potentials as an adult; he must not indicate that he merely wants a convenient place in which to go through withdrawal distress so that he can be rid of his habit for a short time because he has lost his connection, or for some other reason."[68]

The most difficult requirement for the entering addict into Synanon is that he must withdraw "cold turkey"—simply stop using drugs without any possible medical help. If he is able to stop he must live in the community for a minimum of two years. The main feature of the actual treatment is the seminars, where the members meet in small groups several times a week and subject each other to extreme criticism, abuse, and ridicule. The members of each seminar are rotated so that all members of the community come under fire from one another. What this means is that Synanon is like "a mental institution, a prison, or a nineteenth century American utopian community in that one's entire life is lived within its walls. Like monks and nuns, the members give themselves over to the place, but the keys to the doors are always in their hands."[69]

What is nearly unique to the Synanon treatment of the person is that he is treated almost as a non-human and is made to feel completely worthless. This technique is the opposite of the therapy approach where the subject is told that the basis of his problem is his lack of feeling as to his own self worth. In that kind of approach, which is the most common one, he is made to believe that he is a worthwhile person and that his problem comes primarily from the fact that he has failed to realize that. But at Synanon just the opposite occurs as the person's self-contempt and self-hate are developed.[70] The lowness of his worth is drummed into him from the very beginning. The newcomer starts by cleaning out toilets and works his way up to doing the dishes. And at every point those above him are constantly demeaning him to insure his continued humility and debasement.

The beginner in Synanon learns how he is viewed under the most personally painful circumstances. That is when he is trying to "kick" his drug

---

[68] Volkman, Rita and Donald R. Cressey, "Differential Association and the Rehabilitation of Drug Addicts," in Earl Rubington and Martin S. Weinberg, *Deviance: The Interactionist Approach* (New York: Macmillan Co., 1968), p. 411.

[69] Sagarin, *op. cit.*, pp. 143–44.

[70] *Ibid.*, p. 148.

addiction through the "cold turkey" method. He "kicks" on a davenport in the center of a large living room out in the open. Life in the house goes on around him. He learns that his sickness is not important to the men and women who have themselves "kicked" the habit. "In the living room, one or two couples might be dancing, five or six people may be arguing, a man may be practicing the guitar and a girl may be ironing. The kicking addict learns his lesson; these others have made it."[71]

As his treatment moves along the new member of Synanon learns the strong taboos of the group, especially those against drugs and crime. There is a strong taboo against "street talk." For example, how it feels to have a fix, various drug connections, where one took his shoots, or his old drug using associates. Also one must never identify with the criminal "code of the streets" where one is supposed to keep quiet about the criminal activities of his peers. And to even refer to a common citizen as a "square" may lead to a spontaneous lecture, "in heated and colorful terms, on the notion that the people who are *really* square are those that go around as bums sticking needles in their arms."[72] The member is also expected to report any violations of rules by the other members. And if he does not report, and it is found out, more pressure will be put on him than upon the violator, because it is assumed that he knows better. "Thus, for perhaps the first time in his life he will be censured for *not* 'squealing' rather than for 'squealing.' "[73]

The member of Synanon also quickly learns that he has no private self in that others grant him no privacy. The behavior of all members is visible to all others. Not only is what he does seen, but it may also be openly discussed. For example, he may do something one day that will be brought up and discussed the next day during his seminar (or synanon). "The synanon sessions differ from everyday honesty by virtue of the fact that in these discussions one is expected to *insist on* the truth as well as to tell the truth. Any weapon, such as ridicule, cross-examination, or hostile attack, is both permissible and expected."[74]

Synanon has a clearly stated program for distributing the status symbols to the members in return for their conforming to the values of the community. The Synanon experience is organized into a career of roles that represent stages of graded competence. And at the peak are those roles that might later be used in the broader society. Because the member does not have the status of "inmate" or "patient" as in a prison or hospital, he can achieve any position in the status hierarchy. But no member can go up the status ladder unless his "attitude" is correct, no matter what de-

---

[71] Volkman and Cressey, *op. cit.*, p. 415.
[72] *Ibid.*, p. 413.
[73] *Ibid.*
[74] *Ibid.*, p. 429.

grees of skill he might have.[75] So any success must be achieved within the context of total conformity to the values of the Synanon program and individual initiative is of negative value.

The response to the Synanon program usually draws forth strong support or severe criticism. Many have argued that it reaches only a few and doesn't work for many of those. But the leaders of Synanon do not claim to "cure" drug addicts. The contribution that this program makes is that it helps some to stay away from drugs. The statistics on dropouts suggest that the group relations method does not begin to have effect until newcomers are fully integrated into the antidrug, anticrime value system that is Synanon. This means that great time and expense is needed to help those few who are able to stay on and be aided.

It has been argued that in reality the members have substituted a dependence on Synanon to replace their dependence on drugs. Therefore it has been suggested that the program should be seen as a protective community rather than a truly therapeutic community aimed at the eventual reintegration of the patient with the outside world.[76] A more critical view of Synanon has been taken by Sagarin. He suggests that because Synanon is so hostile to the outside world the members develop no real will to get out. Therefore, it may be that Synanon has modified the Alcoholics Anonymous type statement "once an addict always an addict," to "once an addict to narcotics, always an addict to Synanon." It is a convenient modification, one similar to AA's statement that "alcoholism cannot be cured, and one which performs the same function; to keep the individuals tied to the organization, thus preserving its present state and insuring its further growth."[77]

METHADONE

One attempt at curing drug addiction has been through the methadone approach. This approach is based on the fact that sometimes one drug can be substituted for another without producing increased addiction. This approach was used a number of years ago with heroin before it was recognized as a drug of addiction. It was substituted for morphine. Methadone is a synthetic and less active opiate than heroin, and is given to the drug user in decreasing doses. Most of the work with this approach has been done in New York City where applicants are voluntarily hospitalized for six weeks after being examined by physicians and psychiatrists. They are given methadone after their discharge and they are usually still dependent on methadone but no longer on heroin. There is evidence that

---

[75] *Ibid.*, p. 416.

[76] Schur, *op. cit.*, p. 149.

[77] Sagarin, *op. cit.*, p. 158.

the rehabilitation rate is much higher as a result of the methadone approach than through any other treatment program.

However, this approach is still highly controversial and has especially drawn strong opposition from law enforcement groups because in most cases this approach does not resolve the addiction problem but substitutes a legal drug for an illegal one. This is what bothers many law enforcement agencies—because their vested interest is in drug addicts and not with what makes them addicts. Another point of view is that methadone has helped to alleviate the problem by allowing the person to function without the results of increased addiction and thereby helping him become more a productive member of society.

DRUG SUBCULTURES

In this section the interest is in various social settings where persons use drugs. There are some drug addicts who have little or no contact with drug users or drug pushers. For example, one study of physician addicts found they rarely associated with other physician addicts. "They did not have any occasion for doing so, either for the purpose of getting drugs or for passing time or for emotional support. They were solitary about their addiction."[78] However, we will look at several types of drug subcultures, and while they have some factors in common, they are also different in many important ways. The three to be discussed are the addict subculture, marijuana users, and LSD in the college subculture. There are a number of characteristics that all three of these have in common. They typically participate in a group setting with persons they know well rather than with strangers. These relationships usually last for some time. There develops some consensus of values and social cohesion with greater and greater group involvement. The participants view their activity as an important basis for their own identity. "They define themselves, as well as others, partly on the basis of whether they have participated in the drug activity or not."[79] These are values common to many subcultures discussed in this book. Of course, the strength of the subculture for its members will vary widely and one would expect it to be much stronger for the addict than for the marijuana user or the LSD group on college campuses. This difference is predicated on the fact that the addict has a much greater personal commitment and need in his use of his drugs. The various subcultures have contact with many people who are not a part of it. For example, in all high drug-use neighborhoods non-using "squares" live alongside of addicts. And even though drug distribution is closely related

[78] Winick, Charles, "Physician Narcotic Addicts," in Howard S. Becker, *The Other Side* (New York: The Free Press, 1964), p. 267.

[79] Goode, Erich, "Multiple Drug Use among Marijuana Smokers," *Social Problems*, 1969, p. 54.

to the underworld, delinquent gangs as such are not a major factor in promotion of addiction.[80]

THE ADDICT SUBCULTURE

It has been pointed out that the subculture of the drug addict has its symbols of status, its mythology, and to some extent its own language. For example, a "pusher" is one who sells drugs, a "fix" is a drug dose, "horse" is heroin, and so forth. This helps create social solidarity among addicts toward their being outcasts from the broader society. "The addict acquires skills at the necessary transactions to secure drug supplies, often including the skills of some type of professional criminal activity to provide a source of funds for purchasing supplies."[81] Important to all subcultures is the development of rationales to explain who they are to themselves and to boost their morale and lessen their feeling of being isolated. Schur suggests that "drug addicts, like homosexuals, benefit psychologically from knowledge of and contact with others who share his plight."[82]

Regardless of the patterns of interaction that develop in the addict's subculture the reason for its existence is simple—the getting of drugs. His relation to drug sources is the overriding force determining his subcultural membership. "This point is borne out by the experience in Britain, where the availability of drugs eliminates the need for addicts to involve themselves in underworld distribution processes and thus prevents the significant development of an addict subculture."[83] The subculture gives the addict some insurance that he will have contact with several potential sources of narcotics, in case his usual source of supply is blocked. He must be known by others to be an addict in case he needs to approach them for drugs, or for an introduction to a new source of drugs. It is possible that of all deviant subcultures that of the drug addict may be the most utilitarian.

As indicated, very important to the addict subculture are the sellers or pushers of drugs. In one sense they have the ideal product to sell—one where there is always a seller's market with buyer demand based on extreme need and compulsion. They can push their prices to an upper limit because they know the buyers must have what they sell. Schur suggests that in the American system of drug traffic there are at least four classes of sellers. There are *importers* who bring the drugs into the country, and these people are rarely themselves drug addicts. There are the professional *wholesalers* of the drugs, and they too are rarely addicts. Then there are

---

[80] Schur, *op. cit.*, p. 144.
[81] Clausen, *op. cit.*, p. 221.
[82] Schur, *op. cit.*, p. 140.
[83] *Ibid.*, pp. 144–45.

the *peddlers* who may be addicted, and the *pushers* who sell drugs to get the money for their own drug supplies.[84]

The subculture of the addict is illegal because addicts use drugs that are illegal and also because they usually pursue illegal means of getting money to buy the drugs. However, there is no known drug that by itself can be shown to cause crime.[85] In fact the use of drugs may have a negative consequence with regard to most types of crime. For example, in a statement from a joint committee of the American Medical Association and the American Bar Association it is stated that: "Crimes of violence are rarely, and sexual crimes are almost never, committed by addicts. In most instances the addict's sins are those of omission rather than commission; they are ineffective people, individuals whose great desire is to withdraw from the world and its troubles into a land of dreams."[86] As Schur points out, the specific effects of opiates tend to decrease the likelihood of any violent antisocial behavior. Opiates bring about a reduction in sexual desire and long term addiction usually results in impotence.[87]

With the exception of a few physician addicts and some others who have the money, all other addicts in the United States must enter into the subcultural world where the distribution of illegal drugs takes place. The addict is by necessity thrown into contact with drug peddlers and pushers. When crimes are committed by addicts they are usually undertaken to buy illegal drugs. Once again Great Britain provides a contrast because there the addict can get his drugs legally and there is almost no crime associated with drug addiction.[88] In the United States the amount of money needed is great because for some addicts their drug cost may run to a hundred dollars a day.

It is probable that most addicts seek out a subculture as soon as they are hooked because they need the drugs. Just looking for illegal sources of drugs will mean they are usually moving into subcultural contacts. There is a belief that pushers look for non-addicts to hook them and thereby build a market, but this is probably not common. Usually the addict is first introduced to drugs by friends, and after being hooked needs to find a pusher. One writer points out that to hand out free or cheap drugs randomly and hope to hook customers would be uneconomical as well as dangerous because there would be nothing to stop that person from betraying his drug supplier.[89] Between the addict and his drug source there is a vested interest on both their parts to keep away from the police.

As suggested, the subcultural world of the addict has some social system and patterns of defined behavior. Of importance to all subcultures is

---

[84] *Ibid.*, p. 137.
[85] Blum, *op. cit.*, p. 290.
[86] Wakefield, *op. cit.*, p. 9.
[87] Schur, *op. cit.*, p. 121.
[88] *Ibid.*, p. 138.
[89] Laurie, *op. cit.*, p. 33.

the transmission of information. In addict subcultures information about the police, about what kinds of drugs are available, and where to get them is passed on. Information may be sifted out according to consensus concerning the general reliability of various individuals. "In particular, there is a belief that informers can be spotted so that they can be excluded from the grapevine. In some periods, information can be so valuable that it is paid for by the addicted."[90] The accuracy and reliability of the grapevine and general sources of information are basic to the survival of the members and they all have a vested interest in its maintenance.

Because the addict is a deviant and feels rejected by the broader society he turns more and more to the subculture. At the same time the more deeply involved he becomes with drugs the less likely it is for him to associate with straight people. So the gradual immersion of drug addicts in their subcultures is interwoven with the general process by which they have been rejected by the broader "respectable" society. The social image of the addict as a criminal influences both his behavior and his self image. It is of interest that although the physician-addict and the subcultural-type addict are addicted in exactly the same way, their self images are generally very different.[91] Schur also points out that there is a self-fulfilling prophecy which the drug addict gets caught up in. He is aware that respectable people see him as a criminal and he begins to see himself acting as one. As a result he more and more must turn to the drug world for interpersonal support as well as for drug supplies. And as the need to support his habit occupies more and more of his time and energy and as his other worlds recede into the background or fade away completely, addiction becomes a way of life.[92] As the addict becomes more and more immersed in meeting his drug need he often becomes careless about his personal appearance and cleanliness. Consequently, non-addicts may come to define him as a bum and, because he continues to use drugs, conclude that he has no will power or is even a degenerate. The addict is aware of these definitions, and while he may attempt to reject them that may be hard to do because he in part believes them. "They assume importance because they are the medium of exchange in social transactions with the addict and non-addict world in which the addict identifies himself as an object and judges himself in relation to addict and non-addict values."[93]

MARIJUANA USERS

The subcultures that develop here do not have the significance that they do for the addicts, because while the drug used is illegal it is not a

---

[90] Schur, *op. cit.*, p. 143.

[91] *Ibid.*, p. 145.

[92] *Ibid.*

[93] Ray, *op. cit.*, p. 353.

drug of addiction. Therefore, the users do not have a severe need for a drug that is a highly expensive one. There is much less compulsion for marijuana and it is cheaper and easier to get legally. The subcultures develop around the group use of marijuana and their experimentation with it and other drugs.

The first experience with taking marijuana or being "turned on" is almost always a group experience. Goode's study found that only 3 percent in his sample were alone the first time they tried marijuana. Only 5 percent claimed they smoked at least half the time alone, and 45 percent said that they never smoked alone. Marijuana is not just smoked in groups, but it is smoked in intimate groups. "The others with whom one is smoking are overwhelmingly *significant* others."[94] Therefore, marijuana may be described as probably the most social of all drugs.

It is not usual for one to just start smoking marijuana and get high pleasure from it immediately. Rather, an individual will be able to use marijuana for pleasure only when he learns to see it as something that can be used for pleasure. Becker argues that no one becomes a user without first learning to smoke the drug in a way which will produce real effects. One must also learn to recognize the effects and connect them with the drug being used. In other words one must learn to get "high." Furthermore, the person must learn to enjoy the sensations he perceives. With time he develops an interest and motivation to use marijuana which he did not have when he first started. And on completion of this process he is willing and able to use marijuana for pleasure.[95]

Most people who use marijuana do not become heavy users. Using it once in a while does not inevitably lead to its frequent use. In fact, most users either discontinue use altogether, or continue to use it infrequently.[96] These people are not really a part of the marijuana subculture. This is much more common to the heavy marijuana users. Goode describes the consequences of heavy marijuana use. He points out that it implicates the individual in intense and involved social interaction with other heavy users. He also becomes involved in activities related to marijuana use. But most important, his chances are increased as to the likelihood of taking more drugs besides marijuana which the subculture approves of.[97] The most common other drug experimented with by the marijuana subculture is LSD. Of the 204 marijuana smokers Goode interviewed he found that about half had tried LSD. And those who had tried it usually only had one or two experiences. For this group LSD was not a drug of frequent

---

[94] Goode, *op. cit.*, p. 55.

[95] Becker, Howard S., "Becoming a Marijuana User," in Howard S. Becker, *Outsiders* (Glencoe, Ill.: The Free Press, 1963), p. 49.

[96] Goode, *op. cit.*, p. 62.

[97] *Ibid.*, pp. 57–58.

use. Probably more than any other drug in use, the dropoff after the first experience with LSD is precipitous. "There was typically little desire to continue beyond the experimental first few instances."[98] Goode says that experimentation with LSD is a mutual component, with heavy marijuana use, of many drug-using subcultures. In the group there is a certain degree of prestige in having tried a wide range and a large number of drugs.[99] Overall, two-thirds of Goode's respondents (young, white, urban, and high education) had taken at least one drug other than marijuana or hashish at least on one occasion. However, heroin was tried by only 13 percent of the sample, and even with that group extremely limited use was more common than repeated use.[100]

There has also been some evidence of marijuana usage as a subcultural phenomenon overlapping with other subcultures. For example, there has long been an overlap between being a jazz musician and the use of marijuana. In the early days of jazz, around the beginning of the present century in New Orleans, the stimulant most widely used was alcohol. It has been suggested that because alcohol traditionally leads to aggressive and loud behavior this is reflected in the aggressive and loud Dixieland jazz. But in the 1930's the stimulant most frequently used began to be marijuana. During that period jazz was increasingly rejected by the broader society and as a result many musicians grew more alienated. Winick goes on to point out that after World War II the use of heroin became more and more common and the effect is to make the user detached and "cool," which is also a description of much of the jazz of the post–World War II period.[101] It seems clear that drugs have been a part of the experimental music subcultures and continue to be today.

There are also studies that suggest that drug use may be a part of delinquent subculture patterns. Various studies have suggested a close development between drug use and delinquent gangs in the types of neighborhoods in which both would be found and the kind of group context in which both often occurred. This is not to say that gangs and drug use are inevitably related. Many boys who become users of "hard" drugs are less involved in the gang and its activities than are other members.[102] This distinction makes sense when it is kept in mind that marijuana is usually a group activity, while hard drugs are more often used individually and in private.

---

[98] *Ibid.*, p. 52.

[99] *Ibid.*, p. 60.

[100] *Ibid.*, p. 54.

[101] Winick, Charles, "The Use of Drugs by Jazz Musicians," in Walter A. Rushing, *Deviant Behavior and Social Process* (Chicago: Rand McNally and Co., 1969), p. 336.

[102] Short, James F. Jr., *Gang Delinquency and Delinquent Subcultures* (New York: Harper and Row, 1968), p. 108.

LSD in the College Subculture

In Chapter 15 there will be an extensive discussion of militant college students and there will be further discussion on their use of drugs. Here the interest is to briefly point out some factors related to the emergence of the college setting for the use of LSD. For a more detailed analysis of the subcultural characteristics of students the reader should turn to Chapter 15.

There is general agreement among most experts that the use of LSD is primarily located in and around many colleges and university campuses. There are two primary reasons suggested for this. One, the person who is inclined to try the hallucinogenic drugs is different from persons who use opiates or even alcohol. Taking hallucinogens is not so much an escapist habit as it is an act of curiosity and experimentation. The second reason is that knowledge about drugs as well as the substances themselves are more readily available in the campus setting.[103] How many college students there are who have tried LSD there is no way of knowing. It is no doubt more common in the larger, more prestigious schools than in the smaller and less prestigious places.

One researcher estimates that the LSD-type drugs, especially LSD itself, have probably been tried by a million people. However, they are probably being used with any regularity by only a small part, who are for the most part young and intellectually or mystically inclined middle-class persons. It is further suggested that probably no one has "dropped out" completely as a result of using LSD. Rather, it is more likely that individuals already frustrated with the society around them have, along with the use of LSD, disaffiliated themselves from conventional society.[104] But for many who use LSD, at least on occasion, there is a subculture in some respects. That is, the illicit use of LSD has become almost institutionalized. For example, there is a journal called the *Psychedelic Review*. There are also a number of semi-religious groups who use LSD. The best known has been the one centered around Timothy Leary, who has been in constant trouble with the legal authorities. He has, on at least some occasions, advised his followers to renounce the use of hallucinogens.[105] But the LSD subculture has developed a philosophy of its own and this reaches even to its own food and dress on some occasions. In some large cities there are specialized shops for equipment and streetside markets for the basic commodities. In fact there has even been a lecture circuit. It also has world famous leaders, its own martyrs and, "perhaps most significant of all, it has enemies in very high places."[106]

---

103 Sebald, *op. cit.*, p. 467.

104 Fort, *op. cit.*, p. 25.

105 Laurie, *op. cit.*, p. 124.

106 Young and Hixson, *op. cit.*, p. 12.

The federal government has attempted to influence the use of LSD on the college campuses. For example, in 1966 the Food and Drug Administration wrote to 2,000 colleges and universities asking them to institute various measures against the use of LSD such as inspection programs, special counseling, and so forth. But the college and university administrations, by and large, did not rush to cooperate with the federal agency.[107] There were two main reasons for this. One, the government in trying to make the most negative case went beyond what the evidence suggests on the dangers of LSD. This kind of distortion made many of the colleges suspicious. Second, universities usually take a strong negative view towards any group trying to influence how things will be run on the campus. This is a part of the tradition of universities being sanctuaries—sometimes even from the governments of their own countries.

As suggested, in the addict subculture organized crime plays a major role because it is highly profitable. But organized crime has not jumped into the LSD business. There are two major reasons for this. One is that the LSD user is never desperate for a trip as is the heroin addict. He can afford to shop around for a good price and do without when the LSD market becomes tight and more expensive. Second, there is little reason for the well organized crime groups to expose themselves to such a chancy profit.[108]

There has been a great deal of interest in the relationship between LSD and sexual experience. Because LSD is most often used by the young and the highly experimental, it would be logical to assume that one area of experimentation would be the sexual one. There are some who argue that the sexual experience while under LSD is a very different kind of experience. As one writer describes it, "if you fondle a woman's breast she becomes the whole breast and an orgasm feels as though it's spilling right out of you."[109] There have also been some LSD users who have always thought of themselves as completely heterosexual who panic during an LSD "high" because of the belief that their sudden affection for everyone is revealing a latent homosexuality. And by contrast admitted homosexuals sometimes experience a surprising push back toward heterosexual desires.[110]

We conclude by pointing out that the use of drugs is becoming more and more common, but used in a continued setting of conflict. Certainly the idea of mystical experiences that result from drug use is not readily acceptable in the United States. A part of the Western cultural belief is that man is a self-determining force who attempts to control his world by

---

[107] *Ibid.*, p. 18.
[108] *Ibid.*, p. 141.
[109] Laurie, *op. cit.*, p. 123.
[110] Young and Hixson, *op. cit.*, p. 98.

the power of conscious effort and will. Within this framework nothing could be more foreign than the belief in spiritual or psychological growth through the use of drugs. A drugged person is by definition "dimmed in consciousness, fogged in judgement, and deprived of will."[111] In fact the basic belief that the use of drugs might be followed for positive reasons of enhancing one's experience is so contrary to values that if a new drug came along that delivered all the mystical experiences with no ill effects it would be rejected. Such may already be the case with marijuana, which is probably the softest drug, yet is the most savagely attacked of the psychedelics.[112]

This general view that America sees the results of drugs negatively is important, because anything that provides ecstasy, visions, or even happiness and contentment without regard to one's material position poses a real social threat. On economic grounds alone it may be intolerable to many that anyone should receive those satisfactions without having earned them as a reward from society. "If anyone, after an injection or a pill costing a few pennies, were able to sit back and let the world go hang, where would we all be?"[113] This also helps to explain why many believe that all drugs *must* be dangerous and that what they do for the individual is not pleasant, but rather is painful.

But what may be most important in drug use in the United States in the future is the generational conflict. The older generation usually lumps together all drugs as equally harmful and undesirable. The younger generation often knows that some drugs are dangerous but others are relatively harmless. They are also not too influenced by an older generation that criticizes some of the drugs they use, especially marijuana, when they know the older generation is using more dangerous things—barbituates, tobacco, and alcohol. It would appear that in the years ahead there may be a somewhat more tolerant view of at least marijuana among the younger generation.

BIBLIOGRAPHY

BLUM, RICHARD H., *Society and Drugs* (San Francisco: Jossey-Bass, Inc., 1969).

FORT, JOEL, "Social Problems of Drug Use and Drug Policies," *California Law Review*, January, 1968, pp. 17–28.

GOODE, ERICH, "Multiple Drug Use among Marijuana Smokers," *Social Problems*, Summer, 1969, pp. 48–64.

---

[111] Watts, Alan, "Psychedelic and Religious Experience," *California Law Review*, January, 1968, p. 74.

[112] Weakland, *op. cit.*, pp. 360–61.

[113] Laurie, *op. cit.*, p. 46.

LAURIE, PETER, *Drugs: Medical, Psychological, and Social Facts* (Baltimore, Maryland: Penguin Books, 1967).

NOWLIS, HELEN H., *Drugs on the College Campus* (New York: Anchor Books, 1969).

SCHUR, EDWIN M., *Crimes without Victims: Deviant Behavior and Public Policy* (Englewood Cliffs, N.J.: Prentice-Hall, 1965).

WAKEFIELD, DAN, ed. *The Addict* (New York: Gold Medal Books, 1963).

YOUNG, WARREN and JOSEPH HIXSON, *LSD on Campus* (New York: Dell Publishing Co., 1966).

CHAPTER 9

PROSTITUTION

OVER THE YEARS no area of deviance has had more written about it than prostitution. If it is true that it is the "oldest profession" in the world then man has been interested in it since the beginning of time. There have been thousands of books written about prostitution but only some aspects of this behavior can be discussed here. There has been and continues to be some argument about what makes a person a prostitute. For example, some have even argued that a woman who exchanges sex in marriage for material gains is basically a prostitute. However, we will define prostitution as the selling of sex outside of marriage as a vocation. This would mean that an unmarried woman who is given gifts for sexual activities would not be a prostitute so long as that is not her occupational way of life.

We will briefly look at the historical background of prostitution. In most societies of the past, as well as the present, at least some prostitution has been acceptable and often encouraged. In almost all human societies man has been the definer of acceptable behavior. Man has traditionally defined himself as needing sexual outlets based on the belief that he was very different in his sexual needs from women. His assumption was that he needed outlets not only for when he was unmarried but also after marriage because he had greater needs than his wife could be expected to easily satisfy. This means that in many societies in the Western world man not only defined prostitution as something for his own needs but also as the means to help protect his "good" women. There are also broader social factors that influenced the high prevalence of prostitution over time. Kingsley Davis has argued that the rates of prostitution increase when there are barriers to man's sexual freedom. He says that if the age of marriage is high and sexual outlets are quite restricted the rate of prostitution will be high.[1] This is the opposite picture of what is the case in the United States today where the ages of marriage are the youngest in history and the opportunities for sexual outlets outside of marriage are the greatest. As we shall see this has had a great influence on the amount and nature of prostitution as it exists in the United States today.

In the United States it is generally believed that prostitution goes completely against moral and religious beliefs. However, this has not always been true and there are many references historically to religion's taking a permissive and often encouraging view toward prostitution. In some Eastern religions prostitution was a basic part of the religion itself and sometimes involved sacred prostitutes. Henriques has pointed out that to the Western mind the association of sexual intercourse with the worship of the supernatural is at best blasphemous and at worst obscene and degrading. Many other cultures have not made this distinction. "Among the Ancient Greeks, for example, copulation itself was at times regarded as an act of worship. But it is in those societies where prostitution becomes an essential part of the worship of the gods that the most powerful expression of the union of sexuality and religion is to be found.[2] None of the major Western religions have gone so far as to incorporate prostitution into their dogma but many have accepted it at least on occasions. At the beginning of the Middle Ages Saint Augustine believed prostitution to be essential. Saint Thomas Aquinas wrote that prostitution was a necessary evil that prevented seductions and rapes. However, as Western religions became increasingly concerned with "sins of the flesh" the restrictions on all types of sexual expression became greater.

Cultural variation is seen in the early influence of religion on sex in general and prostitution in particular during the early colonial days in America. In the settlements of the south the religious control was less than among the Puritans and it appears that prostitution was much more common there then it was in the north. Yet, even with the strong Puritan restrictions, some areas in New England believed it necessary to introduce legislation against fornicators, bawdyhouses, and "nightwalkers." "And around the time of the revolution, prostitutes were making their way across the ocean to marry the colonists."[3] In the northern states the in-

---

[1] Davis, Kingsley, "The Sociology of Prostitution," *American Sociology Review*, October, 1937, pp. 746–55.

[2] Henriques, Fernando, *Prostitution and Society* (New York: Grove Press, Inc., 1962), p. 21.

[3] Benjamin, Harry and R. E. L. Masters, *Prostitution and Morality* (New York: The Julian Press, Inc., 1964), pp. 21–22.

dentured servants had very few rights and were often at the disposal of their masters sexually. The same thing was also true for the black female slaves in the south. Therefore many of the wealthier men had free access to sexual partners, while the lower class men often turned to the prostitutes. It would appear that prostitution in the early days in the United States was primarily lower-class oriented.

With time prostitution became much more varied in the United States and there developed a level of prostitution aimed at the middle-class and upper middle-class market. It has been suggested that the last half of the 19th century and the early part of the 20th could be called the golden age of the brothel in the United States.[4] That period was also the Victorian era where women were divided into clear cut categories of good or bad. It was the time when the double standard view of sex held by men reached its peak. And many men when they visited brothels believed that they were not only meeting their own needs but were also being considerate of the good women in their lives. They believed that by directing their powerful, uncontrolled sexual needs at prostitutes they were saving their wives from these distasteful functions. Also a visit to the brothel was often much more than just for sexual needs. It was an evening of drinking, dining, cardplaying and masculine company—to be capped off by each showing his masculinity by going off with one of the girls. On this point Kinsey wrote that males of the older generations he interviewed explained how they visited houses of prostitution not only for sex, "but on sightseeing trips and in social groups as well. They were more often involved in the non-sexual activities that occurred in the established houses, such as drinking, gambling, etc. Present day prostitution is more often a matter of dealing with an individual girl who operates on her own."[5]

The "good" and "bad" distinction between women was also reflected during the late 19th and early 20th century by the way prostitutes clearly stood out from other women. They not only lived in red-light districts but they were set apart from middle-class women by their flamboyant clothes, hair styles, wearing of cosmetics, and their use of tobacco, alcohol, and profanity. "The social cleavage between the 'good' and 'bad' women was not only sharp but could be quickly determined by cultural insignia."[6] All of this has changed and today, as Lemert goes on to point out, appearance differences of the prostitute have vanished, "so that to separate her from the society matron, the debutante, or college girl in a hotel lobby is an almost impossible task."[7]

---

[4] Ibid., p. 76.

[5] Kinsey, Alfred C., et al., Sexual Behavior in the Human Male (Philadelphia: W. B. Saunders Co., 1948), pp. 603–4.

[6] Lemert, Edwin M., "Prostitution" in Edward Sagarin and Donald E. MacNamara, Problems of Sex Behavior (New York: Thomas Y. Cronell Co., 1968), p. 82.

[7] Ibid., p. 83.

It was not until about the time of World War I that any real opposition developed to prostitution in the United States. At that time the opposition wasn't so much on moral grounds as it was with an increasing venereal disease rate associated with prostitution. This was seen as threatening to the war effort and therefore patriotism became linked to moralism in making prostitution difficult to defend. However, many houses of prostitution did survive World War I and did not succumb to the forces of anti-prostitution until early in World War II.[8] During World War II prostitution did develop around military bases but was often not based in brothels but on the individual level. Today, houses of prostitution are not very common in most parts of the country. The area where they are most apt to be found today is in the south where the double standard of sex exists in its strongest form in the United States.

In the United States today prostitution is almost totally illegal. The official view taken by all states of the United States is to prohibit it. There has been one exception to the legal bans on prostitution among the states. In the state of Nevada prostitution has been accepted as a way of life since the early mining camp days. At present it is legal in 13 of Nevada's 17 counties. There are about 40 licensed brothels and they do a total annual business placed at between $3 million and $5 million. It is estimated that the girls earn an average of $500 a week, out of which they pay about $200 in room and board and keep the rest.[9] With the exception of the counties in Nevada all prostitution is prohibited and all prostitutes are defined as criminals. The day-to-day practice of prostitution is controlled primarily thorough laws passed by various state legislatures, "which stalwartly resist federal government proposals for uniform legislation in this area, with the result that the prostitution laws differ drastically from state to state."[10] In most states persons who are involved with prostitutes fall under the laws, for example, those associated with them in a business way such as procurers, pimps, and madams. As mentioned above, to be a prostitute is against the law in all states except Nevada, although 27 states do not mention prostitution *specifically* but legally categorize these activities as some type of vagrancy. Maximum penalties seldom go beyond a one-year prison term and in many cases do not exceed six months. In only eight states in the United States is there a statute specifying any punishment for the customer of the prostitute, or making his participation in illegal coitus a crime.

It is necessary to say something briefly about male prostitution. Male prostitutes may be of two types—those who are homosexual and those who are heterosexual. The homosexual male prostitute has been by far the most common over time and still is today. Homosexual temple prosti-

---

[8] Benjamin and Masters, *op. cit.*, p. 86.
[9] *Newsweek*, March 9, 1970, p. 81.
[10] *Ibid.*, p. 376.

tutes existed among the Hebrews and in India. There were boy prostitutes in the early civilizations of Egypt, Persia, Greece, Rome, China, and Japan. (There was probably some Lesbian prostitution but it must have been on a small scale.) It is also known that in renaissance Italy and 18th century France homosexual prostitution was quite common. There is probably more male prostitution in the United States today than ever before. This is in part a reflection of the greater openness of male homosexuals who seek out young sex partners. The boys do not consider themselves to be homosexual and are often a part of juvenile gangs. Male heterosexual prostitutes in the United States have always been rare. This is true when the definition of prostitution's being a vocation is applied. There are some young men who are "kept" by older women but they are much closer to a "mistress" role than that of a prostitute. There are in American folklore, probably developed by men, stories about some men being so good that women seek them out to pay them for their sexual services. But this appears to be based on wishful thinking rather than actual fact.

We next look at what is known about the number of prostitutes and their customers in the United States today. There is some evidence to suggest that since the end of World War II the number of prostitutes and the number of their clients have not changed to any great extent. "On the contrary, what seems to have occurred is a decline in the frequency with which men patronize prostitutes."[11] This suggests that many men still visit prostitutes on some occasions, but turn to them much less because there are more opportunities for sex with women who are not prostitutes. It seems probable that today's younger adult generation is turning much less to prostitutes. This would certainly be expected on the basis of the increased sexual freedom among the younger generation. A recent study of college students around the country found only 4 percent of the boys had experience with a prostitute.[12]

Once again we must turn to the Kinsey data as the best source of information on the use of prostitutes by American men. Kinsey found in his sample that more than two-thirds of the white male population had some experience with prostitutes. Most of them had those relations no more than once or twice a year. Prostitution provided about one tenth of the male's total premarital coital experience.[13] The Kinsey data showed clear differences by social class and the use of prostitutes. The contacts were most common among the lower-class men. "Between 16 and 20, males of grade school level have intercourse with prostitutes 9 times as

---

[11] Esselstyn, T. C., "Prostitution in the United States," *The Annals*, March, 1968, p. 127.

[12] Packard, Vance, *The Sexual Wilderness* (New York: David McKay, 1968), p. 164.

[13] Kinsey, *op. cit.*, p. 599.

often, and males of the high school level have it more than 4 times as often as males of the college level."[14] This distinction no doubt continues to be true today, with lower-class males most often turning to prostitutes.

Men have historically turned to prostitutes for a variety of reasons. We suggest four general groupings of motives or reasons for men seeking out this kind of sexual relief. For any given man the reasons may operate singularly or in various combinations.

1. *Avoid Competition.* There are some men who are not able, or believe they are not able, to compete for women. This may be because they are shy or emotionally very insecure. Some may have severe physical or mental handicaps. In some cases they may be too old. The prostitute provides them a sexual outlet without risk of rejection.

2. *Impersonal Sex.* Some men want to avoid any interpersonal involvement with women. They can pay for their sexual relations and feel no personal or social obligation to the prostitute. This also means they are free of the fear of getting a girl pregnant and being held responsible.

3. *Sexual Peculiarities.* There are some men who have a need for a variety of sexual experiences or of sexual partners. There are also some men who have sadistic or masochistic needs or are addicted to a variety of fetishes. Their needs are very difficult to satisfy without paying for them. Depending on how bizarre or painful their desires are they may even have trouble finding prostitutes to satisfy their needs. Many prostitutes will not engage in various sexual behaviors. For these men, as long as they have sexual peculiarities, it will be difficult to find non-prostitute outlets to take care of them.

4. *Uncomplicated Sex.* Some men want to relax with women where the ordinary conventions are removed. This is where sex is not complicated by explanation or worry about the partner. The male knows his evening will end with sex with no commitment on his part.

PROSTITUTION IN THE UNITED STATES TODAY

In the United States today there is no great social concern with prostitution. This is not to say that prostitution is accepted, but rather that society has lost most of its moral indignation and thus its inclination to strongly condemn it or attempt to do something about it. Society appears to become concerned today when prostitution is linked with some other social problem. For example, there will often be a campaign to reduce prostitution because it is believed to contribute to an increase in venereal disease rates, or after some public outrage when call girls are linked with shady business practices or political manipulations. It appears common for the American public to link prostitution with criminality and shady

---

[14] *Ibid.*, p. 601.

business practices, yet prostitution's closest link to institutions is probably with legitimate, respected businesses.

Prostitution continues to be linked with concerned public reaction often when it is associated with young men in the military forces. During the history of mankind prostitution has always been closely linked with armies. Up until recent times the armies of the world were almost always accompanied by prostitutes who did the cooking and the laundry, as well as taking care of soldiers' sexual needs. In the United States the armed forces have traditionally treated sex with hypocrisy. There is usually an attempt to control the soldier's sexual life as much as possible, but at the same time to keep what is not controlled absolutely quiet. On one hand the soldier is told to live a virtuous sex-free life, but at the same time is officially taught how to use various methods of prophylaxis. The common argument by the military that prostitution must be controlled because of venereal disease is a questionable one. One study during World War II found that a very small proportion of infections in the army were due to professional prostitutes (6 percent); 80 percent were due to amateurs; and a surprising 14 percent were marital in origin.[15]

Of course many military leaders know it would be much better to have military control over prostitution and historically have often suggested it. It was recently suggested by the top army medical officer in Vietnam. General David T. Thomas said, "if the military were permitted to run houses of prostitution as part of the Post Exchange system we could cut venereal disease down to a very, very low figure merely by being able to supervise the operation, if not all the way, at least from the time the soldier goes into the room and from the time he comes out."[16] But his suggestion, as has been the case many times before in the United States, was met with indignation and ridicule. Benjamin and Masters point out that parents often react with the desire to see their sons in the army protected from temptation and seem to believe if there are no prostitutes, there will be no sex. The parents often hold the armed forces responsible for their boys. Yet, even with the military there appears to be less indignation about prostitution than there was only a few years ago. Many moralists would prefer not to be confronted with possible prostitution for the military and then they wouldn't have to react to it. It's when they read a statement like General Thomas's that they feel they must react and then hypocrisy becomes preferable to honesty.

What is the nature of prostitution in the United States today? For the most part the old houses of prostitution are gone and the occupation is less complex and organized today. In the old days a madam might run a house with twenty girls and that represented a complex small business.

---

[15] Benjamin and Masters, *op. cit.*, pp. 52–3.
[16] *The Washington Post*, October 23, 1969.

Today prostitutes work alone or in small groups and have much more control over their career than they did in the past. Writers have described many different categories of prostitutes as they exist today, but for the purpose of discussion the role of prostitutes is divided into two general categories. One is the "street" or "bar" girl. These girls usually sell themselves directly and in person on the marketplace. That is, they are seen and picked out by the customer. The second type of prostitute is the "call" girl who usually makes her first contacts with a customer *without* his actually seeing her. This may be through referral by a pimp or another call girl. These distinctions are not always clear cut and not always appropriate. For example, in some cases a street girl will have a customer brought to her by her pimp and he will of course not see her until he arrives. And sometimes a call girl will work certain cocktail lounges and be picked up there. Another general distinction is that the street girl usually has a lower-middle or lower-class clientele while the call girl has middle and upper middle-class customers. It is also generally true that call girls are more attractive, better educated, and make far more money than do street girls. The primary concern in this chapter is with the call girl.

The rise of the modern call girl came about with the decline of the old madam type of prostitution. The call girl era also appeared to bring in a period when prostitution was more and more an individual undertaking rather than an occupation practiced in close association with others. "The ubiquity of the motel is believed to facilitate prostitution as well as other forms of extramarital sex experience."[17] Less organization to prostitution may also be a result of there being less concern with prostitution today than there was in the past.

The status of the call girl is determined by her attractiveness, financial standing, dress, apartment, manners, and the state in which she keeps her pimp. Her status is also reflected in how she views other prostitutes. Greenwald points out that call girls have more scorn for streetwalkers than does the most puritanical reformer. "They will avoid bars and restaurants that are patronized by girls who, they feel, have inferior status as professionals or whom they consider amateurs."[18] As with any profession the prostitute takes pride in being very good and her success can be measured against what she sees as the failures of the street girls.

Even when a call girl works a bar or cocktail lounge she does so in a manner different from the street girl's. In many large cities there are cocktail lounges that are known to be the hangouts of call girls. In those places solicitation is not directly made by the girl as is usually true for the

---

[17] Esselstyn, *op. cit.*, p. 127.

[18] Greenwald, Harold, "The Social and Professional Life of the Call Girl," in Simian Dinitz, Russell R. Dynes and Alfred C. Clarke, *Deviance* (New York: Oxford University Press, 1969), p. 407.

lower-class street girls. Rather, the call girl sits at the bar and drinks by herself. Many times she will be approached by men who may or may not know she is a prostitute. If the man is trying to pick her up she quickly lets him know that it will cost money because she doesn't want to waste her time on noncustomers. Many of the cocktail lounges encourage the call girls to work there because it is good for their business. Sometimes the bartender or manager of the bar will introduce a potential client who is not too adventurous.[19] Greenwald found that the girls who worked in the cocktail lounges usually started work about four in the afternoon to get the men who stopped in on their way home from the office, and usually continued to work until two or three in the morning.[20] But the most successful call girls never enter a bar to work and make all their arrangements by telephone. Some are on retainers, like a lawyer, to various business firms. This means that they will be available whenever they are needed. But this level of prostitution is carefully covered and there is little actually known about it.

Entering Prostitution

As suggested earlier in the chapter, there has been a great deal of speculation as to the causes of prostitution as a social institution as well as many attempts to explain why girls become prostitutes. Generally the explanations of causes have followed the same patterns as those for attempts to explain such areas of deviance as homosexuality, delinquency, drug use, and so forth. That is, it used to be assumed that girls became prostitutes because they were sinful, but this shifted to their being defined as "sick" in some way. When the cause for becoming a prostitute was seen as sin, the treatment was punishment. But with the causal view becoming "sickness," the way of handling prostitution was seen to be through treatment. It has almost always been assumed that becoming a prostitute was repugnant to the female and she entered *only* because of some forces against her normal will or desires. In other words, the assumption almost always has been that no girl in her right mind and with freedom of choice would enter prostitution. In the United States, as in many other countries, it is commonly believed that many girls become prostitutes against their wills. This is a part of the "white slave" myth which explains the prostitute as a girl who was innocent and was lured under false pretense, drugs, or force. The myth says that these girls were held captive in houses of prostitution and were beaten into submission by mean madams and pimps. They were believed to be constantly moved from city to city, or even from country to country, and eventually would

---

[19] *Ibid.*, p. 405.
[20] *Ibid.*, p. 406.

be sent to a near eastern country never to be heard of again. As Lemert points out, many prostitutes went along with the "white slave" myth. They often found that the story inspired sympathy and discounted their own responsibility for being a prostitute.[21] But there is little evidence that many girls have ever been forced through white slavery into prostitution.

In the United States several theories have developed that try to explain why girls become prostitutes. One of the attempts has been to psychiatrically explain prostitution based upon a Freudian model. Within that framework the prostitute is often described as masochistic or as having an infantile mentality. She was described as being unable to form mature interpersonal relationships and as being emotionally dangerous to the male.[22] A more psychological point of view argues that prostitution is caused by various kinds of childhood experiences. Greenwald says that the prostitutes he studied had "early family experiences of parental conflict, neglect, and rejection. They also had rewarding sexual experiences with older men. These experiences led the girls to see sex as a commodity to barter for personal gain.[23] There is also a social interpretation of the causes of prostitution. This view sees the prostitute as being a victim of her environment or as a person with little or no control over her destiny.

Whatever they are, the causes of entering prostitution are probably very similar to the causes of becoming an airline stewardess or a nurse. Benjamin and Masters have suggested several reasons why a woman might become a prostitute. (1) The economic rewards of being a prostitute are usually far greater than those in many other occupations. (2) The opportunity exists for adventure in what is seen by some as a world of glamour. (3) This work is for some girls attractively easy and undisciplined. So long as they are young and attractive they don't have to put out much effort to make a good living. (4) There are probably a small minority of prostitutes who are so highly sexed that they enjoy many of their sexual activities.[24]

Actually there is a great deal of speculating and theorizing about why women become prostitutes, with little in the way of empirical data. However, one recent study shows that force of any kind is *not* a common cause of entering prostitution. Gebhard found in his study of 127 white female prostitutes that only 4 percent could be said to have been forced into prostitution. And even in those few cases there were some alternative choices. "The female who says her husband or boyfriend forced her

---

[21] Lemert, *op. cit.*, p. 84.

[22] Bryan, James H., "Apprenticeships in Prostitution," *Social Problems*, Winter, 1965, p. 287.

[23] Greenwald, *op. cit.*, p. 406.

[24] Benjamin and Masters, *op. cit.*, pp. 93–4.

to become a prostitute is really saying she chose prostitution rather than lose her mate and possibly experience a beating."[25]

It appears that for most prostitutes the problems they personally encounter center around their affectional relations rather than around any moral guilt about their way of life. The notion that prostitutes go through life upset because of guilt feelings about their sexual morality has been an exaggeration. In fact, it may be that some women who have less need for emotional commitment as well as fewer moral restrictions are drawn to prostitution. Lemert has suggested that prostitution may draw women who are emotionally more self sufficient than others.[26]

The reasons given by prostitutes for entering that profession have very often been discounted or defined as rationalizations. But it would appear that the insights that prostitutes can give about their own occupational choice are as important to consider as other interpretations. Most women say they become prostitutes for very practical reasons. The occupation pays well, the work is reasonably pleasant, they have a fair degree of independence, and a chance of meeting a client they can marry.[27] Gebhard in his sample found that almost 90 percent of the prostitutes listed money as their prime motivation. He also reported that two-thirds of the prostitutes said they had no regrets whatsoever about entering the occupation.[28] The money factor is important in another way. In almost all professions one enters, one must first gain experience and knowledge, and over the years hope to see one's income increase. But with prostitution most often just the opposite occurs. The woman can usually earn big money very soon after starting. This is because even though she may be inexperienced in both sexual and interpersonal techniques her novelty on the market gives her an advantage over her more experienced and better known competitors. "It seems quite likely that the new girl, irrespective of her particular physical and mental qualities, has considerable drawing power because she provides new sexual experience to the customer. Early success and financial reward may well provide considerable incentive to continue in the occupation."[29]

It is a measurement of the strength of moral norms against prostitution that so many girls after seeing the economic rewards of becoming a prostitute as against filling a low paying clerical job will still take the clerical job. The very fact that almost all girls with the lowest income potential never consider becoming a prostitute suggests the continuing strong moral taboos. If the moral controls are weakening then it could be pre-

---

[25] Gebhard, Paul H., "Misconceptions about Female Prostitution," *Medical Aspects of Human Sexuality*, March, 1969, p. 28.

[26] Lemert, *op. cit.*, p. 105.

[27] Esselstyn, *op. cit.*, p. 30.

[28] Gebhard, *op. cit.*, p. 29.

[29] Bryan, *op. cit.*, p. 295.

dicted that in the future more girls would consider prostitution as a real occupational possibility. But the very forces that might allow more girls to consider prostitution are based on greater sexual liberality for the female which makes the need for prostitutes decrease.

There are many girls who drift into prostitution. For example a girl may have been involved in quasi-prostitution for a while, and after a time her activity makes her defining herself as a prostitute inescapable. "A waitress who has been taken on dates by customers from the restaurant where she works and given entertainment or gifts in return for sexual favors may suddenly perceive the bargaining features of the relationships and decide to formalize them through a prostitute's role in order to improve what frequently is a bad bargain from her point of view."[30] In other cases a girl may become a prostitute because others define her as such. This may occur if she is arrested and convicted on the formal charge of commercial vice. For example, if she has a venereal disease she may be given segregated treatment in a clinic along with prostitutes and see herself as such because of her involvement in those settings. These are situations primarily for the lower-class prostitute and are much less apt to be the causes for the call girl's entering the profession.

In American society there continues to be strong resistance to any suggestion that prostitution may be a rational occupational choice for some women. Their choice is constantly defined within the "sick" or "manipulated" categories and this strips them of any occupational self determination. This theme cuts across many other areas of deviant behavior. The delinquent, the drug user, the homosexual, as well as others, are often seen as "pawns" in society. To a great extent this is a reflection of the fact that society cannot accept the notion that what they consider to be deviancy is not accepted as such by all. To recognize this would undercut the universal quality of their notions of wrong behavior— something that many who live in a world of moral universals cannot accept. As suggested, the definers of many forms of deviance insist on a world of total conformity to their values as their basic goal.

PROSTITUTION AS A SUBCULTURE

As in most areas of deviance some persons may function essentially as individuals while many others function as a part of a subculture. In this section the interest is with the subcultural setting of prostitution. Gagnon and Simon believe that the largest proportion of sexual events that may be defined as prostitution are carried out within a setting that may be seen as subcultural. They suggest that the subcultural world "includes as its elements specialized knowledge, language, and relationships

---

[30] Lemert, *op. cit.*, p. 99.

with other persons. Being 'in the life' involves existing inside a prostitute's occupational culture. Most prostitutes exist in social networks consisting of other prostitutes and allied occupational and social roles (e.g., pimps, steerers, the police, customers, etc.)"[31] The subculture also has its historical beliefs or particular folklore that give it a dimension of time. It has been suggested that no other deviant subculture has developed any greater collection of myths and beliefs. "The folklore of prostitution largely concerns the manner in which women become prostitutes, the type of life they lead, and the inevitable culmination of their lives in demoralization, disease, and early death."[32]

Highly important to the folklore of any deviant group is the belief in becoming successful, and this is reflected in the stories about those who have been successful both within the subculture as well as about those who have been successful in escaping it. Among prostitutes it is common to tell stories about women who have married well known politicians or businessmen. There are also many stories about movie actresses who were once "in the game." But not only do prostitutes like to talk about women who have left prostitution and become respectable but they "also seem to treasure the stories of those who descended from respectability to join their ranks."[33] This contributes to the myth that no woman, under the right circumstances, would be immune to becoming a prostitute. Since most of the stories are about prostitutes who have escaped and become successful in the "straight" world it seems to indicate that for most prostitutes the subcultural world is one they would like to leave—at least under some conditions.

Not only do prostitutes have their folklore but there are also many myths about prostitutes. One myth sees the prostitute as a person with a "heart of gold" who is an easy "touch" and who gives most of her money away. There is also an opposite belief that the prostitute hates men and is a cold blooded business woman. The first myth is probably based on the notion that prostitutes give help to the poor families they often came from. Added to this is the fact that they often give up much of their earnings to their pimps. Most prostitutes are probably cold blooded in that sex is their business and they usually want no emotional involvement with their customers. This approach by the prostitute is smart both from a business perspective and from an interpersonal one. Bryan writes, however, that the assumption that "all whores hate men" was not supported in his study of prostitutes.[34]

---

[31] Gagnon, John H. and William Simon, *Sexual Deviance* (New York: Harper and Row, 1967), p. 10.

[32] Lemert, *op. cit.*, p. 83.

[33] Hirschi, T., "The Professional Prostitute," in William Rushing *Deviant Behavior and Social Process* (Chicago: Rand McNally & Co., 1969), p. 201.

[34] Bryan, *op. cit.*, p. 292.

Another common belief about prostitutes is that they are almost all heavy users of drugs. This has in part been supported by the fact that a number of prostitutes have been found to use drugs. However, in many, if not most, of these cases the women are not primarily oriented toward prostitution but rather toward using prostitution to satisfy the role demands of being a drug addict. In other words, the deviant occupation of prostitute is the means to achieve the deviant end of drug use.[35] In his sample of subculturally oriented prostitutes Gebhard found that only 4 percent were ever addicted to "hard" drugs and another 5 percent had experimented with drugs without becoming addicted.[36]

An important aspect of the prostitute subculture centers around the roles and norms directly related to the practice of prostitution. It is the occupational factor that gives the way of life its significance. As with most deviant subcultures, it is this significance which makes the behavior deviant, in this case the profession of prostitution. What about occupational recruitment of prostitutes? When and under what conditions do women become prostitutes?

It has been suggested that there are two model age groupings when women usually enter prostitution. The first period is roughly between the ages of 18 and 22. This is a high entrance age because the young girl finds she is valuable on the market and is offered good money. Secondly, there are probably a minority of women who become prostitutes after the age of 25. It is probable that many women who become prostitutes at the older ages are the ones who enter as a means of satisfying other deviant ends—that is, women who are on drugs or who are alcoholics. There is also evidence that black prostitutes start much younger than do whites (from 3 to 5 years younger).[37] This has probably been true because the black girl has had fewer economic opportunities and because she is less controlled by the traditional sexual morality. There also appears to be an age difference for entrance by types of prostitutes. The street girl, who usually has less education than the call girl, probably starts at a much younger age. This means that a young street prostitute may be a seventeen year old girl while a young call girl might be twenty-one years of age. But even though the call girl may be older when she starts she can generally practice her profession with success much longer than the street girl because she is better able and knows how to keep her attractiveness longer.

The street girls most often become prostitutes by drifting into the profession. As suggested, they often move from amateur to semi-professional to professional status without very much conscious planning. Often these

---

[35] Lemert, op. cit., pp. 105–6.

[36] Gebhard, op. cit., pp. 28–9.

[37] Benjamin and Masters, op. cit., p. 100.

girls tie up with a pimp but are not a part of the prostitute subculture. By contrast many call girls do make a conscious choice about entering the profession and are introduced by becoming a part of the prostitute subculture. The discussion that follows is concerned with the female who becomes a part of the call girl subculture.

The apprentice call girl doesn't have to learn a great deal before she starts to practice. She becomes trained by becoming a part of the subculture, "where she learns the trade through imitation as much as through explicit tutoring. The outstanding concern at this stage is the development of a sizable and lucrative clientele. The specific skills and values which are acquired during this period are rather simple and quickly learned."[38] Bryan also says that despite the girls' protest and their involved folklore the art of being a prostitute is at least initially a low-level skill. "That is, it seems to be an occupation which requires little formal knowledge or practice for its successful pursuit and appears best categorized as an unskilled job."[39]

The apprentice prostitute receives little instruction on various sexual techniques, even though her previous sexual knowledge may have been quite limited. What instruction there is usually centers around having oral sex with the customer. The prostitute learns that in general oral sex is more efficient for her than coitus. This is because coitus allows the man to have some control over his orgasm and he may therefore prolong the act. Besides it is seen as messy and demanding that the prostitute take the time for a douche. By contrast oral sex with the man means that the prostitute controls his orgasm and can bring it about much faster, and it is also seen as less messy. Oral sex is something the customer often wants, so it is necessary for the beginning prostitute to learn some skills in this sexual area. Bryan also suggests that during the training period there is also stress "not to experience sexual orgasms with the client, though this may be quite variable with the trainer."[40]

The structure of the apprenticeship period appears to be common for most prostitutes. The beginner receives her training from either a pimp or from an experienced call girl. "She serves her initial two to eight months of work under the trainer's supervision and often serves this period in the trainer's apartment. The trainer assumes responsibility for arranging contacts and negotiating the type and place of the sexual encounter."[41] Most important about the training period is not so much the learning of skills and techniques but rather the building of a clientele. "For referring the customer, the trainer receives forty to fifty percent of the total price agreed upon in the contact negotiated by the trainer and the customer."[42]

---

[38] Bryan, op. cit., p. 295.
[39] Ibid., p. 296.
[40] Ibid., p. 293.
[41] Ibid., p. 294.
[42] Ibid., p. 295.

The call girl over time tries to build up her practice or clientele. With time most girls get their clients by individual referrals, usually over the telephone, and make their arrangements for sexual contact. The men are usually repeat customers or men who have been recommended by previous customers. Ideally the call girl would like all of her business to be arranged ahead of time, either by telephone or by having someone else set it up. Sometimes if business is slow the call girl may initiate calls. "She doesn't solicit in the usual sense of streetwalking, but she will call a number of men in an effort to drum up trade."[43] While there is competition between call girls for business, they also develop some close relationships. And even in business there is often cooperation among prostitutes. Call girls who have more customers than they can handle will refer them to a friend. The friend will in turn refer some of her extra customers at a future date, or a fee-splitting arrangement may be worked out. Because the girls are in deviant subcultures they know that they must to some extent rely on one another. This dependency may take the direction of mutual aid in a variety of ways. For example, if a girl is sick or in jail her friends will often try to keep as much of her practice as possible for her when she returns.[44] And, too, the girls often live together because it has personal as well as business advantages.

The subculture of the prostitute may be better understood by looking at some of the roles and their meanings. The major role that the prostitute must deal with is that of the customer or "John." The customer is almost always seen as the source of income, the more the better, and that is the basic limit of how he is defined. His economic role governs almost all the kinds of behavior directed at him by the prostitute. The perspective of seeing him almost only in the economic sense is supported by the rationalizations that prostitutes develop with regard to him. Basically the prostitute sees the customer as corrupt. This becomes empirically confirmed for her: when she sees the married man cheating on his wife; when the moralist is secretly betraying his publicly stated values; or when the "John" tries to cheat the prostitute.[45] All of these rationales mean that he is not to be trusted and should be "taken" in every way possible.

But the call girl does have a code with regard to her customers that is based on good business practices and not usually based on any concern for the customer as a person. For example, the call girl will protect the anonymity of her customers. If she runs into a customer in public she will give no sign of recognition unless he does so first. She will not steal from her customers and often will not let them overpay her if she thinks they are doing so because they are drunk. Greenwald goes on to say a "profes-

[43] Greenwald, *op. cit.*, p. 405.

[44] Hirschi, *op. cit.*, p. 201.

[45] Bryan, *op. cit.*, p. 291.

sional call girl will make every effort to satisfy a client even if he has difficulties. When working with groups of men she will not reveal the inadequacies of one of the men to the others in the group, but will praise him."[46] It can be seen that these codes of behavior are good business practices for the call girl.

Earlier some of the reasons why men seek out prostitutes were discussed, but some further elaboration is useful here in terms of how the customer views the prostitute. Frequently the "John" wants the girl to tell her story of how she became a prostitute. This story is often for the prostitute a part of a wide repertoire to choose from in answering a customer. Her story may be an "atrocity tale" of white slavery or at the other extreme may be the equivalent of the proverbial "just lucky, I guess." "The customer, for his part, often attempts to justify his presence to the prostitute. This too, in many instances, takes the form of a hard-luck story."[47] Often both the customer and the prostitute develop stories to try to explain why they are together.

Other roles important to the prostitute subculture are the roles of the "madam" and the "pimp." The madam was traditionally the woman that the prostitute worked for. The madam hired and fired, made the rules, and watched over the activities of the girls on the job. The madam was important in the past when houses of prostitution were important. She ran the house and the girls. She was a boss and had much less interpersonal importance to the prostitute than did the fellow prostitutes or the pimps when they were there.[48] It has been suggested that when the well-being of the prostitute is of primary concern the house system with a madam is the best, because the house provided safety, supervision, and other security benefits such as not even the expensive call girl can always enjoy.[49] The madam was often a different type of person from most of her prostitutes. She was often more intelligent but probably her most important characteristic was her strong ambition for material success. There have been a number of autobiographical books written by ex-madams and they always present themselves as kind-hearted social work types who contributed to the preservation of God, family, and country. But the madam is primarily a role of the past and has little significance to prostitution today. The madam has not been replaced so much as made obsolete by the less formal, more individual prostitution of the street girl and call girl.

A role that brings about as much hostile reaction as that of prostitute is the role of the pimp. Society views the pimp as even lower than the prostitute because he is seen as living off of her earnings. He is not only

[46] Greenwald, op. cit., p. 407.

[47] Hirschi, op. cit., p. 201.

[48] Ibid., p. 203.

[49] Benjamin and Masters, op. cit., p. 240.

seen as a parasite, but as a parasite of the most despicable type, one who feeds off the immoral earnings of a woman's body. In general the views held toward the pimp are based on his real functions. A pimp is basically a prostitute's "man" (lover) to whom she contributes an important part of what she earns as a prostitute. The pimp is also in some cases "her business manager, bodyguard, panderer, and drug connection; but his main function is psychosexual, and his role of lover and recipient of the prostitute's money defines him."[50] A pimp is generally not just a business agent or even a friend because the relationship is typically one of lovers.[51]

There have been many stories about the sexual relationships between prostitutes and their pimps. One common belief is that prostitutes are incapable of reaching any sexual satisfaction with any man and that the pimp uses her but that she gets little or nothing from the sexual relationship. However, it appears quite likely that the average prostitute achieves orgasm at least as frequently as do wives with their husbands. "The attempt to establish frigidity, along with homosexuality, as a common cause of women becoming prostitutes is far-fetched and doctrinaire. When a prostitute is frigid and/or homosexual, the condition is almost always an *effect*—of intercourse too often engaged in, of disenchantment with the male, etc."[52]

The pimp is almost always heterosexual and masculine in appearance and actions, and probably as sexually virile as the average man. His most outstanding characteristic is that he holds high attraction for certain types of women and along with this has the ability to manipulate and exploit those women to his economic advantage.[53] It has been argued that the pimp is a functional necessity for the prostitute, because he watches over her and she in return economically supports him. One writer suggests that the similarity of the pimp-prostitute relationship to the husband-wife relationship, with the *economic roles reversed*, is quite obvious.[54] It has also been suggested that quite simply the pimp is often most important to the prostitute as her "family" and that for the pimp the prostitute is most important as his meal ticket.[55]

It has been suggested that because most prostitutes and pimps come out of the lower middle or lower classes that a lot of the behavior between them can be explained on social class grounds. This interpretation recognizes that social class equals tend to marry one another and may, as well, establish non-marital living relationships. Socially, any man who lives with a woman he knows is a prostitute, when she contributes to

---

[50] *Ibid.*, p. 215.

[51] Bryan, *op. cit.*, p. 289.

[52] Benjamin and Masters, *op. cit.*, p. 221.

[53] *Ibid.*, p. 225.

[54] Hirschi, *op. cit.*, p. 202.

[55] Benjamin and Masters, *op. cit.*, p. 227.

their mutual expenses and he helps her find work, is a pimp. "It is not a case of the man 'creating' the prostitute, nor is it the case of the woman 'selecting' a pimp; her occupation makes them both what they are."[56] As suggested, people who live at the same social class level associate with one another and their behavior will often reflect their particular socialization experiences. Therefore, when a pimp physically beats up the prostitute he lives with, his behavior need not be a reflection of the pimp-prostitute relationship but may be seen as the lower-class way of dealing with a disagreement—the equivalent of a middle-class family argument.[57]

Another common belief about prostitutes, because of the assumption that they hate men, is that many of them are homosexuals. This is also sometimes seen as the reason why many prostitutes do not have pimps. There are several reasons to assume that prostitutes would have a higher potential for homosexuality than other women. One, because they are engaged in a variety of sexual behaviors some would be prone to personally experiment sexually. Second, and related, is that often prostitutes are called upon by customers to perform homosexual acts with one another. While these are usually faked, in some cases the pretended act might lead them to really try it. Third, some prostitutes do dislike men and seek out both interpersonal and sexual satisfactions from other women. However, there are probably far fewer prostitutes who are homosexual than is commonly believed. Gebhard provides some data on this point in his study of prostitutes. He found that almost two-thirds of his sample had no homosexual experience whatsoever, "6 percent had incidental experience (i.e., less than ten events), and 9 percent had homosexual activity only in conjunction with prostitution. This leaves only 24 percent of the prostitutes who had homosexual experience ten times or more for pleasure rather than profit. Of these, only a few had extensive homosexual activity."[58] Gebhard in his study suggests that prostitutes may so effectively compartmentalize their lives that being a prostitute does not seriously interfere with their heterosexual interests, "their orgasmic capacities, or their ability to form affectional relationships with men."[59]

As in any subculture, along with the roles that are defined with regard to one another there are also some general rules and self role definitions. It has been pointed out that the form of deviance tells a great deal about the need for deviant group formation and role interaction. Important to some deviant groups is their instrumentality for the broader society. Do the subcultures provide goods and services through their organization to

---

[56] Hirschi, op. cit., p. 202.
[57] Ibid.
[58] Gebhard, op. cit., p. 30.
[59] Ibid.

meet the demands of others? Prostitution is a good illustration of this instrumental relationship to the rest of society.[60] Therefore, general patterns of conduct are important both for the internal needs of the subculture and for its relationships to the broader society which it *must* deal with. This kind of deviant subculture is different from others because of its needs to maintain its relationships outside. By contrast, homosexual subcultures generally want to avoid any contact with the broader society because they have little to gain and a great deal to lose.

Because prostitution is geared to the outside world it means that prostitutes must make themselves as efficient as possible in dealing with the potential customer market. For example, as is the case in most businesses the seller must set his hours to be most convenient for the customer. This means that the prostitute usually works at night. She will usually set certain hours for business and not accept customers at other hours. However, her hours may be altered given changes in the market demand. For example, in many large cities, such as New York and London, there is a large noon-time and early evening trade.[61]

Often the rules of relationships to the customer become internalized into self role images that the prostitute uses to justify her behavior. For example, the general rule that one gets as much as possible out of a customer becomes a part of a rationalization that the customer is immoral and dishonest and therefore *should* be taken for as much as possible. This also contributes to the self image that prostitution should not be stigmatized and one should not look down upon oneself for being a prostitute. For many prostitutes this appears to be a necessary and therapeutic practice. Bryan suggests that these simple rules help "justify exploitation, sustain what cooperative behavior is necessary for occupational functioning, and reduce both public and personal stigma, real or potential, attached to the actor."[62]

The need for rules and self image concepts is particularly important among prostitutes when they first enter the profession. The fact of the "naming process," of consciously recognizing oneself as a prostitute, is often a traumatic experience. Therefore, the rules and rationalizations that are provided by the subculture are very important. Often the beginning prostitute makes the transition as a result of both push and pull. She feels pushed out of the broader society because she sees that as a hostile or indifferent world. At that time the prostitute often indicates that she had associated with people who meant very little to her or that she had no friends or close family at all. Her violation of the general sexual values is rationalized in two basic ways. "(*a*) Everyone is rotten.

---

[60] Lemert, *op. cit.*, p. 47.

[61] Hirschi, *op. cit.*, p. 200.

[62] Bryan, James H., "Occupational Ideologies and Individual Attitudes of Call Girls," *Social Problems*, Spring, 1966, pp. 444.

Hence, prostitutes are no worse than other people, and they are less hypocritical. (*b*) Society doesn't really scorn prostitutes." But as the authors go on to point out, the rationalizations don't work completely because every prostitute they interviewed expressed some degree of guilt feeling about her activity.[63]

The "pull" factors operating on the beginning prostitute are several. Most important may be the money and the material way of life that they see as highly desirable. But once they are in the prostitute subculture they find available rationalizations that help them to define their roles in a positive way. Many prostitutes believe that they serve important social functions because the human male has a wide and varied set of sexual needs and they in meeting these needs protect both individuals and social institutions. A part of the belief system is that marriages are more enduring because of prostitution. As Bryan describes it, the positive self images about themselves are that they serve as important psychotherapeutic agents, giving comfort, insight, and satisfaction to those men too embarrassed, lonely, or isolated to obtain interpersonal gratification in other ways."[64]

The roles and the rules of behavior within the prostitute subculture are constantly influenced by the fact that its sexual behavior is illegal. This means that the subculture must develop means for dealing with the legal pressures from the wider society. But often it is difficult for the subculture to know what to do because the controls directed at them vary widely over time. Like most areas of illegal deviance prostitution is not treated consistently by legal agencies. So there is always some insecurity and anxiety as to whether the laws will be applied at a given time. Sometimes the prostitute can control the application of the law by paying off the legal authorities to leave her alone. Therefore, the prostitute is in a position to be exploited by the legal agencies as well as those who know she is susceptible to legal punishment or public exposure. "The prostitute's fear of the police is often as much a fear of the publicity or jail sentence which would reveal her occupation to friends and family as it is a fear of punishment."[65] The very fact that she is engaged in an illegal and "immoral" area means that she is potentially open to exploitation by a variety of people. Because she must reveal herself as a prostitute to the customer means she is always gambling in the sense that the customer may create problems for her. This may range from the plain clothes policeman who entraps her on a charge of prostitution to the customer who refuses to pay her, knowing there is often little that she can do. Others who are around her in the work situation may also exploit her. For

---

[63] Jackman, Norman R., *et al.*, "The Self Image of the Prostitutes," *The Sociological Quarterly*, Spring, 1963, p. 159.

[64] Bryan, *op. cit.*, p. 443.

[65] Hirschi, *op. cit.*, p. 203.

example, desk clerks or bellhops in hotels may exploit their knowledge of her identity as a prostitute by demanding money or by becoming non-paying customers.

It does not seem likely that prostitution will ever disappear completely from American society. There will always be some persons who, even in the most permissive society, will never be able to get sexual partners because of age, mental or physical disabilities, or sexual aberrations. But it does appear logical to assume that prostitution will continue to decrease in the United States. All of the indicators are that sexual expression is becoming for many Americans less restricted to the monogamous structure of marriage and less dependent upon an emotional and interpersonal commitment. That is, as more women see at least some aspects of their sex lives as recreational and are willing to participate within that context, men will have less reason to seek out the prostitute for recreational purposes.

There are two main segments of society where prostitution will probably continue to be important for some time. First is in the lower middle and lower social classes where the double standard of sex continues to be strong. Here the traditional reasons for turning to prostitution continue to prevail. Second is the use of the call girl in the world of big business. This is an area where there is very little reliable information, but where clearly the high priced call girl is very important. But in general, it appears that the profession of prostitution is being greatly reduced by the increase in sexual freedom among women outside of marriage.

BIBLIOGRAPHY

BENJAMIN, HARRY and R. E. L. MASTERS, *Prostitution and Morality* (New York: The Julian Press, Inc., 1964).

BRYAN, JAMES H., "Apprenticeships in Prostitution," *Social Problems*, Winter, 1965, pp. 287–97.

BRYAN, JAMES H., "Occupational Ideologies and Individual Attitudes of Call Girls," *Social Problems*, Spring, 1966, pp. 441–50.

ESSELSTYN, T. C., "Prostitution in the United States," *The Annals*, March, 1968, pp. 123–35.

GEBHARD, PAUL H., "Misconceptions about Female Prostitutes," *Medical Aspects of Human Sexuality*, March, 1969, pp. 24, 28–30.

GREENWALD, HAROLD, *The Call Girl: A Social and Psychoanalytic Study* (New York: Ballantine Books, 1958).

HENRIQUES, FERNANDO, *Prostitution and Society* (New York: Grove Press, Inc., 1962).

HIRSCHI, T., "The Professional Prostitute," *Berkeley Journal of Sociology*, 1962, pp. 33–49.

JACKMAN, NORMAN, *et. al.*, "The Self-Image of the Prostitute," *The Sociological Quarterly*, Spring, 1963, pp. 150–60.

CHAPTER 10

MALE HOMOSEXUALITY

IN THE AREA of sexual deviancy the interest in homosexuality has long existed. In recent years in the United States there has been an increasing amount of public awareness and reaction. For the most part the interest has centered around the male homosexual, and that will be the center of attention in this chapter. In the next chapter the focus will be on the female homosexual. Women are treated separately because the social context varies widely and therefore in many respects male and female homosexuality have to be treated as separate phenomena. The first concern in this chapter will be to look briefly at male homosexuality from a historical and cross-cultural perspective.

Homosexuality was widely practiced in antiquity in most countries of the eastern Mediterranean, as it is today, more than in the Western world. Homosexuality was common among the early Greeks and that was due to cultural values about beauty that were idealized around the slim body of the young man in that culture. But with the rise of Christianity homosexuality became more and more tabooed. It is possible that the first theory of homosexuality came into existence during the medieval period when the homosexual was defined as a person in a supernatural state and being possessed of devils. As the years went on he was increasingly seen as the ultimate in depravity and excessive self abuse.

Until well through the 17th century in England there was no special or particular role given to the homosexual, but toward the end of the 17th century there developed the belief that homosexuality was a condition that characterized certain persons and not others.[1] In other words, being a homosexual was seen as a broad social role rather than as simply a sexual act. It is a fairly complex role built around the homosexual desire and activity and this appears to be the way homosexuality is viewed in most of the Western world today, even though countries do vary in their definitions of homosexuals. A majority of European countries do not prohibit homosexual acts between consenting adults. With the exception of one state the negative legal view of homosexuality is the current one in the United States.

A look at cross-cultural views about male homosexuality provides a picture of differential social treatment. In general, it has been found that among mammals there is some homosexual activity, sometimes to the point of ejaculation. This has been found to be true both in wild and in domesticated animals. However, it is rare to find any individual mammals who show an exclusive pattern of homosexual behavior. Ford and Beach in their cross-cultural comparisons found that of all societies where information was available, in 64 percent homosexual activities of some kind were considered normal and socially acceptable for at least certain members of the community.[2] In another cross-cultural survey of American Indian cultures over half of 225 groups accepted homosexuality while 24 percent rejected it.[3]

To say that homosexuality is acceptable in various cultures doesn't necessarily mean it is practiced. Nor does the report of no homosexuality in a society actually mean that none takes place. For example, of the 76 cultures studied by Ford and Beach, 37 percent of them reported that homosexual activities on the part of adults to be totally absent, rare, or carried on only in secrecy. "It is expected, however, that the estimate would run considerably below actual incidence, since this form of sexual expression is condemned in these societies."[4] Also in societies where adult homosexuality is said to be rare there are specific social pressures directed against such behavior. The penalties range from the light sanction of ridicule to the severe threat of death.

Many societies have fallen between the extremes of permissiveness and restrictiveness of homosexuality. In actual fact many societies have been permissive informally while being restrictive formally. There is some evidence that in societies where homosexuality is highly restricted persons turn to homosexuality *or* heterosexuality, but in societies where there

---

[1] McIntosh, Mary, "The Homosexual Role," *Social Problems*, Fall, 1968, p. 188.

[2] Ford, Clellan S. and Frank A. Beuch, *Patterns of Sexual Behavior* (New York: Harper and Brothers, 1952), p. 130.

[3] Pomeroy, Wardell B., "Homosexuality," in Ralph A. Weltage, *The Same Sex· An Appraisal of Homosexuality* (Philadelphia: Pilgram Books, Inc., 1969), p. 4.

[4] Ford and Beach, *op. cit.*, p. 129.

are no strong social sanctions against homosexuality the males are less apt to be either homosexual or heterosexual and more often combine the two activities.[5] It must also be recognized that cultures are rarely ever consistent in their definitions of homosexuality but are very often characterized by internal disagreements. In other words, in any given society there are different people with different views of homosexuality. For example, those who are homosexuals see their activity as a legitimate practice of a minority while psychologists see it as a type of illness (but often with an implied plea for tolerance, as well as treatment) and law-enforcement agencies see it as a crime.[6]

LEGAL VIEWS

The American laws about homosexuality come out of the same background as do most American laws about sexual behavior. They come from the English common law, with strong religious moral overtones. For the purposes of the legal discussion homosexual behavior is defined as sexual behavior between two persons of the same sex. This sexual behavior can consist of simple touching, kissing, petting, stroking the genitalia, mouth-genital contact, and anal intercourse (for the male). This is a simple definition to be used at this time, although later in the chapter there will be a further discussion about defining homosexuality.

None of the fifty states defines homosexuality as a crime *per se*; "the diverse limitations imposed by the states are aimed at punishing the acts employed by homosexuals to achieve sexual gratifications."[7] While it is no crime to be a homosexual, the various states (with the recent exception of Illinois) do have laws against homosexual acts between adults and minors, among adults, and in private as well as in public. "The homosexual, in other words, has no legal outlet for the kind of sex life to which he is drawn; his only alternative to law-breaking is abstinence."[8] Many laws are in existence to protect persons or property against the invasion of others. But this does not appear to be the case with regard to laws against homosexuality. The laws are not to protect persons or property against the "dangers" of adult homosexual activity but rather are for the enforcement of cultural taboos against homosexuality. One writer argues that the laws represent an effort to enforce a morality rooted in religion

---

[5] Pomeroy, *op. cit.*, p. 6.

[6] Petersen, William and David Matza, *Social Controversy* (Belmont, California: Wadsworth Publishing Co., 1963), p. 5.

[7] "The Consenting Adult Homosexual and the Law," *UCLA Law Review*, University of California at Los Angeles, March, 1966, p. 658.

[8] Schur, Edwin M., *Crimes without Victims: Deviant Behavior and Public Policy* (Englewood Cliffs: N.J.: Prentice-Hall, 1965), p. 77.

that is no longer appropriate.[9] However, this is not to say that a definite majority of Americans no longer believe that homosexuality is "bad" and should not be controlled. Most Americans *do* take a negative view, but this doesn't affect the logic of the legal position one way or another. That is, the people of a country may support a point of view that has no logical or rational basis—and they often do.

Given the laws against homosexual activity, how restrictive or harsh are the legal controls? In theory, the laws are very harsh. For example, a number of states provide a maximum penalty for some homosexual offenses of ten or more years in prison. The penalties range from a maximum of one year in New York for a crime against nature with a person over eighteen years of age and where consent was given, to life imprisonment given for the same situation in Nevada. Four states provide a five year *maximum* for sodomy, while four other states provide a five year *minimum* for the same charge. Not only do the penalties vary widely by states, but there is also a wide variation in how homosexual crimes are defined. For example, some states use the term "sodomy," some "crimes against nature," and others use the term "buggery." This also means that some courts define the same types of homosexuality in different ways with different kinds of punishment. For example, some states have defined these laws as applying only to intercourse per anus (the common-law meaning of sodomy), while other states have held the laws to include fellatio. Twenty states have sodomy laws which have been framed to enlarge the common law definition.[10] All of this means that the laws are confused and therefore their application varies widely over time, by location, and by who is doing the applying. This leaves a great deal of discretion not only to the courts but also to the police.

Actually, in the overwhelming number of cases where homosexuality occurs there is no way in which it could be brought to legal attention. And even if it were, in most situations the legal authorities would do nothing about it. In most situations homosexuality involves the consent of the participants and therefore there is no victim to complain to the legal authorities. While in theory the punishments for homosexual activity are harsh, in reality they do not constitute a strong threat to the average practicing homosexual. Schur points out that here, as with the case of abortion, there is the problem of obtaining evidence. "Because there is a willing exchange of services involved, there is no complainant; except, occasionally, in instances when force has been used, and indecent

---

[9] Cantor, Gilbert M., "The Need for Homosexual Law Reform," in Ralph A. Weltge, *The Same Sex: An Appraisal of Homosexuality* (Philadelphia: Pilgram Books, Inc., 1969), p. 88.

[10] *Ibid.*, p. 85.

assault on a homosexual has been made, or a blatant display has taken place."[11]

The legal controls over deviancy are of course applied on two levels. One is the level of abstraction as presented through the formal legal codes and laws and interpreted through the courts, and the second level is the police use and application of the laws. As suggested, there is confusion in the formal laws with regard to homosexuality and how the courts interpret those laws. This means, as is often the case with legal confusion and changing legal views, that the police make many interpretations in applying the laws. The police know the range of legal possibilities they have and they can choose within that range on the basis of a number of factors they see as important. Furthermore, laws may or may not be applied because of lack of police manpower, the belief that police efforts are needed elsewhere, or because the police may feel homosexuality is not an area of great importance and so they leave it alone. It is also true that sometimes the police use homosexuals as informants and therefore will leave them alone. In general the police do not bother homosexuals unless they define them as constituting a public nuisance. The legal study in Los Angeles found that even when the police knew that homosexuals were cohabitating they usually would not initiate any action. In part that was a practical decision because the law was unenforceable in private situations where it was almost impossible to arrest for private homosexual activity without exceeding search and seizure limitations.[12] Generally the police leave homosexuals alone if they are in private or in clubs unless they receive complaints of soliciting or lewd conduct. Actually, as we shall see, decorum is common to places frequented by middle and upper middle-class homosexuals. In Washington D.C. male homosexual arrests totaled 496 in 1960 but only 69 in 1968. "Today, sodomy is becoming as rare a charge as heresy; a lesser charge like disorderly conduct or loitering is customarily substituted."[13]

It has been a common practice in many cities for the police to use "entrapment" methods to apprehend homosexuals. There has often been disagreement between the police and the homosexual as to what constituted "entrapment." The police have generally argued that it is only entrapment if the decoy policeman makes a clear and unequivocal solicitation of the person. Then when the person agrees the police decoy arrests him. But most homosexuals consider it to be entrapment if the decoy uses any dress, gestures, or language that lure the homosexual in any way into a solicitation. However, the trend in many large cities has been for the police to give up almost all entrapment methods. The New

---

[11] Schur, *op. cit.*, p. 79.

[12] *UCLA Law Review, op. cit.*, p. 689.

[13] *The Washington Post*, October 25, 1969.

York police publicly announced abandonment of their entrapment procedures, and this is reflected in that, while in 1965 there were about 800 arrests of homosexuals in New York city, the number fell to about 80 arrests in 1969.[14] The "hands off" policy toward the homosexual reflects a view from the political leaders of the city but often does not reflect the feeling of the policemen. Policemen often reserve a special contempt for deviants; cases of unprovoked homosexual beatings are a part of the records of most large police departments.

The police have always been responsible for who gets arrested as having committed a homosexual act. Legally, both persons engaging in the homosexual act, whether sodomy or oral intercourse, are guilty. But the police often arrest only the active person as committing a homosexual act. The police tend to see the man who is performing the sex act on the other man as "queer," while the man receiving the sexual act is often seen as unfortunate but as having an understandable tendency toward sexual opportunity. To the police the crux of the matter is that the man who is bringing the other man to orgasm is the "real" homosexual while the man being brought to orgasm is not. "To put it another way, the policeman may feel that seeking an orgasm is not really blameworthy even in a homosexual situation, but that being interested in bringing another male to orgasm is unmitigated perversion. We have interviewed many men who disapproved of homosexuality and hotly denied homosexual activity, but freely admitted that they had been brought to orgasm by other males."[15]

According to the *UCLA Law Review* study on homosexuality there are three basic types of people who are picked up by the police for being involved in homosexual acts. The first type is the "cruiser" who is a confirmed homosexual and very often compulsively moves from bar to bar, or who hangs out around public restrooms, aggressively seeking a number of sexual partners. A second type is the homosexual who hangs out around homosexual gathering places and accepts solicitations, but does not himself actively solicit partners. Third, there is the "situational" offender who is usually the passive partner in oral sex, who is approached by the "cruiser," and who accepts "or is induced to make a solicitation for various nonhomosexually motivated reasons including sexual deviation, intoxication, curiosity, or thrill-seeking, and the hope of robbing the "cruiser." For instance, sailors on shore leave exhibit a tendency towards 'situational' violations."[16]

As suggested, there have been some recent attempts to liberalize the laws about homosexuality. Thus far, only one state, Illinois in 1961, has

---

[14] *Newsweek*, October 27, 1969.

[15] Gebhard, Paul H., *et al.*, *Sex Offenders* (New York: Harper and Row, 1965), pp. 324–25.

[16] *UCLA Law Review, op. cit.*, p. 690.

enacted legislation that has significantly altered the legal interpretations of homosexuality. The Illinois laws have no penalties against private, consensual acts of either a heterosexual or homosexual nature. "Only those acts of deviate sexual conduct which are accompanied by force, perpetrated on children, or committed in an open and notorious manner are proscribed."[17] There will be a new and more liberal law in Connecticut in 1971. There have been a number of states that have attempted more liberal laws with regard to sexual freedom, but for the most part they have not been successful. It appears quite possible that in the future more states will accept new sexual laws. All of the laws that have been presented in various states have been very much concerned with the protection of specific societal interests. The concern has been: (1) that all people be free from any kinds of sexual aggressions; (2) that children be carefully protected from any sexual exploitation; and (3) that people be insulated from any public displays of sexual nature.[18]

But one must be careful in suggesting there is any strong trend in the United States in the direction of more liberal laws about sexual behavior in general and homosexuality in particular. With regard to homosexuality the possible legal trends may be seen with reference to sodomy laws. In the period from 1951 to 1965 Arizona, California, New Hampshire, New Jersey, and Wyoming increased their penalties against sodomy. During the same period Arkansas, Colorado, Georgia, Illinois, Nevada, North Dakota, New York, Oregon, and Wisconsin lessened their penalties.[19] These law changes would *not* indicate any very strong liberal trend with regard to homosexuality. One common fear is that if the laws are liberalized there will be a sharp increase in homosexuality. Gagnon and Simon have suggested that greater tolerance of homosexuality through the reform of sex laws would not increase the incidence of homosexuality. But it might allow those males who had not, due to fear of the law, engaged in homosexual contact, to enter into such relationships. "At the same time, there may be a countertendency. The lowering of sanctions and the decrease in stigma may reduce the barrier between the homosexual and heterosexual world, and this may allow some persons in the homosexual world to develop an interest in heterosexual adjustments."[20]

The best available data on the extent of homosexuality in American society still come from the Kinsey study. That study found that about 10 percent of all American men had fairly extensive experiences with homosexuality. However, only about 4 percent of the total male popula-

---

[17] *Ibid.*, p. 668.

[18] *Ibid.*

[19] Cantor, *op. cit.*, p. 83.

[20] Gagnon, John H. and William Simon, "Sexual Deviance in Contemporary America," *The Annals*, March, 1968, pp. 116–17.

tion had an extensive adult commitment to homosexuality.[21] Studies indicate that the incidence of homosexual behavior is high and continues to increase with age among single men while among married men it is low and decreases slightly with age. If the Kinsey figure of 4 percent of all males being extensively homosexual in their adult years is still true then it may be extrapolated that there are between two and three million men who are exclusively homosexual in the United States today. This should be taken only as a crude estimate because the actual figure cannot be known. But what is important is that homosexuality is the exclusive sexual pattern followed by a large minority of American men.

"CAUSES" OF HOMOSEXUALITY

It is doubtful if any other area of human deviance has been subjected to so many attempts to explain its causes as has homosexuality. It appears that, because homosexuality has been traditionally seen as so "abnormal," there has been a feeling of great need to explain it, in part so that "normal" sex can be more securely understood. Homosexuality has presented a challenge to the developing personal and social sciences of the past 100 years. There have been attempts to explain homosexuality by biologists, geneticists, physiologists, psychiatrists, psychoanalysts, psychologists, social psychologists, sociologists, and others. The body of literature in this area is so vast that it can only be very briefly mentioned here.

The attempts to explain the "causes" of homosexuality may be placed into three general groupings: medical, psychological and social. As suggested, historically there have been a number of attempts to define the causes of homosexuality. It was in earlier days seen as sinful and evil behavior, and then later viewed as moral degeneracy. But those approaches are no longer given serious consideration.

Medical Explanations

Under this heading we may briefly consider several medical approaches. For example, there has long been an attempt to explain homosexuality on the grounds of inborn, innate characteristics, that is, the person is born with traits or forces that would make him become a homosexual. However, there has been no research of any significance that supports this approach. Another medical approach has been in terms of hormone treatments for believed deficiencies. But hormone studies have proven almost uniformly negative in finding any differences between homosexual

---

[21] Kinsey, Alfred C., Wardell B. Pomeroy and Clyde E. Martin, *Sexual Behavior in the Human Male* (Philadelphia: W. B. Saunders Company, 1949), p. 640.

and heterosexual individuals, as have various studies of body structure, genital anatomy, and brain injuries. "Studies showing any positive findings in these areas have been poorly done, have had too few subjects or a poor selection of subjects, or have been contradicted by other studies."[22] Yet, there continues to be the belief held by many that some hormonal factors as well as some physical characteristics may indirectly play a part in the development of the homosexual.

The more common medical approach to homosexuality is reflected in the tendency to label it as a "disease" or "illness." This is in part a reflection of a trend in society to apply the concept of illness to many personal and social problems. The view that homosexuality is a sickness implies several consequences. "The first is that those in whom the condition exists are sick persons and should therefore be regarded as medical problems and consequently as primarily a medical responsibility. The second is that sickness implies irresponsibility, or at least diminished responsibility."[23] It has been argued that in using symptoms as a criterion to determine a disease homosexuality does not fit, because in many cases it is the only symptom and the person is mentally healthy in all other respects. There are some cases where psychiatric abnormalities do occur and if, "as has been suggested, they occur with greater frequency in the homosexual, this may be because they are products of the strain and conflict brought about by the homosexual condition and not because they are causal factors."[24] It appears that a disease approach to homosexuality does little to explain causes and contributes little to understanding homosexuality.

PSYCHOLOGICAL EXPLANATIONS

It is here that probably the best known theories about the causes of homosexuality have been developed. This is particularly true with regard to psychoanalytic theories which assert that homosexuality is a form of mental sickness. The psychoanalytic approach is to try to affect the causes of the "sickness" in the homosexual or to help him accept his "sickness" and live with it. In any sociological attempt to understand the causes of homosexuality the psychoanalytic approach is of very little value.

Another psychological approach to explaining the causes of homosexuality sees early childhood experiences as the crucial causal setting. These theories attempt to relate homosexuality to the child's early experiences with his family. Some researchers stress "undue attachment to

---

[22] Pomeroy, op. cit., p. 12.

[23] "Wolfenden Committee," in Edward Sagarin and Donald E. MacNamara, Problems of Sex Behavior (New York: Thomas Y. Crowell Co., 1968) pp. 115–16.

[24] Ibid., p. 117.

the mother, others emphasize unsatisfactory relations with the father, while still others seem to have evidence that both are of equal importance."[25] Another limitation found with this type of approach is that found with all theories that depend on the individual's recall of childhood experiences and call on him for hearsay evidence not only about himself, but also about his parents. To illustrate this limitation Simon and Gagnon point out that recent research in childrearing practices indicates "that two years after the major events of childrearing, weaning, and toilet training mothers fail to recall accurately their previous conduct."[26] If this is true for adults then how much trust can be given to the recall of his childhood by the adult over a far greater span of years?

Social Explanations

There is a psychological assumption that social theories of homosexuality make. This assumption is that there is nothing innate in the sex drive of the individual other than the need for tension release. Therefore the objects toward which the sex drive is directed are a result of social learning. "Young male mammals who have not been previously conditioned will react to any sufficient sexual stimuli, whether these are autoerotic, heteroerotic, or homoerotic in character, and moreover may become conditioned to any of these stimuli."[27] Therefore, homosexuality, as is heterosexuality, is learned through one's social experiences with regard to the sex drive. This means that there is no "natural" sexual pattern, but rather there is the pattern that one learns to satisfy the need of a sexual drive. Whatever the causes for the direction by which one seeks to satisfy his sexual drive, it is done within a dynamic social setting that may variously reinforce or undercut the direction over time. For example, the boy may be socially pushed because he is of slight body build and not able to compete successfully in the world of sports. No social conditions are inevitable, but many may contribute in different and varying ways to a trend already started, or even to starting a trend in the direction of homosexuality.

One writer has argued that it will not be until the sociologist sees homosexuals as representing a social category, rather than a medical or psychiatric one, that we will begin to ask the "right questions about the specific content of the homosexual role and the organization and func-

---

[25] Bene, Eva, "On the Genesis of Male Homosexuality," in William A. Rushing, *Deviant Behavior and Social Process* (Chicago: Rand McNally and Co., 1969), p. 164.

[26] Simon, William and John H. Gagnon, "Homosexuality: The Formulation of a Sociological Perspective," *Journal of Health and Social Behavior*, September, 1967, p. 178.

[27] Churchhill, Waunwright, *Homosexual Behavior among Males* (New York: Hawthorne Books, Inc., 1967), p. 95.

tions of homosexual groups."[28] This approach recognizes that for the committed homosexual, his sexual inclinations are a part of a continuing role he plays and not simply a series of specific sexual activities. The role of the homosexual is not peculiar to himself, but rather is shared with others who are homosexual. As will be discussed in detail it is the very nature of their particular deviance that homosexuals are drawn into interaction with one another.[29] It has been pointed out that the homosexual's sexual object choice has dominated and controlled the views about him and led to the assumption that his sexual choice determines all other aspects of his life. "This prepossessing concern on the part of nonhomosexuals with the purely sexual aspect of the homosexual's life is something we would not allow to occur if we were interested in the heterosexual."[30] Of course, homosexuals vary widely in the degree to which their sexual commitment is the major focus for organizing their lives.

The view of homosexuality as a social role implies a "naming process" for both the homosexual and for others who define him as such. As McIntosh has pointed out the practice of the "naming process" or social labeling of deviants operates in two ways as a means of social control. First, it provides a clear cut and recognized dividing line between permissible and impermissible behavior. Second, it helps to segregate the deviants from others and this restricts their practices and rationalizations to relatively confined groups.[31] Often the deviant sees the social role he fills as a condition which he cannot control. Given this view the homosexual often sees his homosexual role as justified because he cannot move back into the heterosexual world completely. But it is suggested that the homosexual should be seen as playing a social role rather than as having a condition.[32]

What can be said sociologically about the causes of homosexuality? The concern with the basic causes of homosexuality may be overdone. Even if the causes could be distinguished, that knowledge would have limited application to understanding or even influencing the *development* of homosexuality. This is true because often the reason for starting in the direction of some form of deviant behavior has little to do with the influences that occur once the start is made. For example, the initial reason for taking drugs may have little relevance to the developing patterns that make the person into a drug addict. There is a tendency to think of causes as discrete and set in time rather than as being diffuse and

---

[28] McIntosh, *op. cit.*, p. 192.

[29] Schur, *op. cit.*, p. 85.

[30] Simon and Gagnon, *op. cit.*, p. 179.

[31] McIntosh, *op. cit.*, p. 183.

[32] *Ibid.*, p. 184.

changing over time. The research data on homosexuality clearly show it to be a complex phenomenon not only in how it is manifested in individual and social experience and behavior but also "in its determination by psychodynamics, biological, cultural, situational, and structural variables. An 'either-or' position with respect to any one of these variables simply does not account for the extraordinary diversity of the phenomena to be accounted for."[33] There also appears to be general agreement among experts as to two aspects of homosexuality: one, that there exists in some people a homosexual propensity that varies quantitatively in different individuals and can also vary quantitatively in the same person at different stages in his life cycle; and second, that this propensity can influence behavior in several ways, some of which are not clearly sexual, although exactly how much and in what ways are matters for disagreement and dispute among experts.[34]

There is a need to question some of the assumptions made about the causes and directions that homosexuality takes, because with few exceptions the discovery of homosexuality in a person is taken as clear evidence that there exists major psychopathology. "When the heterosexual meets these minimum definitions of mental health, he is exculpated; the homosexual—no matter how good his adjustment in nonsexual areas of life—remains suspect."[35] The image of the homosexual often presented to society is that of those homosexuals the medical practictioner encounters, and these are almost always people with severe problems. On this point Pomeroy, as a practicing psychologist, has said that if his concept of homosexuality were based on what he sees in his practice he would also think of it as illness. "I have seen no homosexual man or woman in that practice who wasn't troubled, emotionally upset, or neurotic. On the other hand, if my concept of marriage in the United States were based on my practice, I would have to conclude that marriages are all fraught with strife and conflict, and that heterosexuality is an illness."[36]

Sociologically, the most fruitful approach to studying homosexuality may center around the notion of social roles. Some roles which have as a basic part the nature of one's sexual inclination also include far more than that. Simon and Gagnon have been the major figures in attempting to develop a sociology of homosexuality. They feel that the problem of finding out how people become homosexual requires an adequate theory of how they become heterosexual. And the patterns of adult homosexuality are dependent on the social structures and values that surround the

---

[33] Hooker, Evelyn, "Male Homosexuals and Their 'Worlds,'" in Judd Marmor, *Sexual Inversion* (New York: Basic Books, 1965) p. 86.

[34] "Wolfenden Committee," *op. cit.*, p. 113.

[35] Simon and Gagnon, *op. cit.*, p. 180.

[36] Pomeroy, *op. cit.*, p. 13.

homosexual after he becomes such.[37] Therefore in the next section the concern will be with the development and significance of the homosexual subculture.

THE HOMOSEXUAL SUBCULTURE

The subculture of homosexuals is found in the large cities of the United States. There are undoubtedly some variations between the different cities with regard to the size and complexity of the subculture. But there are patterns that are common to all cities and those are the focal point of interest in this section. One of the problems in trying to study a deviant subculture is that so much of it is hidden, not only from the broader society but often even from many of the deviants themselves. Hooker has described the homosexual subculture as analogous to an iceberg, where the visible aspects of the subculture are only a small part of the whole and an understanding of the hidden part is fundamental to an understanding of the whole. She writes that in the broad world of homosexuality are to be found men who have "longstanding living relationships with other homosexual men and who rarely, if ever, go to bars or other public establishments because of their sexually predatory and competitive character."[38] In other words, many homosexuals are isolates. For the most part they will not be a part of the discussion in this section because there is little known about them and they are not a part of the homosexual subculture.

What does the homosexual subculture mean in the broadest sense? The subculture implies a continuing group of individuals who share some significant activity and begin to develop a sense of a bounded group possessing special norms and a particular argot. They engage in various social activities that reinforce a feeling of identity and provide for the homosexual a way of institutionalizing the experience, wisdom, and mythology of the collectivity.[39] As Hooker explains it, it is within the context of the subculture in relation to the broader society that homosexuals are able to develop working solutions to problems of sexual performance and psychological gender which cannot be understood in the perspective of the heterosexual world.[40]

Of course all deviant subcultures represent structures built around that which makes the members deviant. The deviance becomes a highly

---

[37] Simon and Gagnon, *op. cit.*, p. 179.

[38] Hooker, *op. cit.*, pp. 100–101.

[39] Simon, William and John H. Gagnon, "Feminity in the Lesbian Community," *Social Problems*, Fall, 1967, p. 217.

[40] Hooker, Evelyn, "An Empirical Study of Some Relations between Sexual Patterns and Gender Identity in Male Homosexuals," in John Money, *Sex Research: New Development* (New York: Holt, Rinehart and Winston, 1965), p. 26.

significant role for the individual. This is similar to the complex of activities that are built around other major roles that the person fills, as around sex role, occupational role, or that of a family member. But for the deviant, the role of deviancy may transcend all other roles in importance not only for him but also for others who know him as a deviant. Therefore, one of the consequences of the deviant commitment to sexual choice becomes of major importance in the organization of the homosexual's overall life style. He may organize his "friendship, leisure time, and occupational adjustments around the homosexual community and around homosexual friends."[41] The subculture becomes a socialization setting not only for the new homosexual but also for those who have been in it for a while. Once individuals enter that life their personal and social identities as homosexuals are continually being defined over time through their interaction with one another. Of course, different people are involved in different degrees within the subculture and are therefore differentially influenced by it.

However great the degree of involvement by the homosexual in the subculture, it must always be recognized that it is only one important influence on his life style. The subculture presents one set of variables, which interact with many other variables, "such as personality dynamics and structure, personal appearance (including body build, gesture, demeanor), age, and occupation, to produce these attitudes, self-concepts, and behavior. Most accounts of gender identity and sex roles in male homosexuals focus on personality traits and psychodynamics, and ignore the important contribution of the shared perspectives of homosexual subcultures."[42] While the stress here is on the influence of the subculture for the homosexual it must be kept in mind that there are other forces, in varying degrees of strength, influencing and shaping his behavior both individually and socially.

Evelyn Hooker's research provides an indication of the various types of homosexuals that will be encountered in an analysis of subcultures. She suggests three general social levels of homosexual types that generally *will not* be a part of the subcultural setting: one, closely knit clique groups formed around pairs of homosexuality "married" persons, or singles, many of whom are married to women; two, larger groups with one or more loose clique structures as a central group along with a number of peripheral members; and three, loose networks of friends who may meet once in a while at various parties.[43]

Because it is the special sexual choice that sets homosexuals apart it is important to look more specifically at the direction the sexual activity

---

[41] Gagnon and Simon, *op. cit.*, p. 116.

[42] Hooker, *op. cit.*, pp. 44–5.

[43] Hooker, Evelyn, "The Homosexual Community," in John H. Gagnon and William Simon, *Sexual Deviance* (New York: Harper and Row, 1967), p. 180.

takes. That is, there is a need to examine the range of homosexuality both as a sexual act and as a sexual activity role of the individual. One basic distinction that is made is between the bisexual and the homosexual. The bisexuals are those that have both homosexual and heterosexual experiences. There are some bisexuals who are that way because they believe that the sexual act is the thing that one does and the gender of the partner doesn't really matter. The sexual experience, not the sexual partner, is what matters. But other bisexuals may be caught in conflict because they can't make a clear choice to go one way or another and this bothers them. Many of these do seek out the homosexual subculture because they see it as providing them with a rationale for their homosexual inclinations.

The term homosexual as it is used here refers to those persons who have made an overwhelming personal commitment for some time to sexual partners of the same sex. This means they are homosexual regardless of the sexual roles during homosexual activity that they choose to play. Traditionally, the role of homosexual was seen as only applying to those who played the female role. The old terms of "active and passive" partners or "masculine and feminine" roles are no longer applicable to many homosexuals. "Instead, the variety and form of the sexual acts between pair members, the distribution of tasks performed and the character of their performance do not permit us to make such a differentiation."[44]

The stereotype of the homosexual continues to be one of a highly effeminate male. He is seen as a person who deliberately acts like, as well as uses the speech patterns and gestures of, the woman. "Blatant displays of effeminacy are viewed with scorn by many male homosexuals; similarly, in some cases it may be an exaggerated display of masculinity that makes one man an object of sexual desire for another."[45] When effeminacy is found in the homosexual male it is probably not due to measurable differences from other males in physical characteristics, but rather in the use of the voice, facial gestures, walk, gait, manner of wearing the hair, and other characteristics.[46]

Not only may there be effeminacy among some male homosexuals but there may also be among others an exaggerated masculinity. There are some male homosexuals who act excessively male and almost caricature the image of masculinity. To further confuse the picture Pomeroy has pointed out that there are "false positives"—"people whose mannerisms, vocal inflection, or way of dress suggests homosexuality even though they have no homosexual tendencies."[47] Pomeroy goes on to say that the relationship between effeminacy and homosexuality is very elusive. For ex-

---

[44] Hooker, "Male Homosexuals and Their Worlds," *op. cit.*, p. 102.

[45] Schur, *op. cit.*, p. 69.

[46] Cory, Donald W., "Homosexuality," in Albert Ellis and Albert Abarbanel, *Encyclopedia of Sexual Behavior* (New York: Hawthorne Books, Inc., 1961), p. 488.

[47] Pomeroy, *op. cit.*, p. 11.

ample "overt homosexual contact was probably more common among the cowboys and the Indian fighters of the west in the 19th century than among any other single group of males in our century."[48]

Furthermore, it is often difficult, if not impossible, to distinguish the homosexual from the heterosexual by various psychological tests. Evelyn Hooker presented to a group of judges, selected on the basis of their clinical expertise, the results of three widely used clinical projective tests that had been given to homosexuals as well as to a group of heterosexuals. The judges were able to distinguish the homosexuals from the heterosexuals on no better than a chance level.[49] The evidence clearly shows that one cannot accurately define the homosexual as a distinguishable type in appearance or even as a personality type, at least on the basis of present psychological tests.

If homosexuals cannot be clearly distinguished on the basis of appearance is it possible to analyze them by the type of sexual activity they engage in? In the broadest sense homosexuality can refer to any kind of sexual activity that occurs between members of the same sex. However the two basic types of sexual activity are oral and anal sexual relations. Many homosexuals view with repulsion sodomy (anal sex) because initially it is very painful and it is only after considerable conditioning that it becomes pleasurable. One researcher estimates that only about 20 percent of all homosexuals engage in sodomy as recipient.[50] So oral sex is the overwhelming activity of male homosexuals. It used to be believed that only the effeminate homosexual used his mouth in providing oral sex while the masculine role partner received the oral sex but never gave it. In fact, many, if not most, homosexuals do have a preference for one way or another *but* are often willing to be either the passive or active partner in oral sex depending on the desires of the partner. It also appears that the beginning and younger male homosexuals most often have oral sex performed on them but as they get older and are involved longer in homosexuality will often turn on at least some occasions to performing oral sex on a partner. This shift over time is reflected in an old homosexual belief that, "today's trade is tomorrow's competition." However, who does what in the sex act is not a clear indicator of the broader sex roles played among homosexuals.

The subcultural world of homosexuality is characterized by a high level of sexual expression with a variety of partners. Therefore, one of the characteristics of the homosexual subculture is the high degree of sexual promiscuity. Hoffman writes that "since the sexual relationships in gay life tend to be transitory, the sexually active homosexual constantly

---

[48] *Ibid.*

[49] Cited in Weisstein, Naomi, "Woman as Nigger," *Psychology Today*, October, 1969, p. 22.

[50] Allen, Clifford, "Sexual Perversions," in Albert Ellis and Albert Abarbanel, *Encyclopedia of Sexual Behavior* (New York: Hawthorne Books, Inc., 1961), p. 804.

needs new partners in order to obtain a reasonable amount of sexual satisfaction."[51] The excessive amount of promiscuity makes it very difficult to estimate the number of different sex partners had by the adult male homosexual. Many homosexuals estimate that they have had hundreds of sex partners and some even place the estimates in the thousands. Gebhard found in his sample of adult males that two-thirds had had over 75 different sex partners. He goes on to point out that part of the reason for the large numbers is that some homosexuals are as interested in the sexual activity for its own sake as they are interested in achieving their own orgasm. In fact they are sometimes more interested in the former. "This is particularly true of the homosexual who is desirious of fellating other males. In one evening he may tally more sexual partners than many purely heterosexual males may accumulate in a lifetime."[52]

There are some general distinctions made within the subculture about the nature of the sexual relationship. The "one night stand" is probably the most common type of homosexual relationship. However, this may take two forms, one of which is the "quicky" which is brief and may range from a few minutes to a few hours. In that situation the partners have probably never seen each other before and usually will never see each other again. A second kind of one night stand is where the couple spend the night or even a weekend together. By contrast an "affair" between homosexuals is seen as a relationship lasting for weeks or months.[53] These types of relationships are very similar to those found between many unmarried men and women.

As suggested, many sexual encounters between male homosexuals involve only a single encounter and they never see each other again. One study found that 60 percent of the sex partners were persons with whom they had sex only one time. And for about 40 percent of the respondents the longest homosexual affair lasted less than one year.[54] Having so many different partners carries with it certain risks. This risk is even greater when the partners are sought in public and semipublic locations. It was found that between a quarter and a third of the homosexual respondents reported having been robbed by a sexual partner.[55]

"COMING OUT"

Highly important to any deviant subculture is what takes place when an individual enters and is accepted by the subculture. In the life cycle

---

[51] Hoffman, Martin, *The Gay World* (New York: Bantam Books, 1968), p. 42.

[52] Gebhard, *op. cit.*, p. 344.

[53] Sonenschein, David, "The Ethnology of Male Homosexual Relations," *The Journal of Sex Research*, May, 1968, p. 77.

[54] Gagnon and Simon, "Homosexuality: The Formulation of a Sociologial Perspective," *op. cit.*, p. 354.

[55] *Ibid.*

of the individual this is a crucial "naming stage." Within the homosexual subculture this is referred to as "coming out"—as presenting oneself as being homosexual at least to the extent of wanting to function at times within the subculture. So coming out is that point when the person sees himself as a homosexual and makes his first exploration into the homosexual subculture. Hoffman says that walking into a homosexual bar for the first time is a momentous act in the life history of the person because for the first time he publicly identifies himself as a homosexual. "Of equal importance is the fact that it brings home to him the realization that there are many young men like himself and, thus, that he is a member of a community and not the isolate he had previously felt himself to be."[56]

When the homosexual first comes out his decision may release for him a great deal of sexual energy. During the initial period he may pursue sex quite indiscriminately and with great vigor and enthusiasm. Gagnon and Simon have suggested that this period is similar to the "honeymoon" view of sex held by the young married couple. That is, sexual intercourse is seen as legitimate and therefore pursued with great energy. However, the high sexual involvement declines as demands are made on the young married couple. "In these same terms, during the homosexual "honeymoon" many individuals begin to learn ways of acting out homosexual object choice that involve homosexual gratification, but that are not necessarily directly sexual and do not involve the genitalia."[57] The same authors also suggest that during the coming out stage there is sometimes a crisis in the degree of femininity to express. There is often a tendency to "act out" in public places in a somewhat effeminate manner. "Thus the tendency is for this kind of behavior to be a transitional experiment for most homosexuals, an experiment that leaves vestiges of 'camp' behavior, but traces more often expressive of the character of the cultural life of the homosexual community than of some overriding need of individual homosexuals."[58]

While coming out implies an entrance into the homosexual subculture it at the same time also implies the leaving behind to some extent of the straight world. This carries with it certain possible risks for the homosexual. It may endanger his livelihood or his professional career. But if he is able to escape those dangers his coming out may have some positive consequences for him in the eyes of the broader society. For example it may absolve him from failure to assume the responsibilities of marriage and parenthood, and it is a way of fending off painful involvements in heterosexual affairs.[59] Once the individual has made the move and is accepted as a part of the homosexual subculture he may find himself a

---

[56] Hoffman, *op. cit.*, p. 14.

[57] Gagnon and Simon, *op. cit.*, p. 356.

[58] Simon and Gagnon, "Homosexuality," *op. cit.*, p. 182.

[59] Lemert, Edwin M., *Human Deviance, Social Problems and Social Control* (Englewood Cliffs, N.J.: Prentice-Hall, 1967), p. 48.

functioning member with a number of shared values and behavior patterns. One area of values in the subculture centers around love and the establishment of extended homosexual relationships.

Probably most homosexuals desire love and permanent relationships. If these values do not seem too important when they are young they take on increasing importance as the homosexual gets older. Most homosexuals distinguish sex and love relationships from those of friendship. They usually try to keep sex separate from their friendships. Many homosexuals have friends with whom they have never attempted to have sex, as well as friends who were once sexual partners but have since moved into nonsexual friendships. Sonenschein also found that while "genital relations between friends were extremely rare, sex play was very common."[60] There is sexual kidding but not actual sexual activity.

It is common to hear the verbalized image that the homosexual is like anyone else except that he chooses a sex object of the same sex. He is said to want long-lasting and monogamous relationships based on love the same as do heterosexuals. He recognizes that many of his relationships do not come close to approximating this ideal of love and permanency of relationship. This the homosexual may argue is no different from the ideal and the reality of the heterosexual world. He often sees that world as one where every husband cheats, there is a high level of wife swapping, and the only thing that holds the marriage together is the social pressure of children.[61] This view helps the homosexual in his rationalization that his world isn't very different from that of the heterosexual.

Gebhard found that deep emotional involvements were commonly reported among homosexuals. In his sample 81 percent said they had loved another male and 63 percent had loved more than one male.[62] As suggested, to find a permanent partner was a common goal for many homosexuals, but was not universal. It did increase after "aging" set in (about age 30), when finding a steady mate became a significant concern.[63] As the homosexual finds his competitive ability on the market decreasing a more permanent relationship becomes even more desirable to him.

There are some homosexuals who do set up fairly permanent relationships and define themselves as being "married." Sonenschein in his study found homosexual "marriages" to be characterized by certain traits. (1) There was usually some sort of ritual, and in most cases it was an imitation of the heterosexual marriage ceremony. (2) There was the using of some of the symbols of the ceremony as in the wearing of wedding rings.

---

[60] Sonenschein, op. cit., p. 73.

[61] Sagarin, Edward, Odd Man In: Societies of Deviants in America (Chicago: Quadrangle Books, 1969), p. 99.

[62] Gebhard, op. cit., p. 347.

[63] Sonenschein, op. cit., p. 80.

(3) There was a tendency to dichotomize social roles. This sometimes was one staying home and being feminine and the other going to work and being masculine. But this was not a typical pattern and described a special type of "marriage."[64] In most cases the division of labor in terms of household duties was based on personal choice rather than any masculine or feminine role differences.[65]

THE HOMOSEXUAL BAR

Important to any subculture is that there be opportunities and settings where the members may meet and interact with one another. The physical setting may also take on a symbolic meaning for the deviant because when he enters the setting it signifies to him that he is among his own kind and he may be open and relatively free in filling his deviant role. Probably the most important subcultural setting for the homosexual is the bar. It has been suggested that the bar provides a natural setting for the homosexual community because most of the homosexual's involvement in his subculture is during his leisure time, and the bar provides the setting for free time sociability. It has also generally been true that because homosexuals have been subject to legal and police pressures they needed a gathering place which was mobile, a place which can open, close, and open again without great loss or difficulty. However, it should be stressed that homosexuals who turn to bars are a minority of all practicing homosexuals. But the bar is important because it is visible and tells us something about general patterns of interaction in the homosexual subculture.

It is quite probable that not only most large cities in the United States, but also in the Western world, have homosexual bars. Of course the number of bars and their freedom from legal intervention varies greatly. For example, in Europe the city of Amsterdam is informally known as the homosexual capital. This is because Amsterdam not only has many homosexual bars and other gathering places, but also because it takes a generally permissive view toward homosexuality. This has proved to be an economically profitable point of view for that country. In the United States the most permissive city with regard to homosexual bars and other activities is probably San Francisco. This is a part of that city's long time permissive attitude toward sexual matters in general, which is also seen in its acceptance of erotic movies, nude dancers, and so forth.

In the various cities the homosexual bars tend to cluster in certain areas. This is in part because of the habits of the clientele, who often like to move from one bar to another during the course of an evening. Hooker

---

[64] *Ibid.*, p. 81.
[65] *Ibid.*, p. 75.

found that in Los Angeles the clusters of homosexual bars are typically found in the following areas: "residential sections with heavy concentrations of homosexuals; beaches or other places of homosexual group recreation or leisure-time activity; public entertainment districts—theaters and so forth; and areas of high tolerance and relative permissiveness toward other forms of deviant behavior."[66] As to how many homosexual bars there are in cities, some indication can be given from figures for two cities. In the middle 1960's in San Francisco there were more than 30 bars that catered exclusively to a homosexual clientele. In the late 1960's it was estimated that there were at least 35 bars in Los Angeles County that catered exclusively to homosexual customers.[67] A few bars encourage heterosexual trade because they come in to "watch" the homosexuals. The homosexuals (and sometimes they put on an act) in those bars are in effect the floor show or entertainment that draws the straight crowd. However, this is not the kind of bar the homosexual wants to frequent as a part of his subcultural involvement.

There also appears in some cities to be a wide range of homosexual bars that are differentiated by various types of clientele. A study in Los Angeles found a variety of homosexual bars such as the S&M (sadists and masochists) clubs and "makeout" bars. Often the owner of the bar cultivates a specific type of homosexual customer and takes steps to keep others out. "One bar owner stated that on rare occasions when non-homosexuals try to enter, he will either ask them to leave or serve warm beer, or turn off the heating system. Further, if homosexuals who are not regular customers try to enter, they will be ostracized by those present. Thus most homosexual bars are quasi-private clubs which create no risk of outraging the public."[68] In most cities the general policy of the alcoholic beverage commissions and the police departments is one of tolerance. In Los Angeles this is true as long as the owners do not allow the occurrence of overt homosexual activities to take place on their premises. In general, the authorities feel that the mere congregation of homosexuals at a bar is not enough to justify any action. But it was found that the policies of the police department towards harassment of homosexual bars did vary, with the larger communities appearing to be more tolerant than smaller communities.[69]

Homosexuals do not congregate in just any homosexual bar, rather they seek out those that are not only convenient but where the atmosphere allows them to feel at ease. Therefore, the successful operation of a homosexual bar calls for skill on the part of the operator. "It requires a

---

[66] Hooker, *op. cit.*, p. 95.
[67] UCLA *Law Review, op. cit.*, p. 689.
[68] *Ibid.*, pp. 689–90.
[69] *Ibid.*, p. 730.

knowledge of the tastes and behavior of homosexual clientele and the ability to create the kind of atmosphere that will attract them in large numbers, as well as the ability to control behavior within limits to which law enforcement officers, passing as ordinary clientele, cannot legally object."[70] The successful bar begins to take on an atmosphere of its own. This is reflected in the same faces that appear in the bar several nights of the week. "Every bar has its cluster of friends who gather to exchange gossip, to look over the new faces, and to spend social evenings in an atmosphere congenial to them, where the protective mask of the day may be dropped."[71]

But the most important function of the homosexual bar is that it serves as a "flesh market." It functions very much like the "socials" discussed in an earlier chapter with reference to "swingers." On a given evening two persons may meet and make arrangements to get together that evening for sexual purposes, or may exchange information to be used at some future date to get together. Hoffman writes that men go for the purpose of finding sexual partners, "and if this function were not served by the bar there would be no gay bars, for, although homosexuals also go there to drink and socialize, the search for sexual experience is in some sense the core of the interaction in the bar."[72] While the "flesh market" aspect of the bars may be their basic reason for existence they do perform other important functions for the homosexual. These bars are also centers where friends can meet and exchange news about the homosexual world. Hoffman suggests that the sexual function of the homosexual bar is illustrated by the way the patrons sit. He says that in a heterosexual bar the patrons' interests are focused on one another as they sit in pairs or small groups. But in a homosexual bar the patrons sitting at the bar usually face away from the bar and look toward the other people in the room and toward the door as they watch for possible sex partners.[73]

Besides the homosexual bars there are other locations or gathering points where homosexuals may come together. These are locations where some subcultural interaction may take place, but which more specifically provide the setting for sexual exchange to occur. The first of these are the public baths found in most large cities. Here the persons are stripped and are judged on their physical attributes. The baths as a homosexual gathering place exist because of the strong tendency among some homosexuals to be highly promiscuous. It is difficult to imagine female homosexuals developing a similar kind of sexual gathering place. Many of the men who go to the baths and have only one sexual experience during that visit will

---

[70] Hooker, op. cit., p. 96.

[71] Ibid., p. 98.

[72] Hoffman, op. cit., p. 51.

[73] Ibid., pp. 53–4.

feel disappointed. Hoffman writes that he once interviewed a young man at one of the baths who "preferred to take the receptor role in anal intercourse and had 48 sexual contacts in one evening, simply by going into his room, leaving the door open, lying on his belly and letting 48 men in succession sodomize him."[74] This is an illustration of the ultimate peak of purely physical sexual interaction with no personal interchange taking place.

Closely related to the use of baths, but much more common, is the use of public restrooms for sexual contact. In the jargon of the homosexual subculture these are referred to as "tearooms." Public restrooms are used because those who know can easily recognize them. "Drives and walks that separate a public toilet from the rest of the park are almost certain guidelines to deviant sex. The ideal setting for homosexual activity is a 'tearoom' situated on an island of grass with roads close by on every side."[75] The tearoom, like the baths, represents the setting where the most impersonal sex takes place. Throughout most of the sexual encounters in the public restroom nothing is said. "One may spend many hours in these buildings and witness dozens of sexual acts without hearing a word. The mechanism of silence goes beyond satisfying the demand for privacy. Like all other characteristics of the tearoom setting, it serves to guarantee anonymity, to assure the impersonality of the sexual liaison."[76] In the homosexual subculture the restroom serves a highly specialized function —a place for the sexual act to occur.

Within the specialized homosexual setting of the tearoom there are really only two roles. One performs the sex act and the other receives it. The one who performs the sexual act on the men who come is the one who is usually seen as being a homosexual. This man is often one who wants a large number of sexual experiences, and he may fellate ten or fifteen men a day. The men who come to the tearooms looking for the sexual act to be performed on them are called "trade" in the homosexual subculture. Many of these men are known as regulars and stop in the restroom almost every day on the way to or from work. Humphreys found that only a small percentage of the homosexuals who hang out in the bars are also found in the restrooms. "The so-called closet queens and other types of covert deviants make up the vast majority of those who engage in homosexual acts—and these are the persons most attracted to tearoom encounters."[77]

It appears that most of the men who seek homosexual release in the tearooms are seeking nothing more than physical sexual release. "They

---

[74] *Ibid.*, p. 48.

[75] Humpheys, Laud, "Tearoom Trade: Impersonal Sex in Public Places," *Trans-Action*, January, 1970, p. 12.

[76] *Ibid.*, p. 13.

[77] *Ibid.*

want a form of orgasm-producing action that is less lonely than masturbation and less involving than a love relationship."[78] But with no verbal exchange it is hard to see that these kinds of sexual activities are any more personal than masturbation. In fact the code of behavior among the "trade" is reflected in there being no friendship groups among those who come to the restrooms. They come in alone, seek out the sexual outlet, and avoid conversation with one another. So impersonality is the keynote of sex in the tearoom.

Humpheys has some data on those who seek out sexual release in the public restrooms. He found them to be uniformly lonely and isolated and with no success in marriage or in work. "En route from the din of factories to the clamor of children, they slip off the freeways for a few minutes of impersonal sex in a toilet stall."[79] While their marriages are nothing special he did not find that they were especially unstable for their social class level. Nor did it appear that any of the wives were aware of their husbands' secret sexual activity.[80] Very few of the "trade" think of themselves as homosexual—certainly not as long as they are receiving the sex—although some as they get older will be the giver in the sex act and may then define themselves as homosexual. It should also be recognized that tearoom homosexuality is risky because it is responsible for a majority of the arrests for homosexual offenses in the United States.

There is one other related type of social situation where homosexuals find their sexual partners. This is where boys, usually part of delinquent gangs, are paid by homosexuals to serve as sexual partners. These boys are often hustlers or prostitutes in the sense that they sell themselves as sexual partners. Very often the older and less attractive homosexual may have to seek out the hustler if he wants a sexual partner. It may also be that "married homosexuals from out of town and ultrasecretive homosexuals who seek the ultimate in anonymity may also be among the hustler's customers."[81]

Albert Reiss, in his study of delinquents and homosexuals, found that the boys functioned as members of gangs and their gang involvement set the patterns for their behavior with homosexuals. The boys could let themselves be used by homosexuals but could under no circumstances show any sexual or personal concern for the homosexual. The boys did not define themselves as homosexuals. They defined homosexuality not on the basis of homosexual behavior but rather on the participation in the homosexual role. "The reactions of the larger society in defining the *behavior* as homosexual is unimportant in their own self-definition. What

---

[78] *Ibid.*, p. 18.
[79] *Ibid.*
[80] *Ibid.*, p. 17.
[81] Schur, *op. cit.*, p. 90.

is important to them is the reaction of their peers to violation of peer group norms which define roles in the peer-queer transaction."[82]

Aging

Of all the personal factors that might worry the homosexual there is probably none more psychologically upsetting for many than aging. Because such great importance is attached to appearing youthful and attractive to successfully compete he often worries as he feels he is losing his youth. In some of the subcultures aging may occur around age 30, and men past that age may be seen as "senior citizens." It is very common for the homosexual to try to postpone getting old by imitating the young. One observer writes that the middle-aged homosexual lets grow long "what is left of his hair, wears beads, body shirts, western vests, and peace emblems, studies the head's manner of movement and speech, and goes right on getting high on alcohol, because he considers drugs unsafe."[83]

Gagnon and Simon have suggested that aging is a life cycle crisis that the homosexual shares with the heterosexual in our youth-oriented society. They point out that while American society in general places an extremely high emphasis on youth, the homosexual community places an even greater stress. But the homosexual has fewer resources by which to meet the crisis of aging than does the heterosexual. "For the heterosexual there are his children whose careers assure a sense of the future and a wife whose sexual availability cushions the shock of declining sexual attractiveness. In addition, the crisis of aging comes later to the heterosexual, at an age when his sexual powers have declined and expectations concerning his sexuality are considerably lower."[84]

As suggested, when the homosexual gets older and becomes less desirable on the sexual market it may be necessary for him to pay for his sexual partners. When the older homosexual can afford it he may have a "kept" younger man. This boy or young man is "kept" in the role of "mistress" and his interest in the relationship is usually materialistic. The young man's involvement with his older partner tends to be superficial and exploitative.[85] Sonenschein found that in the relationships where the young man was being kept by the older homosexual they tended to have limited involvement in the homosexual subculture. This was due to the fear on the part of the older man that his "boy" would be stolen from him, "and on the other hand, to the fact that the other members of the group held a rather low opinion of such a relationship and the in-

---

[82] Reiss, Albert J. "The Social Integration of Queers and Peers," in Howard Becker, *The Other Side* (New York: The Free Press, 1964), p. 207.

[83] Burke, Tom, "The New Homosexuality," *Esquire*, December, 1969, p. 308.

[84] Gagnan and Simon, *op. cit.*, p. 357.

[85] Sonenschein, *op. cit.*, p. 75.

dividuals involved in it. The 'kept boy' however apparently served a social function to his 'keeper' in that the older homosexual liked to occasionally 'show off' his partner and the manner which he could 'keep' him to the rest of the community."[86]

COMMUNICATION IN THE SUBCULTURE

As mentioned, the subculture provides the setting for the passing along of information, gossip, and anything else of importance to the community. Also the direction that language and communication takes contributes to the solidarity of the subculture and helps to dramatize for the members their adherence to the homosexual values. "Thus, the gossip about sex, the adoption and exaggeration of feminine behavior, and the affectation of speech represent ways of affirming that homosexuality is frankly accepted and has the collective support of the group."[87] One of the measurements of the effectiveness of communication within a subculture is how fast it can transmit information. Hoffman points out that one of the characteristics of the homosexual community is that news travels very fast and information as to streets, public parks, and particular restrooms where homosexual contacts may be found is rapidly circulated among the members of the subculture.[88]

As with all subcultures, that of homosexuality develops some specialized jargon. They have borrowed words from the subcultures of jazz, criminals, drug users, and so forth, but have also coined some of their own words. Their language is the language of their special subculture and refers to their roles, values, and activities. While the jargon contributes to the cohesiveness of the group it above all is communicative. The language that is developed centers around the social and sexual relationships rather than around the sexual act itself. "To illustrate this: when, in the subject group, homosexuals talked about sex it was for the most part in the context of *who* had sex with *whom* and *why* that particular relationship might or might not have taken place; it was, in other words, talk about sexual *partners* rather than sexual outlets."[89]

Sonenschein found that a small number of homosexuals he studied had enacted speech patterns that imitated female speech patterns. This was done in several different ways. One, an attempt was made to imitate the verbal sound of female conversation. This was the copying of inflec-

---

[86] *Ibid.*, p. 76.

[87] Leznoff, Maurice and William A. Westley, "The Homosexual Community," in John H. Gagnon and William Simon, *Sexual Deviance* (New York: Harper and Row, 1967), p. 187.

[88] Hoffman, *op. cit.*, p. 45.

[89] Sonenschein, David, "The Homosexual's Language," *The Journal of Sex Research*, November, 1969, p. 285.

tional and stress patterns, but rarely the stereotyped lisp. Two, use of what are often thought of as feminine adjectives—words like "darling" and "lovely" and phrases like "terribly sweet"—was common. Third, feminine familiars like "honey" and "darling" as well as pronouns like "she" and "her" used both as terms of address and reference to males were used. Last, masculine names were feminized. Harry becomes Harriet and David becomes Daisey.[90]

There are other more subtle means of communicating among homosexuals. While it is not true that nonhomosexuals could pick out many homosexuals on sight, it is often true that homosexuals can frequently recognize one another. This is not necessarily because of any physical or even dress characteristics. The signs are shown and picked up when homosexuals are "cruising"—looking to pick up or be picked up. When they are cruising they engage in behavior gestures which immediately identify themselves to each other. "A large part of cruising is done with the eyes, by means of searching looks of a prolonged nature and through the surveying of the other man's entire body. It is also done by lingering in the presence of the other person, and by glancing backward."[91] Or there may be signals transmitted by homosexuals telling what they are interested in sexually. For example, foot tapping is homosexual sign language indicating a willingness to participate in oral copulation.[92]

Another area of behavior for the homosexual about which there is a great deal of speculation, but little empirical data, is the extent to which homosexuals dominate or are disproportionately represented in certain occupations. In fact, in recent years there have been some who have argued that there is a homosexual conspiracy to dominate the arts and other fields. In many artistic occupational fields there are undoubtedly a large number of homosexuals. This appears to be true in such areas as classical music, the theater, interior decorating, and so forth. This may sometimes occur because the individual selects the occupation and as a result finds himself defined as "different" because of his choice. For example, a boy who at an early age develops a strong interest in ballet will often have difficulty in developing a strong masculine self image. But whatever the reasons there does appear to be a high number of homosexuals in certain occupations. It may be that once homosexuals are in certain fields they have a tendency to recruit and encourage those who are sexually like themselves. This is similar to ethnic or religious favoritism found in some occupations. But it seems doubtful that there is a homosexual conspiracy because whatever they are creating or selling does go for the most part to a heterosexual market. That market may be in-

---

[90] *Ibid.*, p. 283.
[91] Hoffman, *op. cit.*, p. 45.
[92] *UCLA Law Review, op. cit.*, p. 692.

fluenced, but could hardly be manipulated as a part of an organized homosexual conspiracy.

As all subcultures are characterized by a high level of conformity this is also often true in such areas as dress styles and other material goods. That is, there develops an "in" knowledge as to what is really right in dress, places to eat, books to read, and so forth. In some of the larger cities businesses have developed that are patronized primarily by the homosexual because of the influence of his subcultural values. It has been pointed out that in New York City there are a number of clothing stores, restaurants, barber shops, tailors, and even some stationery shops "who carry a line of greeting cards for 'gay' occasions." That writer says that "some homosexuals feel enough group loyalty to patronize mainly those establishments considered 'gay,' usually because of their employees, but others are indifferent to the point of calling them 'fruitstands.' "[93] In general those who most strongly identify with the subculture are the ones most apt to support the business outlets run by and/or for homosexuals.

One of the themes of this book has been that deviant activities and subcultures frequently overlap one another. There has often been speculation that the homosexual way of life has a high overlap with those patterns of attitudes and behavior associated with the use of drugs. It has been recently suggested by one writer that most homosexuals under the age of forty are frequent users of marijuana and occasionally of "acid." It is suggested that for those homosexuals in their early and mid-twenties drug use is very common because it has been a part of their growing up experience, but that they used more than their heterosexual peers because drug use annoyed heterosexual adults. "Their heterosexual fellow heads, after all, though properly alienated, did maintain one important allegiance with the system: heterosexuality."[94]

Timothy Leary and other spokesmen of the drug movement have stated that LSD cures homosexuality. There has been some suggestion that LSD does appear to bring about in many homosexuals a new, if somewhat ill-defined and subordinate, interest in the opposite sex.[95] It does seem that today the homosexual tends to be more secretive about his drug use than his sexual interests. This suggests that the relative fears with regard to his deviancy indicates that being caught for drug use has a greater danger than being caught for homosexuality. Of course, the punishments are much more severe for drug use than homosexuality. In general one would expect deviants to be more willing to try other areas of deviancy than would non-deviants. The very fact of being a part of one

---

[93] Helmer, William J., "New York's 'Middle-Class' Homosexuals," *Harpers,* March, 1963, p. 87.

[94] Burke, *op. cit.*, p. 308.

[95] *Ibid.*, p. 312.

deviancy pattern makes one experienced in having made the move of being different—something the non-deviant has not been through.

In summary, what can be said about the homosexual subculture? Basically it provides a social setting where the deviant may find others like himself both for sexual contacts and social reassurance. Because the subculture is the only setting where the homosexual feels he can be himself he often develops a deep emotional involvement which contributes to his willingness to accept the controls of the subculture. The regularity with which he seeks out the subculture members is a clear indication of his dependency.[96] As suggested, there are variations within the homosexual subculture, and one basic one alluded to is between secret and overt groups. The secret ones are based on small, loosely knit cliques. Interaction within the cliques is frequent, and the members generally meet in each other's homes. By contrast, the overt homosexuals gather in cohesive social groups which become the major force in their lives. Their activities in the straight world are seen as peripheral and often empty of any meaning for them.[97] The subculture may vary widely in the significance that it has for a given homosexual over time.

THE MILITANT HOMOSEXUAL

Militancy is usually based in the subculture because of the organizational structure and force it can provide. However, there are some homosexuals who are involved in the new militancy in various ways that are only partly involved in the homosexual subculture. But basic to the new militancy is some organization. This is necessary so that their case is presented collectively and not as isolated individuals. Up until recent years almost all homosexuals in the United States were extremely secretive and the last thing they wanted was any kind of public exposure. As a result they had no way of presenting organized resistance to the forces against them in the broader society.

Among homosexuals the militant movement is usually known as the "homophile" movement. Sagarin has pointed out that no group so large in number and so completely stigmatized has remained so long unorganized.[98] No homophile organization appeared in America until after the second world war. Sagarin suggests that there were several factors that inhibited earlier organizing among homosexuals. One, before World War II the attitude in the United States was negative to social change with regard to sex and particularly with regard to homosexuality. Second was that the concealment of the homosexual encouraged him *not* to organize.

---

[96] Leznoff and Westley, *op. cit.*, p. 186.

[97] *Ibid.*, p. 193.

[98] Sagarin, *op. cit.*, p. 79.

Third, there was no structure to use for the exchange of ideas and values which could lead to an organization. Finally, there were no leaders primarily because those who had the intellectual respect that might allow them to be leaders had the most to lose by giving up their anonymity.[99]

But the above restrictions have been changed in many respects and the greater sexual permissiveness of society created a climate that made possible the emergence of the homophile organizations. The generally new attitudes toward sex meant that even the highly tabooed area of homosexuality could be discussed. The 1960's saw the discussion of homosexuality even in the most conservative of mass media—television. At the present time there are homosexual groups who conduct programs to try to educate the public to a better understanding and tolerance of homosexuality; for example, the Mattachine Society which was started in 1950 in Los Angeles has as its aim the promoting of acceptance of homosexuality by American society. By 1969 there were about 150 known formal and structured voluntary associations that could be called a part of the homophile movement. There were also many small clubs on the periphery of the movement.[100]

As the organizations developed they were not militant. Their early functions were seen as attempting to educate the broader population and to provide counseling for homosexuals. In the 1950's counseling was the main focus of action and this continues to be a major function even in the more militant age. The militant homosexuals, as have other deviant groups, have taken the black revolution as their model. As with all militant groups there is controversy within the ranks of the homosexuals as to the best methods for achieving their ends. Some argue for militant, revolutionary action while others argue for peaceful protests. But what is important is that homosexual militancy has taken to the streets on some occasions. There have been public protests against police raids on homosexual bars as well as against sodomy laws. In Greenwich Village 500 homophiles yelled "Gay power to gay people" and threw firebombs and bricks at police.[101] It seems reasonable to expect that this new openness and militancy will continue to expand in the future. And many homosexuals, whether organized or not, have an enhanced feeling of self worth from knowing there are homophile spokesmen, groups as well as pickets, in front of the White House."[102]

Also basic to the homophile movement is the changing concept that the homosexual has about himself. The organizations try to bolster their members' feelings that they are "as good as anybody else"—which means

---

[99] *Ibid.*, p. 81.

[100] *Ibid.*, p. 87.

[101] *The Washington Post*, October 25, 1969.

[102] Sagarin, *op. cit.*, p. 345.

"as *well* as anybody else."[103] The groups argue that homosexuality is neither a sickness nor a mental disturbance and therefore talking about cures is irrelevant. "Anyone who suggests cure, according to Mattachine leaders, must be a charlatan or a quack."[104] For them the slogan might be "Gay is good" in the same way that "Black is beautiful." This is also seen in the belief that "cure" is irrelevant. One homophile spokesman remarked that he does not see "the NAACP and CORE worrying about which chromosome and gene produces a black skin, or about the possibility of bleaching a Negro."[105]

Exactly what is the position of the new militant homosexual groups? The old question of the 1950's was "Why are we what we are?" But this has given way to the assertion "Here we are, now let's take it from there." In other words the homophile argument is that they don't want rehabilitation, nor cure, nor acceptance of homosexuals as "persons" in distinction from their sexual "acts." The militant homosexual wants to be accepted in society not in spite of homosexuality but together with it. "And he wants himself and his homosexuality, and other homosexuals and their homosexuality, not merely to be tolerated, but to be positive values as worthy contributors to the social order and as a worthy way of life."[106] It would appear that his chance of getting this in the near future is very slight.

THE HOMOSEXUAL SUBCULTURE IN THE BROADER SOCIETY

In this last section it is important to look in more detail at how the broader society views the homosexual. The focus thus far has been primarily from the perspective of the homosexual in his own subcultural setting. Here we will look at some other aspects of the homosexual in terms of the broader society, both from his perspective and from that of the broader society. Also the interest is primarily in the homosexual in general with little special interpretation given to the small militant minority.

Probably few, if any, homosexuals are able to so immerse themselves in the homosexual subculture that they are able to cut themselves off from the broader society. Being a member of the homosexual subculture does not remove them from the social influences of society. Even if the role of homosexual becomes the major role for those in the subculture, it is

---

[103] *Ibid.*, p. 103.

[104] *Ibid.*

[105] *Ibid.*, p. 104.

[106] Gunnison, Foster, Jr., "The Homophile Movement in America," in Ralph P. Weltge, *The Same Sex: An Appraisal of Homosexuality* (Philadelphia: Pilgram Press, 1969), p. 128.

not the only one. Such persons will likely have to interact or be defined according to broader society in some significant areas of their nonsexual behavior. "For instance, the Negro homosexual is a Negro as well as a homosexual; the homosexual lawyer cannot restrict his behavior and identity to that which centers on his sexual orientation."[107] But probably most homosexuals feel they must hide their homosexuality on many if not most occasions, and this builds in a strain in making sure they are filling the proper role in the right social situation. We will look at some of the different pressures that exist on the homosexual in various social settings of the broader society.

As mentioned at the start of the chapter, engaging in homosexual acts is against the law and there is always the danger of getting caught and possibly exposed. The greater the success of the homosexual in the "straight" community the greater the anxiety about getting caught. The fact that his homosexual secret is "criminal" means any exposure may lead to legal consequences—and this increases his personal anxieties. Most homosexuals are able to cope without exposure, but nevertheless the potential for exposure is always there.

Studies indicate that most homosexuals cope very well considering the stigmatized and criminal nature of their sexual interests. One study suggests that only about one in four homosexuals ever has any trouble with the police. In the same study about one third of the exclusive homosexuals had "ever been rolled" and about one in seven had "ever been blackmailed."[108]

In recent years there has been some concern with the homosexual from a combined legal and medical perspective. That concern has been around the possibility of his being a high carrier of venereal diseases. Up until the late 1950's there were no standard reports on male-to-male transmissions of venereal disease. In fact, the American Social Health Association, which accumulates such data from 120 health departments each year, did not request that information until 1967. However, on the basis of scattered reports there had been indications of an increasing spread of syphilis by homosexuals as early as 1955. One recent finding showed that only 7 percent of male patients with gonorrhea admitted to homosexual contact as compared to 57 percent of male patients with syphilis. "There would appear to be no logical reason why the percent of homosexuals should be so much lower among patients with gonorrhea than with syphilis."[109] One reason why venereal disease rates are higher among homosexuals is that their contact rates are twice as high as for heterosexual

---

[107] Sagarin, *op. cit.*, pp. 91–92.

[108] Simon and Gagnon, *op. cit.*, p. 181.

[109] Trice, E. Randolph, "Venereal Disease and Homosexuality," *Medical Aspects of Human Sexuality*, January 1969, p. 70.

patients. That is, homosexuals averaged eight sexual contacts in contrast to an average of four for heterosexual males. Trice found that venereal diseases are usually spread by those homosexuals whose preference is for anal intercourse. Another study concluded that "syphilitic infection is most likely to occur in the male homosexual in the age group fifteen to twenty-nine, who is apt to be highly promiscuous, and whose sexual preference is anal sodomy."[110]

Still another important area of interaction with the broader society for the homosexual is with his family. Simon and Gagnon found that between one-fifth and one-quarter of the exclusive homosexuals they studied reported difficulties of orientation with their families.[111] There are many homosexuals who do maintain close relationships with their families. There is no strong evidence to suggest that the proportion of homosexuals for whom relatives are significant differs from that of heterosexuals. "The important differences rest in the way the relationships are managed and, again, the consequences they have for other aspects of life."[112] This means that often the homosexual must be careful when he is around his family not to give out cues as to his sexual preference and way of life. Simmons reports one homosexual respondent he studied saying, "When I was home watching television with my folks, I'd catch myself saying, "that's a good looking guy."[113] Of course many parents do know about their son's homosexuality and react anywhere from total acceptance to total rejection.

Briefly, how do the institutions of religion, government, and the military treat the homosexual? In recent years there have been some religious groups who have accepted the homosexual, but for the most part organized religion has treated him with rejection. A part of the reaction to homosexuality by religion may be that historically religious groups have often had to deal with it among their own ranks. When homosexuality is found to be true for a lay person it usually means silent shunning, and if found for the clergyman it means a transfer to a different location. But given the changing nature of some religious groups, with an increasing concern with personal and social problems, there will probably be a liberalizing of many church policies with regard to homosexuality in the future. But the changes probably will come from a few of the leaders and not from the more conservative congregations.

The federal government has long had a policy of not hiring homosexuals as well as getting rid of them if they are discovered after hiring.

---

[110] *Ibid.*, p. 71.
[111] Simon and Gagnon, *op. cit.*, p. 180.
[112] Gagnon and Simon, *op. cit.*, p. 360.
[113] Simmons, J. L.; *Deviants*, (Berkeley, Calif.: The Glendessary Press, 1969), p. 82.

This has been done on the argument that the homosexual is a security risk and would be subject to possible influence through blackmail or other forms of extortion. The Civil Service Commission has said that a person who proclaims publicly that he engages in homosexual activities would not be suitable for federal employment. However, the same commission chairman went on to say that homosexual tendencies alone were not sufficient cause for barring employment. "In other words, it's all right to have homosexual tendencies but it isn't all right to exercise them, even in private with consenting adults."[114] However, the liberalizing influence has been reaching the government employment policies. The Federal Appeals Court in Washington D.C. recently declared that a government agency could not dismiss an employee without first proving that his homosexuality would significantly influence the efficiency of the agency's operations.

Finally, one institution in the United States that has always taken a highly repressive view towards homosexuality is that of the military, although historically many armies have not only tolerated homosexuality but have on occasion encouraged it. It is possible that the American military establishment may have over reacted to the homosexual permissiveness of the military in other societies and become strongly repressive in counter reaction.

The rates of homosexuality in the military forces are difficult to estimate. One study of the army shows that from 1960 to 1967 only 8 out of every 10,000 soldiers were discharged for reasons of homosexuality. Of course this number represents only those the army found out about and processed for discharge.[115] Another study of homosexuals who had been in the military services found that about one fifth of them reported difficulties during their military experiences.[116] Apparently a definite majority of homosexuals are able to serve their military careers without being in trouble on that score.

Sheppe, in his research, found that the Navy indicates a sharp decline in the number of official separations for homosexuality since 1966. However, some qualified observers suggest that the decline may be directly related to a concurrent rise over that period in the rates of drug abuse as grounds for separation. In the Armed Forces the investigation and control of drug use has required a great deal of manpower "which might otherwise have been expended in ferreting out homosexuals. There is also far

---

[114] Maddocks, Lewis I., "The Law and the Church vs. the Homosexual," in Ralph P. Weltge, *The Same Sex: An Appraisal of Homosexuality* (Philadelphia: Pilgram Press, 1969, p. 101.

[115] Sheppe, William M., "The Problem of Homosexuality in the Armed Forces," *Medical Aspects of Human Sexuality*, October, 1969, p. 72.

[116] Simon and Gagnon, *op. cit.*, p. 180.

less stigma attached to separations based on drug abuse than to separations based on homosexuality."[117]

The hostile view that the military takes toward the homosexual is reflected in the procedures they use when one is brought to their attention. The individual is abruptly removed from duty, told that he is a security risk until proved otherwise, and subjected to intensive interrogation. "In the course of the matter, it may be implied that the charges against him are airtight, but that such unpleasantness, including courtmartial and possible imprisonment, may be avoided if the individual will only cooperate."[118] This also shows that under the present military regulations, homosexuality is not seen primarily as a medical matter but rather as a legal offense, proscribed and punishable under the Uniform Code of Military Justice. The present policy is that if a person is established as having homosexual activities with a consenting adult in private he is given an undesirable discharge. This is harsh because it makes him ineligible for any G.I. benefits.

In this last section we have been considering some institutional responses to homosexuality. What about general public opinion in this area? Even a professional area such as medicine is far from unanimous in its acceptance of more permissive views for the homosexual. In a recent sample of M.D.'s 68 percent agreed that discreet homosexual acts between consenting adults should be permitted without legal restrictions, while the rest felt they should not. This is a much more liberal position than comes from public opinion in general. A recent Harris poll reported that 63 percent of the nation considered homosexuals "harmful to American life." Another study of traits attributed to the male homosexual found them: "sexually abnormal," 72 percent; "perverted," 52 percent; "mentally ill," 40 percent; and, "maladjusted," 40 percent.[119] As pointed out earlier in this chapter, the role of the homosexual far transcends the sexual choice and influences the view of the total person if he is known as a homosexual. He has all of his roles seen through the view of him as a homosexual. However, there are many variations among groups in the United States in their treatment of homosexuals and often the homosexual seeks out an environment where he runs into the least amount of discrimination. This may be in terms of occupational choice, a city to live in, or a place to go on vacation. As suggested, the most permissive city for the homosexual is probably San Francisco, and that city probably has more homosexuals per capita than any other city.

But even if public opinion in general is not becoming significantly more permissive with regard to the homosexual some changes are taking place.

[117] Sheppe, op. cit., p. 73.
[118] Ibid., p. 81.
[119] Simmons, op. cit., p. 29.

For example, in San Francisco if a homosexual feels he is receiving undue police harassment he is encouraged to go to the police department's community relations division which will usually straighten the matter out. Or recently the State Liquor Authority of New York lifted its traditional ban on homosexual bars and various state courts decided that "intrasexual" dancing, touching, and even kissing were not necessarily disorderly so long as the various sexes refrained from touching one another upon primary sex organs.[120] Finally, in late 1969 the National Institute of Mental Health recommended the repeal of laws against homosexual acts between consenting adults in private and a reassessment of bans by employers against hiring homosexuals. Yet, this recommendation came at the same time that a CBS poll found that two-thirds of all Americans continued to regard homosexuals with "disgust, discomfort or fear."[121]

The future of the homosexual in America is difficult to predict. This is because there is such a wide gulf between some professional belief and argument for greater tolerance and freedom and the prevailing feeling of contempt and disgust found among most Americans. If the homosexual, through his subcultural support and strength, chooses to become increasingly militant for his rights one of two things will probably happen. He might be able to make the general population more sensitive and tolerant of his sexual choice. But more likely, if he becomes militant he will antagonize more "middle Americans" and find the resistance to him even greater. Whichever course is taken the homosexual subculture will continue to have great importance and probably become more and more the rallying point for an even greater proportion of homosexuals.

BIBLIOGRAPHY

HOFFMAN, MARTIN, *The Gay World* (New York: Bantam Books, 1968).

HOOKER, EVELYN, "Male Homosexuals and Their 'Worlds,'" in Judd Marmor, ed. *Sexual Inversion* (New York: Basic Books, 1965), pp. 83–107.

HUMPHEYS, LAUD, "Tearoom Trade: Impersonal Sex in Public Places," *Trans-Action*, January, 1970, pp. 11–25.

McINTOSH, MARY, "The Homosexual Role," *Social Problems*, Fall, 1968, pp. 182–92.

SAGARIN, EDWARD, *Odd Man In: Societies of Deviants in America* (Chicago: Quadrangle Books, 1969).

SCHUR, EDWIN M., *Crimes without Victims, Deviant Behavior and Public Policy* (Englewood Cliffs, N.J.: Prentice-Hall, 1965).

SIMON, WILLIAM and JOHN H. GAGNON, "Homosexuality: The Formulation of a Sociological Perspective," *Journal of Health and Social Behavior*, September, 1967, pp. 177–85.

---

[120] Burke, *op. cit.*, p. 308.

[121] *The Washington Post*, October 25, 1969.

SONENSCHEIN, DAVID, "The Ethnology of Male Homosexual Relationships," *The Journal of Sex Research*, May, 1968, pp. 69–83.

"The Consenting Adult Homosexual and the Law," *UCLA Law Review*, University of California at Los Angeles, March, 1966.

WELTGE, RALPH A., ed. *The Same Sex: An Appraisal of Homosexuality* (Philadelphia: Pilgram Press, 1969).

CHAPTER 11

THE FEMALE
HOMOSEXUAL

THAT there has emerged in the United States an increasing awareness of the male homosexual was discussed in Chapter 9. Also, as suggested, there is not only an awareness of the male homosexual but often strong negative feelings directed at him from the general public. By contrast, when the female homosexual (or lesbian) is mentioned there is often a kind of vague, almost puzzled reaction by many people. That is, people know such women exist but they have never come into contact with them so their knowledge is an abstract awareness and not one based on experience. Also by contrast with the male homosexual there has been much less written about the lesbian and she has rarely been presented through the mass media. So for most Americans the level of knowledge as well as the level of experience is low.

This chapter will be shorter than Chapter 10 because there has been less research as well as serious speculation directed at the female homosexual. However, it is believed that the lesbian should be discussed and analyzed separately from the male homosexual. This is true even though there are some similarities among homosexuals regardless of gender. However, the differences are probably greater than the similarities. The basic similarity is that both groups choose as sex partners members of their own sex. But once that is recognized the similarities are generally not very great. This difference is because basically the male homosexual is a male

285

and the female homosexual is a female in terms of the basic roles by which others see them and they see themselves. And the choice of a same sex partner generally does not significantly change this basic role for either men or women. It will also be seen that within the homosexual setting males are more apt to develop and depend on subcultural involvement than are females. That is, the social context of being a homosexual is more complex and developed for the male than for the female. In the discussion ahead some contrasts will be drawn between the patterns of male and female homosexuals. This should contribute not only to a better understanding of homosexual variations but also of basic sex role differences in the United States.

HISTORICAL BACKGROUND

While the history of man has many references to male homosexuality the references are far fewer to female homosexuality. In the Talmud of the ancient Hebrews the practice of lesbianism was regarded as a trivial obscenity and the punishment was that when the woman chose to marry the ceremony could not be performed by a priest. There is some evidence that lesbianism was common in the harems of Egypt and India where women were herded together and often saw no men other than the husband they shared. Each wife was expected to wait her turn to be sexually satisfied by the shared husband. But many may have turned to each other for sexual release. It may have been that the husband knew of the homosexuality but was willing to overlook it rather than to have his wives more sexually frustrated and possibly creating problems for him.

The first real advocate of female homosexuality in the Western world was Sappho, who lived in the 6th century B.C. She was born and lived most of her adult life on the island of Lesbos. Sappho had several affairs with men and was the mother of one child. She was one of the first persons to argue for the rights of women. Sappho appears to have fallen in love with many of her female students and wrote sensuous poems for them. Those poems later won her great respect and she came to be known among Greeks as the Tenth Muse. Basically the belief that developed on Lesbos was that the admiration of beauty could not be separated from sex and as a result many women took sexual delight in one another.[1] The term "lesbian" has become a universal generic term for the female homosexual and is used as a synonym.

During the medieval period as sexual repression became an important part of religion homosexuality was also condemned. The medieval church found homosexuality sinful for both men and women but the male was

---

[1] Lewinsohn, Richard, A History of Sexual Customs (New York: Harper and Brothers, 1958), p. 60.

obligated to perform penance longer. There have been many time periods in many European countries where some female homosexuality was practiced. For example, lesbianism was fashionable in the court of Marie Antoinette, although whether she participated is not known for sure.

Given the high repression of all forms of sexual behavior in the early days of the United States there is little evidence that lesbianism existed, and if it did it must have been very well hidden. In the early written records of the United States there is little reference to female homosexuality. In fact, in American literature, the female homosexual is ignored throughout the 19th century except possibly for some suggestion in the novels of Oliver Wendell Holmes. Lesbianism appears "for the first time in American literature in explicit fashion in the expatriate writings of Henry James and Gertrude Stein."[2] Up until very recently the lesbian was rarely presented in novels. The few times she was written about she was either presented as an erotic symbol for the satisfaction of the male reader or presented sympathetically as a highly romantic and mysterious figure.

Given the limited references to the female homosexual historically, what is known about her on the cross-cultural level? Ford and Beach found that in only 22 percent of the peoples they studied was there any specific information about female homosexuality. In only a few of those cultures was there evidence concerning the nature of the homosexual practices involved.[3] They also point out that in most societies female homosexuality is given much less attention than male homosexuality. Ford and Beach found that frequently some substitute for a penis is employed, as it also may be in solitary masturbation. They go on to write that "among the Dahomeans, the common practice of homosexuality on the part of women is believed to be a cause of frigidity in marriage. Interestingly, the Haitians put it just the other way; the frigid woman who cannot please her husband seeks another woman as a sex partner."[4] Pomeroy points out that among American Indian cultures 53 percent accepted male homosexuality while only 17 percent accepted it for females.[5] However, there appears to be only one primitive society, the Mohave Indians of the southwestern United States, for whom there were records of exclusive homosexual patterns among the females. That group was also the only one for which there were reports that female homosexuality was openly sanctioned.[6] Because female homosexuality was much less common among

[2] Cory, Donald W., *The Lesbian in America* (New York: The Citadel Press, 1964), p. 48.

[3] Ford, Clellan S. and Frank A. Beach, *Patterns of Sexual Behavior* (New York: Harper and Brothers, 1952), p. 133.

[4] *Ibid.*

[5] Pomeroy, Wardell B., "Homosexuality," in Ralph W. Weltge, *The Same Sex: An Appraisal of Homosexuality* (Philadelphia: Pilgrim Books, 1969), p. 4.

[6] Kinsey, Alfred C., *et al.*, *Sexual Behavior in the Human Female* (Philadelphia: W. B. Saunders Co., 1953), p. 451.

primitive groups, as well as in literate cultures, than was male homosexuality, it should not be assumed that it was due to biological gender differences. The difference is due to the social roles that women have traditionally played and the means in which they have been personally and socially controlled in their sexual experiences. This point will be further elaborated in the discussion ahead.

LEGAL ASPECTS

The laws that exist with reference to the female homosexual are much simpler and less restrictive than those that exist for the male. Basically, the reason is that in most societies homosexuality among men has been seen as far more threatening both in scope and complexity. It is also important that with few exceptions the legal controls over sexual behavior developed in all societies have been the work of men. In many respects the laws about sexual behavior have been aimed at protecting their self interests. For example, in prostitution the male customer is usually protected. In extramarital relationships the woman has more to lose and is more severely condemned than the man. There have been few laws directed against the lesbian because man has rarely ever seen her as a threat in any way. When man has thought about her he has always felt superior to the lesbian and has seen no need to legally constrain her.

Much of the American legal system came from the common law of England and it can be seen that the English legal view of the female homosexual is close to what is found in the United States. For example, when the recent reforms in the criminal law of England occurred which allowed homosexual relations between consenting adults in private, lesbians were never taken into consideration because there were no laws against them in the first place.[7] In fact the Wolfenden report, upon which the above reforms were made, found no case in which a female had been convicted in Great Britain of an act with another female which exhibited "the libidinous features that characterize sexual acts between males."[8]

In many states the sex laws don't apply to lesbians, but in some states the laws are similar to those for the male homosexuals. For example, in New York State it is not illegal to be a female homosexual but it is illegal to perform a homosexual act. Yet, rarely do the women run into the law because most homosexual arrests are made for public behavior. Lesbians are rarely "cruisers" and don't hang around public toilets, where the majority of male arrests are made. According to Kinsey, from 1696 until 1952 there was not a single case on record in the United States of a sustained conviction of a female for homosexual activity. Kinsey also found in his total sample of several hundred women who had homosexual experience

---

[7] Hoffman, Martin, *The Gay World* (New York: Bantam Books, 1968), p. 174.

[8] *The Wolfenden Report* (New York: Lancer Books, 1964), p. 76.

that only three had minor difficulties and only one had serious difficulty with the police.[9]

For the most part the police do not consider lesbians as being a threat because they keep to themselves, are not as promiscuous as male homosexuals, and rarely solicit others. The UCLA study in Los Angeles found that "decoy enforcement is considered too degrading for policewomen. However, entertainment licenses have been revoked as the result of observations of lewd conduct in lesbian bars by male undercover officers."[10] The same study goes on to say that the police view lesbians as much less aggressive than males. As a result their behavior is much less conspicuous than that of males and less likely to offend the public. Thus, "there are a minimal number of complaints concerning female activity."[11] However, there appears to be some increase by police in picking up female homosexuals in recent years. In New York City the police have picked up women for "loitering," a charge applied "for soliciting another for the purpose of engaging in deviate sexual intercourse." Ten women were picked up on this charge in 1968 but a total of 49 women and 69 men have been apprehended on the same charge during the first nine months of 1969."[12] These arrests are probably coming from the most militant lesbians who are insisting on their rights in all areas, including that of soliciting sex partners if they choose to do so. In a recent study of active lesbians in Philadelphia one-quarter said they had been arrested by the police, but usually on a drug or solicitation charge. Twenty percent of them said they had experienced physical aggression from the police. But some of these women were a part of other militant and deviant subcultures and therefore their encounters with the police are often not simply because of lesbian activities. The women may be lesbians, political militants, female militants, and so forth and come into contact with the police in various roles or in combinations of roles.

In the discussion ahead some references will be made to the Philadelphia study just mentioned. Although the sample was only forty women this study is included because there is so little empirical data, and the findings will possibly contribute to some better understanding. The forty lesbians were interviewed mostly in lesbian bars and all openly defined themselves as having at least some homosexual interests. Their average age was 25, and three-quarters of them had never married. The women were also well educated, with one-third of them having graduated from college. This group was basically quite militant and open about its homosexuality.

---

[9] Kinsey, *op. cit.*, p. 484.

[10] "The Consenting Adult Homosexual and the Law, *UCLA Law Review,* March, 1966, p. 693.

[11] *Ibid.*, p. 740.

[12] Nemy, Enid, "The Woman Homosexual: More Assertive, Less Willing to Hide," *New York Times,* November 17, 1969, p. 61.

The point has been made that there are fewer female homosexuals than there are males. In a study done in the 1920's of 1,200 unmarried female college graduates who had been out of college for at least five years, about half of them indicated that they had experienced some intense emotional relations with another woman. About half of that number had experienced some overt physical practices along with their feelings. However, while the figure is not given, it is probable that only a small percentage of the women had sexual experience to the point of orgasm with another woman.[13] The Kinsey study found that at the time of marriage 5 percent of the women had at least one sexual experience to orgasm with another woman.[14] As would be expected, the homosexual experiences of women vary by marital status. Homosexual outlets accounted for 0 percent of the married women, 2 percent of the postmarried women, and 19 percent of the single women.[15] Kinsey also found some variations by education among women having homosexual experience. The percentages having homosexual experience to orgasm by education are: grade school, 6 percent; high school, 5 percent; and college, 10 percent.[16]

It is hard to estimate with any accuracy the frequency of male homosexuality, and even harder to estimate for women. Most lesbianism is hidden because it is less physical and publicly overt. The differences also contribute to a delusion by many that female homosexuality is less common than it is in fact, and that makes the estimating of the rates even more difficult. There are several other reasons for underestimating the number of lesbians. One, usually when an effeminate male is seen he is associated with homosexuality, whether he is or not. But masculine women are not usually defined as homosexual. Therefore, the defining of visual characteristics varies for men and women. Two, because male homosexuals are much more apt to gather in public places they are more visible and the public is more aware of them than it is of lesbians it may rarely see. Three, the male is promiscuous and seeks out openly and aggressively his sexual partners in ways rare for the lesbian. He is therefore seen in his sexually-seeking role. Finally, male homosexuals, because they are more open and aggressive, are given much more publicity in the newspapers.[17]

CAUSES

Most theories about homosexuality have been developed to explain the male and often are applied to the woman as a kind of afterthought. The

---

[13] Davis, K. B., *"Factors in the Sex Life of Twenty-Two Hundred Women* (New York: Harper and Brothers, 1929).

[14] Kinsey, *op. cit.*, p. 488.

[15] *Ibid.*, p. 562.

[16] *Ibid.*, p. 488.

[17] Cory, *op. cit.*, p. 88.

basic assumptions of the medical, psychological, and social theories were discussed in Chapter 9. There are many lesbians who believe that their sexual orientation is a problem and should be taken to the psychiatrist. In the Philadelphia sample 42 percent of the women had received some psychological help. There is probably a strong desire by most lesbians to understand their sexual orientation. Most do recognize that their behavior is deviant, and having some explanation is important to themselves and to others. For example, if the girl accepts the belief that she was born a homosexual then that relieves her and her parents of any responsibility for what she is or for doing anything about it.

One common belief about the causes of lesbianism is that older women seduce innocent younger girls. But Gagnon and Simon found in their study of lesbians that seduction by older women was not mentioned as an experience. They suggest that the real social importance of the image of the older seductress is that it provides a basis for many popular explanations of what "causes" homosexuality and this serves the function of reducing the sense of guilt and shame.[18] This is seen as making the person a victim of circumstances over which she has no real choice.

It seems probable that most lesbians follow a pattern of growing up that is similar to most heterosexual girls. The notion of "extreme" or "special" socialization causing homosexuality is not substantiated by the available research. Gagnon and Simon found that all the women they studied reported some heterosexual dating and mild sex play during their high school years. "Only two carried it to the extent of intercourse, although a larger number indicated that they had experimented with heterosexual coitus after homosexual experiences."[19] It appears that by high school age many young homosexuals are aware of others like themselves in the school. Love reports that homosexuals in Philadelphia say there are cliques of "gay boys and gay girls in every school in the city and intercommunication among them. Even if no one else knows they are there, the youngsters involved do."[20]

Simon and Gagnon have provided the best sociological explanation for the development of female homosexuality. They argue that in most cases the female homosexual follows a conventional female pattern in developing her involvement with sexuality. They go on to say that the organizing event in the development of male sexuality is puberty, while the organizing event for females is that period of romantic involvement that culminates for most in marriage. For females the "discovery" of love relations precedes the "discovery" of sexuality while the reverse is generally

---

[18] Gagnon, John H. and William Simon, *Sexual Deviance* (New York: Harper and Row, 1967), p. 255.

[19] *Ibid.*, pp. 259–60.

[20] Love, Nancy, "The Invisible Sorority," *Philadelphia Magazine*, November, 1967, p. 69.

true for males. "The discovery of their homosexuality usually occurred very late in adolescence, often even in the years of young adulthood, and the actual commencement of overt sexual behavior frequently came at a late stage of an intense emotional involvement."[21] What they are saying in part is that training in love comes before training in sexuality for women. And for most women, including most lesbians, the pursuit of sexual gratification is something distinct from emotional or rational involvement and is not particularly attractive; "indeed, for many it may be impossible."[22]

The above argument suggests that in one sense the lesbian should be defined somewhat differently than the male homosexual. They are both alike in choosing sex partners of the same sex but there are often differences in what is wanted from and with the partner. For the male it is almost always primarily a partner for sexual activity, while this is frequently much less true for the lesbian. This is not to argue that the lesbian doesn't have a strong sexual interest, but rather that her sexual interest is a part of an interpersonal sexual interest. A lesbian then is a woman who feels a strong and recurring need to have sexual relations within an interpersonal context with another woman.

The idea has often been presented that all humans are potential homosexuals, given the circumstances where it could be brought out. This idea assumes that under certain conditions most persons would turn to homosexuality regardless of their negative socialization. If this idea is valid it might be more appropriate for women than for men because homosexuality is less threatening to the woman's basic self image. This idea recognizes that in certain social situations homosexuality may come forth. The situations are not seen as causes, but rather as providing "conditions, learning patterns, and justifications differentially favorable to the occurrence of homosexual contacts and self-concepts."[23] One good illustration of this is the prison "turnout" who enters homosexual activities while in prison but gives it up when he or she leaves that setting. A situation such as the prison provides the setting for women to take on new homosexual involvements. Giallombardo, in her study of women in prison, suggests that the ease by which women may demonstrate acts of affection, both verbally and physically, towards members of the same sex, "may provide a *predisposition* to widespread homosexuality and its ready acceptance under the extreme conditions of isolation in the prison settings."[24]

---

[21] Gagnon and Simon, *op. cit.*, p. 251.

[22] Simon, William and John H. Gagnon, "Femininity in the Lesbian Community," *Social Problems*, Fall, 1967, p. 214.

[23] McCaghy, Charles H. and James K. Skipper, Jr., "Lesbian Behavior as an Adaptation to the Occupation of Stripping," *Social Problems*, Fall, 1969, p. 263.

[24] Giallombardo, Rose, "Social Roles in a Prison for Women," *Social Problems*, Winter, 1966, p. 286.

The isolated environmental setting, such as the prison, with its high rates of homosexuality also develops rationales for new members to help them make the transition. Another study of a woman's prison points out that a folklore develops that is intended to justify and encourage the homosexual adaptation to prison life by new inmates.[25] A part of the rationalization is that the sexual adaptation is seen as temporary and brought about *only* because of the isolated conditions. So those women who turn out in prison "define themselves as *bisexual,* and they expect to return to heterosexual relationships upon release."[26] Often the sexual aspect is made easier because the women see it as a part of an affectional relationship they need. "The overriding need of a majority of female prisoners is to establish an affectional relationship which brings in prison, as it does in the community, love, interpersonal support, security, and social status. This need promotes homosexuality as the predominant compensatory response to the pains of imprisonment."[27]

While there are far more males than females who turn to homosexuality in society this does not appear to be true in prisons. The evidence suggests that a greater proportion of women than men have homosexual experiences while in prison. This would appear to be evidence for the hypothesis that women are less threatened by homosexuality than are men and find it easier to accept, at least temporarily. If this is true one would expect the same greater tendency for homosexuality in other situations where one sex is isolated. At present there is no evidence from other sex segregated institutions that might be applied to this hypothesis.

In general, as with the male homosexual, the causes of female homosexuality are seen as complex and not uniform. As Sawyer points out, homosexuals are coming to be viewed as people who emerge as social beings because of their intrinsic motivations, individual adaptations, and childhood conflicts. But along with this they are also a product of their total and ongoing environment in which there is their family, "peer groups, various legal and societal penalties and sanctions, and subcultural expectations, all of which help to shape the homosexual as he exists in American society."[28] And as with the male homosexual there is little reason to believe that the strongly committed lesbian is very often going to be totally reoriented from complete homosexuality to complete heterosexuality. There seems little likelihood of any "cure" of homosexuality in the sense of changing the nature and the object of the lesbian's sexual desires.

---

[25] Ward, David A. and Gene Kassebaum, "Homosexuality in a Prison for Women," *Social Problems,* Fall, 1964, p. 168.

[26] *Ibid.,* p. 76.

[27] *Ibid.*

[28] Sawyer, Ethel, "The Impact of the Surrounding Lower-Class Subculture on Female Homosexual Adaptations, *Society for the Study of Social Problems,* San Francisco, Calif., August, 1967, p 2.

THE LESBIAN SUBCULTURE

As earlier suggested, the subculture for the female homosexuals is much less important than it is for males. The main reason for this difference is the greater desire for privacy by the women than by the men. In general the women are much less aggressive in all ways than are men. However, for some women the lesbian subculture does exist and does have meaning and therefore it is important to examine what is known about it. In this section the concern is with the subculture in general and there will also be a discussion of two specific groups of lesbians that have been studied. One is a group of lower class black women and the other an occupation group of strippers. These studies refer to specialized groups within the homosexual subculture and are of interest in what they tell about themselves as well as for the general insights they provide into female homosexuality.

What can be said in a general way about the lesbian subculture? For the individuals who participate in it, it serves a number of functions. First, it provides the means for sexual contacts as well as expediting those contacts, but it is nowhere the "flesh market" as is the male subculture. The subculture also provides a source of social support and is a place where the lesbian can express her feelings or describe her experiences because she is interacting with others like herself. The subculture also "includes a language and an ideology which provides each individual lesbian with already developed attitudes that help her resist the societal claim that she is diseased, depraved, or shameful."[29] It can be seen that these ends are basically no different than for the male homosexual, rather the difference is one of degree, with the subculture generally being less important to lesbians than to male homosexuals.

There is some overlap between the male and female subcultures. Sonenschein in his study found that lesbians shared only infrequently in male group activities; the homosexual subculture is in fact a male subculture. He says that the lesbians shared a number of more common terms such as "gay" and "butch," but the word "fluff" (a very feminine lesbian) was their only unique term found in use.[30] In the larger cities, however, there does appear to be a distinct lesbian subculture that sometimes overlaps with that of the male, but is in no real sense dependent on it. The lesbians are probably more influenced by the male homosexuals than the other way around. Simon and Gagnon also suggest that there is one other important difference between the two subcultures. They argue that for the males the emphasis is upon the facilitation of sexual activity while the socialization process is probably of greater emphasis for the females.[31]

Other reasons have also been suggested for the lower involvement of

---

[29] Gagnon and Simon, *op. cit.*, p. 262.

[30] Sonenschein, David, "The Homosexual's Language," *The Journal of Sex Research*, November, 1969, p. 288.

[31] Simon and Gagnon, *op. cit.*, p. 219.

women in the homosexual subculture. One is that the woman who makes a commitment to homosexuality is not as removed or alienated from conventional society as is the man. Her choice and her patterns for pursuing her sexual choice are less recognized and recognizable to the broader society. A second reason suggested by Simon and Gagnon is that the forces of repression that result in differences between males and females during the ages when sexual activity is initiated may also help the female to handle subsequent sexual restrictions easier than the male. "More females than males should therefore be able to resist quasi-public homosexual behavior which increases the risks of disclosure; further, lesbians should be better able to resist relations that involve sexual exchange without any emotional investment."[32]

All of the lesbians that Gagnon and Simon interviewed in their study were a part of a subculture to at least some degree but they concluded that most lesbians avoid such participation. As suggested, the lesbian may have less need. Gagnon and Simon point out that the "lesbian may mask her sexual deviance behind a socially prepared asexuality. Not all categories of women in our society are necessarily defined as sexually active, as, for example, the spinster."[33] In the sexual setting the American society is more permissive for women interacting with each other than they are for men, and this tells us a great deal about why they are differentially treated. Basically, unmarried females, unlike unmarried males, may live together, they may kiss and touch each other affectionately, and they may seek each other's company without attracting any undue notice.[34]

The bar is for the lesbian, as for the male homosexual, the main public center of the subculture. But the number of bars is much less for women than for men. The UCLA study found in Los Angeles out of 15 homosexual bars that 12 were for male homosexuals and 3 for female homosexuals.[35] The bars are different in other ways, as for example there is not much "cruising" in the lesbian bars. One study suggests that the bar is a good place to meet, but lesbians often do not leave together the first time they meet.[36] A recent description of one of the most popular and expensive lesbian bars in New York City points out a notable absence of "drag dykes," the women who imitate men in their dress and manner. In that bar the girls gather, young and middle-aged, white and black, miniskirted and pantsuited. The women talk, drink, and dance, usually with arms around each other's waists or necks.[37]

What are the roles that lesbians play? As the above description sug-

---

[32] *Ibid.*

[33] Gagnon and Simon, *op. cit.*, p. 262.

[34] Gagnon, John H. and William Simon, "Sexual Deviance in Contemporary America," *The Annals*, March, 1968, p. 118.

[35] *UCLA Law Review, op. cit.*, p. 740.

[36] Love, *op. cit.*, p. 67.

[37] Nemy, *op. cit.*, p. 61.

gests they are much less strong than male homosexuals and the stereotype of the masculine lesbian is as far from reality as is the stereotype to the effeminate male. The masculine-appearing lesbian is often called a "dyke" or a "butch" and these are women who usually wear masculine styled clothing and have some male mannerisms. They are fairly easy to identify as homosexuals but they imitate men only to a degree. What these terms imply is that the lesbian is in some observable way appearing like a male. This may be not only through dress and mannerisms but also through body stance, speech, or vocabulary. By contrast the "femme" is a homosexual who appears as feminine as does the average heterosexual woman. She in no visual way appears "different." Of course, the roles of "dyke" and "femme" are not mutually exclusive and many lesbians may fall in between the two types with their various characteristics.

The stereotype of the lesbian also tends to define her as being or wanting to be a "counterfeit man." But the only thing which most lesbians share with men is the gender of the object of their sexual desires. The same point may also be made about the male homosexual's being like women. The mannerisms that are peculiar to the lesbian are less distinguishable than for men. For example, there are fewer behavior gestures and signs which indicate homosexuality on the part of females than males. Also "camp behavior," which is that behavior seen as both outrageous and outraging, appears to be essentially a product of the male homosexual community. There is very little visible avant gardism in the lesbian community.[38] This would also suggest that female homosexuals may be basically more conservative in their patterns of behavior. And this of course tends to be a general characteristic of male and female differences with regard to sexual expression in any kind of social setting.

As with the male homosexual the notion of "passive" and "active" roles in their sexual relations has been exaggerated for the lesbians. The stereotype has been that the "active" sex partner who performs the sex was the "dyke" while the "passive" partner who receives the sexual stimulation was the "femme." But often the lesbians do not define themselves with such simplicity. In the Philadelphia sample half of the female homosexuals defined themselves as "gay" and half as "bisexual." The distinction appeared to be that the "gay" women have completely rejected men as sex partners while the "bisexual" ones have *almost* completely rejected men. The women were asked how, in a permanent relationship with another woman, they preferred to participate sexually. Eighteen percent said "an active role," 21 percent "a passive role," and 61 percent said "both about equally." Most of the lesbians went on to say that while they might have a slight sexual preference the situation and the desires of the partner more often determined whether they were sexually passive or ac-

---

[38] Simon and Gagnon, *op. cit.*, p. 216.

tive. To many lesbians the "passive" and "active" distinction is rejected as appropriate for only heterosexual activity. They often see their sex activity as special or different and not involving anything like a masculine role. A part of this belief is seen in the argument that one woman can better understand another woman in terms of what will sexually satisfy her because she is a woman and therefore has this gender knowledge. The argument goes on to say that lesbianism is based on a knowledge and intimacy between two women that makes it significantly different from anything that can occur between a man and a woman. In fact, this is often the major argument when one woman is trying to persuade another to have sexual relations with her.

Another characteristic of lesbians that distinguishes them from the male homosexual is that they are much less promiscuous. The Kinsey data show that of single females who had homosexual experience half of them had it with only a single partner. Twenty percent of them had it with two different partners. Only 29 percent had three or more partners in their homosexual relations, and only 4 percent had more than ten partners. So the female homosexual record contrasts sharply with that of the male. "Of the males in the sample who had homosexual experiences, a high proportion had it with several persons, and 22 percent had it with more than ten partners."[39] This distinction between the promiscuity of men and women reflects a general sexual difference and not just a homosexual one. That is, heterosexual males who have premarital, extramarital, and postmarital coitus have both a greater number of partners and more frequent activity than do heterosexual females who are also experienced in these areas. To put it another way, males are more promiscuous than females, regardless of the sexual object.

The women in the Philadelphia sample were asked several questions about their type of sexual involvement. Half of them said that they had no "one night stands" in the past year. Lest one might think that a low level of promiscuousness is inherent in the female there were 12 percent in the sample who had "one night stands" with more than 50 different partners in the previous year. For many lesbians, as with male homosexuals or even sexually active unmarried men and women, there is often regret over past sexual experiences. However, there doesn't appear to be any evidence that lesbians are particularly regretful of their sexual choice. Kinsey found that of the lesbians with the most extensive homosexual experience 71 percent said they had "no regrets."[40]

There appears to be little question that lesbians in general have a high desire for permanent relationships. This is a pattern generally common to women regardless of the type of sexual partner. The lesbian, like the

---

[39] Kinsey, *op. cit.*, p. 458.
[40] *Ibid.*, p. 477.

heterosexual female, places a higher stress on interpersonal involvement than on sexual outlet. As a result homosexual relationships between females tend to be more effective, to take place under more stable conditions, and to be viewed in terms of a total relationship. Far more often for men, homosexuality is seen simply as a means of sexual gratification and is a casual impersonal act. However, many lesbians are not able to establish permanent relationships that last for any great length of time. In the Philadelphia sample 70 percent of the lesbians said they had at least one satisfying relationship during the past two years. That doesn't mean that all relationships are satisfying, because only 44 percent characterized themselves as being "very satisfied" with any of their relationships over the past two years. But they nevertheless continue to search for the good relationship. Gagnon and Simon report in their study that almost all of the women they interviewed defined themselves as "women who wanted to become emotionally and sexually attached to another woman who would, in turn, respond to them as women."[41] Those two researchers go on to point out that what often seems to be involved is a kind of nineteenth-century commitment to romantic values. "Their aspirations were fundamentally those embodied in 'the American dream': a comfortable home, an interesting job, access to enjoyable leisure activity, and above all, a sustaining and loving partner."[42]

In Chapter 9 it was suggested that the aging factor for the male homosexual was crucial to him in many ways including an increasing desire for more permanent relationships. It appears that aging is less traumatic for the lesbian because she doesn't operate in the same highly physical setting of competitiveness as does the male homosexual. There is some irony in a society where aging is generally more crucial and resisted more by women insofar as physical attractiveness is concerned that the reverse may be true among homosexuals. This difference is also in part explained because the women do place greater stress on interpersonal factors than do men. In general it would appear that aging is easier for the lesbian to handle psychologically than it is for the male homosexual.

One crude measurement of the importance of the subculture is the extent to which lesbians choose their friends from within that setting. It is in the area of friendships that the male and female homosexual subcultures most often overlap. Gagnon and Simon found that almost all the lesbians they interviewed "included some male homosexuals among their friends; for some of the lesbians male homosexuals constituted their only close male friends."[43] In the Philadelphia sample 85 percent of the lesbians said they had some good friends who were "straight," but in most

---

[41] Gagnon and Simon, *Sexual Deviance, op. cit.*, p. 265.

[42] *Ibid.*, p. 275.

[43] *Ibid.*, p. 273.

cases they were referring to "straight" female friends. The "straight" male is not usually a friend because he is usually seen as competitive. The homosexual male is not only not competitive but is often seen as understanding because of the similarity of his position in society. Often the lesbian in interacting in the "straight" world needs a male companion and the male homosexual can provide this without demands or expectations by either. The extreme illustration of this is when a lesbian marries a male homosexual as a means of social convenience and with no sexual involvement between them.

As with the male homosexual, there is often some risk in having "straight" females as friends. That is, there may be a desire and possibly an attempt to have sexual relations with the "straight" woman. There are also some risks in establishing friendships with other lesbians. As pointed out, the population from which the individual lesbian is likely to select her friends is the same population from which she is likely to choose her sex partners. "As a result, most discussions of friendship were filled with a sense of anticipated impermanence."[44] Therefore, for many lesbians impermanence may be a characteristic of both sexual relationships and friendships.

One area in which there is a great difference between male and female homosexuals is with regard to children. Many lesbians not only want children but have them. Often lesbians will have children from a marriage and keep them after divorce. A woman would have to be quite openly homosexual before the court would not allow her to have custody of the child, because children are almost always placed with the mother. Actually there is no law against placing a child with lesbians and any refusal by the courts probably would be on the grounds of a poor moral atmosphere in the home. There has been some pressure in recent years to allow lesbian couples to adopt children. It is doubtful if this will occur where the women openly state they are lesbians. However, there are moves in some places to allow single women to adopt and this means will be used, with the placement agencies having no knowledge that the woman is a lesbian. It would also appear that when lesbians have children to take care of this also contributes to making the "aging" process somewhat easier to adjust to.

Unlike the male homosexual's case, there are no occupations that are stereotyped as being lesbian occupations. About the only prediction that might be made is that lesbians would more commonly be found in those occupations where women are thrown together and isolated from men either through physical separation or other restrictions against heterosexual interaction. There is one occupation, however, that appears to be overrepresented with female homosexuality. Before examining that occu-

---

[44] *Ibid.*

pation it should be stressed that occupations are important to lesbians because they are not dependent on males as breadwinners. Lesbians appear to be more seriously committed to work than most women and one reflection of this is that they tend to have relatively stable work histories.[45] In the Philadelphia sample 60 percent of the women defined their jobs as "rewarding" while the rest defined them simply as "a way of earning a living." And 70 percent of the women said they had to hide the fact that they were "gay" in their work situations. About a quarter of them said they would be fired if it were found out, but only 6 percent had actually ever been fired. The dangers and the rates of job loss for being homosexual are much higher for men. It would appear that the occupation is another means of helping the lesbian adjust to her being sexually different from other women.

THE STRIPPER

One interesting study on the relationship between the occupation and lesbian practices has been with strippers in burlesque theatres by McCaghy and Skipper. They asked the 35 strippers that they interviewed to estimate the proportion of strippers that had homosexual contacts. The estimates of the girls currently being at least bisexual in their contacts mostly fell within the 50 to 75 percent range. They also found that 26 percent of their respondents had engaged in homosexuality although they did not ask for that information or have prior evidence of the respondents' involvement.[46] The two sociologists suggest there are several social factors that operate within the setting of "stripping" as an occupation that help to explain the high rates of lesbianism.

One social condition was the isolation of the girls from effective social relationships. Many of the girls were not able to maintain any permanent social relationships such as marriages or close friendships. Beyond whatever personal limitations the strippers had there were also severe restrictions based on the nature of the occupation. The girls on tour spent only one week in each city and worked every day of the week, with their working day starting in the early afternoon and not ending until late at night. So one of the universal complaints among them was the loneliness they constantly encountered. This meant they had to turn within themselves for friendships. However, loneliness was not necessarily conducive to homosexuality because the strippers were not only isolated from men but also from women, other than the ones in their troupe. "But strippers find that contacts with males are not only limited but often highly unsatis-

---

[45] *Ibid.*, p. 270.

[46] McCaghy and Skipper, *op. cit.*, p. 265.

factory in content, and homosexuality can become an increasingly attractive alternative."[47]

A second factor that contributes to the homosexuality of the strippers is their disillusionment with men. They often see their male customers as "dirty" and want nothing to do with them. When they do develop any lasting relationships with men during their career "chances are good that they will result in another embittering experience."[48] This is very similar to the pattern of relationships that prostitutes often have with men. Therefore, limited contacts with men along with their wariness tends to sharply hold down their sexual activity. So the opportunity for a warm and close relationship without the hazards the male brings to it becomes attractive. McCaghy and Skipper stress that pressures placed on the girls toward lesbian practices should not be over done. They feel that more important is the fact that opportunities for homosexuality take place in an atmosphere of permissiveness toward sexual behavior. The strippers did not see sexual behavior generally as being right or wrong by any universal standard and many of them "firmly expressed their view that lesbianism and prostitution are easily as common among women outside the occupation as among strippers."[49]

What appears to be the case is that the strippers see themselves in a situation where lesbianism becomes acceptable. The chances are if they could be in a situation where the probability of more satisfying relationships with men could take place they would probably give up their lesbian relationships. This is very similar to what happens to women when they are in prison; lesbianism is seen as an acceptable adjustment based on psychological needs and special social circumstances. What this also suggests is that women are more tolerant and accepting of sexual deviance than are men, at least under certain circumstances. This study is of value not only in pointing out the importance of the situation as a determining factor in sexual deviancy for women, but also in indicating how situational adaptations differ between men and women.

BLACK LOWER CLASS

There is a second study to discuss briefly that also gives some insights into lesbianism. This study analyzes lesbianism as a part of the black lower-class subculture. Ethel Sawyer has studied the impact of lower-class black culture on female homosexual roles. She studied a group of lesbians between 17 and 34 years of age. They were involved in a subculture that

---

[47] *Ibid.*, p. 266.
[48] *Ibid.*, p. 267.
[49] *Ibid.*, p. 269.

centered around bars, taverns, and night clubs that catered to homosexuals and where there was little and sometimes no effort to conceal their deviation from the larger society.[50]

Sawyer analyzes the two basic roles that existed within the homosexual subculture. The women were designated as "studs" or as "fish." The studs are female homosexuals who fill both socially and sexually the role modeled after the masculine one in the broader society. The fish are those who take on the feminine role. She points out that the roles are more than just labels because they carry with them "matters of appropriate dress, mannerisms and behavior, domestic responsibility, attitudes toward homosexuality, the larger society and towards oneself which accompany each of the roles and which serve to distinguish them. These roles are complementary, i.e., a stud and a fish make a homosexual couple."[51]

Sawyer suggests that the term stud probably had its origins with the male animal and was used to describe black male slaves who were used to breed slave children. The term is commonly used in the black lower class by one male referring to another and it carries with it the connotations of virility and sexual prowess. Often the stud in the lesbian subculture is referred to as a "stud broad' to make a gender distinction.[52] The use of the term fish in place of the commonly used term "femme" among lesbians is of interest. The term fish may come from several sources. In some prisons, fish designates a new prisoner and often the fish is someone who is entering lesbianism for the first time. However, Sawyer suggests that fish may have a more direct sexual connotation and may derive its meaning from the nature of the smell which is often believed to come from the female sexual organs. She suggests that this interpretation takes on importance when examined in the context of two other points of concern important to the lesbian subculture. One is that in the sexual area there appears to be an almost "obsessive and compulsive" concern with cleanliness. The second issue centers around mouth-genital contact and the stigma that goes with it. Sawyer found that although oral-genital contact was widespread, generally accepted and performed, there was still a good deal of ambivalence surrounding the activity. "One 'gives head' for instance to those who are clean, one takes a bath and has her mate do so before indulging in mouth genital activity."[53]

As mentioned, the stud role includes far more than simply the direction of participation in the sexual act. Ideologically the stud is the "aggressor, the provider and the protector" and Sawyer says that one often hears this cliche in the subculture uttered by both studs and fish. In

---

[50] Sawyer, *op. cit.*, p. 3.
[51] *Ibid.*, p. 5.
[52] *Ibid.*, p. 6.
[53] *Ibid.*, pp. 6–7.

theory the role of the stud is closely approximated to the male in the broader society. Even many of the double standard values of society have been adopted by them. The studs are the ones who have one-night stands, and go out on the town while the fish remain at home. The studs are the ones who drink large amounts of alcohol while the fish are expected to drink in moderation; "and studs are the ones who may at any point 'let their hair down' while fish are to always exhibit the most 'ladylike' conduct."[54] Often the employment record and economic responsibility of the stud is no different from that of the male in that subculture. Like the man, some studs who are employed do not support their fish. Often the stud uses the male models of "hipster" or "stud on the corner" as a prototype for her behavior. As a result studs "are sometimes inclined to view fish in an instrumental and exploitive fashion, and often cast them into roles of persons from whom they may gain favors, particularly along monetary lines."[55]

Sawyer was also interested in the relationships of the lesbians to their children and a number of the women, both studs and fish, did have children of their own. She found that when studs had children of their own they were more likely to take care of them financially than they were to take care of the children of their fish. But often the studs were capable of developing strong emotional ties to children belonging to their mates. And in most cases the studs did not hesitate to show their feelings for the children. "It is not an uncommon sight to see a stud wheeling the baby carriage of another's child or walk into a home and observe the stud caring for a baby or engaged in play activities with children of their mates."[56] Sawyer's study is important not only in itself but also because it provides a picture of an attempt to develop different patterns under special social circumstances—those of the black lower-class subculture. It may also be seen as another illustration of women's use of and ability to deal with homosexuality in a situation where it is felt to be of some value to them. It is hard to imagine men being able to make the same kind of adaptive use of homosexuality in a similar social situation.

We conclude this chapter by looking a little more at the relationship of lesbianism to the broader society. As already indicated, the female homosexual probably has fewer problems with the broader society than does the male homosexual. Gagnon and Simon point out that the female homosexual "is probably better integrated than the male homosexual into conventional relationships such as the family of origin, work, religion, and conventional leisure time pursuits."[57]

---

[54] *Ibid.*, pp. 9–10.

[55] *Ibid.*, p. 12.

[56] *Ibid.*, p. 19.

[57] Gagnon and Simon, "Sexual Deviance in Contemporary America," *op. cit.*, p. 118.

Similar to men, but to a much lesser extent, there has developed among some lesbians a militancy with related organizations to push for what they believe to be their rights. The largest lesbian organization, the Daughters of Bilitis, was founded in 1955 and named after some 19th century song lyrics that glorified lesbian love. The organization has its headquarters in San Francisco and in 1969 there were four official and five probationary chapters. The purpose is to explore changing some present laws that are believed to discriminate against the lesbian, but they also maintain social clubs where some counseling takes place. The organization is generally known by its initials, the DOB, and it has a few honorary male members whom it calls Sons of Bilitis, or SOB's.[58]

The new militancy of some lesbians is not so much a result of their feeling that they were increasingly being discriminated against as that they should do something about the wrongs they feel have long been directed at them. There is also some evidence of overlap in the militancy of lesbians and some factions of the militant women's liberation movement. This should not be surprising because the female homosexual is a part of two minority groups—she is a woman and a homosexual. There is supersensitivity in the woman's liberation movement to the lesbian charge. The existence of a few militant lesbians within the movement once prompted one of the leaders, Betty Friedan, to complain about the "lavender menace" that was threatening to warp the image of woman's rights. Regardless of the relationship it would seem a good possibility that the aggressiveness of the female homosexual will increase in the near future.[59]

One of the greatest problems for the lesbian appears to be with her family. In the Philadelphia sample of lesbians 50 percent of them said their parents knew they were homosexual, 21 percent said their parents absolutely did not know. Almost half of the respondents said the fear that their parents would find out about them had been a source of concern to them. Gagnon and Simon found in their study that frequently parents suspected or even knew, but decided to ignore the possibility of their daughters' being lesbians.[60] However, it is probably much easier for a parent not to recognize or to ignore a daughter's being a homosexual than a son's.

It seems quite likely that in the future lesbianism, if not more common, is going to be much more open. This would seem to be an inevitable part of women's achieving greater equality. As women attain the right to sexual expression closer to that of the male, that right is going to be

[58] Sagarin, Edward, *Odd Man in: Societies of Deviants in America* (Chicago: Quadrangle Books, 1969), p. 89.

[59] Brownmiller, Susan, "Sisterhood is Powerful," *New York Times Magazine,* March 15, 1970, p. 140.

[60] Gagnon and Simon, *Sexual Deviance, op. cit.,* p. 268.

directed in a number of different directions. As society moves in the direction of a single sex standard for both males and females it will cut across all areas of sexual expression. Therefore, the woman will have greater equality heterosexually and homosexually.

BIBLIOGRAPHY

CORY, DONALD W., *The Lesbian in America* (New York: The Citadel Press, 1964).

GAGNON, JOHN H. and WILLIAM SIMON, *Sexual Deviancy* (New York: Harper and Row, 1967).

LOVE, NANCY, "The Invisible Sorority," *Philadelphia Magazine*, November, 1967.

McCAGHY, CHARLES H. and JAMES K. SKIPPER, JR., "Lesbian Behavior as an Adaptation to the Occupation of Stripping," *Social Problems*, Fall, 1969, pp. 262–70.

NEMY, ENID, "The Woman Homosexual: More Assertive, Less Willing to Hide," *New York Times*, November 17, 1969, p. 61.

SAWYER, ETHEL, "The Impact of the Surrounding Lower-Class Subculture on Female Homosexual Adaptations," *Society for the Study of Social Problems*, San Francisco, Calif., August, 1967.

SIMON, WILLIAM and JOHN H. GAGNON, "Femininity in the Lesbian Community," *Social Problems*, Fall, 1967, pp. 212–21.

CHAPTER 12

DELINQUENT
SUBCULTURES

THERE HAS BEEN a vast body of literature written about many different aspects of juvenile delinquency. Therefore, any attempt to deal with the topic in a single chapter must be highly limited. The intention here is to present a brief discussion of delinquency primarily as it relates to the concept of a deviant subculture. This means that such areas as individual deviancy, where the young person commits an illegal act by himself and without the direct influence of age peers, will not be considered here.

The concern with delinquency is probably about as old as mankind. This is because all societies have recognized that certain kinds of behavior are wrong because they are defined as harmful at least to some. Out of this protective view emerged the social concern with criminal norms and laws and various means for protecting the innocent and punishing or trying to change the guilty. But there probably also developed early in the history of mankind the recognition that not all persons who did things wrong could be defined and treated in the same way. Over the centuries one variation related to the age of the individual, while others were related to the person's mental competency as determined by either mental ability or mental illness. The problem of age and individual responsibility has been confused by the transitional years of growing up to adult maturity. In some primitive societies this was not a problem because the young person was defined as a child, with few rights and obligations, until a certain age and then he was subjected to tests and if he passed he was from that point on defined as an adult. In that kind of society being a child or an adult were separate and not a stage along a line of transition. In the United States it is the pattern that a child up until ten or twelve years of age is defined as being pre-rational in that he is not usually held responsible for his actions. For example, if an eight year old child kills someone he is not held personally responsible for his actions. In most situations by age eighteen the individual is held responsible for what he does (assuming mental competency and in some cases no other mitigating circumstances). This results in the period of adolescence's being one where the individual is only partly responsible. It is for this age period that juvenile courts as well as various types of detention centers are set up to work with behavior based only on partial individual responsibility.

Sociologically, any study of the delinquent must start with the recognition that he is, in effect, a "second class citizen" because he has only partial rights in society. And most adolescents, whether delinquent or nondelinquent, often seek for adult status with all the rights and privileges they see as going with older age. The adolescent, being neither child nor adult, and having no clearly defined roles available to him in the overall culture, has created a loose cultural system to provide some role meanings for his adolescence. This means that there are certain conflict points with the dominant adult cultural system. And the inconsistency of adult definitions of adolescent behavior has also contributed to the emergence of subcultural values. The very fact that the adult views the adolescent with indecision as to appropriate behavior means that the adolescent is treated one way on one occasion and a different way on another. Since the adolescent often desires decisiveness and some precision in role definitions, he consequently tries to create his own roles. When he does, he often demands a high degree of conformity by other adolescents as "proof" of the rightness of his definitions. There is a certain irony in that many adolescents think of themselves as social deviants. What they fail to realize is that their adolescent groups deviate from the adult world, but that the requirements for conformity within their subcultures are extremely strong. And this level of subcultural conformity is just as powerful for delinquent subcultures as it is for nondelinquent ones.

Over space and time the adolescent's behavior varies widely, as does the definition of that behavior. And some of the features of delinquency that are so pervasive in the United States and that have come to be taken for granted as inherent in the idea of delinquency can be absent in other cultures. It is probable that delinquent subcultures have different stresses in different societies and that those could be related to differences in the various social systems of which they are a part. This also helps to stress the point that there is nothing inherent in an activity that makes it delinquent. Furthermore, there is the recognition that what is defined as delinquency varies over time. For example, at one time school truancy was defined as a more serious form of delinquency than it is today. Or one of the most common types of delinquency today did not exist fifty years ago—the stealing of automobiles.

But whatever specific acts are defined as delinquent the general concept has probably been close to universal. "In every society known to us, a certain number of minors have also been transgressors. And, when troubled by the delinquency in their midst, members of every society have sought to account for that phenomenon. The threat posed by 'ungovernable youth' has provoked a multitude of reactions and led to a variety of explanations."[1] There have been few areas of human behavior that have been more extensively studied than that of delinquency. Part of the reason for this is that personal alarm competes with the economic cost. "In a culture where the cash nexus has much to do with shaping morals, 'experts' feel heavy pressure to find a remedy, cut the loss, declare war on crime and stamp it out. Moral and financial accounts are to be settled simultaneously."[2]

As a result of the vast amount of research, almost every social variable believed to have negative consequences has been linked to delinquency. In one sense the concern about delinquency becomes a rallying point around which one may aim at a variety of assumed causes. This means that often attention is directed at delinquency not so much as a problem in itself, but rather because it is seen as the result of other problems of deviance that various groups are concerned about. For example, one may study the relationship of delinquency to broken homes because the delinquency is seen as further proof that broken homes are bad and the broken home is the area of deviancy where the concern rests. This may also be found in studies attempting to causally link delinquency to poverty, racial conflict, and so forth.

Since the concern in this chapter is primarily with juvenile delinquency in the collective rather than the individual sense, the interest is in delinquency as it refers to gang or subcultural forms. From the sociological point of view the interest is not in the individual delinquent and what he does but rather in the overall group, which implies that the collectivity has some qualities beyond the mere sum of the individuals involved. This means that the sociological view is different from the legal one, because in the legal approach of the Western world the weight of legal responsibility is on the individual actor, and not the collectivity as a whole.[3]

---

[1] Rosenberg, Bernard and Harry Silverstein, *The Varieties of Delinquent Experience* (Waltham, Mass.: Blaisdell Publishing Co., 1969), p. 3.

[2] *Ibid.*, p. 4.

[3] Sebald, Hans, *Adolescence: A Sociological Analysis* (New York: Appleton-Century-Crofts, 1968), pp. 354–55.

One major difficulty in any study of delinquency is trying to bring together the various legal meanings. The laws in the different states are very general and often quite vague. For example, in the state of Illinois, a delinquent is described as "an 'incorrigible' growing up in 'idleness,' 'loitering' in the streets at night without a proper excuse, or guilty of 'indecent' or 'lascivious' conduct. New Mexico, as another example, exceeds Illinois in vagueness by making 'habitual' infraction a necessary condition for the definition of delinquency."[4] Furthermore, delinquency is not simply crimes committed by juveniles, because the statutes are so broad they allow juvenile authorities to assume control over all types of adolescents engaged in all kinds of misbehavior. In some cases the laws empower the juvenile court to take jurisdiction of adolescents who show vague conditions such as "immorality," as well as those who are involved in specific areas of misconduct.

It seems clear that most adolescents at some time commit delinquent acts but are not officially defined as delinquents. To be defined as an official delinquent is the result of social judgments, in most cases made by the police. The individual becomes "a delinquent because someone in authority has defined him as one, often on the basis of the public face he has presented to officials rather than of the kind of offense he has committed."[5] This suggests that most adolescents are at some time behavioral delinquents, but to become labeled as such is determined by legal agency decisions. There are many agencies beyond the police who contribute to defining some youths as delinquents. In fact, those who do the defining contribute to many confusions because there are many different conceptions held by the police, social workers, psychiatrists, psychologists, sociologists, judges, and so forth. These different perspectives may lead to redefinitions of an adolescent as "disturbed" rather than "wild" or "insecure" and "in need of love" rather than strong discipline and "a kick where it hurts." "The behavior content of a youth's activities, therefore, may not be as critical in such cases as the interpretations which are placed upon it by others."[6] What is important is that there are a number of different vested interests with different views of delinquents and how they should be treated. This can lead to confusion for the adolescent as well as the broader society.

Regardless of the variety of vested interests the real source for defining most delinquents is the police. The police come upon adolescents doing

---

[4] *Ibid.*, p. 352.

[5] Piliavin, Irving and Scott Briar, "Police Encounters with Juveniles," in Earl Rubington and Martin S. Weinberg, *Deviance: The Interactionist Perspective* (New York: Macmillan Co., 1968), p. 145.

[6] Cicourel, Aaron V. and John I. Kitsuse, "The Social Organization of the High School and Deviant Adolescent Careers," in Earl Rubington and Martin S. Weinberg, *Deviance: The Interactionist Perspective* (New York: Macmillan Co., 1968), p. 132.

something that is against the law and they must decide if the lawbreaking youth should be treated as a "bad one" needing court attention or a "good kid" who needs only a strong talking-to. Once the police make this decision then other agencies may enter if he is defined as needing the attention of the court. For example, "someone must decide whether a youth should be sent to a training school or placed on probation. Someone must judge whether a training-school inmate should be turned loose on parole this week, next month, or at some other time."[7]

When the police respond to the delinquent actions they are usually responding as more than just policemen. They often are responding as individuals who have strong moral values about what they feel to be right adolescent behavior. Because many police come out of lower middle-class backgrounds they usually believe that the adolescent should be seen and not heard and this in itself may make a difference as to whether or not an arrest takes place. In general the police tend to see the adolescents they come into contact with as being of two general types. First, there are those whom they see as "good kids" who do not usually cause any trouble and second are the "troublemakers" who constitute most of the adolescents' groups they have contact with. The police may make even further distinctions among adolescents. For example, among the good kids the police may make a distinction between the "quiet, studious kids who never cause any trouble," and those who are seen as "good kids who cut up a little and need to be warned." The police may also make a distinction between two types of "troublemakers." One group are those they see as "wild kids who need a good kick in the ass," and those considered "real no-good punks" headed for criminal careers.[8]

There are a number of other factors that determine how the police will react to potential delinquents and how they will treat them. It has been suggested that other than the previous record of the individual the most important factor is the youth's behavior toward the police. In the opinion of policemen themselves the demeanor of apprehended juveniles was a major determinant of their decisions for about half of the juvenile cases they processed.[9] The actual cues that the police use to decide the demeanor of the juvenile are quite simple. When juveniles were contrite about their wrongs, respectful to the policemen, and fearful of the sanctions that might be employed against them they were usually seen by the police as basically law-abiding or at least "salvagable." By contrast, youthful offenders who were fractious, obdurate, or who appeared nonchalant in their encounters with patrolmen were likely to be viewed as "would be tough guys" or "punks" who deserved the most severe sanction: arrest.[10]

---

[7] Garabedian, Peter G. and Don C. Gibbons, *Becoming Delinquent* (Chicago: Aldine Publishing Co., 1970), p. 4.

[8] Cicourel and Kitsuse, *op. cit.*, pp. 131–32.

[9] Piliavin and Briar, *op. cit.*, p. 141.

[10] *Ibid.*, p. 142.

The fact that police officers tend to show animosity toward recalcitrant or aloof offenders appears to come from two sources. One is moral indignation that the juveniles appeared to be self-righteous and indifferent about their transgressions. Second was the feeling that the youths did not accord the respect to the police that they believed they deserved. Because the policemen saw themselves as honestly and impartially performing a vital function that deserved respect and deference from the community they often attributed the lack of respect shown them by the juveniles to reflect the latters' immorality.[11]

There is evidence that many police respond to adolescents in terms of their personal stereotypes. For example, compared to other youths, blacks and boys whose appearance matched the delinquent stereotypes were more often stopped and interrogated by policemen. This occurs often even when there is no evidence that an offense has been committed. Also, boys fitting the sterotypes when arrested are usually given more severe dispositions for the same violations than those who did not fit the stereotypes.[12] Therefore, becoming a delinquent, like becoming a criminal, often depends on a series of factors that may have little or nothing to do with the illegal act itself.

How Much Delinquency?

If one tries to estimate the number of young people who engage in acts that could be defined as delinquent the number would be extremely high. In fact, "self-report studies reveal that perhaps 90 percent of all young people have committed at least one act for which they could have been brought to juvenile court."[13] So while it seems that nearly all youngsters engage in acts of misconduct, only about 3 percent of all juvenile court-eligible children (between 7 and 18 years of age) ever get into the juvenile court each year, while about double that number come to the attention of the police. Most of those who get officially processed by the police and the courts are children of working class parents who have engaged in serious and repetitive acts of lawbreaking.[14]

During the 1960's the number, as well as the percentage, of adolescents defined as delinquents showed a substantial increase. For example, in 1960, about 14 percent of all urban offenders were in their teens, but by 1965 this had increased to 21 percent. Actually, most crimes, wherever they are committed, are committed by boys and young men. In looking at the overall years of adolescence it can be seen that about one in every six male youths will be referred to juvenile court in connection with a delinquent act (excluding traffic offenses) before his 18th birthday. "Arrest

[11] *Ibid.*, p. 143.
[12] *Ibid.*
[13] Sebald, *op. cit.*, p. 357.
[14] Garabedian and Gibbons, *op. cit.*, p. 3.

rates are highest for persons aged 15 through 17, next highest for those 18 through 20, dropping off quite directly with increase in age."[15] Put another way, in the period between 1960 and 1965 the teenage population in the United States increased by 17 percent but its rate of delinquency increased by 54 percent. More specifically, there was an increase in delinquency in the suburban areas during the 1960's. Adolescents made up 32 percent of all criminals in the suburban areas as compared to 21 percent in the urban and 19 percent in the rural areas.[16]

The high rates of juvenile delinquency are costly to society because of the necessary detention and treatment procedures. For example, in the 1960's a daily average of around 63,000 youths was incarcerated in juvenile institutions in the United States. Another group of roughly 300,000 were under supervision in community programs through probation and parole. The institutionalized delinquents required approximately 32,000 employees to process and supervise them, while another 10,000 individuals were employed as community correctional agents.[17] It can be seen that just the sheer size of delinquency makes it a costly and complex social problem.

DELINQUENT SUBCULTURES

Given the long and intense interest in juvenile delinquency by sociologists, it is not surprising that many theories have been developed to try to explain the phenomenon. Only some of these sociological theories can be considered in the briefest way with the intention simply to indicate just the main points of the various theories. All of the theories are sociological in concept and see delinquency as a part of a group process.

The earliest sociological theories attempting to explain delinquency came out of the attempts to try to explain the characteristics and the spatial distribution of gangs in cities. "These, in turn, were related to research and speculation concerning structural and growth processes of cities and the influence of different, and sometimes conflicting, cultures in the American melting pot."[18] Ever since the publication of Shaw's famous studies many American sociologists have argued that the most serious forms of male juvenile delinquency "can be described as distinctively subcultural phenomena, manifestations of a deviant peer-group tradition, or way of life."[19] During the same general period Thrasher's work on gangs had a great influence. In essence Thrasher saw the de-

---

[15] Sebald, op. cit., p. 363.

[16] Ibid., p. 364.

[17] Garabedian and Gibbons, op. cit., p. 3.

[18] Short, James F., Jr., Gang Delinquency and Delinquent Subcultures (New York: Harper and Row, 1968), p. 133.

[19] Lerman, Paul, "Argot, Symbolic Deviance and Subcultural Delinquency," American Sociological Review, April, 1967, p. 209.

linquent subculture as the way of life that would be developed as a group became a gang. Bordua suggests that the most important difference between Thrasher and some of the more recent theoretical views of delinquency was that Thrasher saw crime and delinquency as being attractive to the boy and being a good boy as dull. "They were attractive because one could be a hero in a fight. Fun, profit, glory, and freedom is a combination hard to beat, particularly for the inadequate conventional institutions that formed the competition."[20]

ALBERT COHEN

In recent years the most influential sociological theory about delinquency has come from Cohen.[21] In his study he examined what he called a delinquent subculture and saw it as a system of beliefs and values brought about through the process of verbal interaction among young men in similar circumstances. The circumstances were alike by virtue of their positions in the social system, and the subculture constituted a solution to the problems of adjustment to which the established culture provided no satisfactory solutions. The problems were for the most part ones of status and self-respect arising among working-class children because of their inability to meet the standards and expectations of the established culture. "The delinquent subculture, with its characteristics of non-utilitarianism, malice, and negativism, provides an alternative status system and justifies, for those who participate in it, hostility and aggression against the source of their status frustration."[22] Basically, Cohen argued that many working-class boys were forced to develop the delinquent subculture as a way of recouping the self-esteem destroyed by the dominating institutions of the middle class. Rather than concentrating on the gang and its development over time, "Cohen's theory focuses on the way of life of the gang—the delinquent subculture."[23]

RICHARD A. CLOWARD AND LLOYD E. OHLIN

The theory of Cloward and Ohlin is similar to that of Cohen except that they see a variation in types of delinquent subcultures.[24] They argue that all delinquent subcultures emerge because the individuals have lim-

[20] Bordua, David J., "Delinquent Subcultures: Sociological Interpretations of Gang Delinquency," in William Rushing, Deviant Behavior and Social Process (Chicago: Rand McNally and Co., 1969), pp. 27–8.

[21] Cohen, Albert K., Delinquent Boys: The Culture of the Gang (Glencoe, Ill.: The Free Press, 1955).

[22] Cohen, Albert K. and James F. Short, Jr., "Research in Delinquent Subcultures," Journal of Social Issues, 14 (1958), p. 20.

[23] Bordua, op. cit., p. 28.

[24] Cloward, Richard A. and Lloyd E. Ohlin, Delinquency and Opportunity (New York: Macmillan Company, 1960).

ited access to legitimate opportunities. Given the limited access, specific types of delinquent subcultures result from variation in the different means of *illegitimate* opportunity available to lower-class boys. According to this approach there are some communities characterized by politically protected organized crime, and in that setting there exists the fullest access to illegitimate opportunity. In that setting they argue that a *criminal* type of delinquent subculture will predominate. They go on to suggest that in lower-class areas where there is an absence of both illegitimate and legitimate opportunity two other types of delinquent subculture may be expected to develop. One is the *conflict* type of street gang and this includes those boys who are frustrated in their aspirations for big money and who have no effective access to illegitimate opportunity and therefore shift their status goals to being street fighters. The second is the *"retreatist* type of gang which includes boys for whom illegitimate opportunity is similarly unavailable. But unable to use violence because of subjective inhibition, they resort to drug use as they seek status in groups for which the cultivation of inner experience constitutes a dominant value."[25]

WALTER MILLER

Miller argues that gang delinquency is most directly influenced by the lower-class community itself.[26] He says that there is a long established, distinctly patterned tradition with an integrity of its own, rather than a delinquent subculture, which has arisen through conflict with middle-class culture and is oriented to the deliberate violation of middle-class norms. Miller sees the lower-class culture as coming from the shaking-down processes of immigration, internal migration, and vertical mobility. "Several population and cultural streams feed this process, but primarily, lower class culture represents the emerging common adaptation of unsuccessful immigrants and Negroes."[27] Miller sees the focal concerns of lower-class subculture as trouble, toughness, smartness, excitement, fate, and autonomy.

Miller argues that participation in lower-class street gangs produces delinquency in several different ways. First, as with Cloward and Ohlin's illegitimate means, many cultural practices are comprised essentially of elements found in the overall pattern of the lower class which automatically violate specific legal norms. Second, where alternative means to similar ends are available, the illegal means often provide a greater

[25] Kobrin, Solomon, *et al.*, "Criteria of Status among Street Groups," in Short, *op. cit.*, p. 180.

[26] Miller, Walter, "Lower-Class Culture as a Generating Milieu of Gang Delinquency," *The Journal of Social Issues*, 14 (1958), pp. 3–19.

[27] Bordua, *op. cit.*, p. 31.

and more immediate return for a smaller investment of energy than does the legal means. Third, the expected responses to a variety of situations often occurring in the lower-class culture involve the performing of illegal acts.[28] The adolescent street gang also provides the mechanism for the boy to deal with girls as well as to fit him into the all male activity which he will be a part of as an adult. So Miller emphasizes the wide range of activities of a nondelinquent nature that the gang members engage in —because of the desire to be "real men."[29] Miller's view is primarily different from the others in his stressing that the subculture of the delinquent boys comes from the broader lower class and he doesn't really see what they do as delinquents as being significantly different.

Lewis Yablonsky

In his writings, Yablonsky has reacted against the view of delinquent subcultures with their assumed structure and functions.[30] He suggests that one way to view human collectivities is on a continuum of organization characteristics. At one extreme of the continuum there would be a highly organized, cohesive, functioning collection of individuals making up a group. At the other extreme would be a mob of individuals characterized by anonymity, disturbed leadership, motivated by emotion, and in some situations representing a destructive collectivity within the inclusive social system.[31] He goes on to argue that midway along the continuum are collectivities that are neither groups nor mobs. These he calls "near-groups" and they are characterized by some of the following factors: "(1) diffuse role definition, (2) limited cohesion, (3) impermanence, (4) minimal consensus of norms, (5) shifting membership, (6) disturbed leadership, and (7) limited definition of membership expectations. These factors characterize the near-group's 'normal' structure."[32]

Yablonsky applied his concept of the near-group to the study of gang battles in New York City. He argues that the press, public, police, social workers, and others project group conceptions into near-group activities. In their treatment of the aggregates as gangs they attribute to them subcultural characteristics that may not exist in reality. Yablonsky says that most of the young men at the scene of gang wars were actually participating in a kind of mob action. "Most had no real concept of belonging to any gang or group; however, they were interested in a situation which

---

[28] *Ibid.*, p. 32.

[29] Miller, *op. cit.*, pp. 3–19.

[30] Yablonsky, Lewis, "The Delinquent Gang as a Near-Group," *Social Problems*, Fall, 1959, pp. 108–17; reprinted in Earl Rubington and Martin S. Weinberg, *Deviance: The Interactionist Perspective* (New York: Macmillan, 1968), pp. 225–34.

[31] *Ibid.*, pp. 225–26.

[32] *Ibid.*, p. 226.

might be exciting and possibly a channel for expressing some of their aggressions and hostilities."[33]

It is suggested by Yablonsky that to approach a gang as a group, when it is not, tends to give it a structure that did not formerly exist. He says that the gang worker's usual set of notions about gangs existing as groups includes some of the following distortions: "(1) the gang has a measurable number of members, (2) membership is defined, (3) the role of members is specified, (4) there is a consensus of understood gang norms among gang members, and (5) gang leadership is clear and entails a flow of authority and direction of action."[34] So Yablonsky's contribution to the theory of delinquent subcultures is to caution against assuming subcultural characteristics to delinquency simply because it is shared activity.

DAVID MATZA

He too recognizes that subculture is the central idea of the dominant sociological view of delinquency.[35] Matza suggests that the sociological theorists have a remarkably similar picture of the delinquent. That is, the individual is committed to delinquency because of his membership in a subculture that requires the breaking of laws. "The sociological delinquent is trapped by the accident of membership, just as his predecessors were trapped by the accident of hereditary defect or emotional disturbance. The delinquent has come a long way under the auspices of positive criminology. He has been transformed from a defective to a defector."[36]

Matza goes on to suggest that the subculture of delinquency is a delicately balanced set of precepts doubly dependent on extenuating circumstances. Both the performing of and the abstaining from delinquent acts are approved only under certain conditions. He is saying that the delinquent subculture is really of two minds regarding delinquent actions, one that allows members to behave illegally and to gain prestige in that way and the other which shows the impact of conventional precepts of legal conformity.[37] His thesis is that even in the situation of company the commitment to delinquency is a misconception—first of delinquents and later of the sociologists who study them. "Instead, there is a system of shared misunderstandings, based on miscues, which leads delinquents to believe that all others situated in their company are committed to

---

[33] *Ibid.*, p. 227.
[34] *Ibid.*, p. 230.
[35] Matza, David, *Delinquency and Drift* (New York: John Wiley, 1964).
[36] *Ibid.*, p. 21.
[37] *Ibid.*, p. 40.

their misdeeds."[38] Matza believes that the subculture of delinquency is more dependent on and integrated into the conventional society than are most other deviant subcultures. Therefore, he says the key to the analysis of the subculture of delinquency may be seen in its high degree of integration into the wider society rather than in its slight differentiation.[39]

A basic part of Matza's theory is the concept of neutralization. The concept suggests that modern legal systems recognize the conditions under which misdeeds may not be penally sanctioned, and that these conditions may be unknowingly duplicated, distorted, and extended in customary beliefs. So the delinquent's neutralization proceeds along the lines of the negation of responsibility, "the sense of injustice, the assertion of tort, and the primacy of custom."[40] The theory of neutralization is also an explicit denial of Cohen's thesis of a delinquent subculture. The neutralization view suggests that most delinquents are not following a different or subcultural set of norms. Rather, they are basically adhering to the conventional norms while accepting many justifications for deviance. Matza also introduces the concept of "subterranean values" to show that the values behind a large portion of juvenile delinquency are far less deviant than commonly indicated. Subterranean analysis requires the exploration of connections between local deviant traditions in a subculture and a variety of traditions in conventional society. "Subterranean tradition may be defined by specification of key points along the range of support. It is deviant, which is to say that it is publicly denounced by authorized spokesmen. However, the tradition is viewed with ambivalence in the privacy of contemplation and in intimate publics by most conventional citizens."[41] The subterranean values are close to the old code of conduct for "gentlemen of leisure." There is high emphasis on daring and adventure, the rejection of disciplined work and labor, a desire for things of luxury and prestige through the show of masculinity. "It is only the form of expression that differs—the form being labeled 'delinquent.' In essence, it is not the values that are deviant but only the forms of expressing them."[42]

The various theories presented disagree as to whether or not a subculture exists, and when there is acceptance of the general concept they disagree about how it develops its basic structure and what its values are. When one looks at the various theories it seems that the delinquents discussed by Cohen, Miller, and Matza were, in varying degrees, clearly recognizable as once being children. By contrast, Cloward and Ohlin's

[38] *Ibid.*, p. 59.
[39] *Ibid.*, p. 60.
[40] *Ibid.*, p. 61.
[41] *Ibid.*, p. 64.
[42] Sebald, *op. cit.*, p. 372.

delinquents seem suddenly to appear on the scene sometime in adolescence, to look at the world and discover there is little for them.[43] Bordua in his summary of delinquent theories suggests that in general it did not seem like much fun any more to be a delinquent. He says that Thrasher's boys enjoyed themselves by being chased by the police, shooting dice, skipping school, rolling drunks. He goes on to say that Miller's boys do appear to have a little fun but somehow seem generally desperate. "Cohen's boys and Cloward and Ohlin's boys are driven by grim economic and psychic necessity into rebellion. It seems peculiar that modern analysis has stopped assuming that 'evil' can be fun and sees gang delinquency as arising only when boys are driven away from 'good.' "[44] Before examining in further detail the elements seen by many researchers as basic to delinquent subcultures it is necessary to look at some social variables that are commonly thought to be related to delinquency.

RELIGION

Religious values and institutions have traditionally been seen as the antithesis of all kinds of "badness"—including that of delinquency. A part of the American stereotype sees the boy who goes to church and participates in religious activities as a good boy. Frequently, religion in some form has been used as a means for dealing with delinquency through various types of religious therapy and orientation. Yet, it is also clear that often those who get in trouble are also those who appear to be quite religiously active. Therefore, the question may be raised as to the relationship between religious involvement and delinquent behavior.

A recent study of high school students found that those who often attended church were slightly more likely than infrequent attenders to express respect for the police, and were slightly less likely to agree that law violation is okay if you don't get caught.[45] But this study also found that students who believed in the devil and in a life after death were just as apt to commit delinquent acts as were students who did not believe in the supernatural world. And students who attended church every week were just as likely to have committed delinquent acts as students who attended church rarely or not at all.[46] The authors conclude that the church is "irrelevant to delinquency because it fails to instill in its members love for their neighbors and because belief in the possibility of pleasure and pain in another world cannot now, and perhaps never

---

[43] Bordua, op. cit., p. 35.

[44] Ibid., p. 37.

[45] Hirschi, Trovis and Rodney Stark, "Hellfire and Delinquency," Social Problems, Fall, 1969, p. 207.

[46] Ibid., p. 211.

could, compete with the pleasures and pains of everyday life."[47] This study is a good indication that the positive effects of religion on decreased delinquent behavior has been exaggerated.

SCHOOLS

Those years when delinquency is most apt to occur are the years that the person is in high school. The school is crucial if for no other reason than that it has control over the adolescent for so many hours of the day. The high school provides the setting for bringing the young together for functions that extend far beyond those of the formal school system. Undoubtedly, a great deal of delinquency either occurs in the school or is planned for there. Furthermore, there are various types of delinquent acts that are specifically related to the school, for example, truancy and school vandalism. And other more general delinquent acts such as assault, intimidation, shakedowns, rapes, and so forth often occur within the school.

Almost all high schools operate on a set of middle-class beliefs that stress such values as deferred gratification, interpersonal courtesy, respect for the individual and property, and hard work. But for many high school students these values are of no importance and they are in high school only because they must remain there until they are old enough to legally quit. For many of the young people the attractions of life are outside the school. For many boys, to study so as to get a good job is not even a part of the real world he knows. What is prestigeful and important to him are the lower-class values of toughness and immediate, hedonistic pleasures. Therefore, for many lower-class boys, both black and white, the future world implied in the high school system is meaningless as well as seeming to stand in the way of their immediate pleasures and the status symbols that are important to them. In most cases it is the lower-class students who are defined as the troublemakers by the school because from the school's point of view they most often go against the school's values and norms.

Those students who are defined as delinquent by the schools are also defined as such by the police. In fact, when the police officially define a student as delinquent he often becomes defined the same way and at the same time by the school. The "official" delinquent is seen by the school as "disruptive," and being bad for the reputation of the school. So contacts between the adolescent, the police, and the school will have major significance for the adolescent's career as a delinquent within the school system.[48]

Another area in which the school sees itself combating delinquency

---

[47] *Ibid.*, p. 213.

[48] Cicourel and Kitsuse, *op. cit.*, p. 131.

is through athletic programs. This appears to be based on the assumption that physical prowess and high energy can be channeled from delinquent acts into organized athletics. And one study found that among athletes there were fewer delinquents than among nonathletes. The study found that the association was most marked among boys who were blue-collar, low achievers; that is, boys who came out of the lower middle class and were not successful in school often became either delinquents or athletes. There is a possibility that athletics attracts the most conforming types of boys. "Stated differently, the negative relationship between athletic participation and delinquency may not be the result of the deterrent influence of athletics at all, but rather to selection of conformers into the athletic program."[49] Organized sports in the United States not only places great stress on *conformity*, but also tends to stress conservative, traditional values. The players are constantly told that what matters is the team's winning and not the individual performance. But they learn that one gains far more by being a star on a mediocre team than being a mediocre player on a great team. Athletes will usually accept extremely authoritarian control by the coaches not only over their athletic activities but often over many other aspects of life. Given these considerations it may be that those boys who choose sports over a delinquent career may have selected qualities that allow them to be severely controlled and regimented.

SOCIAL CLASS

For the most part the discussion in this chapter has centered around delinquency in the lower middle and lower class. Most of the studies of the past, as reflected in the various subculture theories, have seen delinquency as primarily rooted in the lower class. In recent years there has emerged the strong awareness that delinquency in the middle class is much greater than generally recognized. But to say this is not the same as saying that delinquency is as high in the middle class as it is in the lower class. One obvious reason is that the middle-class young person has less need for delinquency because he has many more material possessions; for example, he is more apt to have legal access to a car.

There are different patterns of delinquency by social class. Generally in the middle class there are less involved expressions of delinquent patterns, and they are probably less deeply rooted than in the lower class. For example, for some middle-class adolescents in school the delinquency patterns may be such activities as vandalism, truancy, drug experimentation, and disruptive behavior in the classroom and school.

---

[49] Schafer, Walter E., "Participating in Interscholastic Athletics and Delinquency: A Preliminary Study," *Social Problems,* Summer, 1969, p. 47.

These behavior patterns are not subcultural in the strict sense "since they are often done by the individual in isolated fashion. They can be called 'normative' because they are common offenses, relatively accepted by the peers, and under certain circumstances even expected and respected by peers."[50] One of the most important differences between lower-class and middle-class delinquency is that the lower-class boy is more apt to engage in activities that will contribute to his sense of manliness and adult status.

One study of lower-class and middle-class delinquents shows some of the differences in their values and their behavior patterns. It was found that lower-class boys defined themselves as tougher, more powerful, fierce, fearless, and dangerous than middle-class boys. By contrast the middle-class delinquents conceived of themselves as being more loyal, clever, smart, smooth, and bad.[51] From an overall perspective it appears that the two classes differed chiefly in that significantly more lower-class delinquents felt themselves to be "loyal and daring comrades."[52]

Another important difference between the two groups was the frequency with which reported and unreported robberies and assaults were committed by members. Of the lower-class delinquents, 84 percent had committed one such offense as compared to only 28 percent of the middle class. Also more of the lower-class boys used weapons and more advocated "stomping." Lower-class boys also regularly carried weapons on their persons more than did middle-class boys.[53] These all reflect a greater involvement in physical aggression among lower-class delinquents.

There were also differences between the two groups of delinquents with regard to their sexual expression. This difference was tied into their different views of masculinity as reflected in their treatment of adolescent girls. "Toughness, callousness, and physical prowess appeared to be dominant for the lower class, while sophistication, dexterity, and verbal manipulation seemed prominent for the middle class."[54] Dating was seen by the lower-class boys as the means to the end of sexual intercourse while the middle-class boys often saw dating as an end in itself involving the fun element of going out. "For the lower class boy, sexual intercourse was to be achieved by the raw force of his masculinity; he would not 'seduce' his date so much as he would 'conquer' her."[55]

Regardless of the social class level of delinquents most of them grow

---

50 Sebald, *op. cit.*, p. 356.

51 Fannin, Leon F. and Marshall B. Clinard, "Differences in the Conception of Self as a Male among Lower and Middle Class Delinquents," in Edmund W. Vas, *Middle-Class Juvenile Delinquency* (New York: Harper and Row, 1967), p. 106.

52 *Ibid.*, p. 107.

53 *Ibid.*, pp. 108–9.

54 *Ibid.*, p. 110.

55 *Ibid.*

up and leave their delinquency behind. Most of them "settle down, marry, go to work, repudiate criminal careers and no more (nor less) seriously violate laws than most of the rest of us."[56] It is important that delinquency, as compared to many other forms of deviancy, is restricted to an age range. While one might become a homosexual, a drug addict, an alcoholic, and so forth during adolescence and remain that type of deviant for the rest of his life, he cannot do so as a delinquent. When he reaches his early adult years he can enter the straight world or the deviant one of criminality. It may be that some of the forces that make delinquency attractive to some adolescents are the very ones that contribute to their wanting to leave. As suggested, the delinquent subculture often gives the boy the sense of being an adult—something he very much wants. But when he becomes an adult he no longer needs the subculture for that status and in fact may find that if he continues in it, it will cost him something in his newly achieved adult recognition.

DELINQUENT SUBCULTURE

Recognizing that there is considerable disagreement as to the extent and meaning of the delinquent subculture, it is still useful to describe it in a general way. Here we are defining a delinquent subculture as consisting of a system of values, norms, and beliefs that influence the behavior of the members. And some significant part of the subcultural behavior goes contrary to the modes of behavior generally defined as the right and proper types of conduct by the broader culture. David Matza has suggested that the subculture of delinquency "is a synthesis between convention and crime, and that the behavior of many juveniles, some more than others, is influenced but not constrained by it."[57]

Cohen and Short have argued that there are five types of male delinquent subcultures. First is the *parent male subculture*. This is the subculture that Cohen describes in his work. It has been described as stressing such values as short-run hedonism and group autonomy. It is believed to be the most common type of delinquent subculture in the United States. They suggest that this is basically a working-class subculture. Second is the *conflict-oriented subculture*. This is the subculture characteristic of large gangs that may have membership running into the hundreds. The size makes it different from the parent subculture, whose members consist of small gangs and cliques. This type of subculture has a territory or "turf" which it defends. The status of the gang is dependent on its toughness. In their other activities they are like the delinquent subculture, for example, in drinking, sex, gambling, stealing, and vandalism, which are prominent activities. Third is the *drug-addict subcul-*

---

[56] Rosenberg, and Silverstein, *op. cit.*, p. 116.
[57] Matza, *op. cit.*, pp. 47–8.

ture. The addict wants no part of the violent forms of delinquency and prefers the income-producing forms of delinquency which are necessary to support his drug habit. So the addict subculture, in contrast to the delinquent and conflict groups, is utilitarian, but this utilitarianism is in support of, and a precondition of, the addict way of life. Fourth is the *semi-professional thief subculture*. This seems to characterize persons who in their young years become robbers and burglars. The first stage of this sequence describes what is called the parent subculture. But most participants here seem to drop out or to taper off around the age of sixteen or seventeen. Finally, there is the *middle-class delinquent subculture*. Cohen and Short assume that middle-class subcultures arise in response to problems of adjustment that are the characteristic products of middle-class life. They further suggest that the qualities of malice and violence will be underplayed here and these subcultures will more often emphasize the deliberate courting of danger and the sophisticated approach to roles centering around sex, liquor, drugs, and automobiles.[58]

Short has suggested that it is important to distinguish between gangs and subcultures. He points out that most subcultures are not carried out just by one particular group and what happens in any group may be more than the values of the particular subculture which bind them together, the point being that most gangs have a dimension to them beyond the subcultural limits. For example, the character of gangs that are involved in conflict depends to a great extent upon their relationships with other conflict gangs—as either allies or enemies—and their reputations among these gangs.[59] All of these gangs are a part of the delinquent subculture, but they each possess some qualities that make them different from each other. In fact, two gangs may be subculturally alike in every significant way, but the very fact that they are different gangs may realistically be the most crucial factor because this may force them to fight each other or work out some accommodation.

As the various theories of delinquency suggest, there is disagreement about the strength of ties in delinquent subcultures. It would seem that different groups will vary widely in the strength of their ties, and a given subcultural group may vary widely over time. For example, if a gang is threatened by other gangs then the strength may be very great because of the need for protection, but these ties may be relaxed during peacetime. It has been argued that internal strengths have less impact among gangs than among most subcultural groups. This argument suggests that gang cohesiveness derives from and is perpetuated by forces mostly external to the group.[60] This view would be supported by the suggestion that threats by other gangs, the police, and so forth would lead to greater

[58] Cohen and Short, *op. cit.*, pp. 24–28.

[59] Short, *op. cit.*, p. 9.

[60] Klein, Malcolm W. and Lois Y. Crawford, "Groups, Gangs, and Cohesiveness," in Short, *op. cit.*, p. 259.

cohesiveness so as to achieve greater self protection. But it might also be that external pressure in certain cases will splinter the subculture. For example, if the police exert strong pressure on a gang some members may feel that the police will leave them alone if they remain apart from the gang. The strength of the subcultural controls over the individual members will be determined by the internal needs that are felt to be met by the group and the external forces that may either splinter or bring together the group.

There is a common belief about gangs, probably helped along by movies and television, that they each have a few strong leaders. A part of the same belief is that the leader is very powerful and the followers will do what he wants when he wants. This is clearly an exaggeration because while there are powerful gang leaders most of the time, the delinquent gang operates with no leadership because none is needed. For example, the many hours spent standing on a street corner don't call for leadership. During these long periods other roles filled by members may be given more attention, i.e., the comedian, the storyteller, and so forth.

But there are times in the life of a gang when leadership does become important and it is therefore useful to look at some variables associated with those who are the leaders. Yablonsky argues that at the center of the gang are the most psychologically disturbed members—the leaders. He says it is these individuals who need the gang the most. So it is the coterie of disturbed leaders who make up the core of the gang and give it its cohesive force. In a gang of about thirty members there may be about five who are the core and provide the leadership.[61] There is generally desire to be a leader when the person feels no sense of importance about the group he is part of. Assuming he has the abilities needed to be a leader, he must also have the motivations. Yablonsky points out that leadership in the gang may be assumed by almost any member if he so determines and emotionally needs the power of being a leader at a given time. "It is not necessary to have his leadership role ratified by his constituents."[62] Probably in most gangs the aspiring leader must also show that he is physically or mentally tough enough. Because "toughness" is so highly valued, one must have a sufficient amount to qualify for the possible roles of the leader.

All subcultures are basically defined through their relationships to the broader society. The various theories of delinquent subcultures recognize that how the delinquents collectively think and behave is based to a great extent on how the broader society defines them and how they *think* the broader society defines them. But one cannot say that the relationship between the subculture and the broader society is simply one of disagree-

---

[61] Yablonsky, *op. cit.*, p. 230.
[62] *Ibid.*, p. 232.

ment. Actually the relationship is subtle, complex, and sometimes devious. This is because the subculture exists within a cultural setting which affects it and which it, in turn, affects. Matza suggests that when it is kept in mind that the conventional culture is complex and many sided then the relationship of the subculture to it can be seen as highly complex and frequently changing.[63]

Probably, as in most subcultures, when delinquents look at the broader world's treatment of them there is a sense of injustice. This is based on their perspective of the legal and police systems. "The role played by the sense of injustice is to weaken the bind of law and thus ready the way for the immediate condition of neutralization—the negation of intent. Neutralization enables drift. It is the process by which we are freed from the moral bind of law."[64] What Matza argues is that the delinquent subculture's reaction to the legal system is not one of ignorance but rather one of antagonism.

Matza suggests that the subculture of delinquency is not highly committed to delinquency. He argues that if there were a high commitment to delinquency there would be much less shame or guilt upon apprehension. This is different from other deviant subcultures; for example, the homosexual or professional thief when he is arrested may be angry, but is often not ashamed. These kinds of deviants are most apt to respond to apprehension with indignation, a sense of martyrdom, and fear of the consequences of their apprehension, rather than any stigma about the apprehension.[65] Many delinquents agree that someone should be apprehended and punished, but not themselves. "Thus, the indignation of the delinquent differs from that of, say, a nationalist rebel. The delinquent's is a *wrongful* indignation."[66] The delinquents' view of the law also reflects this perspective because they direct their antagonism at the officials who run the system. Therefore, their antagonism takes the form of a jaundiced view of officials, "a view which holds that their primary function is not the administration of justice but the perpetuation of injustice."[67]

Also implied about the delinquent subculture is that the members spend time together and engage in some activities together. Most delinquent gangs when they are together may be doing little or nothing— talking, playing cards, and so forth—but for many of them it is important to be together even if their activity is limited. When they engage in illegal behavior they generally do it together. Estimates based on official statistics suggest that somewhere between 70 and 90 percent of ado-

---

[63] Matza, *op. cit.*, pp. 37–38.

[64] *Ibid.*, p. 176.

[65] *Ibid.*, p. 40.

[66] *Ibid.*, pp. 40–41.

[67] *Ibid.*, pp. 101–2.

lescent crimes occur with two or more individuals together. What is important is that their main reason for being defined as a delinquent subculture, their actual delinquent behavior, is shared behavior.

As suggested, the most important value of the delinquent subculture is that of manliness. So being an adult, not through aspirations, but through specific acts of manly prowess, is a prime concern of subcultural delinquents. Therefore, the primary goal is a system of behavior that almost incidentally permits and encourages criminal acts, but essentially pursues the gratification deriving from the license of precocious manhood.[68] Often those acts which define the adolescent as delinquent may not have been pursued for their own sake, but rather for the end of achieving manliness within the delinquent subculture.

The most common means of expressing manliness in the delinquent subcultural setting is through fighting. The fight is the situation where a boy's reputation can be won or lost. The common code is that a boy does not walk away from a fight and often the preliminaries are governed by an elaborately plotted choreography. "You do not provoke the fight; against all reason, you are trapped into it. Beyond a certain point, not to fight is to be chicken, and there is no talking or finessing your way out. Honor calls for a duel with friend, foe or stranger."[69] Often it is only necessary for a boy to fight a few times to prove himself, and if word of his prowess spreads he can often ride on his reputation.

Closely related to fighting is the delinquent boy's involvement with girls as a status giving factor. It may be that fighting over a girl to win her admiration may or may not cause his stock to rise with her; however, "it will almost certainly reinforce his self-esteem and his social standing in a community where fisticuffs, well mastered, is a vehicle for elevation into manhood."[70] Sexual activity for boys in delinquent gangs usually starts at a very young age. Initially girls are seen as primarily objects for sexual play and it is not until the boys become seventeen or eighteen that they show the girls anything resembling respect. Often the sexual involvement by the boys is not on an interpersonal, pair level, but rather a number of the boys with one or more girls. This often occurs as a "gang bang" where a number of the boys will have sexual intercourse with one girl. It also appears that in some gangs there are periods when the boys have little sexual contact with girls. This is because often the boys will use a girl sexually only if she becomes available. Usually after they get a girl they may spend a week or so of intensified sexuality, and then the girl will disappear. Then the boys enter their involuntary celibacy until another willing girl comes along.[71]

---

[68] *Ibid.*, p. 168.

[69] *Ibid.*, p. 166.

[70] *Ibid.*, p. 86.

[71] Rosenberg and Silverstein, *op. cit.*, p. 75.

FEMALE DELINQUENCY

There has been very little research into female delinquency when compared to the studies made of the male. This has been true because there has been much less interest in female delinquency and it is believed to be a minor problem when compared to the male. In part this is justified, because the number of male delinquents is far greater than that of females. In recent years, the ratio of boys to girls appearing in juvenile courts has been about five to one. However, sex ratios vary by different types of delinquency. Boys tend overwhelmingly to be arrested on charges involving stealing and mischief of one sort or another, "while girls are typically brought before the court for *sex offenses* and for '*running away*,' '*incorrigibility*' and '*delinquent tendencies*,' which are often euphemisms for problems of sex behavior."[72] This means that most girls who are defined as delinquent are so because of moral behavior rather than for legal reasons. For most of them their wrong is that they are sexually promiscuous by society's moral standards.

There seems to be some evidence that when girls are a part of a delinquent subculture they are in a male subculture. When this happens the girl is largely dependent on the male with whom she is identified for her status. However, there are some exceptions where delinquent girls do develop a form of a subcultural group. This may be for the purpose of sexual activities, drug addiction, or as counterparts of the male hoodlum gang.[73] In general, Short suggests, when girls are involved in delinquent subcultures their activities are as varied as any male members'. He points out that the participation of girls in drug-use subcultures is extensive. He found that drug-using girls seem especially caught up in a vicious cycle of unsatisfactory interpersonal relations. But even the non-drug users "appear to be swept along by limited social and other abilities, and experience which limits opportunities to acquire those skills or to exercise them is acquired."[74] Girls in the lower class generally have low status in social activities important to males because this is a reflection of a male dominant view of the sexes. So the girl in the delinquent male gang has a second-class membership and has little direct influence on activities defined as important by the male members. Cohen has argued that the subculture of the male delinquent gangs is really inappropriate for the adjustment problems of lower-class girls. This is because at best it is "irrelevant to the vindication of the girl's status as a girl, and at worse because it positively threatens her in that status in consequence of its strongly masculine symbolic function."[75] It would appear that most girls who become a part of the male delinquent gangs do so because they

---

[72] Cohen and Short, *op. cit.*, p. 86.

[73] Sebald, *op. cit.*, pp. 355–56.

[74] Short, *op. cit.*, p. 6.

[75] Cohen, *op. cit.*, p. 143–44.

are willing to accept the secondary status membership. It also would seem that when delinquent girls do violate the norms of society they do not do so because of ignorance or hostility to the norms. Rather they are motivated toward the deviancy because they want to maintain status within the subculture.

One researcher suggests that when the delinquent female is compared with her male counterpart one important difference is related to the extent to which girls possess resources that may be used to manipulate for their own ends in the adult world. "Specifically, adolescent females are more than capable of competing successfully with adult females through the use or promise of sexual rewards."[76] The adolescent boy has little of value, whether morally or legally acceptable, to the broader society. But what the adolescent girl has is prized by many adults, though legally and morally prohibited. She is therefore in the position theoretically of being wanted, and knowing this she can negotiate other ends that are desirable to her.

At the same time the female has more freedom to pursue some activities that are not legally available to the male. For example, the adolescent female who is not old enough to drive can get an older male to take her places. By contrast, the adolescent male restricted to his age peers may often steal a car. It may also be easier for the adolescent girl to drink illegally by being with an older male.[77] In general, the young girl has more social agencies helping her satisfy many of her needs than does the boy.

As indicated, almost all discussion of female delinquency stresses the sexual nature but says little about other aspects. There is little on what her delinquency actually consists of, other than that it usually involves sexual misconduct of some kind. Whatever other aspects of her life there are that might be delinquent are generally overlooked. But it does appear that the sexual delinquency is often used by her as a form of bargaining and even social control. One important research question might be: If one put aside all female delinquency directly and indirectly related to sexual activity, what would be left? It might be that the findings would show that generally female delinquency is really sexual delinquency. If this is true then it is possible that if there continues to be an increasing degree of premarital sexual freedom what is seen as sexual deviancy will decrease. This would result in a decrease in the rates of female delinquency. On the other hand, one might also speculate that as boys and girls become more alike in their behavior patterns more girls will become delinquents in the areas usually associated with males. This might be in such areas as physical aggression, truancy, stealing, and so forth. This

---

[76] Marwell, Gerald, "Adolescent Powerlessness and Delinquent Behavior," in Rushing, op. cit., p. 43.

[77] Ibid., pp. 43–4.

would be consistent with the argument that as females achieve greater equality with males it will be reflected in all areas including deviancy and social problems.

BIBLIOGRAPHY

BORDUA, DAVID J., "Delinquent Subcultures: Sociological Interpretations of Gang Delinquency," *The Annals*, November, 1961, pp. 119–36.

CLOWARD, RICHARD A. and LLOYD E. OHLIN, *Delinquency and Opportunity* (New York: Macmillan Company, 1960).

COHEN, ALBERT K., *Delinquent Boys: The Culture of the Gang* (Glencoe, Ill.: The Free Press, 1955).

COHEN, ALBERT K. and JAMES F. SHORT, JR., "Research in Delinquent Subcultures," *Journal of Social Issues*, 14 (1958), pp. 20–37.

GARABEDIAN, PETER G. and DON C. GIBBONS, *Becoming Delinquent* (Chicago: Aldine Publishing Co., 1970).

MATZA, DAVID, *Delinquency and Drift* (New York: John Wiley, 1964).

MILLER, WALTER, "Lower-Class Culture as a Generating Milieu of Gang Delinquency," *The Journal of Social Issues*, 14 (1958), pp. 3–19.

ROSENBERG, BERNARD and HARRY SILVERSTEIN, *The Varieties of Delinquent Experience* (Waltham, Mass.: Blaisdell Publishing Co., 1969).

SHORT, JAMES F., JR., *Gang Delinquency and Delinquent Subcultures* (New York: Harper and Row, 1968).

VAZ, EDMUND W., *Middle-Class Juvenile Delinquency* (New York: Harper and Row, 1967).

YABLONSKY, LEWIS, "The Delinquent Gang as a Near-Group," *Social Problems*, Fall, 1959, pp. 108–17.

CHAPTER 13

PRISONS

PROBABLY from the time man first felt a need to protect himself from others there has been some way of holding threatening individuals and controlling their possible behavior. This may have represented a more humane stage in man's development because he probably at first destroyed those he had reason to fear, before he was destroyed. Over time man developed procedures for incarcerating his fellow man. And historically as penal systems developed they had three major functions: custodial, coercive, and corrective. In the early Roman law the *Digest* of Justinian established the principle of custodial care through the assertion that "a prison is for confinement, not for punishment." In the countries that followed Roman law the principle that imprisonment was not a legal punishment was dominant for about 1,000 years. It may also be seen that in early England the courts wanted to clear the jails rather than to fill them and so the prisons of the middle ages were primarily concerned with simply holding prisoners while they waited for trial.

In England the earliest prisons were the common jails and they were in theory the king's jails. During the medieval period the jails were not like what we are familiar with today. A jail might be a castle tower, a gatehouse, or a cellar. The first house of correction was set up in London in 1553 and the primary purpose was to bring the offenders around to becoming good citizens by discipline of industry, education, and religious instruction. But during the 18th century the houses became more

330

and more penal institutions and less concerned with corrective functions. This was essentially the tradition that was brought to the early settlements in America.

In the early prisons in America there were no barriers to communication between inmates. The prisoners were held in common areas and no attention was paid to differences in age, sex, criminal history, or mental status. Over the years various prison reformers were shocked by the promiscuity, violence, and organized deviant behavior found in congregate prison systems. As a result they moved to institute a "separate system" of prisons. So in 1791, the Walnut Street Prison in Philadelphia, a small cell house containing sixteen cells, was built. The belief was that the inmates would stop being contaminated by one another and it was believed that religious conversion would occur during the years of enforced meditation leading to the individual's reformation. Over the years the congregate but silent system came to be the accepted type of prison design. These "contained industrial shops, dining halls, and large recreational yards in addition to individual cells. But whenever and wherever prisoners assembled strict silence was enforced."[1]

The development of types of prisons is largely determined by how a society views criminality and how it believes the criminal should be treated. Over the past two centuries in the United States the societal reaction to criminality has been mainly punitive. Punishment for criminals has been pain or suffering which was intentionally inflicted by the state because of the belief that the pain or suffering was supposed to have some value. The programs that were developed to carry out the punitive reaction to crime were seen as correctional techniques. "Physical torture, social degradation, restriction of wealth, and restriction of freedom are among the programs used for inflicting pain on criminals. At present, the most popular techniques of this sort are restrictions on wealth (fines) and restrictions on liberty (imprisonment).[2]

The prison is like the mental institution in that it performs an integrating function for society. There are two principal aspects to the integrating function. One, the prison is expected to restore society to the state of equilibrium and harmony that was its state before the crime was performed. This means that the undesirables of society are removed from society and segregated in the prison. Two, the prison is expected to help with social integration by reducing the occurrence of future crimes. This function is seen as taking place in two different ways. In the first case the crime rates are believed to be kept minimal through the deterrent effects of imprisonment and the fact that imprisoning men reinforces anti-

---

[1] Cloward, Richard A. "Social Control in Prison," in Lawrence Hazebrigg, *Prisons within Society* (New York: Anchor Books, 1969), p. 85.

[2] Cressey, Donald, "The Nature and Effectiveness of Correctional Techniques," in Lawrence Hazebrigg, *Prisons within Society* (New York: Anchor Books, 1969), p. 350.

criminal values of the society responsible for the imprisoning. In the second case, imprisonment is expected to reduce crime rates by changing criminals into noncriminals.[3]

The isolating nature of the prison makes the inmates different in an important way from most other types of deviants. Most kinds of deviants, such as alcoholics, are treated in groups for therapeutic reasons. However, the prison which has been based on isolation and minimal communication between prisoners has been reluctant to recognize the possible therapeutic use of inmate groups. In this situation the punitive function of the prison makes the therapeutic one difficult if not impossible to pursue.

On the broadest level the prison may be seen as representing certain needs of society. In this sense the prison is a service organization, "supported by the community largely for the purpose of maintaining order and not for the production of any goods which yield the individual or the community an immediate economic return. Like most other service organizations (such as mental hospitals and social agencies), the prison is a means of safe-guarding other institutions of the society."[4] In general, society thinks of the prison as performing an important function because it is protecting them against the dangerous threats of some of their members. It appears that the greater the fear a society has toward a given deviancy the greater the autonomy given to those social agencies that stand between society and the deviancy.

The prison itself is a fairly isolated social system, and it can be seen as a caste system made up of those in control and those being controlled. The caste system of the prison is seen as necessary by society. The prison is also given autonomy because it does not compete with any other organization. That is, the prison justifies its existence by fulfilling a legal mandate and this allows those who run it a great deal of latitude. Furthermore, the prison is generally protected from outside scrutiny. "Public cries for reform and shake-ups in the prison system are rarely, if ever, an immediate response to the day-to-day operation of the relatively static prison community, but are usually the work of outside interest groups."[5] In general there is little control by outside forces on what goes on within prisons.

From the point of view of most of those who run prisons the main aim is to maintain order and control over the prisoners. Usually the most efficient way to achieve this is to keep the prisoners from influencing one another in any way that might disturb the order. The belief is that this is best done by isolating the prisoners from one another as much as possible. So there are strong custodial exhortations to "go it alone" which

---

[3] *Ibid.*, p. 351.

[4] Grosser, George H., "External Setting and Internal Relations of the Prison," in Lawrence Hazebrigg, *Prisons within Society* (New York: Anchor Books, 1969), p. 9.

[5] *Ibid.*, p. 11.

are a part of a systematic attempt to reduce the frequency and saliency of interaction between prisoners. By this definition the model prisoner is the isolated prisoner who bothers no one.

In the earlier days physical violence was a common means of controlling prisoners, but under the influence of 19th century penal reform it was pretty much eliminated as a legitimate means of control. So except in certain cases, such as riots, assault, escape, and similar crises, the custodian could not take the life of, or otherwise do bodily injury to, an inmate.[6] However, as will be discussed later, violence is an important part of prison social control, but it is more often between prisoners than between guards and prisoners.

Along with punitive controls the prisons also have rewards that may be used to try to get the prisoners to accept their position with minimal problems for the prison authorities. There are two systems of formal incentives. First are those incentives that provide for an early release from the prison. That is, if the prisoner behaves he may get parole and time off his sentence for good behavior. Second is a kind of formal incentive to provide some rewards while in prison by helping to make the isolated life a little more bearable. This may be done through various degrees of freedom as well as the right to certain privileges.

Some prisons may have the means of controlling the inmate by the threat of sending him to more restrictive prisons. That is, a limited form of expulsion is sometimes employed in penal systems. As a result a difficult prisoner in a minimum security prison can be transferred to a medium or maximum security prison. However, when transfer is employed as a control mechanism "one institution's solution simply becomes another's dilemma. The deviant cannot be expelled from the system as a whole; somewhere, someone must come to terms with him."[7]

The Guard

The guard in total institutions such as prisons or mental hospitals is the person concerned with the day to day operations of the institution. Often the philosophy or ideology of care and custody is seen by the guard as unimportant in light of the chores he must handle each day, but because the guard does stand as the representative of society and the prison administration he brings to his position a great deal of power. Sykes has suggested that the prison community may be best seen as resting in an uneasy balance between two hypothetical poles. "At one extreme all inmates would be constantly secured in solitary confinement; at the other, all inmates would roam freely within the limits set by the wall and its

---

[6] Cloward, op. cit., p. 80.
[7] Ibid., p. 81.

armed guards."[8] In reality, and varying between different prisons, the inmates have a limited degree of freedom and this creates a wide variety of interaction patterns between the guards and the prisoners. As a result the guards and the inmates become involved in a complex pattern of social relationships where the authority of the guard is subject to a number of corrupting influences.[9]

Often the guard has an important choice to make and that is the degree to which he will enforce the rules of the prison. Some guards in the cell-block may rigidly enforce all the rules in the belief that a minor violation of a regulation may be the first suggestion of a serious breach in the control system of the prison. Or, and what may more often occur, other guards may be lulled into forgetting about the possible dangers of their position.[10] Whichever pattern he follows the need for some consistency is important because with inconsistency the guard may be seen as playing favorites and this can lead to increased problems from among the inmates.

It has been argued that the guard is often under pressure to try to achieve a smooth running cellblock not with the stick but rather with the carrot. But this is not always easy because the possible rewards he can hand out are limited. Often the guard has a kind of future favor he wants from the inmates which may influence him to ease up on the enforcement of many of the prison regulations. This is that "many prisons have experienced a riot in which the tables are momentarily turned and the captives hold sway over their *quondam* captors."[11] And if that ever happens he wants to be sure that the inmates will protect him.

In many prisons a lot of the minor chores which the guard is expected to perform each day can be gradually turned over to inmates whom the guard comes to trust. When this occurs it represents an overlap of the formal system of the prison with the informal social system of the inmates. That is, the effectiveness of the inmates' handling of the guards' chores is to a great extent determined by the prisoners' willingness to accept their fellow inmate in that position. And in general, so long as his first loyalty is to his fellow inmates, it is to their advantage to cooperate with him and try to keep him in that position of power.

In general, the success of the prison system is highly questionable. That is, most of the "techniques" used in "correcting" criminals who are in prison have not been found to be either effective or ineffective and are only vaguely related to any reputable theory of behavior or criminality.[12]

---

[8] Sykes, Gresham M., "The Corruption of Authority and Rehabilitation," in William A. Rushing, *Deviant Behavior and Social Process* (Chicago: Rand McNally and Co., 1969), p. 157.

[9] *Ibid.*

[10] *Ibid.*

[11] *Ibid.*, p. 159.

[12] Cressey, *op. cit.*, p. 371.

This can further be seen as we examine in some detail the subcultural world of prisons. In the next section we look at men's prisons and in the last section examine the world of the women's prisons.

MEN'S PRISONS

In general when a man enters prison he leaves behind one world and enters a new one. This is certainly true in terms of physical separation in that his new world is physically confined and all that he can interact with must be found within the prison setting. As in the mental hospital, life is isolated. However, as we shall see, the prison subculture is very much affected by what goes on outside the prison and what the inmates have brought in with them in the way of values and behavior patterns. Most of the values and patterns of behavior brought into the prison must be adapted to the special nature of the isolated, confining world of the prison. Out of this comes the subculture of the prison. First, we shall discuss the prison subculture in general and then look at some of the variations within prison subcultures.

As earlier indicated, prisons are total institutions and one effect of this living style is that it allows only psychological means for "escaping" the prison. As in all total institutions many prisoners fantasize and daydream about the world outside the prison. To the extent that they psychologically escape they are able to resist the socializing of the prison world. One who would be totally socialized to the prison subculture would be a person who concerned himself very little with the outside world, but most inmates think of the prison as a temporary world. Because the subcultures of the prisons are very much influenced by values and behavior from outside the prison they serve as a means of stopping the prisoner from being totally socialized to a prison world. If one of the functions of the prison is to try to socialize the inmates to the world of prisons to attain "corrective or therapeutic" orientations they are usually undercut by the inmate subculture that has a close link to the outside world with its related values and patterns which are the very ones the formal institution of the prison is trying to change or alter.

But to say that a subculture develops in prisons is not to say that all inmates are a part of it in the same way and to the same degree. Very often in prisons inmates react to various situations simply as individuals even though this may create problems for them. This is in part due to a selective factor—that a number of men who are in prison are there primarily because they are not able or willing to conform to any extended set of social restrictions. So for some inmates there may be personal refusal or inability to conform to the formal demands of the prison or the informal demands of the inmate subculture. Of course there are often high costs for those inmates who fail to conform. "Those who dominate others are viewed with a mingled fear, hatred and envy; and the few who manage to retreat into solidarity may well be penalized in the struggle to evade the poverty-stricken existence—both material and immaterial—proscribed by the institution."[13]

The importance of the inmate subculture is recognized by most prison authorities and is often tolerated and even encouraged because it is believed to help make the prison run more efficiently. This is because the prison operates basically not by force or even the threat of force alone, but mainly because of the acceptance of rules on the part of most inmates and their willingness to adhere to those rules. "These rules are partly the official rules of the prison, partly the mores of the inmate culture developed by many generations of convicts to the official code."[14]

When the inmate comes into prison he may have to make some very severe adjustments to the restrictive and isolated world. The degree to which he must adjust may be related to his previous experiences with prisons. At any given time, of all those persons entering a prison a large number have been there before. In fact a number of inmates have been socialized to the world of the prison from a young age. This is true of the large number of adult criminals who spent time in institutions for juveniles. In many juvenile detention centers there exists a form or variation of the adult prison subculture. As a result some of the newcomers to prisons for adults are persons who have been oriented to the prison subculture and who "have found the utilitarian nature of this subculture acceptable."[15]

During the early period when one enters prison the greatest personal problem may be adjusting to the isolation. With time many inmates become involved with others. Studies show that most of the role types found during the middle periods in prison are situations of involvement with others. "The tendency for inmates to become involved suggests that pressures toward involvement are stronger and more keenly felt at a period when they are further removed from the free community."[16] Garabedian goes on to suggest that the extent of inmate solidarity is "likely to depend not on the number of right guys found in the prison population, but rather on the balance that exists between inmates located at the two extremes of the institutional career and those located in the middle periods of confinement."[17]

---

[13] Sykes, Gresham, "The Pains of Imprisonment," in Norman Johnson, *et al.*, *The Sociology of Punishment and Correction* (New York: John Wiley, 1962), p. 137.

[14] Grosser, *op. cit.*, p. 18.

[15] Irwin, John and Donald R. Cressey, "Thieves, Convicts, and the Inmate Culture," in Howard S. Becker, ed., *The Other Side* (New York: The Free Press, 1964), p. 233.

[16] Garabedian, Peter G. "Social Roles and Processes of Socialization in the Prison Community," *Social Problems*, Fall, 1963, p. 151.

[17] *Ibid.*, p. 152.

Closely related to the isolation the new inmate must cope with are the related problems of loss of freedom and material deprivation. His loss of freedom means he must give up the material services and goods that were his outside of prison. Along with this he also loses his heterosexual relationships, "personal autonomy, symbolic affirmation of his value as an individual, and a variety of other benefits which are more or less taken for granted in the free community."[18] In the broader society the individual often gets status from the material possessions that are his. This may be based on the kind of automobile he drives, the clothes he wears, and where he lives. But the material signs of personal status are for the most part removed when he enters prison. Because the material possessions are often so much a part of the person's self concept, to strip him of them may be to threaten him at the basic core of his personality. As a result, whatever the discomforts and irritations of the inmate's way of life he must also carry the "additional burden of social definitions which equate his material deprivation with personal inadequacy."[19]

Because of the restriction of material symbols of success in the prison two kinds of adaptation often occur. These also occur in other settings where the individual must give up most of the material things that were important to him, for example, in mental institutions, or in the military. One attempt to adapt is to talk a great deal about what he had in the outside world. The inmate may tell about all the expensive clothes he owned and the costly restaurants that he went to. A lot of what he says may be fiction, but he often feels it very important to give the impression of having been successful when he was outside. A second kind of adaptation to the lack of material symbols is to place high importance on material goods which might be relatively unimportant in the outside world. For example, to have enough cigarettes or reading material may be a measure of material success in a system where many do not have those things. In other words, if the inmate possesses a few things that most others do not, this may contribute to his sense of individual identity and worth.

Another problem the inmate in prison must attempt to cope with is his aggression. Because many prisoners were aggressive outside of prison they must often curb their aggressions in prison or the consequences can be very severe. Yet when they do, the problem arises as to what prevents them from turning aggression inward against themselves. It has been suggested by Grosser that aggression becomes partly restrained and partly displaced, and projected, "both onto *rats* and other unreliable inmates and onto a variety of outgroups within and outside the walls, thus helping to sustain the hostile attitude of the inmate in-groups."[20] So one

---

[18] Sykes, *op. cit.*, p. 132.

[19] *Ibid.*, p. 133.

[20] Grosser, *op. cit.*, p. 144.

of the functions of the prison subculture is to help provide the means for directing aggression. Sykes and Messinger have pointed out that if a group of prisoners develops a state of mutual antagonism then many of the problems of prison life will become even more acute. "On the other hand, as a population of prisoners moves in the direction of solidarity, as demanded by the inmate code, the pains of imprisonment become less severe. They cannot be eliminated, it is true, but their consequences at least can be partially neutralized."[21]

There is another way in which the external world influences the involvement of the inmate in the subculture, and that is the point in time he has reached in serving his prison sentence. His notion of time and response to the world around him will usually vary by the length of time he still has to serve. And at any point in time the temporal frame of reference of various types of inmates can have various psychological and social meanings.[22] For example, one would expect that for most inmates the extent of conformity to the demands of the prison would be greater the nearer to the time of release.

The concept of "prisonization" has been suggested to describe the central impact of the prison on its inmates. This describes the socialization of the inmate to the subcultural systems of the prison. This is the process whereby the inmate is indoctrinated into those codes, norms, dogma, and myths which sustain a view of the prison and the outside world generally different from what the prison wants, at least to the extent of its wanting to rehabilitate the inmate. The core concept in prisonization is the inmate code or system of norms requiring loyalty to other inmates and opposition to the prison staff, who serve as representatives of a rejecting society beyond the walls.[23] Wheeler further suggests that no inmate can remain completely unprisoned. The very fact of being in prison means the offender is exposed to certain general features of imprisonment. "These included acceptance of an inferior role and recognition that nothing is owed the environment for the supplementing of basic needs."[24]

We now look in more detail at some of the general aspects of the prison subculture. Basically the inmate is faced with the need for physical, social, and psychological survival. He is helped in this with the basic value of endurance in the face of difficult conditions. This is available to

---

[21] Sykes, Gresham M. and Sheldon L. Messinger, "The Inmate Social System," in William A. Rushing, *Deviant Behavior and Social Process* (Chicago: Rand McNally and Co., 1969), p. 135.

[22] Wheeler, Stanton, "Socialization in Correctional Communities," in William A. Rushing, *Deviant Behavior and Social Process* (Chicago: Rand McNally and Co., 1969), p. 145.

[23] *Ibid.*, p. 144.

[24] *Ibid.*

the new inmate as a part of the prison subculture he comes into contact with. The subculture provides him with the means to attain some self-respect and sense of independence that can occur despite "prior criminality, present subjugation, and the free community's denial of the offender's moral worthiness. Significantly, this path to virtue is recognized by the prison officials as well as the prisoners."[25] There are some inmates who are able to survive with little help from the subculture, but most prisoners turn to their fellow inmates on at least a number of occasions.

In prison subculture, as in most subcultures, there may be variation between an individual's stated acceptance of the values and his actual behavior. Studies have found that many of the inmates who deviate the most from the values and norms of the prison subculture are those who are the most vocal in stating their commitment to them. "Much of the answer seems to lie in the fact that almost all inmates have an interest in maintaining cohesive behavior on the part of others, *regardless of the role they play themselves,* and vehement vocal support of the inmate code is a potent means to that end."[26] It would seem likely that those inmates who do the opposite, conform to the subcultural norms but talk against them, would find themselves in severe difficulty. Sykes and Messinger suggest that those inmates who are actively alienated from the other members but continue to give lip service to the subculture are like a manipulative priesthood, "savage in their expression of belief but corrupt in practice. In brief, a variety of motivational patterns underlies allegiance to the inmate code, but few inmates can avoid the need to insist publicly on its observance, whatever the discrepancies in their action."[27]

It has been suggested that there are five basic tenets that make up the inmate code to be found in most prison subcultures. First is not to interfere with the interests of other inmates. This is based on the desire to serve the least amount of time and to do it as easily as possible. Second is to keep oneself under control and not do anything rash. This means that emotional conflicts should be minimized and one should try to ignore the irritants of daily life. Third is the belief that one should not exploit his fellow inmates. This means not to take advantage of others through force, fraud, or deceit. Fourth, there are rules that are concerned with the maintenance of self, for example, the dictum "Don't weaken." This means developing the ability to withstand frustration or threatening situations without complaining. Finally, one should not give any prestige or respect to the guards or to the formal system for which they stand. "Guards are *hacks* or *screws* and are to be treated with constant suspicion and distrust."[28] These basic tenets are not always followed and the in-

---

[25] Sykes and Messinger, *op. cit.*, p. 135.
[26] *Ibid.*, p. 136.
[27] *Ibid.*
[28] *Ibid.*, p. 131.

dividuals may sometimes deviate without severe criticism or punishment by the subculture, but they do provide a value system for most of the inmates most of the time.

We move from the general values and norms of the prison subculture to some of the roles that are commonly found in prisons. The various roles develop around a focal value or set of values and the interrelationships between the various role sets are primary to the prison subculture. There have been a number of different roles distinguished in the studies of prison life. One role is that of the *right guy*. He is seen as the hero of the inmate subculture and his role contributes to the meaning of the various villain roles. The deviants in the subculture are the *rat*, the *gorilla*, and the *merchant*. What is important about the *right guy* is that he serves as a base line, however idealized or infrequent in reality, from which the inmate population can take its bearing.[29] There are a number of characteristics attributed to the *right guy*. He never interferes with other inmates who are attempting to manipulate the formal system. It is also believed that anyone who starts a fight with him had better be prepared to go all the way. If he gets anything extra he shares it with his friends. In his dealings with the prison officials he is clearly against them although he doesn't do anything foolish. Even though he doesn't look for trouble with the officials, he'll go the limit if they push him too far.[30] He possesses all the desirable qualities of the inmate as idealized by the inmate subculture.

The roles that are filled in the prison subculture are also seen in the different interpersonal involvements between inmates. Clemmer suggests role variations on the basis of the degree of involvement with other inmates. First is what he calls the complete "clique man." This refers to a man who is one of a group of three or more men who are very close friends. These men share material goods as well as personal secrets and will accept punishment if necessary to help or support one another. Second is the "group man" who is friendly with a small group of men but who does not completely subject himself to the wishes and acts of those groups. He also mixes freely with other men and with them is friendly at least in a casual way. Third is the "semi-solitary" man. This kind of man is civil with other inmates but never becomes intimate with any of them, nor does he share with them in any way except the most casual. Fourth is the "complete-solitary" man. This kind of man keeps almost constantly to himself and shares nothing with any other inmates.[31] These roles represent a range from interpersonal commitment to individual isolation. Most inmates would define the first, the "clique man,"

[29] *Ibid.*, pp. 131–32.

[30] *Ibid.*, p. 132.

[31] Clemmer, Donald, "Informal Inmate Groups," in Norman Johnson, *et al.*, *The Sociology of Punishment and Correction* (New York: John Wiley, 1962), pp. 113–14.

as the best way of doing time, while the prison authorities would most often prefer the fourth type, the "complete-solitary" man.

Another important role in the prison subculture is that of the various leaders. One study has found a number of characteristics that appear to be common to leaders in prisons. When compared to other inmates the leaders have served more years in prison, have longer sentences still to be served, are more frequently charged with the crimes of violence, and are more likely to be repeated offenders. The same study goes on to point out that more leaders than other inmates are diagnosed as homosexual, psychoneurotic, or psychopathic. "Finally, the institutional adjustments of leaders are marked by a significantly greater number of serious rule infractions, including escape, attempted escape, fighting and assault."[32] In other words leaders in prisons are those who deviate the most from what the formal system of the prison wants. The very fact that they are the most rebellious contributes to their being the leaders because this indicates the strength and willingness to go against the formal prison system.

Another important role in the inmate subculture is that which prisoners give to the guards. Because the guard must interact with the prisoners he will generally be defined as a good or a bad guard, and the inmates constantly attempt to influence him. So good guards are those who often do not report infractions and who pass on forbidden information to the inmates in criticism of the higher authorities. However, this "corruption" of the guard's formal role is generally not due to bribery. There are a variety of pressures in American society to "be a decent guy" and the guard in prison is not immune to them.[33] In many ways the guard is probably closer to the inmate than to those who make policy decisions about the prison. Usually, the inmates and the guards come out of similar social class backgrounds and therefore share many of the same values. Furthermore, some of the values they share go contrary to the formal requirements of the prison, and guards may be inclined to go with the values if they can do so without any great risk. However, it may be that some guards, even though from the same type of background as the inmates, are unsympathetic to the prisoners because they believe that the individual "badness" of the inmates takes precedent over any appeal to similarity of social class background.

The discussion thus far has been about a general prison subculture but there is some debate as to the possible variations in subcultures that may be found in prisons. The argument for differences in prison subcultures is based on the contention that different subcultures have been brought

---

[32] Schrag, Clarence, "Leadership among Prison Inmates," in Norman Johnson, et al., *The Sociology of Punishment and Correction* (New York: John Wiley, 1962), p. 118.

[33] Sykes, "The Corruption of Authority and Rehabilitation," *op. cit.*, p. 158.

into prison in addition to variations that develop within the prison setting. It has been suggested that a great deal of the subcultural behavior of the prison is not peculiar to the prison at all. In reality, goes the argument, there is little real difference between the subculture of the criminal and that of prison. "It seems rather obvious that the 'prison code'—don't inform on or exploit another inmate, don't lose your head, be weak, or be a sucker, etc.—is also part of a *criminal* code, existing outside prisons."[34] It may also be suggested that the prison subculture is close to that of another closed institution—the mental institution. So it may be the closed nature of the institution that leads to the similarities, rather than a specific approach to life and society.

It seems clear that one may visualize a prison subculture as we have described it, and any distinctions that one makes within the subculture do not discount the overall similarities. Two criminologists in a prison study divided inmates into three rough groupings, and while all three were a part of an overall prison subculture, they did have some important differences. The three groupings represented somewhat different orientations and are referred to as "thief," "prison," or "convict," and "conventional" or "legitimate" subgroups.[35]

"Thief" Subgroup. Basically the patterns of adjustment that these inmates make to prison are based on the criminal norms that exist outside the prison. The types who fall into this group are professional thieves and career criminals. For many of these people there are shared values which extend to criminals across the country with a high level of consistency. According to the values of this group, criminals should not betray each other to the police, but should be reliable, trustworthy, cool headed, etc. High status is also awarded to those who possess skill as thieves, "but to be just a successful thief is not enough. There must be solidness as well."[36] For the thief, imprisonment is one of the recurring problems which he must learn to deal with. It seems almost inevitable that he will be arrested from time to time and the subgroup provides him with patterns for dealing with this problem. "Norms which apply to the prison situation and information on how to undergo the prison experience—how to do time 'standing on you head'—with the least suffering and in a minimum amount of time are prepared."[37] The thief subgroup values and information are developed and spread around in various prisons across the United States.

"Prison" or "Convict" Subgroup. These are subgroups which originate in the prisons. The most central value is the utilitarian use of the prison setting. This means that those inmates who are the most manipulative

[34] Cressey, Donald R. and John Irwin, "Thieves, Convicts and the Inmate Culture," *Social Problems*, Fall, 1962, p. 145.

[35] *Ibid.*, p. 148.

[36] *Ibid.*, p. 146.

[37] Irwin and Cressey, *op. cit.*, p. 231.

acquire the available wealth and the positions of influence that exist. This subgroup can be found wherever men are confined, "whether it be in city jails, state and federal prisons, army stockades, prisoner of war camps, concentration camps, or even mental hospitals. Such organizations are characterized by deprivations and limitations on freedom, and in them available wealth must be competed for by men supposedly on equal footing."[38] Irwin and Cressey suggest that the inmates in both the thief and the prison subgroups are conservative in that they want to preserve the status quo. However, their motivations are somewhat different. "The man oriented to the convict subculture is conservative because he has great stock in the existing order of things, while the man who is thief oriented leans toward conservatism because he knows how to do time and likes things to run smoothly with a minimum of friction."[39]

"Conventional" or "Legitimate" Subgroup. The inmates who enter this group are not a part of the thief subculture before they enter prison, and after they enter prison they reject the "convict" subculture. These men present few problems for those who run the prisons and are generally seen as the "ideal" type of inmate. They represent the largest percentage of inmates in most prisons. They may enter various groups within prison such as religious groups or athletic teams, but they are primarily oriented to the problem of achieving goals through the means that are approved in the world outside the prison.

SEXUAL BEHAVIOR

One area of behavior important to any understanding of the relationships between prisoners is that of sexual expression. In a world where the men are cut off from all women they have the choice of no sexual expression, masturbation, or some kind of sexual contact with other men. There has been very little research with regard to the inmates who abstain from sex or who use masturbation as a form of meeting their needs. Most of the research has centered around various types of homosexual patterns found in prison.

Chapter 10 was concerned with male homosexuality and the reader may wonder why male homosexuality in prisons is being treated separately. There are two major reasons for this. First, in male prisons homosexuality is generally not a matter of choice and usually refers to a physical sexual act and not to a role filled by an individual. Second, homosexuality in prison often is not sexually motivated but rather is a consequence of power relationships between men. These two points will become clear in the discussion ahead.

For the inmate who is shut off from women the problem is more than

---

[38] *Ibid.*
[39] *Ibid.*, p. 238.

simply being deprived of potential sex partners. The absence of women removes the important dimension of meaning to a great deal that is important in the male world. "Like most men, the inmate must search for his identity not simply within himself but also in the picture of himself which he finds reflected in the eyes of others; and since a significant half of his audience is denied him, the inmate's image is in danger of becoming half complete."[40] The research clearly indicates that for most inmates the lack of interaction of all types with females is a very frustrating experience and one which weighs painfully on his mind during his time in prison. In the prison there is constant reference to sexual matters. One common theme is the problems of sexual frustration while another is the frequency of homosexuality in prison. Often the inmate is confronted with the possibility of homosexual resolution of his heterosexual frustrations—a possible resolution geared to physical release but often at the risk of psychological guilt and a questioning of his own masculine self image. "And if an inmate has in fact engaged in homosexual behavior within the walls, not as a continuation of a habitual pattern but as a rare act of sexual deviance under the intolerable pressure of mounting physical desire, the psychological onslought on his ego image will be particularly acute."[41]

With the elimination of women to help the man develop his male self role image he is forced to turn to other means. As a result his attempts to define masculinity are forced to an extreme position so that in many prisons the path to achieving masculine status is through "toughness." This path is also found in situations outside of prison. For example, in some lower-class subcultures where a man cannot attain status through an occupation and where his involvement with women tends to be brief and not status-giving, he may also turn to toughness as a means of achieving masculine status and recognition.

All of the related research indicates that homosexuality in male prisons is quite common. The two major roles related to homosexuality indicate the way in which it is viewed and how participating inmates are defined. In general, the extent to which homosexual behavior is seen as being masculine or feminine appears to be the most important consideration and provides the setting for defining sexual perversion by the inmate population. One group are the "fags" and "punks." They are looked down upon because they are seen as having sacrificed their manhood. The second group are the "wolves" who are seen as making a temporary adjustment to the sexual tensions in the male prison. In general the behavior of the wolf is seen as consistent with the cultural definitions of the masculine role. In sexual activity it is the wolf who is performing the act

---

[40] Sykes, "The Pains of Imprisonment," *op. cit.*, p. 134.
[41] *Ibid.*

on the fag or punk. That it, the wolf is active and the fag is passive in sexual relations.

There are some further distinctions in the sexual roles played. The fag is recognized by his exaggerated and feminine mannerisms. That is, he generally pretends to be female in more than just the sex act. By contrast the punk submits to the demands of the more aggressive homosexuals without showing any of the signs of femininity in any other respects. He often fills the punk role because he has no choice.

The stress of the masculinity of the wolf's role is reinforced because many inmates believe that his part in homosexuality implied absolutely nothing on his part. He is seen as one who seeks out a partner to be used for the mechanical act of achieving an orgasm. "Unmoved by love, indifferent to the emotions of the partner he has coerced, bribed, or seduced into a liaison, the *wolf* is often viewed as simply masturbating with another person."[42] The fact that the wolf doesn't see his activity as being homosexual may be in part a reflection of a lower-class characteristic. Various studies have shown that persons in the lower class do not define as homosexual the person who plays the active role in the sexual act. This appears to be much less true in the middle class. In other words, in the lower class, being homosexual depends on who does what in the sex act while in the middle class, being homosexual is more often based on any sexual experience with a member of the same sex. To use the middle-class definition in the prison situation would be to take away one of the few activities that is seen as clearly masculine.

A recent study shows that homosexual rape in prison can occur on *any* inmate if there are other inmates who choose to do so. This was a study of homosexual rapes carried out in Philadelphia prisons and police vans. All men were potential rape victims, but some were quickly selected. For example, practically every slightly built young man sentenced by the court was sexually approached within a day or two after his admission to court. "Many of these young men are repeatedly raped by gangs of inmates. Others, because of the threat of gang rape, seek protection by entering into a homosexual relationship with an individual tormentor."[43]

Those who committed the assaults did not think of themselves as homosexual or even as engaging in homosexual acts. But what was most important in this study was the finding that sexual release was not the primary reason for the sexual aggression. The primary goal of those who carried out the sexual aggression was the conquest and the degradation of the victim. It was repeatedly found that aggressors used such language as "fight" or "fuck," "We're going to take your manhood," "You'll have

---

[42] Sykes, Gresham, "Argot Roles: Wolves, Punks and Fags," in Johnson, *op. cit.*, p. 139.

[43] Davis, Alan J., "Sexual Assaults in the Philadelphia Prison System and Sheriff's Vans," *Trans-Action*, December, 1968, p. 9.

to give up some face," and "We're going to make a girl out of you."[44] Most of the aggressors were men who were members of the prison subculture where most other avenues of asserting their masculinity were closed to them. "To them, job success, raising a family, and achieving the respect of other men socially have been largely beyond reach. Only sexual and physical prowess stands between them and a feeling of emasculation."[45] But what is so overpowering in the prison situation is that homosexual rape is an inevitable consequence for many men. And given the fact that prison strips the inmates of most of the means of achieving masculine status, it may even then destroy for them those few means that are available in prison. That is, the man repeatedly raped loses any sense of masculinity through his lack of strength to resist and is forced into the female role in sexual activity. These kinds of experiences are often so overwhelmingly destructive to the personality of the individual that he is completely stripped of any sense of masculinity.

In concluding this section of the male in prison it should be pointed out that prison experiences directly and indirectly influence the man long after he leaves prison. He is often placed on probation and subjected to close controls over his activities. He may also have trouble getting a job or have to take a job below what he would have if he had not spent time in prison. His prison status is often continued because he is known as an "ex-convict." Like most other deviancies that one leaves, it still carries some stigma. This is true of the ex-mental patient, ex-alcoholic, ex-drug addict and so forth. (About the only "ex" who gains prestige in American society is the "ex-communist.") Also, for many ex-deviants there are social organizations to help them adjust to the world. This is true for those who were on drugs or were alcoholics. But all efforts to form organizations of ex-convicts have met with one serious obstacle. This is the tradition that a prisoner discharged on parole is not allowed to associate with known criminals, which means, among others, ex-convicts. "So that while many officials countenance the self-help movement *in prison*, they oppose its continuation outside."[46]

WOMEN'S PRISONS

In this last section we look at prisons for women and it will be seen that they are different in many important ways from the prisons of men. In recent years there have been two excellent studies of women's prisons that will be drawn on in the discussion that follows. The first was a study

---

[44] *Ibid.*, pp. 15–16.

[45] *Ibid.*, p. 16.

[46] Sagarin, Edward, *Odd Man In: Societies of Deviants in America* (Chicago: Quadrangle Books, 1969), p. 166.

of a woman's prison in California by Ward and Kassebaum,[47] and the second a study of a woman's federal prison located in West Virginia by Giallombardo.[48] The findings of these two studies, done separately from one another, show a remarkably high agreement in their findings.

Women entering prison are defined by those who work with them in a very different way than are new male inmates. The male criminal is usually seen as dangerous to society but the woman is most often viewed as disgraced and dishonored and often seen as pathetic. So the women who commit criminal acts are often regarded as erring and misguided persons who are in need of help rather than as dangerous criminals from whom society must be protected.[49] In the past, and still commonly today, the method of treatment for females in prison is to try to instill in them certain standards of sexual morality and train them to fill the duties of mothers and homemakers. So traditionally women's prisons have tried to surround the prisoners with what were believed to be good influences: "small homelike residences, individual rooms, attractive clothing to develop self-respect, educational classes, and recreation. In addition, the view that criminal women were sinful and misguided had much to do with the development of a benevolent maternal orientation of the staff toward their charges."[50]

Physically, the women's prisons are very different from those of men. The federal prison in West Virginia is approximately five hundred acres of farm, pasture, and woodlands enclosed with wire fences topped with barbed wire. The women live in cottages, each of which is operated as an independent unit with kitchen, dining room, living room, library, and individual rooms for every inmate.[51] The state prison in California does not look like the traditional penitentiary either. There are no gun towers, no stone walls, no armed guards. The grounds are surrounded by a cyclone fence ten feet high and topped with accordion wire. Here the women live in dormitories and most inmates live by themselves in rooms with curtained windows, bedspreads, rugs, and wooden doors.[52]

Most any person put in prison and isolated from the outside world will find the adjustment difficult. But it seems a reasonable argument that the impact of imprisonment is more severe for women than for men because for them a socially isolated life is much more unusual. One concern that is particularly serious for women in prison is the severing of

---

[47] Ward, David A. and Gene G. Kassebaum, *Women's Prison* (Chicago: Aldine Publishing Co., 1965).

[48] Giallombardo, Rose, *Society of Women* (New York: John Wiley and Sons, Inc., 1966).

[49] *Ibid.*, p. 7.

[50] *Ibid.*, p. 8.

[51] *Ibid.*, p. 22.

[52] Ward and Kassebaum, *op. cit.*, p. 7.

their ties with their children. "The male prisoner can serve time with the knowledge that, although the family may experience great difficulty while he is not the breadwinner, the wife can care for the children. The confined mother, however, loses her ability to fill what is, in our society, her most important role."[53] Far fewer men than women in prison are married and far fewer who are parents feel any strong sense of concern for their children.

When women enter prison they do not become a part of inmate subculture like that found in men's prison. The traditional criminal values do not fit the women's prison because those values are concerned with features of imprisonment that are relevant to men but not usually to women. "Women in our society are not prepared to 'play it cool,' 'to take it like a man,' to refrain from 'copping out' or to use force to fight for one's rights, if provoked."[54] So the inmate code is usually met with indifference in the women's prisons. This is not because the women are unexposed to criminal norms and values, but because the values embodied in the code reflect psychological needs and social roles of male prisoners."[55]

When women enter prison they react to the situation from several different perspectives. Most of them bring together several views and influences. First, they must respond to a situation that imposes on them deprivations and restrictions. Second, they sometimes respond within the context of some preparation for that kind of life, that is, to the extent that they have internalized, to varying degrees, the values of delinquent subcultures and of prisoner codes. Third, they react as women. These perspectives work together in providing them with frames of reference which influence behavior in the prison setting.[56] There are variations within the female population with regard to these values. There appears to be greater emphasis placed on solidarity and loyalty by those women who have internalized criminal norms in the community or in previous prison experiences. "Those least likely to support group loyalty and the norms of the inmate code were those women serving time for the once-only offense—homicide—and for 'white collar' offenses, such as embezzlement, forgery, and bad checks."[57] In general, Ward and Kassebaum found in their study little evidence of the differentiated inmate types and the degree of solidarity reported in the studies of prisons for men. They point out that in all interviews the "inmates responded that informing on other inmates was characteristic of almost the entire inmate population."[58]

---

[53] Ward, David A. and Gene G. Kassebaum, "Homosexuality: A Mode of Adaptation in a Prison for Women," *Social Problems*, Fall, 1964, pp. 161–62.

[54] Ward and Kassebaum, *Women's Prison, op. cit.*, p. 68.

[55] *Ibid.*, p. 69.

[56] *Ibid.*, p. 58.

[57] *Ibid.*, p. 48.

[58] Ward and Kassebaum, "Homosexuality," *op. cit.*, p. 163.

Giallombardo suggests that both men and women develop inmate subcultures as a means of responding to the general deprivations of being in
prison, but the nature of the response in the two communities is influenced by the differential participation of men and women in the external
society. She found that cultural definitions and content of *both* men's and
women's roles are brought into the female prison setting and they function
to determine the direction and focus of the inmate cultural system. "These
general features I have suggested are those concerned with the orientation
of life goals for males and females; second, cultural definitions with respect to dimensions of passivity and aggression; third, acceptability of public expression of affection displayed toward a member of the same sex; and,
finally, perception of the same sex with respect to what I have called the
popular culture."[59]

The female inmate in prison, like her male counterpart, quickly learns
there are few escape routes because psychological and physical withdrawal
are not usually effective means for easing the pain of imprisonment. Giallombardo says that women develop a subcultural structure to attempt to
deal with the harmful effects of physical and social isolation. They attempt to develop a world in which they may preserve an identity which
is relevant to life outside the prison. "In this structure, the inmates' orientation is quasi-collectivistic, depending upon where one stands in terms
of homosexual or kin relationships; the degree of mutual aid and the expectation of solidarity decrease as one goes from nuclear members to
proximal relationships to distal relationships."[60]

Another important difference between men's and women's prisons is
that among the women there are far fewer leadership roles to be filled. As
a result the female prison world is much less characterized by struggles
for power. In fact leadership appears to be very diffuse in women's prisons.
What gives the women's prisons their stability is the dynamic mechanism
of "kinship" relationships. This means relatively lasting homosexual relationships are the basic unit of the social structure. There are also clearly
defined social roles that developed as a form of adaptation to the prison
setting. In fact the sharpness with which roles are defined and filled is a
striking feature of the prisons. This sharpness does not occur with the
same degree in male prison subcultures.

Briefly defined and described are some of the roles found in the wom-
en's prisons. "Square" is a derisive name given to the inmate who is believed to be an accidental criminal. This person is usually oriented to the
prison administration and holds "anti-criminal" attitudes. There are "hip
squares" who tend to sympathize with the inmate code and follow some
of the principles. But what makes a woman a "hip square" is that she does
not engage in homosexual behavior, because anyone who does not engage

---

[59] Giallombardo, Rose, "Social Roles in a Prison for Women," *Social Problems*,
Winter, 1966, p. 288.

[60] Giallombardo, *Society of Women*, *op. cit.*, pp. 103–4.

in homosexual activities in the prison in one form or another is automati-cally labelled a square.[61] Another role is the "jive bitch," and she is seen as a troublemaker because she usually creates unrest among the inmates and cannot be depended upon. There is also the "snitcher" who is the female counterpart to the "rat" in the male prison. To accuse an inmate of snitching is the most serious accusation which one inmate can make about another. Yet in women's prisons the inmates do not usually show any great surprise at another inmate's deviating from the restrictive norms about prison affairs. Actually, many deviant acts are overlooked or are not strongly punished. "In contrast to the situation in the male prison, we find the violation of the 'no snitching' norm does not often result in vio-lence."[62] Another role is that of the "pinner" who serves as a lookout. This is an inmate who can be trusted and who will stand up under pressure.

Some inmates become what are called "rap buddies," chosen because they are easy to talk with and because one can assume that what one says will be secret and mutually binding. The "homey" role is about the closest thing to a "blood" relationship that can be found and holds a special place in the thinking of inmates. The homey is an inmate who is from another inmate's home town or nearby community. The two develop patterns of mutual aid, are close to each other, but exclude all homosexu-ality. Giallombardo suggests that the occupants of the homey role are buy-ing insurance for the future. After getting out of prison a homey will not speak negatively about the other's prison behavior to anyone in society.[63]

Homosexuality

The most striking finding in the two studies was the degree of involve-ment in homosexuality and its importance to the prison subculture. On the basis of the two studies it can be estimated that somewhere from 50 percent to 75 percent of the inmates were homosexually involved at least once during their prison terms. However, very few of the inmates practiced homosexuality before they entered prison. About 5 percent of the female inmates had homosexual experience prior to first entering prison. The fe-male homosexual is in a favored position in prison because competition of males has been removed. However, most women who enter homosexual experiences while in prison end them when they leave and return to the heterosexual world. And it must also be stressed that, unlike in the male prisons, women are rarely ever physically forced into homosexual activities.

In general the inmates make a distinction between a "penitentiary turn-out" and a "lesbian." The lesbian is seen as a woman who prefers homo-

---

[61] Giallombardo, "Social Roles," op. cit., p. 277.

[62] Ibid., p. 275.

[63] Giallombardo, Society of Women, op. cit., p. 119.

sexual relations even in the free community. In this respect she is like the fag in the male prison. There is also some evidence that the lesbians are like the male in some other ways. For example, among those few inmates who can be classified as prison politicians and merchants there is a large number who are true homosexuals.[64] Of course, the penitentiary or jail-house turnout receives her introduction to homosexuality in prison and does not see it as basic to her personality.

The question arises as to why so many of the women turn to homosexual experiences. Ward and Kassebaum suggest that the women are faced with a lack of experience in serving time and the absence of conventional sources of emotional support by husbands, lovers, or families. This makes many of them receptive to homosexuality as a means of adjustment when it is offered to them upon their arrival at prison. "Our data clearly indicate that more inmates resort to homosexuality than to psychological withdrawal, rebellion, colonization or any other type of adaptation."[65] As discussed in Chapter 10, it seems clear that homosexuality is much less threatening to the female than to the male. And for the women in prison it is seen as a temporary adaptation to prison life.

As suggested, women are rarely ever forced into homosexual relationships. Yet, force and violence do sometimes develop around homosexuality in prison. The real violence that occurs tends to be around a homosexual triangle. When these fights occur the great fear is not usually for one's life but rather about disfigurement—"the fear that an inmate 'out to get' another will use razor or scissors to disfigure one's face."[66] Often for the women the fears are less about physical threats and more about gossip. So the inmate often fears the consequences of jealousy that may result in vitriolic verbal attacks and she suffers from insecurity in handling the frequent attacks through the "penitentiary darby"—"gossip which takes place at all times on all sides with the prison."[67]

There are two major homosexual roles that are filled in the women's prison. The first is the "butch," "stud broad," "drag butch," or "daddy" who is the aggressive, active sexual partner. Most lesbians fall into this role, but there are also many jailhouse turnouts. The butch wears her hair short, no makeup, her legs unshaven, and she often wears pedal pushers, or if she wears a dress, the belt is worn low on the hips. "Masculine gait, manner of smoking, and other gestures are adopted."[68] Usually this role is accorded prestige by the other inmates because there are fewer of them and they are in great demand.

---

[64] Ward and Kassebaum, *op. cit.*, p. 168.

[65] *Ibid.*, p. 175.

[66] Giallombardo, "Social Roles," *op. cit.*, p. 274.

[67] *Ibid.*, p. 274.

[68] Ward and Kassebaum, "Homosexuality," *op. cit.*, pp. 168–69.

The complementary role to that of the butch is the "femme" or "mommy." The femme maintains a female appearance and ideally plays a more submissive, passive role. She continues to act out many of the female functions performed in outside society and she emphasizes her role primarily through her behavior. She walks with her arms around the butch, embraces and kisses her in public, and allows the butch to speak in her behalf.[69]

Often the homosexual pair are cast in the context of a "marital" relationship in the prison and are so viewed by the other inmates. While this kind of relationship seems to be repugnant to most women when they are in the outside world, the uniqueness of the prison world forces them to redefine homosexual behavior. "For the vast majority of the inmates, adjustment to the prison world is made by establishing a homosexual alliance with a compatible partner as a marriage unit."[70] These marriages are generally monogamous and the inmate who "chippies from one bed to another"—i.e., terminates affairs too quickly—is held in scorn by the others as her behavior is held to be promiscuous. This behavior draws forth words of scorn from the inmates because the ideal cultural pattern in the prison is to establish a permanent relationship."[71]

While the sense of belongingness and the affectional ties are important in a homosexual marriage, the couple is also usually involved in some kinds of sexual activities. In all cases the butch performs sex on the femme, but about one-third of the butches refuse to let the femme reciprocate sexually. In some cases the butches remain clothed during sexual activity. In part this may be to maintain the illusion of masculinity which would be lost by the removal of clothing. In the sex act the role of the femme is completely passive where the butch *"gives work,"* i.e., "engages in cunnilingus, manual manipulation of the clitoris, and breast fondling. While the butch gives work, the denial of sexual gratification for herself is called *giving up the work.* Such self denial militates against becoming obligated to the femme and from developing emotional ties that would be painful to disturb or break."[72] This concern is often a result of the fact that many of the women in the butch role were unsuccessful in having heterosexual relationships that were affectionate, and they continue to have the fear of being rejected again in a homosexual relationship.

This discussion indicates that women's prisons have developed around living patterns similar in many ways to the outside world. This is far more true than is the case for the men's prisons. It seems that prisons for men and women have been both successes and failures. They have succeeded

---

[69] *Ibid.,* p. 284.

[70] Giallombardo, *op. cit.,* p. 282.

[71] *Ibid.,* p. 284.

[72] Ward and Kassebaum, *op. cit.,* pp. 171–72.

in removing the threat of the individual criminal from the broader society but they have failed in significantly reducing the future criminality of the inmates.

BIBLIOGRAPHY

Cressey, Donald R. and John Irwin, "Thieves, Convicts and the Inmate Culture," *Social Problems*, Fall, 1962, pp. 142–55.

Davis, Alan J., "Sexual Assaults in the Philadelphia Prison System and Sheriff's Vans," *Trans-Action*, December, 1968, pp. 8–16.

Garabedian, Peter G., "Social Roles and Processes of Socialization in the Prison Community," *Social Problems*, Fall, 1963, pp. 139–52.

Giallombardo, Rose, *Society of Women* (New York: John Wiley and Sons, Inc.), 1966.

Hazebrigg, Lawrence, ed. *Prisons within Society* (New York: Anchor Books, 1969).

Johnson, Norman, et al., eds., *The Sociology of Punishment and Correction* (New York: John Wiley, 1962).

Ward, David A. and Gene G. Kassebaum, *Women's Prison* (Chicago: Aldine Publishing Co., 1965).

PART II

SUBCULTURAL EMERGENCE
AND SOCIAL CHANGE

CHAPTER 14

MILITANT WOMEN

IN THE LATE 1960's in the United States a new militancy seeking female equality or liberation emerged. The United States has had a long history of feminism that has brought about many significant social changes. But the new militancy has been much more aggressive and demanding than anything that had gone before. To a great extent this is because the female liberation movement has developed from the militancy movement of the 1960's in civil rights, student protests, and the politically radical left. There are many who see the militant women's movement as a temporary fad that will quickly fade away because women really are not discriminated against and have no basis for protest. However, it is argued here that the movement will not fade away and in fact quite possibly may become one of the most important social movements of the 1970's. This argument is based on the contention that there are many ways in which women are still treated as second class citizens and oftentimes as being inferior to men. Female militancy has qualities both of social problems and of social deviancy. In general any second class treatment of the woman represents a social problem, and the more militant ways of dealing with discrimination in the United States have become forms of deviancy. To better understand the roles of women today and the context in which the women's liberation movement operates it is necessary to look at how women have been defined and treated in the past.

357

HISTORICAL BACKGROUND

It has been pointed out in other contexts in this book that almost all societies of the past have been patriarchal, meaning in effect that women have had second class status. If we go back to early Greek civilization it can be seen that the powers the Greek husband had over his wife were no less than what he had over his children. If she had no children he could divorce her. The dowry of the wife became the husband's property during his lifetime and he had the rights to any separate earnings she might acquire. She was under his jurisdiction almost entirely and could not even leave the house without his permission. In the words of Menander, "The life of a respectable woman is bounded by the street door."[1] By contrast the early Roman wife stood in a place of complete social equality to her husband and was seen as having dignity and honor both within the family and the state. She was both honored and subordinated: "She was highly respected, and yet she was given no tangible legal rights."[2]

Whatever status the woman had gained during the Roman period she began to lose with the rise of Christianity. In that period a tendency developed to increasingly restrict the woman's legal and social rights. Women were given no special position or recognition in early Christian teaching. Jesus expressed no new ideas with respect to the position of women. The Apostle Paul advocated that women take a subordinate position to man and over time this became the dominant attitude among early Christian leaders. Therefore, the status accorded to women was a step back compared to what they had had in Rome. With time women were excluded by Christians from any offices. Still less were they men's equals in private life. "In marriage wives were bidden to be subject to their husbands."[3]

Christianity developed an obsession with sexual matters that also placed a great strain on woman. While she had been treated by the Saxons as property, by the Middle Ages the woman was seen as the source of all sexual evil. "It was argued that sexual guilt really pertained to women, since they tempted men, who would otherwise have remained pure."[4] Combining the view of her inferiority to man with her being the repository of sin placed her at a level of inferiority she has never completely recovered from in the eyes of traditional Christian thought. With time, and due to Christian influence, she also came to be legally defined as inferior.

---

[1] Clarke, Helen I., *Social Legislation* (New York: Appleton-Century-Crofts, Inc., 1957), pp. 31–32.

[2] *Ibid.*, p. 35.

[3] Lewinsohn, Richard, *A History of Sexual Customs* (New York: Harper and Brothers, 1958), p. 92.

[4] Taylor, G. Rattray, *Sex in History* (New York: Ballentine Books, Inc., 1954), p. 64.

In the English common law the husband's rights over the wife's personal property were almost unlimited. After the end of the 13th century the common law put the absolute property in the wife's chattels with the husband. She was not even permitted to make a will without the husband's consent. In many respects up until the 20th century the woman had a status not too different from a slave. This was the general state of affairs that existed at the time the American colonies were founded and developed.

The Colonies

For the Puritans, marriage was a very important relationship based upon religious, social, and economic values. A man needed a wife and children so as to survive and prosper. Calhoun wrote that the rigors and the dangers of early colonial life constituted a man's world. "Life conditions allowed a type of patriarchism that found affinity in the Old Testament regime. Views as to proper relations between husband and wife, parent and children, or between man and maid before marriage, came directly from the scriptures."[5] The father's authority could not be openly questioned without implying a questioning of basic religious tenets. Continuous childbearing took a heavy toll of Puritan wives. Great numbers died at childbirth, and the number and close spacing of births, plus the harsh nature of the environment during the early days of settlement, brought about old age and death long before it was chronologically due. The mother also had to live with the expectation of losing many of her children.

The life of the Puritan wife-mother was highly restricted and almost wholly bounded by the interests of maintaining the home. Her social life was often no more than a weekly visit to church on Sunday and a religious "lecture" on Thursday. If a woman did not marry she had little hope of freeing herself from the control of her father or brothers until she could find a job and a place to live outside the home. In the colonies, a woman had to work in some home or another because there were few other jobs for women. Given this choice, the woman, if she could, preferred to marry and work in her own home. Sinclair suggests that the worship of the American home began when the household was the focus of all daily life and the workshop for it.[6]

In many ways early American women were treated almost like slaves. Both the slave and the woman were expected to behave with deference and obedience toward owner or husband. Both had no existence officially

[5] Calhoun, Arthur W., A *Social History of the American Family: Colonial Period* Vol. 1 (New York: Barnes and Noble, Inc., 1960), p. 83.

[6] Sinclair, Andrew, *The Emancipation of the American Woman* (New York Harper and Brothers, 1965), p. 15.

under the law and both had but few rights with regard to education. "Both found it difficult to run away; both worked for their masters without pay; both had to breed on command, and to nurse the results."[7] It is of interest that from the very start the woman and the Negro have been compared in terms of their second class status, and this comparison is as appropriate today as it was during the colonial period.

It was early in American history that the first female rebels appeared. Even though the Puritan women had the generally low status common to women in patriarchal societies, they nevertheless played a significant part in the history of the New England Puritan era. Erikson, in his study of deviance in Puritan society, traces three major "crime waves." Of particular interest is that in all three women played major roles. The first historically important rebellious woman in America was Mrs. Anne Huchinson. She attacked the prevailing views about religion during meetings in her home and argued for the idea of personal and direct contact with God, without regard to church or minister. She was tried and in 1638 was expelled from the church. The second crime wave was the Quaker persecutions of 1656 to 1665, and the first open indication of this trouble was when two Quaker housewives were arrested on ship in Boston Bay. They were taken to jail, stripped of their clothing and searched for markings of witchcraft.[8] The third Puritan crime wave was the Salem witchcraft outbreak of 1692. In the period that followed a number of girls and women were accused, tried, and found guilty of witchcraft.[9] In all three of those early historical events women made their presence strongly felt. These women were seen as deviants or rebels because they went against values of society in a variety of ways, but they were not female rebels fighting for female rights.

THE EIGHTEENTH CENTURY

Women continued to be treated in many respects as second class persons. They received very little formal education because it was a commonly accepted theory that girls were unfit in brain and character to study seriously. It was argued that girls should be taught how to run a household, "and, if suitable how to display the graces of a lady."[10] However, near the end of the 18th century there were voices being heard that no longer accepted the traditional definition of the woman. And if helplessness were one common female adaptation to the world around her, for other women a new militancy was coming to be an alternative. For a few

---

[7] *Ibid.*, p. 4.

[8] Erickson, Kai T., *Wayward Puritans* (New York: John Wiley and Sons, Inc., 1966), p. 115.

[9] *Ibid.*, p. 141.

[10] Sinclair, *op. cit.*, p. 29.

women there was the choice of either barricading herself in the home with the myth of frailty or of struggling to get outside the home and finding some new definitions of femininity.

In 1792, the first comprehensive attack on marriage as it then existed and on the way in which it subjugated women was made by Mary Wollstonecraft in a book called *A Vindication of the Rights of Women*. She did not want to do away with marriage but rather to correct some of the inequalities that existed. She argued that women should have increased social and economic rights as well as greater education so that in marriage they would not have to be submissive, but rather equal to their husbands. Women were also being heard in other areas of protest. In general in the 18th and 19th centuries when voices of protest were heard they were from women. It was primarily women who fought against slavery, against child labor, and against the development of slums. They also fought for schools, libraries, playgrounds, and legislation to protect children. Women have historically been the social conscience of American society.

THE NINETEENTH CENTURY

During the 19th century great changes occurred in the United States. Industrialization meant a change in life patterns with the productive unit no longer the family, but rather the individual going away from the home to work. For some women, where the home had been the setting for all their work, the chance to work in a factory appeared to be freedom. Hard work for twelve hours a day, or more, had been normal for most American women and their tasks had been heavy, endless, and unpaid. For many of them the early factory system represented a semi-skilled and repetitive job which demanded little physical exertion.[11]

As the 19th century unfolded female rebels became increasingly common. The first female rebels were basically rebels who happened to be women. That is, they were not champions of their sex, but rather were champions of themselves. They fought for the right to be treated as individuals, without distinction made by sex. However, they did not consider themselves to be other than exceptions. "They never questioned that the general rule was the rule of women by men. Thus they were not feminists so much as female rebels, made so by the accidents of birth and place and inspiration."[12] The early feminists also saw how the role of lady had enslaved American women because the very definition of a lady was based on inferior status and ability. Yet, many of the early feminists only felt free when they were playing the role of ladies. They never came to terms with this anomaly and as a result feminism in the 19th century remained

---

[11] *Ibid.*, p. 139.
[12] *Ibid.*, p. 32.

primarily a middle-class and ladylike business. "In fact, most American ladies—by their very social position—opposed anything other than safe and mild reforms of a religious or educational nature."[13]

In the decades prior to the Civil War in the United States a changing definition of women had developed on the part of men. The "animal" nature of women came to be stressed less by men, and women came to be seen as more spiritual. So the new explanation for their exclusion from politics came to be not because they were inferior, but rather because of their superiority. They were seen not so much as sinful as too good for the world. As a result their moral value placed them above the nasty business of politics and making money. The men turned over to them the matters of "culture" and the rearing of children. Women were encouraged to believe that their sex gave them a distinct function that was different from and better than the mere getting of money.[14] It is doubtful that very many men really believed that what women did was important. The really important world was their world—the man's world of money making and politics. So they could keep women out of their world and feel sanctimonious about it at the same time.

Despite all the forms of resistance, the woman's rights movement did develop and grow. The factor of industrialization continued to remove many women from the home and freed many of them from the functions they had performed in the past. There were a number of landmarks in the movement. For example, in 1833 Oberlin was the first men's college in the United States to admit women, and four years later Mount Holyoke, the first women's college, was opened. The first woman's rights convention was held at Seneca Falls, New York in 1848. The first to speak out in public for women's rights were Fanny Wright, the daughter of a Scottish nobleman and Ernestine Rose, the daughter of a rabbi. There was great hostility toward those women and the first was referred to as "the red harlot of infidelity" and the second as "a woman a thousand times below a prostitute."[15] The declaration that came out of Seneca Falls brought forth an outcry of revolution and insurrection directed at the women, and the hostility was so great that some of the women withdrew their signatures.

By the 1850's such respected intellectuals as the New England Transcendentalists were aligning themselves with the woman's rights movement. During that period in England the Unitarians and other liberal elements were also becoming involved. In 1869 John Stuart Mill wrote his work, *The Subjection of Women,* which gave the mark of respectability to English feminism. By the 1860's women began to discard their crinolines and slowly slimmed down their skirts until only the bustle was left.

---

[13] *Ibid.,* p. 109.

[14] *Ibid.,* p. 255.

[15] Friedan, Betty, *The Feminine Mystique* (New York: W. W. Norton and Co., Inc., 1963), p. 86.

"Once again they could and did begin to take exercise and play simple games of sport such as croquet and lawn tennis; and unchaperoned they could once again walk arm in arm with men."[16]

However, the major force in the growth of the feminist movement in the 1800's was the slavery issue. So the concern that turned many women into pioneer reformers was less an attack on sexual bondage than an assault on the slavery of the Negroes. In their seeking to free the slaves many radical women became more conscious of their own lack of freedom. "Through helping others, they learned to help themselves. The destiny of American women and American Negroes had been interacting, and still is."[17]

As suggested, the typical man was strongly against the women's rights movement. He was, of course, a double standard male who saw his way of life being threatened and the possibility of some of his conveniences being taken away from him. The man had no desire to change his world but only to increase his rights as a male. On economic grounds he found his world ideal. A subjugated wife, even if cranky, was simpler and cheaper to deal with than an equal before the law who could leave with her property if she wanted or who could sue for redress if mistreated. From the business point of view the woman's low position made good sense to him. So any plea for female education or reform in marriage was often linked with atheism, socialism, abolition, teetotaling, sexual immorality, and other despicable forces by the male.[18]

The male often took on a pious posture in arguing against the woman's rights movement. By supporting the image of the female as submissive, dependent, and inferior he could argue that her basic being was under attack. So he could intone as did one senator in 1866 that to give women equal rights would destroy that "milder gentler nature, which not only makes them shrink from but disqualifies them for the turmoil and battle of public life."[19] Against this image he could then picture the feminists as violating their very nature as women, and the picture they often presented was in sharp contrast to the traditional docile women. Some of the early feminists cut their hair short, wore bloomers, and tried to be like men. So the hostile image held of the feminists came to be one of inhuman, fiery man-eaters who had none of the traditional feminine qualities.

Near the end of the 19th century new forces for women's rights were developing. Over the long run one of the most important developments was higher education for women. In the late 19th century there was the founding and establishing of a number of women's colleges. The rise of

---

[16] Hunt, Morton M., *The Natural History of Love* (New York: Alfred A. Knopf, 1959), p. 332.

[17] Sinclair, *op. cit.*, p. 37.

[18] Hunt, *op. cit.*, p. 331.

[19] Friedan, *op. cit.*, p. 86.

those new colleges created a demand for the services of academic women, and the demand, under the circumstances of the time, created the supply. These schools came about as a result of the great reform ferment that had started in the 1840's and, while slowed down by the Civil War, reached a peak at the turn of the century. "Abolition, women's rights, temperance, prison reform, labor organization—these were only a few of the many causes which had been fostered in the great reform movement. The higher education of women had been one of the many."[20] In the first two decades after the turn of the century many of the elitist women's colleges were in conflict with themselves. "The academic women who staffed them were still for the most part women with causes, still reformers at heart, but action was becoming less attractive than contemplation within the ivy-covered walls. The feeling began to grow that the academic role was not an activist one."[21] But the colleges had provided the rallying point and the training grounds for many of the women involved in women's rights that occurred around the turn of the century.

By the end of the 19th century some women began to believe in an alternative to the traditional role of marriage and motherhood. This came about as customs changed and more women were able to work and support themselves without losing their self-respect. Also during this period some women entered business and moved into the professions. Toward the end of the century essays appeared that argued that for a woman to remain single and support herself was better than to become the wife of a dissipated man. "The rights of lowly and genteel women alike to work provided the means of escape from unhappy or loveless marriages."[22] So while the work pattern was not common for most women it was there and provided the roots for rapid development in the 20th century. But at the same time the battle to keep the woman in the home continued. While anthropology and biology had destroyed the old belief that women were inferior, new arguments developed. Some men contended that immigration and eugenics provided reasons for keeping women in the home. Their argument was that old stock women were needed at home to bear children that would be necessary to preserve and protect the destiny of the nation. Those middle-class women were told how important they were and how they should stay home and bear more superior beings like themselves to compensate for the "inferior" offspring of the immigrants.[23] It is clear that historically whenever one argument against women was destroyed new ones emerged.

---

[20] Bernard, Jessie, *Academic Women* (University Park, Penna.: Pennsylvania State University Press, 1964), p. 31.

[21] *Ibid.*, p. 36.

[22] Hunt, *op. cit.*, p. 333.

[23] Sinclair, *op. cit.*, p. 237.

THE TWENTIETH CENTURY

As suggested, during the 19th century the battle for women's equality was closely linked to the freeing of the slaves. During the 20th century the battle for women's rights was closely linked to the fights for various social reform. The feminist movement was tied in with Jane Addams and Hull House, the rise of the union movement, and the great strikes against intolerable working conditions in the factories. And the final battle for the right of the female to vote was fought primarily by the college trained women.[24] Social reform continued to be seen as something for which women could be concerned. These concerns were linked with man's stereotype of women's being compassionate and impractical creatures. The American man has always underestimated the influence of the woman as society's conscience. A reading of history indicates that man's inhumanity would have been much greater if women had not functioned to force a more compassionate view of the world and human beings.

The most dramatic change in the image of women came after the First World War. This resulted from the upsurge in women's employment outside the home. The 1920's saw the emergence of the white-collar class in the United States and the women were a large part of it. For example, over twice as many women entered the labor force during that decade as during the previous one.[25] But the major event, and one that had been fought for many years, was the passing of the Nineteenth Amendment to the Federal Constitution in 1920. It read that the "rights of citizens of the United States to vote shall not be denied or abridged by the United States or by any state on account of sex." This was an important landmark in the fight for women's rights. However, it did not bring about any great changes in the political life patterns of women.

The 1920's were the period of greatest change in the roles and rights of American women. That decade saw a revolution in morals that was most vividly reflected in the behavior of women. During the 1920's many taboos of the past against women were thrown aside. For the first time women began to smoke and drink in public. As recently as 1918 it was considered daring for a New York hotel to permit women to sit at the bar. But during the twenties, despite prohibition, both sexes drank in public. As Degler points out, in the years since the twenties there have been few alterations in the position of women that were not first evident during that decade. "The changes have penetrated more deeply and spread more widely through the social structure, but their central tendency was then already spelled out."[26]

---

[24] Friedan, *op. cit.*, pp. 97–8.

[25] Degler, Carl N., "Revolution without Ideology: The Changing Place of Women in America," *Daedalus*, Fall, 1964, p. 657.

[26] *Ibid.*, p. 659.

The 1920's were also the period of great change in the sexual behavior of women. It was the period when women began to believe that they had the same rights to sexual satisfaction as did the man. And it was during that decade that the increased frequency of premarital coitus among females occurred. The sexual superiority of the male was no longer an accepted belief for many women as well as men.

Once women had the legal right to vote in 1920 they found that this did not lead to legal equality. This was because there could be no real sex equality until women actually participated on an equal basis with men in politics, occupations, and the family. "Law and administrative regulations must permit such participation, but women must want to participate and be able to participate."[27] Actually in the 1920's the grip of the traditional political machines became even stronger with women voting. This was because the female relatives of every man connected with the political machines were registered to vote. For many of those city bosses the vote of the women was merely a multiplication factor. In fact, women refused to vote against anti-feminists in Congress, and sent them back with increased majorities as their representatives.[28] While the women had the vote they generally continued to use it as their men told them to.

Since 1920 the number of women who have attained positions of power in the federal and state governments has been unbelievably few. There have been only three women elected state governors. Two women have held cabinet rank in the federal government and only six have served as ambassadors or ministers. At the present time the United States has one female senator out of one hundred. And while women hold about one-fourth of all jobs in the federal civil service they hold only 2 percent of the top positions. But this also appears to be true in many other countries, although somewhat less severely than in the United States. For example, even with the Soviet Union's wide base of professional personnel the number of women decreases disproportionately as one goes toward the top in the Soviet hierarchy.[29] Before looking further at the present position of the women's rights movement in the United States it is useful to look at the position of women in other societies, preliterate and literate, and past and present.

PRELITERATE SOCIETIES

In no society are most jobs left to be indiscriminately filled by either sex. Some jobs are always assigned to one sex or the other. However, so-

[27] Rossi, Alice S., "Equality between the Sexes: An Immodest Proposal," *Daedalus*, Spring, 1964, p. 610.

[28] Sinclair, *op. cit.*, p. 344.

[29] Women's Bureau, *1969 Handbook of Women Workers*, Bulletin 294 (Washington, D.C.: United States Department of Labor, 1969), p. 3.

cieties vary greatly in whether a male or a female sex status is paired with a specific occupational status. Preliterate societies sex-typed such jobs as hunting, cooking, crop growing, pottery making, and so forth. But there is nothing inherent in the job which makes it the property of only one sex—that is, which sex fills the occupation is dependent on society's definitions.

There is probably nothing in most occupations that inherently makes them seem glamorous or like drudgery. What makes a job drudgery is usually that it must be endlessly performed with little variation in how it is done. While this is typical of housekeeping in our society it may be typical of hunting in a preliterate culture. In preliterate societies the jobs performed by the women were usually as important as those done by the men. In those societies the women were just as much a part of the world around them as the men. And the economic worth that the society placed on the woman's labor was just as high, and sometimes even higher, than that which was placed on the work of the men.

As the economic and social structure of cultures became more complex men increasingly took over the "important" jobs for themselves. Very often the women were excluded from social gatherings and various public places. Also the honors and the offices of a society became the province of men and women were excluded from them. The strongest proof that most preliterate societies have been male dominated is that they have almost all been patriarchal. And while polygyny has been very common, polyandry was rare among preliterate groups. This difference in acceptance appears to have been based on the potential for jealousy being a major cause for prohibiting polyandry but not polygyny. Men's feelings of jealousy were spared but women's were not.[30]

Stephens found in his cross-cultural analysis of a number of preliterate societies that wife to husband deference customs were commonly practiced while husband to wife deference customs were quite rare.[31] He also found that all societies had premarital and extramarital restrictions that were much stronger on women than on men.[32] Over all Stephens found some near universals among preliterate groups with reference to husband and wife roles. First was a standard division of labor by sex. Second was the "esssential femininity" of some tasks, such as child care, and the "essential masculinity" of other tasks, such as fishing. Third, power and privilege were reflected in the husband's status being either equal to or higher than the wife's, and matriarchies were very rare.[33]

---

[30] Stephens, William N., *The Family in Cross Cultural Perspective* (New York: Holt, Rinehart and Winston, Inc., 1963), p. 46.

[31] *Ibid.*, p. 292.

[32] *Ibid.*, p. 290.

[33] *Ibid.*, p. 305.

WESTERN WORLD TODAY

The treatment of women has changed in most countries of the west. How women are treated in most countries appears to be related to the educational and social class level of men and women. Goode found in his cross-cultural studies that in the lower classes, women had somewhat more authority. This was because the low standard of living gave the women a key position in the family. In the higher classes where the men are better educated, they are often more willing to concede rights and women are eager to demand them. "Men in the lower strata, by contrast, are much more traditional minded than their counterparts in the upper strata, and are less willing to concede the new rights being demanded; but they have to do so because of the increased bargaining power of their women."[34]

But when the countries of the Western world are examined it can be seen that they are changing rapidly, and in some cases women have received greater rights than in the United States. The right of the vote is now common to the woman in most countries. In 1968 women could vote and run for office in 117 countries. There were only seven countries that prohibited voting for women and four others that imposed some limitations. Women have also gained in the number who go on to college. In the 1960's women in the United States and Great Britain made up a little over 30 percent of the college population while in the U.S.S.R. women made up well over 40 percent of the student population. While the proportion remains small in most countries, women in the professions in Sweden, Great Britain, the Soviet Union and Israel have doubled or more over the past twenty years.

In Russia, a woman would be expected to explain why she is *not* working while in the United States the woman is often expected to explain why she *is* working.[35] In the Soviet Union women do not have the domestic help or the household appliances commonly taken for granted in the United States. And the Russian men, like other European men, and unlike Americans, typically do not, and are not expected to, help in the household.[36]

Sweden is probably the country most affected by feminist reform. In 1970, 14 percent of its parliamentary seats and two of its cabinet ministeries were filled by women. Swedish women do such jobs as running cranes and driving cabs and buses. The fathers must support their children, although divorced women are expected to pay their own way. The

---

[34] Goode, William J., "Industrialization and Family Structure," in Norman W. Bell and Ezra F. Vogel, *The Family* (Revised Edition) (New York: The Free Press, 1968), p. 118.

[35] Epstein, Cynthia F., *Woman's Place* (Berkeley, Calif.: University of California Press, 1970), p. 43.

[36] *Ibid.*, p. 103.

schools have compulsory coeducational classes in metalwork, sewing, and child care. The new tax structure of Sweden is forcing many wives to go to work and a start has been made on the development of day care centers. There has been a recent government-ordered revision of textbooks that is expected to start eliminating the stereotype images of both sexes that have traditionally been presented.

The trend clearly has been one where societies have legislated reforms and the legal framework to provide economic opportunity for women. However, there is probably no modern society, with the possible exception of those of the Communist countries, "in which expectations of female-role behavior include a constellation keyed to women's participation in the productive and prestigious work of the economy."[37] In the United States the contribution of women to the economy is seen as secondary to that of men and not equal to their contribution in social worth.

One expert on the family suggests that there will be no family system emerging in the next generation that will grant full equality to women, although the general position of women throughout the world will greatly improve. "The revolutionary philosophies which have accompanied the shifts in power in Communist countries or in the Israeli *kibbutzim* have asserted equality, and a significant stream of philosophic thought in the West has asserted the right to equality, but no society has yet granted it."[38] Goode goes on to argue that it is possible to create a society where full equality could occur, but to do so would call for radical reorganization of the social structure. A new socialization process would need to be developed because families continue to rear their daughters to take only a modest interest in careers in which they would have equal responsibility to men.[39] Girls continue to be reared in most societies to fill the secondary roles they have always filled.

AMERICAN WOMEN TODAY

LEGAL POSITION

Before examining the social roles that women fill in the United States today it is useful to look at their legal position in society. In very few societies have women ever been legally equal to men. In fact, in most societies married women have often been at an even greater legal disadvantage than unmarried women. This has been because the social and legal sphere of married women has been the home and there they were expected to be subservient to the husband and their duty was to care for him, their

---

[37] *Ibid.*, p. 46.
[38] Goode, *op. cit.*, p. 119.
[39] *Ibid.*

children, and their home. While this has changed greatly in the United States the woman is still far from equal to the man within the context of the legal system. The differential laws by sex discriminate against women for two reasons. First, the woman is still seen as not having the ability or rights to do some things that men can do; and second, laws are made to "protect" her on the assumption that woman must, by the nature of her sex, be given special legal protection. An illustration of the first reason is that in three states women may not serve on juries of the state courts, and an illustration of the second reason is that in 16 states (and the District of Columbia) women called for jury duty may claim exemptions for reasons *not* available to men.

A further illustration of legal discrimination against women is that in 42 states after divorce a wife is legally entitled only to what income and property she herself had earned or acquired. This means that only eight states place any economic value on the wife's homemaking servi‌es.[40] The laws related to her "limited" ability as a woman are reflected in the fact that in all states a husband is liable for the support of his wife while in most states the wife is responsible for the support of her husband only if he is unable to support himself.

Some of the most discriminating laws against women exist in areas related to her rights in the work setting. For example, there are in 43 states laws that limit the number of hours that a woman can work, usually to eight hours a day. One consequence of this law is to eliminate the chance for women to earn the higher pay that goes with overtime work. Or in many states there are weight-lifting standards placed on women, and this keeps them off of some of the better paying jobs. Generally the legal restrictions are that a woman cant lift more than 40 pounds, nor is she allowed to push 75 pounds or more. These restrictions on physical effort are often senseless to impose on women because many of them pick up and carry children who weigh more than 40 pounds and do jobs around the house that call for the moving or lifting of heavy weights. These laws categorically reject women from specific job opportunities without reference to individual variations in strength and willingness to fill a certain job.

The most important changes in the legal work rights of women were brought about in Title VII of the Civil Rights Act of 1964. When that act was being written the word "sex" was put into the section that prohibited employment discrimination on the basis of "race, color, religion, or national origin." The word "sex" was introduced facetiously and not because of any serious concern with female discrimination. But the result has been very important to women. The official guidelines to Title VII

[40] Ellis, Julie, *The Revolt of the Second Sex* (New York: Lancer Books, 1970), p. 48.

provide that employers can no longer not hire or promote women on the grounds that their fellow workers or customers would not accept them. Nor can employers classify certain jobs exclusively for males or females unless sex is a bona fide qualification. Employers can no longer establish separate seniority lists based on sex nor label jobs as "light" or "heavy" when that is a subterfuge for the terms "male" or "female." They cannot forbid the hiring of married women if the ruling is not also applied to married men, nor can they place newspaper help-wanted advertisements excluding applicants of one sex and limiting the job to applicants of the other sex.[41]

An examination is now made of the traditional roles of women as they are filled in the United States today. The interest is in looking at the roles of wife, sexual partner, mother, and housekeeper. In the next section an examination will be made of the work role of women and how that role is related to their traditional roles.

WIFE ROLE

The most modern and democratic view of the wife role is within a colleague family setting. This type of marriage is not in reality an association of complete equals, but is based on the notion of the development of specializations within marriage. In different areas, both partners recognize that authority is vested in the role or in the interests and abilities of only one of them. This recognition allows each one to defer to the other in different areas of competence, without loss of prestige. The division of labor in the colleague marriage is not based on a belief of complete differences between the husband and wife roles and often, if conditions demand, one partner can temporarily take over the role of the other. But even in this setting various duties are sex assigned. While a husband might take over the washing of laundry if his wife is ill, as soon as she is well she takes it over in most cases. Even the most democratic marriage is generally one where the husband has more privileges and does more of the things important and interesting to society.

SEXUAL PARTNER ROLE

The middle-class woman grows up being taught that when she enters marriage she has a right to sexual fulfillment. If, in Victorian times it was considered a "vile aspersion" that women were capable of having an orgasm, it is considered in modern times a "vile aspersion" that any woman is incapable.[42] Many of today's marriage manuals emphasize the sexual

---

[41] House Resolution 7152, *Congressional Record*, 110, May 25, 1964, p. 11847.

[42] Sinclair, *op. cit.*, p. 362.

problems centering around the wife's achievement of orgasm. The husband is told that he should control his sexual selfishness to make sure that his wife reaches her sexual peak. Given the importance of need satisfaction in the sexual nature of marriage, modern emphasis on the interests of the woman adds an increasingly important dimension to the problem of sexual adjustment in marriage. One implication of this change is that not only are women increasingly achieving sexual satisfaction, but they are also increasingly conscious of *lack of achievement*.

As more and more restrictions are removed from the woman and she is encouraged to achieve sexual satisfaction, it seems logical that the change in her sexual desires will include the desire for greater frequency of sexual intercourse. Theoretically, the woman's ability to indulge in sexual intercourse is not biologically restricted. In other words, she continues to be sexually limited by social and psychological influences, but as these are altered or removed, the biological restrictions remain few. Because of the loss and modification of inhibiting values, women are moving in a less inhibited direction. One consequence may be that the biological differences with regard to sexual frequency will become more and more important. Some couples may find themselves in a situation where the sexual interests of the wife are greater than those of the husband. But because of the biological limitations on the man, he, unlike the woman, cannot normally, without some interest, function as a sex partner.

MOTHER ROLE

Rossi has pointed out that for the first time in the history of any known society motherhood became a full time occupation for adult women in the United States.[43] In the past it was an impossibility because the woman had far more things to do and more children to look after. Full time motherhood came about as the result of technological development and economic affluence. Once full time motherhood came about women were told how important it was and the fact that mankind had previously functioned without it was forgotten. It seems clear that continuous mothering, even in the first few years of life, is not necessary for the healthy emotional development of the child. What is more important is the nature of the care rather than who provides it.[44]

In fact, there is strong evidence that not only is the full time mother not necessary to the growth of the child but that she may also contribute to severe problems for the child. In a number of cases the etiology of mental illness is linked to inadequacies in the mother-child relationship. It is the failure of the mother which perpetuates problems from one gen-

---

[43] Rossi, *op. cit.*, p. 615.

[44] *Ibid.*, p. 619.

eration to the next that affect sons and daughters alike.[45] Alice Rossi writes that full time motherhood is neither sufficiently absorbing to the woman nor beneficial to the child to justify the modern woman's devoting fifteen or more years to it as her only occupation. "Sooner or later—and I think it should be sooner—women have to face the question of who they are besides their children's mother."[46]

HOUSEKEEPER ROLE

As industrialization developed and the means of taking care of the house increased many women have not reduced their household efforts, but rather have continued to spend as much time on them as before. The American woman has become subject to Parkinson's Law that "work expands to fill the time allotted for it." As cleaning aids have been improved, standards of cleanliness have been upgraded far beyond the thresholds of sanitation necessary for health.[47]

Regardless of the propaganda, housework is basically low status work. This is reflected in a number of ways. Our society rewards occupational efforts with money and yet housework is not within the money economy. In fact it is not always defined as real work. Many women who do not hold income producing jobs will say they don't work—only take care of a house. Among women who work for money, domestic work is at the bottom of the occupational hierarchy. Lower-class girls prefer to work in offices and factories rather than to hire out and care for children and a house. Because they can't get domestic help many middle-class women must do their housework themselves. So the low prestige occupation of housework has become a major specialty of the educated woman.[48]

Another reflection of how many women feel who take care of the house themselves is reflected in what they are willing to pay domestic workers. When it comes time to hire a woman they want to pay her the lowest salary possible. In fact, many women who are quite liberal about increasing the pay of grape pickers are all for slave wages for the domestics they try to hire. As a result they often show their own low assessment of housework by saying that the women should be satisfied with the low pay because it is only housework.

There are also persons of some respectability and influence telling women how important housekeeping is. They change the name to homemaking because that sounds more creative. For example, one female author writes that "homemaking during the early family years is a full-time

---

[45] *Ibid.*, p. 621.
[46] *Ibid.*, p. 624.
[47] Epstein, *op. cit.*, pp. 104–5.
[48] *Ibid.*, p. 42.

job, and that the skills required are probably quite as exacting as those necessary in many of the professions."[49] What the professional skills of homemaking are she doesn't say. It appears that in spite of all the attempts to sell women on housekeeping as a means of life fulfillment it is failing in the middle class. Many women can understand housework as something that has to be done—but not something that will give them any real personal satisfaction. Yet the American system continues to socialize girls to want to grow up to fill the traditional roles. It is difficult to persuade girls during their high school years to look beyond their goals of marriage and a family.

Traditional female roles in the family have been discussed for the middle class. However, there are some sharp differences among women in the lower middle and lower social classes. Most of those women continue to live in a world that is patriarchal—at least when the male is present. For many there is little in marriage that is shared between the husband and wife. For example, Komarovsky found in her study of a working class group that the husband and wife shared little other than the immediate daily tasks and the "impoverishment of life and of personality curtails the development of shared interests."[50] In the sexual realm the great majority of the wives felt that men were more highly sexed than women. And less than a third of the women in her sample expressed high satisfaction with their sexual relations.[51]

In the lowest social class levels frequently the husband participates very little and the wife carries the responsibility for the home and the children largely by herself and seldom participates with her husband in outside activities.[52] As Patricia Sexton writes about the working class wife there is nothing "collective" about her because she is basically unorganized. She is neither a joiner nor a participant. She may be quite religious but is much less likely to attend church regularly than her middle-class counterpart. She is virtually isolated from life outside the confines of her family and neighborhood.[53]

Yet with all the restrictions on the life of lower-class women there does not appear to be a high degree of status frustration among them. They expect to be housewives—that is their reason for being and there is no real alternative. Komarovsky found in her study hardly a trace of the low

---

[49] Harbeson, Gladys E., *Choice and Challenge for the American Woman* (Cambridge, Mass.: Shenkman Publishing Co., 1967), p. 59.

[50] Komarovsky, Mirra, *Blue-Collar Marriage* (New York: Random House, 1962), p. 155.

[51] *Ibid.*, p. 85.

[52] Rainwater, Lee, *Family Design* (Chicago: Aldine Publishing Co., 1965), p. 56.

[53] Sexton, Patricia C., "Wife of the 'Happy Worker,'" in Edwin Schur, *The Family and the Sexual Revolution* (Bloomington, Ind.: Indiana University Press, 1964), p. 274.

prestige that educated housewives attach to that role. Rarely did she find a woman saying, "I am just a housewife." The women did have discontent, but it was not caused by a low evaluation placed on domesticity but rather by normal frustrations of being a housewife.[54] When some of the women did show a dislike for housework they often felt guilty about their dislike of what they saw as the normal female responsibility. "Unlike some college-educated housewives who detest housework, our respondents never say that they are too good for it, that housework is unchallenging manual labor."[55]

MALE-FEMALE DIFFERENCES

Before looking at women in the work force and in occupational careers it is necessary to examine the basic differences between males and females. This is important because so much of the discrimination against the female has been and continues to be rationalized on the grounds of unchangeable, physical differences. The argument here is that almost all significant differences between the sexes can be explained on the basis of differential socialization and that the biological differences have been greatly exaggerated insofar as the differential behavior patterns attributed to them.

It is obvious that men and women are somewhat different as sexual beings and usually perform in complementary ways. However, there is no inherent reason for believing that either sex is dependent on the other for sexual satisfaction. Heterosexuality, as well as homosexuality or solitary sexuality, are adaptations to sexual needs that are made by individuals. The fact that the vast majority of adults prefer heterosexuality as a means of expression is because they have been socialized to do so.

Probably the most important biological difference between the man and woman is the differential reproductive burden. The man is needed only to provide the sperm and he doesn't even have to be present to do that, while the woman in a normal pregnancy and birth must carry the fetus for nine months. In the past the pregnancy period of the woman led to many restrictions being placed on what she could do. However, it seems clear that most women who have no pregnancy complications can work on most jobs with no more than a loss of a week or two for the birth of the child. So there is no reason why many women, if they choose, cannot pursue a career at the same time that they have children. It is common to argue that time off for pregnancy interferes with a career for women. Yet many men must also take time off from a career for illnesses and other reasons and this doesn't usually affect their careers. Or some flexibility could be

---

[54] Komarovsky, op. cit., p. 49.
[55] Ibid., p. 55.

set up to allow women to use vacation time to have children. The point is that there is little that is inherent in the birth experience for women that *necessarily* must restrict them as they have been in the past.

Another common argument for differential treatment of women centers around the fact that the *average* woman is not as strong as the *average* man. That is, she has been excluded from certain jobs because it has been argued that she doesn't have the strength to perform. The range of physical strength among women is as wide as it is among men. This means there are some women who are stronger than some men. Strength, by sex, is not an absolute difference, but a relative one. Many times men are rejected from jobs because they are not strong enough. "For men only" becomes irrelevant, and instead the job requirement should be based on strength to qualify. In that way work would be available to individuals on the basis of abilities, skills, strengths, and motivation regardless of sex. A woman might be turned away from a job because she wasn't strong enough, but some men would also be turned away for the same reason.

It has also been argued that because women do have some physical differences, this results in personality differences based upon their being female. A psychoanalytic view is that there are personality types that represent femininity.[56] Yet there are no personality qualities found in women that are not also found in men. Once again it is a question of relative differences rather than absolute ones. And whatever it means to be a woman is dependent on the socialization experience and what the individual personality brings to bear. Any combination of so-called female personality traits if applied to male and female samples would find them present in some men and absent in many women.

In the United States male and female infants are immediately subjected to different socialization experiences. They are dressed differently and are provided with toys seen as appropriate to their sex. As they grow up social values are often exerted on girls to be more gentle and emotionally demonstrative than boys, but the differential socialization is never total and boys are sometimes reared like girls and vice versa. When that happens the impact of the socialization experience is clear. As they grow up boys and girls learn about their future roles and they quickly learn that the male adult is the adult of greatest prestige and influence. For example, seldom do even educated girls develop a mental picture of a family basking in the glow of the mother's achievement as a scientist or judge unless she is also seen as a good homemaker. No one asks if a male Nobel Prize winner is also a good father. But the headline in a recent article about a female Nobel Prize laureate scientist read, "Grand-

---

[56] Thompson, Clara, "Femininity" in Albert Ellis and Albert Obarbouel, *The Encyclopedia of Sexual Behavior* (New York: Hawthorne Books, 1961), p. 423.

mother Wins Award," as if having grandchildren had some relevance to high professional achievement.[57]

An important part of the assumed difference between males and females has been a part of the American historical heritage. Basically the difference has been intellectualized to be not only inevitable but also desirable. The most powerful intellectual influence has been that of Freud. The propaganda that women should marry early and breed often has prevailed. The psychologists and psychiatrists have replaced clergymen as the authorities. In this century the belief came to be that it was best for a woman to become a mother, not because God said so, but because Freud said so.[58] Freud's view of women was to see them as inferior human beings. The castration complex and penis envy, two ideas basic to his thinking, were based on the belief that women were inferior to men. Freud's view of women reflected the times in which he lived. In his middle-class world there were highly conservative beliefs about the proper roles for men and women in marriage and society. Those views have little validity for the kind of world that exists today. But the Freudian view has continued to be perpetuated. For many years American women have been told through Freudian followers that there can be no greater destiny for women than through their traditional femininity. Women have been told to pity the neurotic, unfeminine, unhappy women who have wanted to be poets or physicians.[59]

Freud's followers have seen women in the same image as he did—as inferior and passive. They have argued that women will only find *real* self fulfillment by affirming their natural inferiority. One of his followers writes that for women there must be a willingness to accept dependence on the male without fear or resentment and that she must not admit of wishes to control or master, to rival or dominate. "The woman who is to find true gratification must love and accept her own womanhood as she loves and accepts her husband's manhood. The woman's unconscious wish to possess the organ upon which she must thus depend militates greatly against her ability to accept its vast power to satisfy her when proffered to her in love."[60]

In recent years both Freudian and some other psychiatric interpretations have lumped the increased employment of women with many social and personal problems. Their working has been linked with increased divorce, more crime and delinquency, and increased alcoholism and schizo-

---

[57] Epstein, *op. cit.*, p. 66.

[58] Sinclair, *op. cit.*, p. 359.

[59] Friedan, *op. cit.*, pp. 15–16.

[60] Lundberg, Ferdinand and Marynia Farnham, "Woman: The Lost Sex," in Edwin Schur, *The Family and the Sexual Revolution* (Bloomington, Ind., Indiana University Press, 1964), p. 230.

phrenia among women.[61] American society has also been inundated with the psychoanalytic viewpoint that believes that any conflict in personal or family life must be treated on the individual level. "This goes with the general American value stress on individualism, and American women have increasingly resorted to psychotherapy, the most highly individualized solution of all, for the answers to the problems they have as women."[62] The psychiatric influence has been such that any problem is seen as individually based rather than socially determined. As a result many women who have felt miserable and unhappy as housewives have defined themselves to be at fault or inadequate, rather than recognize that in many cases they are victims of social situations that cause their problems. All the individual therapy in the world will not change a social situation that is the cause of the problem.

While the Freudian influence in the thinking about keeping the woman in the home has declined in recent years other "intellectual" spokesmen have come along. Both Dr. Spock and Dr. Bettelheim in books and in their advice columns in popular women's magazines argue that women should not be employed during their children's early years. "Thus the mothers not only have difficulty finding good care for their children but they also feel guilty about it."[63] It has only been with the literature of the Woman's Liberation Movement that women are being presented with information that counteracts the traditional views of the woman's place being in the home.

THE WOMAN AND WORK

In one respect the general disregard of the significance of the female in the work force is seen in the fact that women are rarely, if ever, mentioned in the academic literature that deals with work and occupations. When they are considered, it is almost always within the context of the family structure. That is, they are characterized as *still* single, the secondary jobholder in an *organized* family, or the major jobholder in a *disorganized* family.

Women at present are marrying at younger ages than ever, with half of them married by age 20.6, and more of them marry at age 18 than at any other age. But still about nine out of ten women work outside the home at some time during their lives. In general, marriage and the presence of children tend to limit their employment, while widowhood and divorce and the decrease of family responsibility tend to bring them back

[61] Nye, F. Ivan and Lois W. Hoffman, *The Employed Mother in America* (Chicago: Rand McNally and Co., 1963), p. 7.

[62] Rossi, *op. cit.*, p. 613.

[63] Epstein, *op. cit.*, pp. 109–10.

into the work force.[64] The female percentage of the work force has steadily increased over the years. In 1900 only 18 percent of all workers were women, in 1940 it was 25 percent, and in 1968 it had increased to 37 percent.[65] Furthermore, in 1968, 42 percent of all women of working age were in the labor force, and of that group three out of five were married. Put another way, in 1968 37 percent of all married women were in the work force.[66] Among the married women the highest rates of participation in the labor force were where the husband's income did not represent poverty levels, but rather the lower range of middle-income levels. The rate then declined as the husband's income reached higher levels.[67] About two-fifths of all married women and many single women as well were both homemakers and workers. "During an average workweek in 1968, 50 percent of all women were keeping house full time, and about 42 percent were either full- or part-time workers. Most of the remainder were girls 16 to 20 years of age who were in school."[68]

Working mothers with children under 18 years of age represented 38 percent of all mothers in the population and 38 percent of all women workers. Of those mothers who worked (with at least one child under 14 years of age), 46 percent of the children were cared for in their own homes, with 15 percent looked after by their fathers, 21 percent by other relatives, and 9 percent by maids, housekeepers, or babysitters. Another 16 percent of the children were cared for outside their own homes, about half by relatives. Thirteen percent of the children were looked after by their mothers while they worked, and 15 percent had mothers who worked only during school hours. Eight percent of the children were expected to care for themselves, while only 2 percent of the children were in group care, such as day care centers, nursery schools, and after-school centers.[69]

Of great significance about women who work is what they earn relative to the income of men. In 1966, women who were year-round full-time workers had a median income or salary of $3,973, while men had $6,848. Not only is the income of women considerably less than for men, but the gap has been widening in recent years. In 1956, among full-time year-round workers, women earned 63 percent of what men earned. In 1966 they earned only 58 percent of what men earned.[70]

Not only does the working woman earn less than the man for doing the same job but, to compound this area of discrimination, she is also

---

[64] Women's Bureau, *op. cit.*, p. 7.

[65] *Ibid.*, p. 9.

[66] *Ibid.*, p. 3.

[67] *Ibid.*, p. 33

[68] *Ibid.*, p. 12.

[69] *Ibid.*, p. 49.

[70] *Ibid.*, pp. 133–34.

subjected to greater taxes and other working costs. The woman's income is emasculated by the government's refusal to recognize household and child care expenses as essential business deductions. In addition to paying between 20 and 50 percent of her income for domestic help she must also pay income tax on the higher bracket into which her second salary places the family. It is estimated that if a husband earns $10,000 and a wife $5,000 her contribution to the net family income would be only $2,175, and she couldn't afford full-time domestic help with that amount. Or if the husband earns $15,000 and the wife earns $10,000 the wife, after paying for nondeductible domestic help, will add only $650 to the yearly family income.[71]

More specific facts about the American work force and some variables related to women's participation are of interest here. Before the Industrial Revolution most men and women were co-workers on the land and in the home. But the Industrial Revolution removed work for most men from the home and they became both psychologically and physically separated in their work from the home. This same industrial process that separated work from the home for men also provided the opportunities for women to follow men outside the home to work.[72] In one sense the entrance of married women into the work force is a resumption of the part they had played in the past as co-worker with the husband. It should be recognized that the Victorian heritage that a man's work alone should support his family continues to be accepted. When this notion emerged it was a new one in human history—that one sex should support the other entirely.[73]

As mentioned previously, when women began to enter the work force in large numbers the belief developed that their husbands and children were suffering as a result. Nye and Hoffman, in their extensive study of working women, found that there were some problems in the husband-wife relationship associated with the woman's working. This may have been due to the husband's holding to the Victorian view of his being the only family wage earner, and as a result his sense of masculinity was threatened. And it may also have been that some women entered employment because they were dissatisfied with their marital relationship.[74]

Nye and Hoffman found none of the studies they examined showed any meaningful differences between the children of working mothers in general and the children of non-working mothers.[75] Alice Rossi also came to the same conclusion and reports that children of working mothers

[71] Ellis, *op. cit.*, p. 161.
[72] Degler, *op. cit.*, p. 654.
[73] Sinclair, *op. cit.*, p. 356.
[74] Nye and Hoffman, *op. cit.*, p. 385.
[75] *Ibid.*, p. 191.

are no more likely than children of non-working mothers to become delinquent, to show neurotic symptoms, to feel deprived of maternal affection, to perform poorly in school, to lead narrower social lives, etc.[76]

CAREER WOMEN

We now look more directly at women who pursue occupations in the same way as most men, that is, as a potential life work that will be long range for them and to which they will have a commitment. In the past most American women have been interested in jobs and not in careers. This is the primary reason why the United States, with one of the highest proportions of working women in the world, ends up with a very small proportion of its women in such professions as medicine, law, and the sciences. To argue, as many feminists have, that men have opposed and resisted the opening of career opportunities to women is only partially true. The complete truth is that American society in general, including women, has shunned like a disease any feminist ideology directed at high occupational commitment.[77]

An absolute requirement for entering most careers is that the individual have the formal education necessary for qualification. Therefore it is important to look at women in higher education and see how they fare as compared to men. In general, in most families there continues to be a somewhat greater stress on sending the boy to college than the girl. However, once girls enter college their chances of staying in are the same as those of the boy. The college dropout ratio is the same, about four out of ten who enter. However, the reasons for dropping out are different. Boys are more apt to leave school because of academic problems or difficulties in their personal adjustment, while the most common reason for girls' dropping out is to get married.[78]

At the present time just about half of all high school graduates are girls, while in 1900 they represented 60 percent of all high school graduates. The percentage of all bachelor's degrees going to women has been steadily increasing. In 1900 females received only 19 percent but in 1970 it was up to 41 percent.[79] As to higher degrees, there has been little change in the percentage of women receiving masters or doctorates since 1930.[80]

Women have been attracted to specific subject areas for earning their degrees. Jessie Bernard points out that a field like political science, which emphasizes power, attracts or fosters relatively few women, whereas an-

---

[76] Rossi, *op. cit.*, p. 615.

[77] Degler, *op. cit.*, p. 665.

[78] Epstein, *op. cit.*, p. 59.

[79] *Ibid.*, p. 57.

[80] Women's Bureau, *op. cit.*, p. 191.

thropology, "at least where it emphasizes kinship more than kingship, finds much more place for women."[81] Or on the doctorate level, although only 12 percent are earned by women, their share in certain fields has been considerably higher. Women received 20 percent of the doctorates conferred in 1967 in education, in the humanities, and the arts, and 19 percent in psychology. On the other hand, when half of all doctoral degrees conferred in 1967 in the United States were in the basic and applied sciences, the women's share was only 6 percent."[82]

One of the consequences of achieving higher education is a greater interest in entering the work force. Not very many women are going to be satisfied with receiving a higher education and never using it in any occupational way. So the more education that a woman receives, the more likely it is that she will seek employment, irrespective of her financial status. "The educated woman desires to contribute her skills and talents to the economy not only for the financial rewards, but even more to reap the psychic rewards that come from achievement and recognition and service to society."[83] In 1968, 71 percent of all women 18 years of age and over who had completed five years of college or more, and 54 percent of those who had earned a bachelor's degree only were in the work force. The percentage dropped to 48 percent among those who were high school graduates and to 31 percent among those who did not go beyond the eighth grade."[84] A study of 10,000 Vassar alumnae showed that most graduates in the mid-1950's wanted marriage, with or without a career, while in the mid-1960's graduates were strongly insisting on careers—with or without marriage.[85]

What kind of occupations do women enter? Of all the women in the work force a large number of them fall into low skilled clerical jobs. But the women who enter professional careers tend to go into teaching, nursing, social work, and related occupations. These are commonly seen by both men and women as occupations appropriate to the "special" qualities of women. However, the definition of what is appropriate work for men or women changes over time. For example, during the colonial period elementary school teaching was seen as a male occupation, supposedly because women did not have the necessary stamina of mind to educate the young.[86] Or one rarely hears of an American woman dentist, but 75 percent of the dentists of Denmark are women and dentistry is considered to be a female occupation in some South American countries."[87]

---

[81] Bernard, *op. cit.*, p. XX.
[82] Women's Bureau, *op. cit.*, p. 198.
[83] *Ibid.*, p. 9.
[84] *Ibid.*, p. 205.
[85] Ellis, *op. cit.*, p. 8.
[86] Epstein, *op. cit.*, p. 157.
[87] *Ibid.*, p. 158.

The cultural definitions of the professions as linked to one sex or the other are often based on what are believed to be special characteristics of one sex. In illustration, many times women are thought to be good elementary school teachers because as females they are believed to have compassion, sympathy, and feeling for children that men do not have. Or as Epstein points out, in the same way that it has been argued that blacks "have rhythm" and are therefore good jazz musicians so women are said to have "intuition," and a gift for handling interpersonal relations and are therefore encouraged to become social workers.[88] The image of women also includes some noncharacteristics: "lack of aggression, lack of personal involvement and egotism, lack of persistence (unless it be for the benefit of a family member), and lack of ambitious drive."[89] The career woman who is seen as having many of the above characteristics often has been viewed as the antithesis of the feminine woman.

In some occupations consisting of a large proportion of women, men have replaced them in the positions of power and influence. For example, the decline in the percentage of female elementary school principals has been very great. In 1928, 55 percent of the principals were women; in 1948, 41 percent; in 1958, 38 percent; and, in 1968 the figure was reported to have dropped to 22 percent.[90] The belief seems to be that while the woman can be a teacher she is not qualified to administrate the school. In many occupations there appears to be a distinction made which permits women to be the professional field workers, whether it be teachers, social workers or nurses, but when it comes to administration those positions should belong to men. As Epstein points out, "No matter what sphere of work women are hired for or select, like sediment in a wine bottle they seem to settle to the bottom."[91]

Because the career woman, whether married or single, is filling a social role with a great amount of social confusion she is often defined by others in a variety of ways. For example, many housewives see the working woman as a threat to themselves. The career woman is often seen as a competitor for their husbands (the working woman, though deprecated, also seems more glamorous—and often is, because she usually takes care of her appearance and is more interesting). The career also provides an alternative model to the domestic life and may cause the housewife to question her own choice of life style."[92] If the career woman is married and is a mother and gives the appearance of being happy and satisfied with her life she often becomes a severe threat to the woman who has rejected a career and is not very happy with her life.

---

88 *Ibid.*, p. 22.
89 *Ibid.*
90 *Ibid.*, p. 10.
91 *Ibid.*, p. 2.
92 *Ibid.*, p. 120.

Many men react to the career woman with confusion. If the woman is attractive they can't quite cope with her as a nonsexual being. Because so many men are geared to women only as sexual objects they find it very difficult to see them as something more. It is probably also true that most American men are uneasy in the presence of highly intelligent women in a way which they would not be with very intelligent men. But most men probably react to career women as potential threats to themselves and in this sense their opposition is not ideologically based but rather based on vested interest. "Because men typically have more power they suspect and fear encroachment on that power. The situation is, of course, analogous to the fears of whites about retaining job priorities in the face of advancing opportunities for Negroes."[93]

Very often women who choose both marriage and career find their situation to be one where the norms are confused and unclear. There are no clear guidelines for apportioning time and resources between the two major role responsibilities. The ability to handle the roles of wife, mother, and career is still for the most part a matter of individual adaptation. So while fewer career women today are spinsters, among those who marry there is a high rate of divorce. "The proportion of divorced professional women is substantially higher than that of professional men."[94]

Alice Rossi has argued that these problems of different roles can be worked out by what she calls socially androgynous roles for men and women. These would be roles where the two are equal and similar in such spheres as intellectual, artistic, political, and occupational interests and participation. But they would be complementary in only those spheres required by physiological differences between the sexes. "An androgynous conception of sex role means that each sex will cultivate some of the characteristics usually associated with the other in traditional sex role definitions."[95] Rossi goes on to point out that this is one of the points of contrast with the early feminist goals. That is, rather than a one-sided plea for women to adapt a masculine stance in the world, "this definition of sex equality stresses the enlargement of the common ground on which men and women have their lives together by changing the social definition of approved characteristics and behavior of both sexes."[96] This suggestion is based on the assumption that men and women can work out a solution together and that there is no inherent incompatibility between the male and the female that cannot be worked out. However, this is not an assumption that is shared by some of the modern day feminists in the woman's liberation movement.

---

[93] *Ibid.*, pp. 117–18.

[94] *Ibid.*, p. 98.

[95] Rossi, *op. cit.*, p. 608.

[96] *Ibid.*

THE WOMAN'S LIBERATION MOVEMENT

There is a risk in talking about a movement that is emerging because what is happening at a given time can become obsolete a short time later. However, the woman's liberation movement is so important that it should be looked at as it emerges without waiting until it develops further. This movement has a long history and one of the primary purposes of this chapter up until this point has been to provide a background for looking at the contemporary woman's lib movement. Quite simply what the movement wants is complete equality for women, and it wants it fast. This makes its basic aims the same as the black militant movement. The new militant feminism has taken hold in territory that at first glance looks like an unlikely breeding ground for revolutionary ideas: "among urban, white, college educated, middle-class women generally considered to be a rather "privileged lot."[97] As the movement developed in the late 1960's it came out of two primary influences. One was the influence of Betty Friedan's book, *The Feminine Mystique*, published in 1963. The second was the influence on young women of the civil rights and radical left movements.

FRIEDAN'S INFLUENCE

Through the 1950's and into the 1960's there was little in the way of a feminist movement in the United States. During those years no one argued whether or not women were inferior or superior to men; they were simply seen as different. Women during that period were assumed to be happy with being a wife and mother. Given the great influence of psychoanalytic thought it was assumed that if a woman felt frustrated she had a personal problem and if she could work her problem out she could once again be happy doing what women should do. During that period words like "emancipation" and "career" sounded strange and embarrassing; no one had used them for years.[98] It should be remembered that the 1950's were conservative thinking years in American history. It was a period characterized by the political conservatism of McCarthyism, student complacency, and the benevolent paternalism of the Eisenhower years. When Betty Friedan's book appeared it sold in large numbers and brought forth great indignation from the traditional and conservative forces of society.

The major thesis of Friedan's book was that the core of the problem for women was not sexual but rather a problem of personal identity. She

---

[97] Brownmiller, Susan, "Sisterhood Is Powerful," *New York Times*, March 15, 1970, p. 27.

[98] Friedan, *op. cit.*, p. 19.

wrote, "it is my thesis that as the Victorian culture did not permit women to accept or gratify their basic sexual needs, our culture does not permit women to accept or gratify their basic needs to grow and fulfill their potentialities as human beings, a need which is not solely defined by their sexual roles."[99] She went on to say there was growing evidence that woman's failure to develop to complete identity had hampered rather than enriched her sexual fulfillment and this "virtually doomed her to be castrative to her husband and sons, and caused neuroses, or problems as yet unnamed as neuroses, equal to those caused by sexual repression."[100]

Friedan saw the answer to the woman's achievement of a personal identity to be reached through work. She felt that work was the key to the problem because the identity crisis of American women had started a century before, as "more and more of the work that used their human abilities and through which they were able to find self-realization, was taken from them."[101] She goes on to say that one of the first things that women must do is reject the housewife image. "The first step in that plan is to see housework for what it is—not a career, but something that must be done as quickly and efficiently as possible."[102]

In the years following the publication of her book, Betty Friedan was the most influential spokeswoman for the little female rebellion that did exist. The passage of the Civil Rights Act of 1964 made it clear to a number of women that there was a need for a civil rights organization that would speak out for women. In June, 1966, Betty Friedan met with a number of other women and they agreed that an organization would be founded. At that time NOW (National Organization for Women) was founded and its initial purpose was to take action to bring women into full participation in the mainstream of American society and to gain all the privileges and responsibilities that would make them completely equal to men. In August, 1967, NOW organized its first picket line. The members dressed in old-fashioned costumes to protest the old-fashioned policies of the *New York Times* in its male and female help wanted ads. They handed out thousands of leaflets and were for the first time featured on television news and given wide mass media coverage.

The big issues for NOW came to be: (1) the Equal Rights Amendment which has been kicking around Congress since 1923 (this amendment states: "Equality of rights under the law shall not be denied or abridged by the United States or by any state on account of sex)"; (2) abortion law repeal; (3) day-care centers for everyone, and (4) equal em-

---

[99] *Ibid.*, p. 77.
[100] *Ibid.*
[101] *Ibid.*, p. 334.
[102] *Ibid.*, p. 342.

ployment opportunities and equal pay for equal work.[103] The NOW group includes men in its membership so long as they are men concerned about the civil rights of women. However, the more radical groups in the Lib movement do not accept men regardless of whether they are sympathetic to the cause or not.

CIVIL RIGHTS AND THE RADICAL LEFT

The Betty Friedan influence on the woman's liberation movement has had its greatest appeal to older and less radical women. By contrast, many of the younger and more radical women have come out of the civil rights and radical left movements. And some of their terms are a reflection of their past influence. For example, *sexist* is a women's lib term for a male supremist and its similarity to racist is clear. This was inevitable in a movement that drew much of its rhetoric and spirit from the civil rights revolution and that, like America's first feminist movement, evolved out of the effort to liberate blacks.

Yet many of the young women left the other movements because they found that often the men in those groups were as chauvinistic as men in more conservative groups. As "movement women" they were tired of doing the typing and fixing the food while "movement men" did the writing and leading. For example, during the student takeover at Columbia University a call went out for women volunteers to cook for the hungry strikers. One young female revolutionary protested that "women are not fighting the revolution to stay in the kitchen," and the call was amended to ask for *people* to man the kitchen.[104] Many of the movement women were living with or married to movement men who, they believed, were treating them as convenient sex objects or as somewhat lesser beings. This is illustrated in an often quoted statement of Stokeley Carmichael to S.N.C.C. that "the position of women in our movement should be prone." So many of the young radical women felt the men were taking a condescending approach to women's problems while they felt their problems were important and it was up to them to do something about them.

So the radical lib groups are made up of only women, although many of their tactics have been borrowed from the radical left and civil rights groups. It is common in the lib literature to see similarities drawn to the civil rights movement and analogies drawn between the problems of blacks and of women. This, as suggested throughout this chapter, has been a characteristic of the feminist movement in the United States. Morton

---

[103] Ellis, *op. cit.*, pp. 47–8.
[104] Epstein, *op. cit.*, p. 34.

Hunt, in a *Playboy* article, has argued that this analogy is misleading. He says that whites and blacks do not have innate differences that commit them to different roles in education, politics, employment, and so forth. However, men and women can eliminate all role differences "only by ignoring and suppressing a vital part of their inherent natures and by accepting the frustration that results from unmet needs and unfulfilled desires."[105] However, there is no clear evidence of different "inherent natures" and Hunt's arguments in the *Playboy* piece are really those of a male chauvinist, sophisticated, but nevertheless chauvinistic. No one would deny that there is a biological basis for people's being black, but no one argues that it should be treated with a biological solution. In the same sense sex is also a biological fact, but the problem is a social one in the same way as is the problem of race.

There is another way that the radical lib groups are like the militant black groups. Many of the lib women feel that, like the blacks with their Uncle Toms, they are also hampered with an enormous fifth column of women referred to as "Aunt Tabbies" or "Doris Days." Also like the blacks, the militant women are asking that their "hidden history," the study of the feminist movement, be taught in schools and colleges. The intellectuals in the movement are challenging many of the psychologists, sociologists, and anthropologists that have held to the theory that for women their "anatomy is their destiny."[106]

In 1969 and 1970 a wide range of women's lib groups developed. The most conservative is NOW, and the spectrum moves leftward to the highly radical and revolutionary groups. Groups presently in existence besides NOW are FLF (Female Liberation Front), WITCH (Women's International Terrorist Conspiracy from Hell), Redstockings, and so forth. The revolt is growing with rapid speed and "instead of Lucy Stone in bloomers, we have Abby Rockefeller in bare feet, dungarees, and workshirt."[107]

The ultimate goal of the radical groups is revolution. As one radical journal writes, revolution must occur because the condition of female oppression does not "depend on," is not "integrated to," the structure of society; it is the structure. "The oppression of women though similar to that of blacks, differs from it in that it depends not on class division but rather on a division of labor premised on private property and resulting in the family as the primary unit for the function of the economy."[108]

Another radical lib group, the FLM, through their journal, *No More*

---

[105] Hunt, Morton, "Up Against the Wall, Male Chauvinistic Pig," *Playboy*, May, 1970, p. 207.

[106] Ellis, *op. cit.*, pp. 9–10.

[107] *Ibid.*, p. 19.

[108] "I Am Furious (Female)," *Radical Education Project*, Detroit, Michigan (no date), p. 4.

Fun and Games, urges women to leave their husbands and children and to avoid pregnancy. They also want women to dress plain and simple, to cut their hair very short, and to "reclaim themselves" by discarding their husbands' or fathers' names. The journal also urges the women to live alone and to abstain from sexual relations. The FLM women refrain from wearing makeup—though Chap Stick and hand lotion (for karate callouses) are allowed.[109]

All of the lib groups see the present conjugal family structure with its traditional division of labor as destructive to full female identity. Much of the focus has been on trying to alleviate the burdens of housework and get help through free collective child care. The more radical groups such as the FLM have contempt for the family. Roxanne Dunbar, a leader of that group writes: "The family is what destroys people. Women take on a slave role in the family when they have children. People have awful relationships. It's a trap, because you can't support it without a lot of money."[110] Another spokesman writes that marriage, which is made to seem attractive and inevitable, is a trap for female children as well as mothers. "Most women do not grow up to see themselves as producers, as creators—instead they see their mothers, their sisters, their women teachers, and they pattern themselves after them. They do not see women making history."[111] Still another spokeswoman, Ti-Grace Atkinson, said at a conference of the women's lib in New York City that the prostitute is the only honest woman left in America. According to Atkinson prostitutes are the only honest women because they charge for their services rather than submit to a marriage contract which forces them to work for life without pay.[112]

It seems clear that for most groups in the women's liberation movement marriage is a clear definition of a relationship making the woman subservient and secondary. The possible solutions for this can range from ending marriage to modifying it. But what is most important is the belief that marriage implies a secondary status for women. It is clear that many men as well as women believe that a woman in marriage is a second class citizen. For example, in the recent article on the Women's Lib Movement in *Playboy,* Morton Hunt wrote that for the American woman today and in the foreseeable future the most workable answer—"the scheme of life that most nearly fits her own needs and those of the American man—is a combination of marriage and career in which she accepts a secondary part in the world of work and achievement in order to have

---

[109] Ellis, *op. cit.,* p. 54.

[110] *Ibid.,* pp. 54–5.

[111] Limpus, Laurel, *Sexual Repression and the Family* (Boston: New England Free Press, 1970), p. 65.

[112] *Philadelphia Bulletin,* May 29, 1970, p. 2.

a primary part in the world of love and home."[113] This statement is a good example of the kind of male thinking that women's liberations groups of all types are fighting against.

Another role activity which many of the lib women object to is that of motherhood. They rebel against the belief that childbearing and the rearing of children is the fulfillment of a woman's destiny. Limpus writes that this belief is by far the most damaging and destructive myth that imprisons women. Having children is no substitute for creating one's own life, for producing. And since so many women in this culture devote themselves to nothing else, they end up becoming intolerable burdens upon their children, because in fact these children are their whole lives.[114] The women are objecting to the fact that not only is there a mystique about parenthood but that the mystique really equates motherhood with parenthood. People frequently say how important a father is to his children but the empirical evidence shows that when there is no father the children suffer no more psychological problems than when the father is present. However, no one has ever studied those families where there is no mother present and the children are reared by the father. It may be that those children are not significantly different from those reared with a mother.

It is not that most lib groups are opposed to women having children if they so desire. What they object to is the woman's being required to fill the mother role and care for the children. The lib women insist that society should take care of the children. They argue that childcare centers are needed not just for women at the poverty level, but should be put at the disposal of all working women and to be used the same as any other public facility, such as a museum, library, or park. At the present time the United States is the only industrialized country which does not provide childcare services. There are close to four million children in the United States who need supervision while their mothers work and the present facilities can handle less than half a million.

Because most lib groups see themselves as women who have been sexually exploited by men there is a great deal of concern with sexual participation with men and what it means. Yet, in the areas of male-female interaction women have in recent years felt freer to speak of their rights in the sexual sphere than in the social sphere. And as suggested earlier, sexual rights for the woman have been gained and women increasingly have the means of sexual equality. In fact the right of women to sexual equality is now established and even treated as acceptable in the mass media. For example, such conservative national women's pub-

---

[113] Hunt, *op. cit.*, p. 209.

[114] Limpus, *op. cit.*, p. 66.

lications as *Ladies' Home Journal* and *McCall's* carry articles almost every month dealing with some aspects of sex in detailed clarity.[115]

However, the objection that many liberation women have to sex is how it is used as a means of manipulating both men and women by various agencies in society. Much of the resentment results from women feeling they are being treated by men as sexual objects. "Fashion, advertising, movies, *Playboy* magazine, all betray the fact that women are culturally conceived of as objects, and still worse, often accept this definition and try to make themselves into a more desirable commodity on the sexual market."[116] The objection is not that females or males make themselves sexually attractive, but rather that the mass media focus on the sexual attractiveness of the woman and do not present her as a human being.

One writer for the lib movement, a female sociologist, sees the problem of sexuality as a dual one. When she speaks of female liberation she refers to liberation from the myths that have enslaved women in their own minds as well as in the minds of others. "Men and women are mutually oppressed by a culture and a heritage that mutilates the relationships possible between them."[117] She further suggests that the problem of sexuality illustrates that men and women are oppressed together. She argues that women shouldn't become obsessed with freeing themselves from sick male sexuality, but rather, that it is more important for both males and females to free themselves from structures that make them sexually sick. "The male definition of virility which makes women an object of prey is just as much a mutilation of the human potential of the male for the true love relationship as it is the female's."[118] Limpus goes on to say that even though it is the female who experiences the predatory attitude, she as a woman also contributes to it. "We must both be liberated together, and we must understand the extent to which our fear and frigidity, which had been inculcated in most of us from infancy onwards and against which most of us have had to struggle for our sexual liberation, has hurt and mutilated them."[119]

Limpus further points out that the socialization to female sexual repression is so strong that even most highly liberated women cannot completely shake their earlier restrictive sexual training. She observes that even in supposedly radical circles girls can still be labelled "promiscuous." "There are tremendous residual moral condemnations of female

---

[115] Epstein, *op. cit.*, p. 37.
[116] Limpus, *op. cit.*, p. 70.
[117] *Ibid.*, p. 61.
[118] *Ibid.*, p. 67.
[119] *Ibid.*, p. 68.

sexuality in all of us, in spite of our radical rhetoric. A woman, even a relatively sexually liberated one, often finds it hard to approach a man sexually the way a man can approach her."[120]

Probably the most publicized and most important statement about sexual expression made in the women's lib movement was by Anne Koedt called "The Myth of the Vaginal Orgasm." She points out that frigidity has usually been defined by men to mean that women have failed to have a vaginal orgasm. The myth of the vaginal orgasm has primarily been perpetuated by psychoanalysts. In actual fact the vagina is not a highly sensitive area and is not physiologically constructed to achieve orgasm. All physiologically based orgasms in the female come from the clitoris. Koedt points out that men have orgasms primarily through friction of the penis in the vagina, not with the clitoris. "Women have thus been defined sexually in terms of what pleases men; our own biology has not been properly analyzed. Instead we have been fed a myth of the liberated woman and her vaginal orgasm, an orgasm which in fact does not exist."[121] She goes on to say that women must redefine their sexuality and discard the "normal" concepts of sex and establish new guidelines. "We must begin to demand that if a certain sexual position or technique now defined as 'standard' is not mutually conducive to orgasm, then it should no longer be defined as standard."[122] It is also important that from Freud on it has been men who have defined the standards of sexual satisfaction and adjustment for women. Actually the "vaginal orgasm" has been a part of the overall view of many followers of Freud related to the belief in the inferiority of women. The myth of the physical vaginal orgasm is recognized by most sexual authorities today.

The women's liberation movement, like that of the militant black, the militant college student, and the hippie, has been greatly influenced by television. If a group of women interested in the lib movement meet and carry on their session without theatrics they are not covered by the mass media. As a result many people believe that the women's lib movement is made up of nothing more than far-out, deviant types of women. In one sense there develops a reaction against a kind of caricature of the movement. So a common reaction is not to take the movement seriously and to respond with ridicule—which has been the reaction to feminists for decades. However, some men have begun to react to the lib movement with anger and many members are expecting an increased blacklash from men and women.

Women often have reacted to the lib movement with confusion and hostility. What they hear goes contrary to their socialization experiences

---

[120] *Ibid.*, p. 69.
[121] Brownmiller, *op. cit.*, p. 130.
[122] *Ibid.*

as females. Women are often their own worst enemies and are willing to attack one another in ways that men will not do to each other. Women everywhere refer to female "cattiness" and disloyalty. "They claim to dislike other women, assert they prefer to work for men, and profess to find female gatherings repugnant. This set of attitudes constitutes a barrier to women's aiming high in the occupational world."[123] There are also many women who have established careers in male dominated fields who are resentful of the lib movement because their individual success gives them a sense of superiority over other women. Some of these women say they encounter no discrimination. It may be that the men who work with them, as with blacks, show respect to indicate that they are not prejudiced. Many organizations not only have token blacks but also have token women in their employment.

But probably the most hostile reaction to the women's lib movement comes from the many women who have spent a good part of their adult years doing the things that lib women are saying are demeaning and valueless. To a great extent the hostility is a generational one. The middle aged woman who has spent her adult years as a wife, mother, and housekeeper is very threatened by the young woman who tells her that her life has been empty and she is a victim of male viciousness. For her to admit that the lib women may be right is to admit that her life has been a charade. So one can predict increasing resistance and hostility from the majority of American women who are wives, mothers, and housewives.

There is a great deal of disagreement among the various factions of the women's liberation movement on what they want, but most of them want gender difference to become secondary to human equality. That is, all persons are human beings first and male or female second, but what is often overlooked is that full equality may mean equality in areas that are not always desirable. As women have achieved greater equality to men in the United States their rates of alcoholism, drug addiction, and so on have increased. But many women are quite willing to accept these negative possibilities along with the more desirable ones.

It may also be that many women have an idealized image of the freedom of some men, because the only really independent people are those with no interpersonal relationships at all. Yet this is not something that very many persons want. And many of the women in the lib movement who reject husbands and family turn to each other to meet their interpersonal needs. One writer suggests that few of the women she met in the lib movement accepted the notion that life itself was unfair. "Most of them cherish an apocalytic conviction that a society that assumed the drudgery of child-rearing would free women."[124] The question is, to free

---

[123] Epstein, op. cit., p. 125.

[124] Newsweek November 29, 1969, p. 76.

women for what? To fill the jobs that men now fill and often hate? Very few men could be described as creating their own histories by transcending themselves.[125] Many women believe that the fight for total sexual equality is the issue and if it is achieved and women find themselves along with men in undesirable life patterns then the fight can be made for overall human betterment.

BIBLIOGRAPHY

BERNARD, JESSIE, *Academic Women* (University Park, Penna.: The Pennsylvania State University Press, 1964).

BROWNMILLER, SUSAN, "Sisterhood is Powerful," *New York Times*, March 15, 1970, pp. 27–28, 30, 132, 134, 136, 140.

DEGLER, CARL N., "Revolution without Ideology: The Changing Place of Women in America," *Daedalus*, Fall, 1964, pp. 653–70.

ELLIS, JULIE, *Revolt of the Second Sex* (New York: Lancer Books, 1970).

EPSTEIN, CYNTHIA F., *Women's Place* (Berkeley, Calif.: University of California Press, 1970).

FRIEDAN, BETTY, *The Feminine Mystique* (New York: W. W. Norton and Co., Inc., 1963).

LIMPUS, LAUREL, *Sexual Repression and the Family* (Boston: New England Free Press, 1970).

ROSSI, ALICE S., "Equality between the Sexes: An Immodest Proposal," *Daedalus*, Spring, 1964, pp. 607–52.

SINCLAIR, ANDREW, *The Emancipation of the American Woman* (New York: Harper and Brothers, 1965).

WOMEN'S BUREAU, *1969 Handbook of Women Workers*, Bulletin 294 (Washington, D.C.: United States Department of Labor, 1969).

---

[125] Limpus, *op. cit.*, pp. 62–3.

CHAPTER 15

MILITANT STUDENTS

THE DEVIANCE of college students before the 1960's was relatively trivial and the concern minimal. Whatever concern there was developed when students misbehaved at football games or staged "panty raids." And generally their misbehavior was attributed to the inevitable pranks played by college students. But almost overnight, during the 1960's, the behavior of the silent generation of the 1950's drastically changed. No one during the 1950's had any idea of what would happen in the colleges during the 1960's. The militant student of the 1960's and on into the 1970's has had tremendously important social consequences. Not only has he significantly influenced higher education, but he has also been the key force in the developing generational conflict now common to the United States. In fact, the militant college student symbolizes for many older Americans all that they believe to be wrong with youth in America. The student is defined as a deviant who goes against the norms and the laws of society and fails to show respect for the traditional institutions of American society. In this and the following chapter on the hippie movement one can see in detail a theme characteristic of a number of the areas of social deviance and social problems discussed in this book—generational conflict. The first section of this chapter is a brief examination of the historical background of the college student in America.

HISTORICAL CONTEXT

During the first century and a half of the United States, going to college was something restricted to a small, elite group of young people.

Most of them went to college to learn to be gentlemen and to prepare for certain professions. They studied the classics, law, medicine, and so forth. It was not until later years that the sciences came into the curriculum, and much later the social sciences, business, and education became a part of university programs. During those early years some conflict and violence did appear on some college campuses. "Dormitory life in nineteenth century America was marked by violence, rough and undisciplined actions, and outbreaks of protest against the rules and regulations through which faculties and administrations attempted to govern students."[1] But this kind of rebellion was internal to the campus situation and was not usually directed outward to broader social issues.

At the beginning of the present century, approximately 1 percent of those of college age in the United States were attending academic institutions. By 1939 the figure had grown to 15 percent. But in the years following World War II the American university came to be a national institution, so that in 1970 about half of all persons in the college age range were attending institutions of higher learning. (This is in contrast with about 10 percent in European countries.) The figure may reach 70 percent in the 1980's. So one important factor related to the development of student militancy is that there are more students in more different schools, and most of the schools have grown in size.

It was during the 1930's that the first large number of militant university students emerged. That was the time of the great economic depression and people seriously questioned whether the American economic system would be able to survive. The militant students of that period were concerned with survival in a society where many were starving to death and the traditional institutions were inadequate. Therefore, most of the radicals of that time were interested in the political beliefs of socialism and communism. There are two important points with reference to the militant students of the 1930's and the 1960's. One is that many of the militants of the 1960's had parents who were the militants of the 1930's. Second, Lipset suggests that more attention is being focused on the American student movement at present than occurred during the 1930's, even though the movement was large in the thirties.[2]

During the late 1930's and into the 1940's the United States pulled out of the depression and entered World War II. Those events resulted in most persons, including college students, believing that the economic system could work, and also unified the country against a common enemy. This period saw "a widely revered president and an enemy who symbolized

---

[1] Skolnick, Jerome K., *The Politics of Protest* (New York: Ballantine Books, 1969), p. 87.

[2] Lipset, Seymour M., "Students and Politics," in Edward C. McDonagh and Ian E. Simpson, *Social Problems: Persistent Challenges* (New York: Holt, Rinehart and Winston, Inc., 1965), p. 195.

absolute evil" and this "was to affirm the United States as the ethical center of the universe for American liberals."[3]

Following World War II the colleges and universities of the United States underwent the most dramatic change in their history because of the G.I. Bill of Rights, which subsidized the education of millions of service veterans. This had the general effect of democratizing colleges by sending them students from social backgrounds that never before attended colleges. It also introduced the phenomenon of combining marriage and going to college that has continued to be common. The veteran influence also did away with many of the rituals and traditions of various colleges. However, the post-World War II period was not a period of student dissent. The attitude of most veterans was that they had given up a number of years of their lives for the war and they wanted to get their education over as fast as possible and get on with the business of earning a living. This period was the beginning of the great expansion of higher education in the United States.

The early 1950's was a period of isolation, guilt, and fear for many Americans. For many intellectuals during that period "the domestic failings such as racial injustice and McCarthyism were overshadowed by the dismal realities of life behind the Iron Curtain, and especially Khrushchev's validation of the crimes of the Stalin era."[4] In the 1950's the dissidents usually ignored poverty and racial injustice in the United States. The alienated youth of that period was a "rebel without a cause." "His cultural heroes were apt to be 'beats' like Jack Kerouac; if he was intellectually inclined, he drifted to existential writers like Jean-Paul Sartre, whose basic message was the meaninglessness of human existence."[5] During the 1950's there was a common theme for commencement speakers to present and that was to decry the silence and apathy of college students in the face of urgent national and international issues. And it should be remembered that to many Americans the "silent generation" of the 1950's was as much a concern then as the "active generation" is now. But it should be stressed that the student activism of the 1960's appears to be of unprecedented quantity and quality and "compared to earlier activism . . . involves more students and engages them more continuously, is more widely distributed on campuses throughout the country, is more militant, is more hostile to established authority and institutions (including radical political organization), and has been more sustained."[6]

The first major influence on student militarism occurred in February

---

[3] Skolnick, Jerome K., "The Generation Gap," *Trans-Action*, November, 1968, p. 4.
[4] *Ibid.*

[5] Seligman, Daniel, "A Special Kind of Rebellion," in *Youth in Turmoil* (New York: Time-Life Books, 1969), pp. 18–19.

[6] Skolnick, *The Politics of Protest, op. cit.*, p. 87.

of 1960. At that time black students began to attack segregation in public facilities by "sitting in" at segregated southern dime-store lunch counters; and Northern students supported those demands by picketing and boycotting northern branches of those stores. "The success of the southern students' sit-ins led to the formation of the Student Nonviolent Coordinating Committee (SNCC). Northern white student groups formalized their organizations to support the southern movement."[7] By the latter part of 1961 some students were using the civil rights techniques of nonviolent direct action—marches, vigils, and picketing—to protest some parts of American foreign policy. During the early 1960's the thrust of the militant student movement was toward the reform of society rather than of the university. During that period the university was seen as neutral and even a positively valued base of operations. "For many student activists, the university represented a qualitatively different kind of social institution, one in which radical social criticism could be generated and constructive social change promoted."[8]

It was in 1964 that the first major, far-reaching event in the development of the student militancy movement occurred—that was the Berkeley protests. Not long after classes started in the fall of 1964 that campus was hit by a series of protest demonstrations which reached a peak in December with a large sit-in at the administration building that led to many arrests and a student strike. "The Free Speech Movement began, conventionally enough, over suddenly imposed restrictions on students who used the campus to support or advocate off-campus political or social action."[9] That movement had a great significance because through wide publicity it demonstrated the feasibility of involving large numbers of students in overt actions on campus issues.

As indicated, before the Berkeley free speech movement most student activists had viewed campus issues as unimportant when compared to the important issues of the day—especially that of civil rights. Up until that time the only way that a white student could show his commitment to social change was to move off the campus, but the Berkeley events made the campus a legitimate battleground. The great publicity attached to Berkeley showed militant students everywhere that what happens on a campus can matter nationally and even internationally. As Skolnick concludes in his study, the free press movement at Berkeley in 1964 marked the turning point in the American student movement. "The Berkeley uprising gave the student movement a new prominence and evoked a new interest among students and others in university reform and educational innovation."[10] By the following year, in 1965, "student

---

[7] *Ibid.*, p. 89.

[8] *Ibid.*, pp. 90–91.

[9] *Ibid.*, p. 93.

[10] *Ibid.*, p. 94.

left" organizations were found on 25 percent of American campuses and by the end of the 1960's on over 50 percent of the campuses.

The pattern of student protests that followed Berkeley was that of increased numbers occurring most often during the spring months, near the end of the academic year. In many parts of the country this has been due to the warmer weather's allowing the students more freedom to move around. It is also because issues usually develop over the academic year and take months to reach the point of action. This often means that student rebellion is limited to a month or so before the end of the school year. Many times delaying tactics are used by administrations with the knowledge that the school year will end and the students (as well as many of the faculty) will be leaving the campus. Many of the issues of student militancy up until 1968 were local campus issues, although there were also some common themes that cut across campuses, for example, opposition to the Vietnam War, to ROTC, to military research on campus, and so forth. During the first half of the 1967–68 academic year there were 71 separate demonstrations on 62 campuses. By the second half of the year, the number had risen to 221 demonstrations at 101 schools.[11]

The major event of student militancy in 1968 was that which took place at Columbia University. Confrontations on many campuses across the country had been becoming increasingly militant. They were coming to be more than just demonstrations for demands—they were also a show of power. The turning point came with the rebellion of Columbia University in the spring of 1968 when students occupied five university buildings for a week and caused the university to suspend normal operations for the remainder of the semester. There had been campus buildings occupied before Columbia but the assumption had been that when that occurred the causes were related to the particular institution. "With the rising of the slogan 'Two, Three, many Columbias' the similarities of the revolts—the causes, the demands, the mood of students everywhere—are widely recognized."[12]

Certain common characteristics are the occupation of buildings, the greater involvement of community people, fighting the police and national guard, and often a student reluctance to negotiate. "This last has had the anticipated effect of genuine confrontation—that is, the power of the students versus the power of the trustees."[13] Because there has been a similarity and a pattern to many of the activist activities since 1968, this has led to the notion by some that they are nationally coordinated and organized. However, there appears to be little evidence that this is true. While one might argue that the SDS (Students for a

---

[11] *Ibid.*, p. 79.

[12] Grant, Joanne, *Confrontations on Campus: The Columbia Pattern for the New Protest* (New York: A Signet Book, 1969), p. ix.

[13] *Ibid.*, p. ix.

Democratic Society) is involved in many of these activities it is questionable how significant they are—in other words most of the events would have occurred without the SDS. But a conspiracy theory of student riots is tempting for many people because it simplifies and suggests that the students are victims of some insidious outside force. This then distracts from dealing with the questions the students raise and shifts the focus to how they have been manipulated. In the 1950's the Communist party in the United States was seen by many to be behind any critical questioning of the American system, but the late 1960's saw it replaced by the SDS as the bogeyman of all student political deviancy.

The end of the 1960's saw a stiffening of resistance toward the student militants. For example, the early months of 1969 were characterized by a hardening of official response to student protest on many campuses, as "evidenced by the presence of bayonet-wielding National Guard troops at the University of Wisconsin and the declaration of a 'state of extreme emergency' at Berkeley."[14] 1970 saw a developing of more students involved in protest, especially with the Vietnam War and their feeling that President Nixon and his administration had no interest in them and their interests. In 1970 the rallying cries around student participation in curriculum planning and the appointment of faculty were pretty much put aside and the year's turmoil focused mainly on national issues—primarily the war and the internal repression, exemplified to many students by government treatment of the Black Panther Party. 1970 saw the university, as never before, involved in the society around it.

The social concern during the spring of 1970 was shown in the large number of colleges that in effect shut down early, and in many cases eliminated final exams for that semester. This came about as a result of the Cambodian invasion which polarized student sentiment against the war. This resulted in many student protests, one of which led to the death of four Kent State University students who were killed by the Ohio National Guard. This event appeared to polarize the American people even further along social class and generational lines. The polls after the Kent State killings found that an overwhelming majority of Americans believed that the students were essentially responsible for their own deaths. That is, if they had not been protesting, the shootings would not have happened.

Out of the 1960's there developed several major themes or concerns among a number of university students. One was with civil justice, which was primarily focused around civil rights. Two was a desire for more humanization and personalization in international relations. This was expressed in the opposition to the American position in Vietnam and by the initial endorsement of the Peace Corps with its early stress on inter-

---

[14] Skolnick, *op. cit.*, p. 79.

personal relations. Three was with the modernization of the university and its having a more significant relationship to the rest of society. Fourth, cutting across the other three, was an emphasis on individual freedom and self-determination in many actions.[15]

The student activism that emerged late in the 1960's was not restricted to the United States but was found in many countries of the Western world. Many nations have a long history of student involvement in militant political revolution. And in some countries the university is a recognized sanctuary even during a revolution. However, with a few exceptions, in Europe students had not been active in revolts or revolutions in many years. It should also be recognized that student idealism has not always been radical and revolutionary. For example, students were very active in the right-wing movements of the 1930's that led to the rise of fascism in western Europe.

Skolnick has observed that even when student rebellion is directed to the end of progress and change the students do not always express an autonomous rebellion against the larger society. An example was the Czechoslovakian student movement of the late 1960's which was linked to liberalizing movements in that country rather than to any distinct student radicalism.[16] Historically, revolutionary student movements have been mainly a feature of transitional societies. Thus, student revolutionary activity was a constant part of Russian life during the 19th century. The communist movements in China and Vietnam grew out of militant student movements. And in Latin America, student movements have been politically crucial since the early part of this century.[17]

Skolnick also points out that of all the new student movements, that found among the white American students has the least resemblance in its origins to the classical model. By contrast the French student movement resembles the classical model in that it is a part of a call for modernization, and a rebellion "against traditional culture and the archaic forms of authoritarianism that still pervade French society and the organization of its universities."[18] This is also why the student revolution in France in the spring of 1968 was closer to being a total revolution than those that occurred in any other country.

There were not only common themes found in the student militancy in the various countries but also interaction between various student leaders from some of the countries. So there has been cross-cultural fertilization and mutual inspiration in recent campus uprisings. Whatever simi-

---

[15] Shoben, Edward J., "Thoughts on the Decay of Morals," in G. Kerry Smith, *Stress and Campus Response* (San Francisco, Jossey-Bass, Inc., 1968), p. 136.

[16] Skolnick, *op. cit.*, p. 82.

[17] *Ibid.*, pp. 82–3.

[18] *Ibid.*, p. 85.

larity there is between student movements around the world the movements are neither completely spontaneous nor centrally coordinated. But whatever the extent of contacts, the number of student demonstrations in various countries reached its peak in 1968. At that time demonstrations and strikes paralyzed universities in nations as far apart, geographically and culturally, as Japan, France, Mexico, West Germany, Czechoslovakia, Italy, and Brazil.[19] The writer spent the spring semester of 1968 in England and talked to English university students who were quite apologetic because they were not demonstrating when the students in so many countries were.

AMERICAN UNIVERSITIES

It is possible to make only a few general remarks about the types and structures found in American higher education today. Colleges and universities vary greatly in size, degree of freedom, and caliber of faculty and students. For the most part student militancy has been found in the large university of high academic prestige. In this section the concern is with the university in general and a brief look at administrations, faculty, and student bodies. This will provide background for a more detailed examination of militant university students.

The trend in America is to the larger and larger university, and this has a direct relationship to student militancy. Large schools lead to those structures and social features which have come to describe the complex "multiversity." Scott found that school size was the most consistent predictor of student demonstrations. "After size, complexity was second; quality was third and the size of the community was fourth."[20] With the increased pressure due to continue through the 1970's many universities will continue to grow in size. However, many colleges cannot grow much larger without losing their identity, and some have already reached the utilitarian limit in size. There is the belief among many experts that by 1980 higher education will be mainly found in very large institutions in the large metropolitan areas of the United States.

With the limits that seem inherent in expanding the big universities there was a move in the 1960's to assume part of the burden through the rapidly developing junior and community colleges, which by 1970 were more than a thousand in number with over two million students. But those colleges are limited—the student who wants a baccalaureate degree must transfer after two years to a four year college. Often the community college starts out with the idea of giving both academic and applied sub-

---

[19] *Ibid.*, p. 81.

[20] Scott, Joseph W. and Mohamed El-Assal, "Multiversity, University Size, University Quality and Student Protest: An Empirical Study," *American Sociological Review,* October, 1969, p. 707.

jects to its students. But very often many applied courses are dropped as many of the colleges quickly aspire to becoming four year, academic colleges that will give the baccalaureate degree. With a very few exceptions these types of colleges have not been active in student militancy. This, of course, makes them attractive to some people in the community who don't want militant students in their local colleges.

The university is a big business operation. The expenditures for higher education went from $4.5 billion in 1956–57 to $13.2 billion in 1966–67 and is expected to reach $25.3 billion by 1976–77. There are approximately 2,200 institutions of higher education and they employ about half a million people to teach and hold about seven million students. Most colleges and universities are supported by tax money on the local, state, and federal levels. They also depend on endowments, tuition, and various kinds of investment returns. In general the older and most prestigeful colleges such as Wesleyan or universities such as Yale have huge endowments. But the wealthy schools also usually have high tuition rates and many of them receive tax money through a variety of procedures.

Often federal money goes to universities for research and development, but this money goes for the most part to only a few institutions. A congressional study in 1964 found that of the 2,100 universities in the United States, ten of them received 38 percent of the federal funds for research and development. (They were the University of California, MIT, Cornell, Columbia, University of Michigan, Harvard, Illinois, Stanford, Chicago, and Minnesota.) That money often accounted for a large part of the universities' total budgets. "Thus, 80 percent of MIT's funds are estimated to come from the government. Columbia and Princeton get about 50 percent of their money from Washington."[21] But in 1970 many of those schools had to make drastic adjustments to the withdrawal of federal money. Many of the subsidized programs of the 1960's were in the physical sciences and they resulted in the producing of many new Ph.D.'s. Added to this was the introduction of Ph.D. programs in many colleges that never had them before. The number of new Ph.D.'s together with a severe cutback in positions available to them have combined to create something of a crisis in the university. It is an irony that the most prestigeful and wanted new Ph.D. in the 1960's, the theoretical physicist, had a difficult time finding a job in 1971.

Some universities also earn money from consumer products, or at least from the royalties that go with products. For example, Indiana University holds the patents to Crest toothpaste and Rutgers University makes millions in royalties from patents it holds on streptomycin.[22] Furthermore, many of the wealthier universities make money on their

---

[21] Ridgeway, James, *The Closed Corporation: American Universities in Crisis* (New York: Ballantine Books, 1968), p. 5.

[22] *Ibid.*, p. 82.

investments. This led to a new confrontation with some universities in 1970. Namely, if they were holders of large blocks of stocks in various corporations why did they unquestioningly go along with the management decisions of those corporations? In other words, why didn't the colleges as major stockholders try to influence some of the courses of action that corporations were taking? This will probably become an increasing area of student pressure in the 1970's.

When a university takes research money from government or industry or when it is a stockholder in large corporations, many students (and faculty) feel these involvements are rightfully a concern to them. It therefore seems doubtful that there will be any great reduction of conflict as long as universities continue their commitment to supplying research in politically contested areas. This is especially true in the case of war-related government research.[23] Because of student pressure many universities are ending their commitments in these areas.

Basically, the traditional assumption of the university as a neutral institution is being subjected to serious questioning. Neutrality may have described the pretensions of the university rather than its actual uses even in the past. The university is not and cannot be neutral if that means not to be of service to any special social interests. And the university is not neutral in the sense of being equally of service to all legitimate social interests. "In our time, the university is an important cultural and economic resource; it is also much more fully in the service of some social interests than others. The provision of defense research, for example, necessarily aligns the university with the course of national foreign policy and military strategy."[24] As Birenbaum points out, given the "multimillion dollar budgets, extensive real-estate holdings, and future property needs, pretensions about and real connections to the national purposes and welfare, the universities must confront changing views about their institutional responsibilities."[25]

In the past it has been common to describe the university as a community; this often meant a community in the geographical sense and also a community of common ideals and ideas. In their day-to-day operations many universities are communities in providing for their members a kind of welfare state. For example, there is the feeding and housing of students, the regulating of many of their relationships and providing them with medicare programs of their own. "And along with parking lots are athletics and other systems for influencing and shaping the cultural and social lives of those who live there. The more detached and isolated a university campus is from the city, the greater is its need to construct and

---

[23] Skolnick, *op. cit.*, p. 121.

[24] *Ibid.*, p. 114.

[25] Birenbaum, William M., *Overlive: Power, Poverty and the University* (New York: Delta Publishing Co., 1969), p. 39.

maintain the total paraphernalia of a going community."[26] However, when community is used to refer to common interests and values the argument may be made that the university barely resembles a community. Skolnick argues that given that fragmentation of interests, "the university is unable to deal effectively with conflict, whether internal or external; it has been unable to develop new modes of governance in line with its increased and disparate commitments."[27]

One major reason for not talking about the university as a community of common ideas is that there is little that faculties and administration share in common. So the application of the notion of community appears most appropriate to what have been the patterns of control over the lives of the students. The rules on college campuses have been traditionally expressed negatively. Many of the rules are still based on those original prohibitions to protect the student from the temptations of city life. "They seldom state what the people can do, but they elaborately spell out what is *verboten* regarding the consumption of liquor, sex relationships, political activity, etc."[28] Many of these restrictive rules are rapidly being eliminated in a large number of schools.

But what continues to be important about university communities is that they are highly segregated. The style of campus life works against intellectual or social interaction among different people of different ages. The young are with their age peers, as are the older. The grouping of faculty offices by academic disciplines and the disciplines according to the colleges they are a part of discourages communication among people on the faculty. Probably in every faculty dining room in every college there are specific tables where people from English sit and others where the physics faculty eat and so forth. And most faculty move in and out of the community because they don't usually live on the campus and only spend certain hours of certain days there. Birenbaum suggests that the whole campus is wrapped in the principle of separateness and detachment. "A principle designed to impress upon those subject to it an appreciation for their differentness, and upon the public beyond a respect for the alleged objectivity, neutrality, and elite quality of the academic 'community.' "[29] The next section examines more specifically the three major groups that make up the university.

ADMINISTRATION

This refers to all of those who are concerned with the operating policies and day-to-day running of the university. At the top of the power hierarchy

---

[26] *Ibid.*, p. 36.
[27] Skolnick, *op. cit.*, p. 115.
[28] Birenbaum, *op. cit.*, p. 46.
[29] *Ibid.*, p. 37.

is the board of trustees. These are people who are responsible for the general policies and the major decisions that give direction to a university. Very often trustees are indifferent to academic values and are frequently uninformed about issues and problems in higher education. Trustees tend to feel that it is inappropriate for students and faculty to have decision-making power in important academic issues. The average trustee is in his fifties, and almost always white. Over half have yearly incomes of more than $30,000 and over one-third are business executives.[30] In the same study of trustees over two-thirds advocated the screening of campus speakers and over one-third felt it was reasonable to require loyalty oaths from faculty. In the same study 27 percent disagreed with the statement that "faculty members have a right to free expression of opinions." It was further found that "70 percent of the trustees surveyed believed that students and faculties should not have major authority in choosing a university president; 64 percent felt that students and faculty should not have major authority on tenure decisions; 63 percent felt students and faculty should not have major authority in appointing an academic dean."[31]

It is often difficult to get any clear understanding of the university because it remains essentially a secret organization in its operations. As Ridgeway points out, one can find out more about the activities of a public corporation than about a university. "The trustees of universities are invariably self-perpetuating bodies of businessmen who meet in private and do not publish accounts of their activities. In public institutions, where there are more apt to be periodic open meetings of the regents and trustees who are elected or appointed by the state governor, the real business goes on behind the scenes in executive sessions, and the minutes of these backroom deals are either nonexistent or never made public."[32]

It is with reference to trustees that serious questions of power are now being raised. Skolnick feels that foremost to the future of the university is the problem of the "attenuation of the university's autonomy from distant interests, as manifested in the location of decision-making power in the hands of trustees whose values and interests so frequently conflict with those of an academic community."[33] Or on the same point Birenbaum writes that the government of universities is ripe for reform. "The reform must be along cooperative and democratic lines, recognizing that, in a community devoted to the discovery of knowledge and the application of reason, those to be governed should govern themselves."[34]

The amount of power that a university president has depends to a great

---

[30] Skolnick, *op. cit.*, p. 116.
[31] *Ibid.*
[32] Ridgeway, *op. cit.*, p. 2.
[33] Skolnick, *op. cit.*, p. 121.
[34] Birenbaum, *op. cit.*, pp. 106–7.

extent on his board of trustees and the degree to which they use him or he uses them. During the decade following World War II university presidents were often ex-army officers, ex-politicians, and businessmen, but for the most part those types were not successful. The presidents of universities today most often come from administrative positions within universities or from the large foundations. The president is the chief administrative officer, fund raiser, and public image. But in recent years he has often been faced with the problem of dealing with militant students in campus takeovers. For the most part he has not been very successful in that role and as a result it is difficult to find people of high reputation to take the positions of college and university presidents.

Below the president in the university are a wide range of administrative positions. One major distinction may be made between those related directly to the academic functions and those related to the operation of the institution. Basically, the first group deals with students and faculty while the second group is concerned with running a large scale physical operation. The interest here is in those administrators concerned with academic functions. This group is primarily made up of academic deans and their assistants. In the past many deans took that position near the end of their career and had very often been successful men in their academic fields. But this is much less true today when most deans have decided on an administrative career rather than an academic one. Generally a dean is expected to have some credentials as a scholar, and most often they are only minimal. What is most important is that when an academic person becomes an administrator he in effect changes his career. His intentions may be to remain a historian or a physicist along with being a dean, but in reality it rarely happens.

In most universities the administration has a great deal of power because faculties have no interest in many areas. In any university power would be acquired by default rather than through any formal delegation. It is a part of the folklore of administrators that faculties resist change and action. And very often faculties say they have no interest or power in many of the areas where the administration acts. "There is a gentlemen's agreement of sorts to maintain an uneasy peace. Generally the administrators concede the curriculum to the faculty in return for almost everything else."[35]

What is not understood by many people outside the universities is how little power the administration has over the faculty. In most good universities promotions and tenure are decided by a faculty member's departmental peers. The possible threats of the administration toward a faculty member are generally very limited. If he has tenure it is extremely difficult to fire him. He also has operating for him the tradition of academic free-

---

[35] *Ibid.*, p. 74.

dom which allows him among other things the right to be highly critical
—even of the administration of his university. Skolnick suggests that
the lack of power or authority of administrators over their faculties often
makes the faculty appear capricious and irresponsible while the administration seems intransigent and unresponsive. So when the administrators
do speak "it is difficult to know whether they represent faculty or students, trustees, or other interested parties. The 'double-talk' and evasion
about which students so often complain is a standard defense against clear
commitments in a situation where great constraints exist."[36]

The expansion of the universities and colleges during the 1960's saw a
great proliferation of administrative positions. A few years ago a dean of a
college might have one or two assistant deans, but now he often has eight
or ten assistant deans along with two or three associate deans. Over the
last decade the ranks of the administrators have been expanding much
faster than those of the faculty. Hacker writes that he has not heard of a
college or university where the growth rate of the administration is less
than that of the professoriat. "Educational administrators, like their
counterparts elsewhere, are adept at discovering new services they can perform, new committees they can create, new reports they can write."[37]

One of the consequences of the increasing size and complexity of the
administration is that it becomes more bureaucratic in its structure and
operation. This means it is often unable to cope with the unexpected and
unanticipated. As a result many administrators are unwittingly drawn into
conflict with the activist students. The administration comes to be seen by
many students as the impersonal, routinized, punchcard like aspect of
modern society they so strongly dislike. It should be remembered that in
most student confrontations and protest actions it has been the administration that has been the target. And it is not just that they appear bureaucratic, but also that they appear responsible for many of the decisions that
the students object to. For example, the militant students' critiques of
"universities imply that research policy and use of government funds is
largely a matter of administrative decision rather than of faculty desire."[38]

The Faculty

The professor in a large university has a variety of roles. He is generally
expected to be, in various combinations, a good teacher and researcher-
writer, to serve on committees, and to consult outside the university. Not
all are expected to fill all of the roles to the same extent or with the same

---

[36] Skolnick, *op. cit.*, p. 118.

[37] Hacker, Andrew, "The College Grad Has Been Short-Changed," in Christopher
Katope and Paul G. Zolbrod, *Beyond Berkeley: A Sourcebook of Student Values* (New
York: Harper and Row, 1966), p. 206.

[38] Skolnick, *op. cit.*, p. 118.

ability. As suggested, they usually operate in a reward system of promotion and tenure over which they have the major control.

Probably every college and university in the country states that it places important value on good teaching. But generally once that is said there is little done to insure or determine if good teaching does exist (there is no agreement as to what good teaching is or how it is measured). In the universities the young scholar is given little training to be a teacher. In most cases he is given his first class and told to teach it. Any attempts to introduce him to education courses are laughed at by the faculty members in the arts and sciences who view colleges of education with general contempt. With very few exceptions the minimal requirement for faculty status in a university is the Ph.D. This standard is so accepted that it is often used as a status symbol by aspiring colleges seeking higher status. Higher status is believed to be achieved by a higher percentage of the faculty's having Ph.D.'s, although there is usually little concern with where the faculty received their degrees or what they have done since receiving them. In the larger universities the Ph.D. is the union card of admission to first appointment and little more. To get ahead the individual must usually engage in research and writing.

There is one major distinction that can be made between various faculty members and that is an institutional vs. a professional commitment. The faculty member with the institutional commitment generally has committed himself to the institution in which he is a member and expects to stay there throughout his career. He often becomes involved in the operations of the college or university and achieves his recognition from within the institution. By contrast, the professional commitment means that one's primary identification is with his field of academic specialization. He will move from one institution to another if he feels he can pursue his professional career better in the new setting. For him, his reference group is made up of other professionals in his field in various universities around the country or the world. So in the first case the individual's primary identification is with the college or university and his second identification with his academic field, while in the second situation the reverse is the case.

What are important to an understanding of campus conflict are the feelings of many faculty toward the administration. University faculties, and especially those who are most vocal, have little respect for the administration. Birenbaum suggests that "allegations of obdurate stupidity, inefficiency, malpractice, and simple inadequacy of the university's administrators are the cement which hold most faculties together."[39] It is clear that whatever the sources or legitimacy of complaint the "mistrust and animosity between faculties and administrations are very much in evi-

---

[39] Birenbaum, *op. cit.*, p. 97.

dence at many American universities, and this hostility is very little assuaged by a sense of common commitment to the university as a repository of unique values and traditions."[40]

So the feelings of contempt and hostility of many faculty members toward the administration places them close to the students. Generally when the demands of militant students come into conflict with administrative authority the faculty sides with the students. Many times the younger faculty choose to identify with the students. In the past the young faculty member would almost always affect the dress, demeanor, and speech patterns of his senior colleagues, but this is often not the case anymore. Many young college faculty can pass for students in their beards, long sideburns, and general dress. This is increasingly a source of conflict in many universities between the senior and junior faculty.

There are some observers who feel that the faculty involvement and general support of the militant students is dangerous. And there are some who feel that many of the militant students are being directed and manipulated by various faculty members. However, there is no evidence to support this, but there are various reasons for the belief. For example, one writer appears puzzled by the empathy that faculty often feel for militant students. He writes that "on the surface this seems odd because the faculty, which is the university, is obviously a victim of student protest. The faculty's reputation suffers. The worth of the institution that the faculty has triumphantly shaped is called into public question."[41] This writer is in error on several counts. First, no university that has had militant students has suffered in its *academic* reputation. In fact, for some not to have had student rebellion is taken as evidence that the students can't be very good. Second, most faculties don't measure the worth of their institution through public interpretation but through their academic peers. It would appear questionable that faculties have lost much that is important to them through the student militancy. By contrast it is clear that administrations have lost a great deal in both power and prestige.

It should be stressed that faculties do resist student militancy when it begins to enter into their personal domains. Many faculties are quite willing to have students sit in on university and college committees. One important reason is that it helps diffuse administrative power and the faculty knows that in most cases the students will agree with them. Faculties are also generally willing to have students in positions of advising with reference to curriculum matters. But the resistance develops when students want to become directly involved in matters of promotion, tenure, and contract renewal. This is an area where most faculties will strongly resist student involvement in anything other than an advisory capacity.

---

[40] Skolnick, *op. cit.*, pp. 117–18.

[41] Mays, John B., *The Young Pretenders: Teenage Culture in Contemporary Society* (New York: Schocken Books, 1965), p. 149.

The comments thus far have been about faculty members who generally side with the militant students. But in all universities there are a number, usually a minority, who do not agree with any of the demands of militant students. In part this is because there is often an agreement between the political orientation of faculty members and their students, but not always. There may be high agreement in such professional schools as engineering, education, or business where both faculty and students tend to be relatively conservative. In other areas, such as mathematics, biology, or English both the students and the faculty tend to be relatively leftist. "In still others, particularly sociology or political science and especially in the better universities, the students tend to be to the left of the faculty. Where discrepancies between faculty and student orientations exist, the student and the faculty often differ in their conceptions of the subject. Thus, students view some of the social sciences as fields concerned with remedying 'social problems.' "[42]

STUDENTS

At this point a few comments are made fitting the role of students into the overall picture of the university. First, a look at the population out of which the college student comes. At the present time almost half of the American population is under twenty-five years of age and by 1972 the median age of the American voter will be about twenty-six. Beyond their increase in number American youth have attained a kind of solidarity by the fact of attending college. Students are coming to be seen as a group roughly analogous to a social class. "Selective Service deals with them on special terms; advertising identifies them as a distinctive and important 'public target'; they are courted politically, and their moves are acknowledged, sometimes with acceptance and sometimes with retributive outrage, as different from those of older generations."[43]

However, the present generation of college students is a complex one. In part the complexity stems from the large number and variety of "youth" in a society where youth is often extended into the mid-twenties. "No one characterization can be adequate to the drop-outs and stay-ins, hawks and doves, up-tights and cools, radicals and conservatives, heads and seekers that constitute American youth."[44] One important fact about the militant student is that he generally has a high regard for the institution he is rebelling against—the university. In a national survey at the end of 1969 students were asked to rate a number of American institutions. At

[42] Lipset, op. cit., pp. 204–5.

[43] Shoben, op. cit., pp. 135–36.

[44] Keniston, Kenneth, "Youth, Change and Violence," in Edward C. McDonagh and Ian E. Simpson, Social Problems: Persistent Challenges (New York: Holt, Rinehart and Winston, Inc., 1965), p. 107.

the top was the university, which 68 percent gave a favorable rating. By contrast favorable ratings were given the family by 58 percent, the police by 40 percent, and organized religion by 33 percent.[45]

Going to college can meet a wide variety of needs on the part of students. This may include a way to avoid the draft, to get away from parents and have the experience of independence. But for the majority, still, "the student goal is a job, security, a first step on the rung of the commercial ladder, or a graduate-school fellowship."[46] Most important is that going to college is the major dividing line for the future. For example, the college graduate can expect to earn over twice as much money in his lifetime as the person who does not go beyond high school. Not to go on to college generally means that the person is restricted to a way of life that gives him a second class economic life.

The cost of higher education for students is steadily going up. This is a result of more students wanting to go to college, as well as the fact that all items related to higher education are expanding in cost. For the period between 1947–1948 to 1967–1968 the tuition and boarding costs of going to college went from about $900 to $2,400. And for the same periods the average cost went from less than $600 to more than $1,200 in public institutions.[47] One of the consequences of student militancy has been to make various sources of money more difficult to tap for higher education. In many states the basically conservative legislatures have in 1970 cut back on their expected appropriations for education. Added to that was the recession of 1970 that meant that higher education was confronted with severe economic problems.

One other general aspect of the university that is highly important is the graduate students and their programs. In the 1960's most schools that could introduced graduate programs as well as expanded those already in operation. Many schools did this because they felt there was a need for more graduate programs and that they were needed to attract better faculty. But the basic reason was that graduate programs were seen as the best means of achieving higher academic prestige. There were also other reasons. One was that graduate programs provide cheap undergraduate education. For the salary of a professor three graduate students can be hired to teach three times as many students. But as suggested, one unanticipated consequence of these programs was that in the early 1970's their new Ph.D.'s were going on the job market along with those from the older and more prestigeful graduate programs to compete for fewer jobs.

The graduate student during the 1960's played a significant role in

---

[45] *Newsweek*, December 29, 1969, p. 43.

[46] Young, Warren and Joseph Hixson, *LSD on Campus* (New York: Dell Publishing Co., 1966), p. 75.

[47] Birenbaum, *op. cit.*, p. 63.

many of the militant activities on campuses. During that period many of them organized on individual campuses and within their professional associations. With the added employment difficulties developing in the 1970's it seems safe to predict that graduate students may be even more involved in student militancy during the 1970's.

COLLEGE STUDENTS IN GENERAL

The intention here is to discuss college students in a general way to present an overall picture before looking more specifically at the militant college student. One common image that developed in the late 1960's was that most college students were militant. But all the reputable studies show that apathy and privatism were far more dominant than student dissent. And in the overall picture militancy was relatively infrequent within the context of the total number of institutions of higher education and their students. In general the demonstrations were concentrated in the larger universities and institutions of highest academic caliber, "and almost totally absent at teachers' colleges, technical institutes, and non-academic denominational colleges."[48]

Most students who go on to college today are not especially concerned about the education they receive or about the world around them. The millions of young people who enter college are there primarily for career purposes. "Most of today's students are not intellectuals, nor are they capable of becoming so. They do not object to large, anonymous classes. They have no ideas of their own to put forward and they want to be told what they have to know."[49] However, even those students and schools that have not been characterized with militancy do have changes taking place. That is because a measure of student power has been attained peacefully on many campuses where there has been no overt militancy. The main target for change has been an old one, and that was to remove some restrictions on the personal life of the student. Traditionally, the universities took it upon themselves to act in loco parentis, but that is being abandoned. A large number of students in all types of schools believe that their morals—whether they drink or make love, or go to church on Sunday—are none of the university's business.[50] But there still are a few schools left that maintain the restrictive view toward students that was common only a few years ago.

It is possible to get a picture of higher education by looking at some general value areas and what studies indicate are student beliefs or re-

---

[48] Keniston, Kenneth, "The Sources of Student Dissent," in Walt Anderson, The Age of Protest (Pacific Palisades, Calif.: Goodyear Publishing Co., Inc., 1969), p. 228.

[49] Hacker, op. cit., pp. 208–9.

[50] Main, Jeremy, "The 'Square' Universities Are Rolling Too," in Youth in Turmoil (New York: Time-Life Books, 1969), p. 123.

sponses. In the discussion that follows frequent reference will be made to a "national sample." This study was based on a national sample of 2,000 college seniors in 1969.[51] About three-quarters of those students believed that the university is one important symbol of hope in the troubled world. "Only one in five feels that his professors don't really care about the problems of society, and still fewer feel that what they are learning in class is 'silly, wrong, or useless.' "[52] We next look more specifically at various patterns of beliefs and activities common to many campuses.

As suggested, the traditional pattern was that students were watched over and controlled by representatives of the college. In the past this was done, especially with coeds, by placing them in dormitories and other approved housing and subjecting them to restrictions. The most common for the coed was that she had to be in by certain hours and could not have male guests in her living quarters. However, two major changes are occurring on many campuses. One is that the rules are being relaxed in the dormitories and second, large numbers of students are moving off campus. In recent years a successful and highly profitable business has been to build apartment houses and rent them to undergraduate students. In general the trend is away from college dormitories toward off-campus housing.

The citadel of the traditional Joe College, the fraternity, is on the decline on many campuses, including the quiet, non-militant ones. In the past the Greeks, although small in number, were well organized, and often controlled student offices. But this is disappearing and the indication is that fraternities will continue to be of decreasing importance to campus life. "What really puts the fraternities out of joint with their times is their continued refusal, with rare exceptions, to admit Negroes. The fraternities live under the dead hand of their alumni, who make sure the race bar stays up although officially it may have been removed from their constitutions."[53]

Another traditional area common to all types of colleges undergoing change is the intercollegiate athletic programs. The main supporters of the programs, especially football, are the alumni, although football games are well attended by undergraduates. But what is important about athletics in this era of change is that in most types of colleges the coaching staffs overwhelmingly represent a traditional, conservative force on campus. Most football coaches run their operations in exactly the same fashion as does a military commander. The coaches become the most authoritarian, antidemocratic forces on campus, and many of their athletes follow their example. The athletes are subsidized in their studies and are for the most part clean-cut and clean-shaven. They are often housed and fed together

---

[51] Hadden, Jeffrey K., "The Private Generation," *Psychology Today*, October, 1969, p. 32.

[52] *Ibid.*, p. 33.

[53] Main, *op. cit.*, p. 131.

and form a cohesive group. While there is an increasing number of exceptions the "jock" faction tends to be a conservative element on the campus, the "ones that follow the traditional leaders and reject the radicals. Being hired hands, they accept discipline and leave university policy to the authorities."[54] In some schools the athletes have even been used as an informal police force of restriction against militant students. However, it seems clear that an increasing number of athletes are refusing to accept the total and arbitrary control of the coaches, especially as it affects their personal lives. For example, in a number of schools athletes have left programs because they refused to cut their hair according to some restriction placed by their coaches.

Given the patterns of changing life on the campus it is useful also to look at some general values. The national study found no general alienation of college students from their parents. Almost eight out of ten denied that "all my parents care about is how much money I make when I get out. Though 43 percent have parents who feel that college teaches wild ideas, 83 percent say that their parents would be terribly hurt if they did not finish school." Hadden goes on to say that the "irony of the students is not their rebellion but their docile conformity to the stated ideals, if not the example, of their parents and teachers."[55]

There is also strong evidence that many college students think of themselves as patriotic. For example, the national study found that 67 percent of the respondents believed that it is "a young man's duty to serve his country when called, and only 18 percent said they would use any means necessary to avoid serving in Vietnam."[56] Some of the students may be patriotic about serving in the military because they have been able to avoid it. That is, if they were all confronted with going into the armed forces the next day they might not take as strong a position about duty to serve one's country. There is a certain hypocrisy in hearing a high level of agreement about military duty from that group most effectively able to avoid that duty.

The studies all seem to indicate that for most college students religion, at least in the traditional sense, is coming to mean less and less in their lives. There are wide variations in church attendance by students in different types of colleges. In one survey the students at several schools were asked if they had attended church at least once during the previous month. At San Francisco State 36 percent of the women and 41 percent of the men answered "yes," as contrasted with 81 percent of the women and 62 percent of the men at the University of Alabama.[57] Another study was done of 1,062 college students in Philadelphia and their participation

---

[54] *Ibid.*

[55] Hadden, *op. cit.*, p. 79.

[56] *Ibid.*

[57] "Close-Up: Schools," *Playboy*, September, 1969, p. 223.

in anti-war demonstrations. It was found that only 3 percent of the Catholic respondents participated in anti-war demonstrations, while 35 percent of those with no religion did. "Of those responding from the Quaker school 31 percent had demonstrated against the war; of those from the city university, 13 percent; and of those from the two Catholic colleges, 2 percent. Respondents who rarely or never went to church were the most likely to have opposed war by public demonstration; and those who went to church either regularly or more than regularly were the least likely to have engaged in such action.[58] Two-thirds of the students in the national sample felt that "the churches in America have been hopelessly slow in joining the struggle for social justice."[59] The turning away from organized religion by many students does not mean that students are no longer interested in questions of meaning and commitment to life. On most campuses of all types many students are looking for studies relevant to a search for life commitment. Not all students, or even a majority of them, are pursuing the search with urgency, but those who do are far more than the militant left. But the search has little to do with organized religion, as "students are turning away from their churches and instead toward human and social concerns."[60]

The strongest forces for racial equality are also found on many college campuses. But the students' feelings about racial equality are not clear and unprejudiced. Hadden, in the national survey, found that two-thirds of the student respondents felt that they were morally obligated to do what they could to end racial injustice in society. "At the same time, nearly half are unwilling to reject the most latent stereotype in our culture—that of the irresponsible and carefree Negro."[61] There is increasing racial segregation on many campuses. But often this is being brought about by the demands of black militant students for such things as their own rooms in student cafeterias or for their own sections in dormitories. This may contribute to increased conflict between black and white students in the near future.

There is no evidence that a very large number of college students have rejected the American political system. Hadden found that only 14 percent of the respondents agreed with the mildest radical statement that "there is no point in trying to change existing political structure. If one is interested in change he must work outside these structures."[62] Yet, most college students do not take any active part in the political system. For

---

[58] Connors, John F., Richard C. Leonard and Kenneth E. Burnham, "Religion and Opposition to War among College Students," *Sociological Analysis*, Winter, 1968, pp. 218–19.

[59] Hadden, *op. cit.*, p. 35.

[60] Main, *op. cit.*, p. 129.

[61] Hadden, *op. cit.*, p. 32.

[62] *Ibid.*, p. 34.

example, only 12 percent had ever sent a letter or a telegram to a public official; and 5 percent had a leadership role in some political cause."[63]

In many respects college students are generally pro-business. The national sample found that a clear majority of students believed that private enterprise is capable of solving any problem it puts its mind to, including poverty. Many students tend to confirm business in the abstract but are suspicious of incursions upon the inner self. Certainly the positive identification with business as a career has changed greatly from the past. The Hadden study found that nearly two-thirds of the students said they did not plan to take jobs in business if they could do something more worthwhile.[64]

What can be said about college students in general and their beliefs? It seems clear that many college students are withdrawing from institutions and into themselves. The notion of privatism recognizes the ideology that is important because the college generation tends to reject meaning or authority outside of the self. "The new style of privatism not only cries for freedom from established institutions, it fundamentally rejects their legitimacy. Privatism's ideology is altruistic, for it acknowledges the privileges of private existence—as rights—to all men."[65] But many of the students are optimistic about the future. Over two-thirds of them believe that their generation is going to make a better world. But their optimism is tempered; only 13 percent believe that their generation "will create the first society that is truly free of prejudice."[66]

The national study of college students came to five general conclusions on the basis of their interviews. First, college students today are socially aware and idealistic, possibly more so than any previous generation. Second, their idealism often takes the form of contempt for what they believe to be the older generation's hypocrisy. Third, they tend to reject many aspects of the existing institutions. Fourth, for all their idealism students do not have a realistic sense of what their ideals imply in terms of political and social action. It is not clear how committed they are to the ideals, especially when action may be in conflict with their privatism. Fifth, the privatism is ambiguous. "While it tends to be self-centered and anti-institutional, and assumes a high level of materialistic comfort, it develops in many cases an acute sensitivity to others and a determination to conduct their own lives so as to contribute personally to their ideal of a decent society."[67]

It should be stressed that while few college students are militant there

---

[63] *Ibid.*, p. 32.
[64] *Ibid.*, p. 35.
[65] *Ibid.*, p. 32.
[66] *Ibid.*, p. 33.
[67] *Ibid.*

is a high degree of identification by college students with those of their generation who are rebelling. For example, Hadden found that about six out of ten students believed that college administrations brought on student rebellion by being indifferent to student needs. "Seventy-nine percent are sympathetic with the goals of protest, though not always the methods, and 95 percent insist that they are as concerned with university reform as the protest leaders are. The student majority hate hippies and radicals at the student union but still defend them against discipline. Though 57 percent feel that the protest leaders 'give the rest of us a bad name,' a bigger majority (68 percent) do not want these fellow students kicked out of school."[68]

What is highly important about the college generation is that while there are disagreements within that group, they are much closer to each other than they are to those of their generation who do not go on to college. In 1969, *Fortune* magazine had a national survey done with 723 college students and 617 nonstudents between the ages of 17 and 23.[69] They found that noncollege youths take nearly as critical a view of society as college youth. However, the similarities between their opinions cease when the questions turn to philosophical and moral convictions. Noncollege youth may be dissatisfied with the society in general, but they are not willing to cast away the traditional beliefs of their parents. Thirty-eight percent of the college and 64 percent of the noncollege respondents "consider religion very important." Believing that premarital sex is not a moral issue was true of "64 percent of the college respondents as contrasted with only 41 percent of the noncollege respondents. Thirty-five percent of the college and 60 percent of the noncollege respondents believed that patriotism was very important."[70]

MILITANT STUDENTS

As indicated, the number of militant students on campuses represents a small minority. There have been several attempts through surveys to determine the number of students who have been involved in campus militancy. One poll in 1968 found that about 20 percent of all undergraduates had ever been engaged in any protest activity, and most of them only once.[71] A 1969 poll of college students found 36 percent who said they had ever been involved in a campus demonstration.[72] Of course the rates vary greatly by different types of schools. At San Francisco State, 46

---

[68] *Ibid.*, p. 34.
[69] Main, Jeremy, "A Special Report on Youth," *Fortune*, June, 1969, p. 73.
[70] *Ibid.*
[71] Seligman, *op. cit.*, p. 17.
[72] *Newsweek*, *op. cit.*, p. 44.

percent of the women and 59 percent of the men said they had participated in student demonstrations, while at the University of Illinois it was
11 percent of the women and 19 percent of the men, and at the University
of Alabama, 4 percent of the women and 14 percent of the men.[73]

Those who have participated in student demonstrations do not represent the basic core of militant students. One study suggests that behind
the one-quarter to one-third of the college students who have demonstrated there is a small and highly visible activist group of possibly 2 percent of the student body.[74] That percent can become significant in the
large universities. With 2 percent of 2,800 students there are organizational possibilities, but with 2 percent of 12,000 you can fill a fair sized
hall. "Television has also worked to dissipate any sense of isolation among
radical students. Indeed, TV has made it possible to mobilize thousands
of students, from different campuses, in very brief periods of time."[75]

As indicated, the student activist is usually found in the large and most
prestigeful universities. Very often certain universities act as strong attractions for potential student militants, but not particularly because of
their reputations for political radicalism but rather because they are
known for their academic excellence. As Keniston points out, once the
potential militant is on campus he must have the chance to meet and interact with others like himself. They can develop common points of view
and shared policies—"in short, to form an *activist subculture* with sufficient mass and potency to generate a demonstration or action program."[76]
The fact that large numbers of students live off campus contributes to the
development of their militant group. Many may live in co-op housing
where it is possible for them to develop a high degree of ideological solidarity and organizational cohesion.[77]

Not only are potentially militant students attracted to the top universities, but the top universities actively recruit the type of student out of
which many militants develop. Therefore, the possibility of campus demonstrations increased, because at the same time that many of the schools
increased administrative autocracy, administrative bureaucracy, and social
alienation, "they also attracted, recruited and socialized students who were
inclined to change these very structural conditions wherever they found
them in society."[78]

From what has been suggested throughout this chapter it is clear that
some universities are more prone than others to recruit the type of student

---

[73] *Playboy, op. cit.,* p. 224.
[74] Seligman, *op. cit.,* p. 17.
[75] *Ibid.,* p. 21.
[76] Keniston, *op. cit.,* p. 235.
[77] *Ibid.*
[78] Scott and El-Assal, *op. cit.,* p. 708.

who will be a militant. For example, at a school like San Francisco State only 17 percent of the students define themselves as "moderately" or "very conservative," while 42 percent define themselves as "very liberal" or "radical." By contrast at the University of Alabama over 50 percent of the students define themselves as "moderately" or "very conservative" and only about 6 percent as "very liberal" or "radical."[79] It should also be added that often the schools with the most conservative students are the schools that are the most restrictive in their treatment of students. And ironically the most militant students are often found in those schools where there are the fewest restrictions placed over them.

There is a stereotype of the militant student in the United States which does not distinguish him from the hippie. Keniston describes the stereotype of the campus militant as "both a Bohemian and a political activist, be-levi-ed, long-haired, dirty, and unkempt, he is seen as profoundly disaffected from his society, often influenced by 'radical' (Marxist, Communist, Maoist, or Castroite) ideas, an experimenter in sex and drugs, unconventional in his family behavior."[80] Along with the stereotype of what a militant student is, there are also stereotypes of why he is that way. The most common belief is that student militancy is a direct result of the loss of certain traditional American virtues. "The 'breakdown' of American family life, high rates of divorce, the 'softness' of American living, inadequate parents, and, above all, overindulgence and 'spoiling' contribute to the prevalence of dissent."[81] All of these stereotypes have been developed and nurtured by the mass media, especially television.

The stereotypes of the student militant are wrong for a number of reasons, the most important being that there are a variety of different types of student militants. In fact there has been an important change in time as related to the issues that were important to student militants. As indicated earlier, there have been two general stages to the student militancy movement—before and after 1965. During the first stage there was concern about a variety of social issues but the movement generally accepted the legitimacy of the American political community in general and especially the university. But in the second stage "a considerable number of young people, particularly the activist core, experienced a progressive deterioration in their acceptance of national and university authority."[82]

Keniston suggests that possibly the best way to look at campus militants is to see them as falling somewhere along a continuum that runs between two ideal types—"first, the political activist or protester, and second, the withdrawn, culturally alienated student."[83] Keniston goes on to suggest

---

[79] *Playboy, op. cit.*, pp. 223–24.
[80] Keniston, *op. cit.*, pp. 228–29.
[81] *Ibid.*, p. 229.
[82] Skolnick, *op. cit.*, p. 100.
[83] Keniston, *op. cit.*, pp. 229–30.

that the defining characteristic of the new activist is that he participates in student demonstrations and group activities that are concerned with some matter of general political, social, or ethical principle. "Characteristically, the activist feels that some injustice has been done, and attempts to 'take a stand,' 'demonstrate,' or in some fashion express his convictions."[84] The new activists tend to be more responsive than most other students to deprivations of civil rights both on and off the campus, "particularly when political pressures seem to motivate on-campus policies they consider unjust."[85]

One popular explanation of the militant student, and also of many other deviants in American society, is to describe them as alienated from society. But Keniston has argued that this is misleading because many militants have basic commitments to traditional American values. For example, many have strong personal commitments to free speech, citizens' participation in decision-making, and equal opportunity. Often when the militant rejects all or parts of "the establishment" it is because he believes the realities fall far short of the ideals. "And insofar as he repudiates careerism and familism, it is because of his implicit allegiance to other human goals he sees, once again, as more crucial to American life. Thus, to emphasize the 'alienation' of activists is to neglect their more basic allegiance to creedal American ideals."[86] Keniston does believe there are some students who may be described as culturally alienated because they are too pessimistic and opposed to "the system" to want to show their disapproval in any organized public way. When this group shows its dissent it is private. "This is through their nonconformity of behavior, ideology and dress, through personal experimentation and most of all through efforts to intensify their own subjective experience, often through the use of drugs. They generally show a distaste and disinterest in politics and society."[87]

Many of the political student militants practice what has been called the "politics of conscience" which is basically a set of political beliefs that leaves no room for compromise. Often in demands made by the militants there is the assertion that their demands involve a moral issue. "This often means, in practice, that the issue is regarded as not susceptible to resolution by democratic processes."[88] Very often the student militant of the left is like the militant of the right—he is absolutely convinced that he is right in his interpretations and demands. So his arguments for change become more than attempts to alter political procedures—they often are rather a moral crusade. Many student militants have become anti-intellectual and attempt to destroy some of the processes they claim to believe most

---

[84] *Ibid.*, p. 230.
[85] *Ibid.*, p. 234.
[86] *Ibid.*, p. 230.
[87] *Ibid.*, p. 231.
[88] Seligman, *op. cit.*, p. 29.

strongly in. For example, to demonstrate against the Department of Defense or the Dow Chemical Company is legitimate, but to prevent a representative from doing his lawful job, "and to interfere with access to him on the part of other possibly interested students—such activities have too much in common with bans on speakers, the censorship of the college newspaper, or restrictions on the circulation of 'dangerous' library books."[89]

There is often the tendency to see only the militant aspect of the student militant and overlook his role as a student. A large number of militants are very intelligent students and are often learning both in the classroom and through their militant activities. The militant students often study areas that are related to their activist interests (or they may become militant because of the areas in which they study). On most campuses the conservative students are most apt to study engineering or business while the liberal students go into the humanities and the social sciences. "Such selection reflects the extent to which varying political orientations influence students to opt for different career goals. Leftists, particularly those from well-to-do and well-educated families, are inclined to favor academic fields concerned with social and political issues or careers in the arts, social work, scholarship, and public service."[90] The militant student is generally not found among engineers, future teachers at teachers' colleges, or students of business administration. Often the activist sees his educational goals as seeking a liberal education for its own sake, rather than for specific technical or professional preparation. But what is most important is that the militants not only do well academically, but tend to persist in their academic commitments. They drop out less often than most of their classmates, and the militant is generally not strongly dissatisfied with his college education. This may be because many active militants are in the universities that provide the best undergraduate education available in the United States today.[91]

What are the backgrounds of the student militants? A disproportionately large number of them grow up in the east, although many of them attend the top universities of the midwest and far west along with those schools in the east. But most important are the socialization experiences that many of the militants went through. Most of them did not grow up during a period of cynicism but rather were growing up during the complacent years of the Eisenhower administration and during the early idealism of the Kennedy years. Harrington suggests that it may be the unique experiences of the 1950's and early 1960's that gave the militants a distinctive flavor. That is, for some a sense of outrage at having been betrayed by

---

[89] Shoben, *op. cit.*, p. 141.

[90] Lipset, *op. cit.*, p. 196.

[91] Keniston, *op. cit.*, p. 233.

all the father figures of their childhood—which derives from original innocence. And it is also the source of the young radicals' insistence on sincerity and community.[92]

Very often in the past the young radicals were rebelling against their
parents and their parents' values. That has generally not been the case
with student militants. They often come from families with liberal political views and many students say their parents hold views similar to their
own and accept and support their activities as militants. "Thus, among the
parents of protesters we find large numbers of liberal Democrats, plus an
unusually large scattering of pacifists, socialists, et cetera."[93] Keniston
found in his study that when the activists of the left were compared with
active student conservatives, the militants tended to have higher parental
incomes, more parental education, and less anxiety about social status. "In
brief, activists are not drawn from disadvantaged or uneducated groups; on
the contrary, they are selectively recruited from among those young Americans who have had the most socially fortunate upbringing."[94] Other researchers have found that the militants are often psychologically
"healthy." And they are probably "more independent, more mature, more
egalitarian, more dedicated to helping their fellow men, and more responsive to the ideas imparted by teachers than are their inactive peers."[95]

Of great importance, both in number and influence, in the militant
students' groups have been the Jewish students. In the late 1960's it was
estimated that about 5 percent of all college students of all types were
Jewish. But Glazer estimated that among the small number of committed,
identifiable radicals on the most active campuses, probably one-third to
one-half were Jews.[96] Jews are very much in evidence among the broad and
varigated body of student militants. A study of the Berkeley students in
1964 showed that Jews were most likely of all students to be militant. And
at the University of Chicago, of those who protested the release of student
grades to draft boards in 1966, 45 percent were Jewish.[97]

Like many other militants the Jews are frequently the children of generally liberal, enlightened, and prosperous business and professional men.
They also come from families that identify themselves as Jews in religion
or Jews in some ethnic sense. "The students themselves accept this definition. But it is also important that they make nothing of it. Indeed, they

---

[92] Harrington, Michael, "The Mystical Militants," in *Thoughts of the Young
Radicals* (New York: Pitman Publishing Co., 1966), pp. 66–7.

[93] Keniston, *op. cit.*, pp. 232–33.

[94] *Ibid.*, p. 233.

[95] Blum, Richard H., *Students and Drugs* (San Francisco: Jossey-Bass, Inc., 1969),
p. 8.

[96] Glazer, Nathan, "The Jewish Side in Student Activism," in *Youth in Turmoil*
(New York: Time-Life Books, 1969), p. 95.

[97] *Ibid.*, p. 96.

are scarcely conscious of it, and are not aware of it at all in connection with their political activities."[98] Many of them were undoubtedly social-ized to values of militancy and accepted their backgrounds without ques-tion. That is, many of them had radical parents or grandparents. "The parents may even have been victimized by McCarthy (that is, old Senator Joe). Think of that for pedigree and background. Mayflower descent is hard put to compete with it."[99]

For the most part, until the late 1960's, the black student was not in-volved in the militancy of the white student. Up until a few years ago the black student tended to be individualistic, assimilationist, and politically indifferent. However, the drive for black power has changed that. There appear at present to be two streams feeding into the new black protest. One is from the middle classes of the southern black community and the other, increasingly more dominant one, is from the urban ghettos of the North.[100] The black student militant is now the most revolutionary of all the students. In fact his ideas set him apart almost as much from nonstu-dent blacks as from whites. For example, in the *Fortune* study, 61 percent of the black students believed the United States to be racist as compared to 31 percent of the black nonstudents. When compared to white college students on tactics of protest the black is more actively militant. While 79 percent of the whites and 71 percent of the blacks believe that sit-ins are sometimes justified, they differ on other tactics. The destruction of prop-erty is a tactic approved of at least sometimes by only 14 percent of the whites but by 45 percent of the blacks. To assault the police is sometimes felt to be justified by 18 percent of the white and 51 percent of the black students.[101] On many campuses, where there are both white and black students, the militancy movement has become segregated. The blacks pur-sue their ends and don't want the white radicals involved with them. So many white militants find themselves rejected by the black students, the one group they most want to identify with. This is leading to a split among radical students and contributing to new forms of campus conflict along racial lines.

GENERATIONAL CONFLICT

One of the main themes in this book with respect to many areas of deviancy has been the causal impact of generational differences in values and behavior. Therefore it is important to look at the militant student in terms of his parents and their generation. As suggested, the conflict with

---

[98] *Ibid.*

[99] *Ibid.*, p. 99.

[100] Skolnick, *op. cit.*, p. 110.

[101] Main, *op. cit.*, p. 74.

parents is minimized by the fact that the parents often share the same values as their militant college students. But often the generational conflict is not directed specifically at the parents but rather at their generation. In fact the radical parent is often more a deviant to his generation than is the militant student to his generation.

The generation who became parents in the 1940's were really the first post-Victorians. They were born in the 1920's, the period of great social change in the United States. They grew up in a world very different from what their parents had experienced, so that in education, politics, religion, sex and marriage, and child rearing those parents altered a great deal of the dogma by which they had been reared. There was probably far more conflict within the family setting between the militant's parents and the grandparents than between the militants and their parents.

The militant student generation was really the first group in the United States to grow up with "modern" parents, that is, parents who often reared their children under the permissiveness of Spock in a society of affluency and with few material deprivations. Keniston suggests that the influence of the "modern parent" alone "distinguishes the present generation from previous ones and helps create a mood born out of modernity, affluence, rapid social change and violence."[102]

Probably what most bothers many in the parent's generation is that the militant younger generation doesn't seem to respect many of the values of life that they do. This is often the case in many well-to-do families where the son does not respect his father's achievements or authority. That may be because there is no reason for the son to view his father's experience as relevant to his own. "In the world of highly specialized, endlessly reorganized, increasingly internationalized white-collar executives, sons are often not even clear what their fathers *do* all day, and it is usually unrealistic for them to suppose that they might sometime be doing the same thing."[103]

For many middle-class students of today there is a feeling of hypocrisy when they look at their parents. This often centers around what they feel is a discrepancy between what parents say and what they do. Probably the most common criticism centers around the parents' verbal statements on independence and self-determination for their children, because often what the parents say doesn't correspond with their behavior when the children actively seek that independence. "Similar perceptions of parental 'hypocrisy' occur around racial matters: for example, there are many parents who in principle support racial and religious equality, but become violently upset when their children date someone from another race or religion."[104]

---

[102] Keniston, "Youth, Change and Violence," *op. cit.*, p. 107.
[103] Seligman, *op. cit.*, p. 25.
[104] Keniston, *op. cit.*, p. 113.

The studies further indicate that the student militants tend to come from the type of homes where they are encouraged to speak up. Their parents are inclined to cherish self expression over self control and spontaneity and sincerity above caution and restraint. Those are values that make the children critical of their parents even when the parents have a highly liberal background themselves. They criticize their parents "for not doing enough to carry out the liberal and socialist principles they profess and have taught their children."[105] So many parents have become involved in action protests against the war because their children "shamed" them into it.

The generational conflict is also involved in an education gap. In the same way that there are wide differences between college students and noncollege students there is a gap between their two sets of parents. For example, in the *Fortune* study, the respondents were asked "whether it was worth fighting a war to defend a nation's honor" and only 25 percent of the college youth and 35 percent of their parents answered "yes." By contrast 59 percent of the noncollege youth and 67 percent of their parents answered "yes."[106] This supports the suggestion made earlier that at least in some areas parents can be closer to their own children than they are to other parents of their generation. The results of most research findings indicate that "the real generation gap exists not so much between children and parents as between children and what they perceive to be the world their parents' generation made."[107]

The militant youth is often accused of being unrealistic and of not understanding the world around him. Frequently the students of today are called a generation of "romantics." But as Skolnick points out the real "romantics" are often the older generation that waves the flag, "that sees America as a country of manifest destiny saving the world for democracy."[108] He goes on to suggest that the younger generation is actually a generation of realists "who are not willing to kill and be killed unless the cause is unmistakably honorable. In this perspective, the issue today is not what is wrong with the younger generation in trying to overturn established institutions, but what is wrong with the older generations in trying to conduct business as usual."[109]

There have been many attempts by those in the older generation to understand and react to the generational conflict. Probably the most common reaction is one of indignation and anger at a generation that rejects what they believe in and tells them they are wrong for so believing. Cer-

---

[105] Glazer, *op. cit.*, p. 101.

[106] Main, *op. cit.*, p. 74.

[107] Albrook, Robert C., "Parenthood Today Is No Bore," in *Youth in Turmoil* (New York: Time-Life Books, 1969), p. 118.

[108] Skolnick, "The Generation Gap," *op. cit.*, p. 5.

[109] *Ibid.*, p. 5.

tainly this kind of reaction is understandable. But it may also be that many in the older generation react with envy. The young person of middle-class background has been liberated from concerns about material success that dominated the lives of his parents, so that the student can do things that were not done by his generation. A feeling of envy often enters into adults' discussions about the high degree of freedom allowed the college students today.

In the past the behavior of college students often could be laughed at. Parents could patronize their offspring in the past when they were involved in panty raids because only the most puritanical were alarmed. "When frivolity turns to defiance, however, adult responses change correspondingly. Even some who view themselves as liberals are frequently upset by long hair, marijuana and LSD, miscegenation and seemingly unpatriotic antimilitarism."[110]

Often parents want an answer to why their children are militants or engaged in various types of deviance. One common explanation is that of conventional wisdom which says that youth is "naturally rebellious." This view provides comfort for some adults because it indicates that the youth will soon see the light. "Moreover, adults who hold these views need feel no special responsibility or guilt over the rebelliousness of youth, since it is 'inevitable.'"[111] This point of view doesn't distinguish between college pranks and student militancy. It puts together the swallowing of goldfish, panty raids, and protests against the war as being of the same magnitude, but it is clear that the intensity and commitment of many militant students is different from anything in the past. Whether or not they will "grow out of their beliefs" it is too early to determine. But it seems highly likely that the peak of militancy in the life cycle of most individuals will be reached during their college years, and as they get older they get more conservative. To that extent the folk wisdom is correct— but it doesn't explain the intensity of involvement of the militant student as he lives and behaves while in college today. However, a fair number of Americans are holding to an agreeable notion of the generation gap. "The notion is agreeable because it implies that this generation too will eventually come to terms with its elders and their institutions."[112]

As indicated, it is clear that in the United States today there are social class differences in reactions to militant college students. In general the older the respondent and the lower his social class, the greater the hostility to the militant college student. For example, a 1970 Gallup poll asked a national sample if they "agreed or disagreed with college students going

---

[110] Harris, T. George, "The Young Are Captives of Each Other: A Conversation with David Riesman," *Psychology Today*, October, 1969, p. 30.

[111] Skolnick, *The Politics of Protest, op. cit.*, p. 82.

[112] Seligman, *op. cit.*, p. 13.

on strike as a way to protest the country." Among those with some college background 73 percent disagreed, as did 87 percent of the grade school population. Among those 21–29 years of age 73 percent disagreed, as did 88 percent of those 50 and over.[113]

In the minds of many the college student appears to be looking down on the working class and many of its values. That group has less education and less sophistication and is less apt to reject affluency because it hasn't had it yet. "For the not-yet-wealthy, it is disturbing to see that college students are not greedy, are not wanting to strike it rich, but are rejecting the very things for which the less fortunate are striving."[114] Once again it is a question of the values one group thinks are important being viewed as unimportant by a group that already possesses them. And to see that once people are successful they then often reject many values raises questions about the importance of the values. As a result members of the working class often feel they must show that something is wrong with those who reject their values to protect the integrity of their beliefs for themselves.

It is useful to look in more detail at the values common to many militant students. In general modern youth see themselves as a part of a new generation and they tend to identify with their peers as a group and not with their elders. They do not have clearly defined leaders and heroes. "Among young radicals, for example, the absence of heroes or older leaders is impressive; even those five years older are sometimes viewed with mild amusement or suspicion."[115] Receiving widespread criticism from the general community, the militant turns strongly to his peers as a reference group. While the general public criticizes the militant student, he is actively defended and praised by a large part of the academic community. So the university in general is often a part of his overall reference group. "In addition, the active participation of admired faculty members in protests, teach-ins, and peace marches acts as a further incentive of students."[116]

To look at specific values common to militant students makes it clear that they have little commitment to a traditional view of patriotism. In the late 1960's patriotism came to seem square and old-fashioned. "Principally responsible for this transformation is the belief that the U.S. is no longer a society beleaguered by international Communism."[117] While there is generally not a rejection of the political system as such there is often a rejection of the major political parties and their candidates. One

---

[113] "Gallup Poll," *Philadelphia Bulletin,* June 4, 1970.

[114] Harris, *op. cit.*, p. 28.

[115] Keniston, *op. cit.*, p. 108.

[116] Keniston, "The Sources of Student Dissent," *op. cit.*, pp. 238–39.

[117] Seligman, *op. cit.*, p. 20.

study found that about half the militant students studied felt that none of the three presidential candidates in the 1968 election (Richard Nixon, Hubert Humphrey, and George Wallace) held views close to their own. In fact all three candidates ran behind Che Guevara in a list of personalities most admired.[118]

The militant college student, like many college students, is concerned with a personal search for meaning and purpose in life. Because of his convictions there is usually no consolation through religion and so he may feel a strong sense of emptiness. Many do feel a need for a deep and meaningful experience in what they see as an increasingly secular society. "Because the church, as organized religion, seems to reflect so many of the trends in society which they find distasteful, they are attracted to the Eastern religions with their emphasis on mysticism and personal religious experience."[119]

One of the major values of many college students and especially the militant ones is that of meaningful interpersonal relationships. Many of them no longer feel that they are to be found in the traditional settings of the family or religion. They often talk about "personalism" which is the discomfort created by any nonpersonal, "objectified, professionalized and exploitative relationship. Manipulation, power relationships, superordination, control and domination are at violent odds with the I-thou mystique. Failure to treat others as fully human, inability to enter into personal relationships with them, is viewed with dismay in others and with guilt in oneself."[120] With the insistent concern among many students today for developing warm human relationships the militant of today is in sharp contrast with the few rebels of the 1950's. The beats of the 1950's emphasized coolness, romanticized their loneliness and derided togetherness.[121]

The aspect of interpersonal involvement that receives the greatest amount of publicity is that of sexual expression among the young and unmarried. For many in the militant groups there is an importance to moving beyond their inhibitions and puritanism toward what they feel is greater physical expressiveness, sexual freedom, capacity for intimate and close involvement, and the overall ability to enjoy life. "Marriage is increasingly seen as an institution for having children, but sexual relationships are viewed as the natural concomitant of close relationships between the sexes. What is important is not sexual activity itself, but the context in which it occurs. Sex is right and natural between people

---

[118] *Ibid.*, p. 16.

[119] Nowlis, Helen H., *Drugs on the College Campus* (New York: Anchor Books, 1969), p. 26.

[120] Keniston, "Youth, Change and Violence," *op. cit.*, p. 109.

[121] Seligman, *op. cit.*, p. 29.

who are 'good to each other,' but sexual exploitation—failure to treat one's partner as a person—is strongly disapproved."[122]

The notions of sexual expression among militant students are also seen to fit with their beliefs about politics, religion, and so forth. That is, each does what gives himself and others pleasure and some sense of achievement. Therefore, one would expect that persons who are more liberal in their political views would also be more liberal in their sexual views and experience. In a study done by the writer in 1970 a sample of 276 students were asked how they defined themselves politically, and information was also obtained as to their premarital sexual experiences. Of the females who defined themselves as "conservative" or "middle-of-the-road" politically, 57 percent were virgins, while of the females who defined themselves as "liberal" or "radical," only 39 percent were virgins. The same pattern was also true for the males, with 53 percent of those saying they were "conservative" or "middle-of-the-road" being virgins, as contrasted with 36 percent of the "radical" and "liberal" males. Another study indicated the same general relationship. At San Francisco State, of the nonvirgins 55 percent had participated in student demonstrations in contrast with 24 percent of the virgins. The same difference was found in other schools of various political involvement.[123]

One recent value that has troubled many people both within and outside of the student militant group is the use of violence. Many times the militant student takes a stance of nonviolence—but that position must be assessed within a violent world, so that while he may seek to minimize violence his very efforts often serve to bring forth violence on the part of others. Generally confrontations have been arranged by militant students to be "symbolic" rather than disruptive or destructive. While there have been some student militants who wanted physical violence to emerge from confrontations, there is little evidence that that desire was very widespread. "Further, there is little evidence that many students are willing (much less able) to disrupt functioning, attack persons, or destroy property in the university. But they are willing to engage in symbolic protest."[124] Yet, it takes only a few students to bring forth violence if they choose. And it would seem that while most militant students do not want violence, nevertheless it will continue to increase in the future. To a great extent this may be because the broader society will encourage and accept violence by the legal authorities with increasingly less provocation. That appears to have been a partial explanation for the killings at Kent State and Jackson State in the spring of 1970.

This chapter has had as its focus the militant student. As described,

122 Keniston, op cit., p. 109.
123 Playboy, op. cit., p. 224.
124 Skolnick, op. cit., p. 106.

this has been the student who has taken the path of various types of political demonstration. There also emerged in the 1960's another kind of deviant student who has rejected the traditional roles available to students in a university. Keniston describes the demonstrations of dissent of this type as being private; "through nonconformity of behavior, ideology, and dress, through personal experimentation and above all, through efforts to intensify his own subjective experiences, he shows his distaste and disinterest in politics and society."[125] His personal experimentation and search for subjective experience very often comes through the use of various drugs. This deviant student type is the drug experimenter who is often looking for new experiences and develops campus subcultures made up of others like himself. There has been some tendency to lump together the militant student with the drug experimenter, but they are usually (although not always) quite different and distinct from one another.

THE DRUG EXPERIMENTER

One study done on the campus of a large midwestern university in the mid-1960's shows the differences between the militant students and the drug users. In that study the militant students were described as the *politicals*. They were the leaders and followers of the new student left. They devoted a great deal of their time and energy to organizing protest demonstrations and confronting the establishment. They held in low value the introspective hedonism and political individualism of the second group, the drug experimenters, known as *skuzzies* on the campus studied. That group often gave verbal and even body support to the politicals during a crisis, but they were committed to "doing their own thing," which "did not include the hard, collectively organized work of political protest and the weekly publication of the local underground newspaper."[126]

Simmon and Trout found that some of their sample of drug experimenters (skuzzies) had tried the hippie communities away from the campus. Many had returned to the campus, often disillusioned with the drug abuse they had found. But more important, the study found that the skuzzie "wants to 'turn on' and 'tune in,' but not to 'drop out,' at least not completely."[127] They also describe the recruiting procedures into the political and skuzzie subcultures. To become a political all the teeny-boppers need to do is carry signs, go to committee meetings, and drink coffee at the politicals' cafeteria. It was found that often it took only

---

[125] Keniston, "The Sources of Student Dissent," *op. cit.*, p. 231.

[126] Simmon, Geoffrey and Grafton Trout, "Hippies in College from Teeny-Boppers to Drug Freaks," *Trans-Action*, December, 1967, p. 28.

[127] *Ibid.*, pp. 27–28.

two terms to transform a political into a skuzzie. "As a political, the teeny-bopper's grades were, probably, better than average. During his transition from political to skuzzie, his grades usually fall."[128]

Simmon and Trout found that in some respects the freshmen and sophomore skuzzies were very much like their fellow students along fraternity row. Just as the younger Greeks drink more, the younger skuzzies smoke more pot. However, the skuzzie life usually lasts about a year and a half. "The skuzzie tries to find himself through drugs, drinking, sex, and very little work. Other interests come along and he moves on."[129]

Who are the drug experimenters? In the study above it was found that a large number were National Merit scholars and scholarship students. There was a disproportionate number of Jewish students, but only two blacks. Most of the participants came from middle- to upper middle-income families living in urban or suburban areas. Very few were the products of broken homes.[130] Their backgrounds were very similar to the militant students, a part which some of them had filled during their college years. Another study found that students with illegal drug experiences were generally wealthier and older upperclassmen. They were irreligious in contrast to their parents, political left wing and politically active, and in the arts and humanities or social sciences.[131] As Nowlis observes, it appears that most students who use drugs are from an "academic and social elite. And these student drug users are likely to be just as concerned with ethics and moral integrity as are their fiercest critics—although what each group *means* by morality differs."[132]

What are some of the reasons that students give for the use of drugs? Among the commonly given reasons for using drugs are: combatting fear; exploring one's self; achieving religious experience; relieving boredom, elaborating moods, and so forth.[133] Nowlis suggests that adults with their alcohol and tranquilizers and students with their drugs are both reacting to conditions they feel negate human values and human worth. But the main difference is that what the adults use are depressants taken to blunt the pain. "The students' drugs of choice are perceived by at least some of the more serious, rightly or wrongly, as an attempt to strike back at, to seek insight into, to protest what they feel to be the causes of the pain."[134]

Often the public response to the use of drugs contributes to their being used even more. This is true when the publicly stated reasons against drug use appear to the student to be contradictory or hypocritical. "For

---

[128] *Ibid.*, p. 29.

[129] *Ibid.*, p. 30.

[130] *Ibid.*, p. 28.

[131] Blum, *op. cit.*, p. 81.

[132] Nowlis, *op. cit.*, p. xi.

[133] Blum, *op. cit.*, p. 97.

[134] Nowlis, *op. cit.*, p. 76.

example, it is widely assumed that when there is no medically approved reason for taking a drug the individual has no right to take it. A further questionable assumption is also made; since the only legitimate use of a drug is in the treatment of illness, anyone who takes a drug is, *ipso facto* —ill, or criminal."[135] The students who object to both of the above assumptions argue that alcohol is at least as dangerous, but society assesses it in a different way and says that individuals can take alcohol for other than medical reasons and not be considered ill. Drug users "argue that the attitudes toward alcohol should be extended to include other seemingly non-dangerous, non-medical drugs."[136]

As most college students are not involved in the militancy in the universities, so most are not involved in drug use. As Blum points out, any diagnosis of student drug experimentation or activism which says "students are . . ." misses the fact that *most* students are not. "Even the students who are—are by no means—a homogeneous group."[137] Also, generally speaking, college students who do use drugs use only marijuana. Goode found that on the college campus "heroin use involves a very tiny segment of even the drug-using contingent, and its use is distinctly frowned upon."[138] However, Blum found in his research that in the late 1960's a rapid increase in the number of students experimenting with marijuana occurred. "Hallucinogens appear to have been consistently less popular, although their use also has increased. Hard narcotics use is rare."[139] The using of marijuana varies widely on different types of campuses. For example, at San Francisco State 42 percent of the women and 47 percent of the men had smoked marijuana and intended to continue doing so. At the University of Illinois the rates were 2 percent of the females and 9 percent of the males, and at the University of Alabama it was 2 percent of the coeds and 14 percent of the men.[140]

An increasing number of students arrive at college for their first year already familiar with drug experiences. Blum, in a study of an upper-middle class high school, found that 16 percent of the boys and 10 percent of the girls said they had tried marijuana.[141] In the same sample 10 percent of the boys and 5 percent of the girls said they had tried hallucinogens.[142] Blum says that it took about ten years for drug use to shift from older-intellectual-artistic groups to graduate students. But it only

[135] *Ibid.*, p. 24.

[136] *Ibid.*

[137] Blum, *op. cit.*, p. 6.

[138] Goode, Erich, "Multiple Drug Use among Marijuana Smokers," *Social Problems*, Summer, 1969, p. 59.

[139] Blum, *op. cit.*, p. 17.

[140] *Playboy, op. cit.*, p. 224.

[141] Blum, *op. cit.*, p. 325.

[142] *Ibid.*, p. 326.

took an estimated five years to catch on among undergraduates, "only two or three years to move to a significant number of high school students, and, then, within no more than two years, to move to upper elementary grades. This progression is apparent only for metropolitan centers such as the San Francisco Bay area, Los Angeles, Boston, and New York."[143]

Blum and his associates, after their extensive research, predict that student drug use will continue to expand "and that as these students grow older, many forms of drug use now considered deviant or dangerous will become part of what otherwise respectable adults do."[144] Their prediction is based on the assumption that those who are using the drugs on the campuses will be the future leaders in a change-oriented society which is constantly looking for adjustment, pleasure, and personal enrichment."[145] This assumption also implies a class based prediction. There is no indication that the lower middle classes will turn in large numbers to drugs. Therefore, in the future it may be that the higher educated will turn to drugs and the lower educated to alcohol. One consequence for some may be that the increased use of drugs may stop them from developing alcohol problems of a more severe nature.

A great concern has developed about the use of drugs among students by their parents and that generation. Probably most parents are against the use of drugs by their children, but they are uncertain as to the nature and strength of controls that should be exerted. Probably most adults are not eager for massive police action on the college campuses because many of their sons and daughters would be arrested. So in general most universities ignore discreet use of illegal drugs on the campus. If they don't they will be forced into painful policing of the sort "which will arouse new antagonism between students and authorities and which would, if it were to result in arrest of all students actually using such drugs, cut campus populations—at least in some areas—in half."[146]

In some university communities conflict has developed between the university administrators and the legal authorities in the local community. That is, the university is fairly permissive in policing drug use but the community wants to follow restrictive approaches. For some in the local community the opportunity to legally go after students for drug use may be an excuse. As Fort points out, the laws against drug use, particularly those dealing with marijuana, "provide a convenient device for attacking youth and stifling dissent and non-conformity."[147]

Because the use of drugs is illegal the students on many campuses have

[143] *Ibid.*, p. 362.

[144] *Ibid.*, p. 380.

[145] *Ibid.*

[146] *Ibid.*, p. 363.

[147] Fort, Joel, "Social Problems of Drug Use and Drug Policies," *California Law Review*, January, 1968, p. 26.

set up within their subculture the means for using drugs and dealing with some problems that may arise. As a result the university records rarely show any accurate figures about the use of drugs on the campuses. Blum points out that the "examination of official cases reveals that school records, whether academic, disciplinary, or medical, report far fewer cases of distress than students themselves report."[148] In fact, it is rare for any of the ill effects from the use of drugs to come to the attention of school authorities. On most campuses the students either endure their ill effects or have developed informal procedures "so that, as in other folk medical practice, they take care of themselves and one another without calling for a physician."[149]

SUMMARY

In concluding this chapter it is useful to try to assess the basic impact of the militant student on the universities and on society in general. It is probable that most academics would agree that the serious student protest has been of overall value. It has forced changes that are valuable and that probably would not have been brought about otherwise for many years. These have been needed changes in curriculum and a general questioning of policy that existed because it had always been that way. So students have become more influential with regard to university policies and university programs. For example, it has been primarily the influence of students that brought about the development of Black Studies programs in many colleges and universities. The educated youth of any society have to be taken seriously, even when they condemn the society strongly, because they are the future leaders. But what is also special about the present situation in the United States is that no other society in history has ever had to deal with *mass* educated youth. So the impact of this generation of college students for the future direction of the United States is overwhelming.

At the present time it seems reasonable to predict that the number and intensity of student protests will continue to increase. There are a number of reasons for suggesting this. First, because many of the things that concern them are important and are not being solved. The main problems that are under attack by students are the war, racism, poverty, and bureaucracy, and these are areas that many respected observers would agree require major attempts to correct.[150] Second, the students are directly affected by many of the areas they are connected with. That is, they are blacks, or they can go to war, or they are treated often within a

---

[148] Blum, *op. cit.,* p. 166.

[149] *Ibid.,* p. 363.

[150] Lunsford, Terry F., "Activism, Privatism, and the Moral Advantage," in G. Kerry Smith, *Stress and Campus Response* (San Francisco: Jossey-Bass, Inc., 1968), p. 92.

bureaucratic context. Third, the fact that a great deal of their activity is against the law is not a course of action alien to American society. That is, breaking the law is frequently done by many elements of "respectable society." The American society has a long tradition in the use of violence.[151]

However, once it is predicted that campus militancy will probably continue, and even if it is agreed that some possible gains have been made, it is also clear that the costs have been great and could become even greater. As Harris points out, "it is possible that University education may profit from student dissent and political action in the short run—and suffer in the long run through faculty weariness and the triggering of a national backlash."[152] In 1970 there is convincing evidence that the backlash toward college students is strong. The backlash is taking the direction of supporting more drastic measures against student protest through the use of the police and the national guard. For a large number of Americans the legal representatives are expected to use physical force, including killing, if they, the law enforcement agencies, decide it is necessary. The backlash toward students is also taking the direction of reductions of financial support for higher education by federal, state, and local governments. It is also possible that businesses are contributing less because of their increased hostility toward militant college students.

But most important about the public reaction to the militant college student is that it is the focal point for the strong generational conflict that exists today. To many Americans, especially of the working class and older, the college student is seen as selfish, immoral, and an economic parasite who shows no respect for any of the hallowed American traditions. The student often sees the older generation as reactionary, insensitive, and chauvinistic. The evidence clearly indicates that all of these views are becoming stronger and contributing to increased hostility between the generations.

BIBLIOGRAPHY

ANDERSON, WALT, The Age of Protest (Pacific Palisades, Calif.: Goodyear Publishing Co., Inc., 1969).

BIRENBAUM, WILLIAM M., Overlive: Power, Poverty and the University (New York: Delta Publishing Co., 1969).

BLUM, RICHARD H., Students and Drugs (San Francisco: Jossey-Bass Inc., 1969).

GRANT, JOANNE, Confrontations on Campus: The Columbia Pattern for the New Protest (New York: Signet Book, 1969).

---

[151] Ibid., pp. 93–94.

[152] Harris, op. cit., p. 31.

HADDEN, JEFFREY K., "The Private Generation," *Psychology Today,* October, 1969, pp. 32–35, 68–69.

KATOPE, CHRISTOPHER G. and PAUL G. ZOLBROD, *Beyond Berkeley: A Sourcebook of Student Values* (New York: Harper and Row, 1966).

KENISTON, KENNETH, "Youth, Change and Violence," *The American Scholar,* Spring, 1968.

LIPSET, SEYMOUR, "Students and Politics," *Daedalus,* Winter, 1968, pp. 1–20.

NOWLIS, HELEN H., *Drugs on the College Campus* (New York: Anchor Books, 1969).

RIDGEWAY, JAMES, *The Closed Corporation: American Universities in Crisis* (New York: Ballatine Books, 1968).

SCOTT, JOSEPH W. and MOHAMED EL-ASSAL, "Multiversity, University Size, University Quality and Student Protest: An Empirical Study," *American Sociological Review,* October, 1969, pp. 702–709.

SELIGMAN, DANIEL, "A Special Kind of Rebellion," in *Youth in Turmoil* (New York: Time-Life Books, 1969), pp. 13–30.

SIMMON, GEOFFREY and GRAFTON TROUT, "Hippies in College—From Teeny-Boppers to Drug Freaks," *Trans-Action,* December, 1967, pp. 27–32.

SKOLNICK, JEROME H., *The Politics of Protest* (New York: Ballatine Books, 1969).

SMITH, G. KERRY, *Stress and Campus Response* (San Francisco: Jossey-Bass Inc., 1968).

Youth in Turmoil (New York: Time-Life Books, 1969).

CHAPTER 16

THE HIPPIE MOVEMENT

ON THE most general level this chapter can be seen as a logical continuation of the previous one on the militant student. What will be considered here is another way in which a significant number of young people have deviated from the traditional range of expectations available to them. Basically the difference is that the militant student has rebelled against society and attempts to change it in some way, while the hippie drops out of society. The hippie movement first achieved public attention in the mid-1960's, and since that time has developed into a social movement. This chapter is concerned with the initial development of the hippie subculture during the mid-1960's and what has happened to the movement since that time.

The hippie movement as it is used here has been referred to as a "counter-culture" by some writers. But it is believed that that term implies too much—almost as if two cultures function at the same time. It is hoped that the term hippie conveys the sense of both origin and development of a social movement, and not the emergence of a new and basically distinct counter-culture.

The historical roots of the hippie movement, at least in terms of the communal living aspect, extend far back into the past. Probably the pattern of communal living is almost as old as mankind, but there have been periods in history when this life-style caught the imagination and participation of enough people to be called a social movement. Those movements in the past were often tied in with religious beliefs, for example, the Cenobite movement in third century Egypt, Benedictine monasticism in the early Medieval Ages, Franciscan monasticism in the late Middle Ages, the Jesuits of the counter Reformation, the Anabaptists of Lutheran Germany, and the 19th century utopian communities of the United States.[1] At each of those periods in history important changes were occurring in society and the communes were reactions to those changes.

The hippie movement, along with the communal pattern of living, also is based on a rejection of many general values of society. In the United States there is a long tradition of this kind of rejection, for example, "the tradition of revulsion against conforming, unaesthetic, materialistic, unattractive, middle-class America runs through American writing from Melville through the 'lost generation' to the 'beat generation' and has been expressed concretely in the Bohemian subcultures that have flourished in a few large cities since the turn of the century."[2]

In recent American history the hippie movement emerged out of the "beat" generation. Actually, bohemians, beats, and artistically inclined undergraduates who rejected middle-class values have long been a part of the American student scene, especially at the more prestigeful colleges and universities. They represented the only really visible form of dissent during the political and moral silence of American students in the 1950's.[3] They generally had little influence beyond themselves because they were small in number and were not motivated to proselytize or influence the behavior of others. This lack of involvement was characteristic of the beat scene that developed in the 1950's and early 1960's. In that movement people had encounters rather than interpersonal involvements. If the beatnik objected to the world as it existed, the most that he would propose as a program of reform would have been the removal of every social and intellectual restraint on the expression and enjoyment of his unique individuality. "To each his own kicks. Social protest rarely gets beyond the state of hating cops. The beats are notably apolitical."[4]

The hippie movement did not develop under the influence of any single, charismatic leader. Rather it appeared to emerge more as a result of the unrest and frustrations that were felt during the same period of time by a large number of young people. However, if there was an early leader and founder of the hippie movement it was probably Timothy

---

[1] Groutt, John, "The Communal Movement: A View from the Bridge," 1970, unpublished, pp. 3–4.

[2] Keniston, Kenneth, "The Sources of Student Dissent," in Walt Anderson, *The Age of Protest* (Pacific Palisades, Calif.: Goodyear Publishing Co., Inc., 1969), p. 239.

[3] *Ibid.*, p. 232.

[4] Powell, Elwin H., "Beyond Utopia: The 'Beat' Generation: As a Challenge for the Sociology of Knowledge," in Arnold Rose, *Human Behavior and Human Processes* (New York: Houghton-Mifflin, 1964), pp. 365–66.

Leary. But the early stages of the movement gathered momentum around the slogan of *love* "and a rejection of middle-class materialism, hypocrisy, and dishonesty."[5] The hippie movement primarily developed around the San Francisco–Berkeley area in the mid-1960's. As soon as the word spread, a migration to the San Francisco area took place. It has been suggested that the migration reflects in its own way the continuing strong migration of newcomers to the state of California. However, the "go west" theme was narrowed for the early hippies. Going west meant specifically the Bay Area, not Laramie, Wyoming, and rarely Denver or Boulder, Colorado.[6]

As a social movement the hippie scene developed within a mass society where the traditional ties of community and class were weak and where there was a development of identification with one's age-peers. A common result of rapid social change and upheaval or extensive vertical mobility is for generations to split off from each other.[7] So age has been a basic factor in the hippie movement—it was developed by and for the young. In the mid-1960's, as various hippie groups emerged in different cities, the hippie mecca quickly came to be the Haight-Ashbury district of San Francisco.

The hippie movement was given tremendous impetus by some of the agencies of "square" society, especially the mass media. In 1966 television discovered the hippies and by 1970 there was not a major television station, magazine, or newspaper who hadn't devoted time or space to the hippie phenomenon. The term hippie became a part of the American language and has come to mean for most Americans practically anyone who has long hair, a beard, or who dresses differently. But one of the other consequences of the great amount of publicity given to the hippie movement was that it contributed greatly to the recruitment because it made many young people aware of what was going on and where. It should also be mentioned that San Francisco has a long tradition of accepting the deviant, especially if he is profitable. By the summer of 1967 San Francisco was making millions of dollars off the hippies because they had become the major tourist attraction. In fact, they almost put out of business the previous tourist attraction—the topless dancers, waitresses, and shoe shine girls. There is a certain irony in that some of the social agencies the hippies most strongly reject were highly instrumental in contributing to their early success.

While there tends to be general hostility toward all hippies by most Americans today there was initially a high fascination with them. Sim-

---

[5] Yablonsky, Lewis, *The Hippie Trip* (New York: Pegasus, 1968), p. 289.

[6] Carey, James T., *The College Drug Scene* (Englewood Cliffs, N.J.: Prentice-Hall, 1968), p. 18.

[7] Powell, *op. cit.*, p. 362.

mons writes that even as we put down the deviant, he often sparks our desires to be free and wild and leads us to tug against our moral restraints. "Our own Western outlaws, and more recently the beats and hippies, have produced a similar ambivalence in mainstream American society."[8] For many Americans the reaction to the hippies has been a mixture of attraction and revulsion, envy and rejection.

There were many in the mid-1960's who believed that the hippie movement was a temporary thing and would fade away as had many other fads. However, such has not been the case because the roots of the hippie movement are deep within American society. As the years of adolescent dependence are further lengthened, "and as the accelerated pace of technological change aggravates the normal social tendency to intergenerational conflict, an increasing number of young people can be expected to drop out, or opt out, and drop into the hippie subculture."[9] And the influence of the hippie movement may continue to be great on those of the same age who do not actively enter the subculture. "A very large number can be expected to hover so close to the margins of hippie subculture as to have their attitudes and outlooks substantially modified."[10]

THE HIPPIE SUBCULTURE

In this section a general description and analysis will be presented of the hippie subculture. However, the picture presented here is of an ideal type rather than of a specific subculture. That is, the presentation draws upon a number of studies and attempts to put the various findings together to create an ideal picture. It will be clear that there are many variations from the ideal type presented in this section. Also, the picture described here is primarily of the subculture that existed in 1966 and 1967 in San Francisco. The last section of this chapter will be concerned with the changes that have occurred in the hippie subculture since 1967.

The term hippie is derived from "hip." The term roughly means to be emotionally and spiritually wise or in-group "and it has a clever, light and airy semantical connotation. It seems apt for a movement with a gay love-in, colorful, fun, not totally serious ethic."[11] Even though the term hippie has been used by the general public in a derogatory way it is still used by hippies themselves. One recent study found that people do refer to themselves as hippies, and to them being a hippie "means dropping out completely, and finding another way to live, to support oneself physically and spiritually. It means saying no to competition, no to the

[8] Simmons, J. L., *Deviants* (San Francisco: The Glendessary Press, 1969), p. 22.

[9] Davis, Fred, "Why All of Us May Be Hippies Someday," *Trans-Action*, December, 1967, p. 18.

[10] *Ibid.*

[11] Yablonsky, *op. cit.*, p. 290.

work ethic, no to consumption of technology's products, no to political systems and games."[12]

There is a common tendency to lump together those called hippies with those defined as young radicals. However, those two groups are different in several ways. Basically the radical has not given up on his society or his political beliefs and his efforts are aimed at changing that society. However, the hippie has dropped out of a society he believes to be lost or irredeemable. His focus is on the change and development of his personal consciousness. The hippies are apolitical. They reject the capitalist emphasis on "mine," whether it be my house, my money, my gadgets, my child or my work of art. But they also reject the Communist practice of job assignment and restriction of the arts and individual freedom.[13]

There tends to be a strong awareness by hippies that they are different from society in general. This is because they have rejected the social values rather than having been rejected by society, as is true of such deviants as the drug addict, the homosexual, and so forth. The hippies see themselves as a subculture that exists outside of and apart from ordinary, everyday society. "They see their way of living, especially its communal aspects and 'tribes,' as a return to simpler and more primitive social reforms. Importantly, the straight world also tends to see the hippie scene as remote and strange."[14]

In earlier chapters discussing various deviants it was shown that many were deviants in only a few aspects of their total life. For example, the drug addict or homosexual might go through many days' activities and no one would be aware of his deviancy. By contrast, the deviancy of the hippie is something that is almost constantly observable because that is his choice. As a result the life style of the hippie subculture is not just different from the rest of society but it is inescapably and observably different. There have always been many young people (and also some older ones) who have not accepted all the standard middle-class American values and behavior patterns. "But in the past most of them went their different ways more privately and *sub rosa*, individually or in small groups."[15] Often the stress of the hippie movement is on individual behavior, but that behavior occurs mainly on a group level which is different from the usual patterns of American behavior.

Before examining the subculture in some detail it is useful to look at the background of hippies. In most respects their backgrounds are not

[12] Davidson, Sara, "Openland: Getting Back to the Communal Garden," *Harper's*, June, 1970, p. 94.

[13] Bingham, June, "The Intelligent Square's Guide to Hippieland," in Dinitz, Simon *et al.*, *Deviance* (New York: Oxford Press, 1969), p. 420.

[14] Weakland, John H., "Hippies: What the Scene Means," in Richard Blum, *Society and Drugs* (San Francisco: Jossey-Bass, Inc., 1969), p. 343.

[15] *Ibid.*, p. 352.

different from those of militant students. How many genuine hippies there are is very difficult to estimate. Yablonsky, in 1967, estimated that there were about 200,000 core, visible and identifiable hippies in the United States totally committed to that way of life. Along with that number he estimated another 200,000 visible teeny-boppers, part-time summer and weekend hippies. Yablonsky also suggested that in addition there may have been several hundred thousand invisible "Clark Kent" hippies. "There are students, young executives, and professional people who use psychedelic drugs, interact, and closely associate with totally dropped-out hippies, yet maintain nine-to-five jobs or student status. Many of these 'invisible hippies' are potentially total dropouts."[16] So there may be several million Americans, in various degrees, involved with the hippie movement. There is also a constant turnover and even in the 1970 hippie communes Ald observed that the number of new dropouts from society greatly exceeded those members who left the communes. In fact, "the fluidity of the scene imbues its participants with the feeling that they are pioneers and that their collective attempts are but experiments for arriving at the truth."[17]

On the most general level the hippie subculture has been a part of the subculture of poverty. Harrington writes that there is one subculture of poverty in the United States that at times is spirited and enthusiastic. There live the poor who are intellectuals, bohemians, and hippies. "They strive or pose; they achieve or go back to the middle class whence they usually come. But their lives are lived in the midst of physical deprivation and, often enough, of hunger."[18] What is striking about these groups is that outside of religious orders they are the only citizens of the affluent American society who choose to be poor. And yet, even though the intellectual or the hippie share the tenements, the diets, and the work of the poor, they are really not a part of the overall culture of poverty. They have chosen a way of life instead of being victimized by it. "They do not participate in the atmosphere of defeatism that permeates the lives of the truly poor."[19] While the hippie subculture may be characterized by poverty, it has a very different meaning than for those who live in a world where there has always been poverty and there is no chance of participation.

Yablonsky found in his study that three quarters of the hippies came from middle- and upper-class segments of American society. He points out that they voluntarily chose to drop out into scenes that Negroes and other minority groups have been trying to escape from for more than half

---

[16] Yablonsky, *op. cit.*, p. 37.

[17] Ald, Roy, *The Youth Communes* (New York: Tower Publications, 1970), p. 41.

[18] Harrington, Michael, *The Other America: Poverty in the United States* (Baltimore, Maryland: Penguin Books, 1963), p. 83.

[19] *Ibid.*, p. 86.

a century.[20] As discussed in earlier chapters, when the children of the affluent reject those values that many in the lower middle classes are striving for, questions arise for those doing the striving. Therefore, a part of the hostility directed at hippies is for this reason. When those who have say it's not worth having, those that want see their aspirations seriously questioned, rejected, and even ridiculed.

In Yablonsky's sample of 686 hippies he found that over three-quarters of them had graduated from high school and half had at least some college.[21] Almost three-quarters of them reported coming from a family with an income of over $7,500 a year. He also found in his sample that the sex ratio was three males for every female.[22] In terms of religious backgrounds most hippies have few if any ties with organized religions. It is also the case, as with militant students, that a disproportionate number of hippies are Jews. There has been one study of Catholic students who became hippies and it was found that they were moved initially by a crisis of faith and were attracted by the opportunity to avoid their religious community. The Catholic moved from religious solutions to those offered by the hippie subculture. So he must learn new myths outside of a strongly Catholic milieu. "Upon accepting those myths, which necessarily implies that he is considerably involved with others who are non-Catholics or ex-Catholics, he embarks on a new path which, however odd its trappings, finds him bound by the same dimensions of the religious absolute that defined his seeking when it was conducted within a more conventional setting."[23] That is, he changes the values he is committed to—but in both situations a strong commitment is called for.

It is possible to draw from two studies of hippie groups made in Berkeley and in Haight-Ashbury to provide a general picture of the hippie. Generally the members are in the age range of 18 to 25 and are likely to be students or are student dropouts. They are usually the products of the established middle class and are confident enough of their position in society to be able to criticize and react to the faults of society from their perspective. They are metropolitan dwellers who were raised in large cities or in the suburbs.[24] The second study found that most of the hippies were from states outside of California and had been in that state less than a year. That study also found most to have had at least some college education and to be from middle- and upper-class families. They were found to be disassociated from conventional Christianity. "Ninety-six percent had smoked pot and 90 percent had taken LSD. Regarding

---

[20] Yablonsky, op. cit., p. 26.

[21] Ibid., p. 344.

[22] Ibid., p. 345.

[23] Custis, Jack H., "Drugs and Catholic Students," in Richard Blum, Society and Drugs (San Francisco: Jossey-Bass, Inc., 1969), p. 319.

[24] Carey, op. cit., p. 11.

sexuality, 42 percent of the males reported homosexual experiences, as did 24 percent of the females."[25]

An examination of the recruitment and joining of new members into the hippie subculture shows that probably the most powerful recruitment appeals are based on a disenchantment with society and its institutions and the feeling that the hippie subculture offers a better way of life. Yablonsky suggests that many youths drop out of society and become hippies to rationally escape from a society "that undeniably has many plastic, ahuman characteristics. However, many other youths who join the hippie movement do so because they are already in one degree or another emotionally disturbed rejects from the larger society. In a sense, they are displaced persons, refugees, whose emotional condition was produced by a society that has no acceptable solutions for their treatment."[26] The hippie communities around the country provide a network of safe "islands" throughout the society which promise the alienated some amount of security and the feeling of being part of a far larger movement that he can find wherever he goes in the country.

There are many individuals out of other deviant groups that are attracted to the hippie movement, that is, individuals from the peace movement, revolutionaries, political activists, anarchists, homosexuals, drug users, and so forth. Or it may be that some individuals live by shifting back and forth between subcultures. But whatever the reason for entering the hippie subculture the novice tends in his initial involvement to identify very strongly. And while those who have been a part of the hippie scene for some time will admit to many phony and destructive aspects of the life, the novice admits to none. "He is more vocal and perhaps clutching more desperately at the new ideas and philosophy because he has not yet achieved 'the peace of pure involvement.' "[27]

In the value system of the hippie subculture there are two major values, the love ethic and doing one's own thing. The hippie values abhor violence and war and the slogan "Make love, not war" expresses that sentiment. Love is seen as the only valid reason for positive interaction between human beings. And any behavior that might influence or order behavior by other means is seen as evil and doomed to ultimate failure. However, the hippie idea of love is vague and hard to clarify. "It is evident, however, that his 'love' is centered in the individual, connected with one's personal achievement or self-knowledge and realization of harmony with the entire universe."[28] The love ethic is conceived to be at the opposite pole from an American culture viewed as competitive,

---

[25] Blum, *op. cit.*, p. 24.

[26] Yablonsky, *op. cit.*, p. 329.

[27] *Ibid.*, p. 32.

[28] Weakland, *op. cit.*, p. 354.

hostile, and violent. If there is a basic purpose to the hippie movement it is an attempt to achieve a condition of love. "That their aspirations fall far short of their lofty goals may be more of a commentary on the spiritual poverty of the society in which the effort is taking place than on the feeble attempts at love acted out by the young affluent participants in the movement."[29]

The second major value of the hippie subculture is that of "doing his own thing." This value means exactly what it says in that the individual pursues his life as he chooses. This places it in direct opposition to the superordinate-subordinate complex of American society. The right to do one's own thing is a central battle orientation of the hippie movement.[30] This value places the major stress for the measurement of success with the individual rather than with society. Therefore, the status symbols that serve as measurements of success in society are inappropriate to the hippie world.

The time dimension for the hippie subculture is the present. There is little concern for any aspects of the past. So the belief is that life is now and every moment is as valid as any other and whatever pleasures there are to life should be extracted immediately. Therefore there is no reason in forgoing pleasure for hard work in order to realize a pleasure profit at the end of one's lifetime. "Everywhere on the commune scene, pleasure, good feelings, good vibes, are not a means toward any committed end. Pleasure is in itself both the means and the end."[31] The hippie view represents a sharp change from the traditional view of time in American society, as Davis puts it, the shift from what will be to what is, from future promise to present satisfaction, "from the mundane discounting of present feeling and mood to a sharpened awareness of their contours and their possibilities for instant alteration. Broadly, it is to invest present experience with a new cognitive status and importance: a lust to extract from the living moment its full sensory and emotional potential."[32] The middle-class pattern is one of deferred gratification while the hippie belief is in immediate gratification.

When it comes to what one does with his life in doing his own thing the hippie view basically is: all of them are artists. Quite simply their manifesto is that all men are artists and it makes no difference that some are better at it than others.[33] What is important is that the individual honestly seek out for himself and others the best in life that can be achieved without hurting others. When this is achieved then the artist is being

---

[29] Yablonsky, op. cit., p. 286.
[30] Ibid., p. 311.
[31] Ald, op. cit., p. 77.
[32] Davis, op. cit., p. 15.
[33] Ibid., p. 14.

successful and has achieved his ends, and that is the only measurement.

A major part of the belief in doing one's own thing is that the external controls will be minimal or nonexistent, if possible. This is a part of the view which sees the rights and controls of any government as "total insanity." "The assumption that anyone should have real granted power over another person is a complete violation of the hippie ethic of 'doing your own thing' and being a 'free man.' The true hippie is a complete *anarchist*."[34] Yet, with all the talk about total freedom and doing one's own thing the hippie world is marked by its own type of conformity. "This is perhaps most evident in terms of dress and drug use, but the hippie world also has its own moral standards and fixed conception of proper social behavior—in fact, quite rigid ones."[35]

Probably the group closest to having total freedom to do one's own thing to come out of the hippie movement has been the Yippies. The Yippies are present day Dadaists. Dada was always devoted to the destruction of Dada; its principles were often enunciated: The real Dadaists are against Dada. "Everyone is a leader of Dada. No one is a leader of Dada. The Dadaists and Surrealists wanted to kill art, which degenerates inevitably into Culture. But Dada's own gestures were continually being framed off as artifacts and hailed as 'the new art,' so the movement had to keep killing itself."[36] The similarity of the Yippies can be seen in that Abbie Hoffman wrote after Chicago in 1968, "There never were any Yippies and there never will be. It was a slogan YIPPEE! and that exclamation point was what it was all about. It was the biggest put-on of all time." And Paul Krassner wrote that, "the crazies have a rule that in order to become a member one must first destroy his official membership card."[37] What these splinter non-group groups indicate is that the hippie subculture must have some structure and conformity to exist regardless of what some of its members may attempt to argue.

Because the hippie subculture represents a sharp break from the values of the broader society the individual identification with the movement is often very strong. As a result there tends to be an extravagant faith in the movement. Yablonsky found that hippies, especially when they were under the influence of drugs, had "an unshakable belief in the correctness and perfect character of their new life style. *Extravagant faith* is especially characteristic of religious movements, in many respects modern hippies are comparable to the early Christians."[38]

While there is strong faith in the hippie movement there is no interest

---

[34] Yablonsky, *op. cit.*, p. 321.

[35] Weakland, *op. cit.*, p. 354.

[36] Wills, Garry, "The Making of the Yippie Culture," *Esquire*, November, 1969, p. 135.

[37] *Ibid.*

[38] Yablonsky, *op. cit.*, p. 291.

in organized religion. Hippies feel that the spiritual and emotional quality of the religious experience in traditional religious groups has died along with God. They see organized religion in the United States as being outwardly directed in that one is measured by others rather than by himself. As a result the hippie is interested in the inwardly oriented Eastern philosophies and religions. Magic, drugs, astrology, divination (the *I Ching*), transcendental meditation, Eastern mysticism, sensitivity groups all are basically aimed at giving man some sense of control over his individual self. A study done of 18 religious communes over a period of three years found that the belief in the paranormal was virtually an act of faith held by communal inhabitants. "Use of the *I Ching*, Tarot cards, the Ouija Board, and astrology is a common element in the lives of these people. The notion that 'mental vibrations' can influence crops, the weather, animals, and people is taken for granted."[39]

Along with rejecting many of the major values of society the hippies also reject material goods in the sense of accumulation. In the Haight-Ashbury hippie setting there existed such establishments as the Diggers' Free Store that gave things away that were given to them. The anti-materialistic position is evident in other ways. For example, many hippies in the cities engage in panhandling. Their approach is one of easy, and sometimes condescending, casualness, "as if to say, 'You've got more than enough to spare, I need it, so let's not make a degrading charity scene out of my asking you.' "[40] Of course in the United States many material goods have their real significance as symbols of success and when the hippie rejects those material things as unimportant he is once again rejecting those things that many Americans devote their total lives toward achieving and accumulating.

The value system of the hippie centers around a few values and the rejection of many things that are unimportant to him. Because there are few things that he wants and because he stresses the present there is little concern with the future in any planning sense. Basically, most hippie groups are nondogmatic, nonideological, and to a large extent hostile to doctrine or formula for the future. So there are no long range plans and no life patterns laid out in advance. But the stress on not planning is both a strength and weakness of the hippie movement. It is a strength because it is attractive to the members who want to do their own thing, but it is a weakness because it makes the movement extremely difficult to maintain. Their very hostility toward any form of government defeats any effort on their part to achieve as a group. "Consequently, most hippie attempts at communes *without governments* are chaotic failures, at least by American standards of evaluation. Their bitter rejection of govern-

---

[39] Groutt, *op. cit.*, p. 10.

[40] Davis, *op. cit.*, p. 13.

ment and their embracement of total anarchy is thus a major difficulty of the movement."[41]

In general, the more complex and organized a subculture the greater the number of roles. Therefore, in the hippie subculture, with minimal organization, there are few roles to be filled. If the subculture were totally unstructured there would be no roles and everyone would be like everyone else in whatever he did. However, there are some general distinctions that can be made between roles. Yablonsky describes the "high priest" or "philosopher" in the hippie scene. What distinguishes that role from others is that he claims to have reached some level of being tuned-in to the cosmic affinity of man. The high priest believes on some level that there is a God in all people, all things, and that he is part of that unity. "The true hippie priest believes he has achieved his position of ascendency, in part, through the use of drugs as a sacrament."[42]

Also in many hippie settings the role of a leader develops. There are often non-compassionate, physically strong people who fill the leadership vacuum and take over where there has been anarchy. The hippie belief that when everybody simply does his thing order will prevail does not usually work. "The inevitable psychopaths in the group, who have a thin veneer of love on the surface, begin to take advantage and push people around, including the natural, real spiritual leaders in the group."[43] This also reflects the fact that regardless of the honesty of almost all hippies there are often some who are dishonest, consciously or unconsciously, who exploit the group. And because the hippie is committed to the belief in doing one's own thing he will generally tolerate a great deal from others before expelling them from the group.

Yablonsky, in his study, estimated that in the hippie subculture there may be 10 to 15 percent who have the role of high priest or philosopher. He suggests that the novice makes up another 35 percent of the total. That means that, in Yablonsky's view, only about 50 percent of the hippie subculture is pure. "The other half of the hippie world is a conglomeration of people, mainly young people with varied motivations. There are roughly four categories: (1) a new breed of hippie drug addict; (2) 'teeny-boppers'; (3) severely emotionally disturbed people using the hippie world as a sanctuary; and (4) miscellany."[44] In one important sense the hippie subculture is like religion—both are expected to welcome anyone who seeks them out.

The teeny-boppers are important because out of that group come many of the recruits of the future. Initially most of them are part-time, week-

---

[41] Yablonsky, *op. cit.*, p. 322.
[42] *Ibid.*, p. 30.
[43] *Ibid.*, p. 196.
[44] *Ibid.*, p. 33.

end, or summer hippies. The teeny-boppers are teenagers who "make the scene." They have an enormous involvement with the new music; "and with allowances granted by indulgent middle-class parents, they buy the records. They use the drugs on the scene, not for the spiritual purposes, but admittedly for fun and risks."[45] It can be seen that the roles are not many in the hippie subculture and are generally related to the extent of involvement in the scene rather than to any status or power relationship between individuals.

One of the characteristics of subcultures discussed in detail in this book is the development of specialized language or argot by various deviant subcultures. The argot of the hippie subculture is rich and extensive. The argot has been borrowed from other subcultures, often with some slight changes in meaning. The hippie has borrowed in particular from the Negro, jazz, homosexual, and drug addict subcultures. His language is strongly directed towards words and phrases in the active present tense, for example, such words as "happening," "where it's at," "turn on," "freak out," "grooving," "mind-blowing," "be-in," "cop-out" and "split."[46] But many of the hippie terms have been taken over by the broader society and they are even found being used in television commercials. When that happens the subculture usually comes up with new terms, with the meanings for a while limited to the hippies themselves.

Most hippies dress very much alike but this is often because they get cheap, functional clothing that does not allow for variations in styling even if such were desired. But the clothing, along with grooming, sets the hippie apart from conventional society and attenuates any kind of relationship. His dress and appearance symbolize to others like himself that they share certain things, and at the same time symbolize to the outside world that it has nothing in common with him. Hippies are well aware that straight people are upset or offended by what they consider to be the flouting of conventional middle-class norms in dress styles. Probably the attitude toward cleanliness among some hippies most grates upon the middle-class observer because it symbolizes the corruption of "clean" values.[47] It is interesting that while hippie dress patterns have been aped by many in straight society and have been exploited commercially, the important point about dress for the hippie is that usually it is clear that the clothes he wears and his general appearance are unimportant to him. It doesn't matter what he wears, with the result that many in straight society are offended by his rejection of their value that appearance matters.

As suggested, a major hippy value in influencing others is love. This

---

[45] *Ibid.*, p. 34.

[46] Davis, *op. cit.*, p. 15.

[47] Carey, *op. cit.*, p. 64.

means that manipulation is defined as bad and one reacts and affects another through love. However, the hippie generally does not believe that commitment and intense emotional involvement with another person is either positive or desirable. As a result the "personal relationships among the hippies, though pleasant and easy-going, often appear as cool and thin, as essentially transient—not necessarily brief, but never necessarily lasting."[48] There is an important difference between love as seen by hippies and as seen by the broader society in that to most Americans love must be lasting or it is not defined as real or significant love, while for the hippie love is an emotion which may be very intense but is usually short in duration. It does not imply monogamy as it does in the broader society. Carey observes that "to love someone means simply that they 'turn you on,' that you respond to them at a physical level and are attuned to them. The former requirement of romantic love as a prerequisite to sexual intercourse is no longer necessary."[49]

The hippie views of love are also related to views about sexual involvement and commitment. The public image, as developed through the mass media, is that hippies live in one continuous sex orgy. But there is no evidence that this is true, although the hippie values with regard to sex are quite different from those of the broader society. Basically the hippie ideal value is extra-sexual, that is, seeking for a communion of persons more intimate than the sexual connection on a physical plane. "The body is not only an end-purpose but a vehicle for a profounder, all-enveloping force."[50] This describes an ideal value about sex, and actual sexual practices are obviously generally engaged in for the pleasure of the act and are often spontaneous to the occasion. In this respect sex is not practiced with ritual but is more a happening. Because most of the values against sex common to American society are removed, sex is simply a part of the hippie scene. This is generally true only if the person is a part of the subculture because the hippie sex setting is *not* one of free love. "Sex is not free—one must be resonant to the feelings of the potential sex mate. For people fully tuned-in, sex is "free," plentiful, and, from all reports, 'a groove' great in the hippie world."[51]

Ald, after spending some time in hippie communes, observed that his first impression was that there was a great deal of sexual activity, but he realized that "this impression had been heightened because of the obviousness of their sexual acts. They would take place almost anywhere, casually, among people sleeping, dozing, and others talking."[52] Ald also ob-

---

[48] Weakland, *op. cit.*, p. 355.
[49] Carey, *op. cit.*, pp. 25–26.
[50] Ald, *op. cit.*, p. 87.
[51] Yablonsky, *op. cit.*, p. 23.
[52] Ald, *op. cit.*, p. 80.

served that because sexual expression is open and available to the members, there is a reduction in any lustful desire in the hippie communes.[53] There also appears to be much more sexual experimentation among the hippies. That is, homosexuality among both men and women is common and this reflects far fewer restrictions or "hang-ups" among hippies as to what is sexually acceptable. The same basic hippie value applies to sex—what one wants to do, if it does not hurt others, he should do.

Along with the image of the hippies engaging in never-ending sex orgies, there is also the stereotype of them as always being on drugs. This notion, like that about their sexual views, has some basis in truth, although greatly exaggerated by the mass media. It is important to look at the value context in which the hippie chooses to use drugs. He basically turns to drugs when his imagination fails. "Drugs impart to the present —or so it is alleged by the hippie psychedelic religionists—an aura of aliveness, a sense of union with fellow men and nature."[54] Drugs are also used because of alienation from the broader society and the hope that through drugs new dimensions will be seen and achieved. However, there is more than alienation because many in society who are alienated do not turn to drugs. Other things must be present, namely the subculture, so that the person is in a setting where drugs are available and where he is introduced to them by those who are significant others to him.

What are the drugs used in the hippie subculture? Marijuana is a basic staple of the hippie world and is generally smoked in a group. LSD is also commonly used. Yablonsky states that LSD was used by a large majority of all the hippies he met "as their personal key to cosmic consciousness and universal unity. But LSD and 'grass' are viewed by many hippies as the sacraments of their religion."[55] Another study of a hippie community found that there was a general caution about the use of LSD. In that group those that tried it did not take it often—about once or twice a month. "It is an intense experience which must be thought about. Furthermore, they will not aggressively proselytize—though they are eager to talk about it."[56] The studies agree that the amphetamine drugs like methedrine are not commonly used by hippies. "A true hip believer 'puts down' the use of these drugs, which are considered, along with such drugs as heroin, to be a 'bad trip.' "[57]

The use of marijuana is an accepted part of the hippie subculture and is generally not given much thought. In the hippie world the non-marijuana user is a rarity. "Firsthand and secondhand information about

---

[53] *Ibid.*, p. 88.

[54] Davis, *op. cit.*, p. 17.

[55] Yablonsky, *op. cit.*, p. 22.

[56] Carey, *op. cit.*, p. 64.

[57] Yablonsky, *op. cit.*, p. 23.

drugs is so quickly and thoroughly disseminated that even the open-minded non-user can fairly easily determine the effects of various drugs."[58] In fact, very often the hippies read the official and medical statements to see how close the authorities approach "reality," not for any enlightenment. These drug-users in many ways know more than the experts.[59] The hippie view of the social disapproval by the broader society toward marijuana is seen as an absurd tragedy and a "reaffirmation of the reasons for rebellion by those engaged in making their separation from such authority."[60]

Because many hippies are able to handle drugs without physical or psychological problems does not mean that all are free of severe problems. There may be as many as a third of all hippies who are addicted to "speed" in some self-destructive fashion. This is related to the fact that a significant minority of hippies are severely emotionally disturbed people who turn to the hippie community as a refuge from the broader society. In any hippie group there may be a number of persons with severe medical problems that are sometimes intensified by drug use. There are also more minor health problems among other hippies. For example, there is a prevalence of colds, bronchial diseases, and sinusitis. And much of the listlessness and poor health among the hippies can be attributed to malnourishment and inadequate shelter.[61]

The relationship of the hippie to the broader society is a complex one and generally is characterized by hostility from both sides. First, a look at how the hippie views the broader society, and second, how he is viewed in turn. Basically, for the hippie, American society is beyond redemption or is not worth trying to redeem. The hippie's emphasis on the present, love, and doing his own thing, along with the rejection of traditional values, prevents him from undertaking any long range endeavors like education or community organization. He therefore refuses to participate in the "future" orientation so basic to American society. Regardless of whatever real or imagined pathology the middle class assigns to the hippies, it is the middle-class scheme of life that the hippies are reacting against. So *the hip scene is the message,* "not the elements whence it derives or the meanings that can be assigned to it verbally."[62] The hippie subculture sees society as "straight," "rigid," "up-tight," and "inflexible" and accuses it of imposing its outlooks and its institutions on persons who want and need something else or something more.

Because most hippies come out of the middle and upper classes they

---

[58] Carey, *op. cit.*, p. 40.
[59] *Ibid.*
[60] *Ibid.*, p. 41.
[61] Ald, *op. cit.*, p. 104.
[62] Davis, *op. cit.*, pp. 10–11.

have been a part of the system they are rejecting. And furthermore they could have achieved many of the goals held to be most valuable by society. Therefore, they are not reacting against blocked opportunity structures. "In contrast with the traditional delinquent, the new deviants, the hippies, reject the means, the goals, and the values of society."[63] What separates the hippie from most other deviant groups is that not only has he had what is defined as desirable and rejected it, but furthermore refuses the opportunity to return to the fold and have his "sins" forgiven. The hippie is also saying in effect that he doesn't care about the rest of society because they can't be changed. Therefore, you can't change others but only yourself. "A true hippie believer would not get 'hung-up' with heavy game playing, the new left, war protests, or civil rights battles. He simply would strengthen his own perceptions of honesty and truth."[64]

One of the most difficult ideas for members of the broader society to grasp is that the hippie world simply does not care about them. Often the hippie subculture simply wants to be let alone and, when it is criticized by the broader society, it is usually completely indifferent. And once deeply felt moral concerns and criticisms are met with hippie indifference, increased hostility by society is often the result. Too, the hippie subculture often says to the older generation that the only way it can reach the hippies is by turning on itself, which the hippies know is an impossibility for their parents' generation. Yet, this is the counterpart of what many young complain about when they say they can get together with their parents only if it is according to their parents' values and standards. "The standards and evaluations are in opposition, but underlying both positions is the common premise that contact depends on likeness."[65]

In some respects the older adult world has a love-hate relationship with the hippie subculture. There are some who accept that way of life, a large majority who reject it, and the rest who fall somewhere in between. There are some parents who state their opposition to the hippie subculture and yet send money and other kinds of reinforcement to their children. But the strongest feeling for many in the older generation simply may be that of envy and that they are a part of the wrong generation.

In the years since the hippie first came to the attention of the public he has been subjected to increasing harassment by society. In many communities before there is police harassment other methods are often used. For example, rumors about disease, orgies, drugs, thievery, and corruption of the young are often circulated through the neighboring areas. This is sometimes followed by a period of harassment by local "toughs," arson, killing of pets, shooting up the place, molesting of men and women, and

---

[63] Yablonsky, *op. cit.*, p. 320.

[64] *Ibid.*, p. 57.

[65] Weakland, *op. cit.*, pp. 356–57.

damaging of machinery. The fact that drugs are often used provides the police with the reason for busting some of the hippie settlements. Increasingly, the free circulation of drugs is a continuing source of tension in many hippie communities because of the threat of police intervention.

As suggested at the start of this section the intent has been to provide a general picture of the hippie subculture, particularly as it developed in the late 1960's. The hippie subculture, as it existed in San Francisco, ended the summer of 1967 and at that time many believed that the hippie movement was over. However, the movement changed directions in a number of ways and has continued to grow in importance. In the last section the interest is in looking at the direction the hippie movement had taken by the beginning of the 1970's.

THE HIPPIE MOVEMENT IN THE EARLY 1970s

During the developing stages of the hippie movement in the mid-1960's hippies moved into the slum areas in San Francisco, New York, and a few other large cities. Housing could be found cheaply and there were things to be attained free—surplus food, second-hand clothes, and free clinics and services. The cities were also where the drug resources were located. However, before long the slum areas became hostile to the hippies. While the hippies did nothing to change the neighborhoods they were also exploited by drug pushers, other criminals, and desperate or psychopathic individuals. After the summer of 1967 the hippies began moving to rural areas. They took up "voluntary primitivism," which meant the "building of houses out of mud and trees, planting and harvesting crops by hand, rolling loose tobacco into cigarettes, grinding their own wheat, baking bread, canning vegetables, delivering their own babies, and educating their own children. They gave up electricity, the telephone, running water, gas stoves, even rock music, which, of all things, is supposed to be the cornerstone of hip culture."[66] As the hippies moved into rural and semi-rural areas their patterns of life varied more than had been the case in the city. The places they lived ranged from brief, temporary camps to complex, lasting communes. While some live in communes, many hippies have rejected communal living in favor of loose groupings of individuals. For example, some people live alone or in monogamous units, cook for themselves, and build their own houses and sometimes raise some of their own food.[67] The more complex the commune the more it deviates from the basic hippie values of each doing his own thing with minimal planning and organization.

One of the problems all hippies face is that regardless of how much

---

[66] Davidson, *op. cit.*, p. 94.
[67] *Ibid.*, p. 95.

they want to reject the system they must still draw from that system for survival. In the cities the hippies may not enter directly into the economic system but they do draw from it—through panhandling, money from parents, public charities, and so forth. By contrast, many of the rural hippie communes have tried to operate outside the system by raising their own foods and thereby becoming economically self-sufficient. But Davidson found that none of the hippie communes she studied had been able to live entirely off the land. And most of the communes are unwilling to go into cash crops or light industry because where there are no rules there are not enough people to work regularly. She found that "the women with children receive welfare, some of the men collect unemployment and food stamps, and others get money from home. They spend very little—perhaps $600 a year per person."[68]

The problem of work for the sincere hippie, whether he be in a city or the rural area, is what kind of work he can do in good conscience. That is, a major problem is often how to economically survive and keep one's integrity. Hippies therefore find the work of the rural commune attractive. They can devote their efforts to results that will only be used by themselves and will not contribute to the economy of the broader society. When they do have to go into the work force there are some jobs that are seen as acceptable because they are viewed as not exploitable of others. These are mainly jobs in the areas of unskilled labor such as hospital attendant, messenger, or farmhand.[69]

It is also of importance that the rural commune hippie, although often highly educated, does not earn a living in any intellectual capacity. To the hippie the intellect is the technician, "the engineer of systems human and otherwise, whose work, no matter how high its level of scientific or scholarly complexity, acts to confirm and to further (in the name of progress) the dominant culture's objective reality."[70]

Many of the rural communes are faced with the problems of land control. If they rent land they are often thrown off because of local community pressure after they have devoted initial hard effort to developing the land. So for many hippies there has developed the belief that they should own their own land. This is even true in the city where some groups are buying their houses. In part the argument for this is that property is power and the hippie movement needs economic backbone. But John Groutt suggests that a strange contradiction thereby develops for the hippie. "Many of these people have turned down personal economic influence available to them within the system as a means of inde-

---

[68] *Ibid.*

[69] Carey, *op. cit.*, p. 21.

[70] Ald, *op. cit.*, p. 48.

pendent self-determination, but do want the group to have property, which gives a sense of the same."[71]

But whatever the organization, it must be kept in mind that most hippie communes are minimal in structure and significantly different from the broader society in orientation. The general American community is other-directed, with physical design and function of paramount importance. But the new communitarian groups are inner-directed. The hippie's community is himself. Ald points out that this is not an easy adjustment for many incoming communitarian hippies to make. "Many go rather quickly from one place to another in search of that outward sense of order to which they have been accustomed."[72]

In the truly hippie communes failure is practically guaranteed from the beginning. This is because non-aggressiveness or passivity is the general pattern. Therefore materialistic motives, a desire for object possession, "is frowned upon and there is no room for work in the hippie trinity of love-pleasure-joy except as a necessary evil. And, of course, it is precisely this simplistic summation which collides with the reigning work-ethic, that is responsible for the condemnation of the developing hippie communal scene."[73] However, if a given commune does exist for any time certain leaders do emerge and various persons do take on certain responsibilities. This may be nothing more than preparing food for more than oneself or repairing a shelter. The very notion of hippie love, which implies some commitment on some occasions to another, means that some help should be extended. Thus, some persons on some occasions must take initiative which when acted upon is the simplest form of leadership.

It is possible to draw upon Ald's extensive study of hippie communitarians to get an idea of what they believe in. Basically the hip communitarian is a total dropout from society who wants to cut all ties. He insists on the credo of living one's own life and chooses to interact with those of the same belief. But he shuns any long range commitment in or out of marriage. "His sense of community is unique. It dwells on an intimate, non-verbal rapport and rejects the notion of leadership and 'pecking order,' which has traditionally provided the framework for social structuring."[74] But, as indicated, while these beliefs are often sincere they are only approximated in reality. On the broader level Ald found the communal hippie to be highly educated but anti-intellectual. The hippie is the heir of the most affluent of all societies but chooses to reject that affluence. "He is contemptuous of organized religion and yet gives evidence—in his

---

[71] Groutt, *op. cit.*, p. 8.

[72] Ald, *op. cit.*, p. 120.

[73] *Ibid.*, p. 36.

[74] *Ibid.*, pp. 9–10.

own search for expanded consciousness—of being more susceptible to religious sensitivity than any modern generation."[75] The value system of the hippie, like most value systems, is often one of contradictions.

As suggested earlier, there are a variety of different hippie settlements. In the cities there are several new types of hippie communes. There are *crash pads* which are usually apartments or houses rented by a person or group where friends and strangers "crash" the pad. They come and go, stay as long as they like, and may or may not contribute to expenses. By contrast the *cooperatives* are more organized living arrangements, and their motive is practicality. It is cheaper to live together rather than alone, but there may also be political or social agreements of shared values.

Ald, in his study of rural communes, came up with four general types. First was the *collective settlement*, which is well-ordered and work oriented. With few exceptions it is agrarian, conservative, no-nonsense Kibbutzim. Sex is generally open and spontaneous, although monogamous attachments tend to be the rule. The use of drugs is usually limited or forbidden. Second is the *commune*, the most common form of societal living. It is characterized by an open sexuality and unprogrammed or even a deliberately anarchistic structure. In this type drug use is pervasive. Third is the *expanded or extended family*, which may take two different forms, one where married or unmarried males and females enter into open, spontaneous relationships, and the second made up of only married couples. Fourth is the *tribal group*, which has a powerful mystical orientation rooted in unquestioned dominance of an individual of "nuclear personality."[76] Of course, over time individuals may move in and out of all of the above types. They are also all linked loosely together because there has developed in the broad hippie world newspapers, magazines, meetings, exchange of position papers, and economic cooperation which tie them together.

The above four types all involve some structure and some stability, but there are also a number of hippies who at least for some periods of time do not belong to any of the above but rather are nomads. The nomads are almost always heavy drug users and they don't often work. In the cities they exist by panhandling, signing up for food stamps, or selling drugs. They crash at night into the woods, churchyards, empty buildings, and the beaches. (This is one reason why they are usually found in the warmer climates, especially that of southern California.) What is most characteristic of the nomads is that they keep moving, although they have no destination in mind. When they hitchhike they are not heading anywhere in particular. Some stand on the highway hitching in one direction with one thumb and in the opposite direction with the other thumb.

---

[75] *Ibid.*, p. 10.

[76] *Ibid.*, pp. 12–13.

Most of them, like other hippies, come from middle-class backgrounds. They treat sex casually and share everything. But their diets are sparse and unhealthy. Malnutrition is universal and hepatitis is widespread. The nomads are the ultimate dropouts, "a subculture of tuned-out kids who call themselves freaks and who are in some ways more estranged from technetronic America than the Weathermen or the communards or the urban hip underground."[77]

The nomads are important in another way to the hippie movement because they are the ones who become involved with megalomaniacal cultist leaders. Among the nomads there are some who will follow most anyone who wants to develop himself as their aggressive leader. And in the hippie movement there are some persons who become leaders because they are glib and intuitive street psychologists. Ald observed that the commune phenomenon has made available to such persons a very receptive audience and "that they, naturally, gravitate toward such groups. Furthermore, the new communitarian's sensibility—mystically inclined and struggling to alter the traditional reality pattern—is singularly vulnerable to such influences."[78]

The more stable and complex hippie communes are like the broader society in some ways. It is striking that one distinction that tends to remain, with all the stress on equality, is that of sex roles. Davidson writes about one community that the sex roles are well defined and satisfying. "When men actually do heavy physical labor like chopping trees, baling hay, and digging irrigation ditches, it feels very fulfilling for the women to tend the cabin, grind wheat, put up fruit, and sew and knit."[79] This kind of sex role assignment is no different from the broader society and is not based on interest and capability but entirely on sex.

The traditional influences with regard to marriage are also seen in most hippie communes. While many hippies do attempt to break the traditional monogamous love bond which is the basis of the nuclear family, they nevertheless show jealousy, bruised egos, and attempt to assert claims as a result of intimacies that last any length of time. Or they attempt to completely separate sexuality from reproduction, but still the strongly maternal female is commonly found in the hippie communes.[80] Yet, although there are similarities to the broader society, the hippie community is attempting to make very different kinds of relationships based on different value assumptions. For example, the requirement of marriage is removed from the having of children. Ald quotes one young woman who was annoyed with her parents' disapproval of her having a

---

[77] *Newsweek*, July 27, 1970, p. 22.

[78] Ald, *op. cit.*, p. 110.

[79] Davidson, *op. cit.*, p. 100.

[80] Ald, *op. cit.*, p. 89.

child out of wedlock as saying, "We're all married—married to each other from the day we're born." "She was expressing the new breed's awareness of the common bond of humanity and the conviction that the time for the ultimate decision has arrived. Oblivion or utopia."[81]

Of special interest in the hippie community is the rearing of children. It is clear that children are dependent for survival on others and yet the hippie philosophy of doing one's own thing severely undercuts dependency. And because often the hippie is totally committed to seeking his own identity the children are often abandoned for long periods of time. Yablonsky found that the children in the communes he visited were treated as playthings. "They are adored and adorned with affection and trinkets; however, in the communities I observed they are not cared for with the basic necessities of food, clothes, and adequate health facilities."[82] Ald, in his study, found the child to be better off the nearer his commune environment was to the family patterns of the broader society. He found that the commune child develops of necessity a surprising steadfastness in the face of much adult behavior which is ideosyncratic and offensive.[83] "I cannot say that communitarian children are inferior to those raised in the dominant culture. From what I could see, the communal youngster, in spite of the apparent neglect, is healthier or certainly as healthy."[84]

It will be of interest to see what will happen when the hippie children become teenagers. Will they rebel against their way of life and seek something new? It would seem reasonable to believe that such will be the case for many of the children. This has recently been the case in what had been extremely closely knit and internally controlled subcultures of the American Chinese in San Francisco and the Amish in Pennsylvania. The children grow up and forcefully seek to leave their subcultures for the broader society. Davidson found that in the more stable communes there were problems with the children. And some of the members have "started to joke uneasily that their sons will become uptight businessmen and their daughters suburban housewives."[85]

CONCLUSIONS

What kinds of generalizations can be made about the hippie movement? First, because the movement is complex and varied its impact is difficult to assess. The extent and the impact of the hippie subculture—

---

[81] *Ibid.*, p. 96.
[82] Yablonsky, *op. cit.*, p. 196.
[83] Ald, *op. cit.*, p. 91.
[84] *Ibid.*, pp. 93–94.
[85] Davidson, *op. cit.*, p. 99.

"amplified as it is by new drugs, new music, new sexual morality, and a new kind of war—may be, in some respects, unprecedented."[86] Or as one observer has suggested, one great contribution of the hippies is that they are breaking set patterns of looking at things. "They have, at least among the young, been exploding 'old mental associations,' such as 'love leads to marriage, marriage leads to children.' Why? What if they don't?"[87] The hippie appeals of pleasure, self-knowledge, drugs, and hanging loose, along with the new music and art, are so great that this is no longer limited but probably a powerful appeal to many of the young for many years to come.[88] In other words, the greatest influence of the hippies is on the young. They have provided a way of life not previously in existence that may be followed by many.

But there are also other influences of the hippies on the broader society. Their values have been related to those of other persons who have been attempting to develop group relationships that give something greater to the individuals. For example, the same search made by the hippie is seen in the "widespread enthusiasm for 'sensitivity training' groups and even in the increasing use of groups as a therapeutic instrument."[89]

Also of great importance is that the hippie movement has not been limited to the United States but is today found in many parts of the Western world. Davis suggests that it is perhaps the only real cross-national culture to be found in the world today. It is built on "the rag-tag of beards, bare feet, bedrolls, and beads, not on the cultural-exchange programs of governments and universities, or tourists, or—least of all— ladies clubs' invocations for sympathetic understanding of one's foreign neighbors."[90]

It is quite possible that in the United States in the 1970's the major source of domestic conflict will be the generational one based upon militant students and hippies. But also it will be of interest to note what happens to the hippie generation as it grows older. Will it make the move back into the broader society and return to the dominant values? It seems likely that this will happen to some degree, but probably not completely. If that is the case, this hippie generation and the millions influenced by it, at least in some of their beliefs, may become a transitional generation for a future generation who may deviate even further. If

[86] Simmon, Geoffrey and Grafton Trout, "Hippies in College—From Teeny-Boppers to Drug Freaks," *Trans-Action*, December, 1967, p. 32.

[87] Packard, Vance, *The Sexual Wilderness* (New York: David McKay, 1968), p. 15.

[88] Blum, *op. cit.*, p. 23.

[89] Keniston, Kenneth, "Youth, Change and Violence," *The American Scholar*, Spring, 1968, p. 111.

[90] Davis, *op. cit.*, p. 42.

that is the result, the compatibility of generations will be most apt to be among the higher educated and higher social classes. This may lead to reduced generational conflict but greater social class hostility.

BIBLIOGRAPHY

ALD, ROY, *The Youth Communes* (New York: Tower Publications, 1970).

ANDERSON, WALT, *The Age of Protest* (Pacific Palisades, Calif.: Goodyear Publishing Co., Inc., 1969).

BLUM, RICHARD, *Society and Drugs* (San Francisco: Jossey-Bass, Inc., 1969).

DAVIS, FRED, "Why All of Us May Be Hippies Someday," *Trans-Action*, December, 1967, pp. 10–18.

DAVISON, SARA, "Openland: Getting Back to the Communial Garden," *Harper's*, June, 1970, pp. 91–102.

POWELL, ELWIN H., "Beyond Utopia: The 'Beat' Generation as a Challenge for the Sociology of Knowledge," in Arnold Rose, *Human Behavior and Human Processes* (New York: Houghton-Mifflin, 1964), pp. 360–77.

SIMMON, GEOFFREY and GRAFTON TROUT, "Hippies in College—From Teeny-Boppers to Drug Freaks," *Trans-Action*, December, 1967, pp. 27–32.

WEAKLAND, JOHN H., "Hippies: What the Scene Means," in Richard Blum, *Society and Drugs* (San Francisco: Jossey-Bass, Inc., 1969), pp. 343–72.

WILLS, GARRY, "The Making of the Yippie Culture," *Esquire*, November, 1969, pp. 135–38, 266, 268.

YABLONSKY, LEWIS, *The Hippie Trip* (New York: Pegasus, 1968).

INDEXES

AUTHOR INDEX

465

SUBJECT INDEX

This book has been set in 10 and 9 point Electra, leaded 2 points. Part numbers and chapter titles are in Engravers Roman Bold. Part titles and chapter numbers are in Engravers Roman. The size of the type area is 27 by 45½ picas.